TREKKING

H O L I D A Y S

IN INDIA

85
Treks
+ *50* Trekking options

outlooktraveller.com
For updates, packages, news and new destinations, log on to our website
www.outlooktraveller.com

OTHER TITLES FROM OUTLOOK TRAVELLER GETAWAYS

www.outlooktraveller.com

Editorial
EDITOR-IN-CHIEF Vinod Mehta
DEPUTY EDITOR Manju Rastogi
ASSOCIATE EDITOR Lesley A. Esteves
ASSISTANT EDITORS Himanshu Joshi,
Deepa A.
CONSULTING EDITORS Ranee Sahaney,
Lalitha Sridhar, Nagraj Adve

Research
INFO AND RESEARCH COORDINATORS
Julia Dutta, Rani G. Kalra
TREKKING GUIDES RESEARCH Suraj
Wadhwa, Ahtushi Deshpande
RESEARCHERS A. Prabhavati, Aparna
Chandrashekaran, Lakshmi Peri,
Chhandita Chakravarty, Jessica Paul

Design
DESIGN CONSULTANT Shuka Jain
SENIOR DESIGNER Pallavi Narain
Ashish Rozario
DTP COORDINATORS Rajesh K.G.,
Ganesh Shah, Gulshan Sharma

Graphics
Jai Kumar Sharma, Anis Khan

Photography
PHOTOGRAPHER Abhijit Bhatlekar
PHOTO COORDINATORS Tashi Tobgyal,
Kuldeep Kalia

Production
GENERAL MANAGER Anup Dwivedi
SENIOR MANAGER Rakesh Mishra
ASSISTANT MANAGERS Shashank Dixit,
Shekhar Pandey

Business Office
NATIONAL MANAGER Lalit Pramar
NORTH Nikhil Sood, Sugandha Anil
WEST Praveen Meloth
CIRCULATION Sudipto Mookherjee

Printed and published by
MAHESHWER PERI
on behalf of Outlook Publishing (India)
Private Limited from AB-10, Safdarjung
Enclave, New Delhi-110029
Processed & Printed at IPP Limited,
Phase-II, Noida

TREKKING GUIDE
PROJECT and PHOTO EDITOR
Sonia Jabbar

Dear Reader,

It gives me great pleasure to introduce you to an exciting and unusual form of travel. We, at Outlook Traveller Getaways, have compiled a collection of 85 Trekking Holidays in India for you to explore, from hiking across sere trans-Himalayan Ladakh to walking through the dense shola-forested ranges of Kerala. The treks are by and large gentle and can easily be done by the average person on a long weekend break, though we have included some classic Himalayan trails, like the Valley of Flowers in Garhwal, the Indrahar Pass trek in Himachal and the Dzongri trek in Sikkim for the more experienced and adventurous. Those going to Ladakh for the first time may want to throw in a short hike and try Ladakh's 'baby trek' from Likir to Temisgam or the longer, classic trek in the Markha Valley. For wildlife and birding enthusiasts, we have details of the little known Corbett-to-Nainital trail, and the Namdapha National Park hike in Arunachal Pradesh. For our readers in Western and Southern India, if you can't take the time out and head north to the Himalayas, try your own backyard. Mumbaikars can do Duke's Nose in a day and still make it back to their favourite watering hole by the evening. Bangalore trekking enthusiasts can easily climb Brahmagiri or Kodachadri over a weekend.

We believe that trekking should not simply be seen as a sport for fitness enthusiasts, but as an activity that makes us more sensitive to the natural world. In keeping with our commitment to the environment, we have provided interesting snippets on flora and fauna, which will help enhance your knowledge and appreciation of nature.

We welcome you to the very special world of trekking.

VINOD MEHTA

Editor-in-Chief

CONTENTS

INTRODUCTION

THE TREKS

NORTH
LADAKH

HIMACHAL PRADESH

UTTARANCHAL

NORTH-EAST

WEST

SOUTH

10 years of courage and conviction, defiance and cheek and chutzpah... in short, inspired journalism

OUTLOOK

Celebrating 10 Years of speaking out

determination, truth and trials, repartee and riposte,

HOW TO USE THIS BOOK

REGIONS

	LADAKH
	NORTH
	NORTH EAST
	WEST
	SOUTH

How the book is organised

Outlook Traveller Getaways' *Trekking Holidays in India* features 85 treks in various regions of the country, organised geographically in five colour-coded sections (*see right*). The front pages of the book provide information on planning a trek as well as camping and packing tips. Each section opens with a route guide of the region, with details of the road network, followed by the hubs and the treks themselves. Route guides of the trekking trails are also provided

Region or state
Mentions the area where the hub is located, followed by the name of the hub

Must-visits
Lists the major tourist attractions in the hub as well as outdoor activities (for instance, adventure sports) that you can indulge in

Hub Facts
Indicates the hub's location and gives details on how to reach it by air, road and rail. Mentions cost of transport, time required to get there from the nearest railhead/airport, plus the STD code of the place

CHAMBA REGION-Hub DALHOUSIE

Abandoned and disowned by Lahore after Partition, Dalhousie's remains have unfairly been labelled "Dull and Lousy". Yet, a walk around its three malls and wooded loops such as Potreyn Road, Bakrota and Moti Tibba hills is anything but dull. It has as many as five functioning churches, charming British-style country houses that have been converted into hotels, a cemetery painted by the first flood of Tibetan émigrés in 1959.

Dalhousie market square

MUST-VISITS

CHURCHES
Dalhousie's oldest is St John's Church, situated near the GPO. At the other end of the Mall, on Subhash Chowk, is St Francis Church. The best-preserved in Dalhousie is without doubt the church in the Sacred Heart School. Of the others, St Patrick's is the biggest on Potreyn Road, whereas St Andrew's which is in the Cantonment can only be accessed with permission.

A RAJA'S HUNTING LODGE
Roughly 2½ km from Gandhi Chowk is the residence, and now the summer home of the former Rajas of Chamba. Though the property is out of bounds now, the charming road to Jhandrighat is a walker's delight. Subhash Book (2,065m),

▶ **Dalhousie Facts**

• **LOCATION** Spread over five hills at 2,000m, and sandwiched between the Dhauladhar and Pir Panjal ranges, north-east of Pathankot
• **GETTING TO DALHOUSIE By rail** Nearest railhead: Chakki Bank (58 km/ 2½ hrs). Taxi Rs 1,000; **By road** NH1 from Delhi to Jalandhar via Ambala and Ludhiana; NH1A to Pathankot via Dasua. Then state highway to Dalhousie via Chakki (14 hrs). The roads are good except for a section between Jallandhar and Pathankot, where the construction of a new highway is in progress
• **STD code** 01899

160

Subhash Chandra Bose's meditation spot, also falls on this route.

THE WATERFALL WALK
Take a morning walk to Satdhara, said to have medicinal properties in the seven streams that converge on this road 1 km down from Gandhi Chowk), and to Panchpullah, 1 km further on, which offers two waterfalls within touching distance.

CHAMERA DAM
Also called Bhadrakali Lake by the locals, this is an ideal picnic stop en route to Chamba, about 8 km from the bustling village of Banikhet.

WHERE TO STAY
Mehar Hotel (Tel: 01899-242179; Tariff: Rs 550-1,300), on the Mall, is a mid-range hotel run by painter Manjit Bawa's family. Another option is Hotel Manimahesh (Tel: 242155; Tariff: Rs 800-1,500), which is a new hotel run by the HPTDC, near the bus stand; the service is courteous here.
For more hotels and details, see Accommodation Listings on pages 523-524

WHERE TO EAT
No fine cuisine to be had here. But for a wholesome meal of hot tandoori rotis and rajma, head for Gandhi Chowk or the bus stand. Just below the taxi stand, Sharma's Dhaba offers good parathas and vegetable biryani.
INPUTS FROM CHARU SONI

Hubs
Every trek has a hub, the most well-connected destination nearest to the starting point of the trek. On occasion, as in Shimla or Mahabaleshwar, the hub is also the starting point of the trek. Here is where you will find trek support: guides, agents, porters/ ponies and provisions. Most of the hubs have accommodation facilities across various price slabs. A selection of a few hotels is given under the 'Where to stay' sub-head. A more exhaustive list can be found in the *Accommodation Listings* on pages 522-555

Eating info
Highlights the culinary specialities of the region plus the names of popular eateries

Trekking guide
Each trek has a visual guide detailing every point of the trekking trail, with symbols highlighting campsites, rest houses, tea shops, rivers, bridges, peaks and passes. While we have tried to be as accurate as possible, some anomalies may occur and we strongly recommend the use of local trekking guides

Section colour
For instant access, each section has been given a colour (see colour code on opposite page). In the North, Himachal treks have been given a shade of orange while the ones in Uttaranchal have green

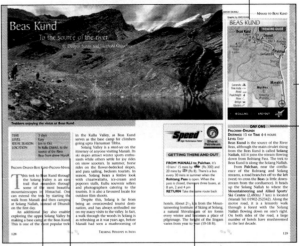

Day-wise info
Each segment describes individual days of the trek in detail. Apart from directions, there's information on the distance covered, the approximate time taken for trekking and the level (for instance, easy or moderate)

Route
Lists the starting point of the trek, the main areas it passes through, and the last point of the trail

Info box
Presents the number of days required to do the trek and the level (whether it's easy, moderate or tough). Ideal season gives you the best time to do the trek. Also provided is its location

Getting there and out
Tells you how to get to the starting point of the trek, from the hub. Also gives you the cost of transport to get there and the amount of time required. The best way of making the return journey is also given

Icons
A tent icon indicates the places where you can camp during the trek. The icon of a kettle highlights tea shops located on the trekking trail

Log hut icon
Indicates a rest house, lodge or hotel on the trekking route

Boxes on myths, history, flora and fauna
Most treks have a short feature about the flora and fauna of the region (see listings on page 573), besides other interesting trivia

11

Section openers
A breathtaking, double-page photo divides the four trekking sections of the book

Route guides
Each region opens with a route guide (not to scale) showing the recommended route with approximate distances, national highways, state roads, airports and railway stations. It also highlights the physical features of the region, such as ranges and passes, as well as hubs and trek points

Back of the book
Provides all the information you need for planning and setting out on your trek, including listings of hotels, tourist offices, mountaineering institutes and trekking agents. There are also sections on health and first-aid tips and weather conditions in the trekking regions covered in this book so that you know what to pack when. A glossary features a collection of specialised terms with their meanings

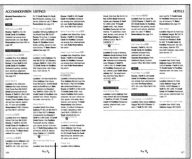

Tourist offices
Information on tourist offices in the states you can trek, along with contact details in the metros

Trekking agents
Region-wise listing of agents you can contact to organise your trek, alpine or sahib-style

Hotel listings
Detailed listing of facilities, tariffs and contact information of hotels, PWD Rest Houses, Forest Rest Houses and home stays located in the hubs and in various points of the trek

Hiring and buying equipment
Location and contact details of places from where you can rent trekking equipment

Health and first-aid
Tells you about training for your trek, what to pack in your first-aid kit and measures to take in case of medical emergencies

Analogue Compass
- Continuos heading
- Displays numeric and cardinal heading
- Allows user to set declination angle based on geography
- INDIGLO® night-light
- WR 50 m

Digital Compass
- Highly accurate digital compass
- Bearings based on 16 cardinal points measured in degrees
- Allows user to set declination angle based on geography
- INDIGLO® night-light
- NIGHT-MODE® feature
- WR 100 m

One for 'off' the road
Presenting the Timex expedition series

Trekking holidays in India
By Sonia Jabbar

Long ago, when the world was young, they roamed the Earth, your ancestors and mine. They trekked far and wide over mountain and desert, grassland and jungle, looking for food and shelter. They navigated by the sun and the stars. They slept out in the open under sheltering skies. They ate when they were hungry, rested when they were tired. For entertainment, they sang songs around the fire and spun a web of stories that was passed on as legend from generation to generation. They knew when the wind brought rain and when it was going to scorch the earth. They knew which plant could be eaten and which could be used to tip their arrows with deadly poison. Life was simpler then. The human being was just one more creature among many who happily ranged the Earth.

Today, stuck in that traffic jam, breathing not air but a deadly cocktail of carbon monoxide and suspended particulate matter, this picture of human life may seem completely inaccessible, a frozen tableau in the dim and distant past. But before you give up all hope and submit to the tragic fate of being a citizen of an Indian metro with all its attendant features (diseased lungs, hypertension, obesity), take a hike. It will change your life, I promise.

WHY HIKE?

Coming down the mountain on the last day of the trek, I am always enveloped in a marvellous sense of well being. My legs feel strong, my backpack no longer weighs down heavily, my stomach muscles have tightened admirably, my skin glows healthily, I almost feel invincible. This feeling actually lasts well into the third week of my return to the city. When I have managed a 17,000-ft pass, forded rivers and successfully navigated my way through unknown terrain, the problems I face in the city are but piffling little setbacks.

THE OUTDOOR SCHOOL

Hiking and trekking are not about climbing summits. Each day is a challenge and pleasure as the land unfolds slowly in front of you, revealing its treasures: a waterfall, a magnificent deodar, a bird you've only recently learned to identify. Here's your chance to recover some of that lost wisdom of your ancestors. Learn to predict weather from looking at the sky, tell the difference between a kite and a lammergeir, learn to live on simple food that you have prepared yourself.... The list of your newly acquired skills can become impressively long.

KNOW THYSELF

When you are trekking for five to seven hours every day, the walking becomes a kind of meditation as you pace your step and your breath. The mind goes into a relaxed and tranquil state, reflecting the solid mountain beneath you and the vast sky above you. Stopping for a break at the top of a pass, you are overcome by a deep sense of oneness with the whole universe. On a hike you can also learn a lot about yourself and your limitations: How do you deal with fears and challenges? Are you someone who gives up easily or do you push yourself to find new strengths? How do you cope with emergencies?

LOSE THOSE UNWANTED POUNDS

Admit it, no matter what the variation in routine, the gym is precisely that: routine, which can get quite boring. Hiking is a wonderful and interesting way to knock off at least two-three kilograms a week. Your body becomes incredibly strong, your stamina increases, and you simply radiate good health. If your kids are turning into TV or Internet junkies, cure them with a regular dose of exercise on the trail.

THE GREAT CEMENTER

There is perhaps no better way of bonding with family, friends or colleagues than by going on a hike together. It's probably that nomadic gene of our ancestors that makes us connect so marvellously well with those we walk. After all, the tribe stuck together when they crossed those mountains and rivers and jungles. The adventure, the exercise every day, climbing a pass together, experiencing the beauty of nature together, cooking and hanging out by a campfire at night, all seem to bring you closer to your loved ones. Introduced to nature in this manner, your children will thank you forever for this precious gift. ✦

Planning your trek
By Sonia Jabbar

Which trek should I choose? When do I go? How do I prepare? These are some of the questions that will arise once you decide to go on a trekking holiday. The kind of hike you end up doing will depend on your level of physical fitness, time constraints and your budget. A person with no trekking experience should not begin with a hike in Ladakh, no matter how attractive it seems. You will be starting at a high altitude and will definitely have a problem acclimatising. Far from your holiday being fun, it could end up being torturous. Hiking is a sport that can last a lifetime. Plan well and enjoy yourself, so that you can enjoy a new and more challenging trail the next time around.

Choose an area you think you would like to explore. Go to that section in this book and read through all the treks carefully. Look at the **IDEAL SEASON** for each trek. If you want to see alpine flowers, for instance, don't take leave from the office in October, you will be disappointed even if you go to the Valley of Flowers.

Check the **LEVEL** of each trek. Although we have taken pains to include mostly entry level or moderate treks, some are tougher than the others. Be realistic, not ambitious. It's better to choose one that will **suit your level of fitness** rather than suffer later.

If you have children, ensure that the trek has **pony or porter support**, or is easy enough for your 10-year-old to do. Look at the number of trekking days involved (**TIME**) and the **number of days** it will take you to get to and from your starting point. In the Sahyadris and in South India, getting to the starting point is fairly easy and fast. In the Himalayas, it's a different story and getting to the beginning of the trek can be an adventure in itself (read the **Getting There And Out** box carefully). If you are a first-time hiker in the Himalayas and are going with the family, it may be a good idea to go to Mussoorie or Shimla, spend a couple of days doing gentle walks and day hikes so that your body gets used to walking four to five hours a day and then do one of the overnight or two-day treks.

Finally, the nature of your trek will depend upon your **budget**.

CAMPING SAHIB-STYLE

During the British Raj, English civil servants, merchants and adventurers regularly fled the heat of the plains for the hills on fishing or shooting expeditions. The 'bandobast' for these trips was phenomenal: shikaris to track animals, skinners, gun bearers, a couple of khansamas to prepare the mulligatawny soups, pot roasts and puddings, bearers to serve, porters, mules and muleteers, sleeping tents, dining tents, camp cots, books and painting material, chairs and tables. The holiday-maker's personal trunk consisted of necessities that ranged from silver shaving kits, cases of wine and cigars to dinner jackets.

Believe it or not, it is possible to replicate the experience — for a price, of course. If you decide to go on a trek sahib-style, just decide where you want to go, call a trekking agency (*see List of Trekking Agents on pages 514-517*) and let them tailor-make a trip to suit you. It can be an all-frills attached trip — in which case, just pack your toothbrush, camera and cheque book — or it could be one where you have a cook and guide rolled into one and a couple of ponies and pony-wallahs. Everything can be discussed and finalised before the trek, including your daily menu. In Ladakh, I've seen a veritable caravan of ponies and horsemen, carrying fresh vegetables and fruits, trailed by a few sad looking goats. These were to be slaughtered en route to provide fresh meat for four French trekkers who had about them all the airs of 19th century explorers in the Taklamakan Desert.

COSTS OF CAMPING SAHIB-STYLE

An organised trek can cost anywhere between Rs 700 and 8,000 per person per day. Your trekking agent will take care of all the little details, but if you want to know why you are paying so much, below is a list of factors your agent will consider when quoting you a price:

Location of trek How far from civilisation is the trek? The more remote, the more expensive it is. If you are trekking in remote Arunachal Pradesh or Ladakh, petrol and diesel are much more expensive in these parts, so transporting food, equipment and hired hands to the starting point of the trek and back will be that much more expensive.

Size of the group A trekking group of four to eight people works best in terms of cost-effectiveness. You will need a guide and a cook and at least two to three ponies or mules on the trek, even if you are one or two people. So, if you can increase your group's number to four, the cost per person comes down and the trek becomes effectively cheaper.

Backpack or daypack People travelling sahib-style don't carry their backpacks, which can weigh upto 20 kg, but just a daypack with the bare minimum: camera, water bottle and parka. If you are travelling this way, a porter or a pony/ mule will carry your luggage. The more you take, the number of porters or ponies will increase. A friend actually takes an extra porter for camera equipment!

Ponies or porters Where possible, try and opt for ponies to carry supplies. They are a better bet than porters as they are able to carry more weight and you don't have to share your rations with them. The more porters you have, the more extra porters you will need to carry their share of food and supplies.

Ponies and mules are turned out loose in the late afternoons to graze. In some parts of Ladakh, especially if the winter snows have been less than normal, the grass may be of poor quality and extra ponies may be needed to carry fodder, making your trip more expensive. If you are **travelling with children**, ensure you have an **extra riding pony** for each child. When they get tired of walking they can simply hop on.

Hired hands Ponies and porters can cost Rs 200-300 per porter/ pony per day, depending on your location. Guides and cooks can cost Rs 150-200 per day plus food. You also need to factor in costs of transporting them to the start of your trek and back to their town/ village. Don't forget to **tip** them at the end of the trek.

Food Fresh eggs for breakfast? A hot meal for lunch instead of a packed, cold lunch? Fresh chicken, fish or meat for dinner? Discuss the menu with your trekking agent. Your costs will depend upon it.

Equipment Do you have your own tents, sleeping bags and mats or is the agency providing them? Costs will also depend on the extra equipment, like dining tents, camp chairs and stools. Try and figure whether they're absolutely essential and how much extra you're being charged for all of this to be carried on the trek. Cut costs where possible.

SLOGGING IT ALPINE-STYLE

If you're doing a trek alpine-style, it means you are carrying all your equipment and food yourself without the aid of porters. Don't be wistful about your tight budget and inability to travel sahib-style. Some of the best treks I have done have been solo. After all, the impulse to do the trek was to get away from the crowd in the first place, so why take it along on the trek?

However, if you decide to do the trek alpine-style, your planning must be meticulous, down to the last detail. If there are four of you, have a planning meeting. Discuss what each one will be carrying. Try and minimise the number of clothes, ipods and cameras that each person is carrying. Is it possible to have one camera between the four of you? Ensure that the food and equipment is distributed equally so that one person doesn't end up carrying a heavier load than the others.

The secret of having a wonderful alpine-style trek is to **travel light**. Check out the route carefully. Is it possible to stay in temples, forest rest houses or village schools en route and avoid carrying a tent? Is it possible to eat at dhabas and not carry a stove? Even if you have to carry a stove, can you plan your meals so that you're not overloaded with unnecessary food?

PLANNING YOUR MEALS

Did you know you can actually survive a few weeks without food as long as you keep the fluids going? You'll be surprised how little your body needs. Most of us who live in the city have a spare tire around the waist that can come extremely handy on a trek. I have done four-five-day solo treks in Spiti and in Ladakh carrying a small stove, some dried fruit and chocolates, a couple of packets of namkeen and Maggi, tea and tsampa (roasted barley flour, the highly nutritious staple of Tibetan nomads) and been none the worse for it.

However, you don't have to be that abstemious when trekking alpine-style. Figure out the menu for each day with your trekking buddies and carry food accordingly. Snacks can be extras that each person carries. Breakfast could be tea/ coffee with porridge (easy to carry and make). Lunch could be Maggi that you stop and make or some khichdi or parathas made early in the morning that you carry and eat cold with pickle. Dinner should be a substantial meal and can be khichdi with some ready-to-eat vegetable that you just need to heat (there's good news for trekkers with new and exciting pre-cooked vacuum-packed dals and vegetables which can be easily carried). Try and pack soups that need hot water added rather than those that need to be cooked (you can save kerosene that way).

Try and see if you can get the guest house or hotel you stay in the night before you start the trek to pack parathas or boiled eggs that you can carry for lunch on the first day. Don't bank on dhabas en route for meals as most chai shops in remote areas stock just tea and biscuits and not much more, unless it's on a pilgrimage route.

COSTS OF TREKKING ALPINE-STYLE

Get four friends together and this could be the cheapest holiday of your life where the biggest expense would be the fare to get to the starting point of the trek. Then, if you have a tent, stove and sleeping bag, factor in the amount you want to spend on food and kerosene and buying supplies for your **first-aid kit** (*see Health and First-aid on page 506*) and everything else is free! Excluding your journey to the staring point and back, you can easily do a trek spending less than Rs 200 per person per day including food. If you get a guide, add a little more.

GETTING FIT

Whether you are trekking alpine or sahib-style, preparing your body for the trek is essential. If I have been lazy all year, I make sure I train for at least a month before I leave, to avoid pain and injuries while on the trek. Try and walk every day to build up stamina. Start with walking an hour and build up to walking at least a couple of hours. Alternate with running for 20 minutes to half an hour every other day. If you live or work in an apartment, don't take the elevator but run up and down instead. Strengthen your abdominal muscles by doing sit-ups. Your butt muscles and quadriceps should be built up with squats and leg extensions. Remember, the fitter you are the more you will enjoy your holiday.

SARKARI REST HOUSES

Though PWD, Forest and other government rest houses dot the rural landscape, there's a catch. Getting a booking in advance may be near impossible. The best bet is to take a chance. If the chowkidar is friendly, or reluctant but hints at *baksheesh*, you're in luck! ✦

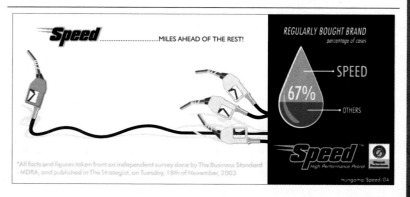

SONIA JABBAR

What to pack
By Sonia Jabbar

What to pack really depends on where you are going, for how many days and the weather you are likely to encounter. If you are trekking in the Himalayas in high altitudes, it's obviously going to be colder than a low-altitude trek in the same season. Are you likely to get snow or rain? (*see Weather on page 556*)

Some areas like the North-East are going to be more humid even in late autumn than in the Central Himalayas or Ladakh. If you are trekking in the Sahyadris in the monsoon to enjoy the lushness of the environs, or in the Valley of Flowers to check out the alpine flowers, well, ensure that your trek doesn't get washed out by packing rain gear and keeping your backpack dry, wrapped securely in a sheet of plastic. Finally, what to pack depends on whether you are travelling sahib or alpine-style (*see page 16*). The former would mean you would have to worry about your personal kit only. The latter would mean your personal kit plus camping gear and food.

If there are four of you, then I would recommend carrying two small tents as it would be far more comfortable than cramming into one big one. One stove, adequate kerosene or stove fuel, one pressure cooker to cook that khichdi quickly and efficiently, one pan for tea, soup and heating pre-cooked vegetables.

TIP If your group comprises more than four people, carry another set of pots, pans, stove and fuel rather than trying to cook for six to eight people on one stove

PERSONAL KIT

Boots Your footwear is the most important gear in your kit. Remember you will be spending five to seven hours a day tramping about in them, so make sure they're comfortable. I suggest you don't pack the brand new pair of New Balance hiking boots you borrowed from your America-returned cousin, even if they had fitted you like a glove at home. Break in all new shoes/ boots before trying them on the trail, or you will rue the day you set foot in them. I personally find most hiking boots too warm for our conditions and where the trail is easy, have preferred to walk in my sneakers.

On difficult terrain, though, it is better to have a sturdy pair of boots. If you are planning to buy a new pair of boots, look for the following: The soles should not be too flexible. If they are, your feet muscles will tire easily. They should only flex a little bit if you push the sole up from the front of the boot. The heel and ankle area should be firm. If the ankle part flip-flops when you push it from side to side, it's no good. You need good ankle support to avoid twisted ankles on the

TREKKING HOLIDAYS IN INDIA

Wrenching Range

The pain and sprain specialist. **IODEX**®

trail. The toe area should feel solid. You are likely to scuff against stones and boulders, particularly on your way down a hill. If there isn't proper protection, you could bruise your toes badly and even lose a toe-nail. Finally, when you slip your feet in, the boot should fit well, not pinch, and you should have adequate room in the front to wiggle your toes. After you purchase your boots, walk around in them for at least a week and only then should you use them on your hike.

Sandals with straps are useful for river crossings. Slip them into your daypack if you know you have a river to cross. This will help keep the boots dry as well as protect your feet from cuts from sharp stones on the riverbed.

Socks This is the second most important item in your personal gear. Calculate one clean pair of socks for each day of trekking. Socks which get stiff with sweat will definitely cause blisters. Socks made of wool or wool mix are a better bet than pure cotton socks, especially in cold weather. Some people prefer to wear two pairs of socks, one thin inner and a thicker outer to avoid blisters. But I personally find this uncomfortable. Try it out for a few days on walks in the park and decide what's more comfortable for you. Carry a couple of extra pairs of clean socks to wear around camp at night.

Thermal underwear In cold weather, this is a blessing. Layer your clothing to stay warm. It's more effective to wear three thin layers than one thick layer. Early in the morning, put on your thermals and a T-shirt over them, followed by a thin sweater or fleece pullover. As the day warms up, you can strip down to the T-shirt.

Shorts In warm weather take shorts to wear in camp at night. I prefer to walk in pants, even in warm weather, to avoid scratches and insect bites on the legs.

WHAT TO CARRY

● T-shirts ● Pants ● Underwear ● Thin sweater ● Fleece pullover ● Jacket ● Raingear or plastic sheet ● Windproof pants and jacket — carry these if you know you will be traversing cold, windy passes ● Thick sweater — I usually pack this when I'm hiking in really cold weather to wear at night around camp ● Sweatpants to wear at night ● Gloves (only required in very cold weather) ● Woollen cap — 90 per cent of body heat is lost through the head and feet. Keep these warm in cold weather and you are sure to be snug ● Woollen scarf — only required in very cold weather ● Bandana or handkerchief — good to wipe sweat, sponge down at a stream, and as an emergency bandage ● Hat or baseball cap — crucial in sunny weather to avoid sunburn ● Sunblock — crucial in sunny weather to avoid sunburn ● Toilet paper ● One empty Bisleri bottle — for those who prefer water to toilet paper. The Bisleri bottle is easier to pack than a mug ● First-aid kit (*see Health and First-aid on page 506*)

CAMPING GEAR

Luggage If you are travelling sahib-style, ask your trekking company whether there will be porters or ponies. If it's the latter, it's better to carry your kit in duffel bags, which are easier to strap to the ponies than backpacks. Take a daypack for your water bottle.

Tent/ Bivouac sack Check for tears and repair before the trek. Clean and air your tent before and after each trek.

Ground sheet A very important item which can be devised by cutting a sheet of thick plastic a little larger than the floor of your tent. This will keep the tent dry in damp weather as well as protect it from sharp stones.

Sleeping bag Sun and air your sleeping bag before each trek. Dry-clean it on your return.

Sleeping mat Either buy a fancy ridged mat from a camping store abroad or devise one by cutting a length of foam a little broader than your sleeping bag. Absolutely essential for a comfortable night.

Stove Test your stove before you go on the trek to check how much fuel it consumes, so you don't end up carrying too much or too little.

Fuel Depends on your stove.

Matches Wrapped in a zip-lock/ securely tied plastic bag; or a cigarette lighter.

Pots, pressure cooker and pans Calculate how many you need according to your daily menu. Also carry **plates, cups** and **spoons**. A **knife** or a **Swiss army knife** will also be useful.

Flashlight It's useful to have a flashlight that doubles up as a lantern. Carry **spare batteries, compass/ GPS** and **camera** and **film**.

Ice axe Only needed if you are trekking in snowbound areas or glaciers.

Gaitors These are only needed if you are trekking in snowbound or leech-infested areas.

FOOD

Plan the dishes on your daywise menu carefully with your trekking buddies. Agree that on Monday morning you will eat A and B for breakfast, C for lunch, D and E for dinner, and on Tuesday, you will eat X, Y and Z and so on. If you prefer porridge for breakfast, don't carry the whole heavy tin, but measure out the required quantity and carry it in a zip-lock bag or plastic. Avoid carrying tinned food as this will only add dead weight to your pack. Be realistic about the quantity of khichdi each person is going to eat every day and carry only the required amount of rice, dal, onions and potatoes. Carry an extra day of rations for emergencies if you are going out to an uninhabited area. Take along dry fruit. It is light and gives you plenty of energy.

TIP If possible, carry dehydrated food as it's light and easy to cook. Dehydrated peas are readily available and you can make your own dehydrated onions, potatoes and tomatoes by slicing them finely and drying them in the summer sun before your trek (remember not to try this in humid weather). You can also do the same with curry/ dhania leaves

FOOD TO PACK: ● Tea/ coffee ● Powdered milk ● Sugar ● Porridge/ dalia ● Salt ● Rice ● Dal ● Small plastic bottle of cooking oil ● Spices ● Atta (if you have the patience to make chapatis and parathas) ● Papad (potato papads are a light, nutritious, tasty addition to the daily fare of khichdi) ● Small bag of pickle ● Packet soup ● Maggi noodles ● Dehydrated vegetables ● Pre-cooked vegetables ● Chocolates ● Biscuits ● Dry fruits ✦

Hiking and camping tips

By Sonia Jabbar

**A campsite below
Chanderkhani Pass**

TIPS FOR THE TRAIL

● **Pace** yourself and don't try and compete with the person in front of you. Start slowly and try and maintain an even pace. Rushing downhill only to crawl up will add to fatigue. If you are carrying your own backpack, try and stop no more than once every hour for 5-10 minutes. If you have only a daypack, then try and **rest** once every two hours for 10 minutes. But this doesn't mean you don't stop for photos or to identify a bird or flower. Remember, the secret of a great trek is **enjoying the walk** and not simply trying to get to the campsite at the end of the day.

● If there is a particularly **tough incline** which seems to go on forever, I set myself small goals: rest for a few seconds every 150 paces. Then as I walk, I count those paces and feel wonderful if I manage to achieve my goal. It's amazing how much distance one can cover this way.

● While **going downhill**, particularly over scree, I find that going slowly and carefully actually makes me even more unsteady. So I take small rapid steps forward, keeping my weight lightly on my toes rather than leaning back into my heels. If there is a particularly sharp decline, especially in snow, use a side step, angling your foot so that it is parallel to the hillside. Then, with each step forward, angle your foot in such a manner that the weight falls on the boot-edge closer to the hill, rather than on the outside, and wedge your boot into the small step that you have created.

● Change into your sandals for **river crossings**. Try and cross rivers early in the morning as, by afternoon, the water levels rise with the melting snow. If the river is fast-flowing, link arms with others and face downstream so that even if you are swept off your feet, you can see what's ahead and have a chance to regain your footing.

- Carry a wide-brim soft hat for treks in hot, sunny areas. Dip it in a cool stream to wet it thoroughly. Then squeeze out excess water and wear to **keep your head cool** for the next few hours. Do the same with your bandana and sponge your neck and arms.

- If you are likely to be **walking in snow**, gaiters can be devised with plastic and elastic bands. Wrap the plastic around your calves from the knee to the top of your boots and secure with elastic bands. Ensure that the plastic goes well over the top of your boots till your laces. This will keep your legs dry and prevent snow from slipping into your boots from the top.

- **Carry dental floss.** This can be used in an emergency to replace anything from broken shoelaces to guy ropes for your tent to securing a splint in case of a broken leg (*see Health and First-aid on page 506*).

- Carry salt in a bag in your pockets, if you are walking in **leech-infested areas** (*see Health and First-aid*)

- Don't think you can make it up that hill? Carry sweets, toffees and dry fruit in your pockets for quick **energy boosts**.

- Carry enough water for the day. Unless you know of springs, try and **avoid drinking untreated water** from mountain streams. In Kinnaur, I was in bliss, drinking water from sparkling mountain streams only to discover, as I climbed higher, that a number of villages had their bath houses on stilts directly over the same streams!

- One can use a few drops of chlorine or iodine (8 drops/ litre or Betadine 4 drops/ litre) to **purify water**, but along with microbes, both kill the taste of water as well. Pregnant women or those with thyroid problems should not use iodine.

- The best way to purify water is to boil some in the morning before starting the trek and then some again in the evening when you arrive at the camp. This should take care of the entire day and night's requirements. Heat kills micro-organisms at temperatures well below the boiling point. Don't waste your kerosene on boiling water for 10-20 minutes. Bringing it to a boil is good enough to kill all bugs.

- Carry some Betadine or iodine to purify water in an emergency, in case you start running short of fuel.

Porters in the kitchen tent

AHTUSHI DESHPANDE

CAMPING TIPS

- Always **check your stove** before you leave. If it's a new stove, try it out at home. Make some tea, porridge, khichdi and boil some water. See how much **fuel** it consumes and calculate how much you will need on the trip. No point

Young hikers learn to pitch a tent

carrying gallons of kerosene that you won't use, but do remember that the higher you go, the longer it takes for water to come to a boil and therefore, the greater will be the fuel consumption.

● Pack your **backpack** intelligently so that the weight is balanced vertically with heavier items on top. Pack heavy things towards the inner side of the backpack, closer to your body, so that the weight does not pull outwards. Keep sandals (if you have a river crossing that day) and other important items in the outer pockets.

● Try and camp in the **campsites** that we have recommended in the guide book. Avoid pitching camp in dry gullies, which may turn into raging torrents if the weather turns. Also, avoid camping under rock faces and cliffs that may have rock falls or avalanches.

● When **pitching a tent**, try and find a well-drained area, not likely to get waterlogged in case of a sudden shower. If you anticipate bad weather at night, dig a two- to three-inch drain around the tent with one end leading off a foot or two, preferably downslope.

● In case you are caught in a sudden thunderstorm, try and find **shelter**: an overhang of the mountain, a small cave, a large rock or tree. The idea is to stay dry, and in the Himalayas, to stay warm. Carry a sheet of plastic in areas likely to be wet. It should be large enough to go over the backpack to keep it dry as well.

● **Personal hygiene** is important on a trek. Men are lucky enough to jump into any mountain stream for a swim. Women should carry a sarong that they can slip into. This can be used as a cover to slip out of your trekking clothes. Find a bend in the river, away from prying eyes and bathe to your heart's content. In case it's too cold or the pace of the trek doesn't allow it, do what I do at the end of each day. After your tent is up, take a mug of warm water, a hand towel and some soap, and zip yourself in. Sponge yourself thoroughly, soaping your groin and armpits. Brush out dust from your hair. Then change into your nightclothes and a fresh pair of socks. You'll be amazed at how the day's fatigue leaves the body and just how refreshed you feel. ✦

TREKKING HOLIDAYS IN INDIA

AHTUSHI DESHPANDE

Iris blooms near a bubbling brook in the Beas Valley

Eco-trekking: Treading lightly

By Sonia Jabbar

Imagine, if in the course of a trek in a pristine part of the country, you dropped two toffee wrappers, your partner left a bit of toilet paper on the trail, your guide set up a campfire each night and your kids collected a small fossil or rock each. Suppose that particular trail attracts a hundred small groups every year, which behaved in exactly the same manner as your group. Now, suppose you returned after ten years, would you find the environs as pristine? Before you grumble to your friends about the devastation, remember two of the two thousand toffee wrappers littered on the track were yours. No matter how small the offence seems, it all adds up. Remember to leave nothing but your footprints.

TIPS TO FOLLOW ON YOUR TREK

● **Travel in groups** of not more than four. Larger groups make a larger mess. If in a large group, walk in a single file on the track rather than abreast to avoid trampling on flowers and ferns.

● **Don't make a noise.** The Great Indian Holiday often means a blaring tape player and lots of screaming and shouting. Remember, you left the city to experience something different. Listen to the wind and the rustling of leaves instead. Others on the trail will thank you.

● **Respect wildlife.** View birds and animals from a distance. Animals find quick movements and loud noises stressful. If you scare them by making a noise, they will tend to avoid that area, spoiling it for animal lovers.

● **Leave areas as you found them.** Camp, wherever possible, at campsites used by others instead of trying to clear the ground for a new campsite.

Trivia on India's biodiversity

- India occupies only 2.4 percent of the Earth's landmass but has over eight percent of the world's known wildlife.
- The Eastern Himalayas are endemic to 3,500 species of higher plants, 20 species of reptiles, 25 endemic species of amphibians and a rich fauna of insects.
- Of the eight species of turtles found in the world, India is home to five species.
- Among the 20,000 species of fishes known, more than 2,000 species are found in India.
- Of the 15,000 flowering plant species in India, over 4,500 are to be found in the Western Ghats.

Brahma kamals amidst alpine flowers

Different species found in India
- Algae 5,000 ● Bacteria 850
- Fungi 1,25,000 ● Molluscs 5,000
- Invertebrates 20,000 ● Insects 59,353
- Fishes 2,546 ● Amphibians 216
- Reptiles 484 ● Birds 1,232
- Mammals 417

Biodiversity is our national heritage and treasure, as valuable as the Taj Mahal. Because different species of plants and animals interact in complex ways to sustain life on earth, if we destroy biodiversity, we may destroy our planet. The Maldives, for example, suffered significantly less damage than other islands because its vast, protected coral reefs absorbed the impact of tsunamis. On the other hand, unchecked atmospheric pollution is giving rise to global warming, which in turn is causing glaciers to melt. Glaciers are the source of rivers. If they disappear, what happens to life on Earth?

- **Save the trees**. Make no open campfires and discourage others from doing so. Where water is heated by scarce firewood, use as little of it as possible. Choose kerosene or other fuel-efficient stoves.
- **Avoid carrying canned food** and leaving tins behind. Leave campsites clean and remember to take back all non-biodegradable litter to the road head/towns for proper disposal. Bury only biodegradable food waste.
- **Human waste disposal:** Insist that the trekking agent carry a toilet tent if you are in a large group. A dry pit toilet of at least eight inches should be dug, filled with soil and covered with rocks once you are ready to leave the campsite. If there are only a couple of you, then find a place at least 200 ft away from rivers and other water sources. Dig a six-inch deep hole (you can even use your pen-knife). Use water

ASHOK DILWALI

Snow trivia

If you looked across a snow-covered area in winter, where would you think the ground would be warmer: in open areas where the snow has blown away or beneath the snow? Believe it or not, it's warmer beneath the snow, which acts as insulation, protecting plants by keeping the temperature around 0°C.

rather than toilet paper to clean up. After you are done, cover it up with earth and stones. You can urinate anywhere as it has little impact on soil or vegetation.

● **Tampons and sanitary napkins:** Proper disposal of tampons and napkins requires that they be placed in plastic bags and taken out. Do not bury them because they don't decompose readily and animals may dig them up.

● **Do not use detergents and soaps** at streams and springs. Carry water away from the source to wash up. Better still, use mud from the river to clean pots and pans. Fallen leaves may be used as a scrub.

● **Do not pluck flowers**. Do not take away cuttings, seeds and roots of plants.

Can you guess how long it will take for these things to biodegrade?

Banana peel	3-4 weeks
Paper bag	1 month
Plastic bag	1 million years
Cotton rag	5 months
Woollen sock	1 year
Aluminium can	200-500 years
Leather shoe	40-50 years
Styrofoam cup	Eternity
Tin can	50-100 years
Wood	10-15 years

WITH INPUTS FROM MANDIP SINGH SOIN

Finding your way

By Sonia Jabbar

Nearly all treks described in this book are some distance away from civilisation. There are no road signs on the trail telling you where you have to go. In some areas such as Ladakh and Spiti, you may walk the whole day without coming across another human being. In such a situation, how do you find your way? Who do you ask for directions? What do you do when you see a fork in the trail? These may cause some consternation when you are walking. After all, the last thing you want on a holiday is to get lost in the middle of nowhere.

The first thing we recommend, especially for those new to trekking, is to hire a guide from your starting point. This will not only make your walk tension-free, but a good guide will also point out birds, animals and plants that you may miss out on, as well as enlighten you on local legend and lore, all of which will make your holiday deeply rewarding. But even if you get a guide, you should learn how to find your way. You are walking in the mountains and at the mercy of Mother Nature, and must be mentally prepared for all eventualities.

In the old days, before compasses, maps and fancy equipment, our wandering ancestors navigated over land and oceans armed only with the knowledge of the sun, stars and wind. They didn't do too badly, considering the vast distances that were covered and explored long before we were born. Before you run out and buy that fancy GPS for hundreds of dollars, hold on. You may not need it. Learn how to use this book and follow a few tips and you can be pretty sure you won't get lost in the wilderness.

• Read the trek carefully before you set out on holiday, especially the Day One, Day Two... sections which describe the trail. Look at the trekking map and try and form a mental picture of the trail.

• Make a photo-copy of the trek you are opting for and the map, put it in a zip-lock or plastic bag and keep it on you at all times during the trek for ready reference.

• Like all maps, the top of the page is north, the right side is east, the left side is west and the bottom of the page is south. If Day One starts at the top of the page and ends somewhere below the starting point on the left of the page, you are walking in a south-westerly direction. If Day Two continues a little below that point and then veers to the right of the page, you know you have to walk south for a bit before turning east. Remember, as you walk south, you will turn to your left to turn east.

• When speaking of a river, notice we advise you to walk on the 'left bank' or 'right bank'. These terms do not necessarily correspond to the left or right side of the valley. Always check whether you are walking up or downstream. If you are walking downstream, then the left bank corresponds to the left of the valley and the right bank to the right of the valley. However, if you are walking upstream on the left side of the valley, you are actually walking on the right bank of the river.

● Try and remember all the important features of each day. Ask yourself the following questions: Towards which general direction will I be walking today? What are the major features I will encounter (river, glacier, pass), so that I can use them as landmarks to get my bearings? We have tried to provide a lot of detail about the trail:

Illustrations by JAYACHANDRAN

landmarks and compass bearings. Study them carefully. If there is a river, you are supposed to encounter after walking an hour, and three hours later you still haven't hit it, I suggest you backtrack immediately and try again!

● You may be puzzled by our description of a day as long and tiring, whereas on the map it may look relatively shorter than the other days. This is because the maps are simplified and are not topographical maps showing you the contours of mountains. When you actually start walking, you may discover that the short distance on the map to the top of the pass may actually have a number of switchbacks, zigzagging across the mountain and adding to the distance and time. In mountainous regions, you also have what is known as 'dead ground'. This is ground located in dips in the land between you and a higher point in front of you, which you cannot see from where you are standing, and which adds enormously to distance and time. So, read the section for the day and don't just rely on the map.

● In most treks, the distance in kilometres is approximate as it's extremely difficult for the authorities to measure distances up and down narrow trails. The time given for each day is also an average, and is the measure of how long it took the author to walk it. You may be a stronger walker, in which case you may be able to complete a 7-hr walk in 5 to 6 hrs. Or you may end up taking 10 hrs to do the day because you stopped at a little mountain shrine and spent an hour trying to photograph a spotted forktail. You should time the first day of your hike to get a sense of your average walking speed, and whether you are walking faster or slower than the author of the trek, and plan the following days accordingly. If you know the 5-hr day was actually a 7-hr long one, make sure you start your trek early the next morning.

• Reading through the book, you will notice we have used compass bearings rather than directions: in most cases the text will say head 'north-west' rather than 'to the left'. This is because it's always assumed that the walk can be done from the opposite direction as well. In this case, if we followed the left/ right convention, you would be walking in the opposite direction and get hopelessly lost.

• Using a compass to navigate: A compass is an instrument that is able to detect the weak magnetic force generated by the spinning of the earth. There are different kinds of compasses available in the market to varying degrees of sophistication, but all of them indicate through the needle — that rests on a pivot — the direction north. Keep your compass flat on your upturned palm and let the needle come to rest. It will settle at the magnetic North Pole. Suppose it points directly in front of you, then, east will be to your right, west to your left and south behind you.

• If you don't have a compass, you can learn to navigate by the sun. This is how I like to find my way on a trek. Each morning, make a mental note of the point where the sun rises and mark that on your mental map as east. Suppose the point is towards a mountain range to your left and a little in front. Now, if the trail you are supposed to take goes a little towards that direction and then slowly starts turning right, you should know that you started out walking towards the east and then moved south-

wards. When you get into camp, mark the point where the sun sets and put it down in your mental map as west.

• Since India is located in the Northern Hemisphere, the sun resides in the southern sky. You can locate the north by looking at the mountains around you. If they are all bathed in sunshine in the middle of the day, then these are the south-facing slopes and north is on the other side. At noon, if the sun is in your face and your back is in shade, then you know you are facing south.

• At night, you can find which way is north by locating the North Star. This is a fun exercise to do, even if you're not lost in the darkness and even if you have a reliable guide. Locate the Big Dipper. The two stars at the edge of the cup opposite the handle will point towards the North Star, Polaris. The moon, too, is a useful navigational tool. Like the sun in the Northern Hemisphere, it resides in the southern sky, rising in the east and setting in the west.

Happy navigating! ✦

Capturing the trek
10 great photo tips
By Ashok Dilwali

Never underestimate the picture possibilities, so carry more film than you expect to use. Trekking trips will take you to remote, sparsely populated areas, where there are no shops to replenish film stock. The film should be fresh and if you can, try a test process before you leave, especially if it's a film you haven't used before.

● Before your trip, check your camera to make sure everything is working smoothly: the shutter mechanism, aperture diaphragm in your lenses and the exposure meters. Never borrow cameras from friends. If you do, check their functions before the trek. Taking chances with untried equipment can lead to bad pictures. A sound knowledge of your equipment is a must. You have to know what it can and cannot do for you. One of the great photographers of India, the late Mitter Bedi, carried his Hasselblad manual with him even when he was at the peak of his career. He always said one needed to know one's camera intimately for its strengths and weaknesses.

Photographs by ASHOK DILWALI

Looking up the Bhilangana Valley

*L*ife is one

Incredible Journey...

**The Bandarpoonch massif dominates the landscape between
Gangotri and Har-ki-Dun Valley**

● Develop the habit of studying other people's photographs. A discerning eye should be cultivated to be able to analyse good photography. Today, innumerable websites on the Internet offer you a chance to look at other people's work. Check out travel photography sites and magazines. Before heading for a particular destination, try and see how that place has been shot and what new possibilities you can explore. Study the existing material before you actually get there. A good photograph gives just the right 'juice' or the 'inspiration' to go out there and do good work.

● Equipment tends to feel heavier and heavier with each passing minute, so carry the bare minimum you are sure you will use. I always try and hire a porter for my two camera bags but often find that when I need a special lens at a crucial moment, the porter is a km or two behind or ahead! Wear a camera jacket or a jacket with several pockets for film and filters. A small umbrella or a polythene rain protection sheet will prove useful in sudden showers. Try and carry a light tripod. They can improve your pictures in two ways. First, they stabilise the image, so that you can use a smaller aperture, giving you a greater depth of field. Second, you may get better compositions with the camera resting steadily on a tripod.

● Every lens should have a UV filter, especially in the mountains, where the air is rarefied and the UV rays are stronger. This filter also doubles as a protection against dust and accidental knocks against hard surfaces. A polarising filter will make the sky look an attractive deep blue. But you should only use one when the sun is on your left or right and not behind you. Avoid gimmicky filters.

● Try and avoid the typical "Yes, we were there" kind of pictures. Nothing can be duller for your friends! Look for new angles when shooting landscape. Try and capture people unawares instead of making them pose in front of the waterfall, snow peak or temple. A photograph should "say" something. A plain and simple shot does not convey much. A successful image is one that "holds" your attention, or else it's nothing but a dull statement. Never be scared or shy of experimenting with imagery. It invariably turns out to be a learning experience.

● Try and shoot early in the morning or late in the afternoon. The best pictures happen when the low angles of light create shadows, which lend 'depth' to an image. For early morning pictures, be prepared to leave the warmth and comfort of your sleeping bag and brave the early morning chill.

● Mountains often present problems of contrast that film simply cannot deal with. A typical scene may have snow peaks and bright skies with dark rocks or forests underneath. Both elements need different exposures and the contrast ratio may be higher than what the films permit. Choose what is more important and set the exposure accordingly. Two aids that can help to sort out contrast are the Gradual Neutral Density Filter (which is a pain to use) and Photoshop software on a computer, which can be used later to darken areas at the base. Always bracket your exposures. If, for example, you are getting a reading of f11/ 250, also shoot the same frame using one stop under (f16/ 250) and one stop over (f8/ 250). The world's best photographers also bracket for the best possible exposure. Film is the cheapest thing on an outing.

● Predicting weather in the hills is difficult business. What is certain is that good weather will be followed by bad and vice-versa. Instead of just waiting for good weather, try experimenting. Storms, clouds and rain present photo opportunities of a different kind. The play of light and the elemental forces in the mountains can end up making the most memorable images.

● Keep a record of everything you shoot and make notes of what you did. After processing, you should check what you did and try to figure out how it can be improved in similar circumstances in the future. ✦

NORTH

N

S

Graphic by RAZA KHAN

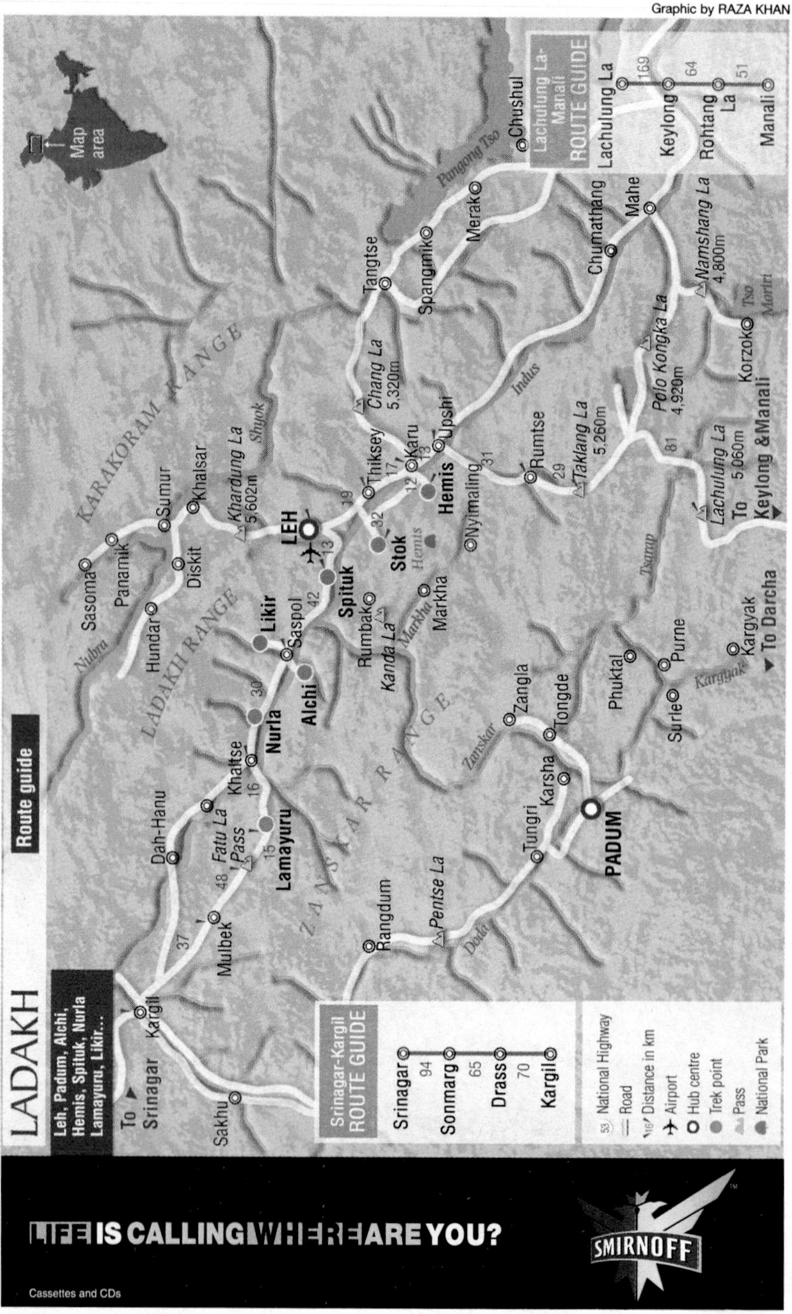

Map area

LADAKH

Leh, Padum, Alchi, Hemis, Spituk, Nurla Lamayuru, Likir...

Route guide

Chushul

Punong Tso

Merak

Spangmik

Mahe

Chumathang

KARAKORAM RANGE

Sasoma

Panamik

Sumur

Khalsar

Diskit

Hundar

Nubra

Shyok

Khardung La
5,602m

LEH

Chang La
5,320m

Thiksey

Karu

Upshi

Hemis

Rumtse

Taklang La
5,260m

Namshang La
4,800m

Tso Moriri

Korzok

Polo Kongka La
4,920m

Lachulung La
5,060m
To
Keylong &Manali

Tangtse

Indus

Nyimaling

LADAKHI RANGE

Likir

Saspol

Spituk

Stok

Rumbak

Kanda La

Markha

Hemis

Marcha

Nurla

Alchi

Zangla

Zanskar

Tongde

Phuktal

Purne

Kargyak

To Darcha

Kargyak

Surle

Dah-Hanu

Khaltse

Fatu La
Pass

Lamayuru

Z A N S K A R   R A N G E

Tungri

Karsha

PADUM

Rangdum

Pentse La

Doda

Mulbek

Kargil

Sakhu

To
Srinagar

53 National Highway
— Road
Distance in km
✈ Airport
O Hub centre
▲ Trek point
Pass
National Park

TRIBHUVAN TIWARI

The view from Leh Palace

This could be Tibet. The vast land, dry and desiccated, swells and billows into great tiers of snow-crested peaks. Arching over it is a sky, pure blue, benign, sheltering. The Indus bisects the floor of the valley. In summer, it is a sullen grey, silt-laden, sometimes turning to violet. In autumn, it is at its most graceful: turquoise and aquamarine waters weaving through golden banks of tall poplars and tumbling willows. Crumbling old monasteries that are perched on rocky promontories command the barren, empty vistas. Dominating Leh from its vantage on the northern crag is the Leh Palace, a diminutive Potala. In the late afternoon, the wind picks up, riffling the prayer flags, carrying snatches of the deeply-intoned homage to Manjushri.

Being in Leh is a real treat, especially when returning from trekking in a remote area. This 17th century capital of the Namgyal Empire is the epicentre of Ladakh. The mountains, snow-capped peaks and fortress-like monasteries provide a dramatic backdrop to the many roadside cafes, restaurants, beer bars, carpet and curio shops, and trekking and rafting agencies. Monks, Ladakhi traders and Tibetan refugees jostle with tourists from all corners of the globe in the small but colourful bazaar, giving Leh the bustling yet laid-back air of Kathmandu of the seventies.

Ladakh is full of trails that connect remote villages spread across ancient trade routes, and there is no better way to absorb this fascinating land and its culture than to trek through it. But remember, even the 'easy' treks of Ladakh and Zanskar are difficult as all of them start at over 4,800m, and many have passes over 3,000m. A successful trek in Ladakh requires you to acclimatise well. Spend a few days in Leh, go for gentle walks and get used to the altitude before you set out on your trek.

MUST-VISITS
LEH PALACE
The imposing nine-storey Palace of Sengye 'Lion' Namgyal dominates the city. Explore its dark passages, making

SONIA JABBAR

Celebrations at a Ladakh festival

your way to the top floors to get a brilliant view of the Indus Valley. Further up beyond the palace is the **Tsemo Gompa**.

SHEY (14 KM E)
The old capital of the Ladakhi kings, it is a pretty spot with numerous chortens and graceful willows that dip their leaves into a pleasant artificial lake. There are extensive remains of a fortress on the hill and a palace, incorporated into which is a temple with a handsome copper and gold Shakyamuni Buddha. Some 300m away is the **Thiksey Monastery**, which houses a huge three-storey Maitreya Buddha.

LAMAYURU (120 KM W)
On the spectacularly beautiful Leh-Kargil Road lies the earliest surviving monastery of Ladakh, known as Yung-drung, or the Swastika. Its site, perched on a rocky promontory high above the Lamayuru Village at the bottom of the valley, is said to have been chosen by the Kashmiri yogi Naropa in early 11th century.

ALCHI (68 KM W)
The most celebrated of the monasteries associated with the Tibetan Translator, Rinchen Zangpo, is one that fell into disuse, probably around the 16th century. Sitting on the high southern

bank of the Indus, in a lush, quiet oasis across the road from Saspol is the ancient centre of learning, **Alchi Choskhor** (a religious enclave). One can happily spend the whole day, if not a few, studying the frescoes and loafing under its verdant apricot trees.

RAFTING ON THE INDUS
Choose a sunny morning to spend floating down the Indus **between Phey and Nimoo**. The rapids provide mild thrills to an otherwise relaxing day. Bookings can be made from one of the many adventure agencies in Leh Bazaar (see *Trekking Agencies Listings on page 514*). Combine it with a picnic lunch and a trip to Alchi.

THE HIGH-ALTITUDE LAKES
Set like sapphires in the otherwise dry, barren landscapes are the two beautiful high-altitude lakes of **Tso Moriri** and **Pangong Tso**. Home to many birds and animals, both require Inner Line Permits (see *Leh Facts alongside*) and 2-day jeep journeys to get there and back.

NUBRA VALLEY
To the north-east of Leh, across the **Khardung Pass**, lies the Nubra Valley nestled between the tall Saltoro and Karakorum ranges. This was the ancient trade route between North India and the Central Asian cities of **Yarkand** and **Khotan**, which existed until 1949, when Communist rule in the Central Asian lands put an end to it. Dominated by sand dunes, Bactrian camels, wild roses and hot springs at **Panamik**, Nubra is truly worth a visit.

WHERE TO STAY
Leh abounds with places to stay, with almost every second house being converted into a guest house. Tariffs range from Rs 300-3,000.

Among the high-end options is WelcomHeritage's **Shambha-La** (Delhi Tel: 011-26561875, 26850438; Tariff: Rs 2,100-2,800 including meals), with its heated rooms and lovely views.

Hotel Lharimo (Tel: 01982-253345; Tariff: Rs 1,365-2,350) on the Fort Road has a restaurant and beer bar. **Hotel Dreamland** (Tel: 252089, 250606; Tariff: Rs 450-850), located on Fort Road amidst a quiet courtyard, has a helpful travel desk. **Oriental Guest House** (Tel: 253153; Tariff: Rs 100-600) offers personalised hospitality, and excellent food for breakfast and dinner. *For more hotels and details, see Accommodation Listings on page 531*

WHERE TO EAT

The Leh area has restaurants, cafés and bakeries catering to all budgets, that run the entire range of cuisines from authentic Tibetan fare (as an outcome of a large refugee population) to European to Kashmiri to Israeli. **Tibetan Kitchen** (momos and thukpas) on Fort Road and **Amdo Café** (spring rolls, fried noodles and fried rice) at the Main Market are two of the best places to gorge on Tibetan and Chinese dim sum delicacies. You'll also find a profusion of Continental and Mughlai eateries in Leh. Chefs at **Dreamland Restaurant, Summer Harvest** or **Hotel Ibex** (on Fort Road) can dish out everything from sandwiches to aromatic biryanis. For authentic Kashmiri, there is the rista at **Budshah Inn** near the Jama Masjid.

Views from the Shanti Stupa
RAJESH THAKUR

→ Leh Facts

● **LOCATION** In the heart of the cold desert expanse of Ladakh, in the trans-Himalayan eastern region of Jammu and Kashmir, at 11,500 ft (3,505m)
● **GETTING TO LEH By air** From Delhi (Jet Airways daily), Chandigarh, Srinagar and Jammu by Indian Airlines and Alliance Air **By rail** Nearest railhead: Jammu Tawi (680 km). Proceed on NH1A to Srinagar by bus (10-12 hrs, Rs 250) or shared taxi (8 hrs, Rs 350 per head). From Srinagar, Leh is a scenic 434-km drive, which takes 2 days by bus (Rs 515) or taxi (full Rs 7,500; shared Rs 1,500 approx) via Kargil (night halt) **By road** Ladakh is connected to Delhi by two routes — via Srinagar-Zoji La Pass, and via Manali-Rohtang Pass-Baralacha La. Both the routes are open between June and October. Both drives, though long and punishing, are arguably the most beautiful road experiences. Carry extra fuel as there are few petrol pumps for the better part of the way. Himachal Roadways, J&K Roadways and HPTDC operate buses early morning from Manali (473 km; 2-day drive with halts at Sarchu and Pang; shared taxi Rs 1,800) during the season. HPTDC runs a direct Delhi-Leh bus via Manali (3-day drive; Rs 1,500)
● **STD CODE** 01982
● **PERMITS** For visits to the 'Inner Line' areas of Nubra Valley, Pangong-Tso and Tso-Moriri, permits must be acquired from the Collector's Office in Leh, situated at the far side of the Polo Ground. Easy to get, these week-long permits can also be organised by local operators for Rs 50. Carry at least 5 photocopies of the permit, which have to be deposited at checkpoints en route
● **TOURIST OFFICES** ● J&K Tourism, Leh. Tel: 01982-252297, 252094 ● J&K Tourism, Kargil. Tel: 01985-232721, 232266

Most restaurants have multi-lingual menu cards! You could cool off with a beer in almost all the restaurants. For those who avoid alcohol, there is the great Seabuckthorn (locally called Tse-Tse Leh berry) juice. Rich in Vitamin C, it is produced by a local women's co-operative and makes for a great thirst quencher. If you are adventurous, you can ask your hotel to arrange for some *chhang*, the local rice beer.

INPUTS FROM SONIA JABBAR

Spituk Monastery stands proudly against the stark backdrop of the Indus Valley

RUPIN DANG/ WILDERNESS FILMS

Spituk to Stok
Exploring the Hemis National Park

By Sonia Jabbar

SPITUK-ZINGCHAN-RUMBAK-STOK LA-
CAMPSITE-STOK

TIME	4-5 days
LEVEL	Moderate
IDEAL SEASON	Mid-Jun to late Sep
LOCATION	South-west of Leh

In 2002, while I was covering the Kashmir Assembly elections, I had five days between two phases. Instead of just squandering them in Srinagar, I felt they would be better spent clambering up mountains in Ladakh. My friend Javeed, who runs Dreamland Treks and Travel, suggested I try the Spituk-Stok 'baby trek'. But I realised later that there are no baby treks in Ladakh, even if you're travelling club class, sahib-style, accompanied by guides and ponymen.

I had always been snooty about the big 'bandobast' that happens around treks in Ladakh, having walked alpine-style in the past without any fuss. But I was to be pleasantly surprised. My guide was a young Ladakhi lad, and the ponyman an old, retired Tibetan drunk. Together they made a great team and I must confess it was lovely to be woken up with bed tea and have the luxury of camp set up at the end of the day, replete with evening tea and pakoras.

I saw plenty of birds and wildlife on the short walk and hadn't realised until then quite how wonderful the Hemis National Park (covering 4,400 sq km) was. The other thing that had escaped my notice until much later was the Himalayan Homestays experience. This programme, supported by UNESCO, is essentially designed to protect the snow leopard. The Himalayan Homestays generates additional income for locals from trekkers and tourists, which helps to compensate for the loss of livestock killed by snow leopards and other predators. With income from tourism that highlights wildlife viewing, local

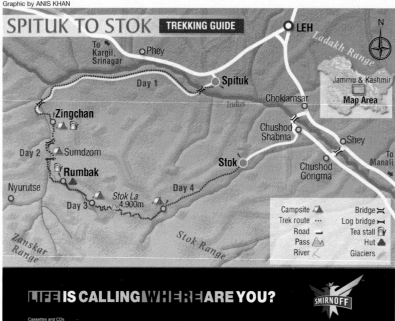

Graphic by ANIS KHAN

SPITUK TO STOK — TREKKING GUIDE

GETTING THERE AND OUT

FROM LEH to Spituk, it's 8 km/ 20 mins by 🚕 (Rs 180) or half an hour by 🚌 (Rs 10). Buses ply between 7.30 am and 9 pm. You can also ask the taxi to drop you beyond Spituk Pharka Village at the point opposite **Phey Village** (12 km/ 40 mins/ Rs 280), which is on the other side of the Indus. Or catch the 8 am bus (runs only on Mondays and Saturdays) to Phey Village **RETURN** Get picked up at **Stok** (17 km/ $^1/_2$ hr/ taxi Rs 750) for Leh via a trip to **Stok Palace**. Or catch a bus to Leh (Rs 10). Only two buses daily at 9.30 am and 6.30 pm

people have a reason to conserve the snow leopard, rather than kill them.

For a small fee you can stay in clean rooms with a Ladakhi family on this route and explore the Hemis National Park accompanied by trained nature guides who will draw your attention to plants and flowers, birds and animals. Who knows, you may even get lucky with a sighting of the elusive snow leopard.

For further details on the Ladakh homestays programme check out himalayan-homestays.com. Also see *Himalayan Homestay Facts on page 47.*

DAY ONE
SPITUK-ZINGCHAN
TIME 4-6 HOURS
LEVEL MODERATE-EASY

The trek traditionally starts at the bridge over the **Indus** about a kilometre west of **Spituk Village**. However, a jeepable road slated to connect Spituk runs nearly all the way to

45

SONIA JABBAR

Autumn colours enliven the trail near Rumbak

Zingchan and if you get your taxi to drop you 7 km down the road to the point opposite **Phey Village**, you can skip the 2-hr long hot walk over unchanging scree-filled landscape (particularly after the **Spituk Pharka Village**). From this point, it is a pleasant walk along the descending road in a south-westerly direction along the Indus, on your right, until you arrive at a fork where a swift flowing stream joins the Indus from the left. Walk into the valley due south, across the bridge, which can be a pleasant resting point. A walk of a couple more kilometres will bring you to a road sign: 'Jhingchan to Rumbak Road 1.00 km'. Look out for the log bridge here — nothing more than a few poplars lashed together — which often gets washed away. If there is no bridge you will have to ford the thigh-deep stream. After crossing the stream, find the path heading south-east which climbs suddenly onto the hillside to **Zingchan Village**.

There are two campsites here — one just before you climb up and one past the village down by the stream called the **Daisy Campsite**. I preferred to walk a little further for an hour, crossing the stream once more on a bridge, past a **Forest Checkpoint** with a sign welcoming you to **Hemis National Park**. Continue up the well-defined path, crossing the nallah at least four times before you arrive at **Sumdzom**, marked by a stone chorten with prayer flags and a grove of willows and wild roses. There are good camping options here.
♦**Entry fee to Hemis National Park** Rs 20 per person per day

DAY TWO
ZINGCHAN-RUMBAK
TIME 4-5 HOURS
LEVEL MODERATE
From Sumdzom walk upstream on the left side (true right bank) crossing the stream twice over sturdy wooden bridges. Then climb steadily uphill as the path moves due south-east until it

Wild roses

Found in the Western Himalayas from Pakistan to Nepal on rocky slopes in arid areas at 1,500-4,100m, the wild rose (*Rosa webbiana*) is a deciduous shrub. The plant can grow to a height of 2m. It flowers in June and the seeds ripen from August to October. The flowers are hermaphrodite (have both male and female organs) and are pollinated by bees.

The fruit is up to 25 mm in diameter, but with only a thin layer of flesh around the seeds. This may be eaten raw or cooked. Care must be taken while eating, as there is a layer of hairs around the seeds just beneath the flesh of the fruit. These hairs can cause irritation to the mouth and digestive tract if ingested.

The seed is a good source of Vitamin E and can be ground into a powder and mixed with flour or added to other foods as a supplement. Watch out for the seed hairs again! The fruit of many members of this genus is a very rich source of

OTTO PFISTER

vitamins and minerals, especially in Vitamins A, C and E, flavanoids and other bio-active compounds. It is also a fairly good source of essential fatty acids, which is quite unusual for a fruit. The wild rose is being investigated as a food that is capable of reducing the incidence of cancer and also as a means of halting or reversing the growth of cancers.

comes out of the narrow gorge into a broad valley which serves as a junction. Straight in front is the **Kandala Nallah**, along which there is a path leading to high pastures. On your left or north is the path that leads up to Rumbak Village past a tea-stall. And up ahead, crossing the nallah and to the right is the path leading to **Nyurutse** and the **Kandala Base Camp**.

Rest a while at the tea-stall. You may want to photograph the plentiful wild flowers, especially straight ahead along the Kandala Nallah.

Walk up past the tea-stall heading east into the broad valley. The first fields and houses of **Rumbak Village** appear fairly soon. If you have booked a homestay at Rumbak then, head over to your lodge and spend the next couple of days exploring the **Hemis**

→ **Himalayan Homestay Facts**

● **Overland Escape** is the designated Homestay Coordinator in Leh, Ladakh
Contact: Tundup Dorjee, Raku Complex, Fort Road, Leh-194101. Telefax: 01982-250858; Email: overland@sancharnet.in

● **Homestay Booking Agent**
Snow Leopard Trails, Hotel Khanglachen Complex, Leh-194101
Tel: 01982-252074, 252355
Email: leopard@nda.vsnl.net.in

National Park. If you are continuing on the trek, I would suggest camping ahead, closer to the **Stok Pass**. Walk up the valley climbing a gentle gradient for about 1$^1/_2$ hrs and then climb steeply up onto the plateau on your left. You will find a flat campsite where you can spend the

Bharal or blue sheep

The female of this species live with their young in large herds of 15-200. The males range in smaller groups of four to five. Measuring 80-90 cm at the shoulder and weighing 40-70 kg, the bharals (*Pseudois nayour*) live in slate-blue shale country and have coats to match, so they can be difficult to spot, but for their white legs and bellies. In summer, their coat becomes red-brown, while adult rams are dark brown with smooth curving horns. The bharal lives in crags and cliffs and forages in alpine meadows. It is a shy creature and when it feels threatened makes a squirrel-like "chirr-itt" alarm call.

OTTO PFISTER

night. I had a surprise visit by a couple of friendly shepherds with their big mastiffs, who appreciated the dinner I shared with them.

DAY THREE
RUMBAK-STOK LA-CAMPSITE
TIME 4-5 HOURS
LEVEL TOUGH

Today is a difficult day on the trek, as you will ascend the 4,900-m Stok Pass also known as the Namlung La. If you are fit and have camped at the plateau just under the pass as I did, you should have no problem climbing up to the pass. I climbed steadily and made it in less than $1^1/_2$ hrs. From the campsite walk up east for 10 mins and on your right you will find a path zig-zagging up the mountain. At first it looks quite steep. Don't worry. It soon crosses over the cleft to the left and heads up east at a less troubling gradient all the way to the pass.

The **Stok La** is marked by prayer flags and has excellent views to the north and south. But it is quite windy. When I was there in early October it was freezing cold and all plans to hang out and brew a cup of tea were quickly abandoned. We went sharply down the track leading north-east down the mountain. The track is in poor repair and crumbling in parts, so be careful as you descend into an arid valley. Soon you will follow a swiftly flowing stream on its left bank as the path broadens. There are stunning rock formations on your left and right.

⚠ There are quite a few campsites just $2-2^1/_2$ hrs from the top of the pass once the valley turns northwards and broadens. Take your pick and settle for the evening.

DAY FOUR
CAMPSITE-STOK
TIME 4 HOURS
LEVEL EASY

Today is an easy day going downhill all the way. Follow the stream on its left bank as it heads north. The path is broad and easy. You will find willows and wild roses growing on islands in the middle of the stream which grows quite wide as you approach **Stok**.

Visit the **Stok Palace**, residence of the king of Ladakh after he was deposed by General Zorawar Singh of Jammu in 1842. The Stok Palace has an interesting museum with ancient war implements and old thangkas. ✦

Likir to Temisgam
Ladakh's baby trek

By Sonia Jabbar

TIME	4 days
LEVEL	Easy
IDEAL SEASON	Late May and late Sep
LOCATION	West of Leh in the Sham area

Photographs by SONIA JABBAR

Heading downhill from Phobe La

LIKIR-YANGTHANG-HEMIS SHUKPACHEN-ANG-
TEMISGAM-NURLA

You won't find an easier trek than this in Ladakh. The passes are all below 4,000m, and the distances between places are relatively short. Plus, there is the added bonus of the Himalayan Homestays Programme (*see page 47*), offering accommodation in village homes, which means you don't have to lug tents and equipment all the way. This is also probably the only trek in Ladakh one can safely do alpine-style, without porters and guides. But on the other hand, you could also make this a safe adventure holiday for the entire family, with smaller children having the exciting option of riding on ponies. Ask your trekking agency about this option.

The Sham area of Ladakh is quite dry and hot and although you can trek this route anytime from the beginning to end of Ladakh's tourist season (late May-late September), I would suggest planning it either during the beginning or towards the end to avoid the hotter middle months.

When I trekked this route in the late nineties, the link road from Likir to Temisgam was just being built. Today, it is a full-fledged 'pucca' road, albeit with little traffic. So much of the journey can be done comfortably following the road all the way except on Day Three between Hemis Shukpachen and Ang. Of course, you can take brief excursions on the short-cut tracks made by the villagers throughout the trek.

Since it takes only an hour and a half from Leh, set out for Likir after lunch and visit the Likir Monastery and either pitch a 🛖 tent in the campsite under the monastery for the night or try the ⛺ **Gyabcho Guest House**. It has a pleasant garden and rooms with attached baths.

Founded between the 12th and 13th centuries, the Likir Gompa was first associated with the Kadampa order of Tibetan Buddhism. In the 15th century, it was taken over by the

Graphic by ANIS KHAN

LIKIR TO TEMISGAM   TREKKING GUIDE

newest Tibetan school, the Gelugpa (Yellow Hats) and today belongs to the Dalai Lama's younger brother, Ngari Rinpoche. The present monastery was built after a fire destroyed the older one in the 18th century. The main du-khang houses the scriptures and has nothing out of the ordinary. A smaller du-khang has a small puja room upstairs, near the private apartment of the head lama. In this room are a number of beautiful images framed in elaborate wooden carvings, as well as some magnificent thangkas, both old and new.

DAY ONE
LIKIR-PHOBE LA-CHAGATSE LA-YANGTHANG
DISTANCE 9 KM **TIME** 4-5 HOURS
LEVEL MODERATE
Although the distance today is short, the route is hot, without any shade or water and you must traverse two passes, so start early with water bottles

GETTING THERE AND OUT

FROM LEH to Likir, it's 60 km/ 1¹/₂ hrs by 🚕 (Rs 775) or 2 hrs by 🚌 (Rs 40). There are a number of buses between 5.30 am and 3.30 pm **RETURN** Get picked up at **Nurla** (80 km/ 2 hrs) and either return to Leh by taxi (return fare Rs 1,600) or by local bus (Rs 52/ 3 hrs) at 8 am **TIP** Book your taxi in Leh as none available in Nurla, unless you get lucky

filled. For Ladakh, these passes are low, but do not underestimate them. I huffed and puffed all the way with a 15-kg backpack, ran out of water and

Dawn breaks over Hemis Shukpachen, a pretty Ladakhi village

had to struggle up the **Chagatse La** (3,630,m). It was not very pleasant!

From Likir, take the road heading west up to **Phobe La** (3,580m). The climb is gentle and you will top the pass in an hour. From the pass, you can scramble down the short-cut tracks and meet up with the road below, avoiding the longer loops of the jeep road. The road continues west to Sumdo, a small settlement where you can stop for 🍵 tea. Just before Sumdo, you will need to cross the stream over a bridge.

From Sumdo, follow the main road that climbs steadily upwards, winding its way to the west for a little over an hour. From Chagatse La it is another 30 mins down. The village of **Yangthang** (3,630,m) is on your left

Collecting valuable fodder for winter

through the fields. ⛺ The camping area is near the main stream, but why don't you try one of the 🏠 Ladakhi homes for the night.

If you reach early and have the energy, check out the **Ridzong Monastery**, which lies about an hour south of Yangthang. This quiet, secluded gompa is over a hundred years old and nestles in a narrow gorge.

DAY 2

YANGTHANG-TSERMANGCHEN LA-HEMIS SHUKPACHEN
DISTANCE 8 KM **TIME** 2-3 HOURS
LEVEL EASY

Today is an easy walk despite the pass because both the approach and the descent are of gentle gradients. From Yangthang Village, head back through the fields onto the road that brought you here and turn left, or west. The road heads north, descending for a bit, crossing a stream before climbing up west again to Tsermangchen La (3,750m). Take a break at the pass before heading down to **Hemis Shukpachen**. The village, named after the grove of cedars (*shukpa* in Ladakhi) is one of Ladakh's prettiest. There are plenty of sparkling streams surrounded by shady willows and large barley fields that add the much

51

Royle's pika

OTTO PFISTER

Besides the cute marmots you see peeking up from burrows in the ground, you see another adorable creature on this trek: Royle's pika (*Ochotona roylei*). The pika is also known as the 'whistling hare' due to its high-pitched warning cry.

This is the most common pika of the Himalayas, found from Ladakh to Kumaon in altitudes between 2,400 and 4,300m. This mammal resembles a large guinea pig and has a rufous grey body, chestnut head and shoulders and upper back. It also has a reddish-purple throat and light to dark grey underparts.

It does not make its own burrows but uses existing burrows, and is active at dusk and dawn. Because it cannot hibernate, fresh grass is collected for storage and becomes hay, providing warm bedding and food. It is not uncommon for pikas to steal hay from other dens; the resulting disputes are usually exploited by neighbouring predators like ferrets and large birds.

needed dash of green to the otherwise desolate, rocky mountains.

🏠 ⛺ Book your stay with the **Himalayan Homestays** *(see page 47)* or camp out near one of the brooks.

DAY THREE
HEMIS SHUKPACHEN-MEBTAK LA-ANG
DISTANCE 10 KM **TIME** 3 HOURS
LEVEL EASY

Again a fairly easy day if you don't lose your way as I did. I set off in a splendid mood early in the morning, following a small irrigation stream due west and saw a track going steeply up the hill to the left. I assumed this was the path and still whistling off tune, climbed and climbed right to the top, where the track simply disappeared! It took me a while to realise that this was the local high pasture, that the track was a mere goat-track and that I should give up and head right back. From the top I was able to see the real track, rather wide, which moved between two hillocks west of the village, past the old **chortens**. Follow this track (there is no road as yet between Hemis Shukpachen and Ang) moving west-north-west through a rather ravaged landscape, until it veers south and climbs steeply up to the **Mebtak La** (3,750m), marked by prayer flags. From the pass head down the gorge to **Ang**, a charming village with apricot orchards.

🏠 ⛺ Choose between the comfort of a **Himalayan Homestay** or camping out.

DAY FOUR
ANG-TEMISGAM-NURLA
DISTANCE 8 KM **TIME** 3 HOURS
LEVEL EASY

Today is the last day and very easy as it's downhill all the way on the main road. You will probably meet up with lots of villagers from **Temisgam** heading to **Nurla** on the main highway to catch a bus to Leh. If you don't feel like walking all the way to Nurla, you may even ask your trekking agency (or the Leh Taxi Stand) for a taxi pick-up at Temisgam or hop onto a local bus or truck. ✦

Lamayuru to Alchi
Among the ancient monasteries

By Dawa Tsering

The mountains around Lamayuru at dusk

TIME	5-6 days
LEVEL	Moderate to Tough
IDEAL SEASON	Mid-Jun to late Sep
LOCATION	West of Leh, moving west to east

Speed
High Performance Petrol

Bharat Petroleum

LAMAYURU-WANLA-HINJU-SUMDHA CHENMO-SUMDHA CHUN-STAKSPI LA-ALCHI

I am a Ladakhi. As a young boy I used to accompany the sheep from our lands in Chilling to the grazing pastures on the Lamayuru-Alchi route. That's how I got to know these tracks so well. Later, I literally decided to cash in on this experience by guiding hikers on this and many other treks in Ladakh. On this route there are three passes (*las*) to cross. There are *las* to the left and right of every part of this trek. One understands why Ladakh could have had no other name but this one, La-tags, meaning land of many high passes.

Lamayuru has a camping ground below the awesome escarpment on

GETTING THERE AND OUT

FROM LEH to Lamayuru, it's 125 km/ 6 hrs by 🚙 (Rs 2,500). Or catch the daily Leh-Srinagar (5 am) or Leh-Kargil (5.30 am) 🚌 (Rs 100-200) for Lamayuru. You can even negotiate a ride on the many trucks that run between Leh and Kargil (Rs 100-200 is reasonable). There are two roads from **Khaltse** to Lamayuru on the Indus. Use the **Wanla Gorge route** as that is impressive

RETURN Get picked up at **Alchi**, take a taxi (return fare Rs 1,500) or a bus (Rs 32) to Leh (67 km/ 2-2¹/₂ hrs). You can also take a taxi (Rs 3,200) to **Kargil** (163 km), from where one can carry on to **Srinagar** (367 km)

Lamayuru: Thirsting for knowledge

Nearly 120 km west of Leh, on a spectacularly beautiful road, lies the earliest surviving monastery of Ladakh, known as **Yung-drung**, or the Swastika. Its site, on a rocky promontory high above the village at the bottom of the valley, is said to have been chosen by the Kashmiri yogi, Naropa, in the early 11th century. Later, the monastery was expanded and embellished by Rinchen Zangpo. Naropa, a great scholar and debater at the Nalanda University, suddenly realised that all his knowledge was merely theoretical. He left the university and wandered alone in search of his guru, whom he believed to be Tilopa, one of the 84 Mahasiddhas.

What he saw when he finally found him did little to inspire confidence: the mad, bedraggled yogi was frying a fish for his dinner, which would have probably been acceptable to the devout Buddhist pundit, had the fish not been alive! Scandalised by this behaviour, the would-be disciple attempted to beat a hasty retreat, when a scornful Tilopa

snapped his fingers, upon which the fish returned unharmed to the lake. Having successfully demonstrated the illusory nature of the universe, Tilopa shooed the awed pundit away. But Naropa's entreaties prevailed and he lived and practised with his master for 12 years before becoming adept in tantra himself. He wrote the famous treatise, *The Six Yogas of Naropa*, and became the guru of the Tibetan yogi, Marpa, who in turn taught Tibet's most celebrated yogi, Milarepa, who in turn taught Gampopa, the adept who established the Kagyu School of Tibetan Buddhism.

Although the interior of the main temple, the du-khang of Yung-drung, is somewhat less dramatic than many other monasteries, one feature makes the visit worthwhile. Ask the monk on duty to show you **Naropa's Cave**. The mouth of the cave is behind a glass wall, but it is still thrilling to flash a torchlight and catch a glimpse of the place where the great soul meditated.

The oldest part of the complex is below the du-khang and is in disrepair. Ask a local to show you the way or you may get lost in the narrow dark alleys. On entering the temple, you may be surprised to see a life-sized image of Vairochana Buddha. This image was worshipped extensively during the life of the translator, Rinchen Zangpo. The other Dhyani Buddhas occupy subordinate positions. There are murals of mandalas and tantric deities, worn by the passage of time. The carved doorway is somewhat like the ones at Alchi. The monastery belongs to a sub-sect of the Kagyu school, the Drikung Kagyu.

SONIA JABBAR

PRASHANT PANJIAR

A pensive monk at the ancient monastery of Lamayuru

which perch the huge 11th century monastery and its guest house. There are several guest houses (book through your Leh agent) and restaurants in Lamayuru; visitors and trekkers pass this way even in November. The yellow loess formations around Lamayuru are most impressive and part of the route takes you past them. At the other end of the trek lies the 11th century temple complex of Alchi. Do spend time here to enjoy the ancient, magnificent frescoes. If no buses or taxis are available at Alchi, walk to Saspol on the other side of the Indus, across a silver-painted girder bridge.

LAMAYURU TO ALCHI   TREKKING GUIDE

To Srinagar
Atitise
Khaltse
Indus
Nurla
Ladakh Range
Lamayuru
Lamayuru
Sumdo
Likir
Saspola
Jammu & Kashmir
Map Area
Day 1
Wanla
Alchi
3,150m
Basgo
Nimmu
Pritikingi La
3,506m
Shilakong
Shilla
Panji La
3,400m
Day 2
Hinju
Day 5
Indus
Stakspi La
4,950m
Zanskar
To Padum
Ripchar
Day 3
Sumdha Chu
Kongske La
4,900m
Sumdha Chun
To Leh

Campsite ⛺	Bridge ✕
Trek route ···	Tea stall 🛖
Road —	Hut ▲
Pass △	Monastery ▲
River ⌇	Glaciers

Sumdha Chenmo
3,900m
Day 4
Sumdha Do
Zanskar Range
To Chilling

Alchi: Array of divinities

The most celebrated of the monasteries associated with the translator Rinchen Zangpo is **Alchi Chos-kho**r (religious enclave), that fell into disuse probably around the 16th century. The murals so remarkably preserved at Alchi are very different in style from the Tibetan-influenced art, which prevails in the entire Himalayan region. Since Buddhist art was effaced from Kashmir and Northern India, first by a resurgent Brahmanism, and later by Islamists, Alchi is perhaps the best example of what must have once been the Kashmiri style of Buddhist iconography. The Alchi complex consists of two main temples: the **Du-khang** and

DAY ONE	DAY TWO
LAMAYURU-PRITIKINGI LA-WANLA	WANLA-HINJU
TIME 4-5 HOURS	**TIME** 5-6 HOURS
LEVEL EASY	**LEVEL** EASY

This is a short but hot march. Better to do it early or later in the day. From **Lamayuru** (3,450m) the path goes down to the stream, then turns south-east up a side valley at the chortens and prayer flags. The track then winds its way up through a barren gorge of yellow loess clay, to the **Pritikingi La** (3,506 m) pass. Descend steeply eastwards into the Shillakang stream, then turn downstream past **Shilla Village** and a 30-min walk will bring you to the big village of **Wanla** (3,200m).

There is a guest house and a few tea-stalls here. Explore the monastery, which is supposed to date from the Lamayuru period.

Follow the jeep track upstream (hot and dusty) for 2 hrs towards **Panji La Pass** where the trail splits. The right path goes south to Padum (Zanskar) up the **Wanla River**. The left track to Panji La (3,400m) Pass leaves the Wanla River and goes high above the village and then descends to rejoin the **Ripchar** stream after 30 mins. Another hour's walk brings you to **Hinju** (3,750m).

There are several campsites beyond the village near *pullus*. These are camping grounds where water is available.

Down **Yapola Nallah** from Panji La is a route that goes south to Photaksar and thence to Padum.

the **Sum-tsek**. The Du-khang, or assembly hall, is the main area used by monks for ceremonies and pujas.

One enters the Alchi Du-khang through a court with colonnaded verandahs into a small dark chamber dedicated to the figures of the Panch Tathagathas. More delightful perhaps, are the painted scenes of secular life, adorning either side of the main entrance. To the left, at the eye level, is the **royal drinking scene**. Notwithstanding the alcohol, their majesties sport large halos. Below, to the right, is a **battle scene**. On the right of the door is an unusual tree, said to be the **Tree of Enlightenment**. The **Sum-tsek**'s architecture is unparalleled in the entire Himalayan region. Its mud walls rise three storeys high, housing the giant figures of three four-armed Bodhisattvas. In the centre is **Maitreya Buddha**, four and a half metres tall, coloured terracotta red. He is flanked on the left by **Avalokiteshvara**, white in colour, and on the right

by the yellow Bodhisattva, **Manjushri**.

Besides these are four smaller structures: The **Temple of Manjushri**, with four clay statues of the Bodhisattva, rather garishly restored. The **Lotsawa Lha-khang**, built in the 12th century with the central image of the Buddha flanked by Avalokiteshvara and Rinchen Zangpo. The **Lha-Khang Soma** contains murals of a later and contrasting style to the splendour of the older buildings. In addition, there are three **Ka-ka-ni chortens**, or stupas, through which one can walk. These chortens are hollowed from the inside and decorated with murals. Two of them show Rinchen Zangpo together with Kashmiri teachers.

TIP Carry a flashlight, as the interiors of the Alchi complex have not been provided with electric lights for fear of damaging the paintings. Without one, the excursion to Alchi is useless. Photography is not permitted inside, so don't bother with cameras unless you are satisfied photographing the exteriors

SONIA JABBAR

Ladakhi devotees at Alchi

DAY THREE
HINJU-KONGSKE LA-SUMDHA CHENMO
TIME 4-5 HOURS
LEVEL MEDIUM

It's a relatively easy climb for 2 hrs above Hinju through several summer pastures. At the shepherds' shelters, the path leaves the stream and climbs steeply for another couple of hours. The views from the **Kongske La** (4,900m) top are worth it. Looking east-south-east behind a subsidiary mountain range can be seen the attractive peaks (around 5,900m) of **Alam** and **Palam**. To the south are the peaks of **Zanskar**, west the peaks above **Suru** and **Batalik** near Kargil, and north, over **Khaltse**, the **Nubra-Shayok** peaks. The descent of the pass is gentle for about 15 mins over snow and ice (if early in the season), then steep down along the **Sumdha**

Lush fields near Alchi

as it flows down. Stay on the main trail that involves four river crossings. Then after about 3½ hrs, towards the left, lies **Sumdha Chun** (3,850m). Between two large boulders turn up into the side valley, towards the north-east, at a large willow growing up against a sheer rock face. The main path continues down to the Nimmu Road. It is another hour's walk up to Sumdha Chun, which has a beautiful **gompa** from the Alchi era, numerous metal workers, who had originally come from Nepal 200 years ago, and a few small ▲ campsites.

DAY FIVE
Sumdha Chun-Stakspi La-Alchi
Time 7 HOURS
Level TOUGH

The climb to the pass is difficult, as it is steep. It can take 4 hrs or more to ascend the scree-laden path. Climb up the valley north-east of the village along a small tributary, to a **campsite** and *pullu* — the last place to get water before the pass. Follow the stream gully to the head of the valley. From here, the preferred direct route goes left or right of the crags to a rock band, traverses left below the band and crosses the shoulder to the top.

The route is tough, with the last section over rocky ground only marked by cairns. The reward is the wonderful view from the top of **Stakspi La** (4,950 m). The descent to the north is sharp over rocky terrain towards the central spur, then crossing the river twice to the grazing grounds and pullu.

▲ ▲ It's another 3 hrs to Alchi, so consider camping here if tired. Otherwise, carry on to the many guest houses and 🍴 restaurants at **Alchi** (3,150m), which has a famous 11th century monastery with amazing frescoes still intact.

For hotels in Alchi, see Accommodation Listings on page 530 ✦

Chu to the *pullus* for another 2 hrs. ▲ The camp at **Sumdha Chenmo** (3,900m) is just below the vast grazing ground amidst hundreds of yaks, sheep and goats. Be careful of the ferocious sheep dogs that accompany their masters. It is possible to follow the Sumdha Chu to its confluence with Zanskar and then get out at **Nimmu** on the Srinagar-Leh Highway.

DAY FOUR
Sumdha Chenmo-Sumdha Chun
Time 5-6 HOURS
Level EASY

The trail, moving south-east, crosses many grazing areas with many stream crossings. If water levels are low, stay along the river; if high, traverse the southern cliffs for about an hour and a half. The path divides 45 mins after leaving **Sumdha Chenmo** at a bridge. The right path goes to **Chilling** towards the **Zanskar River**, and the left path goes into the gorge. Don't cross the bridge but follow the stream

Markha Valley
On the beaten trail

By Sonia Jabbar

SPITUK-ZINGCHAN-KANDALA BASE CAMP-
SKIU-MARKHA-THUJUNGTSE-TSIGU-NYIMALING-
SHANG SUMDO-HEMIS

TIME	6-8 days
LEVEL	Moderate to Tough
IDEAL SEASON	Mid-Jun to late Sep
LOCATION	South-west of Leh, between the Stok and Zanskar ranges

The campsite at Zingchan

Photographs by SONIA JABBAR

With every second shop in the Leh Bazaar being a trekking agency offering the Markha Valley Trek alongwith the less strenuous jeep journeys into Nubra or Pangong, you may be forgiven for thinking this is a breeze. It is not. At Markha, a Swiss couple stumbled into my campsite begging for food and the use of my ponies to carry their overweight backpacks. Just before dinner at Tsigu, I was roused from my tent by a terrific commotion from the English camp. Turned out that the travel agent who had offered them such a great deal didn't feel obliged to provide full rations, and all they had left was flour and onions with two hard trekking days still to go. Needless to say, I was obliged to rescue everybody. Still, I would recommend this trek, particularly if you time it to avoid the peak tourist season, as it gets very crowded. And get yourself a guide at Leh.

The trek itself is thrilling. It's set in part in the beautiful Hemis National Park, with two 4,800-5,000m high passes to cross. There are waist-deep rivers to ford too. This trek satisfies the most demanding of adventurers. Add to that the pleasure of campsites set among aromatic shrubs and wild roses. You can spot bharal (blue sheep), nearly totally disguised on the bare mountains. Or chuckle at the antics of the phia (marmot) as you end up enjoying quite the perfect holiday.

DAY ONE
SPITUK-ZINGCHAN
TIME 4-6 HOURS
LEVEL MODERATE-EASY

The trek traditionally starts at the bridge over the **Indus** about a kilometre west of **Spituk Village**. However, a jeepable road slated to connect Spituk runs nearly all the way to Zingchan and if you get your taxi to drop you 7 km down the road to the point opposite **Phey Village**, you can skip the 2-hr long hot walk over unchanging scree-filled landscape

Meadow near the Rumbak crossing

(particularly after the **Spituk Pharka Village**) From this point it is a fairly pleasant walk along the descending road in a south-westerly direction along the Indus on your right, until you arrive at a fork where a swift flowing stream joins the Indus from the left. Walk into the valley due south, across the bridge, which can be a pleasant resting point. A walk of a couple more kilometres will bring you to a road sign: 'Jhingchan to Rumbak Road 1.00 km'. Look out for the log bridge here — nothing more than a few poplars lashed together — which often gets washed away. If there is no bridge you will have to ford the thigh-deep stream. After crossing it, find the path heading south-east which climbs suddenly onto the hillside to **Zingchan Village**.

🏕 There are two campsites here — one just before you climb up and one past the village down by the stream called the **Daisy Campsite**. I preferred to walk a little further for an hour, crossing the stream once more on a bridge, past a Forest Checkpoint with a sign welcoming you to **Hemis National Park**. Continue up the well-defined path, crossing the nullah at

GETTING THERE AND OUT

FROM LEH to Spituk, it's 8 km/ 20 mins by 🚕 (Rs 180) or half an hour by 🚌 (7.30 am-9 pm, and run every half-hour; fare Rs 10). You can also ask the taxi to drop you beyond Spituk Pharka Village at the point opposite Phey Village, which is on the other side of the Indus River (12 km/ 40 mins; fare Rs 280)

RETURN Get picked up at **Shang Sumdo** (52 km/ 1½ hrs; taxi Rs 1,250) or **Martselang** (47 km/ 1 hr; taxi Rs 1,000) and include a trip to the Hemis Gompa (taxi Rs 1,200). Last Leh bus (fare Rs 30) leaves from Shang Sumdo at 12 pm

TIP Always call a travel agency before setting the exact dates. Sometimes summer comes early and the passes open quicker, and sometimes the winter may set in early, causing an autumn trek to be scuttled

least four times before you arrive at **Sumdzom**, marked by a stone chorten with prayer flags and a grove of willows and wild roses. There are good camping options here.
♦**Entry fee to Hemis National Park** Rs 20 per person per day

DAY TWO
ZINGCHAN-KANDALA BASE CAMP
TIME 5-6 HOURS
LEVEL MODERATE-TOUGH
From Sumdzom walk upstream on the left bank (true right bank), crossing the stream twice over sturdy wooden bridges. Then climb steadily up the hill as the path moves due south-east until it comes out of the

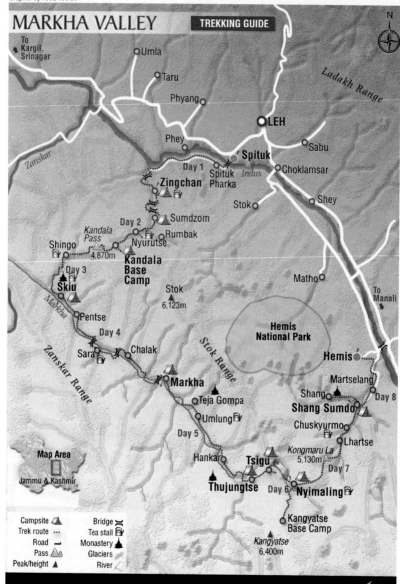

Graphic by ANIS KHAN

MARKHA VALLEY

TREKKING GUIDE

N

To Kargil, Srinagar

Umla

Taru

Phyang

Phey

LEH

Sabu

Spituk

Day 1

Spituk Pharka

Indus

Choklamsar

Zanskar

Zingchan

Stok

Shey

Sumdzom

Day 2

Rumbak

Kandala Pass

Nyurutse

Shingo

4,870m

Kandala Base Camp

Stok 6,123m

Matho

To Manali

Day 3

Skiu

Hemis National Park

Pentse

Day 4

Chalak

Stok Range

Hemis

Sara

Zanskar Range

Martselang

Day 8

Markha

Morkha

Teja Gompa

Shang

Shang Sumdo

Umlung

Chuskyurmo

Day 5

Hankar

Tsigu

Lhartse

Kongmaru La 5,130m

Day 7

Thujungtse

Day 6

Nyimaling

Map Area

Jammu & Kashmir

Kangyatse Base Camp

Kangyatse 6,400m

Campsite	⛺	Bridge	✕
Trek route	···	Tea stall	🏠
Road	—	Monastery	🔺
Pass	△	Glaciers	
Peak/height	▲	River	

Chortens in the village of Chalak in the Markha Valley

narrow gorge. Straight in front is the **Kandala Nallah**, along which a path leads to high pastures. On your left, or east, is the path which leads up to **Rumbak Village**. And up ahead, crossing the nallah and to the right is the path leading to Nyurutse and the Kandala Base Camp. This junction is a pretty spot with wild flowers and a tea shop, a perfect resting place. Follow the Nyurutse path as it climbs steadily southwards. **Nyurutse** is a tiny hamlet and you can rest here, but see if you can press on for another hour that will bring you to a 🏕️ parachute-tent tea shop (shops in tents that come up during the season).

🏕️ There are plenty of camping spots right after Nyurutse and even after the tea shop, but if you are a small group then head up south-west to the **Kandala Base Camp** for the night. This is a small flat piece of land with a water source. It commands very nice views of the valley below, besides cutting short the sharp climb up to the pass the next morning.

DAY THREE
KANDALA BASE CAMP–SKIU
TIME 7-8 HOURS
LEVEL TOUGH

Set out early, particularly if you have camped below the Kandala Base Camp

last night as today is a long day. The trek up to the **Kandala Pass** (4,870 m) takes a little under 2 hrs of steady climbing from the base camp. Follow the path south around the hill and then, instead of going straight up the pasture, find a path to the right or west which zigzags up to the pass marked by prayer flags. Look out for marmots en route. From the pass, a well-defined path leads down to **Shingo**. This is a surprisingly long descent on a well-defined path, taking around 2 hrs to the 🏕️ parachute tea shop.

From Shingo, head south along the village wall and as you come out into open fields, look for a path to your left or east, which heads steadily downhill in a south-easterly direction through a narrow gorge filled with wild roses. The path to Skiu is very well defined except that you have to cross the **Shingo Nallah** at least four times. It's a shallow stream except in one or two places and it's pleasant to get one's toes wet. From Shingo, it should take you no more than 3 hrs even if you factor in a longish lunch break. **Skiu**, situated in the **Markha Valley**, which runs west to east, is a fascinating place with ruins of ancient monasteries.

🏕️ There are two campsites here at Skiu. One, a small one as soon as you enter the village, and another more favoured one, just past the village by the **Markha River**. One can have a lovely rest day here, bathing at the river and doing a side trip westwards into the **Zanskar Gorge** to the small village of **Kaya**.

DAY FOUR

SKIU-MARKHA
TIME 6-7 HOURS
LEVEL MODERATE

If you have rested the day before, today will be relatively easy as you are walking on more or less level ground in the **Markha Valley**. From the second campsite, head a few hundred metres north to the edge of the pasture and find a broad path going east. After a few kilometres, you will come to a broken bridge across the river. Do *not* cross but continue walking upstream,

heading east, into the thicket of willows and out. You will be walking either at the base of the hill or on a path cut into its side. About 7 km from Skiu, the path climbs up and abruptly confronts a high, but sturdy wooden bridge across the **Markha**. From here, it is a couple of kilometres to **Sara** where one can stop for ☕ some hot tea and refreshments.

Soon after, the path descends to another solid bridge crossing over to the true right of the valley into the village of **Chalak**. The path then climbs steadily eastwards up to a ridge which has some very weathered, large Mani walls, some painted red, replete with prayer flags and bharal horns. Descend to the valley floor, crossing a small, swift stream and continue eastwards on the true right of the valley for about an hour. Then cross

Stinging nettles

I tend to pluck leaves of plants I find interesting. Just before I arrived at the Kandala Base Camp, I saw some small bushes and thought, aha! mint tea would be lovely after the long walk. I reached out for the leaves and in a second realised my mistake a bit too late. Nursing my hand in the camp, I discussed the nature of the plant with my guide who informed me that Ladakhis harvest nettles (*Urtica dioica*) in the late summer, dry it and use it in soups through the winter when green vegetables are scarce. Milarepa, Tibet's wandering meditator, lived on nettles for decades, so much so that his skin turned green!

Growing between 30 cm and 1.5m, nettles are widely used by herbalists. The leaves have proven to be beneficial for allergic sinus problems. It's also used as a diuretic, anti-arthritic, anti-rheumatic and anti-bacterial agent. It's used as a CNS depressant in the treatment of anxiety and sleep disorders and as an antispasmodic. An extract of the roots has been shown to reduce suffering that is associated with enlarged prostrates. It is considered to relieve the symptoms rather than the enlargement itself.

A project in Nepal actually makes cloth out of stinging nettles. The giant stinging nettle, *Girdardinia diversifolia*, is a perennial plant that grows much taller than humans. It grows in partially shaded areas and is harvested near the end of the monsoon. The workers use their teeth to separate the bark from the stalk, and soften the fibres by cooking them for several hours in ash. Then they mix the fibres with white clay to lighten the colour, and finally spin the fibre into thread, which is woven into cloth.

Indian ants the size of foxes dig up gold

OTTO PFISTER

If there were broadsheets in Alexander the Great's time, this would have been the dominating headlines, for Megasthenes, Alexander's brave general, was the author of this tale and was backed up by a historian of no less a stature than Herodotus. What actually happened was a case of language confounded: The sands along the Indus River were once rich in gold. While digging its burrows, the Himalayan marmot would sometimes throw up gold-rich sand, which was then sifted by traders from Baltistan. Megasthenes confesses that he hadn't actually seen the ant but only its skin brought into camp by his Macedonian soldiers. The skin of the *cheentee* (ant in Hindi) was actually the skin of the *chipa* or *phia* (marmot in Ladakhi)!

The Himalayan marmot (*Marmota himalayana*) is an adorable mammal and one can spend hours watching its antics. Found from 4,000m to the upper edge of the vegetated zone (5,500m) in the mountains of Nepal, parts of India, and Tibet, it eats roots and shoots, lives in burrows, and hibernates there through the winter. Most marmots are highly social, and use loud whistles to communicate with one another, especially when alarmed.

the cold, thigh-deep, swift **Markha River**. Ensure that your guide picks the shallowest spot and helps you cross to the true left of the valley. A couple of kilometres later the path descends to a bridge.

🏕 There is a walled campsite here as well as across the bridge, closer to the **Markha Village**, fort and monastery. Spend the evening exploring these.

DAY FIVE

MARKHA-THUJUNGTSE-TSIGU

TIME 7-8 HOURS
LEVEL TOUGH

Today is a long day, particularly if you are camping at Tsigu. From the campsite, skirt the hill, past the primary school (no need to climb up the main path to the fort), cross the small stream and head east past the fields. After a few kilometres you will find a bridge across the river. Ignore this and continue on the path up the rise and down onto the river bed. The **Markha River** traces a wide 'U' so it

Yaks graze at the Nyimaling pastures

needs to be crossed twice within a couple of hundred metres. The river is deep and swift, so ensure that you have help while crossing. Climb up the bank, past Mani walls, heading in a south-easterly direction, passing the

Prayer flags adorn Kongmaru La Pass for a safe crossing

Teja Gompa and climbing gently up to the ☕ tea-stall at Umlung.

From here, the clearly defined path continues in a south-easterly direction, first climbing a small rise and then dropping down to a large, flat plain with some fenced fields. The **Kangyatse Peak** (6,400m) dominates the landscape. Continue until you reach the small settlement of **Lower Hankar**. **Beer** is usually available here! From here the path runs downhill to the river and sharply veers to the left or north and leads up a very steep slope up to a ridge which has the remains of an old fort. From here the village and fields of **Upper Hankar** lie before you. Follow the path down into the valley eastwards, until the path veers left or north into a narrow gorge, then east and upwards again to **Thujungtse**.

🔺 If you are a large group, then it is better to camp here. If not and you aren't entirely wiped out, then walk another hour for **Tsigu** that is located in a cirque with a couple of small tarns. The views from here are spectacular. Walk uphill, north-east through a braided stream, and right (east) around a hill. There is a path that moves up to your left. Do *not* take that. Walk straight up (north), up the valley in front of you, keeping to the right of the valley until you come to a fork that moves right. Do not take this. Look to your left (west) instead and find a path zig-zagging steeply up to the top. On the ridge you will find the clearly defined path going northwards to the campsite, only 10 mins away.

DAY SIX
THUJUNGTSE-TSIGU-NYIMALING
TIME 1 ½-3 HOURS
LEVEL EASY

Nyimaling is a beautiful, broad, grassy valley with plenty of drinking water. If you have stopped at Tsigu for the night, then you can do the side trip from Nyimaling to **Kangyatse Base Camp** on the same day. If you are walking from **Thujungtse**, it may be too tiring. Either way, you may want to factor in another rest day here.

🔺 From Tsigu find the well-defined path heading east in a series of switch backs until you come down into the broad valley with a ☕ parachute-tent tea house marking the **Nyimaling campsite**.

The welcome sight of the final camp at picturesque Shang Sumdo

SIDE TRIP TO KANGYATSE BASE CAMP
TIME 4-5 HOURS

From the Nyimaling campsite, take your guide and head due south, ascending gently over pasture land for a couple of hours until you reach the snow line, marking the base camp of the mountain. Pack a picnic lunch with a thermos of coffee. Head back the same way.

DAY SEVEN
NYIMALING-SHANG SUMDO
TIME 7-8 HOURS
LEVEL TOUGH

Across the stream to the north are a few homes, which make up the village of **Nyimaling**. Find the path that goes past them ascending steeply to the **Kongmaru La** at 5,130m, marked by prayer flags. It should take you 2-3 hrs to the top. From here the descent is sharp and treacherous and many pack animals have been lost because of carelessness. A little over an hour should bring you to **Lhartse**, a small, but dusty campsite where you can take a break. From here, follow the path along the small stream. This flows into a narrow gorge where you must watch for rock fall. There are some places where the path disappears and you have to clamber over boulders. Do not

be tempted to climb the shepherds' paths on the true right of the gorge. Stick to the left as the gorge broadens and look out for a well-built paved path on the left that climbs the side of the gorge. Look out for bharal. Stop for ☎ chai at **Chuskyurmo**. Then continue north, past the picturesque village of **Chokdo** and on to **Shang Sumdo** where there are many ⛺ campsites. For those in a hurry, a jeepable road to Shang Sumdo means that you can actually be picked up here.

DAY EIGHT
SHANG SUMDO-HEMIS
TIME 3-4 HOURS
LEVEL EASY

Spend the early morning exploring the side valley and the **monastery of Shang**. Then set out along the jeepable road to **Martselang**. Here, leave the main road, and head west on a path which goes over the scree slopes all the way to **Hemis**. However, this is a very hot and boring walk and I would get the taxi to meet me at Martselang, and drive up to the Hemis Monastery instead. After visiting the monastery in Hemis, which also has a ☎ dhaba where you can have some chowmein, continue on to Leh. ✦

Crouching between the formidable peaks of the Great Himalayan Range and the Zanskar Range, Zanskar was — until recently — one of the most inaccessible places in the world. It is a large area of about 5,000 sq km made up of two valleys, the Stod, which connects up with the Suru and Kargil, and the Tsarab, which follows the Zanskar River up north.

Somewhat breaching its aura of mystery, the Government of India built a road of sorts in the late 70s connecting this once 'Hidden Himalayan Kingdom' to Kargil. But it is still cut off from the rest of the world for seven months of the year by its severe northern winters and, even when open, attracts only those with adventurous spirits. The 234-km journey from Kargil to Padum, though physically punishing, takes one through the Suru Valley, which amply compensates with its stunning beauty. Turn a corner and confront the majestic twin peaks of Nun (7,135m) and Kun (7,134m); turn another corner and witness the mighty Gangri glacier literally tumbling into the Suru River.

Padum itself is no more than a scattering of small, whitewashed buildings in a vast plain with a tiny population of about 1,500 and gaining in reputation as a hub for fascinating treks in the region. Pack-horses, guides and limited supplies can be procured for the trek south into Himachal via Darcha; the trek south-west into Kishtwar via the Omasi La; and the treks north into Lamayuru or Hemis over the Zanskar Range. These expeditions may also be combined with visits to the many ancient Buddhist monasteries that dot the landscape.

MUST-VISITS

ANCIENT HISTORY
Check out the ancient 8th century rock carvings on a boulder near the river. Hire a jeep and visit the **Tongde** (20 km), **Zangla** (35 km), **Karsha** (17 km)

→ **Padum Facts**

● **LOCATION** South-west of Leh and south-east of Kargil, in the Zanskar region between the Great Himalayan and Ladakh ranges at 3,531m
● **GETTING TO PADUM By air** Nearest airports: Srinagar (463 km); Leh (465 km). From either of these places, travel to Padum via Kargil by road **By rail** Nearest railhead: Jammu Tawi, 756 km. Proceed on NH1A to Srinagar by bus (10-12 hrs, Rs 250) or shared taxi (8 hrs, Rs 350 per person). Your next stop is Kargil (229 km/ 7 hrs by taxi, 9 hrs by bus) via the Zoji-La. Taxi Rs 3,000; bus Rs 200 **By road** From Kargil, it is 234 km/ 15 hrs to Padum via the Suru Valley, Panikhar and Rangdum. Buses and taxis: There is a bus to Padum every other day at 3 am. The trip to Padum takes 2 days with an overnight halt at Rangdum. Taxi Rs 7,500

In Panikhar, there is the good JKTDC Tourist Bungalow with rooms for Rs 150. The JKTDC Tourist Bungalow at Rangdum has very, very basic rooms for Rs 100 per person
● **STD CODE** 01983
● **TOURIST OFFICES** ● J&K Tourism, Padum. Tel: 01983-245017 ● J&K Tourism, Kargil. Tel: 01985-232721 ● J&K Tourism, Leh. Tel: 01982-252297, 252094

and **Bardan** (12 km) monasteries. Of these, Karsha is the largest and wealthiest, with 500-year-old frescoes.

RAFTING ON THE ZANSKAR
In summer, a few professional rafting companies organise 7-day rafting trips on the Zanskar River which includes **Grade II-IV rapids**, ending where the Zanskar meets the Indus near Alchi (*see Trekking Agencies Listings on page 514*).

WHERE TO STAY AND EAT
Unlike Leh, or even Kargil, Padum has only limited accommodation and eating places. You have to choose between the **J&K Tourist Bungalow** (Kargil Tel: 01985-232721/ 266) and the few private, basic guest houses. We also recommend **Hotel Ibex** (Tel: 09418002171/ Kargil Tel: 245021).
For details, see Accommodation Listings on page 532

INPUTS FROM SONIA JABBAR

Padum to Darcha
The lost valley

By David Ducoin

Photographs by DAVID DUCOIN

Crossing a stream near the huge monolithic rock, Gombu Rangjum on Day Seven

TIME	9 days
LEVEL	Easy to Moderate
IDEAL SEASON	Jun to Sep
LOCATION	Lugnak Valley, south-east of Zanskar, to Lahaul in Himachal Pradesh

PADUM-SHILLA CAMP-RERU-CHANGPA TSETAN-PURNE-PHUKTAL-PURNE-KARGYAK-SHINGO LA BASE-RAMJAK-PAL LHAMO

Padum to Darcha is an easy trek and very convenient for a first-time trekking experience in the trans-Himalayas. There is only one pass, which is quite rare in this area, and many villages and campsites,

so if you want to make it in 10 days or more, it's quite easy to organise. The only steep bit you have to encounter will be on the day you cross the Shingo La (5,050m), but if you start from Padum rather than the reverse route, it won't be as tough as you get acclimatised well before reaching the pass. If you do the trek from Darcha to Padum, it can be tough and dangerous as you start at 3,300m and zoom up to 5,050m in the first three trekking days. Bad acclimatisation can lead to altitude sickness, which is decidedly unpleasant and therefore to be avoided.

This trek will lead you towards Lugnak, the valley south-east of Zanskar, used by locals historically for trade between Lahaul in Himachal and

Graphic by ANIS KHAN

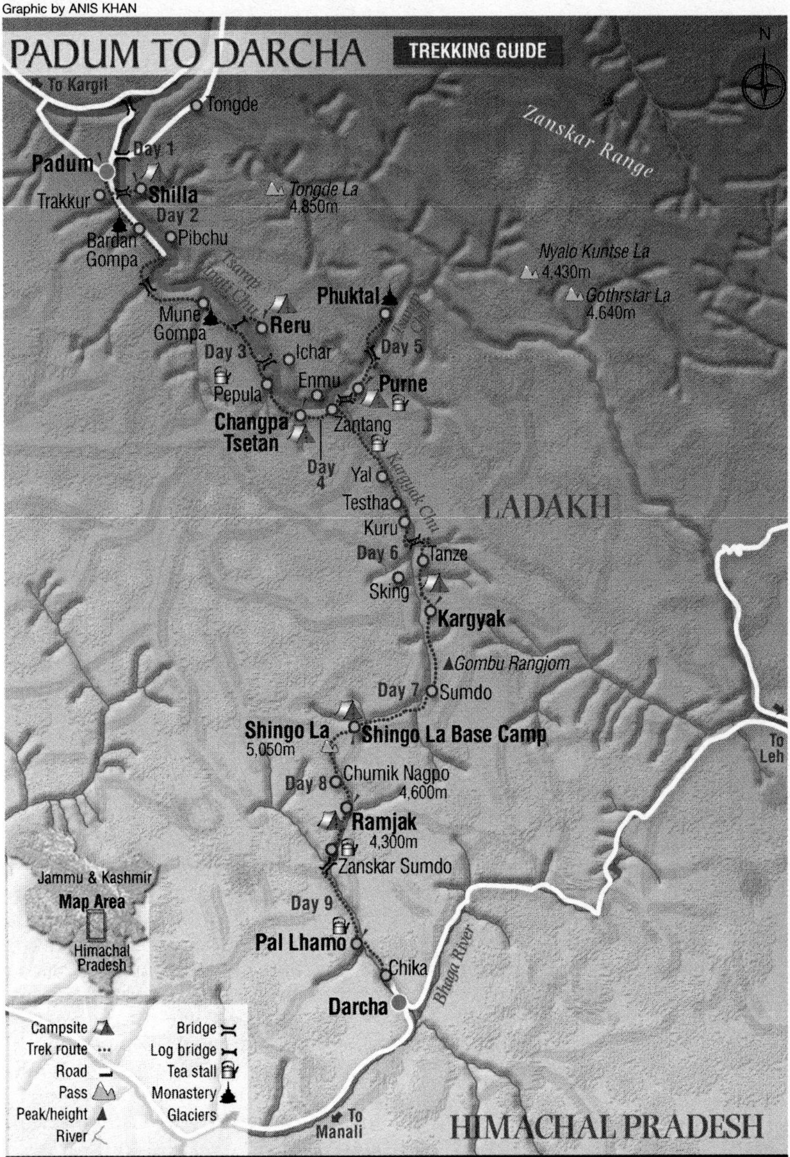

PADUM TO DARCHA TREKKING GUIDE

N

To Kargil

Padum Day 1 ○ Tongde

Trakkur ○ ● **Shilla**

Bardan ○ Pibchu
Gompa Day 2

Zanskar Range

△ *Tongde La*
4,850m

Mune ▲ ○ **Reru** **Phuktal** ▲
Gompa

Day 3 ○ Ichar Day 5

Pepula ▢ Enmu ○ ○ **Purne** ▢

Changpa ▲○ ○ Zantang
Tsetan

Nyalo Kuntse La
△ 4,430m
△ *Gothrstar La*
4,640m

Day Yal ○
4
Testha ○

Kuru ○ **LADAKH**

Day 6 ○ Tanze ▲

Sking ○

Kargyak Chu

● **Kargyak**

▲ *Gombu Rangjom*

Day 7 ○ Sumdo

Shingo La ▲ ○ **Shingo La Base Camp**
5,050m

Day 8 ▢ Chumik Nagpo
4,600m

▲ **Ramjak** 4,300m

▢ Zanskar Sumdo

Jammu & Kashmir
Map Area

Himachal
Pradesh

Day 9 ▢

Pal Lhamo ○

○ Chika

● **Darcha**

Bhaga River

To
Leh

Campsite △	Bridge ✕
Trek route ···	Log bridge ✕
Road ↵	Tea stall ▢
Pass △△	Monastery ▲
Peak/height ▲	Glaciers △△
River ∠	

To
Manali

HIMACHAL PRADESH

Monks at Phuktal Monastery doing the annual whitewashing of chortens

Zanskar. Many children from Lugnak Valley today go to school in Manali as schooling in Zanskar is quite poor and the connection with Manali is easy. The Himalayan jewel of Phuktal monastery is half way from Padum to Darcha. After that, you will meet the magnificence of the Gombu Rangjom rock surrounded by yaks grazing in pastures full of wild flowers.

If you connect this trek with the Lamayuru-Padum trek, you can make this a great 20-day experience. This is a classic and beautiful trek and if you want to do it, I advise you to not wait forever. Do it within the next five years before the road-building exercises in the region destroy Zanskar's aura of the 'lost valley'.

DAY ONE

Padum-Shilla Camp
Time 1 1/2 hours
Level Easy

Before starting the trek, if you have the time it's really worth visiting places in the Zanskar Valley like the old, impressive monasteries of Tongde, **Zangla**, **Karsha** and **Sani**. You can do it in a small 4-day trip or even in one day by jeep. In **Padum**, you will find shops, restaurants and even basic guest houses (Ibex Hotel is the best place in town).

TIP If you are camping in Padum, there are risks: watch out for thieves who could whisk away money, cameras and trekking equipment if you aren't careful!

A better option is to camp across the river facing **Shilla Village**. There is a dirt road, so you can ask to be dropped here to start the trek, or you could hike the short distance from Padum. Go through the upper and older part of town heading south. Find the road following the **Tsarap River** and follow it upstream for 1 1/2 hrs. You will then see a **mani wall**, grassland and clear water.

If you are lucky and there aren't a couple of other trekking groups crowding the place, this makes for a perfect campsite. On the other side of the river, you will see Shilla Village with a beautiful waterfall.

DAY TWO
SHILLA CAMP-RERU
TIME 5 HOURS
LEVEL EASY

From the camp, keep to the same jeepable road heading south-east. Walking a little over an hour will bring you to **Bardan Gompa**, a Kagyu or Red Hat monastery linked to Hemis, which is worth visiting because of its enormous prayer wheel. Continue on the road to **Mune Gompa**. Just after Bardan there is a new wooden bridge and a little further perhaps the last rope bridge you will find in Zanskar. **Don't use it** as it's difficult to know when it will finally collapse and everybody uses the new one! Around the bridge is a stony landscape and if you look carefully you will find some **prehistoric carvings** on stones, which prove that Zanskar was inhabited by ibex-hunting nomads thousands of years ago. Two more hours along the **Tsarap River** leading over a plateau will lead you to Mune Monastery.

🏕 There is a nice campsite just before the gompa if you're tired and want to quit for the day.

From Mune you can avoid the road and find a short-cut on the plateau till **Reru Campsite**, which is before the village just near a small reservoir.

DAY THREE
RERU-CHANGPA TSETAN
TIME 6-7 HOURS
LEVEL MODERATE

The good news of the day is that, from now on, you walk on a path that

Prehistoric rock carvings near Shilla

Bharat Petroleum

GETTING THERE AND OUT

FROM LEH to Padum (465 km), it's a 2-day journey by 🚌 (fare Rs 470; 5.30 am) or 🚙 (Rs 12,000), with Kargil as the stopover for the night. A Leh-Kargil taxi costs Rs 3,700 and Kargil-Padum Rs 7,400
RETURN From **Darcha**, take a bus (Rs 200) or taxi (Rs 5,000) to **Manali** (145 km), a 7-hr drive. Arrange taxi in advance from the trekking agency

won't have a truck or jeep passing through. Keep going east-south-east following the **Tsarap River**, up and down through a dark rocky landscape. There will be some stream crossings. On the other side of the river is **Ichar Village** with its fortress. There's a wooden bridge and a rope bridge below the track.

🏕 ☕ Carry on up on the track to **Pepula** where there is a tea shop and a large campsite of grey sand. The place is quite dusty and windy, so it's better to keep on going for an hour until **Changpa Tsetan**, which is a better option since it has two houses and a good campsite in the fields.

DAY FOUR
CHANGPA TSETAN-PURNE
TIME 4 HOURS
LEVEL MODERATE

Cross the small stream and head east keeping the Tsarap River on your left all day. On the other side of the river you will see **Enmu Village**. Walk past the villages of **Surle**, **Kalbok** and **Zantang** with its ☕ tea shop. After the confluence of the Tsarap and Kargyak rivers, cross the bridge and go up

Zanskari grandfather and grandchild out for a walk near Kargyak

north-east to **Purne Village**. 🏕 🍴
There are two houses and a nice
campsite, which can be quite busy in
peak tourist season. All trekkers prefer
to camp here so that they can head to
Phuktal the following morning. There
is a nice waterfall just beyond the
camp, towards the fields.

DAY FIVE

PURNE-PHUKTAL-PURNE
TIME 4-5 HOURS
LEVEL MODERATE
From the camp, take the path going
up north towards **Kangsar** (one
house only) and walk through the
Tsarap Gorge along the Tsarap River.
When you reach the bridge, go right
if you want to start by visiting the
village (30 mins) or cross the bridge
on the left and you will discover the
fabulous gompa nestled in the cliff.

This **Gelugpa Monastery** was first
built in a cave on the cliff and the
later additions were almost beehive-
like accretions. On the upper side is
an old juniper tree that dominates
the entire valley. If you keep hiking
up the cliff towards the juniper, you'll
find a path going to Shade Village (2
days away) and Tongde Gompa via the

Tongde La (5,200m). This is a nice and
remote trekking option, possible only
in September when the water level is
low enough to cross the rivers.

At **Phuktal**, the monks are very
friendly and accustomed to visitors.
They can arrange lunch and even 🏕
sleeping quarters at the gompa. The
cave has a water point, that only men
are allowed to visit. Allow $1^1/_2$ hrs for
the return journey.

DAY SIX

PURNE-KARGYAK
TIME 6-7 HOURS
LEVEL MODERATE
It's a long but easy day today. Head
back south to the bridge on the confluence of Tsarap and Kargyak rivers.
Then head south-east along the
Kargyak River towards **Yal Village**,
after which you cross the big village of
Testha. Thereafter, continue straight
down to **Kuru Village**. After the
village, head down to a bridge and
cross the Kargyak River, and continue
walking south-east. Cross **Tanze**, a
quiet but important village. It is
another 4 hrs to Kargyak from here. In
June or July, you will cross a number
of summer camps called **Doksa** with

lots of yaks. If you stop in one of them you may get a chance to taste *jo*, curd made of yak's milk.

⚠ The best place to camp is opposite Sking Village, 45 mins before Kargyak, just after the confluence of two rivers.

DAY SEVEN
KARGYAK-SHINGO LA base
TIME 6 HOURS
LEVEL MODERATE
Suddenly the valley is wider and greener than in the past week of trekking. Remain on the same side of the valley (left bank) and walk south-east to **Kargyak** (45 mins) until you see the **Gombu Rangjom**, a monolithic rock that you keep on the left. The path is very clear.

⚠ Cross the river and there is a good campsite here, but I would advise you to soldier on for one more hour moving south-west to the **Shingo La Base Camp**.

The explorer's grave at Darjeeling

SWAPAN NAYAK

Alexander Csoma de Koros
(c. 1790-1842)

Having received the promise of a stipend from a friend to support him during his travels, the young Alexander Csoma de Koros set out for the East, walking from **Nagyenyed** in Hungary to **Darjeeling**, traversing **Arabia**, much of **Central Asia** and **Ladakh** en route. The impetus for de Koros to undertake this incredible hike was the romantic belief that the origin of the Hungarian people was to be found in the remote land of Yarkand, beyond **Ladakh** and the **Karakoram mountains**.

He made his way to Tibet, where he spent four years in a Buddhist monastery studying the language and Buddhist literature, but made little progress. He visited Bengal and got employed in the library of the Asiatic Society, which possessed more than a thousand volumes in Tibetan. Also known as Sikander Beg, the Armenian, or Phyi-glin-gi-grwa-pa (Tibetan for 'foreign pupil'), de Koros arrived in 1823 at **Phuktal Monastery** in Zanskar, to study the then unknown Tibetan language. For 16 months, the Hungarian and the monk, Phuntsog, laboured in a freezing cell, eating only tsampa (ground barley and water). His efforts paid off as the first Tibetan-English dictionary was published in Calcutta, in 1834. He later contributed many articles to the *Journal of the Asiatic Society of Bengal* and published an analysis of the *Kangyur*, the collection of Buddhist sacred texts.

Meanwhile, his fame had reached Hungary, and procured him a pension from the government, which, with characteristic devotion to learning, he devoted to the purchase of books for Indian libraries. He spent some time in Calcutta, studying Sanskrit and several other languages. In early 1842, he commenced his second attempt to discover the origin of the Hungarians, but died in Darjeeling of malaria on April 11, 1842, his quest unfulfilled. Csoma de Koros rejected the accepted wisdom linking the Hungarians to the Finns, saying that the theory stank of fish oil.

Grecian juniper

The juniper is an evergreen tree, which grows up to 20m. It is in leaf all year and the seeds ripen in October. The scented flowers are dioecious (individual flowers are either male or female, but only one sex is to be found on any one plant, so both male and female plants must be grown if seed is required) and are pollinated by wind. The plant is not self-fertile. It requires dry or moist soil and tolerates drought. The juniper is found in the inner dry Himalayan ranges, 1,500-4,200m, from Nepal to Afghanistan.

OTTO PFISTER

In Ladakh, the juniper is considered holy and no sane person would dare to think of cutting it. It is believed that people who break this law are plagued by spirits afterwards.

Juniper twigs and needles are also used for fumigation. Sprinkling needles over pans full of glowing charcoal produces a very aromatic smoke that is believed to clean the atmosphere, ward off diseases and evil influences. The juniper needle is vital in traditional Tibetan incense. The juniper is also used in Tibetan medicine to treat kidney diseases and put in water along with four other plants for baths to treat joint pains, and to brew chhang (Tibetan beer).

DAY 8

SHINGO LA BASE-SHINGO LA-RAMJAK
TIME 7 HOURS
LEVEL TOUGH

Stay on the left side of the valley, going up slowly. The ascent is not so steep and quite easy if you start smoothly. The only problem can be snow on the path, in which case ensure that you have competent guides who can steer you through bad weather. Just before the pass you have to cross snowfields, which will take an hour or two. **Shingo La** is marked by cairns and prayer flags and, at 5,050m, is the highest point of the trek. The views are fantastic but the place is cold and windy. After the pass, the track goes on for half an hour at the same altitude, crossing a torrent (sometimes it's knee-deep). It then starts a steep descent on a path full of rocks and scree for 2 hrs to **Chumik Nagpo** (⛺ camp possibility at 4,600m) and 3 hrs more to **Ramjak** (⛺ better camp at 4,300m).

DAY 9

RAMJAK-PAL LHAMO
TIME 7 HOURS
LEVEL MODERATE

Today is the momentous day that we leave the rocky landscape of Zanskar and enter **Lahaul**, the vista gradually becoming green. It is a gradual descent on an easy path southwards, crossing a bridge at Zanskar Sumdo, where you can take a break at the ☕ tea shop. Then cross a few streams barefooted and follow the river till you are in Pal Lhamo, where there is a good ⛺ camp and ☕ tea shop.

Cross on the left bank again (good bridge) and after 2 hrs you reach Chika where the road starts. If you asked for a pick-up, the jeep or bus can come up to here, otherwise follow the road down to Darcha to catch a bus to Manali.

For hotels in Padum, see Accommodation Listings on page 532 ✦

HIMACHAL PRADESH Route guide

Chamba, Dharamsala
Dalhousie, Manali,
Sangla, Shimla, Tabo...

N

JAMMU AND KASHMIR

Map area

To Leh

Udaipur
Chenab
Keylong 21
Kunzum La
Hanse Kiato
CHAMBA
46 Khajjiar
DALHOUSIE
Bharmour Rohtang Pass 50 Kibber
Dharamkot Solang Gulaba 62 Batal 38 18
Ravi 51 Kaza Dhankar
McLeodganj Palchan Spiti 22 7 Gompa
MANALI Attergo TABO
DHARAMSALA 10 38 Palampur 21 Naggar 20 5 32
Gaggal 20 Katrain Chanderkhani Pass Poh Sumdo 24
Bir 21 51 Yangthang
38 Kullu Jari Kasol National Park Puh 35
Jogindernagar 29
56 Bhuntar Puh
Mandi 22 Aut Katgaon 61
Hamirpur 19 26 Banjar Kalpa 22
40 Pandoh 20 Bagi Pul Chaura 20 Recongpeo
Sundernagar Jalori Pass Jeori 40 16 Karchham
21 Khanag Nirmand 23 1 32 Wangtu
44 Janjheli 22 19 Rampur
Karsog Ani 17 Sarahan
Bilaspur Sutlej 52
94 Narkanda 34 Hatu SANGLA
PUNJAB SHIMLA 30 Theog
Sutlej 49
To Rupnagar
Amritsar 40 Solan
55
Chandigarh Panchkula
1
47
22
HARYANA
64 Ambala 192 To Delhi (Shimla to Delhi 334 km) 72

53	National Highway
	Road
10	Distance in km
	Railway Line
	Railway Station
	Airport
O	Hub centre
●	Trek point
△	Pass
●	National Park

Photographs by GIREESH G V

Snow blankets Shimla in winter

Once the summer capital of the British Raj, Shimla is today the full-time capital of Himachal Pradesh. Though the erstwhile 'most fashionable summer resort' in all of India has certainly declined, you can still count on gorgeous Himalayan views and exciting excursions to the countryside around. The salubrious air and scenic views act as a balm, helping you ignore the scars of modernity as you succumb to the charisma of Shimla's enduring past.

MUST-VISITS

THE MALL
Check out the famous and crowded Shimla Mall and its promenade, at the end of which is the romantic rendezvous favourite, the **Scandal Point**. Enjoy Shimla's indoor **roller-skating rink** and open-air **ice-skating rink**.

THE SEVEN HILLS
Many Elizabethan and Edwardian edifices still stand, spread across the seven hills of Shimla. The old, historic and magnificent mansion **Manorville** is now a guest house of the All India Institute of Medical Sciences. **The Holme**, once the studio-cum-residence of painter Amrita Shergill, is also nearby. Visit the **Himalayan Aviary** right below the State Guest House. Oak and rhododendron

forests lead to the **Squire House**, near the impressive **Viceregal Lodge** on the Observatory Hill. India was once ruled from this colonial mansion, which today houses the Indian Institute of Advanced Studies. Lower down is the **Gaiety Theatre**, once the social centre of town; it still hosts excellent plays.

You can inspect the artefacts at the **Himachal State Museum** atop the Inverarm Hill. Cross over towards the **Grand Hotel** on Bantony Hill, former residence of Governor-General William

→ Shimla Facts

- **LOCATION** High up in the picturesque Shimla hills at an altitude of 2,100m, Shimla is in southern Himachal, 334 km north of Delhi
- **GETTING TO SHIMLA By air** Jubbarhatti Airport (25 km/ 1 hr), but weather routinely disrupts air traffic in this region. Taxi Rs 300-400 **By rail** Nearest metre gauge railhead: Shimla; nearest broad gauge railhead: Kalka (92 km/ 2$\frac{1}{2}$ hrs). Taxi Rs 800 approx up to the lifts. Or catch the metre-gauge toy train from Kalka to Shimla for a memorable 6-hr rail journey **By road** NH1 from Delhi to Ambala is a dream. The Zirakpur-Shimla Highway has been improved and makes for a much faster drive now. Breakfast at Giani's Dhaba after Kalka
- **STD CODE** 0177

Christ Church at night

Bentinck. The home of the former rulers of Sirmour is now the **Police Head-quarters**, also on Bantony Hill. Walk past the now deconsecrated **St Andrew's Church** towards the Roman Catholic **St Michael's Cathedral**. On Elysium Hills, **Auckland House**, once the residence of Lord Auckland, is now a school. **Jakhu** is the tallest of Shimla's seven hills. It's crowned by the **Hanuman Temple**. The most sublime of Shimla sunrises is to be had from here. **Christ Church** is also here. There is also the **St Mary's Church** and **Rothney Castle**, once home to ornithologist and founder of the Indian National Congress, A.O. Hume.

WHERE TO STAY

A wide range of accommodation across all budgets is to be found here. Many of Shimla's hotels are housed in heritage buildings. Remember to book well in advance in season.

Exhaustively renovated a few years ago, **The Cecil** (Tel: 0177-2804848;

Tariff: Rs 6,500-10,000) is easily one of the most luxurious resorts in the mountains. The **Chapslee** (Tel: 2802542; Tariff: Rs 5,500-7,500) is also a very exclusive hotel. Formerly home of the seven viceroys, there is Himachal Tourism's historic **Hotel Peterhoff** (Tel: 2652538; Tariff: Rs 1,200-3,500).

HPTDC has another property, **Hotel Holiday Home** (Tel: 2612890-97; Tariff: Rs 500-2,400), on Cart Road. A cheaper heritage option is **Madan Kunj** (Tel: 2811837; Tariff: Rs 700-1,750), once the summer residence of the governor of Burma. **Woodville Palace** (Tel: 2623919; Tariff: Rs 2,200-7,000) is a beautifully maintained former royal home.

Springfields (Tel: 2621297; Tariff: Rs. 2,950-4,600) is spread over 4 acres. A delightfully outdoorsy option is **Camp Potter's Hill** (Tel: 09418065001; Tariff: Rs 1,600-2,600), spread over 100 acres of forest, 5 km west of Shimla. Another option is **Woodrina** (Tel: 09816069315; Tariff: Rs 900-1,500).

For more hotels and details, see Accommodation Listings on pages 528-530

WHERE TO EAT

Instead of local cuisine, butter chicken and tandoori rotis dominate menus everywhere in Shimla. What little can be had of Himachali cuisine, you'll find at Himachal Tourism's **Goofa** and **Aashiana** restaurants, both on the Ridge. These are hygienic and serve Indian food at reasonable rates.

For the non-fussy, a curious Tibetan-Indian mix of tasty Chinese food is available almost everywhere. Excellent Continental cuisine may be found in some of the fancier heritage properties like the impressive Wildflower Hall at Mashobra. Go for old time's sake to the multi-cuisine **Devicees**, once known for its fine Western food. The multi-cuisine **Baljees** is among the best here. Street food and dhabas are commonplace in Shimla. The ubiquitous **Barista** and **Domino's** (Tel: 2808572, only takeaway) also have outlets on the Mall. ✦

Outdoors

Adventure   Trekking

Camping   Cycling

Riding   Hiking

It's late in the afternoon- 3pm.
So much left behind &
so much yet to be discovered...

The anticipation of wordless secrets yet to be explored. A hunger for triumph yet to be shared. Breathe in & let go of yourself, your dreams & your troubles. There are still, few such places... that make you touch life.

KOTI RESORTS
S I M L A

DELHI: Ph: 51767253; Mobile: 9810104696   CHD: 0172-2600655; Mobile: 9814123104, 9417132151
e-mail:koti resort_adventure@ rediffmail.com

Shimla Day Hikes
Footloose in the summer capital
By Deepak Sanan and Minakshi Chaudhry

GIREESH G V

TIME	1 day
LEVEL	Easy
IDEAL SEASON	All year round except monsoons
LOCATION	In and around Shimla in the Rupshu region

Seven hills of Shimla wake up to a sunny morning

The best way to get to know Shimla is to walk on some of its quiet roads. In spite of a lot of construction in recent years, some of these roads still retain a certain charm. They bring out the stark contrast between Simla, the erstwhile summer capital of British India and Shimla, the present-day capital of Himachal Pradesh. There are enchanting experiences to be found in deodar and oak woods, pleasant weather, deep blue skies, the play of shade and light as you walk through groves of trees and new vistas opening up after every curve.

It is a pleasure to explore this hill town all year round. On a bright winter day, when you venture out all wrapped up in woollens, your breath condenses. The chill necessitates frequent stops at roadside dhabas for a glass of hot, sweet and strong tea. In summer, the pleasant cool winds are a welcome relief from the scorching heat of the plains. Autumn is wonderful with deep blue skies and wild flowers. The old oak, horse chestnut and rhododendrons shed their older leaves amidst the majestic conifers. The monsoons are a good time to be here if you don't mind a little dampness. This is the time when the town is at its quietest, not too many tourists, gentle rain and mist and, when the skies clear, the most awesome sunsets.

A walk on the lawns of the Indian Institute of Advanced Studies (the former Viceregal Lodge) on a rain-washed, foggy afternoon can be a wonderful experience. On these walks, you can stop and sit in the rain shelters with sloping tin roofs or on

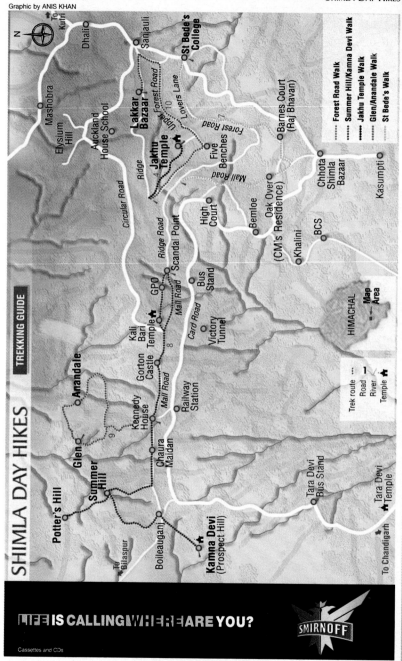

SHIMLA DAY HIKES

Graphic by ANIS KHAN

TREKKING GUIDE

To Kufri

Dhalli

Sanjauli

St Bede's College

Mashobra

Elysium Hill

Auckland House School

Lakkar Bazaar

Forest Road

Lovers Lane

Upper

Jakhu Temple

Ridge

Five Benches

Forest Road

Barnes Court (Raj Bhavan)

Circular Road

Mall Road

Chhota Shimla Bazaar

Kasumpti

Ridge Road

Scandal Point

High Court

Bemloe

Oak Over (CM's Residence)

Khalini

BCS

GPO

Bus Stand

Mall Road

Card Road

Victory Tunnel

Anandale

Kali Bari Temple

Gorton Castle

Mall Road

Railway Station

HIMACHAL

Map Area

Kennedy House

Chaura Maidan

Glen

Summer Hill

Potter's Hill

Tara Devi Bus Stand

Tara Devi Temple

Boileauganj

Kamna Devi (Prospect Hill)

To Bilaspur

To Chandigarh

Trek route
Road
River
Temple

········· Forest Road Walk
········· Summer Hill/Kamna Devi Walk
▪▪▪▪▪▪ Jakhu Temple Walk
▬▬▬▬ Glen/Anandale Walk
········· St Bede's Walk

N

Photos GOPINATH S

Cricket on the Ridge

roadside parapets — not because you are tired but because it is a pleasure to just sit and watch the mists rising and settling around you.

Delicious hot food like rice, rajma, karhi, chapatis and stuffed parathas, besides a variety of other cuisines are available at dhabas and restaurants, all over Shimla and its suburbs like Summer Hill, Boileauganj, Chhota Shimla, Sanjauli, Dhali and Mashobra.

FOREST ROAD WALK
DISTANCE 10 KM **TIME** 3-4 HOURS
LEVEL EASY
Start at the **Ridge** and head north to **Lakkar Bazaar** and then turn east for Sanjauli (3 km). At **Sanjauli Chowk**, turn to your right (south-west) and move up a narrow road ascending steeply up the **Jakhu Hill**. This road leads to the boys' hostels of **Indira Gandhi Medical College**. The climb ends at the point where the road forks. Take the road going left (south). The road to the right leads to the hostels and then back to Lakkar Bazaar. Called the **Upper Forest Road**, the left hand road heads towards Indus Hospital. After about a kilometre, there is another bifurcation, follow the road going up to the right. It leads to a place called **Five Benches** (no benches there now). At Five Benches, three roads branch off.

Shoppers at the bazaar

One road goes to **Jakhu Temple** (climbs up to the right, or north), the other to **Ramchandra Chowk** (goes straight and descends south-west) while the third one goes to **Rich Mount** (descends to the right, or north). Follow the road to Rich Mount, a residential area, and then on to Dream Land Hotel before descending back to the Ridge visible below.

Attractions en route include chana-kulcha and tikkis at **Sita Ram and Son**, the famous snack shop at Lakkar Bazaar. Enjoy the view of snow-clad Himalayan peaks to the north-west as you walk past the Indira Gandhi Medical College Hospital (popularly called Snowdon Hospital). Bask in the silence, birdsong and dappled sunlight on your way to Five Benches, and finish your walk, with mouth-watering chaat on top of the Ridge, at **Taka Bench**.

SUMMER HILL/ KAMNA DEVI WALK
DISTANCE 8 KM **TIME** 3-4 HOURS
LEVEL EASY
From the **Mall Road**, you have two options going west: one, to take the road going past the GPO towards the **Kali Bari Temple**. After the temple, descend to the Mall Road near the Railway Board building. The second option is to walk the length of the Mall Road, and reach the **Railway Board building**, past the State Bank of India. On the way, the headquarters of the ARTRAC (Army Training Command) is to your left.

Take the road to the right of the imposing building of **Gorton Castle**. It is now the Office of the Auditor General of Himachal Pradesh. The walk then goes past the Himachal Legislative Assembly (**Vidhan Sabha**) building and reaches **Chaura Maidan** across from the

Cecil Hotel, the oldest of the Oberoi Hotel properties. A number of small roads branch off from Chaura Maidan, including one heading straight up to the **State Museum** at Inverarm. The main Mall heads north-west to Summer Hill; follow it to reach the **Indian Institute of Advanced Studies**. This neo-Elizabethan building was completed in 1888 and became the residence of the British Viceroy (who earlier stayed at Inverarm).

Visit the institute and then head to **Summer Hill** (turning right at the institute gate, the road on the left goes to Boileauganj). The road winds around to a crossroads at the entrance to the **Himachal Pradesh University**. An option here is to descend west for a short distance to the University Boys Hostel and carry on into the pretty forest area of **Potter's Hill** for a lovely hike.

The route to **Boileauganj** and Kamna Devi is a sharp turn southwards, at the university entrance crossroads. The road joins the main Shimla-Mandi Road at the beginning of **Boileauganj Bazaar**. Directly across, a small road ascends to the left (west), to head up to the small **Kamna Devi Temple** (2,176m), commanding a view of the whole of Shimla Town upto the Jakhu Hill on the east, and the gradually descending hills of Arki to the west.

OTTO PFISTER

Himalayan tree pie

The Himalayan tree pie (*Dendrocitta formosae*) has a black forehead, grey coloration from the crown to the nape, a dark chestnut back and scapulars, and black wings with white specks. Their rumps and upper tail coverts are grey, and their tails are long and black. Himalayan tree pies also have dark, chestnut brown faces, throats and upper chests, ashy brown lower chests and white abdomens.

Himalayan tree pies have a loud, resonant voice and often make a series of short, hoarse calls that sound like "ga er, ge li o". Often seen alone or in small groups, this tree pie usually lives in trees, on flatlands, and in the upper levels of broad-leaved forests in middle-altitude regions. When flying, their wings produce a wave-like movement. Himalayan tree pies are commonly found in forests at the base of mountains, at low and middle altitudes.

Attractions include the **State Museum** at Chaura Maidan, the **Aviary**, the IIAS (with tea in the institute canteen), HPU with lunch at any of the small dhabas, sunset at Kamna Devi.

JAKHU TEMPLE WALK
Distance 4 km **Time** 3 hours
Level Easy

Start at the Ridge and climb east up to Hotel Dreamland, and then to **Rothney Castle**. A proper road leads to the **Hanuman Temple** on **Jakhu Hill** (2,453m). Legend claims that Hanuman had tarried here when he was carrying the *sanjeevani booti* (the miracle herb) to cure Lakshman, who was injured in a battle with Ravan. Descend the same way or wind down to **Five Benches** on the Forest Walk described earlier.

Himalayan weasel

The Himalayan weasel (*Mustela sibrica*) is found above an elevation of about 2,000m, up to about the treeline, in forests, dry sandy slopes and even in low-lying wet areas. It has reddish-copper fur with a body length of about 30 cm, and a tail about 15 cm long. It is found in dense forests from 1,500-5,000m, and also lives close to villages. The Himalayan weasel is a bold and good hunter.

RUPIN DANG/ WILDERNESS FILMS

Apple harvest near Shimla

TRIBHUVAN TIWARI

GLEN/ ANANDALE WALK
Distance 9 km **Time** 4-5 hours
Level Easy

Start from the **Mall** and walk west to the **Vidhan Sabha**. Follow the road going down to the right (north). Past the HP State Electricity Board Office and a concrete rain shelter, the road turns right to descend to the **Anandale Meadow** (a golf course now), while a broad path goes on straight before descending left to the **Glen**.

ST BEDE'S WALK
Distance 7 km **Time** 2-3 hours
Level Easy

Start from the Mall heading southeast to **Chhota Shimla**. The road goes past **Oak Over**, official residence of the chief minister. Take the road going left, leading to **Raj Bhavan** (the erstwhile Barnes Court), the governor's residence. It was in this historic building that the 1972 Shimla Agreement was signed between India and Pakistan. At the entrance of Raj Bhavan, take the road going left (north-east) to Nav Bahar. This road is known as the **Lovers Lane**. It is a quiet road winding through oak and conifer trees, past **Churail Baori** (the witches' spring) to the crossroads above **St Bede's College**. From here, you can take a bus back to Shimla, if you don't feel like walking. ✦

The
Châlets Naldehra
Pine Log Homes

A boutique mountain resort, 22 kms from Shimla, The Chalets is set against a backdrop of a verdant deodar forest. It offers accommodation in quaint pinewood log cottages. The Naldehra Golf Course is just 300 m away.

The Chalets at Naldehra is everybody's dream locale. The log homes are quaint with a small bedroom which opens into a living room with a working fireplace and extends into the dining room. However the romance is completed only by the staircase winding up into a second bedroom with sloping roofs. Small lawns and independent entrances add to the ambience. For those who want to imbibe more than just the peace and serenity, who want to more than just introspect, The Chalets has an activity room with a pool table, table tennis, carrom and indoor games. Also a haven for outdoor enthusiasts, it offers dayhikes and picnics in the adjoining forest, horse riding, golf just 300m away at the 9 hole golf course and whitewater river rafting. Evening barbecues and bonfires under the night sky followed by lip-smacking dinners are an almost perfect way to end the day.

For reservations and more information contact us at :

The Chalets, Naldehra
Phone: 0177-2747715
Cell: 9418062002
Fax: 0177-2747562
E-mail: contact@chaletsnaldehra.com
Website : www.chaletsnaldehra.com

The Caravan, New Delhi
109, 1st Flr, K-138, Kalkaji
Phone: 011-26451482, 26478096,
9810672006.   Fax: 011-26478096
E-Mail: info@travelthemes.com
Website: www.travelthemes.com

Hatu Peak

The Gorkha battlefield

By Deepak Sanan

TIME	1-2 days
LEVEL	Easy
IDEAL SEASON	May-Jun and Sep-Nov
LOCATION	In Shimla District, close to Narkanda, 64 km NE of Shimla

A colourful temple adorns the crest of Hatu Peak

NARKANDA-HATU-NARKANDA

For the rulers of the erstwhile hill states, Hatu Peak was of great strategic importance because of its commanding position. It was accepted as a boundary between the states. The Gorkhas captured it early in the 19th century and established a fort at the top of Hatu Peak. Later, the British ousted them from the Hatu heights.

Narkanda (2,708m), at the base of Hatu, offers a spectacular view of the snow-capped peaks of the Himalayas. It stretches from the Srikhand Range in the east to the Kinner Kailash Range of Kinnaur in the north-west, and all the way across to the peaks of the Tons and Yamuna catchment in Uttaranchal.

Hatu is famous for its ski slopes. A sub-centre of the Mountaineering and Allied Sports Institute at Manali (*see Mountaineering Institutes on page 521*) runs adventure activities here, and ski equipment is available in winter. Thanedar and Kotgarh near Narkanda form the apple heartland of Himachal. Samuel Stokes, an American, introduced apple cultivation here in 1905.

This is an easy walk of 7 km (one way) to Hatu Peak and you can be back at Narkanda, easily, on the same day. But if you want to experience the thrill of the Hatu Ridge at night, take a tent along and camp out.

NARKANDA-HATU-NARKANDA
DISTANCE 14 KM **TIME** 6-8 HOURS
LEVEL EASY
Hatu Peak is located 7 km east of Narkanda, on a jeep road. It's best to follow this road. Take a few easy short-cuts across the switchback turns. From

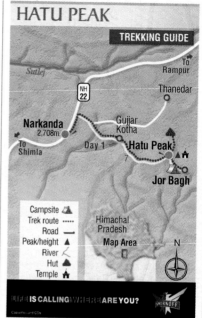

Graphic by ANIS KHAN

HATU PEAK

TREKKING GUIDE

Sutlej

To Rampur

NH 22

Thanedar

Narkanda 2,708m

Gujjar Kotha

To Shimla

Day 1

Hatu Peak

Jor Bagh

Campsite ⛺
Trek route ·····
Road ——
Peak/height ▲
River ∕
Hut ⛺
Temple ⛩

Himachal Pradesh

Map Area

N

LIFE IS CALLING WHERE ARE YOU?

GETTING THERE AND OUT

FROM SHIMLA to Narkanda, it's 64 km/ 2 hrs by 🚙 (Qualis Rs 1,500, Indica Rs 1,000 return fare) or 3 hrs by 🚌 (Rs 55). Taxis charge extra for waiting. Buses, both state and private in the ordinary and deluxe categories, ply very frequently on this route. The first bus leaves Shimla at 5 am and the last at 9 pm. NH22 makes for smooth driving all through

RETURN Take the same route from Narkanda to Shimla

the **Narkanda Bazaar**, take the road going east to Thanedar. It meanders through a rich conifer forest. Less than a half hour along the **Thanedar Road**, at the further end of a little saddle on the ridge to our right (south), a small road branches off, heading a little south of east. A signboard indicates that the road leads to Hatu Temple.

The entire walk is through a mixed forest covering the whole range of high-altitude conifers: blue pine, deodar, fir and spruce interspersed with the broad-leaved moru. Then come the kharsu oak, rhododendron, walnut and horse chestnut. Shaded for the most part, the climb can still make one thirsty. However, water is not available on the trail, so carry enough from Narkanda.

Every year, a fair is held here in May and several small dhabas and bustling 🍵 tea shops come up for a few days. At all other times, you have to carry your own provisions.

Red-billed blue magpie

The red billed blue magpie (*Urocissa erythrorhyncha*) is said to be a relative of the crow. It occurs in a broad swathe, from the Western Himalayas, eastwards into China and Vietnam, among evergreen forest and scrub in predominantly hilly or mountainous country. The head, neck and breast are black with a bluish spotting on the crown. The shoulders and rump are a duller blue and the underparts are a greyish cream. The long tail is a brighter blue (as are the wing primaries) with a broad white tip. The bill is a bright orange-red as are the legs and feet and the ring around the eye. Vocal mimicry is very apparent in this species and its calls are very varied, but the most usual are a grating rattle and a high-pitched whistle, a little like a flute.

RUPIN DANG/ WILDERNESS FILMS

DEEPAK SANAN

At a Gujjar kotha en route to Hatu

The route heads east up the gradually ascending ridge. Half-way up is a **Gujjar kotha** (temporary shelters of Gujjars who come here to camp with their herds in the summer) with a little pond reflecting the tall trees, the peaks beyond and the blue sky above. **Hatu Mata Temple** is located at the top of a long ridge with a more or less north-south orientation. At the northern edge of the ridge is a small shelter constructed by the PWD. From here, you can enjoy a 360-degree panoramic view. The snow-capped Himalayan peaks extend in a wide arc across the northern horizon while the hills and valleys of **Rohru**, **Theog** and **Shimla** spread out on the south and east. The villages of **Kumarsain**, **Kotgarh** and **Nirmand** can be seen amidst dense forests, terraced fields and apple orchards.

An hour's walk south-east past the temple, and then through a forest dominated by oak trees, gets you to the grassy meadows of **Jor Bagh**. The place is ideal for camping if one decides on a night out.

For hotels in Narkanda, see Accommodation Listings on page 528 ◆

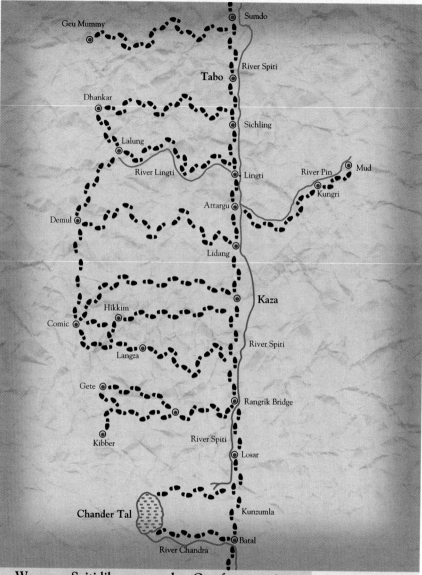

Sumdo

Geu Mummy

River Spiti

Tabo

Dhankar

Sichling

Lalung

River Lingti

Lingti

River Pin

Mud

Attargu

Kungri

Demul

Lidang

Kaza

Hikkim

Comic

River Spiti

Langza

Gete

Rangrik Bridge

Kibber

River Spiti

Losar

Chander Tal

Kunzumla

Batal

River Chandra

We cover Spiti like no one else. One foot at a time.

If you're looking to go trekking in the glorious Himalayan region of Spiti come with Banjara. We are the only camping and trek organisers actually based in the Spiti region. Our in-depth local knowledge, two fully equipped retreats in Kaza and Tabo, and comprehensive arrangements come together to make your trek a unique trip that few can boast of. Come explore Spiti with us, we promise you an experience you'll never forget.

Banjara Camps & Retreats, 1A, Hauz Khas Village, New Delhi - 16, Ph: 011 26861397, 011 26855153, email: info@banjaracamps.com, www.banjaracamps.com

Janjheli-Shikari Devi

Through the ancient hunting grounds

By Deepak Sanan
and Minakshi Chaudhry

The terraced slopes of picturesque Janjheli

JANJHELI-SHIKARI DEVI-JANJHELI

TIME	2-3 days
LEVEL	Easy
IDEAL SEASON	All year except Dec-Jan
LOCATION	In the Beas and Sutlej valleys of Mandi District

Janjheli is a picturesque valley with forested mountainsides sloping down from ridgelines. It's dotted with pretty flower-bedecked meadows. The British wanted to develop the area as a hill retreat but the Raja of Mandi did not approve of their plan. The abode of Goddess Shikari stands atop the highest point in the area. Legends aver that the Pandavas built the temple while wandering in the Himalayas during their exile. Arjun apparently saw a deer in the forest below the ridge but, surprisingly, failed in his attempt to bring down the animal. Realising that the deer must be a manifestation of some divine power, the brothers prayed to the divine power to reveal itself. Navdurga appeared before them and asked the brothers to install her at an appropriate place. The Pandavas then built a temple for the goddess on the peak, and she came to be known as Shikari Devi, the Goddess of the Hunt.

The temple is roofless. According to local lore, the goddess does not permit construction of a roof and all attempts in this direction have failed given the strong winds that buffet the peak. Animal sacrifice is practised at the temple. During the *navratras*, a fair is held here, which attracts a large number of devotees from the surrounding valleys.

DEEPAK SANAN

Experience Octane

The Hi-Octane High Performance petrol from Bharat Petroleum.

Bharat
Petroleum

GETTING THERE AND OUT

FROM MANDI to Janjheli, it's 92 km/ 3½ hrs by 🚗 (Rs 1,200) or 5½ hrs by 🚌 (Rs 95). The road passes through the picturesque Gohar region of Mandi with Chail Chowk and Bagsiad as main stops on the way **Delhi to Mandi** (454 km) Taxi 12 hrs/ Rs 6,000; bus 13 hrs (HPTDC Delhi-Manali bus Rs 550, ordinary Rs 275)
RETURN by the same route or take the other options at the end of the trek

This easy trek can be completed at a leisurely pace in three to four hours. The walk is shaded and is mostly on a

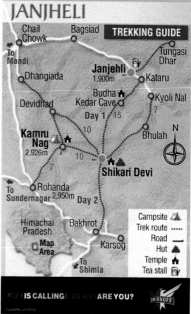

Graphic by ANIS KHAN

jeepable road. From the top, at Shikari Devi (2,950m), several options are available. One can come back by the same route or go down south-west to Devidhad. Or descend south to Chindi/ Bakhrot to reach Karsog Valley from where one can board a bus to Mandi or Shimla. It is also possible to trek to Kamru Nag from Shikari Devi and then trek down to Rohanda on the Karsog-Mandi Road. Alternatively, you can descend to Janjheli (1,900m) from Kamru Nag. All these are one-day treks.

DAY ONE
JANJHELI-SHIKARI DEVI
DISTANCE 15 KM **TIME** 5-6 HOURS
LEVEL EASY
There are two trails from Janjheli that lead to the temple. Both pass through a thick forest of blue pine and oak.

OPTION 1
This is the better option, though slightly longer. It follows the jeep

Himalayan yew

The Himalayan yew (*Taxus wallichiana*) is widely but sparsely distributed along cool temperate belts between 2,600 and 3,300m in the Western Himalayas. It is a temperate conifer tree and the leaves yield the much sought after anti-cancer drug, taxol. Traditionally, the bark of this plant was used in butter tea and medicines and its wood as timber in various regions of the Himalayas. However, due to its excessive collection for use in anti-tumour and anti-cancer drugs, its population has vastly reduced.

SANJEEVA PANDEY

road almost all the way to the temple. The gradient of the ascent is less taxing and there are several short-cuts, which can reduce the distance. The road heads south through the mixed forest of oak and pine that serves as a habitat for numerous wild animals, including the black bear. The road stops about a kilometre short of the temple, from where a path climbs steeply south to a small ridge. At the ridge, the path turns right and levels out to reach a sarai just below the temple.

The **roofless temple** commands a 360-degree view. Kullu District is to the east and north while Mandi and Shimla districts spread out in the other two directions with the **Sutlej Valley** dividing the two districts in the south. The view from the top is stunning. Range upon range of hills appear to roll away endlessly into the distant skyline. On a clear morning, the high snow-covered Himalayan ranges on the Kullu side seem close at hand. A 15-min descent leads to the ▲ 2-room **Trekkers' Hut** (for

The open-air Shikari Devi Temple with stunning views

BIRBAL SHARMA

PARK WOODS, SHOGHI
A VILLAGE RESORT
In 20 acres of wilderness
17kms short of SHIMLA

An offbeat rustic forest retreat amidst an emerald pine forest at 5700 feet and set on a ridge amidst unspoilt wilderness. The panoramic views of the forest and valley around and the mountains beyond makes it a delightful locale. Lawns, gardens, thatched double decked restaurant, a variety of recreational and adventure activities promise to add pleasure and luxury to an adventurous and rejuvenating holiday. Accommodation is a mix of bamboo huts and deluxe swiss cottage tents. All units have heating, comfortable full size beds, attached bathrooms, electricity. The obstacle course, jungle treks, rock climbing and rappelling intersperse the sojourn with adventure. For the more intrepid, moonlit trails and overnight survival camping are a must do. Also a great location for team-building corporate offsites and group adventure programs.

bookings contact DFO Kullu, Tel: 01902-222510), visible from the top. It is reasonably furnished with beds, basic furniture and a kitchen stocked with fuel wood.

OPTION 2

This trek is via the **Budha Kedar Cave**. It involves a steep climb and is tiring. The trail takes off south-west from Janjheli, passes through several small villages and enters a forest with some fine chir pine, oak and blue pine trees. It then climbs south leading to the Budha Kedar Cave, with a cave

Cheer pheasant

Dull in comparison to other pheasants, both sexes of the cheer pheasant (*Catreus wallichii*) have long grey crests, and buff and grey plumage, with black bars. The tail is long and barred buff, grey and brown. Females are very similar to males, though they lack spurs, and are slightly smaller in size. The cheer pheasant is an endangered species frequenting open habitats in the Himalayan foothills of Pakistan, India and Nepal. It is found in forests at an altitude of above 1,000m, especially in the hill slopes with steep rocky cliffs, long grass and scattered trees. Overhunting and habitat destruction has caused rapid depletion of populations.

OTTO PFISTER

temple alongside a stream. Beyond the cave the climb continues through a picturesque landscape before climbing steeply to a ridge, where there are a few **Gujjar kothas**. Here the trail turns left and ascends to the temple sarai. This path can also be used to descend from the temple. An early start in the morning makes the journey easy and enjoyable. The forest is rich in both flora and fauna including bears, therefore one should not travel after dark.

DAY TWO

SHIKARI DEVI-JANJHELI

To return to Janjheli either follow one of the two options described above in reverse. Or choose from the ones described below.

RETURN OPTIONS

SHIKARI DEVI-BAKHROT
DISTANCE 15 KM **TIME** 3-4 HOURS
LEVEL MODERATE

OPTION 1

Descend southwards to **Bakhrot** on the Karsog-Mandi Road. The steep trail is well defined and passes through a beautiful valley with some ancient temples. **Karsog** is a sub-divisional headquarters with bus services to both the district headquarters at Mandi and the state capital Shimla.

OPTION 2

From **Shikari Peak** it is also possible to trek the 10 km to **Kamru Nag** (2,926m) in 3-4 hrs on a defined trail that traverses many small ridges but does not involve many steep ascents and descents. The thickly forested terrain makes this a fine walk heading east from the temple past a ridge-top helipad. From Kamru Nag there is the option of descending to **Janjheli** (10 km/ 4 hrs) or **Rohanda** (7 km/ 2-3 hrs). Rohanda is on the Karsog-Mandi Road.

Kamru Nag is a powerful local deity and the temple is on the edge of a lake.

TREKKING HOLIDAYS IN INDIA

The road to Janjheli winds its way through flower-bedecked meadows

Every year, on 14th and 15th June, a fair is held here, which is attended by thousands of people. There is a tradition that the offerings (often gold/silver ornaments and coins) are immersed in the lake located on the level ridge top.

You can camp here in **Kamru Nag** if you want, and proceed to Janjheli or Rohanda the following day.

OPTION 3

Just past the ridge-top helipad near the Trekkers' Hut, a path descends steeply into another southern valley sloping away from the flanks of the **Shikari Devi Range**, to the Forest Rest House at **Devidhad** (10 km/ 3 hrs). For bookings contact DFO Goher on Tel: 01907-250267/ 268; or Senior District Magistrate on Tel: 250262. Devidhad is connected to Chail Chowk by the Karsog-Mandi Road.

TREKS AROUND JANJHELI

Bhulah, 10 km on the motor road from Janjheli (or a 7-km trek) is a set of breathtakingly beautiful meadows. The metalled road passes through the villages of **Kataru** (1½ km) and reaches **Sangalwara** and **Kyoli Nal** villages (4 km). These are located near the **Bakhali Khad**. From here a dirt road heads to **Bhulah**. Carry tents and necessary provisions if you intend camping out.

Budha Kedar, a short trek from Janjehli (2-3 hrs away to the south), is steeped in myth. It is said that imprints of Bhima's knees were left on a giant boulder when he knelt to stop an escaping bull. The bull escaped, but its tail got caught in a cave nearby. The 'tail' can still be seen in this cave, whereas the 'head' of the bull can be seen at Kedarnath in Uttaranchal, with the body trapped in the earth between these two places.

Tungasi Dhar (3,600m) was chosen by one of the Rajas of Mandi for an observation tower to keep watch over Kullu. Though the highest point in the region, this strategic post gradually lost relevance. It is said that condemned prisoners were once pushed down from the cliff and their shrieks could be heard till Janjheli. This practice stopped when the British took over the hills.

Approach the fort through **Janjheli Village** and climb a steep 3 hrs (7 km) to the east. From here, there is also a trekking route to **Garagushaini** and then to **Banjar**.

The drive from Delhi to Sangla in the Kinnaur region takes all of two days. The first night you halt at Shimla, then you continue the next morning on NH22 towards Narkanda, perched precipitously high above the Sutlej Valley. At Karchham, you leave this dry, dusty valley and take the road climbing steeply above the Baspa, its crystal-clear blue-green waters flowing over craggy rocks. Then suddenly, without any warning, you enter the wide, open Sangla Valley and believe you have stumbled into the heart of the Swiss countryside. Dominated by the impressive snow-clad Kinner Kailash peak, the valley is thickly forested with tall deodars and the stately *chilgoza* (pine). The tiny hamlet of Sangla is lovingly spread out along the Baspa amidst fields of buckwheat and apple orchards.

Chitkul blanketed in snow

ADVENTURE

Go **river crossing** but with professional and experienced operators.

WHERE TO STAY

Options are very limited in Sangla, which is why you must plan well in advance or you might just be left out in the cold!

The **Banjara Camps** (Tel: 01786-242536; 011-26861397; Tariff: Rs 3,300) outfit, located in Batseri Village on the banks of the Baspa River, has 18 Swiss-style tents with attached bath and h/c water. The **Mount Kailash Guest House** (Tel: 242390, 242527; Tariff: Rs 300-1,000) has a restaurant. The **PWD Bungalow** (DC Office Kinnaur, Tel: 01786-222227; Tariff: Rs 200), near the bazaar, is a 2-roomed affair. The caretaker will rustle up basic dal-chawal. Carry your own provisions.

It's a 1-hr walk to the 2-room **Forest Rest House** (DFO Kinnaur, Tel: 01786-223358; Tariff: Rs 250).
For more hotels and details, see Accommodation Listings on page 528

→ Sangla Facts

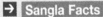

- **LOCATION** In Kinnaur District, at 2,679m, Sangla is 227 km from Shimla
- **GETTING TO SANGLA By air** Nearest airport: Shimla (9 hrs, taxi Rs 3,500 one-way) **By road** Four-wheel drive recommended for this journey from Shimla to Karchham on NH22. At Karchham, turn right up the ridge to Sangla Valley. Daily bus for Sangla from Shimla's Lakkar Bazaar (dep 7.45 am, arr 8 pm; Rs 181). Or, take the Recongpeo deluxe bus from Chandigarh (dep 6.30 am, arr 7.30 pm; Rs 250) for Karchham. Get a pick-up or take a local jeep to Sangla
- **STD CODE** 01786

MUST-VISITS

HERITAGE

The impressive **Kamru Fort** was once the bastion of the Rajas of Rampur Bushehr, who were coronated at the **Kamakshi Temple**, perched on a hillock high above the village.

FISHING

The Baspa River is home to both the rainbow and brown trout. Fishing without a permit is illegal. Obtain one (Rs 100) from the Fisheries Department here.

WHERE TO EAT

Chances are you'll be eating wherever you're staying. There are a few tea shops and dhabas, which dish up the usual fare, including the Tibetan momos and *thukpa* (noodle soup). The lucky might even find a bowl of Chinese-style soup. **Banjara Camps** will, at a pinch, welcome walk-ins for buffet meals.

INPUTS FROM ANJALI ABHYANKAR-ROY

In Sangla we have more than one way to make your trek memorable.

With a fully equipped base in Sangla since 1994, Banjara Camps and Retreats know the region like nobody else. We can take you on treks that few have seen, provide you the comfort and conveniences few can match and leave you with stories that others will envy.

Banjara Camps & Retreats, 1A, Hauz Khas Village, New Delhi - 16, Ph: 011 26861397, 011 26855153, email: info@banjaracamps.com, www.banjaracamps.com

The Sangla Kanda Trek
For holiday-makers at Sangla

By Deepak Sanan

Photographs by SUMAN DUBEY

TIME	3 days
LEVEL	Moderate
IDEAL SEASON	Jun to Sep
LOCATION	In the Baspa Valley of Kinnaur District

The verdant trail to Sangla Kanda's emerald green pastures

SANGLA-SANGLA KANDA-DAMBAR
KANDA-SANGLA

If you are planning a holiday in Sangla and wish to throw in a bit of exercise and adventure, this short trek is ideal for you. This way, you can savour the beauty of the pastures of Sangla Kanda without the exertion of the Rupin Pass trek. Enjoy the Kanda over the afternoon after climbing up from Sangla. Spend the night at (or near) the Trekker's Hut here and climb north-west the next day to cross the Shivaling Pass back towards the Baspa Valley. Once across, stroll down to the trekking hut at Dambar, the pasture of Chansu Village. If time is not at a premium, spend another night watching the moon over Raldang Peak, due

north across the Baspa Valley. From Dambar take the steep track to Chansu Village and Ruttrang Bridge, to reach the motor road 3 km below Sangla.

DAY ONE
SANGLA-SANGLA KANDA
DISTANCE 10 KM **TIME** 4 HOURS
LEVEL EASY

From the motor road at **Sangla**, various paths descend through the village. Cross the **Baspa Valley** by a sturdy footbridge below the Forest Rest House, located just above the Baspa left bank. From here, a footpath climbs steeply south-west through deodar and blue pine. The Baspa Valley is visible below till the crest of the ridge is crossed. Across is the famed expanse of **Sangla Kanda** (3,600m), sloping

Red fox

OTTO PFISTER

With its dog-like face, bushy, white-tipped tail and red coat, the red fox (*Vulpes vulpes*) is the quintessential fox. Valuing its privacy, the red fox usually keeps to itself, hunting at night when few are out and about. However, during the winter mating season, the male comes to stay with the vixen and cubs, in the dens. For two weeks after giving birth, the vixen relies on the male to bring her food while she nurses their cubs. By summer, red fox cubs are ready to leave and go out on their own. Red foxes can run at speeds of more than 30 miles per hour when chased, and are good swimmers.

gradually from west to east before dropping sharply to the Rukti stream on the left. The **Rukti**, a left bank tributary of the Baspa, meets the latter just above Sangla near the hamlet of **Anmoshiresh**. The path continues south-west through single crop fields climbing gradually to reach pasture land as one approaches the head of the **Rukti Valley**.

Graphic by ANIS KHAN

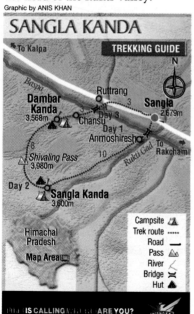

SANGLA KANDA

TREKKING GUIDE

To Kalpa

Baspa

Ruttrang

Dambar Kanda
3,568m

Chansu

Day 3

Sangla
2,679m

Day 1

Anmoshiresh

To Rakchham

Rukti Gad

Shivaling Pass
3,980m

Day 2

Sangla Kanda
3,600m

Himachal Pradesh

Map Area

Campsite
Trek route .....
Road ——
Pass
River
Bridge
Hut

PHONE IS CALLING WHERE ARE YOU?

🦙 **Shepherd shelters** and a basic 🏔 **Trekker's Hut** are an alternative to camping out for the night — but the sheep droppings and mites make tents an infinitely superior alternative.

DAY TWO
SANGLA KANDA-DAMBAR KANDA
DISTANCE 8 KM **TIME** 3 HOURS
LEVEL EASY

From the camp at the upper end of Sangla Kanda, traverse north-west and back towards the Baspa Valley, along the grassy slopes of the mountain

Bharat Petroleum

GETTING THERE AND OUT

FROM SHIMLA to Sangla, it's 227 km/ 9 hrs by 🚙 (Sumo/ Qualis Rs 3,500) or 11 hrs by 🚌 (Rs 105). There is only one bus to Sangla, at 7.15 am. If you miss the direct bus, take a bus to **Karchham** (every 30 mins between 6 am and 10 pm), 18 km short of Sangla. Local jeep (last at 5 pm) charges Rs 20 per person from here to Sangla
RETURN Take the same route back to Shimla. Return bus at 6.30 am

Chilgoza pine

Found in the dry inner valleys of the north-west Himalayas, the chilgoza pine (*Pinus gerardiana*) is an evergreen tree found at altitudes of upto 3,000m. It grows to a height of upto 82 ft. It is in leaf all year, in flower from May to June, and the seeds ripen in October. The flowers are monoecious (individual flowers are either male or female, but both sexes can be found on the same plant), and are pollinated by wind. The crown of the tree is usually deep, wide and open, with

ASHVINI GAUTAM

long, erect branches, but they become narrower and shallower in dense forest. The chilgoza pine's bark is very flaky, peeling to reveal light greyish-green patches. Leaf secretions inhibit the germination of seeds, thus reducing the number of plants that can grow beneath the tree. In Afghanistan, this species is cultivated for its edible seed, and efforts are underway to expand its economic utilisation in India. The seed, rich in oil, is an important local food source and is considered a great delicacy.

separating Sangla Kanda from the **Dambar** pasture of **Chansu Village**. Climbing gradually and curving north, the route ascends to the ridge crossing it at **Shivaling Pass** (3,980m). The pass overlooks the spread of the Sangla bowl below. Across, further

south, is the panorama of the **Kinner Kailash Range** with **Raldang's** sharp spire (5,499m) most prominent. The descent north to Dambar Kanda is not very steep and the ⛺ **Trekker's Hut** (not in good shape) at **Dambar Kanda** (3,568m) is visible from the top.

Ponies graze at Dambar pasture

DAY THREE
DAMBAR KANDA-SANGLA
DISTANCE 6 KM **TIME** 2 HOURS
LEVEL EASY

The descent to **Chansu Village**, 800m below, is steep — but quickly accomplished by those with good mountain legs. Initially, along the grassy slopes, it enters steeper rock faces and scattered forest half-way down. The roadhead lies at **Ruttrang Bridge**, 3 km from Sangla, and just below the reservoir of the recently completed 300 Mw Baspa II Hydel Project. Sadly, it drains the Baspa of its might, and one can no longer experience the magnificence of its precipitous tumble below Ruttrang.

For hotels in Sangla, see Accommodation Listings on page 528 ✦

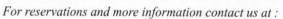

Rupi-Bhaba Wildlife Sanctuary
A wilderness high

By Deepak Sanan

Photographs by DEEPAK SANAN

TIME	5-10 days
LEVEL	Easy to Moderate
IDEAL SEASON	May-Jun, Sep-Oct
LOCATION	North of the Sutlej Valley, Kinnaur District

CHAURA-RUPI-BARA KAMBA-SALARING-SAK KANDA-KATGAON

Apricot blooms near the sanctuary

The Rupi-Bhaba Sanctuary on the right bank of the Sutlej occupies the greenest corner of Kinnaur. Backed by the Srikhand Range, its valleys allow free access to the monsoon travelling up the Sutlej. Rupi-Bhaba also has the greatest altitudinal range among Kinnaur's three sanctuaries (1,200-6,000m). This enables you to see vegetation ranging from the sub-tropical to the alpine, and a wide range in fauna, all in a day and a half's march.

Down by the Sutlej, large-leafed, gnarled trees of melotus, and the smaller span of the ficus, exist in strange proximity with the chir pine. At one or two places there are even groves of banana trees. Warm, subtropical growth gives way to cooler mountain vegetation near the villages — oak, blue pine, temperate fruit trees (birdcherry, wild apricot, peach and pear) and, on occasion, the deodar. Further up, spruce and then fir predominate and finally, high-altitude oak and birch take over as the limits of the treeline are approached. The pasture country beyond is rich and extensive, attracting flocks from great distances, especially the wide spaces of the upper Bhaba Valley.

Near the Sutlej, the goral, an antelope, is the herbivore most fre-quently sighted. Further up is the habitat of the ungainly serow, then the majestic tahr and dainty musk deer and finally, near the Spiti border, is blue sheep and ibex country. The carnivores here are mostly from the feline family. Leopards are the largest of this clan and have for company the leopard cat and the lynx. In the lower areas, the black bear is greatly feared while in the upper reaches, the brown bear prowls the pastures — with only an occasional straying snow leopard from Spiti to share his supremacy. Smaller carnivores include the marten and the fox. For bird life, the sanctuary's major boast is the

Graphic by ANIS KHAN

TREKKING GUIDE

RUPI-BHABA WILDLIFE SANCTUARY

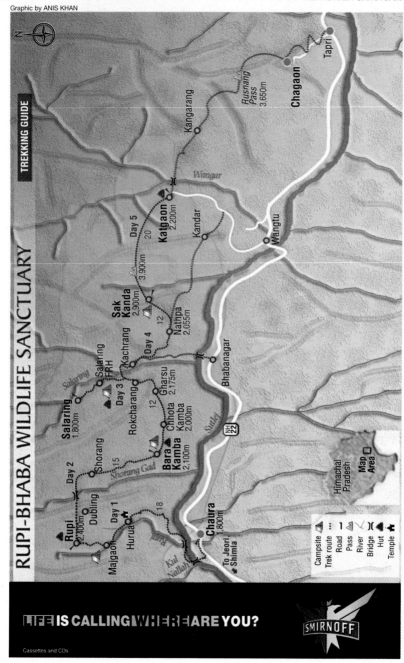

Tapri

Chagaon

Rusnang Pass 3,650m

Kangarang

Wangur

Katgaon 2,200m

Kandar

Day 5

20

Wangtu

Sak Kanda 2,900m

3,900m

Kachrang

12

Nathpa 2,055m

Day 4

Salaring FRH

Gharsu 2,175m

Bhabanagar

Salaring

Salaring 1,800m

Day 3

Rokcharang

Chhota Kamba 2,000m

12

Sutlej

NH 22

Day 2

Shorang

Bara Kamba 2,100m

Himachal Pradesh

Map Area

Dubling

Day 1

15

Shorang Gad

Rupi 2,400m

18

Majgaon

Hurua

Chaura 1,800m

Jhind

Kul Nallah

To Jeori Shimla

Campsite
Trek route
Road
Pass
River
Bridge
Hut
Temple

Walnut

Walnut is the common name given to twenty species of deciduous trees in the genus *Juglans*. The compound leaves of walnuts are spaced alternately along the branches. Each leaf is divided into an odd number — usually from 7 to 23 — of small yellowish green leaves. Walnuts are monoecious, with male flowers borne in long, unbranched, drooping catkins and female flowers borne singly or in short spikes. The walnut fruit is a nut, borne singly or in pairs, and enclosed in a solid, non-splitting green husk. The edible, oil-rich nut kernel is enclosed in a thick, hard, ridged, black shell. Black walnut heartwood is heavy, hard, strong and durable, with a chocolate-brown colour prized by furniture manufacturers and many other industries.

Western Himalayan horned tragopan. Other pheasants likely to be seen include the monal, the kalij, the koklash and, sometimes in the lower reaches, the chir. Also present, in the upper areas, is the snow cock.

With only a limited road network, the Rupi-Bhaba Sanctuary has to be explored on foot. For the real wildlife enthusiast, it is worth moving from village to village, keeping additional days for forays up the various side valleys. This route stays close to the Sutlej River but covers the catchment of every tributary, starting with the Rupi and moving eastwards through the Shorang and the Salaring and ending in the Wangar. You can trek anywhere between five and ten days, depending on the time available for making forays up the different valleys in the sanctuary.

To get to the starting point of Chaura, drive from Shimla to Rampur or Jeori, as they offer a greater choice in accommodation. Head to Chaura the following morning. Chaura also has a Forest Rest House and, if you like, you could try and get a room there, or camp on its grounds. This would allow you to make an early start the next morning.

DAY ONE

CHAURA-RUPI
DISTANCE 18 KM **TIME** 6-7 HOURS
LEVEL MODERATE

Take the path from the motor road at **Chaura** (1,800m) down to a footbridge that spans the **Sutlej**. The 1,100-m climb on the Sutlej right bank is best tackled in the cool of early morning. Reaching the hamlets of **Rupi** (2,400m) under a mid-day sun can become a pitiless, sweat-stained ordeal.

Once across the footbridge, the trek moves upstream, along the right bank of the Sutlej, for about 1 km. Cross the **Rupi stream** near its confluence with the Sutlej, and climb the hillside on its left bank. A right bank path is shorter but this relentless climb, with no water en route, is best avoided. On the main bridle path, there are two springs. The first is near the bridge over the Rupi stream and the second in a boxwood grove half-way up the main climb (the water is sweet but not too clear). After almost 3 hrs of climbing, the pretty temple of **Hurua**, atop a little knoll, heralds the arrival of **Rupi Valley** habitation.

The path now moves right (north) into the Rupi bowl on a gentle gradient. A little over a kilometre beyond the temple, the Rupi stream is crossed. A steep climb on its right bank enables one to reach **Nalling** and **Majgaon** hamlets. Rupi is about 1 km further north-east from Majgaon. It has a beautifully located ⛺ **Forest Rest House** where one can camp overnight. If you have an extra day, you can visit the **Bampa pasture** located above the treeline, immediately behind the rest house. The steep climb will definitely be rewarded with monal sightings en route, besides the additional possibility of seeing tahr and bears.

DAY TWO

RUPI-BARA KAMBA
DISTANCE 15 KM **TIME** 3-4 HOURS
LEVEL EASY

From Rupi to Bara Kamba (2,100m), moving east to the **Shorang Valley**, there are two options — an uphill, forest path that descends to cross the Shorang stream by a footbridge, and a newer path reaching the Shorang much lower downstream and crossing the stream by a *jhula* (a metal basket slung from a steel rope). The latter path is a shorter and more direct route to Bara Kamba but the forest path is an infinitely superior option for the die-hard nature lover.

Bara Kamba shepherd

Bharat Petroleum

GETTING THERE AND OUT

FROM SHIMLA to Rampur, it's 116 km/ 5 hrs by 🚙 (Rs 1,550 to 1,950) or 6 hrs by 🚌 (Rs 100). Plenty of buses leave from the Lakkad Bazaar Bus Stop (Tel: 0177-2811259) through the day and night daily
Rampur to Chaura is 34 km via Jeori (23 km). Take any Recongpeo bus, easily available, for Chaura (3 hrs/ Rs 50). Rampur taxis charge approximately Rs 600 for the $2^{1}/_{2}$-hr drive to Chaura. Alternatively, negotiate with the Shimla taxi
RETURN Take a taxi (Rs 3,500/ 8 hrs) or a bus (Rs 185/ 10 hrs) from **Katgaon** (204 km). There are three buses during the day — 5.30 and 6.30 am and 1.30 pm via Wangtu, en route to Shimla
TIP Rupi is the wettest valley of Kinnaur. Travel before or after the rains

From the rest house, the path circles southwards out of the **Rupi Valley**, moving back towards the Sutlej on more or less even contours. Then ascending the pine and spruce-clad ridge behind **Dubling Village** (visible below the path), it descends sharply on the farther (eastern) side to a bridge on the **Shorang**, below the hamlet of the same name.

The views up and down the **Sutlej Valley** are great all the way to the ridge top and, on the way down, there is a definite possibility of spotting bears feeding on wild fruit in the shaded gullies. Once across the bridge *do not* climb up to the Shorang houses. The more or less level path runs along the Shorang left bank,

Serow

SATYA PRIYA G BHALLA /WFIL ARCHIVE

This odd-looking creature with a goat-like body and donkey-like ears, stands about 3.5 ft at the shoulder. The serow (*Naemorhedus sumatraensis*) has a stocky body, thick neck, large head and ears, and short limbs. Its horns are stout and conical, pointed backwards, and present in both sexes. Serows are generally coloured black or reddish chestnut, with white on their limbs. Mostly solitary, they can be found between 1,800 and 3,000m. Since the serow is related to the goat, it possesses the same ability to jump from rocks and climb steep areas. In addition, it has the special ability of climbing trees that grow on the cliffs. When alarmed, the serow emits a hiss or whistling scream and bounds away.

leaving the stream far below as it tumbles precipitously to reach the Sutlej River. The last kilometre or so of the 5-km distance from the bridge ascends gradually through the fields of **Bara Kamba**, past the village, to a little rocky spur commanding great views of the Sutlej Valley. You can try the **Irrigation and Public Health Department Rest House** here or pitch tent.

TREKKING OPTIONS

For those with time to explore the **Shorang Valley**, it takes at least 2 days to walk to the base of the **Kamba Khango Pass** leading to the upper **Bhaba Valley**. Worth it for wildlife enthusiasts, who can catch a glimpse of the entire range of wildlife in the valley, from goral to ibex. For those with less time, part way up maybe almost as satisfying. A day's march until just beyond **Dumti** (2,705m), at the confluence of two major tributaries of the Shorang, will provide opportunities of sighting the serow, tragopan, bear, marten and leopard en route. Basic provisions can be obtained in all the villages but there is no habitation up valley beyond the **Shorang hamlet** — so all

The pretty little hamlet of Salaring in the secluded Salaring Valley

Rupi women sit around a typical Kinnauri kitchen

provisions and camping gear have to be carried beyond here. One cannot take loaded animals up the Shorang so it may be necessary to hire porters in Bara Kamba.

 Camping is possible at **Dumti** and at many places in the pastures beyond along the eastern tributary of the Shorang that leads to the Kamba Khango Pass. The route is straight-forward and a guide is not essential.

DAY THREE
BARA KAMBA-SALARING FOREST HUT
DISTANCE 12 KM **TIME** 3 HOURS
LEVEL EASY

If one has taken time off to explore the innards of the Shorang Valley, there is a kind of 'find your own path along shepherd trails' alternative in moving on to the smaller valley of **Salaring** (1,800m). Climb the ridge behind the hamlet of Shorang traversing east across the pastures of the Kamba villages and descending to the Salaring stream.

If you haven't done Shorang and are starting from Bara Kamba, the easier, more travelled route is along the village paths heading east, via the villages of **Chhota Kamba** (2,000m) and **Gharsu** (2,175m).

The other option to Salaring is to take an old forest inspection path, which stays just above these villages. Moving up the main Sutlej Valley, this forest path traverses east along steep hillsides, leaving the village of Chhota Kamba below. About 2 hrs out of Bara Kamba, the path climbs over a small spur to come up above the village of **Gharsu**, still in the main Sutlej Valley. It then circles left (north) away from the Sutlej and into the Salaring Valley.

Salaring is the most secluded of the three smaller valleys in the Rupi-Bhaba Sanctuary. Invisible from the road, it's tucked between the Shorang and the Bhaba valleys. About 40 mins from Gharsu, one comes to the hamlet of **Rokcharang**, above the right bank of the Salaring stream. From here, a path descends a short distance to a *jhula* crossing over the Salaring stream. Do not cross. A path moves north up the right bank of the Salaring, from the *jhula*, to a small  **forest inspection hut** located about a kilometre away where one can stay or  camp overnight. Less than an hour's walk up the left bank, brings up the tiny hamlet of **Salaring**, located at a meeting point of two

Farmers of the Rupi Valley harvest a crop of barley

tributaries. With an extra day to explore Salaring Valley, one can move up the valley the next day. The valleys on either side offer the best chances of spotting musk deer.

DAY FOUR
SALARING FOREST HUT-SAK KANDA
DISTANCE 12 KM **TIME** 4 HOURS
LEVEL EASY-MODERATE

Go back to the *jhula* over the Salaring and cross to the right bank. On the other side, the path ascends gradually south towards the main Sutlej Valley. Barely a kilometre away is **Kachrang**, with 12 households, the largest habitation in Salaring Valley. If you want to head back home from Kachrang, it is possible to go down south to a *jhula* over the Sutlej and climb up to National Highway 22 on the other side, just beyond Bhabanagar, 180 km from Shimla.

The path from Kachrang towards **Sak Kanda** (2,900m) climbs left (east) gradually coming out on bare, steep slopes, which tumble down to the Sutlej. Traversing these slopes eastwards up the Sutlej, it reaches **Nathpa** (2,055m). Nathpa is strung out in a long, narrow line. It stretches more than 300m along the bare slopes, ending close to a spruce forest.

Heading up to the top of Nathpa, the path cuts through the spruce trees to the single crop fields of Sak Kanda. Located on the shoulder of a spur sloping towards the **Sutlej**, Sak Kanda overlooks the catchment of the **Kandar Nallah**. This is the smallest of the independent valleys terminating on the Sutlej, in the **Rupi-Bhaba Sanctuary**.

There is no rest house at Sak Kanda but the fallow fields offer plentiful sites for camping out.

DAY FIVE
SAK KANDA-KATGAON
DISTANCE 20 KM **TIME** 8-9 HOURS
LEVEL DIFFICULT

The forest path from Sak Kanda to Bhaba was earlier constructed to circle above **Tholach Kanda** and move north-east into the **Bhaba Valley**. But the erosion in one **Pagal** (lunatic) **Nallah** has made this route impossible now.

The walking track to the Bhaba climbs steeply from Sak Kanda itself, crossing the 3,900-m ridge top in a north-easterly direction through forest and pasture. The bowl of the Bhaba Valley is clearly visible from the top. The descent is steep and long. While many footpaths criss-cross the route through forest and pasture, one just needs to stick to the ones leading down (east).

They come out either directly at the **Electricity Board Rest House** at **Katgaon** (2,200m), located on the

Wangar right bank, or in one of the two villages of **Bai** or **Kafnu**. The rest house is between the two villages, and within a couple of kilometres of easy walking from either.

Those not keen on the ridge crossing from Sak Kanda, have an easier option to reach the Bhaba Valley. Crossing over from Sak Kanda to Tholach Kanda, one can descend towards the Sutlej, on the ridge edging the left side of the **Kandar Valley** to reach a now abandoned rest house built by the electricity board. From here, an old project road descends south in a series of zigzags to join up

Carved entry of the Bhaba temple

with the 17-km **Wangtu-Katgaon Link Road**. This road offers the option of a lift or bus ride as it climbs north into the Bhaba Valley.

TREKKING OPTIONS

The Bhaba Valley is the most extensive one here. The pastures in its upper stretches are famous. If time permits, trek over the **Pin-Bhaba Pass** to Spiti, and the pastures of **Mulling**, **Kara** and **Tiya** en route.

An alternative trek to get back into the Sutlej Valley is also available. A kilometre or so below the rest house at **Katgaon**, a bridge crosses over the **Wangar stream** to the left bank and a path traverses right along the hillside, past a couple of small hamlets to enter the valley of the **Kangarang tributary** of the Wangar. Moving east into the valley, the path circles up and around to the south at the head of the valley. A steep ascent brings up the **Rusnang Pass** (3,650m), crossing into the main Sutlej Valley high above the large village of **Chagaon**. Prepare for a 7- 8-hr tiring walk on this stretch. From Chagaon, a motor road leads down to **Tapri** (7 km) on NH22, from where regular buses or taxis can take one to Shimla.

For rest house bookings in Rupi and hotels in Rampur, see Accommodation Listings on page 528 ✦

Photographs by JITENDER GUPTA

piti confounds your under-standing of space in classic Brechtian stlye — it is here that you will find moonscapes on earth. And ancient monasteries that hang off cliffs as old as time. The valley, stretching over 100 km, is dotted with small villages and tiny hamlets, and is home to a population of less than 10,000. Those accustomed to the gentle slopes of the mountains, filled with pines and poplars, will see a different face of the Himalayas here. This terrain, with its barren landscape and looming rock faces, is stark, naked and awe-inspiring.

On the left bank of the Spiti River, Tabo's complex of nine temples and cave shrines represents the oldest contin-uously functioning Buddhist enclave in India. While Tabo is approached from Shimla, Kaza, the administrative centre of Spiti sub-district, is a really slow, joint-loosening, 200 km-in-12 hours drive from Manali.

From Kaza, a road (19 km) to the north-east goes to Kibber (4,205m), once part of the overland salt trade. It also claims to be the highest village in the world but that honour actually goes to Gette, at 4,270m (7 km east of Ki).

MUST-VISITS

THE TABO MONASTERY COMPLEX
Members of the royal dynasty of Purang-Guge of western Tibet founded Tabo. The most fascinating part of the

Tabo nestles in the Spiti Valley

monastery, undoubtedly, is the 10th century **Tsuglakhang**. Apart from the murals that adorn the walls and ceilings, it houses a number of wall-mounted stucco clay sculptures for which it is particularly famous.

THE TABO CAVE SHRINES
On your left, as you approach the Tabo Monastery from Kaza, are the small, natural caves above the road, which were an integral part of the 10th century monastic complex.

KI (54 km)
Probably founded in the 13th century, this is the largest monastery in Spiti. Ki is best reached from Kaza (7 km) and has about 300 lamas in residence. Set at 4,116m, this gompa belongs to the Gelugpa school of Tibetan Buddhism.

DHANKAR (23 km)
Once the capital of the Spiti waziri, Dhankar is now simply a tiny village. The early 16th century fort-monastery **Dhan-kar Gompa** (3,890m), which once also served as a jail, is wedged between the pinnacles of a razor-sharp spur of crum-bling rock and alkaline deposits. Today, it has about 150 lamas in residence, a collection of Buddhist scriptures, a four-bodied Dhyani Buddha, murals of Medicine Buddhas and protector deities.

PIN VALLEY NATIONAL PARK (43 km)

This untrammelled valley south of Dhankar (675 sq km with a buffer zone of 1,150 sq km) is home to the ibex and snow leopard. The most important monastery in this valley, which has Spiti's only concentration of Nyingmapa Buddhists, is the 600-year-old **Kungri Gompa**, 2 km off the main road near Gulling. Accommodation is limited. Access from Kaza is by bus, which will take you as far as Sagnam Village.

WHERE TO STAY

IN TABO

Banjara Retreat (Tel: 01906-233381, 011-26861397; Tariff: Rs 3,000 with meals) has 10 rooms with attached baths and running h/c water, and a restaurant. **Tashi Khangsar** (contact Subodh, Tel: 223346/ 77; Tariff: Rs 350-500) has 4 rooms, with hot water on request, and camping options for a small fee. Bookings are on arrival. The **Monastery Guest House** (Tel: 223403; Tariff: Rs 200-300) has some rooms with attached baths but no hot water. There are 2 double rooms but you want to avoid the common toilet. There's also a 10-bed dorm at Rs 50 per bed. Bookings on arrival.

IN KAZA

The Banjara Resorts' **Kaza Retreat** (Delhi Tel: *see above*; Tariff: Rs 3,000) is on the same terms as at Tabo. **Sakya's Abode** (contact Tshering, Tel: 01906-222254; Tariff: Rs 500-700) has 12 rooms with attached baths and h/c water. It serves buffet meals at about Rs 150 and breakfast at Rs 100 per head. At **Hotel Khangsar** (contact Bir Singh Bodh, Tel:

Pure lines of the Tabo Monastery

→ Tabo Facts

● **LOCATION** Between Kinnaur in the east and Lahaul in the west, in the Spiti Valley, at a height of 10,000 ft, on the banks of Spiti River, close to the Indo-Tibetan border, 365 km north-east of Shimla, 30 km from NH22 (Sumdo) and 248 km from Manali
● **GETTING TO TABO By road** The Hindustan-Tibet Road (NH22) takes you well over half the distance from Shimla to Tabo. From the half-way mark at Karchham, it's a picturesque 165-km drive to the monastery. During the monsoons the road can close due to bad weather and landslides, so check before leaving Shimla. The Rohtang Pass north of Manali is an alternative, getting you into the Spiti Valley via the Kunzum La Pass, then on to Losar, Rangrik and Kaza to Tabo. Taxis (Sumo) charge Rs 6,500 one way from Shimla. Only one bus (22 hrs) leaves Shimla daily, at 10.30 am (Rs 317) with night halt at Recong Peo. Taxi from Manali charges Rs 5,000 for the 8-hr journey. Two buses leave Manali for Kaza (9 hrs/ Rs 170) and Tabo (11 hrs/ Rs 205) respectively, between 5 and 6 am daily
● **STD CODE** 01906

222275-6; Tariff: Rs 500-700), choose one of the 4 rooms with geysers. Meals extra as per order. Bookings on arrival. *For more hotels and details, see Accommodation Listings on pages 530 (Tabo) and 525 (Kaza)*

WHERE TO EAT

This is no gourmet heaven. Eating in Tabo (and Kaza) is limited to very basic fare: generic North Indian (dal-chawal-roti-subzi, with generous helpings of green 'salaad') or the Tibetan thukpa-momo-thentuk routine. **Sakya's Abode** in Kaza has a sparse Spitian menu for its more adventurous guests. **Layul Café** serves generous proportions of the popular kiyu (square noodles-potato-tomato-onion stew). In Tabo, the **Millennium Monastery Restaurant** offers variations of the same. The best thing about eating in these parts is your accelerated, hyperactive metabolism, making you relish almost anything that's dished out.

INPUTS FROM ANANYA DASGUPTA

Bird's eye-view of the Dhankar fields by the Spiti River

Spiti Left Bank
Celestial mountains
By Deepak Sanan

POH-DHANKAR-LALUNG-DEMUL-LANGZA-
TASHIGONG-KIBBER-LADARCHA-KIATO

TIME	5-7 days
LEVEL	Easy to Moderate
IDEAL SEASON	Jun to Sep
LOCATION	This trek is in the Spiti sub-division of Lahaul and Spiti District

I lived in Spiti for over two years and visited many of the villages covered by this trek. It has gifted me a veritable treasure of memories. The Poh Rest House, with its scenic view, is forever associated with the smiling visage of Dorje Chhering, the caretaker. He always managed to rustle up delicious meals from the limited material at his disposal in Spiti's wilderness. Lalung was a village I visited in winter after the first snowfall of the season cloaked the valley in white. I remember it not as much for the beautiful Ser Khang in the old monastic complex, as for the warmth of salt tea laced with yak butter that we drank on a sun-bathed terrace that afternoon.

Demul, on the other hand, is up in the pastures. It's reached after a sapping climb linked to the song and laughter of a fun-filled summer evening. Komik is all about masked lama dances of the Tangguid Monastery Festival in the chill of early October. Langza, always dominated by the majestic backdrop of the Chau Chau Kang Nelda, the Snow Princess of the celestial bodies, was where I picked my first rock fossils.

For those who venture on these trails, every windswept hamlet still has a smiling, grimy face to soften the awe-inspiring bleakness of the landscape. This is a week-long trek for those with the time and inclination

Graphic by ANIS KHAN

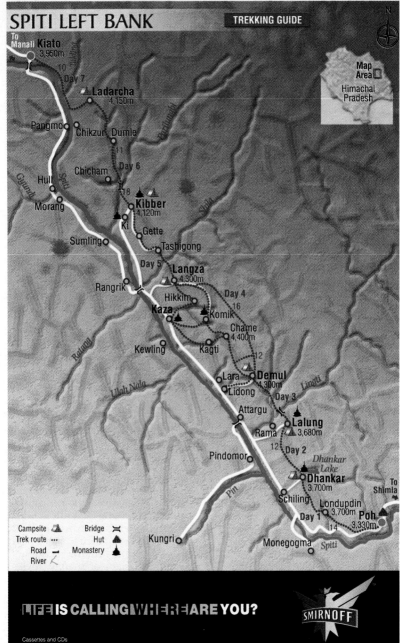

SPITI LEFT BANK

TREKKING GUIDE

To Manali
Kiato
3,950m

10

Day 7

Ladarcha
4,150m

Pangmo

Chikzur Dumle

11

Chicham Day 6

Hull

Morang

8

Kibber
4,120m

Ki

Gette

Sumling

Tashigong

Day 5

Langza
4,300m

Rangrik

Hikkim

Day 4

16

Kaza

Komik

Chame
4,400m

Kewling

Kagti

12

Lara

Demul
4,300m

Lidong

Day 3

Attargu

Lalung
3,680m

Rama

Pindomor

12 Day 2

Dhankar
Lake

Dhankar
3,700m

Schiling

Londupdin
3,700m

To Shimla

Day 1

Poh
3,330m

14

Kungri

Monegogma

Spiti

Map Area
Himachal Pradesh

Campsite	Bridge
Trek route	Hut
Road	Monastery
River	

to savour the many attractions en route. It can, however, be shortened for those with less time, as at every stage a motorable road connects the night halt point.

Misty heights of Dhankar Monastery

DAY ONE

Poh-Dhankar
Distance 14 km **Time** 4-5 hours
Level Easy

Since you will only get to Spiti from either Shimla or Manali in the late afternoon or evening, stay overnight at ▲ **Tabo** and get a taxi to Poh the following morning.

Though **Poh** (3,330m) has a beautifully located **rest house** — to spend a last night before beginning a week's camping out — getting a room

Bharat Petroleum

GETTING THERE AND OUT

FROM TABO to Poh, it's 8 km/ 15 mins by [car] (Sumo Rs 200) and 30 mins by [bus] (Rs 9) on a metalled State Highway 30, located in the Sham region of Spiti **Kaza to Poh**, it's 37 km/ 1 hr by taxi (Rs 800 approx) and 1½ hrs by bus (Rs 25)

RETURN Two buses (Rs 145/ 8 hrs) leave **Kiato** for **Manali** daily at 6.30 and 8.30 am. Alternatively, get picked up at Kiato by taxi for **Kaza** (book from your guest house in Tabo or Kaza). Or stop a bus or truck heading to Kaza **Kaza to Manali** Taxi charges Rs 4,500 for the 10-hr trip. Buses (11 hrs/ Rs 156) leave at 4 and 6 am **Kaza to Shimla** Taxi charges Rs 7,500 for the 2-day trip (412 km). One daily local bus (Rs 350) available at 8.30 am and the same bus leaves from Tabo (Rs 315) at 10.30 am

may be difficult. Reservations can be made at the PWD Office in Kaza. On the first day's walk to **Dhankar**, located to the north-west, high above the left bank of the Spiti River, the initial 5 km are along the motor road to Kaza.

We move past aged junipers, protected from the axe by divine intervention (they belong to the gods). The road heads west up the **Spiti Valley** and moves onto a long, sloping bank called the **Poh Maidan**. Climbing gradually, one stays with the motor road till the other end of this terrace. Then walk up the steep, smaller bank above, due west. Stumpy junipers, thorny seabuck-thorn, wild roses and dusty ephedra, which grow even on the driest slopes, enliven the Poh Maidan.

Across the Spiti Valley, numerous silvery streaks fed by the **Sopona Lake** course down the steep slopes, breaking the brown monotony with refreshing vegetation. Crossing a low ridge brings up a sudden patch of verdure. This is the two-house hamlet of **Londupdin** (3,700m), high above the left bank of the **Nipti Nallah**. The two **Mane** villages are visible across the Spiti River. The green of their irrigated fields contrasts sharply with the background — immense slabs of sharply angled, grey rock and brown and yellow slopes reaching up to an offshoot ridge of the **Manerang Peak**.

Crossing the tiny **Nipti stream** midway between a series of small waterfalls the path, still heading north-west, traverses by the side of another vast terrace. Then passing another little patch of cultivation, the track climbs gradually to meet the link road from Sichling to Dhankar. A somewhat steeper climb through the fields of **Dhankar Village (3,700m)** takes one up to the new monastery building. Even an easy, first day's pace should enable one to complete the 14-km walk in about 5 hrs from **Poh**. It will still leave time for the hour's climb to the **Dhankar Lake**, located in the arid pastures north of the village. Camp can be struck on the periphery of the fields near the monastery.

DAY TWO

DHANKAR-LALUNG
DISTANCE 12 KM **TIME** 4 HOURS
LEVEL EASY

From **Dhankar**, good walkers can easily make **Demul**, the easternmost village of the upland pastures of **Bhar**, the same day. But new arrivals to Spiti shouldn't climb so rapidly to 4,300m. Besides, exploring the monastery complex at **Lalung** (3,680m) should definitely be on the agenda. Best then to make Lalung —

about a 3-hr walk away — the night halt point on Day Two. It is more or less a level walk, initially winding west around dry, south-facing slopes with the wide valley of the many-channelled **Spiti River** below. The **Pin River**, emerging from a narrow valley on the opposite side, also widens out before meeting the Spiti. Between the Pin and the Spiti, the long, flat triangle of **Pindomor**, with its profuse green cover, is a refreshing change for the eyes.

Above the extensive flats of **Subling Maidan** (a little less than half-way to Lalung), the path turns north into the **Lingti Valley**. Soon after, one can meet up with the link road taking off from the Sumdo Kaza Road far below, for the last few kilometres to Lalung. Below, on one's left, the Lingti Valley opens out. The hamlet of **Chabrang** can be seen across on the right bank. The much larger **Rama Village** is just below. Beyond Chabrang, huge terraces, smudged with green young trees, mark the entrance to the steep valley leading to Demul. Soon **Lalung** is visible. The green fields spread down to the Lingti, over 200m below.

Embellished clay icons at Lalung Monastery

Changmurti horses at Demul

Camp can be made near the entrance to **Lalung** or down below, close to the **Lingti River**, after visiting the monastery complex.

DAY THREE
LALUNG-DEMUL
DISTANCE 12 KM **TIME** 6 HOURS
LEVEL MODERATE

Lalung to Demul (4,300m) requires crossing the **Lingti River** heading north-west through the fields below the village. Once over the foot bridge and having passed (still heading west) the hamlet of **Sanglung**, located on a terrace above the Lingti left bank, the route lies up the narrow valley of the **Demul stream**. A steep climb of over 600m, up cliffs of sedimented slate, brings up the more gradual, turf-covered slopes of the pasture land. The hills now ascend in gradual undulations to over 300m above Demul, visible a short distance away. To the left (south), the Demul Link Road traverses the slopes, which end abruptly in steep rock faces that drop down to the main **Spiti Valley**. Looking back towards the Lingti, **Manerang** towers in the distance while, closer at hand, **Kamelang** dominates above Lalung. Up the **Lingti Valley**, snow-covered peaks mark the divide with the **Gue Valley** to the east.

Immediately north, across a deep valley that descends rapidly from the pastures, is a high, beautiful snow-covered ridge running west to **Chau Chau Kang Nelda** (6,303m). The pastures are a vast ocean of rolling green. There is soft, mossy grass (nema) near the water. Elsewhere, there is a low, even growth of bush, surviving on the moisture of late melting snows. Near the stream, south of **Demul** is a good place to camp for the night.

DAY FOUR
DEMUL-LANGZA
DISTANCE 16 KM **TIME** 6-8 HOURS
LEVEL EASY

The sun rises early in Demul and in the short, busy summer the residents are up even earlier to make the most of it. Even an impromptu night of song and dance (a must to honour even unexpected guests) does not warrant a late morning. Not a minute of daylight is wasted in order to gather and store for the winter months. To be

Dawn breaks over Chau Chau Kang Nelda

Himalayan snow cock

Also known as Ram chukor/ chukar (*Tetrogallus himalayensis*), native of the lofty mountains of Asia, this pheasant is a large, overall gray partridge with a white face and throat. It has a brown band below the eye that extends on to the neck forming a collar. Its upper breast has black streaks, the flanks are grey, streaked with black and white. Females are similar to males but lack tarsal spurs and have more buff on the face. The snow cock feeds on grasses found on slopes around 3,000m high.

OTTO PFISTER

up with the lark for Demul residents can mean an enjoyable, long day meandering over the pastures before reaching Langza for a night halt.

The direct route, covering some 16 km, heads north-west, up the slopes behind the village, past the source of the Demul stream, and over the ridge. Down the other side is a long, gentle traverse around the upper edge of a huge, marshy, green bowl, sloping to the cliffs behind **Lara**, located on the Spiti left bank. (An alternative route lies north from Demul. Circling the ridge behind the village, you must move back south to join the direct route above Lara. It is a longer walk but with a more gradual ascent and a more extensive and delightful view of the pastures.) Then, across a little hump, are the soft, mossy tussocks of the **Chame Meadow** (4,400m). It is possible to run down south-west to **Kaza** from here in less than 3 hrs, via the one-house hamlet of **Kagti** (4,100m).

Spitian lama at a festival

DEEPAK SANAN

The more westerly path to Langza climbs gently out of Chame, to the upper catchment of the Kaza stream. A vast amphitheatre of rolling downs, dipping gradually to a sudden drop at the southern end, meets the eye. At the upper (northern) end is the village of **Komik**, on top of which is the new **Tangguid Monastery** (4,450m). From Komik, one can follow a motor road, circling above **Hikkim Village** (4,360m) to reach **Langza** (4,300m) across a low ridge. More exciting and offering superb views of the **Chau Chau Kang Nelda** is the higher ridge above **Hikkim**. Approached up the diagonal slopes north-west from the monastery, therefore leaving Hikkim on the left, the route climbs over 250m higher, to reach Langza from the north-east.

Fossils are scattered in abundance on the slopes behind Langza. With luck, one can pick up a few ammonites on this stretch.

117

Trans-Himalayan trade

Ladarcha was the site of Spiti's annual barter trade fair in the old days before the motor roads reached Spiti, and the Tibet border closed post the Sino-Indian war of 1962. Barley was Spiti's main trading item in those days. From Kullu and Rampur came cloth, sugar and iron goods. These were bartered with the sheep, pashmina wool, yaks, *churpe* (a hard, whey cheese) and semi-precious stones brought by the nomadic herdsmen of Changthang and Rupshu, and the traders of Tibet.

LAXMI MURTHY

ROUTE OPTION

Demul-Langza One can move north from Demul and then turn west across gently sloping grassland instead of taking the southern track on the Chame route. You will enjoy spending some time here with the *dokpas* (shepherds), tending milch cattle and putting together butter for the long winter months. Climbing gradually north-west, the trail slips over the ridge separating the **Lingti** catchment from that of the **Shilla Nallah**. Close up, in the shadow of **Chau Chau Kang Nelda**, the route bypasses **Komik** and **Tangguid**. Then heading south-west along the gentle contours of an irrigation channel once over the little ridge, it reaches **Langza** directly.

DAY FIVE

LANGZA-KIBBER
DISTANCE 18 KM **TIME** 8-10 HOURS
LEVEL MODERATE TO TOUGH

Those chary of the somewhat tougher march the next day can head for the comforts of **Kaza** down a 10-km link road from **Langza** (4,300m). Hardier souls face a steep descent north-west into the gorge of the Shilla stream and an even longer ascent still heading north-west to the small, six-house village of **Tashigong**. The 700-m climb is killing but the reward lies in stepping on hallowed ground since His Holiness the Dalai Lama camped here for many days in 1983. A motor road crosses the low ridge on the Spiti side (south) and gentle slopes across this ridge lead west down to **Gette Village**. From Gette, an option for those wishing to cut short the trek and reach the main valley quickly is a switchback trail leading straight down precipitous cliffs to **Ki Monastery** 500m lower. The road runs on to **Kibber** (4,120m) about 5 km away to the north-west.

⚠ Camp can be struck short of **Kibber** or a little way across it at the edge of the village fields.

DAY SIX

KIBBER-LADARCHA
DISTANCE 11 KM **TIME** 3 HOURS
LEVEL EASY

From Kibber, off to the right (north) is the route to Ladakh over the **Parang La**. Directly opposite lies the village of **Chicham** (4,150m), across the gorge-like valley of the **Parilungbi tributary**

Entrance to Kibber Village

of Spiti. The sixth day out of Poh requires moving in a semi-circle north, around the ridge behind Chicham, to the justly famous meadows of Ladarcha.

The route from Kibber leads down to the **Parilungbi Gorge** along a motor road. Across a bridge, it heads north-west into the

Porters at a campsite

valley of a smaller tributary, that is descending from the Ladarcha (4,150m) side. The path crosses to the right bank of this stream very soon. It then climbs up the valley north-west leaving Chicham behind way to the left. Near the hamlet of **Dumle**, the narrow valley becomes a gentle declivity and the grass-covered, turf country of the pastures follows soon after. Climbing gradually from Dumle, the path winds back west towards the **Spiti River**, bringing up Ladarcha within an hour.

At over 4,000m, **Ladarcha** is a vast sweep of gentle slopes, carpeted with the low bush and mossy grass of the upland pastures, and one can ▲ camp almost anywhere. It is an easy 3 hrs from Kibber to Ladarcha. The afternoon is free to go searching for the Tibetan snow cock and the blue sheep, on the surrounding hillsides.

DAY SEVEN
LADARCHA-KIATO
DISTANCE 10 KM
TIME 3 HOURS **LEVEL** EASY

The last day's walk takes one back to the main **Spiti Valley** along the **Ladarcha-Kiato Road**. On the left (south-west) is a low rise, only barely more elevated than the meadows. It marks the edge of steep cliffs, which drop down to the river. Descending south-west to the riverside terraces, the road moves north-west up the left bank of the Spiti. Downstream is the tiny, isolated hamlet of **Chikzur** and across the **Spiti River**, the larger village of **Pangmo**. Climbing gradually, past bizarre totems carved into the erosion-prone sedimentary soil by snow melt run off, one approaches the **Takling tributary** of the Spiti. Once you have negotiated the short, steep descent and then the steep ascent north on the far side of the ravine, it is less than an hour to **Kiato** (3,950m).

▲ With more than half a day to spare one can get a bus or truck to **Kaza** or move on up the Spiti, to spend the night at **Losar Rest House**.

For rest house bookings, see Accommodation Listings on pages 526 (Losar) and 528 (Poh) ✦

Once a tranquil base to the best treks in the Himalayas, Manali has transformed into a bustling marketplace today. Every now and then, you will come across an Israeli roaring past on a dusty Bullet, telling the world that he's survived the Leh-Manali Road, and Nepali porters scurry up and down the street trying to get their trekking groups organised. But traverse the bridge across the swirling waters of the mighty Beas River, look up and all around — the majestic Pir Panjal, Parvati and Bara Bhangal ranges cradling the town will mesmerise you.

→ Manali Facts

● **LOCATION** At the confluence of the Beas and Manalsu in Kullu Valley, Manali is 274 km from Shimla, 2,050m above sea level and 565 km N of Delhi

● **GETTING TO MANALI By air** Nearest airport: Bhuntar (50 km/ 2 hrs), serviced by Indian Airlines and Jagson Airlines. Hire a taxi (Maruti Van Rs 800) or request your hotel for a paid pick-up (Rs 1,500 approx) **By road** Long hill drive (which begins at Kiratpur) from Delhi. Set off at daybreak, or even in the pre-dawn hours. Highway driving right through. The drive up the Beas after Pandoh is gorgeous. HPTDC Transport runs an overnight luxury bus (Rs 560; dep 7 pm, arr 10 am) and a Volvo coach (Rs 770; dep 7 pm, arr 8 am) from the Himachal Tourism Janpath office (see *Tourist Offices Listings on page 518*). Himachal Roadways runs deluxe (dep: 8.25 pm; Rs 580) as well as ordinary (dep: every hour after 1.30 pm till 10 pm; Rs 350) buses from ISBT, Kashmere Gate. The roadways has a well-connected network linking Manali with all the major towns within Himachal and also Chandigarh

● **STD CODE** 01902

Photographs by DILIP BANERJEE

MUST-VISITS

HADIMBA TEMPLE
Deep within the virgin forests of the Dungiri Van Vihar, the temple is a beautiful wooden structure built in pagoda style, dating to the 16th century.

VASHISHT
A dip in the hot sulphur springs at Vashisht, just 3 km from Manali, can be a thoroughly rejuvenating experience.

OLD MANALI
The original settlement with beautiful old wooden houses is now a hippy enclave full of inexpensive guest houses. You may want to visit the temple in Old Manali for the law-maker, Manu. If you're in the mood for a completely idyllic time, take the left fork past Old Manali, and sit quietly on the banks of the Manalsu.

DRIVE TO ROHTANG PASS
The 51-km climb up to the 3,980m high pass is formidable. Happy picnickers don't realise that 'Rohtang' means 'pile of corpses' in Tibetan. Many of these corpses belonged to those crossing over to the Lahaul Valley, connected to Manali and the rest of India by the pass.

NAGGAR
Naggar, 28 km from Manali, is host to the **Roerich Art Gallery** in what used to be the home of the Russian artist Nicholas Roerich and his wife Devika

Genuine Italian pizzas and pastas served near Hadimba Temple

Residents of Old Manali

Rani. There's also the 12th century **Gauri Shankar Temple** and the **Chatar Bhuj Temple** dedicated to Vishnu. In case you decide to stay the night, the 500-year-old **Hotel Naggar Castle** (Tel: 01902-248316; Tariff: Rs 250-1,500, dorm Rs 75), now a heritage hotel, is a delight with its old courtyard, wraparound verandahs, an art museum and not-to-be-missed views of the valley.

WHERE TO STAY

The sheer number of hotels in Manali means that even if you don't book in advance you are sure to get a room, and one that suits your budget.

Snow Crest Manor (Tel: 01902-253351-4; Tariff: Rs 2,300-9,300), a little away from the main Manali town, is a good option. **Banon Resorts** (Tel: 253026, 252490, 253994; Tariff: Rs 2,000-5,900), in the midst of apple orchards, has a playground for kids, a gym for grownups, indoor games, a designer bar and a multi-cuisine restaurant.

HPTDC's **Log Huts and Hamta Cottages** (Tel: 252407; Tariff: Rs 1,650-4,000), about 2 km away from Manali, claim to have the best views of snow-capped Himalayan peaks. Bright, sunny and full of Bohemian artistic detail, **Johnson's Lodge** (Tel: 253764, 253023; Tariff: Rs 1,000-3,500) is popular with domestic and foreign tourists alike.

On the banks of the Beas are **Manali Resorts** (Tel: 252274, 253174; Tariff: Rs 1,600-3,500) and the HPTDC budget option **Hotel Beas** (Tel: 252832; Tariff: Rs 250-650) that overlooks the river.

En route to Rohtang is **Whispering Rocks** (Tel: 256092, 256180; Tariff: Rs 1,600-2,700) which has a kids' park, a restaurant and a bar. In Raison, on the banks of the Beas, is the HPTDC-run **Adventure Resort** (Tel: 240516; Tariff: Rs 650), which offers huts and a base for trekking and other adventure activities. In Kullu proper, HPTDC has **Hotel Sarvari** (Tel: 01902-222471; Tariff: Rs 450-1,500 and Rs 75 per dorm bed) that has a dorm and deluxe rooms in its new wing and also a restaurant.
For more hotels and details, see Accommodation Listings on pages 526-528

WHERE TO EAT

You can never get gastronomically bored in Manali. Among its best restaurants is **Johnson's Café** on Circuit House Road. Go there for well-made pasta, salads and the house speciality — grilled trout. **Mount View Restaurant** on the Mall has good momos and also serves apple cider that is best during season (September-October). **Chopsticks**, also on the Mall, serving Tibetan and Chinese fare, is another favourite for its hot spring rolls. But be sure to visit the **German Bakery** opposite Nehru Park, a quaint shop selling baked goodies from banana chocolate cakes (the cakes here are divine!) to peanut cookies, croissants and coffee. Pick up home-made yak or cheddar cheese. Those diehards who prefer to stick to Indian can go to **Swamiji's Madras Café**, which does good Southie thalis, or to **Himalayan Dhaba** for North Indian sabzis. They're both on the Mall.

INPUTS FROM RISHAD SAAM MEHTA

Bhrigu Lake
Pool of the gods

By Deepak Sanan

Set sapphire-like at the crest of the mountain is Bhrigu Lake

TIME	2 days
LEVEL	Moderate
IDEAL SEASON	Jul to Oct
LOCATION	Above Manali in Upper Beas Valley in Kullu District

GULABA-BHRIGU LAKE-GULABA

If you want to experience a high-altitude trek and do not have much time on hand, try going to Bhrigu Lake. At 4,270m, Bhrigu can be reached in a day from Manali. It is possible to return on the same day though I would recommend you stay overnight. Bhrigu is a prominent lake of the Kullu region, located to the right (8 km south-east) of the Rohtang Pass.

Legend holds that Bhrighu Rishi meditated here, and that many local gods of the Kullu Valley visit to take a dip in its sacred waters. Most prominent among them is Guru Vashisht, who travels to the lake at least once in a two- three-year cycle. He announces his plan to visit the lake about a month in advance through a medium (*also see page 170*). Elaborate preparations are made after that and many devotees accompany him on the trip. Villagers of the area go to the lake every year on the 20th day of bhadon (August-September) as the day is considered auspicious.

A natural forest of fir, spruce, moru and the higher altitude kharsu oak trees surrounds Gulaba, from where the trek starts. During the early 1960s, swatches of the forest were cleared under a mechanised logging scheme. Later, fir, spruce, maple and poplar were planted and the latter, faster growing trees, are now dominant in these stretches. Carry all necessary provisions, including camping gear and food supplies, as nothing is available after you start walking from Gulaba, which boasts of a couple of ☕ tea shops.

DAY ONE
GULABA-BHRIGU LAKE
DISTANCE 14 KM **TIME** 6-8 HOURS
LEVEL MODERATE

The trail takes off at the **14th Mor** to the right (east) from the road and starts climbing through forest and pasture. Horse chestnuts, spruce, fir and a few birch trees alternate with pastureland through the route, which climbs steeply. After a climb of nearly an hour one reaches a shepherd campsite on the crest of a ridge from where the track turns right and heads up

Graphic by ANIS KHAN

BHRIGU LAKE — TREKKING GUIDE

south through a thick forest. **Kolang Nallah** can be seen from here and the path lies along the nallah through the narrow **Kolang Valley**.

The path then descends right (south) to cross the Kolang Nallah

Taking a break on the climb up

Hi-Speed DIESEL — Bharat Petroleum

GETTING THERE AND OUT

FROM MANALI to 14th Mor (near **Gulaba**), on the Manali-Rohtang Road, it is 22 km/ 1/2 hr by 🚙 (Rs 300) or 45 mins by 🚌 (Rs 20). Buses available from 5 am-8 pm. The Border Roads Organisation has a small camp at **Gulaba**. The trek starts from the camp but it's not a clearly identifiable track. Many trails lead up the slopes and it is best to have a local guide to identify the proper path. One may lose precious time in locating the lake without a guide and possibly miss reaching it altogether **RETURN** the same route to Gulaba **TIP** Hire a guide at the Institute of Mountaineering and Allied Sports (Tel: 01902-252206/ 342) in Manali or from any of the registered travel agents

Lammergeier

OTTO PFISTER

Lammergeiers are common in the Himalayas and other northern mountains. Their wide wingspans, which can measure up to 2.75-2.85m, allow them to live in remote mountain strongholds at altitudes up to 7,500m Typically, lammergeiers nest in caves, ledges and low rocks rising from planes. The bird can swallow whole bones up to the size of a lamb's femur. It has the habit of carrying tortoises and marrow-bones to a great height, and dropping them on stones to obtain the contents, and is therefore called bone-breaker. For the most part, however, the lammergeier is a bird of unashamed cowardice, ready to take advantage of any animal in distress, incapable of defending itself against a creature half its own size and frightened at the wink of an eyelid. There is, however, nothing uncouth about a lammergeier. It is sinister, yet magnificent and dignified.

Forests above Gulaba

over a temporary log bridge. (In case the bridge is washed away, the nallah can be forded easily.) After crossing the nallah there is a steep ascent south-east to a ridge (to the right of the Kolang Valley) that takes nearly 2 hrs. Beyond the ridge is a camping ground where it is possible to find Gaddi shepherds with their large flocks of sheep.

A little ahead to the east is the easily crossed **Chor Nallah** followed by a climb in an easterly direction to reach **Bhrigu Lake**. The climb is strenuous as it gains altitude quickly resulting in a drop in the temperature and levels of oxygen. So take your time, climbing slowly and steadily.

Located almost at the top of the mountain, the lake is in the recess of two ridges and can only be seen when actually reached. It's oval-shaped and not very large.

The ridges around the lake offer a 360-degree view of the ranges around. Peaks of the **Pir Panjal** and **Dhauladhar**, the **Lahaul** triangle between the **Chandra** and the **Bhaga** rivers and even the more distant mountains in **Spiti** can be seen from here. After the sun sets, it can get pretty cold and windy, so carry your woollens. On the other hand, the star-lit sky on a clear night is worth the stay. And with the vista of snow peaks shining in the moonlight, the day's strenuous climb becomes a distant memory.

Local tradition forbids camping near the lake but there is enough space to pitch tents a short distance from the lake. Choose a place with a good view.

DAY TWO
BHRIGU LAKE-GULABA
DISTANCE 14 KM **TIME** 4-5 HOURS
LEVEL EASY
Return on the same route and board a bus at Gulaba. ✦

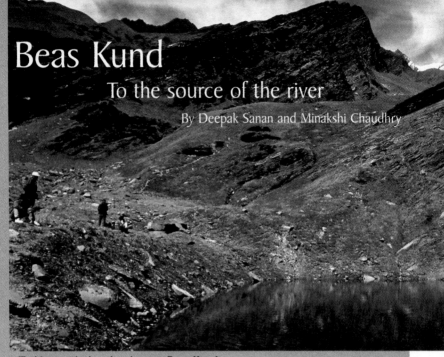

Beas Kund
To the source of the river
By Deepak Sanan and Minakshi Chaudhry

Trekkers enjoying the vistas at Beas Kund

TIME	3 days
LEVEL	Easy
IDEAL SEASON	Jun to Oct
LOCATION	In Kullu District, to the source of the River Beas from above Manali

PALCHAN-DHUNDI-BEAS KUND-PALCHAN-MANALI

This trek to Beas Kund through the Solang Valley is an easy trail that meanders through some of the most beautiful mountainscapes in Himachal. One can extend the trek by starting the walk from Manali and then camping at Solang Nallah, instead of Dhundi, on the first day.

An additional day also enables exploring the upper Solang Valley by making a base camp at the Beas Kund. This is one of the most popular treks in the Kullu Valley, as Beas Kund serves as the base camp for climbers going upto Hanuman Tibba.

Solang Valley is a *must-see* on the itinerary of anyone visiting Manali. Its ski slopes attract winter sports enthusiasts while others settle for joy rides on snow scooters. In summer, horse rides on the flower-bedecked slopes, and para sailing, beckons tourists. In season, Solang bears a festive look with chaatwallahs, ice-cream and popcorn stalls, Kullu souvenir sellers and photographers catering to the tourists. It is also a favoured locale for outdoor film shoots.

Despite this, Solang is far from being an overcrowded tourist destination, and has always enthralled me on my many visits to the valley. In fact, a walk through the woods in Solang is as refreshing as it was years ago, before Manali had seen a mushrooming of

Graphic by ANIS KHAN

BEAS KUND

TREKKING GUIDE

Beas Kund 3,540m

Day 2

Dhundi 2,800m

Day 1

To Rohtang Pass

6

Solang Nallah

15

Hanuman Tibba 5,930m

Palchan

Ski Centre

Shanag

Beas

Manali 2,050m

Campsite ▲
Trek route ·····
Road —
Peak/height ▲
River ⟨
Bridge ⋈
Glaciers

Map Area ▢

Himachal Pradesh

N

GETTING THERE AND OUT

FROM MANALI to Palchan, it's 10 km/ 15 mins by (Rs 300) and 20 mins by 🚌 (Rs 8). There's a bus every 30 mins in summer when the **Rohtang Pass** is open. When the pass is closed, there are three buses, at 8 am, 2 and 4 pm
RETURN Take the same route back

hotels. About 2¹/₂ km from the Mountaineering Institute of Skiing at Solang, a natural Shivalingam of ice forms every winter and becomes a place of pilgrimage. The height of the lingam varies from year to year (10-18 ft).

DAY ONE
PALCHAN-DHUNDI
DISTANCE 15 KM **TIME** 4-6 HOURS
LEVEL EASY

Beas Kund is the source of the River Beas, although the main rivulet rising from the Beas Kund is called **Solang Nallah**, till it joins the stream flowing down from Rohtang Pass. The trek to Beas Kund is along the Solang Nallah.

From **Palchan**, near the confluence of the Rohtang and Solang streams, a road branches off to the left (west) to cross the **Beas** (a little downstream from the confluence). It heads up the Solang Nallah to where the **Mountaineering and Allied Sports' Ski Centre** (2,480m/ 7 km) is located (Manali Tel: 01902-252342). Along the motor road, it is a leisurely walk through a forest with the Solang Nallah flowing down on one's right. On both sides of the road, a large number of hotels have mushroomed in the last decade.

OTTO PFISTER

Raven

Found in a variety of habitat, from treeless tundra to coastal sea banks, rocky cliffs, mountain forests and desert canyons to open plains, ravens are the largest member of the crow family. Ravens are, on an average, 24 inches long, with a wingspan of 46-56 inches. Their colour is all-black with a metallic shine of purple or violet that is noticeable in certain light conditions. The bill is large and stout. In flight, the tail appears wedge-shaped, which distinguishes it from crows.

The common raven's scientific name *Corvus corax* means 'raven croaker'. Noted for their calls, ravens have a wide repertoire of vocalisations. They are strong fliers and are considered among the most intelligent of all birds. Like crows, they can learn to imitate a variety of sounds, including the human voice. Ravens eat rodents, insects, grain, fruits, bird eggs and refuse. They consume much carrion, especially in winter, and will even prey upon sick and injured animals.

From the car parking area (near the ski centre) a well-trodden path heads north-west to **Dhundi** (2,800m/ 8 km). The trek passes through a mixed forest of blue pine, deodar, spruce, fir and wild walnut trees. The path ascends gradually over a stone strewn trail before descending to cross to the Solang Nallah left bank over a temporary wooden bridge. Thereafter, the track climbs up still heading north-west to reach the **Dhundi** camping ground. The **Hanuman Tibba Peak** dominates the horizon to the west during this climb. A jeep road also goes up to Dhundi where the **Snow and Avalanche Study Establishment** (SASE), Manali, has a study unit.

⚠ One can camp anywhere near the abandoned Border Roads Organisation camp or SASE's study unit. Enough water is available nearby.

DAY TWO
DHUNDI-BEAS KUND
DISTANCE 6 KM **TIME** 3 HOURS
LEVEL EASY

The trek from Dhundi starts along the left bank (north side) of Solang Nallah. It climbs up, turns right, or north, and descends to ford a side stream. The Solang Valley narrows down in this stretch. The trail ascends due west to a ridge, turns right and climbs steeply for about 2 km before crossing a log bridge to reach **Bakkar Thatch pastures**, surrounded by birch trees. Splendid views of the **Dhauladhar** and **Pir Panjal ranges** can be seen from here.

After Bakkar Thatch the trail continues on the right (south side) of Solang Nallah, and winding up, turns round a ridge to the north before dropping down to **Beas Kund** (3,540m), a small lake at the edge of a ground. The terrain around Beas Kund suggests that the area was once filled with glaciers that have receded over the years.

Throughout the climb, **Hanuman Tibba** (5,930m) is a towering presence on the west. From Beas Kund, apart from Hanuman Tibba, one can see **Ladakhi Peak, Shiti Dhar** and **Manali Peak**. A difficult 10-hr walk to the south-west can enable a trip to the base camp established by climbers attempting Hanuman Tibba.

A traffic jam on the bridge over the Beas

Deodar

Standing tall and erect with horizontal, table-like branches, the deodar (*Cedrus deodara*), or cedar, is the state tree of Himachal Pradesh. They may attain a height of over 115 ft, and a diameter of 42.65 ft has been recorded. The majestic deodar is a highly sacred tree of the hills. It takes its origin from two separate words, *deo* (*devta* or god) and *daru* (tree), and is considered to be the tree of gods. It is known to be most sacred to Lord Shiva, and can be found in excellent state of preservation, as sacred groves near temples dedicated to him.

AHTUSHI DESHPANDE

Both topography and local belief favour camping some distance away from the Beas Kund lake. Locals believe that it is a bad omen to camp by the Beas Kund. In general, camping or living close to rivers or lakes is not favoured in the hills, possibly because of the havoc that flash floods or a sudden rise in water levels can cause. It's also possible that these myths have arisen to prevent shepherds camping near the lake with their flock, and polluting the water source. Observe the sentiment, and camp away from the lake so that the lake's pristine condition endures. Camp can be established on the western or northern side of the lake. Water is available on both sides.

DAY THREE
BEAS KUND-SOLANG NALLAH
DISTANCE 14 KM **TIME** 4-6 HOURS
LEVEL MODERATE
Return by the same route. Take a taxi from Solang Nallah to Manali. ✦

Naggar to Malana

Painter's muse

By Deepak Sanan and Minakshi Chaudhry

GIREESH G V

Naggar Valley blooms in myriad colours during springtime

TIME	3-5 days
LEVEL	Easy
IDEAL SEASON	May to Nov
LOCATION	In Kullu District, in the Beas Valley, crossing from Naggar to the Malana tributary

NAGGAR-RUMSU CAMP-CHANDERKHANI PASS-
MALANA-JARI

This is an easy 3-day trek with the scope for varying the duration to suit one's time. It is taxing but not impossible to reach Malana (2,652m) from Naggar in one day, or one can camp for a day near the pass. An additional day in Malana can also be worthwhile to study the unique village customs and traditions. Malana has many interesting stories associated with it. Some

people claim it is the oldest democracy in the world, while others trace the remote village to a wandering group of soldiers from the army of Alexander the Great.

The attractions on this trek are many: Naggar — an enchanting village with a majestic little castle (now a heritage hotel also housing a museum), a pass crossing, and the exotic Malana Village. Keep an eye out for rich bird life, particularly the kalij pheasant. For me, it also has some unforgettable memories. Chanderkhani was one of my earliest treks. And on the first morning, climbing up from Naggar, I learnt the peril of gorging on unpasteurised milk obtained from the Gujjars. Later, having lost our way over the Chanderkhani, we stumbled into an isolated Malana *dogri* (part-time home in fields) and experienced the wonderful hospitality that simple rural folk provide to complete strangers (even when communication is limited to sign language!).

Naggar was the capital of Kullu State till 1660 AD. A wooden temple to Tripura Sundari, the presiding deity of the region, is located here. The Devi travels all over the area in procession with her followers, and goes as far as Malana. The other prominent temples to be found at Naggar are the Gauri Shankar Temple, the Murlidhar Temple of Thawa and the temple dedicated to Vishnu.

The Russian painter, poet and philosopher Nicholas Roerich lived here for many years. The small art gallery in his old home offers a glimpse of his mystical interpretation of the Himalayas.

GETTING THERE AND OUT

FROM MANALI to Naggar, it's 26 km/ 40 mins by 🚗 (Rs 500 approx) or bus 🚌 (Rs 20). There is a bus every half hour to Naggar between 8 am and 6 pm
RETURN From **Jari**, take a taxi (Rs 1,000) or a bus (Rs 90) to Manali (71 km/ $2^1/_2$ hrs). There is a bus every half hour, from 7 am to 6 pm

Naggar is a picture postcard village with terraced fields, thick forests and superb views. Located on a wooded slope, it commands a magnificent panorama of the valley, with the

DAY ONE

NAGGAR-SHILLU PATHAR
DISTANCE 11 KM **TIME** 4-6 HOURS
LEVEL EASY
Graphic by ANIS KHAN

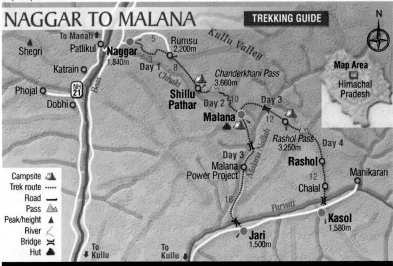

White-crested kalij

Locally known as the kalij pheasant (*Lophura leucomelana hamiltoni*), this is a resident bird of the Himalayas and North-East India. Its elegant plumage is a rich mixture of steely black and white. The white-crested kalij is found most commonly between 900 and 2,100m. It can also be spotted lower down in winter and in the upper reaches in summer. Kalij pheasants are surprisingly omnivorous, eating almost anything from bamboo seeds to small snakes and lizards, but have a special fondness for termites, figs and bamboo seeds. Besides the wing-whirring display, kalij pheasants perform

OTTO PFISTER

a fairly simple lateral courtship, spreading and shaking the tail, expanding the facial wattles, waltzing around the female and making clucking or booming noises. When alarmed, both sexes utter a long, squealing whistle, which is often followed by loud and deep clucking notes.

Rohtang Pass to the north and **Kullu** and **Bajaura** to the south.

A broad footpath takes off to the right (east) from the **Roerich Art Gallery** and passes through a mixed forest of blue pine and deodar trees. The nearly 3-km steady climb takes about an hour to reach Rumsu Village (2,200m), east of Naggar. Alternatively, one can choose the jeep road leading to **Rumsu** (5 km), which climbs gradually through the mixed forest. Rumsu is a big village by hill standards. There are a few government institutions including a health sub-centre, a few provision shops, a temple and apple orchards. A forest inspection hut is located a little away from the village.

Chanderkhani Pass is located south-east of Rumsu Village. From the village a broad, clear and defined path frequently used by locals, leads south-east through forest to the pastures of **Stelling** (2 km) and **Ghalkrari** (4 km). After Ghalkrari, bhojpatra (birch) trees replace the oak and conifer.

Making Himachali caps

GIREESH G V

The track climbs further through grazing grounds to reach a place called **Shillu Pathar** (5 km). One can camp anywhere in these pastures after Rumsu but covering 5-6 km (1-1$^1/_2$ hrs) from Rumsu is recommended. Water is available at many places and one can camp at a convenient place near a water source.

DAY TWO
SHILLU PATHAR-CHANDERKHANI PASS-MALANA
DISTANCE 10 KM **TIME** 4-5 HOURS
LEVEL EASY

The entire trek offers excellent views of snow-covered mountains and wide valleys. From the Shillu Pathar campsite, the track climbs gently over grassy slopes, and heads south-east to reach **Paror**, a place held sacred by the villagers of Rumsu and Malana. Idols of local gods mark the place. From here, one can carry on to **Dhalakda Pathar** (moving stone), a water point. This section is almost on the ridge of the Chanderkhani Range. From the top, one can see

LIFE
IS CALLING
WHERE
ARE YOU?

SMIRNOFF

Cassettes and CDs

Bara Bhangal Range to the west, **Pir Panjal** to the north, and **Parvati** to the east.

Unlike many passes in these mountains, the last stretch to the top of this pass is easy; in fact the track traverses the ridge gently for quite some time. It is important though to cross the **Chanderkhani Pass** only where cairns (a heap of stones piled up as a memorial or as a landmark) mark the pass, since it is easy to lose one's way in bad weather.

The descent to the village of Malana (4 km) is steep when compared to the ascent to the pass. The path turns slippery and risky during the rainy season, from July to August, when tall, wet grass obscures footholds. Two clearly marked trails, both frequently used, descend steeply south-east through thick conifer forests to reach the village.

Malana has its own code of conduct for outsiders. In the village, outsiders are expected to remain on defined paths. Visiting temples or even touching temple walls or stone slabs is prohibited. Violation of the rules results in a fine. At many places, there are boards displaying warnings.

The village today has an aloof and dirty look, quite at variance with the friendliness of my hosts of long ago. The strict customs and stand-offish behaviour of the villagers can put one off. In recent years, the fame of the Malana cannabis has also brought unwelcome habits and, occasionally, unsavoury visitors.

▲ ⛺ Outside the main village, on the south side, there are a few guest houses and a tented colony where board and lodging is available.

DAY THREE

MALANA-JARI
DISTANCE 16 KM **TIME** 5-7 HOURS
LEVEL EASY

A steep but well-defined path goes down south from Malana to Jari. The path descends for nearly half an hour through fields, to enter a forest where deodars predominate. Then it drops down sharply to the south-east for nearly 2 hrs, to a small concrete bridge over the **Malana Nallah**. At one time, this stretch had no path. The harrowing descent through the rocky walls of the **Malana Gorge** added to the mystique of the region. Even today, the path has some hairy stretches. From

Shepherd with his flock on the high pastures of Malana

the bridge onwards, the grade is gentle, descending south-west along the left bank of the Malana stream. An hour's walk brings one up to the dam site of the **Malana Power Project.** 🍴 Here, a few dhabas provide food and tea.

A jeep road to **Jari** (1,500m/ 10 km) connects the dam site and, with luck, one may pick up a taxi on its way to Malana or the dam site. Alternatively, one has to walk on to Jari. Follow the road (take short-cuts wherever possible) that goes down south to a bridge across the **Parvati River** near the power house of the Malana Project. On crossing the bridge, leave the road and follow a footpath to reach **Jari** on the **Kullu-Manikaran Road.**

TREKKING OPTION
FROM MALANA TO KASOL OVER RASHOL PASS
For the more adventurous, this is a good option to cross one more pass before reaching **Kasol Village** on the Kullu-Manikaran Road. From Kasol, board a bus to **Manikaran,** the picturesque pilgrimage centre just 4 km upstream along the Parvati River from here.

DAY ONE
MALANA-CAMPSITE
DISTANCE 12 KM **TIME** 4-6 HOURS
LEVEL EASY
The bridle path crosses Malana and heads north before it turns right (east) to descend to Malana Nallah, crossed over a wooden bridge. It then climbs south-east through fields and village *dogris* (summer houses). The steep descent to the bridge, followed by a steep climb, can be quite tiring. After crossing the fields, the trail passes through a thick forest of deodar, spruce and fir, with high-altitude oak in the higher reaches. ⛺ Camp is best struck in the pastures when the forest thins out. Small streams provide water in the area.

Little Malana citizens near the temple

DAY TWO
CAMPSITE-RASHOL-KASOL
DISTANCE 12 KM **TIME** 4-6 HOURS
LEVEL DIFFICULT
It is an hour-long climb south-east to the top of the **Rashol Pass** (3,250m) from the campsite. On the other side the path goes down south-east through a thick conifer forest. Descent is difficult with certain sections being very steep. Negotiate with care.

Rhododendrons appear in large numbers near **Rashol Village.** There is a cave shelter 1 km short of the village. A proper footpath descends south from Rashol Village for about 2 hrs, till **Chalal Village** on the right bank of the beautiful **Parvati River.** From here, the track goes down to cross the river over a wooden bridge and then climbs up the other side to reach **Kasol** (1,580m) on the Kullu-Manikaran Road.

For hotels in Naggar, see Accommo-dation Listings on pages 527-528 ✦

Jalori Pass
Iris country
By Deepak Sanan and Minakshi Chaudhry

Purple irises carpet the hillsides at Jalori Pass

TIME	3-8 days
LEVEL	Easy
IDEAL SEASON	May to Nov
LOCATION	Inner (Beas left bank) and Outer Seraj (Sutlej right bank) area of Kullu District

Jhibi/ Ghyagi-Shoja-Jalori Pass-Saryolsar-Khanag

The beauty of the ridge line separating the Inner and Outer Seraj was first extolled by Penelope Chetwode, daughter of the Commander in Chief of the British Army in India in 1931. She accompanied her mother on foot and horseback from Shimla to the Rohtang Pass via the Jalori Pass. She returned to India in 1963 to trek the entire distance once again. Her book, *Kulu: The End of Habitable World,* describes this journey. Commenting on her journey to the Jalori Pass from the Khanag side, she says: "The following day we had an easy climb to the top of the pass in the cool of the early morning and in addition to the usual flowers and shrubs I saw huge numbers of sinister cobra plants (*Arasaema wallachiana*), their purple-striped sheaths curving over like cobras about to strike. The whole of this area used to be a haunt of the two most beautiful species of the Himalayan pheasant: the green and purple Monal and the red-crested Tragopan, but although we kept our eyes open for them we were disappointed as we saw none."

Photographs by ASHOK DILWALI

Graphic by ANIS KHAN

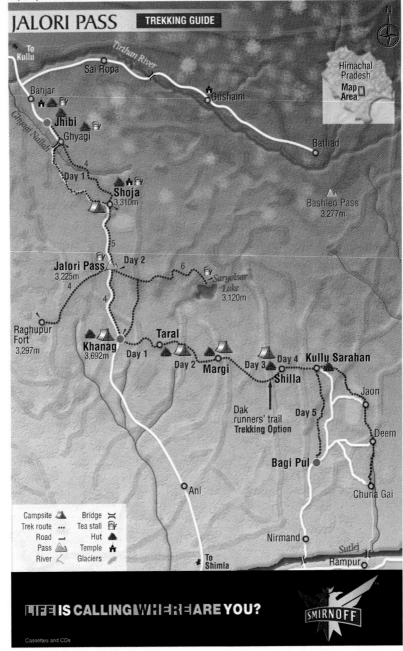

JALORI PASS

TREKKING GUIDE

To Kullu

Sai Ropa

Tirthan River

Gushaini

Banjar

Himachal Pradesh
Map Area

Ghyagi Nallah

Jhibi

Ghyagi

Bathad

4

Day 1

Shoja
3,310m

Bashleo Pass
3,277m

5

Jalori Pass
3,225m

Day 2

6

Saryolsar Lake
3,120m

4

4

Raghupur Fort
3,297m

Taral

Khanag
3,692m

Day 1

Day 2

Margi

Day 3

Day 4 **Kullu Sarahan**

Shilla

Jaon

Dak runners' trail
Trekking Option

Day 5

Deem

Bagi Pul

Ani

Chuna Gai

Nirmand

Sutlej

To Shimla

Rampur

Campsite ⛺	Bridge		
Trek route ···	Tea stall		
Road —	Hut		
Pass	Temple		
River	Glaciers		

Cobra plant

GANESH SAILI

Also known as cobra lily (*Darling-tonia californica*), the red-veined, yellowish green, hood-like leaf has a purple-spotted appendage resembling a snake's tongue. The entire plant has the appearance of a striking cobra. Streams flowing through mountain meadows present an ideal habitat for this remarkable species of the pitcher plant family.

Found all over the Himalayas from Kashmir to Sikkim, this lily grows on moist open slopes between 2,000 and 3,400m. It flowers in June. The flowers are hermaphrodite (have both male and female organs) and are pollinated by bees and flies. It is a greedy plant, inhibiting the growth of nearby plants, especially legumes.

This is a day's walk for a regular trekker but it can be extended to even three or four days for those with the time and the inclination to camp out. It's described as a two-day walk here.

Banjar has both government rest houses and a few private hotels and lodges. The staring point, Jhibi, has a small rest house, and Ghyagi boasts of both a rest house and a few private guest houses. Many people know of Shoja now, and reserving rooms in the rest houses or hotels may be difficult in summer, so book well in advance. Saryolsar Lake and the fort

Bharat Petroleum

GETTING THERE AND OUT

FROM MANDI to Banjar, it's 79 km/ 2 hrs by 🚐 (Rs 1,000) and 2¹/₂ hrs by 🚌 (Mandi to Aut Rs 50; Aut to Banjar Rs 15 by bus/ shared taxi). Regular bus service 7 am onwards. It is best to start walking from Jhibi or Ghyagi, 6 and 8 km away respectively, on the road to Jalori from Banjar **RETURN** From **Khanag**, come to **Ani** (25 km), by taxi (1 hr/ Rs 700) or bus (1¹/₂ hrs/ Rs 23). Buses run between 10 am and 6 pm **Ani to Shimla** is 119 km/6 hrs. Taxi charges Rs 3,000, bus Rs 107

of Raghupur near Jalori Pass are still relatively unknown. On my first visit to Jalori, over two decades ago, I walked over the pass unaware of the existence of either the lake or the fort. On my second visit I walked to Saryolsar. It was only on my third visit that I got to hear of Raghupur and the rest house at Takrasi.

DAY ONE
JHIBI/ GHYAGI-SHOJA
DISTANCE 6-10 KM **TIME** 4 HOURS
LEVEL EASY

The motor road from Jhibi to Ghyagi climbs gently south through exquisite forests of blue pine and deodar. Beyond **Ghyagi** there are two options: one is to follow the motor road (8 km) till Shoja. The other is to climb up a steep footpath (4 km) that winds its way up south, through the forest, along the **Ghyagi Nallah**. With the increase in altitude, the mixture of rhododendron, ban oak, horse chestnut, blue pine and deodar becomes

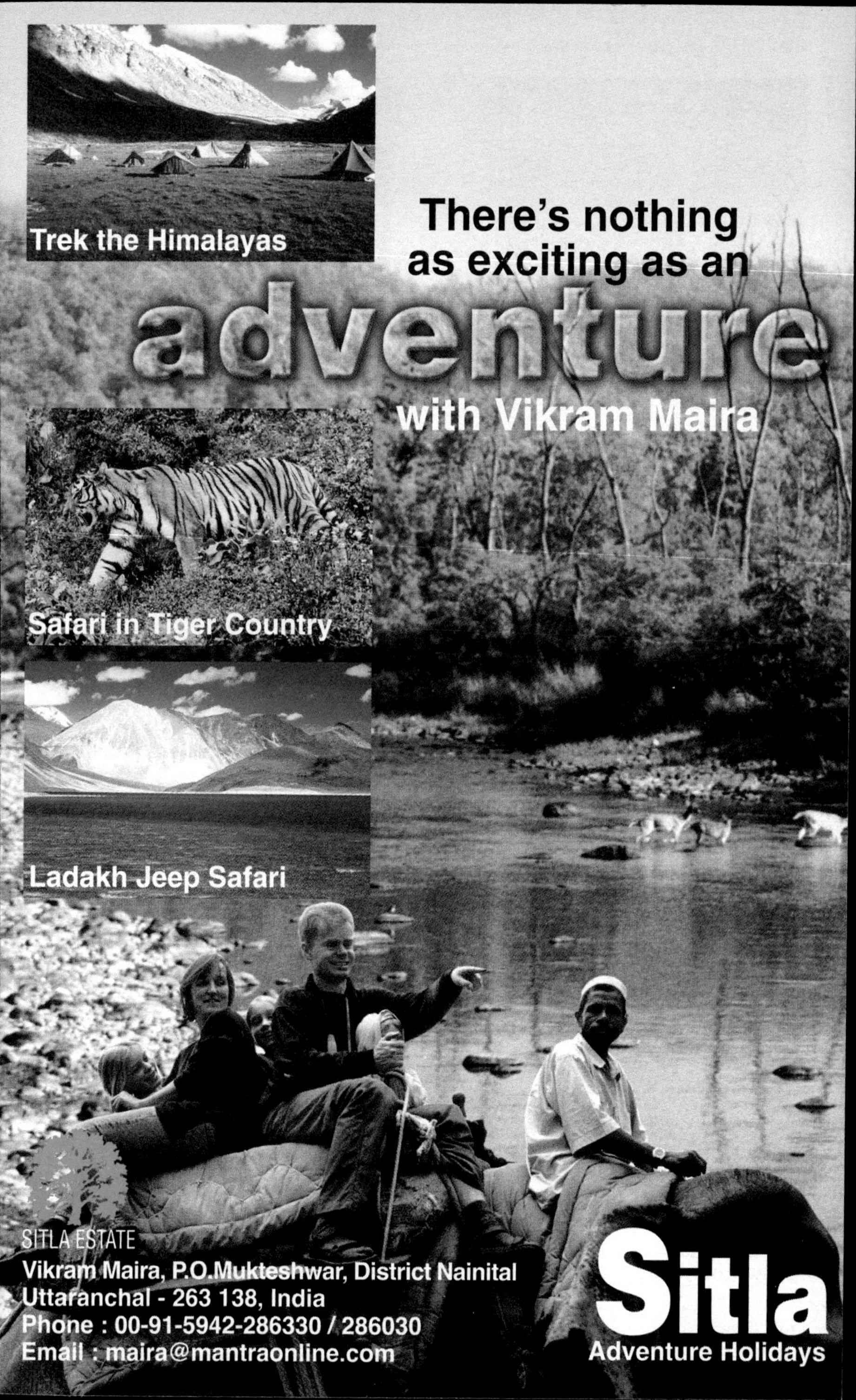
Trek the Himalayas
There's nothing
as exciting as an
adventure
with Vikram Maira
Safari in Tiger Country
Ladakh Jeep Safari
SITLA ESTATE
Vikram Maira, P.O.Mukteshwar, District Nainital
Uttaranchal - 263 138, India
Phone : 00-91-5942-286330 / 286030
Email : maira@mantraonline.com
Sitla
Adventure Holidays

On the trail from Jalori Pass to Saryolsar Lake

interspersed with spruce, moru and then fir, as the Shoja rest house is reached. **Shoja** is a picturesque village with a few modest hotels here offering basic facilities.

🔺 Try the **Banjara Retreat** at Shoja. Though the real treat is to be able to get bookings (from the PWD or Forest Department in Kullu) in the ideally located rest houses above the village. The old **PWD Rest House** located higher up offers better views.

<table>
<tr><td colspan="1">DAY TWO</td></tr>
</table>

SHOJA-JALORI PASS-KHANAG
DISTANCE 16 KM **TIME** 6 HOURS
LEVEL EASY

A climb to the south from Shoja takes one to the top of the **Jalori Pass**, 5 km away. The route is along the motor road past a mixed forest of spruce, fir, kharsu oak and rakhal trees. Grassy meadows characterise the pass. After May, irises literally carpet these grasslands. Wild rose and larkspur also abound on the hill slopes between Shoja and Jalori Pass. The pass itself is not very wide but the surrounding heights offer panoramic views of the **Dhauladhar** and **Pir Panjal** ranges.

🔺 There are many small dhabas at the top of the pass that provide food and even a place to stay.

A gentle, almost level walk of 6 km through forest dominated by kharsu oak leads eastwards from Jalori to **Saryolsar Lake** (3,120m). The small lake is revered on both sides of the ridge and numerous pilgrims trek up in the summer months from the

Skiing is believing...
...there's a heaven on earth.

Gulmarg in winter, is a place dreams are made of! A thick carpet of snow
covering everything in sight, the rush of adrenaline, the sound of your heart accelerating
as you speed down a slope and feel on top of the world.

If you have never skied before, Gulmarg - the Alps of yesteryears is the best and most affordable place
for you to learn. Established in Gulmarg in 1927, the Ski Club of India offers a variety of choices.
For experts there's a 3 km long ski run - the best off-piste skiing round the world. For beginners there's
a gentle slope of 200 mts with accommodation, skiing lessons and equipment readily available.
For non-skiers there's a lot of fun and sun in the snow. After all unlike the Alps,
Gulmarg enjoys sunny weather, even in winter!

Kashmir
PARADISE ON EARTH

Jammu and Kashmir Tourism Development Corporation conducts special package tours with/without skiing.

Visit us at: http://www.jktourism.org For further information, contact or write to J&K Tourist Offices at: **New Delhi** Tel. 23345373 Fax: 23367881
Mumbai Tel. 22189040/22344073 Fax: 22186172 **Kolkata** Tel./Fax: 22285791 **Chennai** Tel./Fax: 28235958 **Ahmedabad** Tel./Fax: 25503551
Hyderabad Tel./Fax: 24734806 **Jammu** Tel. 2548172 Fax: 2548358 **Srinagar** Tel. 2452690/2452691 Fax: 2479548

JWT.5040.2003

Iris

OTTO PFISTER

Found in the Himalayas from India to Bhutan and western China, in alpine pastures at elevations of 3,500-4,200m, the iris (*Iris kemaonensis*) is a perennial, growing to 45-50 cm. It flowers from May to June, a deep lilac to purple with a central tuft of yellow hairs that are called 'beards'.

Though stunningly beautiful, many plants in this genus are thought to be poisonous if ingested, so caution is advised. The roots are especially likely to be toxic. The iris can cause skin irritation and allergies in some people.

Both the flower and seeds are used in Tibetan medicine. They are said to have an acrid taste. The flowers are said to have a cooling potency, and are analgesic and ophthalmic, being used in the treatment of tinnitus, pain in the ears and weakening of eyesight. The seeds, on the other hand, have a heating potency. They are also analgesic and anthelmintic and are used in the treatment of colic pain due to intestinal worms, hot and cold disorders of the stomach and intestines, and pain below the neck and shoulders.

surrounding villages. There is a route even to **Bathad**, the starting point of the climb to the adjoining **Bashleo Pass**. A couple of ☕ tea shops at the northern end of the Saryolsar Lake offer refreshment through the summer season.

About a third of the way back towards Jalori, a steep, well-defined path heads down south through oak and meadows to **Khanag**, about 4 km away on the motor road to **Ani**. Khanag has a pretty ⛺ **PWD Rest House** for a night stay or, one can take a bus or taxi down to Ani.

An option from Jalori Pass is to visit the ruins of **Raghupur Garh Fort** (3,297m), located about 4 km to the right (south-west) of the pass. The fort walls are visible from the pass. It takes a short descent and then a steep climb to reach there.

Occupied by the Gorkhas in their great foray across the Western Himalayas in the early 19th century, the fort was abandoned when the British Army routed them.

The hilltop location commands great views. From **Raghupur**, it is possible to descend south through the oak forest to the village of **Takrasi** (5 km), where an old forest house has played host to Pandit Jawaharlal Nehru, India's first prime minister. From Takrasi, a 7-km motor road leads to Khanag.

THE DAK RUNNERS' TRAIL

TIME	5 days
LEVEL	Easy
IDEAL SEASON	May to Nov
LOCATION	Sutlej right bank in the Outer Seraj area of Kullu District

Views near Khanag

KHANAG-TARAL-MARGI-SHILLA-KULLU SARAHAN-BAGI PUL

This old bridle path passes through tiny hill villages existing in a beautiful time warp. It was the route on which forest dak runners carried official and personal letters in the old days. Trekkers can embark on this exciting journey after Khanag instead of going down to Ani. The old route had eight stages from Khanag to Rampur. It's a gentle walk along the forest paths through **Taral, Margi** and **Shilla** up to **Kullu Sarahan** (4 days). It involves staying at altitudes of over 2,000m throughout, with rest houses at every nine odd kilometres.

🏕️🏔️ **Forest rest houses** at Taral, Margi and Shilla are booked by the Divisional Forest Officer, Ani (office at Luhri, approximately 100 km from Shimla, on the right bank of the Sutlej). These rest houses are not well maintained and trekkers may have to camp in the rest house compound. But all of them are located in idyllic surroundings. However, the **PWD rest houses** at Kullu Sarahan and Khanag are well maintained.

From Kullu Sarahan you can trek to **Bagi Pul**, connected by a motor road. Bagi Pul offers an exit to Shimla via NH22 across the Sutlej.

GETTING OUT from Bagi Pul

There is a regular bus service from here to **Shimla** (152 km/ 7 hrs/ Rs 138). Last bus leaves at 6 pm. Local buses available for the tehsil headquarters at **Nirmand** (17 km/ 1 hr/ Rs 13). At Nirmand, buses and taxis are available for **Rampur** (19 km/ 1 hr / Rs 13 by bus). The Nirmand-Rampur stretch is in poor condition

For rest house bookings and hotels, see Accommodation Listings on pages 522 (Banjar), 524-525 (Jhibi, Khanag, Kullu Sarahan), 527-528 (Mandi, Margi, Shilla), 530 (Shoja, Taral, Takrasi) ✦

Once a quiet retreat of the British Raj, Dharamsala was radically transformed by events in distant Tibet in 1959. The invasion by China and the subsequent exile of the Dalai Lama and many thousands of his subjects transformed Dharamsala into a shabby mirror of its original home on the other side of the Himalayas, with monks and monasteries, the summer palace and temple.

Dharamsala (divided into lower Dharamsala and the upper, McLeodganj 9 km away) is today a curious mishmash of cultures: Tibetan and Kashmiri curio shops, pizzerias vying with tandoori dhabas, Tibetan hippies and American monks, prayer gongs and Hindi film songs, quaint English and Jalandhar mod... the disconnected yet familiar culture of Kovalam and Kathmandu.

→ Dharamsala/McLeodganj Facts

- **LOCATION** Surrounded by a stretch of the Dhauladhar mountains, overlooking the Kangra Valley in west Himachal, Dharamsala (1,387m) is 9 km from McLeodganj or Little Tibet
- **GETTING TO MCLEODGANJ By air** Nearest airport: Gaggal (21 km/ 1 hr), serviced by Jagson Airlines. Taxi Rs 400 **By rail** Nearest railhead: Chakki Bank (84 km/ 3^1/$_2$ hrs). Taxi Rs 1,300. Buses (Rs 70) also available **By road** From Delhi, drive to Una via Chandigarh and Kiratpur; then to Amb and over the Beas to Kangra; from here Dharamsala is 21 km
- **STD CODE** 01892
- **TREKKING RESOURCE** Regional Mountaineering Centre, Dharamkot Road; Tel: 221787. Provides information on mountain climbing and trekking in the Kangra and Chamba valleys

MUST-VISITS

THE TIBETAN CIRCUIT

No trip to McLeod is complete without a trip to the Dalai Lama's **Namgyal Monastery**, and the **Tsuglakhang**, his temple. **Norbulingka**, in Siddhbari (14 km), is modelled on the Dalai Lama's summer palace outside Lhasa. This complex, built in the early '90s, houses

a temple and an atelier for traditional wood carving, sculpture and thangka paintings from old masters. **TIPA** is the impressive performing arts institute, which offers performances of Tibetan opera and theatre on Dharamkot Road.

BHAGSUNAG

The Bhagsunag shrine and waterfalls is a short distance from town, dotted with bakeries and cafés.

CHURCH OF ST JOHN-IN-THE-WILDERNESS

A couple of kilometres from McLeodganj, on the Dharamsala Road, is a charming stone church in a deodar grove, with exquisite stained glass windows. It was built in 1852 by the British.

WHERE TO STAY

Chonor House (Tel: 01892-221006, 221077; Tariff: Rs 1,400-2,200) is centrally located between the Namgyal complex and McLeodganj, set amongst tall deodars and a lovely terrace garden. **Hotel Bhagsu** (Tel: 221091-92; Tariff: Rs 800-1,650), close to the market, is run by the HPTDC, and has great views. **Pemathang Guesthouse** (Tel: 221871; Tariff: Rs 660-990), opposite Bhagsu Hotel in McLeodganj, has a restaurant that offers veg international cuisine. A cheaper option in McLeod Bazaar is **Ashoka Guest House** (Tel: 221763; Tariff: Rs 80-400).
For more hotels and details, see Accommodation Listings on page 524

WHERE TO EAT

The multi-cuisine restaurant at **Chonor House** serves excellent food. It's also one of the few places you can get fresh coffee. **Mcllo Restaurant** in the main bazaar has Indian, Chinese, dosas, soups, shakes and sandwiches on its menu. **Namgyal Café** in Namgyal Monastery is known for its excellent pizzas and cakes. **Hotel Tibet's** restaurant serves the best Chinese and Tibetan food.

INPUTS FROM SONIA JABBAR

Enjoy Dal Bukhara,
the way the early frontier warriors did.

Under the wide open skies

History tells us that the Dal Bukhara was originated and perfected by the early frontier warriors in open pots under the star studded sky.

What better way is there to enjoy this delicacy than on a trek in the great outdoors? Except now you don't have to cook it for 18 long hours over burning coals. Simply buy a Kitchens of India Dal Bukhara, heat and eat.

A feast for the senses

SAVOUR OUR OTHER DELICACIES: [● MIRCH KA SALAN • PANEER DARBARI]
[● CHICKEN DARBARI • MURGH METHI • CHICKEN CHETTINAD]

For further information email us at kitchensofindia@itc.co.in

Triund and Indrahar Pass
In high places
By Deepak Sanan and Minakshi Chaudhry

Fog descends upon the Triund Forest Rest House

TIME	2-5 days
LEVEL	Moderate
IDEAL SEASON	May to Jun. Sep to Oct
LOCATION	Indrahar Pass lies across the Dhauladhar Range between Kangra and Chamba districts

McLeodganj-Triund-Lahesh Cave-Indrahar Pass-Chatta Parao-Kwarsi-Hilling-Choli

If you're holidaying in McLeod-ganj, and if you just have one night to camp out, or want to do a day hike, then go up to Triund. It's a pretty three- to four-hour walk to the top. Of course, if you want to be more adventurous you can go over the Indrahar. This is the most frequented pass across the Dhauladhar, and is known by several names: Laka, Indrahar and Kwarsi.

I crossed it on my way to Bharmour in November 2002. At 7.30 am, on a cold morning late in autumn, there was not a whiff of wind at the top. The Kangra Valley was spread out below like a green and brown checked carpet. Silver lines marked the streams, picked out by the rays of the morning sun as they sliced the checkerboard in crazy patterns. We spent nearly two hours at the top, basking in the warmth of the sun, absorbing the surreal view of a serene and quiet world in the valley below. A Gaddi whom we met just below the pass guided us to Nag Dal. The nearly one-and-a-half-hour trek to the left of the pass lay over snow and boulders and we followed the footprints of a bear till the lake.

A large number of Gaddi shepherds choose this pass for their seasonal migration. For those seeking the

Graphic by ANIS KHAN

GETTING THERE AND OUT

FROM McLEOD to Dharamkot, it's 2 km/ 10 mins by 🚙 (Rs 40). No 🚌 on this narrow uphill climb

Dharamsala to McLeod is 9 km/ 25 mins by taxi (Rs 100) and $\frac{1}{2}$ hr by bus (Rs 9). There is a bus every half hour between 7 am and 8 pm. Shared taxis available (Rs 7 per head)

RETURN From **Choli** on the Holi-Chamba Road, take a taxi (Rs 200) to Kharamukh (20 km/ 1 hr). From Kharamukh, take a taxi (2 hrs/ Rs 800) or bus (3 hrs/ Rs 40) to Chamba (70 km), which is well connected with Pathankot (115 km)

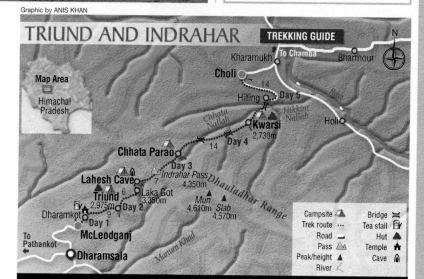

TRIUND AND INDRAHAR   TREKKING GUIDE

N

Map Area

Himachal Pradesh

Kharamukh — To Chamba — Bharmour

Choli
14
Hilling — Day 5
Chhata Nallah   Hikkim Nallah   Holi
Kwarsi
2,730m
14   Day 4

Chhata Parao
Day 3
Lahesh Cave
Indrahar Pass
7   4,350m   Dhauladhar Range
6   Laka Got
Triund   3,350m
2,975m   Day 2   Mun   Slab
Dharamkot   9   4,610m   4,570m
Day 1

To Pathankot
McLeodganj
Manuni Khad
Dharamsala

Campsite ⛺		Bridge ╳	
Trek route ···		Tea stall ☕	
Road ═		Hut ⛺	
Pass ⛰		Temple ⛩	
Peak/height ▲		Cave ⌂	
River ≺			

Monal pheasant

The Himalayan monal pheasant (*Lophophorus impejanus*) is found in high altitudes of up to 4,000 ft. Found in mountain ranges from Afghanistan, the Indian Himalayas to North-East India, Bhutan, Southern Tibet and Burma, usually in open coniferous or mixed forests with bamboo. The monal grows to 2-2½ ft, usually weighing between 1½ and 2½ kg. Their variegated feathers in blue, red, gold and yellow allows one to distinguish males from females who have a duller appearance. The long tail is brown and the head has a crest of upright feathers. The female is smaller than the male, with brown feathers and no crest. Like many animals in Asian forests, loss of habitat is the largest threat to this pheasant's survival, making it an endangered species. Hunting males for their crest of head feathers has been an increasing problem over the past few years, and hunting these birds for food continues to decrease wild popula-

RUPIN DANG/ WILDERNESS FILMS

tions. Most of the monal's day is spent foraging for food, consisting of seeds, berries, tubers, shoots and insects. They are excellent diggers, using their long, curved beak to dig up to 10 inches under the ground. These pheasants are most often found in pairs or small groups. Four to six pairs can be found in a half-mile radius.

The monal is extremely communicative, using both body displays and calls. The wide range in their calls allows them to differentiate between contentment, aggression, alarm and advertising for a mate. The males have intricate displays signalled by bobbing the crest on their heads and fanning their tail feathers.

The breeding season for the Himalayan monal pheasant is April through June. Although the male will make contact calls in the dawn throughout the year, during these months his vocalisations take place throughout the day. The male does not assist with the rearing of young, but may remain close to defend the female and offspring from predators.

thrill of standing on top of a high pass, Indrahar presents the perfect option, and they can return the same way to Dharamsala. The track is well marked, there is no need for a guide and even a lone trekker can safely venture up and return in two days of hard walking.

DAY ONE

McLeodganj-Triund
Distance 9 km **Time** 4 hours
Level Easy

Though you can drive the 2 km to **Dharamkot** from McLeod, it's nicer to walk. A number of yoga and meditation centres have been established in the forest-clad serenity of the Dharamkot area. With a bit of luck, it is possible to spot leopard and *pij* (wild goat). In winter, even the monal has been known to descend to this belt.

Galu Devi (2,130m) at Dharamkot has a small temple and a water point. From here the track ascends northeast through a mixed forest of oak and rhododendron. Triund is famous for its views, and is a popular walk with visitors to Dharamsala and McLeodganj. The well-trodden route is, therefore, peppered with 🍵 tea shops and dhabas from spring till the onset of winter. Wending one's way

AHTUSHI DESHPANDE

Breathtaking views at the Triund campsite

through a 'Magic View', a 'Scenic View' and even a 'Snowline Café', the path ascends sharply in the last stretch to **Triund** (2,975m).

Triund's majestic views include the peaks of **Mun** (4,610m), **Slab** (4,570m), **Rifle Horn** and **Arthur's Seat** up in the Dhauladhar, and the wide sweep of the valley below. Both birdwatchers and stargazers are also well rewarded in Triund's environs. There is one fly in the ointment: water can be scarce at Triund and the source is a kilometre below the **Triund Ridge**, down a steep and narrow path on the western side. This is the only source and the track to it is slippery and risky in the monsoons. Post-monsoon, the volume of water decreases considerably and, at times, it goes dry. In that case one has to go further down in the same direction to get water.

There is no permanent habitation at Triund but a **Forest Rest House**, located on a subsidiary ridge of the Dhauladhar, can be booked in Dharamsala. Nearby rock shelters (to the right) can be used in an emergency. For those carrying their own tents, there is ample space to camp out in the grassy meadows. During the trekking season, a couple of dhabas spring up to cater to traffic but their prices can appear rather exorbitant to humble pockets.

DAY TWO
TRIUND-LAHESH CAVE
DISTANCE 6 KM **TIME** 3 HOURS
LEVEL EASY

It is a moderate, northbound ascent starting behind the Forest Rest House for the first hour and a half, shaded by oak and fir. Somewhat steeper going thereafter brings up **Laka Got** (3,350m), a small, grassy camping ground marked by a trekking shelter in a ruined state. From here, the trail turns to the right (north-east), goes up a small ridge and then turns to the left (west) to climb up north to reach **Lahesh Cave** (3,500m), a natural rock shelter that can house 20 people. It takes less than an hour to reach the cave from Laka Got.

An added attraction near the cave is a small waterfall. There are a number of other huge boulders that can serve as emergency shelter for four to five people. But in this boulder strewn maze, it is easy to miss the cave without a guide. While crossing the pass in 2001, when we reached the Lahesh Cave, we saw two people waving at us from a distance. We signalled them to come over. They were from New Zealand and were on their way to Bharmour. They had tried locating the cave, and had found some place to spend the night under a rock mistaking it for Lahesh Cave!

DAY THREE
LAHESH CAVE-CHHATA PARAO VIA INDRAHAR PASS
DISTANCE 7 KM **TIME** 6-8 HOURS
LEVEL MODERATE

Steady climbing can bring up the pass in 3-4 hrs. The track lies up a steep rock face ascending north over steps both natural and man-made. The narrow width is rendered somewhat hazardous in the rains as numerous streams course down the face. Post-monsoon, most of these go dry and present no difficulty. In general, it is inadvisable to cross the pass after midday as the weather on this pass is unpredictable and visibility can reduce drastically in a very short time. It's best to wait out such periods because it is easy to lose one's way in such conditions.

Jungle trail through forests

A small rock temple embedded with trishuls marks the **Indrahar Pass**. Local travellers and Gaddis usually stop to pray for a safe crossing. In clear weather, both the **Pir Panjal** and the **Great Himalayan ranges** are visible from the top. The view of the **Manimahesh Kailash** is particularly rewarding after the stiff climb.

The descent to **Chhata Parao**, a small camping spot with a rock shelter (3,700m), is taxing because it's along a trail obscured by thick grass. From the top the trail goes down left (west) in easy steep steps through the rocks, for about a hundred feet. It then takes a further turn to the left, goes down a bit before taking a right turn and dropping steeply north to Chatta Parao. The trail lies on the left side of the gully, formed by the glaciers and avalanche cones below the pass.

After going down for nearly 2 hrs, a vertical rock face on the right side of a side stream is to be negotiated. Mercifully, the Gaddi shepherds have cut steps in the rock face making it a little easier for even the faint-hearted. After crossing the stream over boulders, the trail enters the pasture. A huge rock overhang marks the 🔺 **Chhata Parao campsite** and there's sufficient space nearby to pitch tents.

On the left of **Indrahar Pass** are a few glacial lakes and bears can occasionally be spotted here in autumn. The larger **Nag Dal** is located further on the left of the pass. Tucked away in a niche on the barren slopes, it is not visible from the track and the services of a guide are required to visit it. The lake remains frozen till mid-July.

DAY FOUR
CHHATA PARAO-KWARSI
DISTANCE 14 KM **TIME** 4-6 HOURS
LEVEL MODERATE

The path down follows the **Chhata Nallah**, staying on its left side for a few kilometres, then descending steeply to cross Chhata Nallah over a

School kids on the easy hike up to Triund

wooden bridge. This is an easier crossing than the small streams encountered earlier. The trail climbs to the left and crosses a landslip area before descending gradually to a side stream crossed on a *trangari* (wooden log bridge). From here, the track turns left and a steep ascent through conifer forest leads to a ridge offering the first view of **Kwarsi Village**. The path descends for nearly half an hour to reach the Trekker's Hut and then turns right to enter the village.

The route after **Chhata** is well marked but has its hazards. In May, the hard snow in the hollows can be treacherous and in the rains, slush and the thick vegetation can be irksome. Though, the riot of wild flowers on the slopes is compensation enough.

Kwarsi (2,730m) is set amidst fine groves of deodar and blue pine. It has a few shops and a *nag* temple, which is worth a visit. Kwarsi rooftops are a pleasing sight in autumn with corn cobs, tomatoes and grass spread out to dry for the winter months.

🛖 🏔 Kwarsi boasts of a **Trekker's Hut** and a **Forest Rest House**. The rest house, located beyond the village, has not been in use for many years but is an ideal place to camp.

DAY FIVE

KWARSI-HILLING AND CHOLI
DISTANCE 14 KM **TIME** 4-6 HOURS
LEVEL EASY

From Kwarsi, the mule path to **Hilling Village** has a few tricky sections. After the village, the bridle path crosses the fields and then drops down left through a thick deodar forest. After about 30 mins, a 100-metre stretch cut into the rock-face can present problems for the faint-hearted: *the one-foot wide path hangs over a precipitous drop!* The descent is steep till **Hikkim Nallah** is crossed over a permanent wooden footbridge. Thereafter the track is gradual (mostly on the road), passing through Hilling and **Lamu** villages to **Choli**. Hilling has been connected by a jeep road to Choli. However, not many vehicles ply on this section.

For rest house bookings in Triund, see Accommodation Listings on page 530 ✦

GIREESH G V

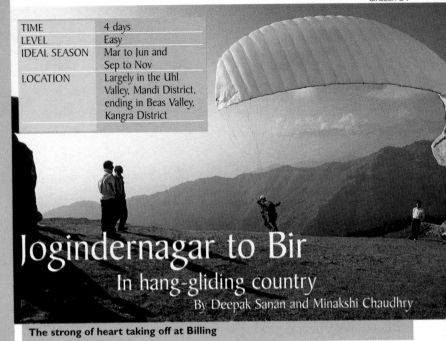

TIME	4 days
LEVEL	Easy
IDEAL SEASON	Mar to Jun and Sep to Nov
LOCATION	Largely in the Uhl Valley, Mandi District, ending in Beas Valley, Kangra District

Jogindernagar to Bir
In hang-gliding country
By Deepak Sanan and Minakshi Chaudhry

The strong of heart taking off at Billing

JOGINDERNAGAR-WINCH CAMP-BAROT-KOTHI KOHR-BILLING-BIR

Easily accessible, Barot is located in the Nargu Wildlife Sanctuary, deep in the Valley of Uhl (a right bank tributary of the Beas River). Favoured by anglers, the Uhl and its tributary, the Lamadug, abound in rainbow trout. Barot is also the site of the intake reservoir of the Shannon Hydel Power Project, designed and executed by Colonel Betty in 1925. The hillsides are thickly forested with deodar, oak, blue pine and spruce. Small villages, located along fast-flowing mountain streams and tiny terraced fields, present a charming picture to the visitor.

This is a four-day trek, which can be altered to suit one's convenience. A two-day walk brings one to Barot, from where it is possible to take a bus/ taxi back to Jogindernagar. Extending one's stay in Barot by a day or two makes it possible to explore the surrounding Chhota Bhangal region.

Several one-day treks are also possible from Barot. You can visit the temple of Bardharni Devi, or trek to Billing, the hang glider's paradise. You could also explore the villages of Polang, Bhujling, Kothi Kohr and Baragaon in the surrounding Chhota Bhangal region. It is also possible to take an easy walk up the pine slopes along the haulage trolley track.

Other walks include visiting the villages of Baragaon (14 km) and Rajgunda (18 km), up the Uhl River, or Lohardi (6 km), Polang (13 km) and Bhujling (13 km), up the Lamadug stream. These villages retain the beautiful, traditional wooden houses of old, unlike the concrete monstrosities that have overrun more accessible areas.

TREKKING HOLIDAYS IN INDIA

If you're interested in more rigorous walking and some great views, it is possible to trek up to the base camps of the Thamsar and Makori passes that link Chhota and Bara Bhangal areas. Palachak, Panihardu and Bherpal Got en route to the Thamsar Pass, and Nanwani Got and Thangkar Got en route to the Makori Pass, are scenic pastures where one can set up camp.

DAY ONE
JOGINDERNAGAR-WINCH CAMP-BAROT
DISTANCE 11 KM **TIME** 4-6 HOURS
LEVEL EASY

Walk from **Jogindernagar** to **Hara Bag** (5 km) on National Highway 20, heading south to Mandi. Alternatively, take a bus to this small village with terraced fields. There is a ☕ tea-stall here, where one can have a decent breakfast before starting out on the trek. Seek directions from the villagers and follow a well-trodden path going

Graphic by ANIS KHAN

GETTING THERE AND OUT

FROM MANDI to Jogindernagar, it's 55 km/ 1½ hrs by 🚗 (Rs 600) or 2½ hrs by 🚌 (Rs 42) on Pathankot-Mandi NH20. Regular buses between 5.15 am and 8 pm **Delhi to Mandi** (454 km) is a 12-hr drive. Taxi (Indica) Rs 6,000 approx, deluxe bus Rs 440
RETURN From **Bir** take a taxi (Rs 1,000 approx) or a bus (Rs 60) to **Mandi** (71 km). While from Bir there are only two buses, from **Bir Morh** (5 km) regular buses are available from 5.30 am-5.30 pm. Take the same route back to Delhi

Chir pine

SONIA JABBAR

Pines are natives of tropical as well as temperate climates. They are found abundantly in the Himalayas. This evergreen three-needled pine is mainly found on dry hill slopes between 1,200 and 1,800m. This is one tree that doesn't elicit joy when it multiplies, as the chir pine (*Pinus roxburghii*) ends up suppressing other plants.

The pine tree does not have the capacity to retain water, which has resulted in the drying up of springs, creating a scarcity of drinking water. It has no canopy and no undergrowth, thus leaving the mountain slopes fully exposed to erosion by rain and wind.

Pines bear seed at a very early age. They seed plentifully and almost every year. The seed is much lighter than that of the deodar and, consequently, is easily carried by the wind and scattered all over the place. Where circumstances are favourable, i.e., with the help of sufficient water and light, it reproduces itself in great numbers. This is the cause of ecological succession of pines over other trees in the Himalayas.

north up to the Winch Camp (6 km). The path is moderately steep as it climbs in a series of zig-zags up the hill.

Winch Camp (2,000m) offers panoramic views on the southern side, where small villages of Kangra and Mandi districts dot the **Beas Valley** below. The views towards the north are limited. From Winch Camp a level walk of 3 km runs parallel to the trolley track, to the left of the **Ghoghar Dhar** ridgeline. The northern Barot side is covered in a dense forest of deodar and oak. The trail goes down north-east through a mixed forest of deodar, oak and chir pine. It is a comfortable descent on a well-defined path into the **Uhl Valley**. Alternatively, one can choose to stay at the neck of the ridgeline. There are many places to pitch tents here.

From Jogindernagar, it is also possible to take a ride in the haulage trolley up to the neck (2,250m). Prior permission has to be obtained from the Resident Engineer (Jogindernagar Tel: 01908-222085) or Sr Engineer (Tel: 222068) of the Shannon Project, at Jogindernagar. If you like, take in this thrilling ride. Photography is not allowed at the project sites and the rule applies to the trolley too.

Music at the monastery at Bir

TRIBHUVAN TIWARI

An additional day at the **Barot PWD Rest House** is highly recommended. You can take any of the lovely day hikes mentioned in the introduction above. Plus, the chowkidar is a great chef and his rajma, masala aloo curry and the locally available fresh trout are worth trying out.

DAY TWO
BAROT-KOTHI KORH
DISTANCE 8 KM **TIME** 2-3 HOURS
LEVEL EASY

Barot is located at the northern edge of Mandi District bordering the Chhota Bhangal region of Kangra just above the confluence of the Uhl with the Lamadug. The Lamadug divides the two districts at Barot with the Uhl at this point entirely in Kangra District. Across a bridge over the Lamadug, on a road heading north-west from Barot, is

Red jungle fowl

OTTO PFISTER

According to Darwin, the red jungle fowl (*Gallus gallus*) is said to be the original "chicken" from which all domestic chickens are descended. It is the only wild fowl that can crossbreed fertilely with the domesticated species. It is yellow-headed with a red comb and wattles, and its multicoloured plumage resembles a jester's costume. The female is slightly smaller and less brightly coloured. The polygamous male is aggressive and completely chauvinistic, taking no part in nest building, incubation or the care of the young.

the **Multhan Village** in Kangra. There are a few offices and a Forest Rest House here. On the other side of Multhan flows the Uhl. **Kothi Kohr Village**, further north-west up the Uhl, is linked by a motor road that goes on to Baragaon (14 km). This road is a part of the Barot-Billing Road currently under construction. A walk along this road, which runs upstream through a thickly wooded conifer forest on the left bank of the Uhl, is truly superior to a vehicular journey on it.

Kothi Kohr is a small village that has a couple of tea-stalls, which double up as provision stores. There is enough space to pitch tents here.

DAY THREE
KOTHI KOHR-BILLING
DISTANCE 13 KM **TIME** 4-5 HOURS
LEVEL EASY

Follow the road upstream along the River Uhl till **Baragaon** (6 km). The road ends at a point where the link to Rajgunda is still under construction.

From Baragaon, a bridle path descends to the left to cross Uhl River, flowing down from the **Thamsar Pass** located far up to the right (north). After crossing a wooden bridge, the path turns left, leaves the Uhl below and climbs up to reach the sizeable village of **Rajgunda** (2,625m/ 3 km from Baragaon). From this village, the route follows the road track that heads south to Billing (2,800m) climbing gently high above the Uhl right bank till it reaches the **Slater Ridge** crossing into the **Beas Valley**. From here, a gentle descent takes one down to Billing. It takes about 2 hrs to cover this stretch through a mixed forest.

Billing, a world-famous paragliding site, has a **Forest Rest House** with a commanding view. The surrounding green carpet-like grass is ideal for camping. There is no habitation at Billing, though seasonal tea shops/ dhabas come up in summer to cater to the itinerant traveller.

JITENDER GUPTA

The magnificent Dhauladhar Range seen from Billing

DAY FOUR

BILLING-BIR
DISTANCE 14 KM **TIME** 3-4 HOURS
LEVEL EASY
There are two options to reach Bir (1,525m).

OPTION I
Follow the motor road (14 km) south-west downhill. This is a leisurely walk with great views of the Kangra Valley.

OPTION 2
The old route, a short-cut, is through a mixed forest and is very steep, cutting short the distance by about 6 km. To take the short-cut, follow the jeep road connecting Billing and Bir till the first turn from where the footpath drops down south. It is easily identifiable. The trek ends short of the market at Bir, meeting the jeep road.

Bir is a Tibetan settlement with a monastery and bazaar, where Tibetan handicrafts are available. You'll also find people from the Bara Bhangal area, as most of them migrate to Bir during the winter. Stay overnight at Bir or head back to Mandi.

For rest house bookings and hotels, see Accommodation Listings on pages 522 (Barot, Billing and Bir) and 525 (Jogindernagar) ✦

Dalhousie market square

A bandoned and disowned by Lahore after Partition, Dalhousie's remains have unfairly been labelled "Dull and Lousy". Yet, a walk around its three malls and wooded loops such as Potreyn Road, Bakrota and Moti Tibba hills is anything but dull. It has as many as five functioning churches, charming British-style country houses that have been converted into hotels, a cemetery spread over nine terraces, a beer brewery (now in ruins) and rock frescoes painted by the first flood of Tibetan émigrés in 1959.

MUST-VISITS

CHURCHES

Dalhousie's oldest is St John's Church, situated near the GPO. At the other end of the Mall, on Subhash Chowk, is St Francis Church. The best-preserved in Dalhousie is without doubt the church in the Sacred Heart School. Of the others, St Patrick's is the biggest on Potreyn Road, whereas St Andrew's which is in the Cantonment can only be accessed with permission.

A RAJA'S HUNTING LODGE

Roughly 2½ km from Gandhi Chowk is the residence, and now the summer home of the former Rajas of Chamba. Though the property is out of bounds now, the charming road to Jhandrighat is a walker's delight. Subhash Booli (2,065m), Subhash Chandra Bose's meditation spot, also falls on this route.

THE WATERFALL WALK

Take a morning walk to Satdhara, said to have medicinal properties in the seven streams that converge on this spot (1 km down from Gandhi Chowk), and to Panchpullah, 1 km further on, which offers two waterfalls within touching distance.

CHAMERA DAM

Also called Bhadrakali Lake by the locals, this is an ideal picnic stop en route to Chamba, about 8 km from the bustling village of Banikhet.

WHERE TO STAY

Mehar Hotel (Tel: 01899-242179; Tariff: Rs 550-1,300), on the Mall, is a mid-range hotel run by painter Manjit Bawa's family. Another option is Hotel Manimahesh (Tel: 242155; Tariff: Rs 800-1,500), which is a new hotel run by the HPTDC, near the bus stand; the service is courteous here.
For more hotels and details, see Accommodation Listings on pages 523-524

WHERE TO EAT

No fine cuisine to be had here. But for a wholesome meal of hot tandoori rotis and rajma, head for Gandhi Chowk or the bus stand. Just below the taxi stand, Sharma's Dhaba offers good parathas and vegetable biryani.

INPUTS FROM CHARU SONI

→ Dalhousie Facts

● **LOCATION** Spread over five hills at 2,000m, and sandwiched between the Dhauladhar and Pir Panjal ranges, north-east of Pathankot
● **GETTING TO DALHOUSIE By rail** Nearest railhead: Chakki Bank (58 km/ 2½ hrs). Taxi Rs 1,000; bus Rs 40 **By road** NH1 from Delhi to Jallandhar via Ambala and Ludhiana; NH1A to Pathankot via Dasua. Then state highway to Dalhousie via Chakki (14 hrs). The roads are good except for a section between Jallandhar and Pathankot, where the construction of a new highway is in progress
● **STD CODE** 01899

LIFE IS CALLING WHERE ARE YOU?™

SMIRNOFF

Cassettes and CDs

ASHOK DILWALI

Dalhousie-Khajjiar-Chamba
Through enchanting glades

By Deepak Sanan and Minakshi Chaudhry

Terraced fields glow neon-green near Chamba

TIME	3 days
LEVEL	Easy
IDEAL SEASON	May to Nov
LOCATION	Chamba District, north-west Himachal Pradesh

DALHOUSIE-KALA TOP-KHAJJIAR-CHAMBA

Lt Col Mapier of Magdala first conceived of Dalhousie as a sanitarium in 1851. Since the sanitarium was founded during the tenure of Lord Dalhousie as Governor General of India, it bears his name. Nobel laureate Rabindranath Tagore stayed at Snowdon, located on Upper Bakrota Road in the town, and Subhash Chandra Bose spent seven months here beginning May 1937. Pandit Nehru, who visited Dalhousie in 1954, wrote, "One of the finest hill stations in India is Dalhousie from the point of beauty, climate and agreeable surroundings." It is known for the long level walks around its five hills (Bakrota, Balun, Kathlag, Patryn and Tehra). Among these, the circular walk on the Thandi Sarak and Garam Sarak, connecting Gandhi Chowk and Subhash Chowk, is the most popular.

My first trip from Dalhousie to Chamba was in 1995 and it yielded an unforgettable image. We started late from Dalhousie in a car and, only a few kilometres out of town, we came across a full grown leopard sprawled in the middle of the road. Disturbed by the light and sound he raised himself from the road and, with a disdainful flick of his tail, ambled off into the forest.

I did not comprehend what Kala Top meant till I reached there. The deodar trees are so thick and tall that

Graphic by ANIS KHAN

DALHOUSIE-CHAMBA

TREKKING GUIDE

[Map showing the Dalhousie-Chamba trekking route with locations including: Ravi, To Tissa/Rajpura, Duggada, To Pathankot, Lakkar Mandi, Kala Top 2,440m, Chamba, Dalhousie 2,039m, Alha, Dain Kund, Sultanpur, Mayari, Gala, To Bharmour, Khajjiar 1,920m, with Day 1, Day 2, Day 3 trek markers]

Campsite ⚠
Trek route •••••
Road ▬
River ≺
Hut ▲
Tea stall ☕

🗺 Map Area

Himachal
Pradesh

N

GETTING THERE AND OUT

FROM PATHANKOT to Dalhousie, it's 95 km/ 3 hrs by 🚗 (Rs 1,200) and 4 hrs by 🚌 (Rs 80). Frequent buses to Dalhousie. At Banikhet, the main highway leads to Chamba while a link branches off to Dalhousie (7 km)
RETURN Take a bus from **Chamba**, the district headquarters, to Pathankot or Dharamsala. **Pathankot**, the railhead, is 115 km/ 3^1/$_2$ hrs by taxi (Rs 2,200) and 4^1/$_2$ hrs by bus (Rs 130)

all one sees on looking up are the dark treetops shutting out the sky. Khajjiar is a picturesque green alp set in the midst of handsome deodar trees. Its fame is justly earned but it is also true that the crowds can detract from its serene charm at the height of the tourist season.

The temple of Khajji Nag is dedicated to the serpent of Khajjiar. Legend has it that a renowned sage lived at this beautiful spot. One day, a powerful serpent saw this enchanting glade and decided to make his home here. The sage resisted but lost the ensuing battle. On his defeat the sage is believed to have told the serpent *"kha aur ji"* (eat and live), giving rise to the name Khajjiar. A small temple dedicated to Hadimba is located nearby.

This trek can be completed even in a day. But don't be tempted into doing that. This is a trek that should be done

Common leopard

OTTO PFISTER

The leopard (*Panthera pardus*) is dispersed over a wider area today than that of any of the other large cats. It is one of the roaring cats, capable of producing a deep sawing roar similar to that of the jaguar. The leopard coat pattern has a clear yellow coat with dark spots or rosettes. Some leopards' coats may vary in colour, and the jet black melanistic type is also popularly called the 'Black Panther'.

The leopard's remarkable adaptability to different environments is an indication that it is basically an unspecialised animal, favouring forest and forest boundary habitats where it can utilise trees for protection and observation platforms. Its compact body, with the graceful trademark tail dangling elegantly from a tree like a velvet rope, is the image that captures the essence of this most powerful carnivore. Leopards prey upon cattle, dogs and even small children, earning the dubious reputation of being maneaters. In India and South-East Asia its numbers have dwindled mainly due to hunting for its prized fur and through loss of natural habit because of the human population explosion.

by those seeking a leisurely walk and not the thrill of crossing a high pass or visiting a remote region. One should allow at least three days to enjoy the natural beauty of the region. The route passes through one of the finest deodar forests in India. The walk is either along the motor road or very close to it, so it can be terminated at any stage by switching to the buses/ taxis plying on the road.

DAY ONE
DALHOUSIE-KALA TOP
DISTANCE 13½ KM **TIME** 4-5 HOURS
LEVEL EASY

Start from Dalhousie (2,039m) after an early breakfast and follow the vehicle road going east to Khajjiar (22 km/ 1,920m). The road meanders upwards to **Alha** (7 km), a pretty spot with terraced potato fields. Alha has a small rest house on a hilltop and the road approaching it serves as a ski slope for beginners in winters.

From Alha, the road winds up east to the **Lakkar Mandi Wood Depot** (3 km). The main road drops down further east to Khajjiar and a dirt road to the left heads off for the Forest Rest House tucked inside the **Kala Top Wildlife Sanctuary** (3½ km). The metalled road to the right goes to **Dain Kund** (4 km from Lakkar Mandi), a high point offering a panoramic view of the Pir Panjal Range.

♦ **Entry fee for sanctuary** Rs 100, to be obtained from the Forest Checkpost, Lakkar Mandi **Forest Rest House Permit** Contact Divisional Forest Officer (Wildlife), Chamba; Tel: 01899-222639

🔺 🛖 Trekkers can stay either at the **Forest Rest House** or opt to camp around Lakkar Mandi.

The Kala Top Sanctuary (2,440m) area is the habitat of a variety of fauna including the leopard, black bear, goral, barking deer, monal and koklash pheasant and the chakor. The rest house in the sanctuary is ideally

The charming Kala Top Forest Rest House

located amidst a thick grove of conifers. If not short of time one can profitably stay another day to explore the surroundings and enjoy the view from Dain Kund.

DAY TWO

Kala Top-Khajjiar
Distance 12½ km **Time** 4-5 hours
Level Easy
There are two options from the Kala Top Rest House to Khajjiar.

Option 1
Follow the charming bridle path managed by the Forest Department from the rest house to Khajjar. This gradual descent of 11 km takes about 3 hrs, heading south-east through a thick and lovely forest of deodar, oak and rhododendron. Carry a picnic lunch and choose from the many charming spots for a lunch break.

Option 2
Retrace the route to Alha, and follow the vehicle road that curls down south-east to Khajjiar. The last couple of kilometres are a sharp plunge down the forested slopes to the lush green meadow of **Khajjiar** with its little lake in the middle (shrinking with a growing silt load and vegetative growth in recent years).

Once famous as a royal retreat for golfers and polo players, it was named

165

Ban oak

SONIA JABBAR

Found between 1,200 and 2,400m all along the outer Himalayas (except Kashmir) from Pakistan to central Nepal, the ban oak (*Quercus incana*) is an evergreen tree, also known as the blue-jack oak. It is a moderate to large tree, growing to 25m and prefers dry hillsides. Its leaves are a leathery, dull green on top, with grey, felted texture underneath, and serrated on the edges. Young trees have a bluish tint.

Its seed is about $2^1/_2$ cm long. It can be dried, ground into a powder and used as a thickening agent in stews, or mixed with cereals to make bread. The seed contains bitter tannins. These can be leached out by thoroughly washing the seed in running water though many minerals will also be lost. It can take several days or even weeks to properly leach whole seeds. One method was to wrap them in a cloth bag and place them in a stream. Leaching the powder is quicker. A simple taste test can tell when the tannin has been leached. The roasted seed may be used as a coffee substitute.

The seeds are also used medicinally as astringent and diuretic. They are used in the treatment of gonorrhoea, indigestion, diarrhoea and asthma. Any galls produced on the tree are strongly astringent and can be used in the treatment of haemorrhages, chronic diarrhoea and dysentery.

A mulch of the leaves repels slugs, grubs, etc, though fresh leaves should not be used as these can inhibit plant growth. The leaves, unfortunately, make good fodder and hence are ruthlessly lopped by locals, inhibiting the growth of the tree. The wood, though hard and red-brown in colour, warps and splits badly when it is seasoned.

the Switzerland of Himachal Pradesh by the Swiss envoy in 1992, becoming the 160th tourist spot in the world to be christened mini-Switzerland!

🔺 Accommodation at Khajjiar includes a standard hotel of the state tourism corporation, a government rest house and a few private hotels.

DAY THREE
KHAJJIAR-CHAMBA
DISTANCE 10 KM **TIME** 3-4 HOURS
LEVEL EASY

Follow the road going north-east to Chamba for about 2 km till **Mayari Gala** from where a broad bridle path goes down left (north-east). Mayari Gala is at a sharp right turn near a ☕ tea-shop. This steep bridle path passes through mixed forest of deodar and blue pine and a number of small hamlets. **Chamba town**, located on a plateau on the right bank of the **Ravi**, is visible from a considerable distance. The bridle path joins the motor road (Sach Road) near Sultanpur, which is 5 km from Chamba.

For rest house bookings and hotels in Dalhousie, Chamba, Kala Top and Khajjiar, see Accommodation Listings on pages 522-525 ✦

Chamba provides a sharp contrast to Dalhousie, the colonial hill resort of the British, because of the way it has cherished ancient Indian heritage and traditional customs. However, over the years, the influx of people from the plains has changed both the topography and the ethnographic profile of the ancient capital of Rajput kings. Its famed temples, weathered and stripped of the intricate wood-carved edifices, first by the British and then by the Archaeological Survey of India, are mere shadows of their former selves.

Lakshminarayan Temple complex

→ Chamba Facts

- **LOCATION** In the north-west corner of Himachal, bordering J&K, 50 km north-east of Dalhousie
- **GETTING TO CHAMBA By rail** Nearest railhead: Chakki Bank (114 km/ $3^1/_2$ hrs). Taxi Rs 1,300. Buses (5 hrs/ Rs 80) run every $1^1/_2$ hrs **By road** Drive to Pathankot via Jallandhar on NH1 or via Anandpur Sahib, Una and Hoshiarpur. From Pathankot to Chamba via Banikhet, it's 124 km/ 4 hrs
- **STD CODE** 01899

MUST-VISITS

TEMPLE VISITS

Chamba's ancient shrines are worth a visit. Of the lot, the **Lakshminarayan Temple complex** is the largest. The **Gauri Shankar Temple**, which faces the gateway to the complex, dates back to the 11th century. Also visit the nearby **Bhuri Singh Museum**. North-east of Lakshmi Narayan is the **Brajeshwari Devi Temple**. Another interesting temple is **Bansi Gopal** (also referred to as Radha Krishan) **Temple**, where you can view a number of stone panels. Most temples bear erotic panels on the outer walls. Next to the colonial Fire Station is the 11th century **Hariraya Temple**, dedicated to Vishnu. A steep, 1-km trek from the bus stand (by road or stairway) is **Chamunda Devi Temple**, from where you can view the entire Chamba town. The intricately carved wooden temple was built by Raja Sahil Varman, the town's founder.

WHERE TO STAY

There are very few hotels to choose from. HPTDC's **Hotel Iravati** (Tel: 01899-222671; Tariff: Rs 600-1,200) is a large hotel in the middle of town, with reasonably clean loos. The service is friendly. Also offers authentic Chamba cuisine, to be ordered in advance. Its budget wing, Champavati, has dorms at Rs 75 per bed.

A few steps from the bus stand, the comfortable **Hotel Aroma Palace** (Tel: 225577; Tariff: Rs 500-3,000), offers a comfortable stay and an interesting view of the Raj Mahal. **Himalayan Orchard Hut** (Tel: 222507/ 607; Tariff: Rs 350-650), situated in village Rulpuli Panj-la towards Sahoo, roughly 12 km from Chamba, offers village tourism at its most charming. Perched at 1,325m, the clay and mud house accommodation offers neat and clean rooms. Also tents in season. Surrounded by fruit trees, vegetable fields and a pool (!), it provides a unique opportunity to unwind in a mountain village atmosphere.

For more hotels and details, see Accommodation Listings on pages 522-523

WHERE TO EAT

The *chaugan* has quite a few dhabas where you can eat the regular Himachali dal, rajma and chawal. Some offer non-veg. It's best, however, to depend on the hotel you're staying in. Some restaurants offer *chamba madhra* (a combination of rajma, dahi and ghee served with rice).

INPUTS FROM CHARU SONI

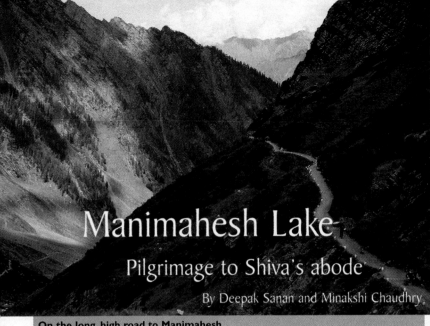

Manimahesh Lake
Pilgrimage to Shiva's abode

By Deepak Sanan and Minakshi Chaudhry

On the long, high road to Manimahesh

TIME	3-4 days
LEVEL	Easy
IDEAL SEASON	Jun to Oct
LOCATION	Bharmour region of Chamba District

HADSAR-DHANCHO-GAURI KUND-
MANIMAHESH LAKE-GAURI KUND-HADSAR

The sacred lake of Manimahesh (4,115m), reflecting the image of the Manimahesh Kailash towering above, draws the faithfuls by the tens of thousands at the time of the annual pilgrimage. My first trip in September 1997 was two days after 80,000 people had thronged the area — leaving the route strewn with disposable cups and plates, fruit peel and soft drink bottles, while the northern end of the lake was choked with polythene bags and plastic waste. But volunteers were already at work to clear the rubbish and I was told that they always do a satisfactory job. Since then, I have been to the lake 21 times and experienced its magic in different seasons. Early in summer, snow still blankets the paths above Dhancho. But the clear blue sparkling water of the half-frozen lake is a special sight, and worth the weary trudge through the snow. There is the additional possibility of sighting the monal pheasant at this time.

Manimahesh Lake, at the base of Mount Chamba Kailash (5,775m), is said to be the abode of Lord Shiva. Traditionally, pilgrims used to start from the Lakshminarayan Temple at Chamba (996m) and covered the 87-km route in seven stages, on foot. Now, most take a bus or taxi ride up to Hadsar. You can stay overnight at Bharmour (65 km from Chamba) and taxi up to Hadsar the next morning to start your trek. Ideally, the trek should be done in three days. At the time of Manimahesh Yatra (August/

September, stretching over two weeks from Janamashtmi) many people do the entire stretch of 26 km in a single day, but this is extremely taxing, and we don't suggest you try it.

The easiest time to trek is a couple of weeks before the yatra. During the yatra, the 7th century Chaurasi Temple complex in Bharmour offers the opportunity of witnessing gaddi rituals, but the crowds can be overpowering. During the yatra, tented accommodation is available at Dhancho, Jumaru, Sundrasi, Gauri Kund, Goth and the lake. Several dhabas and free *langars* also come up at these places. Rates are reasonable with food priced at Rs 25 per meal and a night stay at Rs 50 per person. The Mountaineering Institute Sub-Centre, Bharmour (Tel: 01895-225036; *see Listings on page 521*), also provides tented accommodation at Rs 50 per person (with sleeping bags and ground sheets).

Speed ™
High Performance Petrol
Bharat Petroleum

GETTING THERE AND OUT

FROM BHARMOUR to Hadsar, (17 km/ 30 mins) charges Rs 250, shared taxi and Rs 15. Bus service is frequent **Chamba to Bharmour** (65 km/ 4$^{1}/_{2}$ hrs) Taxi costs Rs 1,500 and bus Rs 50. Buses run regularly 8 am to 5 pm

RETURN Take the same route back — Hadsar to Chamba via Bharmour. The last bus leaves Hadsar at 5 pm

Photographs by ASHOK DILWALI

Manimahesh Lake

Myths and legends

Dhancho Falls Legend maintains that Lord Shiva had hidden behind this waterfall to avoid the demon, Bhasmasur. Gaddis believe that the gods do not permit anyone to climb the **Manimahesh Kailash Peak**. Two rock projections on the western side of the peak are said to represent a sadhu and a Gaddi, who tried to reach the top but were turned to stone.

Gauri Kund It is said that Goddess Parvati used to bathe here. Women are supposed to take a ritual dip in its waters. Men are expected to perform their ritual cleansing at the nearby Shiv *katori*, said to have originated from Lord Shiva's feet.

Manimahesh Lake During the yatra on Radha Ashtami, the Chelas (oracles or mediums through whom the gods speak) cross the lake in a spectacular display of mesmerised devotion. The Chelas belong to Sachuin Village in Bharmour and claim their descent from Trilochan Mahadev — who is said to have accompanied Lord Shiva to the lake as a porter (and stayed with him underneath the lake for six months).

The Chelas, dressed in traditional Gaddi attire (Chola, Dora, Tope), arrive at the lake in a special procession, chanting Lord Shiva's name. First they perform a parikrama of the lake, offer prayers and sacrifice a goat. Then they wade through the freezing waters of the lake. As soon as the Chelas reach the opposite bank of the lake, devotees rush towards them — the first to touch a Chela receives priority in securing answers to queries addressed to the lord. The Chelas then sit on a specially made platform, to answer queries of devotees.

MANIMAHESH LAKE — TREKKING GUIDE

To Kunngli

N

Bharmour
13
Hadsar 2,100m
Tos Ka Goth
Gauri Nallah
Budhil

To Chamba 65 km

Dunali
6
Day 1
Dhancho 2,900m

6
Sundrasi
Day 2
Gauri Kund 3,600m

Manimahesh Kailash 5,775m

1
Goth 3,700m

Manimahesh Lake 4,115m

□ Map Area
Himachal Pradesh

Legend	
Campsite ⛺	Bridge ✕
Trek route ···	Log bridge ✕
Road —	Tea stall ☕
Peak/height ▲	Hut ⛺
River ∕	Temple ⛩
Glaciers ∕	

DAY ONE

HADSAR–DHANCHO
DISTANCE 6 KM **TIME** 2-3 HOURS
LEVEL *Easy*

Drive to **Hadsar** (13 km/ 30 mins). A well-marked track starts from the eastern end of **Hadsar Bazaar** (2,100m). The concrete path turns right (south), just short of the tourist sarai managed by the PWD, and continues south along **Gauri (Manimahesh) Nallah** flowing down from Manimahesh. After about a kilometre (at **Goi Nallah**), it turns westwards and climbs sharply to **Dibri**, a water point. It gains height thereafter and reaches **Tos ka Goth**, a small resting place under fir (*tos*) trees. A couple of small ascents and descents follow before reaching **Dunali**. Here, the path turns left to

A kaleidoscope of colours near Bharmour

cross the Gauri Nallah over temporary wooden bridges, after which a steep climb to the right leads to **Dhancho** (2,900m). Where the tree line ends at Dhancho, there is a sloping pasture marked by rocks and big boulders at the lower end. Check out the huge **Dhancho Waterfalls** at the Gauri Nallah. ⛺ Camp at the tented sarai or pitch your own tents.

DAY TWO

Dhancho-Gauri Kund-Manimahesh Lake
Distance 8 km **Time** 4-6 hours
Level Moderate
There are three options to reach Gauri Kund (3,600m) from Dhancho. I recommend Option 1, as this is the most frequented route, and better maintained than others.

Option 1

The main path to the lake goes past a pre-fabricated structure and dhabas that spring up at Dhancho in summer, before it turns right to cross **Gauri Nallah** over a wooden bridge, and then climbs steeply on the left bank of Gauri Nallah. Going past the top of the waterfall, the path turns left (north) after about a kilometre and crosses another wooden bridge over the Gauri Nallah. Thereafter, it ascends gradually along the right bank of the nallah. En route, two spots with some open space named **Jamaru** and **Sundrasi**, acquire temporary dhabas during the yatra. Sundrasi also has a **medical post**.

A kilometre after the dhabas at Sundrasi, the track forks. The route on the left moves west and follows a long switchback east before crossing two avalanche cones to reach Gauri Kund. This is the most taxing and tiring stretch of the day's walk as the barren, tree-less landscape and thin air makes the climb difficult. A water bottle is a prized possession.
TIP Warning! Watch out for loose stones falling from above at a couple of places on this stretch

Gauri Kund, a pond in a glacial depression, is the place where women are expected to take a dip on their way to Manimahesh. After Gauri Kund, the track crosses Gauri Nallah to the left bank over a narrow wooden bridge, turns right and climbs up through an open pasture called **Goth** (3,700m) to

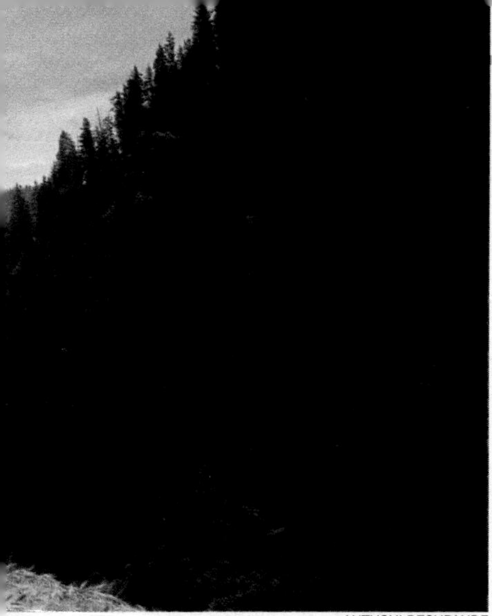

AHTUSHI DESHPANDE

Manimahesh Lake (45-60 mins). **Manimahesh Peak** is visible on the left. The lake has a small roofless temple on its southern side.

One can camp by the side of the lake, or at the prefabricated structures and sarais at **Goth** and **Gauri Kund**. The structure at Goth is dismantled by the end of October. There is sufficient space to pitch tents on both sides of **Gauri Nallah**.

OPTION 2

A new track was laid from Dhancho to Gauri Kund in 2002. It takes off from the main path described above, before Gauri Nallah is crossed below **Jamaru.** It goes straight to Gauri Kund, climbing up on the left side of Gauri Nallah. The ascent on this path is gradual but there is no drinking water available.

OPTION 3

This is the oldest route (through **Bandar Ghati**) that climbs on the right bank of Gauri Nallah. Earlier it was so tough that, at certain points, it required crawling on all fours. But now it has been improved considerably. It turns left (north) from the sadhu-sarai at **Dhancho**, climbs at a very steep grade in a series of short switchbacks before taking a right turn (east) to traverse a rock face. It goes on to meet the main trek (Option 1) below **Jamaru**.

DAY THREE

GAURI KUND-HADSAR

DISTANCE 13 KM **TIME** 4-6 HOURS

LEVEL EASY

The return journey of 13 km can be done in a day on the same route. Try to reach **Hadsar** by late afternoon as taxis or buses do not ply in the evening. Or stay overnight at **Dhancho** and head to Hadsar the following day.

For rest house bookings in Bharmour and hotels in Chamba, see Accommodation Listings on pages 522-523

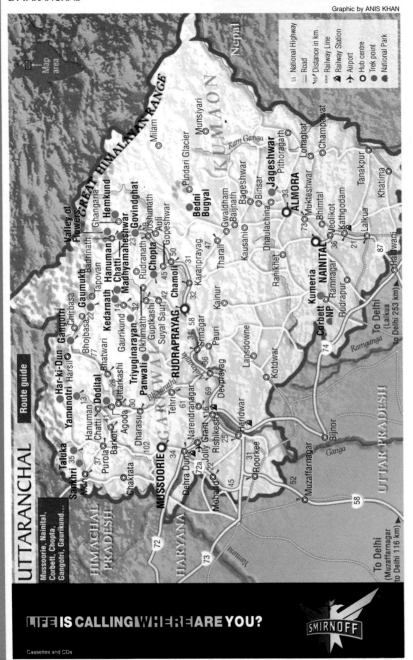

Graphic by ANIS KHAN

UTTARANCHAL
Route guide

Mussoorie, Nainital,
Corbett, Chopta,
Gangotri, Gaurikund...

53	National Highway
	Road
16	Distance in km
	Railway Line
	Railway Station
✈	Airport
◉	Hub centre
●	Trek point
	National Park

LIFE IS CALLING WHERE ARE YOU?

SMIRNOFF

Cassettes and CDs

TREKKING HOLIDAYS IN INDIA

The livin' is easy at Pine Retreat

Though not as pristine as it once was, Mussoorie has always been a great getaway for mountain walkers with an eye for sylvan beauty and a nose for the unspoilt trail. Only 50 yards from Landour's busy chowk, a path leads northwards through fine conifer to the spring at Kharapani where the mountain vista opens onto dramatic limestone cliffs that fall into the Aglar Valley. It is the steepness of the Mussoorie range that has preserved an amazing wealth of flora and fauna and the richness of bird life. It is also Mussoorie's institutional character that has helped slow down municipal encroachment on the forests.

The avian population is rich in these still fairly dense neighbouring jungles. Garhwal boasts some 400 varieties of birds. The most characteristic bird song to start the day in Mussoorie is the thrilling trill of the electric blue Himalayan whistling thrush, which will nest in any limestone crag at the back of your house for generations.

MUST-VISITS

The Mall

Mussoorie's Promenade, the Mall, straddles a precipitous ridge, extending from Cloud's End in the west to Rockville (the 'Haunted House') in the east. Officially, the Mall begins at Gandhi Chowk (better known as Library Bazaar) and ends at the Clock Tower, where Landour Bazaar starts.

Kempty Falls

Though we don't recommend it, most tourists include an excursion to Kempty Falls (15 km), an hour's drive away on the Mussoorie-Yamunotri route (return taxis Rs 350). This once was a lovely spot, but is now a long, scruffy bazaar, littered with plastic bags and garbage. It's bursting with tourists in summer and traffic jams are routine. Better to carry on down to the Yamuna and find a quiet spot to picnic along the river bank.

WHERE TO STAY

There are over 250 hotels and guest houses in Mussoorie and, except for the peak period of high summer, you can take your pick. A majority of them crowd both ends of the Mall.

The **Claridges Nabha** (Tel: 0135-2631426; Tariff: Rs 3,950-4,950), on Barlowganj Road, was the summer resort of the Maharaja of Nabha. With just 20 rooms and a gym, it offers all the comforts one can ask for.

The **Savoy Hotel** (Tel: 2632120/ 010; Tariff: Rs 800-2,500) is a rambling Victorian edifice near the Old Library. Most of its 100-odd rooms offer a lovely view of the Himalayas. **Padmini Niwas**

Photos TRIBHUVAN TIWARI

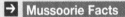
Glitter at the Tibetan market

The main market at Mussoorie

(Tel: 2631093; Tariff: Rs 750-5,400) is another old colonial bungalow, facing the Doon Valley. **Cloud's End Forest Resort** (Tel: 2632242; Tariff: Rs 400-3,200) near Park Estate has panoramic views. **Jaypee Residency Manor** (Tel: 2631800; Tariff: Rs 5,500-12,000) in Barlowganj is among the best options in Mussoorie. **Kasmanda Palace** (Tel: 2632424; Tariff: Rs 2,300-3,000) offers horse riding, arrangements for rafting, paragliding, treks, birdwatching and horse safari, with advance notice.

For more hotels and details, see Accommodation Listings on pages 535-536

→ Mussoorie Facts

● **LOCATION** In the Garhwal Hills at an altitude of 2,000m, spread on a ridge 34 km uphill of Dehra Dun
● **GETTING TO MUSSOORIE By air** Nearest airport: Jolly Grant, Dehra Dun (58 km/1³/₄ hrs). Taxi Rs 850 **By rail** Nearest railhead: Dehra Dun (34 km/45 mins). Taxi Rs 450. Contact Comfort Tours, Gandhi Road, Dehra Dun; Tel: 0135-2656062 **By road** Good motorable roads from Delhi to Mussoorie. It's a 7-hr drive through sugarcane and mango country via Roorkee, Chhutmalpur and Dehra Dun. Semi-deluxe and ordinary buses (8¹/₂ hrs/ Rs 160) available from ISBT Kashmere Gate
● **STD CODE** 0135
● **TREKKING RESOURCES** Choose a reputable local trekking agency (*see Listings on page 514*) if you want your Mussoorie trek organised sahib-style. **Trek Himalaya Tours**, near the Mussoorie Ropeway, run by Neelamber Badoni, provides personalised service and creative itineraries. Neelu's expedition sirdar, "Chillie", enjoys the title of best-loved guide in the Garhwal

WHERE TO EAT

Mussoorie is not a great place for eating out in spite of the fact that Andy Verma, now listed as one of Britain's top ten Indian cooks, ran a bakery here for a few years.

The upmarket **Four Seasons** provides good Indian and Chinese cuisine, and is clean and comfortable; a pleasant place to take the family. Some hotels, such as **Jaypee Residency**, have decent restaurants. The **Padmini Niwas Hotel** provides excellent Gujarati meals, vegetarian of course.

Green in Kulri Bazaar is another old vegetarian restaurant, always crowded. Good South Indian food can also be found in Landour Bazaar. Near the Clock Tower, the little **Golden Restaurant** caters to different tastes. **Whispering Windows** in Library Bazaar may have lost some of its old ambience, but is still popular. **Kwality**, above the old Rialto Cinema, continues to be a favourite perch for people-watching.

The **Writer's Bar** at the Savoy, with its many historic associations, is worth a visit. It may lack modern amenities, but it still has some character. **Hakman's** is another relic of the past, bringing back memories of late night dances, cabarets and beauty contests.

INPUTS FROM BILL AITKEN

View of the beautifully forested Pari Tibba Ridge from Mussoorie

The Pari Tibba Ridge Circuit
In fairyland

By Bill Aitken

Woodstock Bypass-Company Bagh Village
(near Barlowganj Jaypee Residency Hotel)

TIME	1 day
LEVEL	Easy
IDEAL SEASON	Oct to Apr
DISTANCE	12-15 km
LOCATION	East of Landour Bazaar

Situated on the eastern flank of Mussoorie, the modest height of Pari Tibba, the 'Hill of the Fairies', is compensated by its girdle of thick oak and deodar forest. Walking this circuit in April is particularly special, with the rhododendrons in bloom and the oak in purple new leaf. From October onwards, you get a front seat view of the spectacular Mussoorie winter line. It enflames the horizon when the setting sun leaves a unique, lingering band of gold, crimson and purple light along the length of the Doon Valley, from the Ganga to the Yamuna.

Fern addicts should note this area has a fabulous 120 species, ranging from the red-bearded Christmas to the light green Bible. Their inves-

tigation, however, involves the serious risk of leech bites in the rains. Note that the village milk deliverymen give these slopes a wide berth from July through September, when the leech count is phenomenal. Salim Ali's classic, *Indian Hill Birds*, will be much in demand to sort out the varieties of thrushes, laughing and whistling! I was under the impression I had been buzzed by a silent, low-flying eagle until I got home and checked. I discovered that it was the wide mottled span of the eagle owl that caused me to duck as he brushed my head, closely investigating the

Graphic by ANIS KHAN

MUSSOORIE DAY HIKES

TREKKING GUIDE

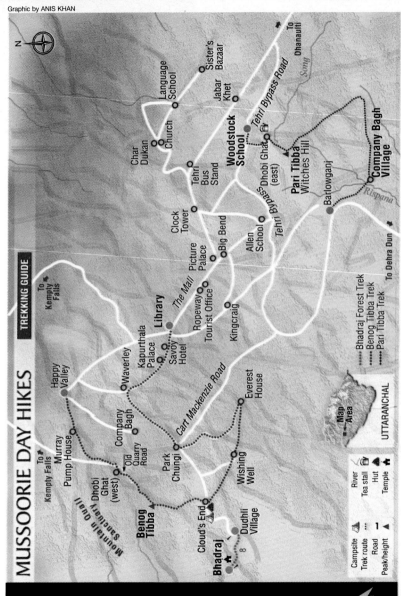

N

To Dhanaulti

To Kempty Falls

Sister's Bazaar

Jabar Khet

Language School

Char Dukan

Church

Tehri Bus Stand

Tehri Bypass Road

Song

Woodstock School

Dhobi Ghat (east)

Pari Tibba
Witches Hill

Company Bagh Village

Tehri Bypass

Barlowganj

Rispana

Clock Tower

Big Bend

Allen School

To Dehra Dun

Picture Palace

The Mall

Library

Ropeway
Tourist Office

Kingcraig

Kapurthala Palace

Savoy Hotel

Waverley

Happy Valley

Cart Mackenzie Road

Everest House

Bhadraj Forest Trek
Benog Tibba Trek
Pari Tibba Trek

Murray
Pump House

To Kempty Falls

Company Bagh

Old Quarry Road

Park Chungi

Wishing Well

Map Area

UTTARANCHAL

Dhobi Ghat (west)

Benog Tibba

Mountain Quail Sanctuary

Cloud's End

Dudhli Village

Bhadraj

8

Campsite	River
Trek route	Tea stall
Road	Hut
Peak/height	Temple

LIFE IS CALLING WHERE ARE YOU?

SMIRNOFF

Cassettes and CDs

179

The magical world of ferns

SONIA JABBAR

● Ferns, of which there are now about 12,000 species, have been on our planet for more than 300 million years. In the Carboniferous Period (about 369-280 million years ago), they grew abundantly; the period was known as the 'Age of Ferns'. Most ferns of this period became extinct but, later, some evolved into our modern ferns.

● Ferns are unlike other plants and have complex structures. What we think of as leaves is arbitrarily called the 'frond'. It is divided into two main parts, the stipe (leaf stalk or petiole) and the blade (the leaf-like part).

● Unlike leaves that arise from stems, fronds arise from rhizomes. Rhizomes are also not uniform in size or character. Sometimes they can be inconspicuous or even underground and, at other times, may even grow to 36 ft in height and 2 ft in diameter, as in the case of some tree ferns.

● Ferns are plants that do not produce seed, but propagate through dust-like 'spores'. Sporangia, small capsules found on the underside of fronds, produce spores. Spores contain oil droplets and sometimes chlorophyll, in addition to their nucleus. Ferns drop millions, often times billions of spores during their lifetime, but very few ever land in a spot suitable for growth.

● The spore that is fortunate enough to find the right conditions then starts to grow by cell division. It forms green, heart-shaped plants that measure about half an inch and lie flat on the soil. They then grow male and female organs on their undersides. The male organ produces spermatazoids, which will swim via a droplet of water to the egg produced by the female organ. The fertilised egg then grows into a fern.

Experience Octane

The Hi-Octane High Performance petrol from Bharat Petroleum.

Bharat Petroleum

GETTING THERE AND OUT

TO GET to Woodstock, use the Tehri Bypass (before entering Mussoorie at Kingcraig) or, if you want to do this in reverse, take the road immediately below it to get to **Barlowganj**. are available at both the Kulri and Library ends of town **RETURN** Take a taxi, or walk, from Barlowganj to Mussoorie, a steep 4 km

intruder in his domain. Wonderful stands of trees of mixed (including flowering) species characterise the banks of the Rispana. But thickets of the rampaging white wild rose creeper should be given a wide berth in the summer months.

TIP Carry a large water bottle, a stout stick, unobtrusive clothes with pockets to cart away food wrappings, sun hat, torch, umbrella (if it's the rainy season) and notebook. These are junk-free trails. Let's keep them that way

THE TREK

From the bypass motor road at **Woodstock**, the distance to the top will only require 2 hrs if you follow the short forest road to **Dhobhi Ghat**, the last place for basic refreshments and drinking water. Stick to the climbing forest jeep road to **Chamalsari**, on the east side of **Pari Tibba**, and follow its gentle ascent for 2 km, where a gap between two peaks is visible. There is a well-trodden village path running down westwards between them. This path is used as a village short-cut to **Company Bagh**. It will take you past some encroaching settlements where villagers graze their buffaloes above the village of **Khetwala**. A straight and even steeper descent to the Arnigad/Rispana stream will culminate in a pucca canal wall along which you can walk (if you have a head for heights). It leads to **Company Bagh**.

To climb Pari Tibba, leave the first peak behind you and look for a trail ascending the second hill to the south (on your right). It is a short and easy climb to the top of **Pari Tibba** but the views are not extensive because of forest growth. You may notice the ruins of old buildings, which are said to be the remnants of an early settlement of the British who were driven out by constant lightning hits. Hence, '**Witches Hill**', used by the students of Woodstock. You will also see the line of large educational campuses that run down the opposite side of the valley, parallel to your ridge route: Wynberg Junior School, Allen Senior School, St George's College (which has the bonus of a chiming clock) and Oakgrove (Railways) School. Using these as constant markers, you can gauge how far down the ridge you have walked.

From the top of Pari Tibba, choose your descent as near to the ridge crest line as possible. This is rough country with some craggy limestone outcrops that have caves — villagers claim they were once bear lairs, so don't be too adventurous in looking for short-cuts. Stick to the crest line of the ridge, which is pathless for much of the way. Follow, as closely as possible, the undulating, descending ridge southwards for another 4 km through untrammelled oak jungle until you come to the end of the jungle marked by a stone wall and a clearly defined bridle path crossing the ridge. `WARNING` Don't continue on further south or you'll finally end up in the Doon Valley!

At the gates of Woodstock, Mussoorie's finest school

TRIBHUVAN TIWARI

Blue whistling thrush

Found in the Himalayas upto 4,000m, in thick forests, usually near fast-flowing streams, the blue whistling thrush (*Myophonus caeruleus*) measures to about the size of a pigeon. It is a dark, purplish-blue bird, with bright blue spots and a yellow bill. The shoulders, tail, forehead and wings are also a bright blue colour. The wings are spotted white. The blue whistling thrush's song is clear and has an almost human quality. Lt Col R.S.P. Bates, described by Salim Ali as India's first bird-photographer, wrote lyrically of the bird, "Be the sun shining in a cloudless sky or the rain lashing in furious gusts, if a blue whistling thrush is there, its penetrating and pleasurable song will be heard. We have seen a bird on the nest with heavy rain drops splashing off its plumage, singing at the top of his voice while we took shelter from the storm under the over-hanging boulder on which its nest was placed."

OTTO PFISTER

If you look over the stone wall, you can spot the roofs of **Chamalsari Village** lower on the eastern slope. Take a sharp right turn and follow the **Chamalsari-Company Bagh** bridle path, which descends at an easy gradient west, then north-west, all the way to Mussoorie via Company Bagh and Barlowganj. **Barlowganj** is a steep climb of 1 km above Company Bagh, and motorable

RUPIN DANG/ WILDERNESS FILMS

The top of Pari Tibba

in theory. The whole circuit should take 6-7 hrs, if you stop to picnic — on the climbing circuit, all alone, I've done it in less than 5. A hot bath afterwards, with salt added to the water, is recommended to avoid dehydration.

In places, note that the dividing ridge between the **Song** and **Rispana** rivers is sheer and rocky, and a strong walking stick is recommended. You are as likely to meet a wild animal as a human being on this trek, since it is too far from any village for sickle-wielding fodder-cutters to penetrate. If you wish to see or hear wildlife, walk softly and don't talk. *Kakar* (barking deer) snooze in the day and you may startle both them and yourself by gate-crashing their bower. Respect boundary markers. Stick to village right of ways and follow the country code. Friendliness on the trail gives better returns than aloofness — villagers whose curiosity has been satisfied will turn out to be useful allies in a crisis. Make it a habit to carry back your own litter. These are thirsty mountains: always keep your water bottle topped up. Don't expect to buy much beyond biscuits in village shops, so stock up in Mussoorie Bazaar. ✦

INCREDIBLE SUNRISE BEHIND VIRGIN SNOW PEAKS

TAMING A TERRIFYING TORRENTIAL RIVER

A MOUNTAIN TRAIL THAT LEADS TO ANOTHER WORLD

BRILLIANT BLUE LAKE IN THE MIDDLE OF NOWHERE

it's all just words till you get there.

The outdoors can't be described. You have to experience the adventure, out there. And no one takes you out there quite like the Great Indian Outdoors team. Totally focussed on genuine adventure travel, GIO brings you a range of breathtaking activities in the incredible Himalayas of Garhwal, Kumaon, Himachal Pradesh, Ladakh and the North East. Needless to say, every activity is professionally managed and expertly executed to let you have the adventure of your life.

GIO
Great Indian Outdoors
www.greatindianoutdoors.com

To know more, call: Delhi 26891626, 26897573, 30935998 Bangalore 51253024
or mail us at info@greatindianoutdoors.com

Trekking • Rafting • Mountaineering • Overland Safaris • Snow Trekking & Camping • GIO Camps

Tangerine/GIO/01OL

TIME	1 day
LEVEL	Mix of the easy and energetic
IDEAL SEASON	Oct to Apr
DISTANCE	15-20 km
LOCATION	West of Library

The Benog Tibba Circuit
Hiking through historical Mussoorie

By Bill Aitken

The hills of Benog that once was the site of a charming observatory

LIBRARY-CLOUD'S END-BENOG TEMPLE-
MOUNTAIN QUAIL SANCTUARY-DHOBHI GHAT-
MURRAY PUMPING STATION-TIBETAN SCHOOL-
LIBRARY

This is a long, full-day hike, rich with historical, environmental and botanical insights that will delight the historian as well as the nature lover. The walk takes one past the fine colonial building of Savoy Hotel (the biggest in the Himalayas) and the exotic but authentic French lines of a chateau, beautifully preserved by the Maharaja of Kapurthala, but not open to the public. The road doubles back at Modern School and brings you to Waverley Convent (known locally as Kala Pushta), one of Mussoorie's oldest and most famous girls' schools. The motor road walk from Waverley to Park Chungi is a level 3 km that passes through unspoilt jungle preserved by virtue of belonging to private estates. In the nick of time, the Supreme Court banned resort developers from axing these forests.

For the student of geology, it is fascinating to study how the motor road has been cut through wavy layers of tectonic activity. Every few inches of pink or yellow or purple band of rock or sediment on the roadside banking represents millions of years of painful upthrust, from what was once the floor of the Tethys Sea. The spread of the Doon Valley, that looks so serene in its security, is actually being pushed under Mussoorie, causing the hill station to rise a few centimetres each year. The moral, if you are a pessimist, is not to buy land in Doon for your retirement years. Optimists point out that at the present rate of slide, Dehra Dun can look forward to another 50 million years of existence!

Near the old chungi is Leopard's Lodge, a ruin that marks the residence

It seems hard to believe that lime-stone trucks once ran up and down the sheer mountainside of Benog. A for-tuitous scientific misunderstanding stopped the suicidal quarrying that broke all environmental laws. Benog happens to be the last fix of Col William Lambton and Sir George Everest's epic Great Trigonometrical Survey of India (a scientific feat never equalled). Translated into popular myth, it was believed that, somehow, the miners were undermining India's most crucial international boundary pillar. A public outcry saved Benog from the fate of Hathi Pao (adjoining Everest's Estate) that was literally decapitated for its limestone, consid-ered amongst the purest on our planet. So frenetic and irresponsible was the urge to quarry it that all eco-sense was abandoned and the Supreme Court had to intervene to enforce a ban.

This eastern flank of Benog has now been declared the Mountain

of the famous Delhi commissioner, Fraser. His brother, Baillie, wrote the classic, *Journal of a Tour Through Part of the Snowy Range to the Sources of the Jumna and Ganges* (1820). The building of Cloud's End bungalow, isolated and immaculately girdled by oak forest, was supervised by one of the first mem-sahib travel writers, Fanny Parkes, in 1838. The Hon Emily Eden noted in her diary that Ms Parkes was socially not much to write home about, but if her social sins were scarlet at least her books are still read. William Dal-rymple has just edited a selection of her travels, which are remarkably sympathetic to the Indian way of doing things. The present proprietor of Cloud's End Forest Resort has made a sincere attempt to create a resort that combines its original ambience with latest eco-friendly regard for the sur-roundings. There is an outdoor restau-rant that functions during the Mus-soorie season.

Prayer flags above the Tibetan School

185

The grand old colonial building of Savoy Hotel

Quail Sanctuary and, thankfully, new plantations have sprung up to obscure the limestone roads. The mountain quail was last sighted here in the 1880s. This area was to have hosted Dr Salim Ali's last expedition but he passed away before it commenced. It is believed that this bird species, assumed extinct, has since been re-sighted in another area of Uttaranchal.

Everest's successor as Surveyor General, Sir Andrew Waugh, had built a tiny, charming observatory on the shoulder of Benog (where the summit clump of trees begin) to mark the momentous "last fix" of the greatest survey ever made. This was fairly intact 20 years ago. Recently, a hotelier ignorant of the building's provenance, knocked it down to use the stone for a bland new temple to Jwala Devi (who has nothing to do with this part of Garhwal). Such well-meaning vandalism is the bane of Uttaranchal tourist development, where an international site of extraordinary scientific significance has been all but obliterated by locals of limited cultural horizons.

THE TREK

This day trek involves walking between 15 and 20 km. This means a long day, but only half that distance if you use transport to and from Cloud's End. If you wish, you can start from the Library (**Kitabghar**), a fine Victorian building maintained by Hugh and Colleen Gantzer, which presides over **Gandhi Chowk** at the western end of Mussoorie's Mall. It is a 6-km walk to **Cloud's End** and you can avoid this by catching a taxi (the motorable road gets progressively rougher), but to do this is to miss out on a well-forested, mainly level ridge walk, west of Mussoorie. Alternatively, you can knock off 2 km of the town section by catching a cycle rickshaw to Company Bagh, a former botanical garden and now a picnic spot, where you can have your photograph taken in a 'hilly dress' complete with guitar (if romantically inclined) or eyepatch (if in a villainous mood). Most useful for the hiker are its dhabas, where you can stock up on aloo paratha.

To get your trekking money's worth, walk on the main road from

TREKKING HOLIDAYS IN INDIA

Everest: The man and the mountain

Remembered long since his death, because of the world's highest peak bearing his name, Sir George Everest was the British Surveyor General of India from 1830-1843. He was a humourless individual having the knack of putting everyone's back up. But since he was a genius, his antisocial habits have been glossed over. He was a worthy successor to Col William Lambton, the unsung Yorkshireman who mapped most of the sub-continent in an unparalleled feat of inch-perfect measurements, and died before his life's mission could be completed.

Sir George purchased the Everest Park in 1833, and married only when he returned to England, advanced in years in 1843. Old Mussoorie citizens have long concluded that the *bibikhana* on his estate was not ornamental! Amusingly, when I took a photograph of the *bibikhana* in 1984 and wrote about it in *The Statesman*, a former Surveyor General, along with Mr Gibson of the Doon School, visited the site and hotly denied that a *bibikhana* ever existed. In the meantime, the building, with its elegant oval lights, was knocked down to build a cowshed! Everest's original Survey office was acquired by the government 20 years ago, but is bare of any fittings and remains totally neglected. Everest himself is said to have lived in a smaller house, overlooking the Doon (now a ruin), called Logarithm.

The story of Mount Everest has little to do with the man. After Everest's retirement in 1843, the Survey of India continued under the direction of his assistant, Captain Andrew Waugh. Earlier called Peak XV, it was considered to be much lower than the Kangchendzonga, declared in 1840 to be the highest peak in the world. Earlier, in the 17th and 18th centuries, the Andean peak, Chimborazo, was considered the highest at 20,561 ft (6,310m). In 1809, the Nepal Himalayan peak Dhaulagiri (26,810 ft/ 8,172m) was declared the ultimate. It was only in 1852 that the Great Trigonometrical Survey of India measured Everest's elevation as 29,002 ft (8,839.81m).

Apparently, one day, the Survey's chief computer, Radhanath Sikdar, a Bengali mathematician, burst into Waugh's office exclaiming, "Sir, I have discovered the highest mountain in the world." The official announcement was delayed until 1856 in order to check and recheck the height of Peak XV. Averaging several readings taken at a distance of some hundred miles, the peak's height turned out to be exactly 29,000 ft (8,839.20m). But fearing that the round figure might look as if it had been made up, Waugh arbitrarily added 2 ft to the peak's height. This figure remained the officially accepted height for more than one hundred years. It was adjusted by a mere 26 ft to 29,028 (8,847.73m) in 1955.

Some geographers expressed reservations about having Everest's name bestowed on the peak, arguing that the mountain should retain its local name — Chomolungma (Mother Goddess of the World) in Tibetan — the standard policy of geographical societies at the time. But after much debate, the mountain received its official name in 1865, in honour of Everest.

Mount Everest's official height was revised recently, when on May 5, 1999, a climbing team possessing state-of-the-art satellite measuring devices measured the summit to stand officially at 29,035 ft (8,849.87m).

LIFE IS CALLING WHERE ARE YOU?™

SMIRNOFF

Cassettes and CDs

Boys playing in the compound of the Tibetan School

Himalayan goral
or ghural

This is a goat-like animal that can be found in mountainous regions at an altitude of 1,100-4,000m. The greyish-brown coat develops thick, shaggy wool in winter. Both sexes have short pointed horns, about 6 inches long. About $4\frac{1}{2}$ ft long, and $2\frac{1}{2}$ ft high, the Himalayan goral (*Nemorhaedus goral*) weighs upto 80 pounds. It is remarkably sure-footed and can move at high speeds even over near-vertical terrain. If faced with danger it 'freezes' and then, suddenly, runs if the danger gets too close. Gorals are well camouflaged, and thus are very difficult to spot, especially when they are still.

OTTO PFISTER

the Library, past the **Savoy Hotel**. The road doubles back at **Modern School** and brings you to **Waverley**.

Just beyond the gates, you get an overview of the route that lies way ahead. To the west, stands the solitary peak of **Benog Tibba**. Note that the high ridge motor road curving towards it is on a fairly gentle contour. Also visible is your return route, culminating in the yellow roof of the **Happy Valley Tibetan Monastery**. Now note the sheer plummeting eastern face of **Benog**, and hope your knees will be warmed well enough to tackle it by the time you get there. From Waverley to Park Chungi is a beautiful, level, 3-km forested road.

At **Park Chungi**, there is a shop and piped drinking water. The shortest way to **Everest's Park Estate** — which occupies the ridge overlooking the **Doon** — is to follow the overgrown, quarry road uphill, taking appropriate short-cuts to cut off the corners (like all pragmatic hill people). Ignore the misleading signposts that suggest access to Everest's house is best along the Cloud's End Road. If you go by this route (which actually advertises a private camping site outside Everest's Estate), you will have to retrace your steps, involving a 2-km climb.

Mussoorie trees

A common shrub found along the 10-mile ridge on which Mussoorie sits is the masuri plant (*Coriani nepalensis*). Many believe that the plant gave its name to the town when an early visitor, who asked a herder the name of the ridge, was given the name of the plant. Incidentally, when the British first came to the Doon, their main task was to deal with powerfully entrenched dacoits. As a matter of fact, all local people pronounce Mussoorie as 'Mansuri', as popular lore has it that the ridge was named after the hideout of a robber called Mansur.

The oak too is a hardy native of the Mussoorie

SONIA JABBAR

hills. It is resistant to fire but much depleted by the hand of British forest managers, who preferred to clear it and plant deodar for commercial profit. Worse, in the vicinity of villages, fodder cutters' sickles hack oak trees to death. Whole branches are lopped to feed the leaves to stall-fed milch buffaloes. Three varieties occupy their own altitude niches — banj (*Quercus incana*) that grows between 1,800 and 2,400m, moru, that is to be seen between 2,000 and 2,700m, and kharsu, between 2,300 and 3,500m. They are all marked by healthy undergrowth. Entering an oak forest after stretches of pine is like passing from barren tracts to an oasis!

The ridge walk to **Cloud's End** from **Everest's Estate** is another 3 km through pristine jungle. At Cloud's End, turn north, descending to a narrow saddle straddling limestone cliffs. Then, swing east to traverse a well-aligned path (3 km) up the southern, bald face of the mountain known to the British as 'Ben Og'. **Benog** gives great views of the snow peaks and the **River Yamuna**. The northern face is so steep and thickly forested that it hosts the ghoral, a mountain goat once quite common in these hills, but today almost extinct.

From **Benog**, you can either return via **Cloud's End** and the motor road to Mussoorie, or make an adventurous descent down the eastern face (facing Mussoorie) by a *pagdandi* (faint footpath) to the old limestone quarries. Continue down near-vertical roads, built for high-geared limestone trucks that once zigzagged crazily to **Dhobhi Ghat**, famous for its gushing water springs. A sheer climb through dense forest will take you back up to **Park Chungi**, the old toll barrier at the western limits of Mussoorie.

From **Dhobi Ghat**, one of Mussoorie's least visited and most magical corners (not to be confused with Woodstock Dhobhi Ghat), a motorable road runs to the main Kempty Falls-Mussoorie Road. To avoid the long detour, opt for a 1-hr climb up the eastern flank of Mussoorie's **Happy Valley** (following the pipeline) through forest. It will bring you to the **Murray Pumping Station**, with its still-working colonial era machinery. There is a jeepable road to **Company Bagh**, but it is just as quick to keep ascending by the original bridle path to emerge at the **Tibetan Central School**. There is a reason for the big Tibetan settlement here, mostly built in the authentic Tibetan style. When the Dalai Lama first fled Tibet, he took up his residence here, at **Birla House**. From **Happy Valley**, a level, well-forested motor road returns you to the **Library** after 4 km. ✦

Photographs by NEELAMBER BADONI

Bhadraj Forest and Temple
The milkman's trail
By Bill Aitken

The house of India's second Surveyor General, Sir George Everest

MUSSOORIE LIBRARY-CLOUD'S END-DUDHLI-
BHADRAJ TEMPLE-CLOUD'S END-MUSSOORIE

TIME	1-2 days
LEVEL	Moderate
IDEAL SEASON	Apr or post-monsoons
LOCATION	West of Library

The most extraordinary feature of this trek is the freakish contrast between the thickly forested northern slopes and the totally bare grassland, which characterises the southern slopes. A line appears to have been drawn by a ruler, down the dividing ridge. Though bizarre, the effect of contrasting green tones is beautiful. It conceals Mussoorie's unique secret, the interplay of geological and climatic factors.

This walk actually overlooks one of the world's most exciting tectonic plate boundaries. The Great Himalayas rear up on the one hand and the Indian plains on the other, the latter slipping inexorably under the former.

If you are short of time and want to skip Day One of the trek, then take a taxi to Cloud's End and start hiking from there. The walk takes one to the village of Dudhli, which, as the name suggests, provides buffalo milk for Mussoorie. The villagers, except for a water problem, are comparatively well off. In the old days, even until 10 years ago, they would spend the whole day walking into Mussoorie and back. Now, with bank loans for jeep taxis, they can deliver the milk in a fraction of the time. Mussoorie milk is famous for its (in)consistency — it thins or thickens according to season. As the tourist numbers grow in summer, the milkmen would have us believe that the same number of buffaloes obligingly provides a matching increase in supply!

The hill of the Bhadraj Temple peaks in a rounded grassy summit, which falls away steeply. Though the surface is parched for almost nine months of the year, this first serious uprise of the Himalayas catches exceedingly heavy monsoon rainfall, allowing for luxuriant grass on the slopes. Mussoorie gets an average of 220 cm of rain annually, of which 160 cm falls in only 70 days. Alas, man has not assisted nature. Colonial commercial policy and Mussoorie's allure as a luxury hill station has led to the weakening of the tree cover. Both fodder and firewood demands have taken their toll on the surrounding landscape.

Like most hill-top shrines, the Bhadraj Mandir has been hideously 'restored' in cement and its ancient character totally defaced. But the devotion remains genuine and the village pujari feels proud that a large, faceless barn has replaced a small building of character. A practical point in the pujari's favour is that, painted white, this larger structure can be spotted by the villagers at greater distances. The idols inside are intriguing and are said to reflect Buddhist influences, which once were very present in these tracts bordering the Yamuna. The main festival occurs in August when offerings of milk are made. This explains the huge mound of little discarded medicine bottles that the villagers reuse to carry their offerings of milk. The mela is a grand affair and has been provided level ground for stalls, and even a helicopter pad.

The great bonus of this hike is that a cool breeze accompanies you all the way, even in the hot months, since the higher you climb, the cooler is the wind on your face. The views, whether to the snows in the north, or over the Shivaliks in the south, are expansive, and the shady path through the oak jungle a constant pleasure.

Milkmen from Dudhli on their daily hike to Mussoorie

TIP If you take a taxi from the Library (west) end of Mussoorie, it will cost half as much as hiring one from Picture Palace at the eastern end. By taking a cycle rickshaw along the Mall for 2 km (between the Ropeway and Library), you can save Rs 300!

DAY ONE

MUSSOORIE-CLOUD'S END VIA BENOG TIBBA
DISTANCE 12 KM **TIME** 5 HOURS
LEVEL EASY

The first day's walk from Mussoorie can take in **Everest Estate** and an ascent of **Benog Tibba**. Three hours there and back from Cloud's End, the night can be spent at ⛰ Cloud's End Resort, which also offers ⛺ camping

facilities (Tel: 0135-2632242; Tariff: Rs 400-3,200). *For more on Cloud's End, see pages 184 and 536.*

DAY TWO

DUDHLI-BHADRAJ TEMPLE-DUDHLI
DISTANCE 16 KM **TIME** 8 HOURS
LEVEL MODERATE

If you don't want a long slog to **Bhadraj Balaram Temple** from Cloud's End, then get a taxi to drop you to the village of Dudhli, 4 km away. You can arrange to have him pick you up later at an appointed hour. Cloud's End also has a Gypsy service for its clients. From Dudhli, follow the ridge westwards up to the crest at **Bhadraj**, a long and punishing ascent of 8 km. Don't go up the bald ridge,

Cloud's End Forest Resort on a sunny winter morning

TREKKING HOLIDAYS IN INDIA

Wormwood

Among the many herbs to be found in the grasslands is *Artemisia parviflora*, an aromatic, bitter-tasting plant with elegantly designed leaves that form part of the ayurvedic repertoire. Scientists refer to this as an 'invasive weed' and, in English, the family is disparagingly referred to as wormwood or mugwort. Rudyard Kipling identifies the lama in *Kim* as having arrived from the hills by virtue of the clinging smell of *artemisia* to his robes. Kipling also describes how, later, the lama, leaving Kim panting behind, strode purposefully

to gain the cool air of the Mussoorie hills, from whence they followed the Yamuna drainage to cross over the Great Range into that of the Sutlej.

Artemis is the Greek hunting goddess, Diana, whose famous temple at Ephesus (where her breasts were worshipped) was criticised by St Paul. She is an essentially female lunar force, the goddess of herbalists and midwives, animal loving, passionate and outspoken. Interestingly, her August festival is echoed in Garhwal by the Nanda Devi celebrations in honour of the Great Mother Goddess.

which separates the completely treeless southern face of the range. Follow instead the prettier, winding path just inside the forest, which clothes the northern slopes.

Both slopes north and south fall away steeply, and the higher you climb the thicker the forest is, though the oak trees all appear to be much less than a hundred years old. This probably explains why the bird life doesn't seem as active as in the older jungles. Pass a forest bungalow, which also explains the present thick

foliage. Without forest guards, the demands of the village buffaloes for this free fodder would see these comparatively young trees decimated in a matter of years.

The climb up from Dudhli to the temple will take 3 hrs and, by noon, you would have picnicked and be well on the return descent to Dudhli and back to Cloud's End. If you can get a foothold on the milk delivery jeep, you can do Bhadraj and back to Mussoorie in just a day, a 36-km round trip. ✦

Nag Tibba
The classic Mussoorie hike

By Bill Aitken

Great Himalayan views from Nag Tibba

MUSSOORIE-AUNTER CAMPSITE-NAG TIBBA-
MUSSOORIE

TIME	2-4 days (70-km round trip)
LEVEL	Moderate
IDEAL SEASON	Oct to Apr
LOCATION	East of Mussoorie

This satisfying circuit used to be a classic three-day trek but now, with motor roads reaching the furthest village, you can be at the base of the mountain in a morning's jeep ride from Mussoorie. However, the fact remains that four good reasons for doing this trek are still valid: Nag Tibba is a few feet short of the magical 10,000-ft mark. The mountain's mixed oak and deodar forests are dense and isolated, and host to a rich variety of bird and wildlife. It has a romantic association with Heinrich Harrer's best-selling *Seven Years in Tibet* as he escaped, in 1944, from a Dehra Dun prisoner-of-war camp. And it possesses a unique cultural identity where the Garhwali lifestyle, traditionally based on reverence for the Ganga, has been influenced by her younger sister, the Yamuna. The village of Lakhamandal on the Yamuna is reckoned to be the site of the Mahabharata incident in which the Kauravas tried to immolate the Pandavas in a palace made of lac. The Yamuna Valley also had a vibrant Buddhist period, and one of the best preserved Ashokan edicts is to be found at Kalsi where the Mussoorie hills taper off.

You don't really need porters for this trek unless you are a group that wishes to savour the flavour of camping out. Many doss down in the village primary schools overnight, or head for the Gujjar grazing sites to sleep out under the stars on Nag Tibba. These nomads are now being "resettled" (read banned and displaced), by the government, from their traditional calling, and have nowhere to go in winter since their grazing lands in the Doon have been converted into a sanctuary. They are extremely hospitable and make for another highly rewarding cultural study. Their dignity and integrity deserves to be emulated, not destroyed.

WARNING Bears are for real here and no villager will venture on to Nag Tibba except in the full light of day

DAY ONE
MUSSOORIE-AUNTER CAMPSITE
DISTANCE 25 KM **TIME** 8-9 HOURS
LEVEL EASY
TIP If you don't want to do the 25-km slog to Aunter, you could taxi to

Graphic by ANIS KHAN

NAG TIBBA

TREKKING GUIDE

Himalayan black bear

SWAPAN NAYAK

A denizen of temperate forests at elevations between 1,200 and 3,700m, the Himalayan black bear *(Ursus thibetanus)* has long, black fur with a distinct white patch on the chest that is often crescent-shaped. It can grow up to 7 ft in height, and prefers to live in steep, forested hills. The bear's ability to balance proficiently on its hind feet means, sadly, that it is often captured and trained as a cub — to dance for human amusement.

The Himalayan black bears are more carnivorous than their American counterparts, although only a small part of their diet is made up of meat. This includes small mammals, birds, fish, molluscs and carcasses. They also feed on grass, fruits, berries, seeds, insects and honey. In autumn, they fatten up for the winter by feeding on nuts. This bear is known to be notoriously aggressive towards humans and there are numerous records of attacks and killing of humans. This is mainly due to the fact that they are more likely to come into contact with humans, and they will often attack if surprised. So if you come across one, stay very quiet.

Suakholi, 11 km away, or walk part way and/ or accept offers of a lift from any milkman's jeep that passes

Start from the **Tehri Road Bus Stand** at the eastern (Landour) end of Mussoorie, or use the bypass that runs below it. Ruskin Bond's Ivy Cottage overlooks this scene and occasionally the author throws open his casement and gives a good imitation of Nelson Eddy at his baritone best. Also, Jeet's

workshop nearby hosts the very first building in the hill station. Follow the well-wooded Tehri Road past the **Woodstock Estate**, which opens out on to great views of the snow peaks to the north, as well as clear vistas of the

The green-backed tit

OTTO PFISTER

Found in the mountains at altitudes between 1,000 and 4,000m, this pretty little bird, measuring 12 cm, is very colourful. It has a yellowish-green back, greyish rump and upper tail coverts, dark yellow abdomen and brownish-black wing feathers with blue edges. With the exception of the cheeks, auriculars and napes, the green tit's (*Parus monticolus*) black head and neck is mixed with shimmering blue feathers. It has distinctive white patches on the cheeks and a black stripe on the centre of its lower belly, which is narrower on females than on males. Green-backed tits make a variety of beautiful calls. Their diet consists primarily of insects, and they are often seen alone or in pairs, searching for food amongst tree branches.

Doon Valley. (If you know where to look, you can even see the world's most beautiful peak, **Changabang**, from this road.)

In March, the wine-coloured rhododendron trees are in bloom. Walk along this mainly level ridge road for 11 km until you come to the village of **Suakholi**. Keep an eye open for short-cuts. Turn north at the last ☕ tea shop and head down sharply on the old British *cheh-footiya* bridle path through pleasant forest that gives way to austere pines as you approach the junction of **Thatyur** on the **Aglar River**. The descent is for 5

The trail near Aunter

km, and so steep that you can do it in less than an hour. A motor road also links Thatyur with Suakholi; so, on your return, it is less wearying to board a jeep taxi up this incline.

There are three routes to Nag Tibba from Thatyur, all of which head north. The shortest and steepest is via the bridge over the Pali stream (1 hr from Thatyur), climbing westwards to the village of **Mangalori** (another hour). From Mangalori, a steep and rough path leads directly on to Nag Tibba's south-western flank where, after yet another strenuous hour, you join the main forest bridle path. It winds up leisurely from the village of **Aunter**, situated at the south-eastern foot of the **Nag Tibba massif**. From here, it is a short walk to the first evening's ⛺ camping site.

Aunter is the second, and easier, route. From the bridge, you continue to head due north for two hours, following the **Pali stream** on a gentle ascent to the base of the dark forested Nag Tibba. Dense stands of deodar sway magically to remove your tiredness. Aunter, like Mangalori and Deolsari, has houses of character, and friendly people. ⛺ The best camping site is about half-way up on the southern face of the mountain, where local shepherds and itinerant Gujjars graze their sheep and buffalo respectively

PARVIN SINGH   Trekking Holidays in India

Slate roofs top the homes of Mangalori

SUMAN DUBEY

(though they use separate watering holes). The bridle path from Aunter continues up, but less coherently, all the way to the western shoulder of the summit ridge where the British had built a bungalow. It's now in ruins.

The third but much longer approach, which would render a 2-day trek into three or four, avoids crossing the stream and tends eastwards, bringing you to the village of **Deolsari**. It adds 10 km to your

Nag Tibba outing. The village has a magnificent wooden pagoda-style temple, set in a gloomy forest. The British built a dak bungalow here since this serviced the official route over the mountain to **Uttarkashi** (hence Heinrich Harrer's rendezvous on Nag Tibba with other prisoner-of-war escapees). You can spend the night at Deolsari and walk the next morning for an hour westwards, skirting the magnificent forest at the

Heinrich Harrer: Fact and fiction

Harrer was known amongst all mountaineers as a Nazi ideologue who had climbed the Eigerwand, not out of love for the Alps, but for the greater glory of Hitler's master race. However, they kept his secret out of regard for his physical bravery. Unwisely, in his old age, Harrer criticised the totalitarian regime in Lhasa. The Chinese responded by publishing, from the Berlin archives (maintained with Teutonic meticulousness), Harrer's early career as a Nazi youth leader whose ancestry had been checked against any

Jewish inputs before he was married off to a similarly certified blonde Nordic maiden! Harrer's story, that as German prisoners of war they had created a sensation when they arrived in Lhasa, is fiction. The sensation was caused not by their nationality but by their poverty, because a party of well-heeled Nazis had already been sent to Tibet as spies. (Others were sent to Sarnath disguised as Buddhist monks.) One can hardly blame Harrer for not spilling the beans. As a spy, he could have been shot!

Camping

Kayaking

Horse Safari

Trekking

Cycling

Rafting

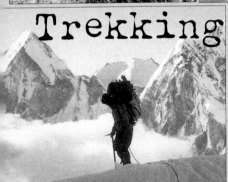

Photos SUMAN DUBEY

Sheep enjoying the green pastures near the summit of Nag Tibba

base of Nag Tibba till you reach **Aunter**, which is plumb under the main massif. From here, there is a village short-cut that runs up the eastern face but the jungle is so dense that a guide is recommended. In fact, he will be indispensable during certain seasons to point out the water sources.

A winding forest bridle path from Aunter announces the official mode of ascent and runs along the southern face of the mountain. It gives a good view of Mussoorie's "backside" as well as delivers you to a **Gujjar camping site** half-way up. As noted, this is the place to 🏕 camp on your first night halt unless you prefer the more easily found water at **Aunter**. On the way, you cross the ridge running up from Mangalori. From Mangalori to the Gujjar grazing flats will take some 4 hrs. From Aunter, much less, because of the evenly graded trail (**Aunter** is on the eastern side of the ridge and **Mangalori** on the west).

Aunter is remarkable for its extraordinary, tall stone tower temple reminiscent of the fortified style found in Lahaul. Enormous boulders form the base of this temple, which was formerly dedicated to a local deity and now — thanks to the Mahabharata on television — is passed off as a form of Shiva. Until recently, it was fashionable in the upper Yamuna region to worship the Kauravas and villagers still sport the name of Duryodhan Singh. The village women (when they visit Mussoorie) dress in a distinctive style — crinoline printed skirts, tight, colourful, long jackets, and a bandana, along with heavy silver ornaments (fashioned in Landour Bazaar). The villagers make for friendly — if talkative — companions on the trail. They are quite used to trekkers asking the way, and are accustomed to acting as guides.

DAY TWO
AUNTER CAMPSITE-NAG TIBBA-MUSSOORIE
TIME I HOUR TO SUMMIT AND 5-7 HOURS RETURN
LEVEL MODERATE

Arrival at the top of **Nag Tibba** is a bit of an anti-climax after the sumptuous stretch of jungle you have traversed to get there. From your overnight **Gujjar Camp**, it is only an hour, but very strenuous going (3 hrs from Aunter). The path is overgrown and becomes steeper and more obscure as you ascend towards the 10,000-ft mark. You pass the **Nag Devta Temple**, a tiny wooden replica of the Deolsari Pagoda,

Maut on Yamuna

An annual festival in the Yamuna and Aglar rivers, called Maut, involves the stunning of fish, which float to the surface. Thereafter, the villagers are able to pick them easily out of the water. The substance thrown into the water is the powdered root of a climbing legume (genus Derris), which is also used as an insecticide. Its active ingredient is the toxic rotenone. This annual mass catching of fish has social, if not religious sanction, though it is against the spirit of the angler's code. Curious visitors from Mussoorie travel down to the Yamuna Bridge in August, to swell the throng of villagers who view the spectacle as a blessing from the river goddess. Yamuna Mai is considered in local mythology to be not just the sister of the Ganga but also of Yamraj, the god of death.

which has water nearby. Eventually, reach the site of the ruined bungalow sited for a snow view. From here, you have to force a way eastwards up the steep and densely forested summit ridge. There is hardly any view from the top because of the growth. In fact, the summit gives one as unromantic a jolt as the truth about Heinrich Harrer's book on escaping to Tibet.

The tough last bit of the hike to Nag Tibba is not helped by the fact that you occasionally hear thumps and snorts from the undergrowth as some heavy animal (wild boar or bear?) blunders out of your way.

For a good description of the wildlife on Nag Tibba, read Stephen Alter's book, *All The Way To Heaven: An American Boy Growing Up in the Himalayas.* Steve knows the area like the back of his hand. Formerly, musk deer were known at this altitude, but have been driven higher by the trappers. The Himalayan black bear is not uncommon hereabouts and, if faced by one, it is recommended you run downhill since Bruno has short forepaws that make downhill running difficult — at least in theory! The presence of bears can be easily detected by broken oak branches, which the animals use to build a nest.

Trees with the bark rubbed off at the base may be the sign of an even more dangerous customer when riled — the wild boar that tends to frequent muddy water holes, of which Nag Tibba has quite a few. From **Thatyur**, to the top of Nag Tibba takes nearly 8 hrs but, while getting down, using the short-cuts and availing of the increasing transport opportunities, you can be back in Mussoorie much sooner. Indeed, you can be back in Delhi (via the Shatabdi from Dehra Dun!) the very same evening. On your return, take this southern short-cut and give Aunter a miss. Or tarry another night at Aunter.

If you have chosen to go by the **Deolsari** route, you would 🏕 camp at the village on your first night and your second night's camp would be the Gujjar's grazing grounds above Aunter. Day Three would start with an ascent of the peak followed by a transport-assisted return to Mussoorie. Or, you could choose to do an overnight at Aunter, returning to Mussoorie on Day Four at a leisurely pace. ✦

Deolsari Temple in the forest

Ruinsara Tal and Har-Ki-Dun
Lake of the Yakshas in the land of Kauravas

By Rakesh Shukla

AKRANT VICHITRA

Taluka Village sits happily within its colourful fields

TIME	6-10 days
LEVEL	Easy to Moderate
IDEAL SEASON	May to mid-Jun, mid-Sep to mid-Oct
LOCATION	North of Dehra Dun towards Purola, District Uttarkashi

SANKHRI-TALUKA-SEEMA/ OSLA-RUINSARA TAL-DEBSU THACH-HAR-KI-DUN-OSLA-SANKHRI-TALUKA

This adventure is perfect for a first hike. There's easy walking, over a major portion along river waters. Up above are azure blue skies, on your right and left loom dense forests of chestnut, deodar and sycamore. You walk along sparkling, playful, flowing streams and waterfalls. And even the climbs are at a gentle gradient!

The trek moves largely in the Supin River Valley, which is really the upper catchment area of the Tons. The Supin becomes the Tons (a tributary of the Yamuna) when it meets the Rupin Nallah, lower down at Netwar. Open meadows in the middle of forests beckon you to camp, and the whole area is teeming with life: parakeets, cuckoos, owls, minivets, bulbuls, tits and thrushes. You may also spot the monal pheasant, koklass pheasant, western tragopan, steppe eagle, golden eagle, the Himalayan snowcock and bearded vulture. The area falls within the Govind Wildlife Sanctuary, home to 11 mammals and 150 bird species. The upper reaches have been declared as a national park for the protection of the elusive snow leopard.

TIP Guides for Ruinsara Tal and Har-ki-Dun cost approximately Rs 200, pony Rs 500 and porter Rs 175 a day

Graphic by ANIS KHAN

RUINSARA TAL AND HAR-KI-DUN TREKKING GUIDE

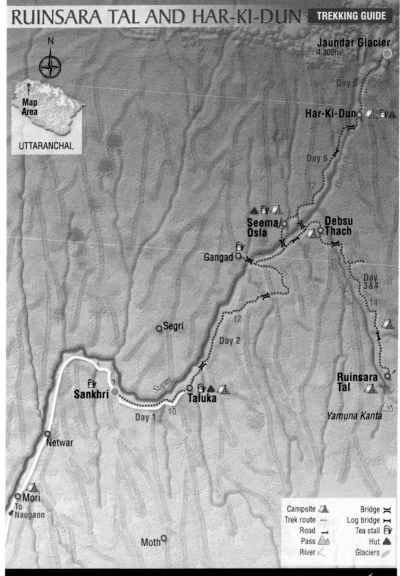

N

Map Area

UTTARANCHAL

Jaundar Glacier
4,300m

Day 6
4

Har-Ki-Dun

Day 5
12

Seema/Osla
Debsu Thach

Gangad

Day 3&4
14

Segri

12

Day 2

Ruinsara Tal

Yamuna Kanta

Sankhri

Taluka

Day 1   10

Netwar

Mori
To Naugaon

Moth

Campsite	Bridge
Trek route ···	Log bridge
Road	Tea stall
Pass	Hut
River	Glaciers

RUPIN DANG/ WILDERNESS FILMS

The unusual Duryodhan Temple at Osla

The people of the area practise customs that may seem strange to the plains-dweller: instead of valorising the Pandavas of the Mahabharata, the Kauravas are worshipped here. You will find temples dedicated to Duryodhana! Polyandry, too, is not uncommon, but given the dominant morality in the rest of the country, villagers now feel sheepish to talk about it. This is also the route that the eldest Pandava Yudhishtara is supposed to have taken after the Mahabharata war, traversing the Swargarohini mountains on his way to heaven.

There are many options to get to Sankhri, the starting point of the trek. If you have your own car or taxi you can stay overnight at Mori and drive one hour the next morning. If you are bussing it, you will have to take a taxi from Purola to Sankhri. If you are short of time you can even skip Day One and drive to Taluka, stay overnight, and start trekking the following day.

♦ **Sanctuary fee** Indians Rs 30 per person, foreigners Rs 350 per person for 3 days, with an additional fee of Rs 20 and Rs 175 respectively for each additional day

DAY ONE

SANKHRI-TALUKA
DISTANCE 10 KM **TIME** 5-6 HOURS
LEVEL EASY

There is a jeepable road from **Sankhri** to **Taluka** along the **Supin River**. However, streams overflow, boulders fall or jeeps conk out. Last year a bridge over a little stream collapsed, with a jeep marooned on the other side! It's a gentle walk, and you have all the time in the world to look around as you saunter. There is no tension over whether you will reach by dark. You certainly will! For those unused to physical exertion, it's a nice warm-up for the trek.

There are a couple of dhabas at **Taluka**. The **Forest Rest House** overlooks the Supin River and has views of the beckoning mountains in the east. It's a bit primitive, with no geysers or running water, but it's

Scarlet minivet

It's found in the lower Himalayas upto 2,700m. Also known as the orange minivet, the scarlet minivet (*Pericrocotus flammeus*) has brilliantly coloured feathers, from scarlet to bright orange. The males have black heads, black shoulders, wings and central tail feathers. While females have grey heads and bright yellow bodies, black wings and central tail feathers. The scarlet minivet measures about 20 cm or 8 inches including the tail, which is nearly half as long as the entire body. The song of the scarlet minivet is described as a pleasant whistling sung in flight or perched. The minivet feeds on a variety of creatures, which it scares out of foliage by beating its wings hard and flushing out the prey.

OTTO PFISTER

GETTING THERE AND OUT

FROM MUSSOORIE to Sankhri, it's 161 km/ 7¹/₂ hrs by 🚗 (Rs 3,000). There are no direct 🚌 to Sankhri; you must change at Purola (55 km/ 2¹/₂ hrs). Taxi from Purola to Sankhri Rs 1,500, shared taxi Rs 40
Dehra Dun to Purola Highland Transport Company runs a non-stop bus from Dehra Dun to Purola (5 hrs/ Rs 90) via Mussoorie, Yamuna Bridge. It stops for a few minutes at Mussoorie's Kingcraig and Library bus stops between 7.40 and 7.45 am and reaches Purola around 11.30 am. Though taxis, trekkers and buses ply on this route, be prepared for indifferent road conditions between Purola and Sankhri
RETURN From **Sankhri** sumos ply through the day to Purola from where you can get taxis or buses for Mussoorie and Dehra Dun. Opt for the direct Highland Transport bus (dep 1.30 pm) from Purola to Dehra Dun

charming and the only place to consider. The tariff is Rs 200 for Indians and Rs 500 for foreigners per room. If it is full, you could always try the **Garhwal Mandal Guest House**. A couple of dhabas complete the picture. You can stay at Taluka or carry on along the river for about an hour and pitch your 🎪 tent at a small meadow, at the confluence of a small tributary and the Supin. However, do enquire about the state of the trekking route before you proceed further.

DAY TWO
TALUKA-SEEMA/ OSLA
DISTANCE 12 KM **TIME** 6-8 HOURS
LEVEL EASY-MODERATE
It's best to start after a good breakfast and ask a dhaba to pack aloo-parathas for lunch. There is a short descent to the river followed by level walking on the path heading east along the river for about 40 mins, which brings you to a bridge. Cross the bridge and you are in the small meadow. Two paths branch out — one goes up the mountain, and the other goes left along the river. Head north-east, up the river. This is easy, level walking, keeping the river to your left. Then the path turns

east and starts climbing up the mountain. It's a gentle gradient as the track meanders through green forest. If you have started early, there is no need to hurry and you can savour the sights and sounds of the forest. Walk uphill

Campers at Ruinsara Tal

for about an hour, then there's a slight descent to a cute bridge over a stream, and then another 30 mins of climbing up. Another half hour of almost level walking brings you to the gentle descent for **Gangad Village**, with houses across the river perched on the hillside. ☕ Hot tea awaits you at a small dhaba. Sadly, no food is available. Pull out the aloo-parathas and pickle from your backpack and dig into them!

For **Seema/ Osla** (a village that has two names!), re-cross the river, and continue walking upriver for

another couple of hours of easy walking. There is a little uphill climb at places. Landslides, rains and fallen trees necessitate small detours at times. You start passing cultivated fields as you near Seema/ Osla Village. 🏠 There is a **Forest Rest House** and a **Garhwal Mandal Guest House** and two dhabas for ☕ tea and food. The village is across the river with houses clinging on the steep hillside. If you have the energy, just an hour's walk east will bring you to a large pleasant meadow called **Debsu Thach**, where you can ⛺ pitch your tent. However, there are no dhabas here and you will have to cook your own food.

DAY THREE
SEEMA/ OSLA-RUINSARA TAL
DISTANCE 14 KM **TIME** 8-10 HOURS
LEVEL MODERATE

Start early, recrossing to the left bank of the **Asi Ganga**. Heading north-east along the river, you cross a little bridge, which frequently gets washed away! It is only a small stream, with convenient boulders to cross if the bridge is missing. As you turn a bend, barely 200m later, look north. There is an enchanting little waterfall emerging from tree-fringed mountains. Climb along the river for another 500m until you come to an intersection. The path branching off towards the north-west will take you

Marsh marigolds

Found in the Himalayas (2,400-4,000m), from Pakistan to Bhutan, the marsh marigold (*Caltha palustris var.himalensis*) is a hardy perennial. It grows in grassy meadows and damp ground near streams created by melting snow. Its large, shining, rounded and fine-toothed leaves, and clusters of bright and pale yellow flowers, which grow 3-4 cm across, can help identify the marsh marigold. The fruit consists of a small cluster of beaked follicles.
RUPIN DANG

There's level ground, complete with a convenient drinking water source. There is an open rectangular structure with a tin roof and low walls, ideal to set up your stove. On the return you may want to pitch your ▲ tent at **Debsu Thach** instead of Seema/ Osla.

Look for a path between the trees, going down through the forest to the east of the meadow. The path is tricky and the gradient is steep. The forest is thick with lots of leaves on the ground. If it has recently rained, as it often does, it is quite slippery. However, this is a short stretch. You can hear the roar and, within 30 mins, you are at a picturesque bridge across the **Ruinsara Gad** or stream. Cross and take a short biscuit break by the water, which careens, cascades and leaps playfully amongst the boulders at terrific speeds.

There is a moderate climb through the forest as the path goes south-east, taking about 45 mins. A small descent and then it's easy, level walking with the Ruinsara Gad flowing below for company. You may encounter short patches where the path has vanished because of a small landslide or has gotten washed away. These stretches have to be negotiated carefully as slipping means about a 100-ft fall on to boulders by the river! A couple of hours of easy, level walking brings you to a nice open space

across the river and onwards to **Har-ki-Dun**. If you are doing Har-ki-Dun on the return, then this is the route you must take. Another 30 mins of a moderate climb brings you to a tempting meadow, **Debsu Thach**.

Premier adventure trips in the Indian Himalaya

919811103831,919868244275 aquatera@vsnl.com

with a shelter ideal for a lunch break. Shortly after the path begins to climb. The gradient is moderate, mostly with a few steep patches.

Then the path goes level along the mountainside, traversing pretty little waterfalls, and a stream, which must be crossed. Descending at a gentle gradient for another 30-40 mins brings you to the level of the river bed. It is water-logged and marshy, but with a clear path going south-east. About an hour on this track will bring you to a stream. The log bridge is often washed away and the path among the rocks is not so clear. Looking for a likely place to cross may easily take half an hour. If it is late, it's better to camp here and walk up to the lake the following morning.

Once across, there is a 30-min moderate climb followed by level walking on a path for another half-hour. The trail passes a hut-like structure and brings you to the lake nestling at the base of the mountains. Even if you have pitched camp overnight en route, you should still make it bright and early the next morning to the **Ruinsara Tal**. The clear waters fringed by reeds and a warm sun invite you for a swim in the lake. Pitch your tents by the lake. A day's stay, relaxing at Ruinsara, is a must!

To the south-west is **Yamuna Kanta**, the pass which takes you to Yamunotri, and rated a difficult trek. To the east is the majestic **Bander-poonch Peak** (6,387m). Walking about 2 hrs south-east from the lake brings you to **Kiarkoti** with the over 6,000m **Swargrohini Range** to the north. The views of **Dhumdhar Kandi** (5,873m) to the east, and **Kala Nag** (6,387m) and **White Peak** (6,102m) to the south-west are spectacular.

DAY FOUR
RUINSARA-DEBSU THACH
DISTANCE 12 KM **TIME** 5-7 HOURS
LEVEL EASY

AKRANT VICHITRA

Except for some short bits, this stretch is mostly level or descending. It's an easy trek. Even if you start at 8 in the morning, you can reach **Debsu Thach** latest by about 4 pm. If you have provisions left, pitch camp in this pleasing meadow for the night. Watch the last rays of the sun light up the tree-tops. Or go for short walks in the forest around. You can, of course, avoid the hassle of cooking, opt for pushing on to **Osla/ Seema**, check in at the rest house and get food from the dhabas. From here, you can retrace your steps back to **Taluka** on Day Five, and **Sankhri** on Day Six, or continue to **Har-ki-Dun**.

DAY FIVE
DEBSU THACH-HAR-KI-DUN
DISTANCE 12 KM **TIME** 7-8 HOURS
LEVEL EASY-MODERATE

From **Debsu Thach**, head back to the point mentioned earlier on Day Three, from where the path heads to the right, or north-west. The path descends towards a bridge across the river. It may take time to traverse this stretch because it gets muddy just near the bridge and it is wiser to negotiate the slippery terrain cautiously. Once across the bridge, a level 30-min walk

Massive snow peaks dominate the horizon at Har-Ki-Dun

between wheat fields brings you to the path going north-east. The sun is already quite fierce by now. A 2- 3-hr moderate climb brings you to the meadow at the top. Rolling grass and alpine flowers greet you and provide an ideal setting for a lunch break. This is the grazing pasture land of the **Seema/ Osla Village**. As you look east, down below you can see the **Ruinsara Gad** and the cute bridge, which took you to **Ruinsara Tal**.

It takes another couple of hours of pleasant, leisurely walking to cross the meadows and arrive at a sparse forest. About an hour on this track brings you to an open tin-roofed structure where you can stop for a biscuit break. Then the track heads down a moderate slope, bringing you to a small stream with a rickety bridge. Climb down, cross and then climb up for about 30 mins. Another hour of easy walking brings you to the playful **Har-ki-Dun Gad** with the water cascading around boulders. There is a sturdy wooden bridge, which you cross, and a short climb brings you to a nice ⛺ camping place if you want to pitch your tent. Or walk another 15 mins and you are at the 🏠 **Forest Rest House**.

As you look north you see snow-covered mountains. Down below, you see a stream with a number of rivulets, triangular sandy delta patches and green grass. If you have the energy, the climb down through the sparse bushes is well worth the treat!

DAY SIX
HAR-KI-DUN-JAUNDAR GLACIER-HAR-KI-DUN
DISTANCE 4 KM **TIME** 2-3 HOURS
LEVEL MODERATE
Spend a day resting at Har-ki-Dun, going on short walks and enjoying the vistas or, if you're still up for exercise and stiff climbing, you can head north-east up the valley 4 km to the **Jaundar Glacier** (4,300m). This may require technical skills and it may be better to walk up just a couple of kilometres there and back.

DAY SEVEN-NINE
HAR-KI-DUN-OSLA-SANKHRI-TALUKA
Return the same way to 'civilisation'.

For rest house bookings, hotels and private camps, see Accommodation Listings on pages 534 (Har-ki-Dun), 535 (Mori), 538 (Seema/ Osla) and 539 (Taluka) ✦

Dodital Trek
Angler's paradise

By Anurag Mallick and Mohit Satyanand

Tranquil setting of the crystal clear Dodital

TIME	4-8 days
LEVEL	Moderate to Tough
IDEAL SEASON	Mar to Oct; Jun to Jul best for angling
LOCATION	In Uttarkashi District, between Asi Ganga and Hanuman Ganga, along the Yamuna

SANGAM CHATTI-AGODA-DODITAL-SIMA-
HANUMAN CHATTI-YAMUNOTRI-SAPTARISHI
KUND-YAMUNOTRI-HANUMAN CHATTI

The pursuit of the Rainbow Trout, the quest to reach Ganesha's far-flung birthplace, a high-altitude lake and a hike along a spiritual superhighway — the Dodital-Yamunotri Trek offers the high of a lifetime. Set amidst lofty heights and at an elevation of 3,310m, Dodital is like a shimmering emerald set in the crest of majestic mountains: mysterious, beckoning and divine. Dense woods of oak, pine, deodar and rhododendron fringe the lake and the crystal clear waters are full of spectacular fish like the Himalayan golden trout. Trout was introduced here about a century ago, transforming Dodital into an angler's paradise. The trek leads through tranquil country, gurgling streams with crystal clear waters, and dense alpine forests, all blending together like a vast green sequinned robe.

TIP Get fishing permits from Uttarkashi before heading out to Kalyani

From Uttarkashi, it's a 15-km drive along the curves of the Asi Ganga via the little settlement of Gangori to Kalyani (1,829m) and Sangam Chatti, where the trek starts. The river has been channelled to feed the Kalyani Trout Hatchery, which breeds and releases not just trout, but various other fish into the stream. Kalyani to Agoda is a gradual climb through woods, fields and villages, on a mule track, while the trek from Agoda to Dodital takes you through thick forests. The trail goes through a few passes, waterfalls and meadows until you reach Dodital, from where the route to Yamunotri takes you through high-altitude grasslands and dense virgin forests.

Graphic by ANIS KHAN

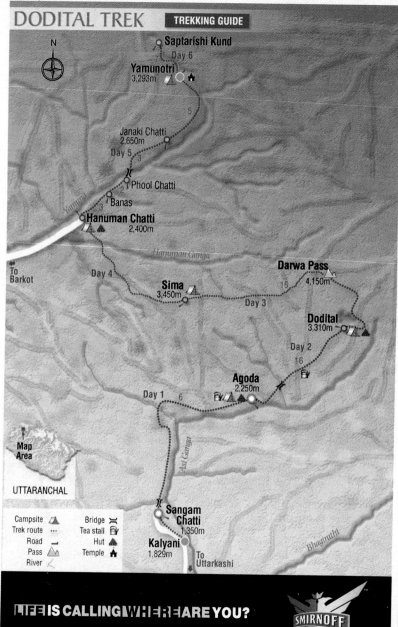

DODITAL TREK   TREKKING GUIDE

N

Saptarishi Kund

Day 6

Yamunotri
3,293m

Janaki Chatti
2,650m

Day 5

Phool Chatti

Banas

Hanuman Chatti
2,400m

To
Barkot

Day 4

Darwa Pass
4,150m

16

Sima
3,450m

Day 3

Dodital
3,310m

Day 2

16

Agoda
2,250m

Day 1   6

Asi Ganga

Map
Area

UTTARANCHAL

Bhagirathi

Campsite	Bridge
Trek route	Tea stall
Road	Hut
Pass	Temple
River	

Sangam
Chatti
1,350m

Kalyani
1,829m

To
Uttarkashi

Amaranthus fields aglow on the trail to the lake

TIP This trek can be done with older children who, if they get tired, have the option of hopping onto ponies, which may be hired at Kalyani

DAY ONE
SANGAM CHATTI-AGODA
DISTANCE 6 KM **TIME** 3 HOURS
LEVEL MODERATE

From **Kalyani**, either drive or walk a little further to Sangam Chatti (1,350m), the base of the trek. Cross the bridge over the small stream and begin your 6-km trek to **Agoda**, heading due north. The track climbs steeply, moving through forest. The last bit of climb can feel a little strenuous and the village huts visible at the top seem tantalisingly out of reach. At Agoda you can hear the faint gushing of the Asi Ganga down below. There are no dhabas or hotels at Agoda (2,250m) but the hospitable

locals provide (at very nominal cost) food and ▲ campsites to pitch tents. Ask for Balbir, a local, who has assisted school trips and led several treks himself. Food is usually Pahari staple — brown rice, pahari rajma, delicious thick chapatis and saag-pahari aloo. After letting the food settle down a bit, you can go down to the river in the late afternoon. It's a good 30-min zigzag hike along the edges of step fields down to the river. Make sure you do the uphill climb back to Agoda while there is daylight so you can watch the sunset as you pitch tents for the night.

DAY TWO
AGODA-DODITAL
DISTANCE 16 KM **TIME** 6-8 HOURS
LEVEL MODERATE

From **Agoda**, it's a long winding walk of 16 km due north-north-east to

GETTING THERE AND OUT

FROM UTTARKASHI to Sangam Chatti (Kalyani), it's 15 km/ 45 mins by 🚕 (Rs 200) or 1¼ hrs by 🚌 (Rs 15) **Delhi to Haridwar** is 203 km/ 5 hrs by road. Taxi Rs 2,600; deluxe bus from ISBT Kashmere Gate, Rs 127. It's 4½ hrs by rail (Shatabdi, Rs 465) **Haridwar to Uttarkashi** is 173 km/ 6 hrs by taxi (Rs 1,500) or 8 hrs by bus (Rs 150). The main route to Uttarkashi via New Tehri and Dobata no longer exists; instead head left directly via Bhaldiana
ALTERNATIVE ROUTE
Mussoorie to Uttarkashi via Dhanaulti is 125 km/ 4 hrs by taxi (Rs 800) or 5 hrs by bus (Rs 80)
RETURN From **Hanuman Chatti** you can either get to Haridwar (taxi 9 hrs/ Rs 3,500; bus 11 hrs/ Rs 160) via Chamba and Narendranagar or drive down to **Mussoorie** (taxi 4 hrs/ Rs 800; bus 5 hrs/ Rs 80) via Barkot
TIP You can break journey at Uttarkashi for the night, going to and coming back from the trek

Dodital. The trail is broad, well defined and runs through forests on either side. Since the gradient is not very steep, it's a fairly moderate walk, except towards the end. On the way you encounter villagers returning with herds of cattle and some **Gujjar encampments**. There are no villages in between but you can find a few ☕ tea stalls for the odd break. Sometimes, you can find pahari women carrying baskets of ripe pears, which you can trade for peanuts. A couple of pears and you're all set for the next leg.

We got into high country, and walked along grassy hillsides and cliffs with 500-ft drops, into forests of deciduous oak, which blended into spruce forests along the ridges. At what was roughly the half-way mark, we came to a picturesque bridge to the right, a good place to stop for lunch. From the bridge, you turn right, cross **Manghi** and walk through rich forests of oak, deodar and rhododendrons until you go past the final incline to reach **Dodital**.

There are a couple of shacks to the left, and after crossing a small bridge, you come to the **Forest Rest House** set in a clearing. And then you see the lake. Set against a stunning backdrop of hills, from where a mountain stream feeds it, Dodital is crystal clear. You can actually see the famed trout swimming about in huge numbers. It is after these trout (*dodi* in the local language), that the lake is

Spotted forktail

There are five species of forktails found in India. If you're lucky you may sight a couple of these on the Dodital route. Found along streams in thick, damp forests, the spotted forktail (*Enicurus maculatus*) is a bulbul-sized bird with, yes, a white spotted black back, black head, wings and tail. The under parts are snow-white, as is the strip across the forehead and the band across its wings. The deeply forked, black tail has white tips. The bird is shy and only if you are patient can you spot it dipping into streams for insects and small fish.

RUPIN DANG / WILDERNESS FILMS

called Dodital. It's believed that Lord Ganesh was born here. You can find a small, unattended temple, dedicated to him, on the left bank of the lake. The cement and tin shelters on the edge of the lake — the government's gift to tourists — have all the charm of postal department inkblots on a beautiful picture-postcard.

You can either camp out or opt for accommodation in the **Forest Rest House**. You can easily spend a few days at Dodital splashing about in the lake, fishing (carry your own rods, tackle and flies) or exploring the lovely surroundings. The only help you can get from the local dhaba-walas is *atta* as bait and help in cooking your fish, perhaps at the cost of a small piece of fish. When you've had your fill, you have the choice of returning to Kalyani the same way, or of continuing onwards to Yamunotri.

DAY THREE
DODITAL-DARWA PASS-SIMA
DISTANCE 16 KM **TIME** 6-7 HOURS
LEVEL TOUGH
If you can get your hands on some pahari aloo and get lucky with the tackle early morning, you can have a hearty fish and chips breakfast and then commence on the 2-day trek to Hanuman Chatti. From Dodital, the climb to the north-west is steep, and it's a long hike for the day, so it's advisable not to leave if the weather looks like it may take a turn for the worse. Being a straight enough route, with few diversions, a guide isn't that essential. The path, which is clearly a misnomer, starts from the lake's feeder stream and passes through dense forests before emerging on a trail close to the upper realms of the tree line.

Ascend the alpine **Darwa Dhar Ridge** (4,115m), the watershed of the Ganga and Yamuna river valleys. This stretch really tests your skill in crossing mountain streams and you have no less than seven opportunities to perfect the art! After the last of these crossings, you finally leave the stream and take a sharp left, or north-west, heading to the top of the range. Cross the tree line and pass the foot of the **Darwa Glacier**, finally reaching **Darwa Top** (4,130m), where you come to a good campsite.

216

Some people may take 2 days to get here and you can camp virtually anywhere on the route near any of the many water sources.

When we crossed **Darwa Pass** (4,150m), we were greeted with magnificent views of **Bandarpoonch** (Monkey Tail, 6,316m) and the **Swargarohini Range**. Continue walking further west and gradually descend through the **Hanuman Ganga Valley** into 🏕 **Sima** (3,450m), where you can camp for the night.

DAY FOUR

SIMA-HANUMAN CHATTI
DISTANCE 18 KM **TIME** 4-6 HOURS
LEVEL EASY

Sima, Seema or Shima, as it is variously (mis)spelt, is a small stop that marks almost the mid-point between Dodital and Hanuman Chatti. Though the distance from Sima to Hanuman Chatti is 18 km, you must come down 1,050m, making the walk fairly gradual. You can trek the distance in as little as 4 hrs. From Sima, you descend north-west on a slightly downhill trail to the Hanuman Ganga River and then to the pilgrimage town of **Hanuman Chatti** (2,400m). We encountered a colourful mix of pilgrims, babas and a touring party of some adventure club. If you have overstayed at Dodital or for some reason want to cut short your journey, you needn't go further north to Yamunotri. There are regular buses plying between Hanuman Chatti and Uttarkashi or Mussoorie. We stayed overnight in the 🏕 **Travellers' Rest House** at Hanuman Chatti.

DAY FIVE

HANUMAN CHATTI-YAMUNOTRI
DISTANCE 13 KM **TIME** 4-6 HOURS
LEVEL EASY

Hanuman Chatti is a multitude of mules, porters, ramshackle shops and labourers perpetually re-laying the road. Porters and ponies are available at Hanuman Chatti and their rates are fixed by the District Magistrate before the start of every yatra (pilgrimage season). From Hanuman Chatti, you can trek on the spiritual superhighway 3 km north to **Banas** (Narad Chatti), 2 km further to **Phool Chatti**, 3 km to **Janaki Chatti** (2,650m) and the final 5 km to **Yamunotri**, the confluence of Hanuman Ganga and Yamuna rivers. Located at an altitude of 3,293m, the most westerly of the four 'dhams' in the Himalayas, Yamunotri is also the

AKRANT VICHITRA

Bejewelled Gujjar girl

least trafficked. Lest you summon up a picture of an idyllic communion with nature along the upper valley of the river, let me clarify that you will be far from alone. The source of the Yamuna is an important pilgrim destination, with its fair share of mules and 'dandis' (palanquins), frail women in wispy cotton, and sun-blackened ascetics with hollowed eyes.

The **Yamunotri Temple** is set in a tight, steep valley, dominated by views of the **Bandarpoonch Peak**. The entrance to the shrine is guarded by

Trout

Photographs by VINAY BADOLA

Brown Trout

Though Dodital might be just about 10 acres in area, it holds a population of brown trout the likes of which you will rarely come across in your life. Quite like the Indian railways, the passion for cricket, the love for tea and the Indian babu, the British are responsible for the trout as well. Sometime around 1890, Morrison, a far-sighted Englishman, was employed by the Maharaja of Tehri, whose lands included Dodital. Morrison saw the potential of Dodital and had it stocked with brown trout. Guarded by these lofty heights, over the years Dodital blossomed into a lush aquatic cornucopia. Today, Dodital is without

Rainbow Trout

parallel for its population of brown and Himalayan golden (rainbow) trout.

Whereas the brown trout are in greater numbers and hence easier to catch, the shining red-spotted Himalayan golden trout remain relatively elusive. The fish has spotted flanks, with bright red spots inside darker circles, and flashy tail fins with swirls of dayglow orange, earning it the name rainbow trout. Locals, however, prefer to call it something that sounds like 'troat'. Taxonomically, the rainbow and brown trout are totally different species, but both co-exist in the same waters and feed on the same fare. What makes the Dodital trek special is not the thrill of grappling with the rainbow trout, but the effort in getting there.

tanks (or kunds) of steaming water channelled in from thermal springs. Pilgrims variously cook their rice in the tanks, rinse themselves of their sins, or, like me, consider the scene awhile before deciding that ablutions in the glacial stream are more hygienic.

The offspring of Surya and the twin sister of Yama, the Lord of Death, the dark-coloured Yamuna wields such cleansing power it would put any modern power-packed detergent to shame. It's believed that anyone who bathes in her dark waters is spared a tortuous death. Tired after the 13-km but exhausting trek, we stayed overnight in the rather basic ⚠ **Travellers' Rest House**, before

making our way back the next day, after darshan at the temple.

DAY SIX
YAMUNOTRI-SAPTARISHI KUND-YAMUNOTRI
DISTANCE 7 KM **TIME** 10 HOURS
LEVEL DIFFICULT

The actual source of the Yamuna is perched high above the temple, a glacial lake on the **Kalinda Parvat**. The ascent is more than 1,000 vertical metres, and not easy of access. When we attempted it in early May, the shepherds' paths were narrow and encrusted with ice, and our 'experienced' guide wasted 2 hrs bush-whacking in the scrubby slopes above

TREKKING HOLIDAYS IN INDIA

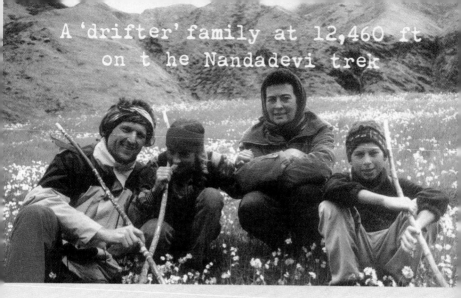

A 'drifter' family at 12,460 ft on t he Nandadevi trek

Drifters don't seek other 'tourists'. They'd rather chat up local shepherds on the meadows

Canned food is for tourists. Drifters savour fresh meals cooked in quaint Himalayan kitchens

Drifters choose to camp on the glacier environs near a snow covered peak.... Never in a hurry to get anywhere fast

They value the meticulous care and friendly vibes of the trek guide

ASHOK DILWALI

Pilgrims at the Yamunotri Temple complex

the temple. By the time we emerged on to the ridge leading to the source, the afternoon rain came pelting down, and the consensus was that we retreat to our camp near the temple complex. Most pilgrims satisfy their piety with the immersion in the kund, and worship at the shrine. I wouldn't — even if you don't make the source of the river, the climb takes one away from the squalor of the shrine, and the ridge above yields aerial views of virginal alpine meadows — the unnamed and beautiful *bugyals* of the region.

DAY SEVEN
YAMUNOTRI-HANUMAN CHATTI
DISTANCE 13 KM **TIME** 4 HOURS
LEVEL EASY

According to a local legend, the **Yamunotri Temple** must be built every few years and the sudden floods and heavy snow ensure that it lives up to this legend. There are several hot water springs adjacent to the temple precinct, the most prominent of which is the **Surya Kund**. Pilgrims immerse rice, gram and potatoes tied in a piece of cloth into the springs, which takes only a few minutes to cook. It is then offered to the deity and later distributed as prasad. Going by the unabashed quantities we had, by no stretch of imagination could it be called prasad. It was a full-fledged meal and rolling down like a sack of potatoes, we set off on the return trip to Hanuman Chatti.

On the way, we visited the **Someshwar Temple** at **Kharsali**, 1 km across the river from **Janaki Chatti**. This was one of the oldest shrines in the region and we paid homage to Yamuna's father Surya, the Sun God. After the 13-km downhill trek to Hanuman Chatti, depending on your schedule or how tired you are, you can either stay overnight in the ▲ **Travellers' Rest House** at Hanuman Chatti or drive back to Haridwar, from where Delhi is 200 km. You also have the option of stopping by at Mussoorie.

For rest house bookings and hotels, see Accommodation Listings on pages 532 (Agoda) and 534 (Hanuman Chatti) ✦

Gangotri-Gaumukh and Beyond
To the source of the Ganga

By Mohit Satyanand

GANGOTRI-CHIRBASA-BHOJBASA-GAUMUKH-
TAPOVAN-BHOJBASA-GANGOTRI

TIME	5 days
LEVEL	Easy to Tough
IDEAL SEASON	May-Oct
LOCATION	North-eastern part of Uttarkashi District

Devotee at Gaumukh

The Ganga, the holiest of the holy rivers, revered by Hindus over millennia, springs from an expanse of ice measuring 8 km by 24 km, the Gangotri Glacier. This is the source of the Bhagirathi, which joins with Alaknanda to form the Ganga at Devprayag. From Devprayag, the river flows 2,480 km to the Bay of Bengal.

The first time I approached the snout of Gaumukh, I was confused and more than a little disappointed. Where was the glacier, the virginal river of ice, its blue highlights glistening in the clear mountain air? Where the Bhagirathi began was a vertical face of mud and rubble, some 300 ft high, bridging the mountain slopes rising on both banks. We drew closer, and I began to detect the flecks of white under the surface of mud and grime. Only gradually could I discern the true nature of the sight before me — a crossection of the glacier, 250 to 270 ft of compacted ice, which had filled, and had shaped, the valley of the infant river.

I heard a crashing sound and turned just in time to catch sight of a chunk of ice, as large as a Maruti 800, tumble into the river. Only then did I lose my sense of disappointment, and begin to marvel at the scale of the scene before me. At the very top of the glacier, like a crust of crunchy chocolate on a vanilla bar, was a 30- to 50-foot layer of mud and rock, the debris dragged down the mountains by the inexorable flow of glacial ice.

To the left, in the north, were the towering vertical faces of the Bhagirathi massifs. Across the Bhagirathi, in the south, the scree slopes swept up into the distinctive pyramid of a Shivaling, topped by its signature overhang. And, at eye-level, was the little entrance to an icy cavern, the mouth of the glacier — Gaumukh. Crafted in opaque ice of white and green, the glacier issued from its dark

221

recesses the little trickle that has for millennia drawn to it the waters of a thousand streams and the faith of countless millions.

I broke off an icicle from a freshly disengaged chunk of glacier and sucked at it. A random thought conjured up the vast dimensions of the arc of time — this ice has not known the fluidity of water for a few thousand years. I quenched my thirst with a great sense of humility.

DAY I
GANGOTRI-CHIRBASA
DISTANCE 8 KM **TIME** 3-4 HOURS
LEVEL EASY

Bharat Petroleum

GETTING THERE AND OUT

FROM UTTARKASHI to Gangotri, it's 105 km/ 3 hrs by 🚗 (Rs 600) or 4 hrs by 🚌 (Rs 80). Buses available daily during season, between 5 am and 1 pm **Haridwar to Uttarkashi** via Bhaldiana is 173 km/ 6 hrs by taxi (Rs 1,500) or 8 hrs by direct buses (Rs 150), which run between 4 and 7 am. Haridwar is well connected to Delhi (203 km/ 5 hrs) by trains and buses (see *Getting There and Out on page 215*)
RETURN Take the same route back from Gangotri to Haridwar (276 km) via Uttarkashi. Taxi 11 hrs/ Rs 3,500. Buses (12 hrs/ Rs 200) operate between 5 am and 1 pm from Gangotri. If you miss the direct Gangotri-Haridwar bus (between 5 and 6 am), get your connection from Uttarkashi
TIP Opt for direct/ chartered buses as local buses are overcrowded and halt frequently en route

Before you set out on the trail from Gangotri (3,046m), you might like to take in the sight of the kund or trough, where the **Bhagirathi River** crashes into a limestone basin polished into fluid sculpture. Popular custom decrees that you visit the **Ganga shrine** half a kilometre upstream before taking to the pilgrim trail that runs above the temple, and begins in the last stands of forest at the edge of the road into town. It is a well-maintained path, hugging the river on its path from east to west. The forest thins rapidly, and one is soon in a landscape of brown and grey, relieved by the stream below, and the symmetrically framed views of the mountains in front.

The traditional first stage of this walk is to **Bhojbasa**, 13 km away. But since the starting altitude is considerable, progress is slow, and if one is unsure of acclimatisation, it may be prudent to do the half-stage, to **Chirbasa** (3,350 m), where a small group of chirs (pine) is a relief in an otherwise desolate landscape. On both sides of the trail, **dhabas** offer simple fare, as well as a carpeted platform to sleep on and an ample supply of quilts. ⚠ If you want to tent for the night, go down to the river, where there is charming camping to be had among groves of freshly planted silver birch. There is also a **forest bungalow**, too decrepit to offer any shelter, but with a water-point and flat grounds well suited to a cluster of three or four tents.

DAY TWO
CHIRBASA-BHOJBASA
DISTANCE 5 KM **TIME** 2-3 HOURS
LEVEL EASY
Above Chirbasa, the valley widens, and offers views of snow-clad peaks in the south. It is a gentle walk to **Bhojbasa** (3,800m), running virtually due south-east along the river, the **Bhagirathi** peaks ever a beacon to the source of the river.

TREKKING HOLIDAYS IN INDIA

Himalayan silver birch

Found between 2,800 and 3,800m altitude, the Himalayan birch (*Betula utilis*) has the whitest bark of any birch. Growing to about 15 ft, the silver birch is a very attractive tree, especially in autumn, when its russet leaves are in elegant contrast to the silver of its bark. At this time particularly, the bark will be peeling, and odds are, you'll find some bits scattered about. The bark is a fine, slightly brittle material, and tends to curl. But once you unroll it, you'll find that the orange underside is extremely smooth and a delight to write on.

Before paper came to the Indian sub-continent, manuscripts were written on this bark — the 'bhojpatra'. Bhojbasa is named for the tree, though, there are more silver birch trees on the banks of the river near Chirbasa, named after the Himalayan pine tree, or chir! In the last decade, a group of environmentalists established bhoj nurseries around Bhojbasa, but growth at these altitudes is slow, and when I last visited, in 2002, they were still more bush than tree.

The bark also has medicinal uses: an infusion is found to be antiseptic and carminative. It has been used in the treatment of hysteria. It is also recommended as styptic (to stop bleeding) and to stop any purulent discharge, and is used to clean wounds. Ayurveda also uses birch in many formulations for obesity and other disorders of lipid metabolism.

Graphic by ANIS KHAN

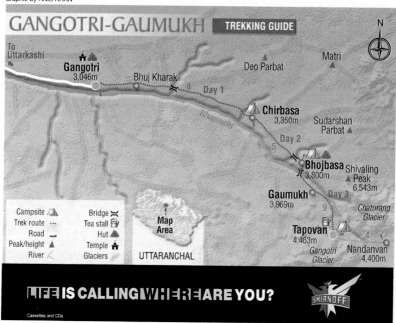

Myth of the Ganga

The Goddess Ganga, daughter of the sacred mountain Meru, wife of Shiva, was asked to reside in heaven to soothe the gods. Once, King Sagar lost 60,000 sons whose tormented souls could only be released by the cool waters of Ganga. Many of Sagar's descendants attempted to propitiate the goddess but it was only Bhagiratha who, after severe austerities, persuaded her to come down to earth. However, the impact of her fall was to be so severe that it could be borne by none other than Shiva himself. Bhagiratha meditated again and finally obtained Shiva's consent. At last, the river came down and fell into Shiva's matted hair, and from there, down to earth. Marking the site is the present-day temple at Gangotri. Then Bhagiratha led the way to the souls of his ancestors and the river followed. They finally reached the spot where the ashes of the 60,000 sons lay. Where they were liberated, an ocean formed. The spot is marked by Sagar Island, where the River Ganga today flows into the Bay of Bengal.

SANJEEV SAITH

Autumn colours at Chirbasa

AKRANT VICHITRA

🔺 🔺 Bhojbasa is the widest point in the upper valley, and camping here at night offers magnificent moonlit views of the Bhagirathi peaks. For those who don't want to light up their stoves, there's an excellent langar at **Lal Baba's Ashram**, or more commercial fare at the **GMVN** establishment, which also offers solar lighting and hot baths.

Typically, pilgrims will do Gangotri-Bhojbasa in one stage, tick off Gaumukh on the second and return to Bhojbasa for the night, completing the return walk to Gangotri on the third. But, a bit more mindful of acclimatisation when with mixed groups, I prefer to do it in easy stages; get in some sun and sand on the riverside, and make sure everybody is in good shape for the haul up to Tapovan.

Jeep safaris in Ladakh, treks all over the Himalaya. White water rafting in comfort at our base camp on the Ganga. Or with high adventure on the Zanskar & other expedition rivers. Our trips are personalized & special.

OUTDOOR ADVENTURES INDIA PVT.LTD.
PH: 91 124 2563648 / 49
Email: oai@touchtelindia.net WEB:raftindia.com

Camping in Shivaling's shadow at Tapovan

DAY THREE
BHOJBASA-GAUMUKH-TAPOVAN
DISTANCE 9 KM **TIME** 4 HOURS
LEVEL EASY-TOUGH

The first four kilometres upstream from **Bhojbasa** are surprisingly flat, and though the valley narrows, the path runs smoothly above the river, and is fringed by a grassy meadow. With about a kilometre to go, the terrain turns rocky, and one has to pick one's way through rocks and boulders, down to a sandy beach sheltered by enormous piles of granite. Incidentally, the beach is a great place to ⛺ camp.

Scour the water's edge for shards of ice, or follow the broken path along the river's edge to the very foot of **Gaumukh** (3,969m), and look up at **Shivaling Peak** (6,543m) almost vertically above. In autumn, the water is a shallow stream of grey-blue, and you could wade out to the middle. In summer, it is a more substantial stream of muddy brown, and one is well advised to keep to the banks.

As one approaches the glacier, the path becomes a bit tentative, and if one wants to make the trip to **Tapovan** (4,463m), it is best to leave Gaumukh before noon. Despite the shifting nature of the route, the orientation is quite clear, and little piles of stone on the higher rocks regularly mark the trail. Climb up the northern side of the glacier (the right bank), till you gain its surface. Turning south, cross the glacier towards the slopes on the opposite side of the valley. Snaking through the rocks and debris that are its surface, it is hard to remember that one is actually on a major glacier. Once you have reached the southern (left) bank of the river valley, the path is more clearly marked — a steep climb of almost a thousand feet to the meadows at the base of Shivaling. This is Tapovan, an exquisitely watered spot from which the fabled peak appears to sweep up in a wave of scree, granite and snow.

⚠ It is an idyllic camping spot; alternatively, a couple of babas have establishments where you can spread your sleeping bag for the night. Simple, wholesome food is also forthcoming. On my first trip to the region, I left my tent and cooking gear at Bhojbasa, and the absence of any luggage other than my sleeping bag made the trudge to Tapovan much easier.

DAY 4
TAPOVAN-BHOJBASA
DISTANCE 9 KM **TIME** 3 HOURS
LEVEL MODERATE-EASY

It's time to trace the trail back. It's downhill all the way till **Gaumukh** and the next 4 km are almost flat. If you're feeling fit, walk another 5 km till Chirbasa, to spend a night exploring the banks of the Ganga. If you manage to reach Chirbasa, the next day will be easy as from here, it is a short hop of under 2 hrs to Gangotri, allowing plenty of time for a drive to **Uttarkashi**, and the dubious charms of civilisation.

DAY 5
BHOJBASA-GANGOTRI
DISTANCE 13 KM **TIME** 4-5 HOURS
LEVEL EASY
From Bhojbasa, start early so that you are in **Gangotri** by noon and then reach **Uttarkashi** by late evening.

TREKKING OPTIONS FROM GAUMUKH
Crossing the glacier again, one can press on to **Nandanvan** (4,400m) — a journey I have not done. Though only 4 km, it is a path strewn with boulders and not so heavily trafficked. You would be well advised to retain a guide for the journey, or for the expedition to **Vasuki Tal** (6 km) at the base of the **Vasuki Peak** (6,792m).

For rest house bookings and hotels, see Accommodation Listings on pages 533 (Bhojbasa), 534 (Harsil, Gangotri) and 539 (Uttarkashi) ✦

Morning rituals at the Chamunda Devi Temple

Jim Corbett may have put Rudraprayag's name on the map for man-eating leopards, but it's difficult to imagine anything wilder than a tabby cat prowling around in the thin scrub covering the surrounding hills. What is of breathtaking magnificence though is the swirling confluence of the

→ Rudraprayag Facts

● **LOCATION** In Garhwal, on the confluence of the Alaknanda and Mandakini rivers, 140 km north-east of Rishikesh
● **GETTING TO RUDRAPRAYAG By rail** Nearest railhead: Haridwar (164 km). Taxi 6 hrs/ Rs 1,500; bus 8 hrs/ Rs 150. Direct buses (5 am-7am) are run by the Tehri Garhwal Motor Owners Corp (Tel: 0135-2430008). Book a day in advance to avoid the over-crowded and unreliable local bus connections. Avoid the local shared cabs for the same reason **By road** Take NH58 from Delhi to Rudraprayag via Haridwar, Rishikesh, Devprayag and Srinagar. The highway is good but it's a long and tiring drive that will take you more than 12 hrs. Direct buses only to Haridwar from Delhi
● **STD CODE** 01364

Alaknanda and Mandakini rivers around which the town has grown.

If you like, you could consider a trip to the fabled ski resort of Auli (162 km). It's connected to Joshimath by a cable car ropeway that traverses 4 km uphill.

MUST-VISITS
The **Koteshwar Mahadev Temple** on the banks of the Alaknanda is less temple, more cave, adorned by ferns and moss. The devout can observe hundreds of spontaneously generated Shivalings carved out of rock by the patient dripping of water. It is a charming spot even for non-believers.

Equally charming are the **Rudra-nathji** and **Chamunda Devi** mandirs, overlooking the confluence of the two rivers just across the bridge at Rudraprayag. Shri Rudranathji is described as the meditation place of the great mediator and troublemaker, Narad Muni. Just below, you will find the goddess watching over the union of the rivers from her modest temple. She is taken care of by a delightful old mataji, Prem Giri, of the Juna Akhara, who, if in the mood, can be a veritable library of myth and folklore.

WHERE TO STAY
Just off the Joshimath Road, 3 km after Rudraprayag, **Hotel Monal Resort** (Tel: 01364-233901; Tariff: Rs 1,600-3,500) is a new, large and pleasant hotel. Probably the best of its kind along the entire Rishikesh-Joshimath route, it offers a children's playground, machan and a restaurant. The **GMVN Tourist Rest House** (Tel: 233347; Tariff: Rs 110-1,400), bang in the middle of Rudra-prayag, is another option.
For more details, see Accommodation Listings on page 538

WHERE TO EAT
Only dhabas available at Rudraprayag, but Monal has a nice restaurant overlooking gardens.

INPUTS FROM SONIA JABBAR

HIMALAYAN HIDEAWAY

Surrounded by a mixed forest of sal and bamboo ringle, overlooking the Ganga, the Himalayan Hideaway is located in the Shivalik foothills, the gateway to the Garwhal Himalaya.

This nine room boutique lodge is scattered over a sloping acre and comes complete with an Ayurvedic massage center. The lodge is ideal if you are looking to escape from everyday life and enjoy a quiet weekend in the hills. If it's a more indulgent experience you are seeking , you can choose from an extensive menu of massages that we offer or even a candle lit dinner by the Ganga. For the adventurous there is a range of sporty activities such as rafting, hiking, kayaking, rock-climbing and fishing.

HIMALAYAN HIDEAWAY

AN IDEAL GETAWAY ANY TIME

Picture this! Over 20,000 sq meters of pristine silver sand surrounded by thick jungle with the emerald waters of the Ganga flowing by. This is the HIMALAYAN RIVER RUNNERS Ganga Base Camp- The first and the largest of its kind and the only one offering a host of activities to stir body and soul.

White water rafting, kayaking, angling, bird watching, rock climbing, hiking - choose your activity or combine them in the experienced hands of the best Indian and International Guides.

Himalayan
RIVER RUNNERS

Himalayan River Runners (India) Private Limited, N-8(F.F), Green Park Main, New Delhi -110016 Tel: 011-26852602, 26968169 fax: 2686 5604 Email: riverrun@vsnl.com Website:hrrindia.com

Panwalikantha
On the meteor trail
By Mohit Satyanand

Summer blossoms at Panwalikantha

TIME	4 days
LEVEL	Moderate to Easy
IDEAL SEASON	Monsoons
LOCATION	In Rudraprayag District, Garhwal Himalayas

Triyuginarayan-Maggu Chatti-Panwali-Kinkhola Khal-Triyuginarayan

For me, like many others, monsoon flowers in the Himalayas meant the Valley of Flowers. One August, on the eve of my second trip there, I received news that a bridge into the valley had collapsed. Determined to find another, equally rewarding, monsoon trip into the mountains, I discovered that Uttaranchal is dotted with 'bugyals', or high alpine meadows. They have a short, accelerated cycle of green, between June and September; and in mid-August, the lush grass is dotted with wildflowers of every hue.

And so we found ourselves in Panwalikantha. Situated on the south-western end of a ridge in the Kedarnath region, there are two ways to approach Panwalikantha. The one we took begins at Triyuginarayan, the temple town marking the spot where Shiva is said to have solemnised his wedding to Parvati. You can stay overnight at Sonprayag 10 km away, or Guptkashi (37 km) which offers more accommodation options. The other route begins at Ghuttu, 62 km north of Tehri. But the access from the latter, southern axis, is a lot steeper, popular as "*Ghuttu ki chadhai, German ki ladai*" (easier to face the German Army than to do the steep climb of Ghuttu!)

In any event, the walk from Triyuginarayan is a hugely satisfying one. On the first day, you climb through lush forests, populated, my wife convinced our son, with hobbits and elves. You go past waterfalls and brooks, and into a bowl ringed by snow peaks. On the second, you walk a stone path bordered by unending gardens sloping into distant valleys. Horses and sheep graze in the mist, lammergeiers circle overhead and, close at hand, snow peaks flirt with the monsoon clouds. No matter where you choose to rest, a spring of crystal clear water is within reach.

Photographs by MOHIT SATYANAND

WARNING If you want to see monsoon flowers, be prepared to get wet

DAY ONE
TRIYUGINARAYAN-MAGGU CHATTI
DISTANCE 8 KM
TIME 4-5 HOURS
LEVEL MODERATE

You can see the notch of **Maggu** high above **Triyugi** (1,982m), off to the south and west. The track, deeply rutted

On the wooded trail

by the monsoon run-off, is a steady gradient through the village, past the school, and into the commons on a shoulder above it. From here, it turns right (more westerly) and submits to the forest.

Even in the monsoons, the broad, cobbled path holds up well, and takes one steadily up through a paradise of vegetation — ferns, grasses and fungi at

Graphic by ANIS KHAN

the ground level, towering trees overhead. There's plenty of water en route. If you take a short break after an hour and a half, your refill should keep you going up to a charming wooden bridge, under which a crystal stream rushes, fresh off a waterfall to your left. It's a lovely spot for a picnic, with fallen tree-trunks, soft cushions of grass, and a little island where the stream divides for a short stretch.

Twenty minutes later, the vegetation thins, rhododendron shrubs make their appearance, and you know **Maggu Chatti** (3,086m) is around the bend. There is enough flat land for a ⛺ camp, a stream close by, and abandoned shelters offer plenty of cover for cooking.

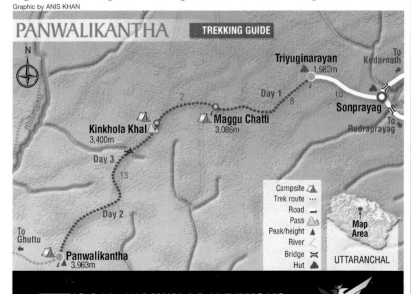
PANWALIKANTHA **TREKKING GUIDE**

N
Triyuginarayan 1,982m
To Kedarnath
Day 1
Sonprayag
To Rudraprayag
Maggu Chatti 3,086m
Kinkhola Khal 3,400m
Day 3
13
Day 2
To Ghuttu
Panwalikantha 3,963m

Campsite ⛺
Trek route ···
Road —
Pass
Peak/height ▲
River
Bridge
Hut

Map Area

UTTARANCHAL

Taking a break by a brook

DAY TWO
MAGGU CHATTI-PANWALIKANTHA
DISTANCE 15 KM **TIME** 6-8 HOURS
LEVEL MODERATE

Climbing gently out of **Maggu Chatti**, the path pulls south. Like a camera tracking away from a scene to reveal more and more of it, you are witness to a growing panorama of Great Himalayan peaks, **Meru**, the **Gangotri Range** and the **Kedar Dome**.

Maggu virtually marks the tree line and from here on, shrubs and flowers dominate the slopes around. Half an hour out of camp, there is a series of switchbacks up to the 'khal' or pass of **Kinkhola**, at 3,400m. It's a great place to perch and take in the morning's walk and the undulating line of the snows. And, on the return, it is a more scenic ⛺ camping spot than Maggu.

But it's a long walk to **Panwali**, and the day's delights have just begun, so head south now. All day, the trail snakes up and down the knife-edge of the ridge, a stony ribbon through the vast acreage of green. There are at least two points

Bharat Petroleum

GETTING THERE AND OUT

FROM RUDRAPRAYAG to Sonprayag, it's 68 km/ 3 hrs by 🚙 (Rs 500) or 4 hrs by 🚌 (Rs 50). Triyuginarayan, the penultimate village on the Kedarnath route, is a rough 5-km ride from Sonprayag (taxi Rs 100, one-way). The dharamshalas in Triyuginarayan are clean and welcoming, but I prefer to overnight in **Suyal Saur**, some 45 km down the valley **Rudraprayag to Guptkashi** is 40 km/ 1 1/2 hrs by taxi (Rs 450) or 2 hrs by bus (Rs 20)

RETURN Take the same route back to Rudraprayag and Haridwar

where you have to trudge up a little knoll, to the next spur of green.

Always heading south-west, about half-way into the day's walk, the ridge broadens into meadows, where Gujjars graze enormous herds of sheep and goat, watched over by bear-like dogs. Looking west, over the **Bhilangana Valley**, you can spot the settlement of **Gangi**, on the **Khatling trail**.

By early evening, you should be in a gentle cleft under the ridge. It seems a good place to ⛺ camp, but do head on up to the main meadow of **Panwalikantha** (3,963m), less than 2 km away.

Marked by a clump of Gujjar shelters and a decrepit ashram, the meadows are vast and rolling, so camp where you please. If you are there in mid-August *and if* the skies are clear, look out for the 'shooting stars' of the Perseids, the spectacular meteor showers that peak on August 12 each year.

The fascinating world of fungi

Fungi are organisms that lack chlorophyll or the green colouring that promotes photosynthesis in plants. There are some 45,000 species of fungi in the world, ranging from the common black mould (*Aspergillus niger*) that attacks exposed food, to hard-to-get-rid-of skin fungi in humans, to the valuable *Penicillum notatum*, a source of penicillin, to the mushroom in your soup. Perhaps because they lack chlorophyll, fungi must have already elaborated food to survive. Given carbohydrates, most fungi can synthesise their own proteins and vitamins. This makes some mushrooms extremely rich food sources. The Shitake mushroom, used in China for the last 6,000 years, is rich in a compound called lentinan. This is known to boost the immune system, and is used against the flu, other viruses, and boosts the immune system of people with HIV. It is also beneficial for those with gastric tumours.

But many, many species of mushrooms are poisonous and can hospitalise a healthy adult or kill a small child or frail adult. A few species will kill *anyone*. You should desist from picking and eating them in the wild unless you are thoroughly trained in identifying them. If you have kids along on the walk, ensure that they stay away from them.

The Amanitas may be among the most beautiful of all mushrooms, but they can be fatal for those who eat them. The Death Cap, Amanita phalloides, and the Destroying Angel, Amanita verna, as well as several other amanitas, contain amatoxins, which are horrific and deadly poisons. Also poisonous are the LBMs ('Little Brown Mushrooms'), which are very hard to identify. Several species of Lepiota contain amatoxins; all of the Lepiotas should be avoided, including the parasol mushroom, Macrolepiota procera. Best to leave all wild mushrooms alone.

Eating as little as two ounces of an amatoxin-containing mushroom like Amanita phalloides can lead to liver failure and death. Typically, symptoms are delayed for 6-12 hrs after eating the mushrooms, after which the victim experiences severe abdominal cramping, vomiting and diarrhoea. Then, there is a period of apparent remission, in which the victim feels better. This period can last for two to three days and the victim may well decide that medical attention is no longer required. During this period of false remission, however, the victim's liver is being destroyed by the amatoxins. By the time liver failure occurs, there are few options remaining aside from a liver transplant. Without a transplant, death occurs within a few days.

WARNING No antidote exists for the amatoxins

AHTUSHI DESHPANDE

ASHOK DILWALI

Perseids:
Meteor showers

At the peak of this shower, hundreds of meteors streak across the sky *every hour*. In that one night at Panwalikantha, on the 12th of August, I saw more 'shooting stars' than I have seen in my entire life — before and after. Striking the earth's atmosphere at speeds in the range of 200,000 km per hour, these meteors are tiny particles of dust that vaporise long before they hit the earth. But they sure go out in a blaze of fire.

The debris of the periodic comet, Swift-Tuttle, the Perseids are the best meteor shower of the year. When the comet whizzed close to the earth, in 1992, its proximity to the sun vaporised part of its icy core. This added to the cloud of debris and, in August 1993 and 1994, the meteor showers were particularly intense

— observers in the US and Europe counted as many as 500 Perseids in an hour. Those in the Southern Hemisphere are not well placed to spot the Perseids but, in India, four factors will govern your ability to enjoy the phenomenon:

● the absence of monsoon clouds
● distance from 'polluting' city lights — darker skies make for better viewing
● phase of the moon — in 2004, for example, a new moon on August 12 meant darker skies
● greater elevations will lead to less atmospheric diffraction of light

And if you miss the Perseids this year, don't worry: they have been as regular as clockwork for 2,000 years now!

DAY THREE
PANWALI-KINKHOLA KHAL
DISTANCE 13 KM **TIME** 5-6 HOURS
LEVEL EASY

If you absolutely can't spare a day to explore the meadows, take your time heading back the ridge to **Kinkhola Khal**. Set up 🏕 camp on the level meadow on the northern side, in the lee of a high knoll. But if you want a grandstand view of a Himalayan sunset, walk down to the pass and onto the opposite hill.

Dusk at Panwalikantha

DAY FOUR
KINKHOLA-TRIYUGI
DISTANCE 10 KM **TIME** 4 HOURS
LEVEL EASY

Retrace your steps back to Triyugi.

TREKKING OPTIONS

Panwali lies on the old pilgrim trail from Kedarnath to Gangotri. You can map many routes out of here. If you want to retrace the old route, you would head south to **Ghuttu**, then west to **Budha Kedar**, and gradually veering north, getting into the Ganga Valley at **Lata**. Or, from Ghuttu, you could do a sharp turn to the north and head for **Khatling Glacier**. The latter trail offers many possibilities — **Shastru Tal** in the west, or an exit at **Kedarnath** by way of **Masar Tal**, **Painya Tal** and **Vasuki Tal**.

For rest houses and hotels, see Accommodation Listings on pages 534 (Guptkashi) and 538 (Sonprayag, Suyal Saur) ✦

Club Group of Hotels in Uttaranchal

Cliff Top Club
Auli , Distt Chamoli
Uttaranchal
Ph- 01389 – 223217 – 20

Alpine Club
Near Aurobindo Ashram
Ayarpatta Hill , Nainital
Uttaranchal
Ph- 05942 236254

Mountain Club
61 June Estate, Bhimtal
Uttaranchal
Ph- 05942 – 248295

Bhairav Devta, the guardian deity of Kedarnath

Kedarnath

Shiva's abode

By Mohit Satyanand

GAURIKUND-RAMBARA-KEDARNATH-
GAURIKUND

TIME	2-3 days
LEVEL	Easy
IDEAL SEASON	Early May-end to Jun, late Sep-end to Oct
LOCATION	In Rudraprayag District, Garhwal Himalayas

I t's like walking into the very heart of a flower," my mother said, as we ascended the Mandakini Valley, fold upon fold of greening hills unfurling like petals around us. One final gasp up the last slope and, suddenly, the centre opens up — a substantial meadow criss-crossed by tiny streams, dotted with little yellow flowers. A kilometre away, the dark stone of the shrine has a massive sense of gravity to it, a delightful contrast to the vaulting slopes of the mountains behind. At night, the temple is a looming shadow, the Kedar massif a glistening wall of ice and, above, the stars are icy pinpricks of light. Heaven meets earth, water meets stone and, if you believe in such things, mortal man meets the cosmos.

Located within the Kedarnath Wildlife Sanctuary, the ancient Shiva Temple is one of the many said to have been built in the 9th century by the Adi Shankaracharya (what a walker he must have been!). The Rawal, or high priest at the shrine, is in the long line of the Nambudiris established by him, and the pilgrimage, believed to be one of the four most essential in the Hindu tradition, is an ode to faith. Though a trekker would classify the climb as easy, it is a respectable ascent, from 1,800 to well over 3,400m.

View the trek through the eyes of a Tamilian widow, clad in white and wearing insubstantial woollies. Hear her gasp for breath at every step, look at the plastic chappals she is wearing, and remember you are looking at the grit-equivalent of you and me climbing Everest without oxygen. This is devotion you have to respect.

This ardent faith has its roots in legend, or as is usually true in India, many legends, and it scarcely matters which one you subscribe to. The most popular one is that the Pandavas, victorious heroes of the Mahabharata, sought forgiveness from Lord Shiva for having killed their own kin, the Kauravas. Not wanting to discuss metaphysical issues with the likes of Bhima, Lord Shiva transformed

Kedarnath Temple

himself into a bull. Bhima saw through the disguise and catching up with him in the vicinity of Kedarnath, threatened Shiva with physical violence. Shiva dove into the ground, leaving his hump on the surface. The lingam worshipped at Kedarnath is the manifestation of this hump.

Graphic by ANIS KHAN

GETTING THERE AND OUT

FROM RUDRAPRAYAG to

Gaurikund, where the trail begins, it is 73 km/ 3 hrs by 🚙 (Rs 600) or 4 hrs 15 mins by 🚐 (Rs 50), available 5 am-4 pm. Places to stay en route are at Agastyamuni, Phata and Sonprayag. I would recommend the GMVN facility at **Suyal Saur**, a cluster of tiny cottages on the banks of the Mandakini, past Chandrapuri. From here, Gaurikund is about 50 km/ 2 hrs by road (taxi Rs 300, bus Rs 20). It leaves ample time to find porters, ponies, palkis, etc. You can also walk to Rambara, which is as much of a first-day ascent as I would recommend for most

RETURN From **Gaurikund**, get your direct bus connections between 5 and 7 am to Haridwar (237 km). Bus 12 hrs/ Rs 200; taxi 10½ hrs/ Rs 3,800

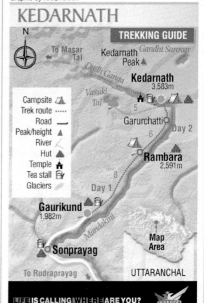

KEDARNATH

N

TREKKING GUIDE

To Masar Tal
Kedarnath Peak ▲ Gandhi Sarovar
Dudh Ganga
Kedarnath 3,583m

Campsite ⛺
Trek route •••••
Road ——
Peak/height ▲
River 〰
Hut 🛖
Temple ⛩
Tea stall ☕
Glaciers

Vasuki Tal
5
Garurchatti
6
Day 2
Rambara 2,591m
8
Day 1

Gaurikund 1,982m

Mandakini

Map Area

Sonprayag

To Rudraprayag

UTTARANCHAL

Taking the easier route to salvation

GAURIKUND-RAMBARA
DISTANCE 8 KM **TIME** 3-4 HOURS
LEVEL EASY

The walk to **Kedarnath** is along a cobbled, well-maintained path, called a *cheh-footiya*, or six-footer, in the local parlance. Referring to the width of the path, this charming nomenclature has its origins in the Public Works Department (PWD) classification of construction projects.

Today, the *cheh-footiya* is a busy thoroughfare. Every couple of kilometres, there is a cluster of stalls selling candy, fizzy drinks and bottled water, and offering the ubiquitous ☕ chai and simple vegetarian food. There are streams and watering points all the way up, all except the river–water itself being quite uncontaminated. So this is a route, like most popular pilgrim routes, where one can travel extremely light.

SONIA JABBAR

Oak

Oak (*Quercus*) is any of a large variety of trees or shrubs that bear acorns. There are more than 600 species of oaks around the world. Some oaks never become taller than small shrubs, while others reach heights of more than 30m.

In the Western Himalayas there is a predominance of ban oak, *Quercus incana*, kharsu oak (*Q. semecarpifolia*) and moru oak (*Q. dilatata*). The kharsu oak, also known as brown oak, is found in altitudes upto 3,600m. The leaves have a coppery tinge in autumn and winter and look very pretty under clear blue Himalayan skies. The edge of the leaf may be serrated or smooth and is suitable for feeding caterpillars of the tassar silkworm. The moru oak is a large evergreen tree of the Western Himalayas and Nepal, growing on cool, moist slopes between 2,000 and 2,750m. The leaves are similar to holly. Oaks grow slowly and usually do not bear acorns until they are about 20 years old. Most oaks live for 200-400 years and are an important source of lumber. Oak wood is heavy, hard and strong, and it has a beautiful grain.

The wood and bark of some oaks contain tannin, a bitter substance used in the preparation of leather. Cork comes from the bark of certain oaks. Acorns are an important source of food for wildlife. The leaves of Himalayan oaks are used as fodder and hence, are ruthlessly lopped, resulting in odd-looking, stunted trees.

Himalayan musk deer

Looking like a cross between a dog (because of its long canines) and a rabbit (because of its Bugs Bunny ears), this is the only deer with a gall bladder, a musk gland and no facial glands, all of it pointing to the deer (*Moschus chrysogaster*) being an evolutionary primitive. Called *kastura* in Hindi, the deer stands not more than 50 cm at the shoulders and weighs only 13-15 kg. It can be identified by its thick, bristly brown coat, speckled with white on the flanks, white stockings and a bare tail, which nestles in thick rump hair. The adult male has a gland under the abdominal skin that secretes musk. This is highly prized as an aphrodisiac and perfume and has led to large-scale poaching of this unusual creature.

OTTO PFISTER

Gaurikund (1,982m) is a shanty town of pilgrims, porters, ponies, shops, dhabas and dharamshalas. You begin your trek along a rocky corridor through this mess. But after a while, nature reasserts herself, and the path seems unchanged from when E.S. Oakley described it a 100 years ago as being, "narrow and steep, wind(ing) along the ledge of rock above the deep glen of the Mandakini... the river roars with hollow sound far below, often hidden from view, the tops of the cliffs and the slopes being clothed with noble forest."

The forests of bamboo, oak and rhododendron are still dense and alluring. Both sides of the valley yield waterfalls and, if you are lucky, transient rainbows. Between the unremitting ascent and the changing views of the infant Mandakini River, this is a walk worth savouring at a leisurely pace. The trail eases a bit at **Rambara** (2,591m) and, with some flat patches around, you can find a place to

Campsite on the pastures above Kedarnath

DIETER REEB

camp away from the swelling crowd. Or you can succumb, as I have sometimes done, to the temptations of a pucca roof, and inhabit a room in a dharamshala.

DAY TWO

RAMBARA-KEDARNATH
DISTANCE 6 KM **TIME** 3 HOURS
LEVEL MODERATE

Leaving behind the settlement of **Rambara** (2,591m), the broad, rocky trail is a series of switchbacks that climb well above the tiny valley to the next ridge. By now the air is thinning, and progress is slow, but never daunting. The trees yield to dwarf rhododendron and, as you approach **Bhumiadar**, there is a splendid waterfall cascading into the gorge.

Until now, the snow peaks have been hidden from view. But once you crest the path at **Garurchatti**, and find yourself in the **Kedar Valley**, you get both the feeling of having arrived in a high place and of being dwarfed by what lies beyond — great banks of moraine and snow, and the towering **Kedarnath massif**. Underfoot, the ground is a lush green turf, drained by myriad tiny streams. Oakley commented on the profusion of violet auriculas around the temple, and I

remember clumps of yellow flowers from my childhood visit. But today, **Kedarnath** (3,583m) is virtually a township, cluttered with eating houses, hostelries and shops selling religious memorabilia.

Once again, you have the choice of dossing down in one of these structures, or striking out on the trail north, and relishing the stars and crisp air of a Himalayan summer night.

DAY THREE

KEDARNATH-GAURIKUND
DISTANCE 13 KM **TIME** 4 HOURS
LEVEL EASY

It's an easy walk down to Gaurikund, with ample time to cover a substantial road journey out. Or, you could walk up-valley, to **Gandhi Sarovar**, a tiny lake, 1 km away, where Mahatma Gandhi's ashes were immersed.

A more strenuous expedition is to **Vasuki Tal**, some 5 km along a goat track. I haven't been up this trail, so can only say that the terrain is somewhat unstable and moraine-ridden, so you would be well-advised to get a local guide to assist you up this path.

For GMVNs, see Accommodation Listings on pages 534 (Gaurikund), 535 (Kedarnath) and 538 (Rambara) ✦

If there's a golfing heaven on earth...

J&K TOURISM

The lure of lavish landscapes. The great sense of exhilaration as you tee off amidst a vast green expanse, merging with majestic mountains and the deep blue splendour of the Dal lake. Embellished with varied flora, apple trees, poplars, pines, oaks and chinars. **The Royal Springs Golf Course, Srinagar.** Designed by the renowned Robert Trent Jones, Jr. Truly, a golfer's paradise.

For further information contact J & K Tourist Offices at : New Delhi Tel. 011-23345373, Fax: 011-23367881. Mumbai Tel. 022-22189040, Fax: 022-22186172. Kolkata Tel. 033-2285791. Chennai Tel/Fax: 044-28235958. Ahmedabad Tel/Fax : 079-25503551. Hyderabad Tel/Fax : 040-24734806. Jammu Tel. 0191-2548172, Fax: 0191-2548358. Srinagar Tel. 0194-2452690-91, Fax : 0194-2452361. Website: http//www.jktourism.org

Madhyamaheshwar
At Chaukhamba's feet
By Mohit Satyanand

Photographs by MOHIT SATYANAND

The ancient temple of Madhyamaheshwar

TIME	5-8 days
LEVEL	Easy
IDEAL SEASON	Oct-Nov (mid-Aug for wild flowers)
LOCATION	Madhyamaheshwar Ganga Valley, Rudraprayag District

UNIANA-BANTOLI-MADHYAMAHESHWAR-BUDHA
MADHYAMAHESHWAR-BANTOLI-KANCHANI TAL-
MADHYAMAHESHWAR-UNIANA

Situated south-west of Kedarnath and part of the Kedarnath Wildlife Sanctuary (one of the world's richest bio-reserves), the Madhyamaheshwar Temple is a close copy of Tungnath, its sibling to the south. But at 3,000m, it is some 600m lower, and still below the tree line, with clumps of oak scattered around the meadow. On the ridge above, gorgeous groves of silver birch (*bhoj*) and dwarf rhododendron are home to a small tribe of plump monal pheasants. In the monsoon months, the alpine meadows around Madhyamaheshwar are said to be home to over a hundred species of wild flowers.

The toothless Andhra-born priest in charge of the temple claims it is 5,500 years old, but historians suggest it may have been built about 1,500 years ago. There is an older, tiny shrine on the ridge some 250m above Madhyamaheshwar. This is little more than a pile of stones with a large black lingam, a small yoni of more recent provenance, and a tiny brass bell which I rang with exuberance, as I looked up at Chaukhamba (7,138m) to the north.

Called 'Budha', meaning ancient, the location of this shrine is reason enough to make the trek to Madhya-maheshwar. Chaukhamba and its appurtenant peaks tower above the ridge, reaching into the depths of perfect autumn skies. Tiny ponds fringed with ice reflect every snow-field and overhang every granite wall and cornice — a vision that will make you circle the shrine once more, ringing the tiny bell with joy.

Interestingly, there is some etymological confusion about the name of this destination. Literature refers to it as 'Madhya-M....' or the middle Kedar. This would seem to square with the notion that it marks the spot where Shiva's navel was manifested. However, the locals all refer to it as 'Madd-m....' (the sound suggested by the two 'ds' resists transcription into English) — implying a drunken god. Without intending to be irreverent, I would suggest this is

Graphic by ANIS KHAN

GETTING THERE AND OUT

FROM RUDRAPRAYAG to Okhimath, it's 45 km/ 2½ hrs by 🚙 (Jeep Rs 400) or 3 hrs by 🚌 (Rs 30). Change here to a local jeep-taxi for Uniana (15 km/ 1 hr/ Rs 200). Part of the road is metalled but it soon deteri-orates into a lurching, rocky track on which I would rather not drive. If you need to, spend the night at Okhimath, at the GMVN. We stayed at the Pintoo Lodge, Uniana

RETURN From **Uniana**, head back to Okhimath and Rudraprayag. Buses are infrequent on this route, so you might want to go by local jeep instead

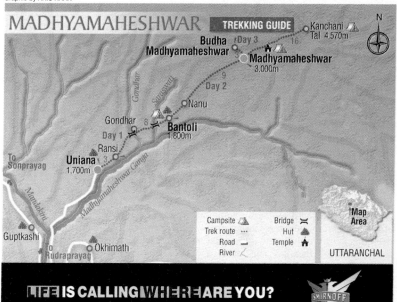

Waterfalls and forests near Gondhar

of the forest, levelling out in time to meet a stream of water cascading down a smoothened sheet of black granite. Barely 50m later, a steel bridge spans a crashing waterfall, marking the low point of the trek. From here, the path climbs along the right bank of the river, offering lovely views of waterfalls and forests as it rises to **Gondhar**.

This large settlement is the traditional halting place on the trek but you should walk a bit longer. Less than a kilometre later, another bridge spans the **Saraswati River** just as it merges into the **Madhyamaheshwar stream**. This is an idyllic spot, and if you climb 10 mins from here, you will reach the ⛺ **Vishwa Lodge** at **Bantoli** (1,800m), where you will find clean rooms, exhilarating views of the river, and a tantalising glimpse of the **Mandani Peak** (6,193m) to the west.

much more appropriate — there is exuberance at the spot that suggests an intoxicated joy; whether with a vision of nature or by ingesting its produce is quite irrelevant.

DAY ONE

Uniana-Bantoli
Distance 11 km **Time** 5 hours
Level Easy

The jeep track fades shortly outside **Uniana** (1,700m) but work is afoot to extend it to **Ransi**, some 3 km away. Threading north-east along the valley of the Madhyamaheshwar Ganga, this stretch is gently uphill, and somewhat dusty. After Uniana, the terrain becomes more idyllic, and the path gradually descends into the forests along the river. About 7 km into the day's walk, there is a succession of switchbacks through the densest part

DAY TWO

Bantoli-Madhyamaheshwar
Distance 9 km **Time** 4-5 hours
Level Moderate

From **Bantoli**, the path continues north-west as it rises steadily past **Khatara** (1 km) to **Nanu** (2 km). Especially in autumn, this is walking at its best — a consistent tug at the calf muscles, a well-graded path, changing views of grassy slopes, emerald streams, dense forests and shimmering snows in the north. After Nanu, which is another possible night halt, the primarily oak forest grows darker. It is a bit of a trudge but, mercifully, the altitude is not yet dizzying. If you don't stop too often, you should find the level ground of the last kilometre well before lunch-time.

The path exits from the forest as it rounds the mountain to emerge at the Madhyamaheshwar (3,000m) meadow. The cheery temple sits in the small depression at the far end and a small cluster of establishments ⛺ offer good clean food, warm rooms and plenty of bedding.

Snow-clad Chaukhamba and its mirror image

DAY THREE
MADHYAMAHESHWAR-BUDHA MADHYAMAHESHWAR AND BACK
DISTANCE 3 KM **TIME** 2-3 HOURS
LEVEL EASY

It shouldn't take more than an hour to gain the top of the ridge lying to the north-west of the temple. If you're young and strong and you made an early start, you could easily do this on Day Two. But both clouds and winds tend to build in the afternoon, marring the views and making a prolonged stay unpleasant. Whereas, if you are up at the ridge by mid-morning, it hosts a delectable meadow, with plenty of spots from which to admire **Chaukhamba**, look downstream to **Uniana**, or wait for the monals to flutter out of the *bhoj* groves. In my opinion, the ridge deserves the better part of a day.

DAY FOUR
MADHYAMAHESHWAR-BANTOLI
Retrace your steps to Bantoli.

DAY FIVE
BANTOLI-UNIANA
And to Uniana. Return by jeep to Okhimath or Suyal Saur. Or if you are fit enough, take a guide and try the trekking option mentioned below.

TREKKING OPTION
DAY FOUR
MADHYAMAHESHWAR-KANCHANI TAL
DISTANCE 16 KM **TIME** 6-8 HOURS
LEVEL DIFFICULT

You definitely need a guide for this rather strenuous stretch to Kanchani Tal. I have not been there myself, but by all accounts the lake at 4,570m due north-east of Madhyamaheshwar is worth the effort. The path leads out from behind the temple to **Kanchani Khal** (4,200m) and then beyond to the ⚠ **Kanchani Tal** (lake) where you can set up camp.

DAY FIVE
Rest day.

DAY SIX
Return to Madhyamaheshwar.

DAYS SEVEN AND EIGHT
Return to Uniana.

For GMVN hotels, see Accommodation Listings on pages 538-539 (Okhimath and Suyal Saur) ✦

Tungnath and Chandrashila Peak
Pinnacle of the Panch Kedar

By Mohit Satyanand

The magnificent snowline views from Tungnath

TIME	2 days or more
LEVEL	Easy
IDEAL SEASON	May to mid-Jun; Aug-Sep for viewing flowers in full bloom
LOCATION	Chamoli District, Garhwal Himalayas

CHOPTA-TUNGNATH-CHANDRASHILA PEAK-CHOPTA

The highest of the Panch Kedar, Tungnath is estimated to be 3,660m above sea level. Ironically, it is also the easiest to reach. You can have breakfast at Chopta (3,000m), tread steadily up the impeccably maintained *chehfootiya* (6-foot wide trail), have your darshan, and be back for lunch. Honest, I have done exactly that with my nine-month-old son in a pouch strapped to my chest. But that's definitely not making full use of a splendid opportunity to enjoy aerial views of the alpine meadows around Chopta, to admire the stone sculpture around the medieval temple, or to extend your walk up to Chandrashila Peak, which, at 4,130m, is a vantage point any eagle would vie for.

Equally pertinent, unless you have already been walking in the region, these are respectable altitudes, and I would suggest you invest a couple of days in acclimatising instead of rushing on and off them. You could do worse than taking long rambles in the wild meadows and forests near Chopta and observing the wonderful bird life (76 species have been recorded in this area).

DAY ONE

CHOPTA-TUNGNATH
DISTANCE 3¹/₂ KM **TIME** 2-3 HOURS
LEVEL EASY-MODERATE
If you're even moderately acclimatised, you can make the temple in 3 hrs. It is

GETTING THERE AND OUT

FROM RUDRAPRAYAG to Gopeshwar, it's 74 km/ 3 hrs by 🚗 (Rs 400, negotiable) or $3^1/_2$ hrs by 🚌 (Rs 60). From here, **Chopta** (39 km) lies on the crest of a road that runs from Gopeshwar via Mandal down to Okhimath, before meeting the Rudraprayag-Kedarnath route. A jeep-taxi (Rs 300) should have you there in $1^1/_2$ hrs and a bus (Rs 20) in 2 hrs

ALTERNATIVE ROUTE

Rudraprayag to Okhimath is 42 km/ $1^1/_2$ hrs by taxi (Rs 300, shared taxi Rs 30). From Okhimath, Chopta is 30 km via Dugalbitta, 1 hr by taxi (Rs 200) or $1^1/_2$ hrs by bus (Rs 20). There are two buses from Gopeshwar to Chopta (12.30 and 1.30 pm) and two from Okhimath to Chopta (7.30 and 8.30 am)

RETURN the same way from **Gopeshwar** or **Okhimath** to Rudraprayag. Buses leave Chopta for Gopeshwar (9.30 and 10 am) and Okhimath (1.40 and 2.30 pm)

Graphic by ANIS KHAN

TUNGNATH

TREKKING GUIDE

N

Thali

Chandrashila
Day 2 Peak 4,130m
$2^1/_2$

To
Dugalbitta,
Deoriya Tal,
Okhimath
Tungnath
$3^1/_2$ 3,660m
Day 1

Chopta
3,000m

To
Joshimath

Gopeshwar

Campsite ⛺
Trek route ·····
Road —
Peak/height ▲
River ⧸
Bridge ⋈
Hut ⛺
Temple ⛩
Tea stall ☕
Glaciers ⩘

Chamoli

To
Karanprayag

Map
Area

UTTARANCHAL

a delightful walk, with the feel of a day picnic. The first half-hour climbs through a forest of conifers and rhododendrons, ferns and lichens, and the smack-on view of **Bandarpoonch**, with the **Kedar massif** off to the west is quite surreal. As the switchbacks begin, and the forest recedes, you get a feel of the **Chopta meadows** you have left behind. On both sides of the path, there are broad swathes of grassy slopes, with tiny clusters of gorgeous wild flowers, wild rosemary and berries.

Half-way up, there are a couple of shacks where you can stop for a ☕ tea and a packet of biscuits. From here on,

Golden bush robin

SUJAN CHATTERJEE

Measuring about 6 inches in length, the golden bush robin (*Tarsiger chysaeus*) is a bright orange-yellow bird found usually in pairs, hopping about in thickets. Males have an olive brown crown, mantle and wings and a prominent black mask from the top of the beak across its eyes. Females are olive, with buff eye ring and ochre-yellow below.

ASHOK DILWALI

Legend of Tungnath

Tungnath is the second of the Panch Kedars, beginning with Kedarnath in the west, and travelling east towards Kalpeshwar.

MOHIT SATYANAND

Most of the legends regarding the origins of the Panch Kedar have Shiva transforming himself into a bull as he did not want to engage in conversation with Bhima. One belief is that when Bhima discovered Shiva, the latter dived underground to escape. Another belief is that Bhima was so enraged at Shiva's refusal that he severed him into several parts. According to this, each of the Kedar temples marks the point where one of Shiva's body parts fell to the earth — Kedarnath for the bull's hump; Tungnath for the arms and chest; Rudranath for the face; Madhyamaheshwar for the belly and Kalpeshwar for Shiva's prodigious locks.

the path drives a steady gradient up the western flank of the hill. In the distance, you can see a cluster of

buildings below the path. This is a research centre for aromatic plants that lies off the path, which now begins to double back urgently, to make the final ascent to the temple.

Just before you get to Tungnath, there is a tiny **Ganesh Temple** perched on a rocky spur. Right after the monsoons, the hills here are covered with forget-me-nots, buttercups, anemones and wild strawberries.

As the path flattens, a flight of about 50 stairs veers sharply off to the left. At their head, a small kund signals that you have reached hallowed ground. You then pass through a corridor of eating and dossing houses before arriving at the temple courtyard, through the arch decked with bells.

Built of solid granite slabs, the **Shiva Temple** at **Tungnath** resembles the ancient temple of Bageshwar and Jageshwar. Guarding the entrance is Shiva's bull, Nandi. Images of the Pandavas and Adi Shankaracharya grace the sanctum sanctorum. 'The

Rhododendrons in full bloom on the snowy slopes of Tungnath

Himalayan griffon

This huge, bulky, khaki-coloured vulture is truly a mountain bird. Found in the Himalayas and in Central Asia, like all vultures this one too has an almost naked head and neck, surrounded by a dun-coloured ruff. With a wingspan of nearly 3m, the Himalayan griffon (*Gyps himalayensis*) is an impressive flier.

It is seldom the first to get to a carcass, as it is mostly attracted by the presence of ravens and bearded vultures. A voracious feeder, it is said that a group of Himalayan griffons can strip the carcass of a yak in two hours. It is very aggressive when feeding, but can be kept off by wolves and other carnivorous mammals.

This bird seldom breeds below 1,200m and may even be found at altitudes in excess of 6,000m. The nests, in small colonies of generally not more

RUPIN DANG/ WILDERNESS FILMS

than half a dozen, are scattered over cliff faces. The nests are sometimes those abandoned by other vultures, or sometimes built by the birds themselves, starting quite small and growing with use over the years. One egg is laid, between late December and May, depending on the area and altitude.

The inviting waters of Deoriya Tal near Chopta

ASHOK DILWALI

arm of Shiva' sits bang in the middle, a dark one-foot high lingam. Outside, there are two smaller temples dedicated to Parvati and Vyas.

A few lodges offer basic accommodation but, if you want, the grasslands below the temple offer infinite camping possibilities.

DAY TWO

TUNGNATH-CHANDRASHILA PEAK-CHOPTA

TIME 4-5 HOURS
LEVEL MODERATE

Start early and climb as fast as you can for the views from the top before it gets cloudy. Backtrack down the stairs to the Chopta path, and turn left (northwards) on the clear trail.

No longer paved, it narrows as it rounds the Tungnath hill, and, you have to clamber a bit as the terrain turns rocky. But it's not dangerous in any way, and suitable for all ages. In fact, even in autumn, you can find tiny icicles in the shadows, which the children in my party used for mock sword-fights!

Soon, the grass reasserts itself, and you can head off the beaten track and walk on soft soil, exploring the various views on either side. The path, always visible, heads straight up. You should crest the tapering slope in less than 2 hrs out of Tungnath.

Legend has it that the deity Chandrama (Moon) spent a long time on the peak in penance. Rama, too, is supposed to have meditated here to atone for killing Ravana, a Brahmin. But even if you are a non-believer, the place offers many rewards. **Chandrashila Peak** is a broad summit, strewn with cairns, and offering plenty of ledges for a gentle lie-back, a sharing of chocolates, and, above all, deep, high and wide views of the **Mandakini** and **Alaknanda valleys** and the white giants that water them: **Chaukhamba**, **Bandarpoonch**, **Kedarnath**, **Nandadevi**, **Gangotri**, **Neelkanth** and several other peaks.

You can roll down the hill to Tungnath (our kids did that quite literally) in an hour, have tea and breakfast, and return to Chopta in another hour-and-a-half. The day is still wide open, and you have ample time to explore the **Mandal Valley**, or **Deoriya Tal**. Or head back to the Mandakini Valley road on the route back to the plains via Rudraprayag.

Alternatively, stay in Gopeshwar for the night, or keep the Mandakini company for one more night at the **Suyal Saur GMVN**, 45 km away on the Guptkashi-Rudraprayag Road. The **Dugalbitta PWD Inspection Bungalow** is beautifully located but difficult to get bookings.

For rest houses and GMVNs, see Accommodation Listings on pages 534 (Dugalbitta, Gopeshwar) and 538 (Okhimath) ✦

Mt. Misery

The pain and sprain specialist. **IODEX**®

Rudranath and Kalpeshwar
Stepping stones to Shiva

By Mohit Satyanand

The sentinels of Uttaranchal stand guard over the devout on pilgrimage

TIME	5 days
LEVEL	Moderate
IDEAL SEASON	Oct to Nov
LOCATION	Chamoli District, Garhwal Himalayas

HELANG-DEVGAON-KALPESHWAR-DEVGAON-DUMAK-PANAR-RUDRANATH-PANAR-SAGAR

The Panch Kedar are traditionally visited in a long arc sweeping from north-west to south-east — Kedarnath, Tungnath, Madhyamaheshwar, Rudranath and Kalpeshwar. Religious belief has it that one must pay one's obeisance in full measure to Shiva, receive his blessings, and only then proceed to Badrinath for a darshan of Vishnu.

Ever the iconoclast, I did the last two in reverse, beginning from Kalpeshwar and then cresting two high ridges before walking to the vertiginous setting of Rudranath. The two days from Kalpeshwar to the high meadows at Panar are demanding, with long, remorseless climbs, sometimes through dense forest. But the paths are usually well defined, the villages en route extremely charming and the views from the ridge between Panar and Rudranath (with 360-degree views of the inner Himalayas) unmatched. Looking south, one can see the Alaknanda carving its way down to the plains, and the hazy blue contours of the foothills. Immediately below, the valleys between Gopeshwar and Mandal are a dense, dark green. And, in a grand arc sweeping from south-east to north-west, there are insider views of Nanda Devi and her sentinels.

When I took this trail late one autumn, the pilgrims had retreated before the oncoming winter, the seasonal shacks along the ridge had been pulled down and, in the early morning, the frost was thick enough to be mistaken for snow. Most days,

Photographs by AHTUSHI DESHPANDE

GETTING THERE AND OUT

**FROM RUDRAPRAYAG to
Helang**, it's 100 km/ 3½ hrs by 🚙
(Rs 1,500) or 5 hrs by 🚌 (Rs 80). For
a wider range of accommodation, spend
the night at **Joshimath** and drive back
14 km (20-25 mins) in the morning for
a 3- to 4-hr walk to **Devgaon Village**
RETURN From **Gopeshwar** take a
taxi to Haridwar via Rudraprayag (240
km/ 8 hrs/ Rs 2,800). If you're using a
bus (3½ hrs/ Rs 55), plan to spend the
night in Gopeshwar. We hired a Tata
Sumo (Rs 2,200 one way) and reached
in time to make the overnight train
from Haridwar

Graphic by ANIS KHAN

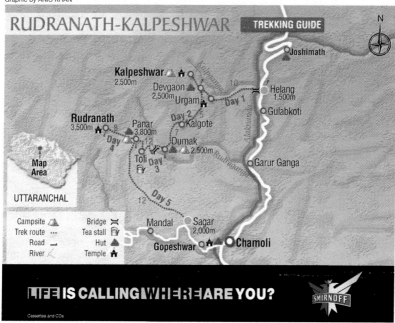

Yellow-throated marten

OTTO PFISTER

Known as *chitrola* in Garhwal, martens are found in moist decid-uous forests, in hilly areas up to 2,500m. Weighing up to 3.5 kg and measuring 40-60 cm in length, the yellow-throated marten (*Martes flavigula*) has a yellow and black head and back, a deep canary yellow throat, and a bushy black tail. They are agile tree climbers, though they run clumsily on the ground. They den in tree hollows and behind rocks.

we had the path to ourselves and at night, we felt we were the only beings privileged to see the stars with such dazzling clarity.

The Rudranath Temple is a tiny, squat structure, which was locked for the winter but the older shrines — with stone idols arrayed under towering granite — were guarded by ravens. Shrines such as these are strongly animistic, situated at 'power-spots' that clearly dominate the landscape. They speak of a deep awe for nature, and the admission of humility when confronted by forces and manifestations that could not be understood, far less controlled.

The traditional route is from the Mandal-Gopeshwar Road. But this involves an unremitting ascent from 1,500 to 3,300m, something I would

not recommend. A third option is from the same axis, beginning at Mandal, from where it is an easy 6 km to Anusuya. The next day, you would trek to Rudranath. Only 12 km, the trek takes you up to Nayla Pass (roughly 4,000m), and then down to Rudranath (approx 3,500m). The third day would be a short one, to the meadows at Panar. Thereafter, you would follow my route in reverse.

DAY ONE
HELANG-DEVGAON-KALPESHWAR-DEVGAON
DISTANCE 10 KM **TIME** 4-5 HOURS
LEVEL EASY

At Helang (1,500m), cross the Alaknanda via a road bridge, on a path which clashes with a road under construction. By the time you read this, a metalled track will snake its way along its feeder, the **Kalpganga**. As we climbed the switchbacks through the soft green forest, labourers were at work to buttress the more substantial shoulders that are required for a motorable path. Within an hour, we had climbed well above the gurgling water, the forest was denser, and the walk decidedly more strenuous.

Exactly 2 hrs later, the forest yields to an idyllic sight of flowers, fruit trees and terraced fields, and a concrete arch proclaiming that you have arrived at **Urgam**. The latter is both a village and a panchayat, consisting of three villages — of which your desti-nation is likely to be the last one. For the next 3-odd km, the path climbs more gently, alternating between forests of oak and pine, and views of open fields falling down to the river far below. At **Devgaon** (2,500m), two guest houses offer adequate shelter for the night, and **Rajinder Singh Negi's** establishment extends to meals served in their home.

If you want to camp, take the gentle path towards **Kalpeshwar** (2,500m), where you will find ideal

Fodder stacked for winter in the village homes en route

sites just above the river, within hailing distance of the temple. Or, if you have dumped your rucksack in the village, it is an easy stroll of 45 mins up the valley, across the river on a suspension bridge, and a short clamber up the opposite hill-face to the rock shelter that is the last, and lowest, of the **Panch Kedar**.

DAY TWO

DEVGAON-DUMAK
DISTANCE 12 KM **TIME** 6-8 HOURS
LEVEL MODERATELY DIFFICULT

The path ascends due south from the village, almost at a perpendicular to the Kalpganga. Marching steadily through the higher reaches of the village, it takes you to the **Urgam Temple** in just over an hour. It's a good place to stop for a bit, take a picture of the valley spread below and refill your water. And, if you have the heart for it, to orient yourself to the lofty notch in the forest that marks the midpoint of today's walk.

From here, you strike into the forest. Oriented south-west, the path is reasonably well defined. It reappears

even if you lose it, in the shade of gigantic chestnut trees. Some have fallen and it is a charming scramble over them, around gigantic boulders and through ferns and fungi. But the climb gets steeper and steeper and the forest seriously dense with khirsu oak as you trudge up to the pass. If you walk steadily, it should take 3 hrs to the pass, marked by the mandatory little temple. Rest a while on the grassy shoulder to your right, before you begin the sharp descent to **Kalgote**, about an hour and a half away. This is a very clear path.

As you approach the village, the **Alaknanda Valley** opens up below you. If you stay on the upper path, to Dumak, **Kalgote** is a gorgeous table-top of houses and fields, against the valley floor, shimmering its way to the plains. From here, it's still a long march to Dumak (2,500m) — about 7 km. Much of it is level, through picturesque light forest, often bordered by pasture land and fields of amaranthus. But there are a couple of climbs, and the last hour or so seems to last forever. For my pains, I was rewarded with the rare sight of a monal pheasant — only the second one I have seen in 20 seasons of Uttaranchal walking!

Dumak is a large village, arrayed along a flat road stone. 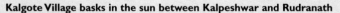 **Mr Bhandari's** family will provide you lodgings for the night, but if you intend to ⛺ camp, look for a spot just above the stream, about three-quarters of a kilometre short of the village.

DAY THREE

Dumak-Panar
Distance 12 km **Time** 6-8 hours
Level Difficult

The day begins with an incredibly stony, narrow path plunging down to the river, the **Rudraganga**, at least 500m below the village. Shortly after, the path levels just above the river, turns left, or south-west, to cross a bridge over limpid emerald pools and little falls of flashing light.

For the next couple of kilometres, it is a gentle climb along shallow rivulets under shady trees, and along tussocks of grass, to the vast meadows at **Toli**. In the season, ☕ tea-stalls offer refreshment but we had to fire up our stove in the lee of abandoned cowsheds. This was before climbing up, above the truly alpine lake, a turquoise mirror to Himalayan peaks, and into the forest ranging up the western slopes.

The path is often tentative and I would tend to advise using a guide as there are few landmarks, and you could get lost. In autumn, water is sparse, so we were well advised to keep our bottles full. About $2^1/2$ hrs into the trudge, there is a welcome respite when the terrain levels off, and you traverse a small, bare meadow with lightning-hit trees. Keep to the left or west till you recover the path, and resume the ascent that becomes steeper. It's at least another hour of thinning air and thinning vegetation, till the sharper light signals the top of the ridge.

From here, the path snakes around the mountain to your right or north, above the sharply sloping meadows of **Panar** (3,800m), to the *gufa* or cave where pilgrims traditionally found shelter.

Perennial springs a couple of hundred feet below the path offer congenial ⛺ camping, but we found our way into the 🏠 army hut, locked and abandoned for the winter, but, by commonly understood local code, offering easy access through appropriately rigged windows. This is a great site to orient yourself to the peaks of the Uttaranchal — **Bandarpoonch, Trisuli, Nanda Ghungti, Nanda Devi**. And to the stars, if you can handle all the dazzle!

Kalgote Village basks in the sun between Kalpeshwar and Rudranath

MOHIT SATYANAND

The Largest Adventure Travel Company in India.
Established in 1982 by Col.N.Kumar (of Everest fame) in collaboration with
MERCURY TRAVELS & THE OBEROI GROUP OF HOTELS

ON OFFER :
- Trekking all across the Indian Himalayas including, Bhutan, Tibet and Nepal.
- River Rafting in more than 15 rivers all over India and Nepal.
- Luxury tented camps in Rishikesh, Ladakh, Dam Damma Lake and Tons Valley.
- Self drive Jeep & ATV tours in Rajasthan and Ladakh.
- Climbing Courses and Expeditions.

For :
- Corporate Incentive and Training Programs.
- Schools-Outdoor Leadership Programs.
- Family Getaways for all age groups.

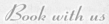

Book with us
Because...................!
We are the Oldest, Most experienced and the safest Adventure tour operator in the country.

WINNER
NATIONAL TOURISM AWARD 2004
for the Most Innovative Tour Operator of India
Awarded by Ministry of Tourism, Government of India.

MERCURY HIMALAYAN
EXPLORATIONS

Jeevan Tara Building, Parliament Street, New Delhi-110001
Phone : +91-11-23346209, 23362008, 23340033, Fax : +91-11-23742013, 26196082
E-mail : info@himalayanadventure.com
Web site : www.himalayanadventure.com

Designed by : *ACE VISION* : # 91-11-22440782, 09811014828

DAY FOUR
PANAR-RUDRANATH-PANAR
DISTANCE 16 KM **TIME** 6-7 HOURS
LEVEL EASY

Don your windproofs when you set out on this path oriented due west, a narrow ridge between the **Mandal forests** to your left and the high peaks to your right. Typically, you would not have fully acclimatised to the height, so it is slow going, but mercifully, there are few stiff gradients. The walk is generally ascending for the first 3 km. A pile of stones, littered with burnt-out 'agarbattis' and their colourful packets, marks the high point of the walk. It's a spot where pilgrims stop to pay homage to their ancestors.

Less than 2 km later, a path climbs sharply to the left, up a lush green slope. Mercifully, this is not your route to Rudranath, but the way in, over the **Nayla Pass**, from **Anusuya Devi**. You have to climb down to meet it at a water-logged meadow. The next couple of kilometres are more or less flat. The path ducks under a brow of rock, a clump of young silver birch stands on a little meadow to your right, and at eye-level is the tiny cluster of buildings that is **Rudranath** (3,500m).

You have to climb down to the kund or tank where you wash your hands and feet, before trudging up the steady incline to the narrow ledge of the Rudranath shrines. The ridge to your left blocks the western aspect, but to the north and east, the **Bandarpoonch Range** towers some 3,000m above, while the valleys are a dark maw some 2,000m deep.

🔺 Return the same way to camp at **Panar** for the night.

DAY FIVE
PANAR-SAGAR
DISTANCE 12 KM **TIME** 4-5 HOURS
LEVEL MODERATE

My recurrent thought as we slipped and slid down the stony path due south-east was only this: thank

Bansinarayan, en route to Rudranath

Rudranath we're not doing this in reverse! Progress is rapid and, in less than an hour, the sparse shrubs and occasional bamboo yields to forests.

Sagar (2,000m) is almost always in view, but it seems tantalisingly elusive. Depending on your footwork, it's at least 3 hrs before you reach level ground, a stream that's nearly level and the first children grazing their water buffaloes. The outlying fields of Sagar begin shortly thereafter and the path often narrows to a series of rocky steps threading through the village.

When the roofs turn flat, the paint a garish green, and plastic bags appear, you know you have returned to 'civilisation'. The road from Mandal to Gopeshwar is not heavily trafficked, but there is a thoughtful bus shelter and, soon enough, a jeep-taxi (Rs 100 one way) will stop and give you a 5-km ride to the Gopeshwar bus-and-taxi-stand for Rs 5 apiece.

For GMVNs and hotels, see Accommodation Listings on pages 534 (Gopeshwar) and 535 (Joshimath) ✦

The Valley of Flowers
A ramble in Eden

By Mohit Satyanand

SHASHANK GUPTA

TIME	4 days
LEVEL	Moderate
IDEAL SEASON	During the monsoons, Jul-end Aug
LOCATION	In Bhyundar Valley of Chamoli District

GOVINDGHAT-GHANGARIA-BHYUNDAR VALLEY-GHANGARIA-HEMKUND-GHANGARIA-GOVINDGHAT

In 1931, Frank S. Smythe was one of six British mountaineers who climbed Kamet. On his return to the plains, he crossed the Bhyundar Pass, standing at 5,086m, "with the intention of exploring the mountainous region at the sources of the two principal tributaries of the Ganges, the Alaknanda and Gangotri rivers." The next day, Smythe descended to "lush meadows… embowered amidst flowers. The Bhyundar Valley was the most beautiful valley that any of us had seen. We camped in it for two days and we remembered it afterwards as the Valley of Flowers" (*The Valley of Flowers,* Frank S. Smythe, Hodder and Stoughton, 1947).

The first flower that Smythe noticed in some profusion was the primula, coloured "a blue so intense it seemed to light the hillside…. At the most it stood six inches high, but its flowers were enormous for its stature, and ample in number — sometimes as many as thirty to the beautifully proportioned umbel." His camp, he recalled, was surrounded by flowers — white anemones, golden nomocharis (which resemble lilies), marigolds, globe flowers, delphiniums, violets, eritrichiums, blue corydalis, wild roses

Flowers and mist adorn Bhyundar Valley

and rhododendrons. Higher up, near the moraine, were saxifrage, yellow and red potentilla, geranium, asters and gentians, so many that "it was impossible to take a step without crushing a flower".

The valley had long held a place in local legend, and was called Nandan Kanan — the garden of Lord Indra. But Smythe's name stuck, and the Valley of Flowers it is. Though the Himalayas are home to countless alpine meadows, called *bugyals* in Uttaranchal and *thach* in Himachal, the Bhyundar Valley has come to occupy the popular imagination as *the* place to see alpine blossoms in the Himalayas.

If you stand at the foot of the valley, grassy meadows run down to the cleft of the stream, which, even in August, is still fringed by ice. On both sides, green slopes turn to dark rock as they vault into deep blue skies. Rising gently, the valley ends as a notch on the horizon, crested by the snows of the Rataban (6,166m) and Nilgiri (6,474m) peaks. And underfoot, the flowers that give the valley its name.

Mercifully, you don't have to climb Kamet to get to the valley — the next time Smythe visited the region, it was via Joshimath, which is today a major army station, and on the Badrinath route.

DAY ONE
GOVINDGHAT-GHANGARIA
DISTANCE 13 KM TIME 4-5 HOURS
LEVEL MODERATE

GOPINATH S

PHOTOS SURESH BABU

Few of the many flora which deck the Valley of Flowers

The garden of Eden

Smythe recorded some 262 species of flowers in 1937 and 29 more were added to the list a few years later. You will find anemones, geraniums, marsh marigolds, primulas, potentillas, geum, asters, lilium, ranunculus, corydalis, inula, Brahma kamal, campanula, pedicularis, arisaema, morina, impatiens, bistorta, ligularia, anaphalis, saxifragus, sibbaldia, thermopsis, trollius, codonopsis, dactylorhiza, cypripedium, strawberry, epilobium and rhododendrons. Many of the flowers found here have medicinal value. The valley remains in bloom for three months while its floral composition keeps changing every few days. By September, the blooms start to fade and, for the next five months, remain dormant over winter when the valley is snowbound.

Apart from the flowers, you are likely to come across many butterflies and, if you are lucky, you may even spot the musk deer, blue sheep (bharal), Himalayan bear, Himalayan mouse hare and the elusive snow leopard.

The bird life in the valley is rich and varied, and you are likely to sight the fire-capped tit, black-throated tit, red-headed bullfinch, fire-fronted serin, striped-throated yuhina, pink-browed rosefinch, dark-breasted rosefinch, speckled wood pigeon, Himalayan tree creeper, yellow-breasted greenfinch, rufous-bellied niltava, rufous-vented tit, brown dipper and monal pheasant.

Govindghat (1,828m) is a humongous parking lot, catering to the thousands of Sikh pilgrims threading up to **Hemkund Lake** (locally known as Lokpal). The pilgrim traffic, and those catering to it, completely dominate the landscape and the walk is an unending ribbon of stalls, providing ⛾ tea, refreshments, full-fledged meals, phone calls and, as you climb higher, even massages!

Leave your transport on the right bank of the **Alaknanda**. The ascent begins as soon as you cross, and join the cheerful groups heading up to **Ghangaria** — now also known as **Govind Dham**. Tracing the path of the **Lakshman Ganga**, the mule track climbs past terraced fields and vegetation, to the hamlet of **Pulna** (3 km).

From here, the trail is a little wilder, and more forested, with occasional glimpses of snow peaks, and of the cascading waters that feed the Alaknanda. The 7 km from Pulna to **Bhyundar**

Enchanting waterfalls near Pulna

Village are a steady ascent and, mercifully, the altitude is moderate, so your lungs should have no problem coping.

Shortly after Bhyundar, the trail crosses the **Laxman Ganga**, over a bridge elevated by giant boulders. The going is somewhat harder now, but Ghangaria is only 3 km away.

🏕 During the short season (Jul-Sep), **Ghangaria** (3,050m) can be enormously crowded. You can always find a place to shelter — including a **Forest Rest House**, **gurudwara**, and associated dharamshalas. But if you want some solitude, there is ample 🏕 camping both before and after Ghangharia.

Graphic by ANIS KHAN

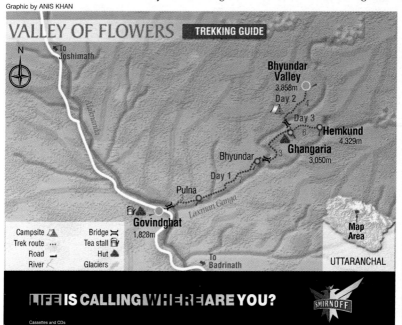

Wild profusion of blooms carpet the path into the Valley of Flowers

SURESH BABU

DAY TWO

**GHANGARIA-BHYUNDAR VALLEY-
GHANGARIA**
DISTANCE 8 KM **TIME** 7-8 HOURS
LEVEL EASY

Lokpal or Hemkund

Believed to be the place where Lakshman meditated, the lake is also called Lokpal, another name for Lakshman. However, the Sikh name derives from yet another appellation: Himkund, or Lake of Snow. Hindu pilgrims often visited the lake on their way to and from Badrinath. And in 1936, a Sikh religious scholar determined that this was the very lake the 10th Sikh Guru, Gobind Singh, had described as being a place of meditation in past lives. By 1939, a small gurudwara had been built on the lakeshore in token of this belief, which was expanded in 1974. Since then, Hemkund has come to occupy a significant place in the religious topography of the Sikh faith.

ATUL SHARMA

Leave Ghangaria with the stream of pilgrims heading to **Hemkund**. You need to veer left (north-west) as they climb east to the lake. The trail is well marked, and is a delightful ramble as it climbs gently through a coniferous forest, before dropping down to a bridge, shack and check-post that

Speed **93** ™

Experience Octane

The Hi-Octane High Performance petrol from Bharat Petroleum.

**Bharat
Petroleum**

GETTING THERE AND OUT

**FROM RUDRAPRAYAG to
Joshimath**, it's 114 km/ 4 hrs hrs by 🚗 (Rs 1,500) or 6 hrs by 🚌 (Rs 95), on the Badrinath Road via Chamoli
Joshimath to Govindghat is another 20 km (taxi Rs 300/ 45 mins; bus Rs 20/ 1 hr) on this route
RETURN the same way from **Govindghat**. This narrow road from Joshimath to Govindghat is one-way only and traffic is governed by 'gates', time slots that regulate departure in each direction, so look for the earliest time at which you can leave. Direct buses (Rs 260/ 13 hrs) to **Haridwar** between 4 and 7am. Taxis charge Rs 3,000 for the 11-hr run

Conservation of the Valley of Flowers

From the summer to the monsoons, high-altitude meadows across the Himalayas attract shepherds. Writing in 1937, Smythe noted their presence in the **Bhyundar Valley**. During this trip, Smythe made extensive collections of plants, seeds and bulbs, setting the trend for several English botanists who made collections over the subsequent decades. Following Independence, from the 1950s onwards, Indian naturalists conducted their own field trips into the valley. Our national bureaucracy saw it as a botanical treasure trove to be protected.

In 1982, the Bhyundar Valley was declared a national park. This meant that camping in the valley was henceforth banned, and grazers were now excluded from its grassy slopes. The floral heritage of **Nandan Kanan** was saved forever. But not quite, for over the next decade, scientists noted a marked reduction in the flower population. Meanwhile, the weeds flourished. Luckily, someone observed that cattle grazing in Himalayan meadows tend to eat the weeds, not the flowers. And so, the ban on grazing, designed to protect flowers, had ended up endangering them. The grazers are back, though regulated, and so are the flowers.

mark the official beginning of the **Valley of Flowers** (Bhyundar Valley, 3,858m). Pay your entry fee (Indians Rs 30, foreigners Rs 150 — for 3 days) here and climb up a rocky trail. The forest is now behind you, and the flowers begin to appear.

As the trail levels out and turns right (east), you begin to get a sense of the valley. To the right, just below the trail, a marble slab marks the death of Margaret Legge, a botanist from Edinburgh who fell to her death here in 1939: *"I will lift mine eyes unto the Hills from whence cometh my strength."*

The valley is exquisite and it seems a shame not be able to spend the night here — depending on the weather, snow bridges may still span the river below, and scrambling up-valley, crossing its numerous feeders, is a delight. If I were to visit the valley again, I would 🏕 camp, not at Ghangaria, but as close to the valley as permitted, and spend a couple of days savouring its delights. In any case, do try and reach there early — both to catch the morning dew on the blossoms, as well as to make the most of the day.

DAY THREE
GHANGARIA-HEMKUND-GHANGARIA
DISTANCE 6 KM EACH WAY **TIME** 4 HOURS EACH WAY
LEVEL HARD

Crossing the bridge over the Hem Ganga once again, head east up the heavily-trafficked path. It is a challenging ascent, but derive some strength from the perseverance of the thousands of pilgrims who make the climb uncomplainingly.

And, if you have done the Valley of Flowers trip the previous day, you will be better acclimatised than most others. If you nevertheless feel drained when you reach the glacial lake (4,329m), you could try joining the more abiding in faith, who swear by the restorative powers of a dip in its chill waters.

DAY 4
GHANGARIA-GOVINDGHAT
DISTANCE 13 KM **TIME** 4-5 HOURS
Return the same way.

For GMVNs and hotels, see Accommodation Listings on pages 534 (Ghangaria) and 535 (Joshimath) ✦

Bedni and Ali Bugyals
In Trishul's shadow

By Mohit Satyanand

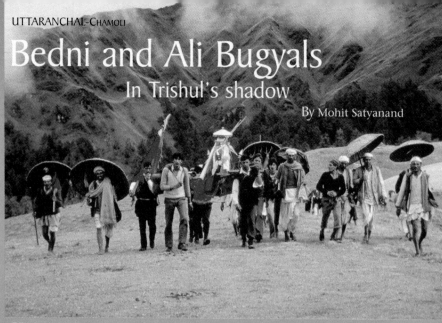

Pilgrims on the annual yatra at Ali Bugyal

TIME	4 days
LEVEL	Moderate
IDEAL SEASON	Monsoons, Jun-Sep
LOCATION	Between the Bedni and Kali Gangas in Chamoli District

LOHAJANG-WAN-BEDNI-ALI-BEDNI-LOHAJANG

This has got to be one of the most romantic spots in the Himalayas — acres and acres of meadow scooped out of lush mountainscape, a steep ridge arching up into the dusk, and above it, the enormous western flank of Trishul. From this perspective, and scarcely 5 km away, every snowfield and crag of Trishul is visible, every cornice and crenellation. And as the sun sets in the deep valleys to the west, its vast wall of snow and granite turns gold against a darkening sky.

One of the larger *bugyals* (meadows) in Uttaranchal, Bedni is also a major way-station on the Nanda Raj Jatra, a ritual procession held every 12 years. Beginning in the Brahmin village of Nauti in Garhwal, the procession is joined by villagers from across Kumaon and Garhwal. The origins of the yatra are deeply mystical and symbolic, and feature a four-horned ram set free to return to Nanda Devi. At the practical level, it is supported by the government and is marred by concrete structures, lots of bandobast, and crowded trails reduced to slush. For a romantic like me, this is the very antithesis of a trip into the flowered munificence of the *bugyals*, so I can safely say that I will not visit Bedni in 2012!

The twin *bugyal* of Ali is an easy day's walk, and can be visited on the return to the plains. Or, if one wants to explore country further north, 'do' Ali on the way up, and then continue on to the somewhat macabre Roopkund. If you have a couple of weeks, especially in autumn, I would highly recommend a walk into the gentle villages of the Nandakini Valley, before striking north to the Kuari Pass, and finally emerging north of the highest chain of the Greater Himalayas, in the region of Auli and Joshimath.

DAY ONE

LOHAJANG-WAN
DISTANCE 5-6 HOURS **TIME** 10 KM
LEVEL EASY

From the pass at **Lohajang** (2,133m), the clearly marked road leads northwards to Wan (2,439m), hugging the left (western) side of the valley as it heads down into it. Beginning as a wide stone-paved path, it narrows as it begins to thread through the valley floor, fringed by shrub and deciduous forest. The ascent that follows is gradual, and the path is always close to water. Within 2 hrs, you are at a tiny plateau in a forested cup. This is a good ⛺ camping spot if you have made a late start, and looks up at the path from Bekhal Tal to Wan.

Graphic by ANIS KHAN

About 7 km out of Lohajang, the low scrub fades, and one is in a pastoral valley with signs of grazing and scattered habitation.

The path runs along the western bank of a shallow stream. Rounded rocks strewn across the valley give one the sense that this must once have been a more substantial river. In short order, one is in view of **Wan**, and the path crosses the stream via an elevated bridge. The main path heads straight into the village, and affords intimate views of life in remote habitation. But, if you have no shopping to do, you could take the steep path to the right which stays south of the village, and leads to the compound of the **Wan Forest Rest House**, which is above, and to the east of the village.

Either way, you will encounter a small clump of imposing deodar, among the finest I have seen in the Kumaon region — this is already a well-noted phenomenon, recorded in

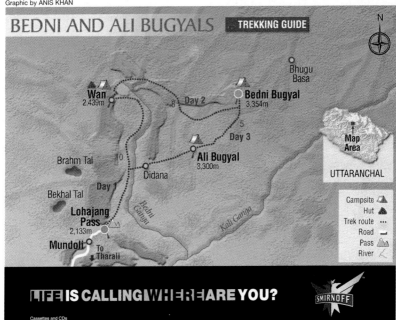

Grand display of the west face of Trishul as seen from Bedni Bugyal

the *Himalayan Gazetteer*, written in the middle of the 19th century.

 Good camping is to be found in the vicinity of the **Forest Rest House**. Or, if you still have the legs for it, head north-east, another half-hour up the trail, to a thrusting spur on the bald ridge above Wan. It has water for the camper and lovely light at dusk, and, on a clear day, offers views of the top-most vanilla bits of Trishul.

DAY TWO

WAN-BEDNI
DISTANCE 8 KM **TIME** 4-6 HOURS
LEVEL DIFFICULT

Once you have climbed the ridge above Wan, the trail switches back, from north-east to north-west, and sharply down the eastern aspect of the hill. Half an hour later, you will find yourself in a moist, fern-shaded glen, watered by the **Bedni Ganga**. It's a great place to stop, fill water, and take a deep breath for the long push through the forest.

The trail is oriented more or less due east, but given the steep gradient, switches back constantly. In the monsoons, it is often slushy, but always eminently navigable. Deep and dark, the mix of oak and rhodo-dendron is standard for these altitudes in Uttaranchal, but the varieties of fungi is not, and I have never seen growths as attractively, virulently orange as in these parts.

About 3 hrs up from the river should bring you to a clearing, popu-lated by wild flowers and weeds. Alas, this is not Bedni, yet! The trail bears south from here, before swinging north again, making you huff and puff up a stony outcrop.

About half an hour later, a higher trail seems to be suspended at a per-pendicular above. Bear left (west) here, on a gentler gradient. The pasture of **Bedni** (3,354m) lies just behind the cliffs to your north-east. The path takes you around them and deposits you in the middle of a substantial

GETTING THERE AND OUT

FROM RUDRAPRAYAG to Karanprayag, it's 30 km/ 1 hr by 🚙 (Rs 200) or 1¹/₄ hrs by 🚐 (Rs 20), if you're planning to come by way of Garhwal. Spend the night at Karanprayag, then head east along the Pindar to **Tharali** (47 km). From here take a jeep to **Mundoli** (1 km from **Lohajang**). Taxi from Karanprayag to Lohajang (80 km/ 3 hrs) is Rs 1,000; bus (3¹/₂ hrs) Rs 40

FROM ALMORA to Gwaldham, it's 95 km/ 3¹/₂ hrs by taxi (Rs 400) or 5 hrs by bus (Rs 60), if you're approaching Bedni from the Kumaon side. Buses are few and uncomfortable on this stretch **Gwaldham to Lohajang** is 50 km/ 2 hrs by taxi (Rs 400) via Tharali and Mundoli. Spend the night at Gwaldham at the GMVN. If you don't have private transport, you may need to change jeeps at Tharali

RETURN From **Lohajang** take the same route back via Gwaldham or Karanprayag to Almora or Haridwar

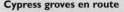

Cypress groves en route

meadow, cascading down from the snows of **Trishul** and **Nanda Ghungti**, and into the valleys to the west.

🏕 🏔 Shelter is to be found in **shepherds' huts**, and the camping is divine.

DAY THREE
BEDNI-ALI-BEDNI
DISTANCE 10 KM **TIME** 4 HOURS
LEVEL EASY
If you climb out of Bedni, you can see Ali (3,300m) laid out in the south-west, and it seems a 5 mins paraglide away. You can visit it in a leisurely day trip from your camp at Bedni.

You need to head back in the direction of **Wan**, but instead of climbing down the rocky outcrop to the west (your right), head straight on the more level path to the south. I haven't done the walk, but I believe you do have to descend a bit before climbing up to Ali. ⛺ Return to **Bedni** for the night and camp. ⛺ Alternatively, if you spend the

Climbing Trishul

ASHOK DILWALI

At 7,120m, Trishul is certainly not the tallest mountain in the Indian Himalayas. But it occupies a special place in climbing history.

In 1907, when Dr T.G. (Tom) Longstaff led a multinational team to its summit, it became the first peak over 7,000m to be climbed. Accompanying him to the summit were Brocherel and the Nepalese climber, Kabir Burathoki. Naturalist, geographer and explorer, Tom Longstaff had explored the region two years earlier, and looked into the Nanda Devi Sanctuary from the south. When he returned in 1907, he forced a passage from the north, skirting Changabang,

and his team climbed Trishul from the North Face.

To place Longstaff's achievement in perspective, one must record that it was to be another 30 years before any other mountain of this height was climbed.

In 1951, Gurdial Singh, a master from Doon School led an Indian team to the peak. Harish Kapadia, climber and chronicler of the Himalayas, asserts that Indian climbing came of age when Gurdial Singh and his colleagues crested Trishul. The current generation of Himalayan climbers seems to echo this sentiment, and today, Trishul is the most frequently climbed '7,000-er' in the Himalayas.

A mouse hare at a shrine at Bedni

night at **Ali**, you can bypass Wan, and join the Wan-Lohajang trail about 6km ahead of Wan at **Didana**.

DAY FOUR

BEDNI-LOHAJANG
DISTANCE 20 KM **TIME** 7-8 HOURS
LEVEL MODERATE
Retrace your steps to civilisation.

TREKKING OPTION

DAY ONE

LOHAJANG-BEKHAL TAL
DISTANCE 8 KM **TIME** 5-7 HOURS
LEVEL MODERATE

DAY TWO

BEKHAL TAL-BRAHM TAL-WAN
DISTANCE 10 KM **TIME** 6-8 HOURS
LEVEL MODERATE

If you're fit, you might like to begin with a climb to **Bekhal Tal**, a pristine lake set in a meadow north-west of the Lohajang Pass, 8 km away (about 5 hrs). I haven't been myself, but Manoj, who accompanied me on my first trek in the area, has convinced me that it is a diversion well worth the effort.

Get hold of a local guide from Gwaldham or Lohajang to show you the way.

For GMVN hotels, see Accommodation Listings on pages 534 (Gwaldham), 535 (Karanprayag) and 539 (Wan) ✦

NAINITAL

Naini Lake

Photographs by TRIBHUVAN TIWARI

Beloved of the British, Nainital was Jim Corbett's home for many years, and he talks about the town very fondly in most of his books. Though Nainital has expanded and the surrounding forest that once teemed with bears, tigers and deer has thinned down abysmally, the soul of the place remains. Set amongst the towering peaks of the magnificent Kumaon Himalayas, this lake resort surrounded by pine trees also has many interesting walks along quaint forest trails in the neighbouring woods.

MUST-VISITS

Naini Lake

Hindu mythology has it that the deep green lake is one of the emerald green eyes of Parvati, Shiva's wife. A rowboat ride around the lake costs Rs 120. Alternatively, you can hire a small yacht at Rs 80-120/ 30 mins from the Nainital Boat Club (Tel: 05942-235318). Several shops line the edge away from the water and here you can browse for shawls, local handicrafts, honey, fruit juices and pickles.

Snow View

A thrill for kids and adults alike is the ropeway Aerial Express to Snow View (2,270m). You get majestic views of the Himalayas dominated by the sacred Nanda Devi. Round trip fare: Rs 65, but you have to return within an hour. Timings: 9 am-5 pm. Horses and ponies also available. By foot, it's a rather steep 2-km climb.

WHERE TO STAY

Hotels are best booked in advance during the summer holidays, Dussehra and Diwali. During off-season, discounts are offered. **Manu Maharani** (Tel: 05942-237341-8; Tariff: Rs 3,500-6,500) near Uttaranchal's High Court in Grasmere Estate, Mallital, is expensive, but offers splendid views. Nearby is **Hotel Langdale Manor** in Langdale Estate, Mallital (Tel: 235447; Tariff: Rs 900-1,400).

The **Claridges Naini Retreat** (Tel: 235105; Tariff: 3,200-6,000) is splendid in terms of the great comfort, peace and quiet it offers. **Hotel Krishna** (Tel: 231646; Tariff: Rs 1,200-2,400) is right on the Mall, overlooking the *tal*. A little less expensive options are KMVN's **Sarovar Tourist Rest House** (Tel: 235570; Tariff: Rs 1,000-2,100) and Hotel **Pratap Regency** (Tel: 235865/ 866; Tariff: Rs 1,000-1,750).
For more hotels and details, see Accommodation Listings on pages 536-538

WHERE TO EAT

Nainital is dotted with numerous restaurants and some well-stocked watering holes. We recommend tikki-in-a-bun at **Laxmi** on the Mall, washed down with chilled lassi or hot special masala chai. Clamber up to **Machan** on the Mall and tuck into Hakka noodles,

---

→ **Nainital Facts**

● **LOCATION** Capital of India's lake district, and close to Corbett National Park, Nainital (1,992m) lies in the Kumaon Himalayas
● **GETTING TO NAINITAL By rail** Nearest railhead: Kathgodam (36 km/ 1 hr). Taxi Rs 250, bus Rs 25 **By road** The drive up to Nainital on NH24 (till Rampur) and then NH87, is the most convenient option. Buses ply regularly from Anand Vihar ISBT, New Delhi
● **STD CODE** 05942
● **TOURIST OFFICE** KMVN Sarovar Tourist Reception Centre, Near Bus Station, Tallital. Tel: 05942-235570 (see *Tourist Offices Listings on pages 520-521*)

---

burgers, pizzas, sandwiches and cutlets. Hardcore vegetarians should beat a path to **Shiva Restaurant** in Barra Bazaar, always packed with hungry hordes stuffing themselves with North Indian regulars. Those who love sweets should make a beeline for **Heritage Restaurant** where the aroma of baking goodies fills the air.

INPUTS FROM RISHAD SAAM MEHTA

ALMORA

This nearly 500-year-old town, once famous for its pretty paved roads and wooden houses with elaborately carved façades, continues to be on the traveller's map because it is the hub for dozens of excursions to scenic retreats, trekking routes and pilgrimage centres nearby.

MUST-VISITS

Discover the art and culture of the Kumaon region at the **Gobind Vallabh Pant Public Museum** near the bus stand. **Bright End Corner** is the place to 'eat the air' and watch the sun rise and set over the hills. Visit the enchantingly located **Chitai Temple**, a good 8 km from Almora. Drive down to Kosi (13 km), where you cross the river before making a 1¹/₂-km trek up the mountainside to the **Katarmal Sun Temple** complex.

WHERE TO STAY

Kalmatia Sangam (Tel: 05962-233625; Tariff: Rs 9,800 for 2N/ 3D, inclusive of all meals) has tastefully designed cottages, located at Kalmatia Estate. Enjoy the views of the peaks from here. The resort organises safaris, guides, hiking, trekking, yoga and meditation. **Deodar Resort** (Tel: 233025) at Papparsalle, up the road from Almora, with only a few rooms is a home away from home. Be warned, you will put on weight because of the irresistible food. The **Gollu Devta Tourist Rest House** (Tel: 230250; Tariff: Rs 300-600) and **Snow View Resort** (Tel: 233650; Tariff: Rs

→ **Almora Facts**

● **LOCATION** Almora is spread across a 5-km ridge atop Kashaya Hill in the Kumaon, 1,645m above sea level and 49 km from Ranikhet

● **GETTING TO ALMORA By rail** Nearest railhead: Kathgodam (91 km/ 3 hrs). Taxi Rs 600; bus Rs 150
By road Take NH24 from Delhi to Rampur, NH87 to Kathgodam via Rudrapur, and then Ranikhet-Almora Road to Almora via Bhowali. Regular bus services from ISBT Anand Vihar, New Delhi

● **STD CODE** 05962

● **TOURIST OFFICE** KMVN Regional Tourist Office, TRH, Almora Tel: 230250 (*see pages 520-521*)

Sadhu at the Chitai Temple

2,500-2,800), which has a restaurant and travel desk, are both in Papparsalle.

Or, if for some reason you prefer to stay in Almora, there is the **KMVN Tourist Bungalow** (Tel: 220588; Tariff: Rs 200-300) on Almora's main road. *For more hotels and details, see Accommodation Listings on pages 532-533*

WHERE TO EAT

There's not much on offer in Almora. Most hotels, Deodar aside, offer a standard menu for residents and some of them may even agree to feed non-residents on prior notice. If you're not over-fussy about what and where you eat, try the **Shikhar Restaurant** that is more like a super dhaba, serving mostly Indian food. For vegetarian, try **New Glory** and **Madras Café**.

INPUTS FROM RICHA LAHIRI

A bend in the Kosi near Kumeria

Corbett Park-Nainital
In Carpet Sahib's country

By Anurag Mallick, Sumantha Ghosh and Vikram Singh

TIME	5-6 days
LEVEL	Moderate
IDEAL SEASON	Nov to Mar
LOCATION	Kumaon foothills of Nainital District

KUMERIA-AKASHKHANDA-KUNJKHARAK-VINAYAK-PATHARIYA-NAINITAL

Unlike most treks that are done in summer, this trek is best enjoyed in winter as high-altitude birds migrate to lower regions and the forests are in bloom. This trek has an altitudinal variation of 450 to 2,500m, allowing for diverse bird and mammal life. An astounding 650 bird species have been reported here and the assemblage of mammals is equally impressive, the most notable being the elusive serow.

The hike, through beautiful natural surroundings, takes us along old pony trails, scenic campsites and old British colonial forest bungalows. Starting from the right bank of the Kosi River, the trail moves through dense broadleaf forest rich in wildlife, and across shallow streams. As we gain altitude, the vegetation and landscape around us go through considerable changes, and one moves through conifer forests of oak and pine that open onto scenic valleys and gorges. The hike finally ends at a temperate forest higher up that offers spectacular views of the icy Himalayas. What is quite remarkable is the ever-changing biodiversity, rich wildlife and the dramatic difference in forest types each day.

For those with kids, this can be an adventurous family holiday. The best

274

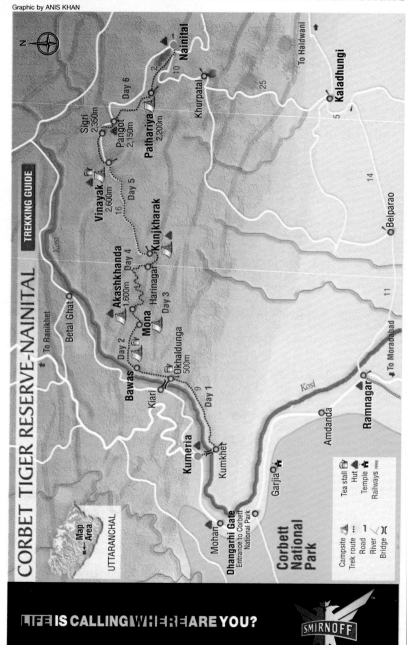

TREKKING GUIDE

CORBET TIGER RESERVE–NAINITAL

Nainital

To Haldwani

Kaladhungi

Day 6

Sigri
2,350m

Pangot
2,150m

Pathariya
2,200m

Khurpatal

Belparao

Vinayak
2,600m

Day 5

Kunjkharak

Akashkhanda
1,600m

Day 4

Harinagar

Mona

Day 3

Betal Ghat

Day 2

To Ranikhet

Okhaldunga
500m

Kosi

Bawas

Kiari

Day 1

Kosi

To Moradabad

Ramnagar

Amdanda

Kumeria

Kumkhet

Garjia

Mohan

Dhangarhi Gate
Entrance to Corbett
National Park

Corbett
National
Park

UTTARANCHAL

Map
Area

Campsite		Tea stall		Hut	
Trek route	...	Temple		
Road		Railways		
River				
Bridge	)(			

GETTING THERE AND OUT

FROM DELHI to Ramnagar

(Corbett), it's 244 km/ 6 hrs by road and best done in your own vehicle. Stop at **Gajraula** for lunch because, after you take the sharp U-turn to the left on the Moradabad Bypass, there are no proper dhabas on the Ramnagar route **Ramnagar to Kumeria** (35 km/ 1 hr) Drive past the forest barrier at Mohan (25 km) towards Ranikhet till you reach Kumeria (10 km from Mohan). Possible night halts here are Quality Inn or the Forest Rest House at Mohan

TIP Ramnagar is the last place to refuel on this route. If you want to drive around, make sure to tank up when you reach Ramnagar, and also when you are heading back to Delhi

Delhi to Kumeria by 🚙 is 7 hrs/ Rs 5,000. 🚌 run day and night from ISBT Anand Vihar to Ramnagar (7 hrs/ Rs 132). Or catch the daily overnight 🚂 Corbett Park (Ranikhet) Express (dep 9.30 pm, arr 5 am) from Old Delhi Railway Station for Ramnagar and head straight to Kumeria for the trek. Book a jeep taxi in advance for Kumeria

RETURN From **Nainital** take a taxi (6$\frac{1}{2}$ hrs/ Rs 4,000) or bus (9 hrs/ Rs 162) to **Delhi** (310 km). Or catch an overnight train from **Kathgodam** (36 km/ 1 hr from Nainital)

naturalist of the Corbett National Park. Wild animals abound and the city-dweller could get into trouble. The keen eye, ear and knowledge of your well-informed guides transform a normal hike into an insightful, exciting and safe adventure

DAY ONE

KUMERIA-BAWAS

TIME 5-7 HOURS

LEVEL EASY

The trek begins at **Kumeria** from where a suspension bridge over the Kosi leads to the trail that cuts right through the relatively large riverside village of **Kumkhet**. Cross the village and walk up the irrigation canal, which runs parallel to the river for

way to organise this would be to get your trekking company to hire ponies from Kumeria for the entire duration of the hike, giving your children the option of riding or walking whenever they feel like it.

WARNING Always hire a local guide or a

A perfect picnic spot in an enchanting glade beyond Akashkhanda

about 30 mins till the head of the canal. From here, turn right to climb uphill through a narrow broken trail that merges with a fire lane leading to the village of Okhaldunga (500m). You are basically following the Kosi upstream in a north-easterly direction. **Okhaldunga** is 9 km or about 3 hrs from Kumkhet. You could stop here for lunch at the banks of the Kosi, a short detour via a path which cuts through the fields on your left. You will find a bridge leading across the river to the village of **Kiari**. If time is a premium, you could even get your taxi to drop you to the roadhead at Kiari and start your trek from Okhaldunga.

Soon after crossing Okhaldunga, you will be walking on the new road which connects these parts to Betalghat. About 2-3 hrs along the road that meanders high above the **Kosi**, you will arrive at **Bawas**. There is a small and very basic ☕ tea-stall here. ⛺ Camp can be made in one of the fields, or by the river.

DAY TWO

Bawas-Mona
Time 3-5 hours
Level Difficult

The path leads past the hamlet of Bawas and turns right or south-east into a narrow valley. The next few hours are simply a long slog up the cobbled path as it zig-zags steeply up to **Mona** through dense lantana bushes. Since this is the only access for the villages above, you will probably pass pack-horses carrying supplies. It can get quite exhausting by the time you reach the small, but pretty village of Mona, nestled between terraced fields. The verandah at the primary school of **Mona** may be used to 🏕 camp for the night. But if you walk a little further due east, you will descend to a small perennial stream, by which you can 🏕 camp for the night.

DAY THREE

MONA-AKASHKHANDA
TIME 2-4 HOURS
LEVEL MODERATE-DIFFICULT

Cross the stream over the bridge and climb steeply up a pony track which heads past some terraced fields and a few houses. You can take the easier trail on the left, meandering along the contours of the hill, or take the shorter, much steeper track, which climbs up directly behind the houses. Slowly, the

Crossing over to Kumkhet

bush gives way to pines till you arrive at the old 🏚 **Forest Rest House** at **Akashkhanda** (1,600m). Being miles away from road, the bungalow is seldom visited by tourists or even forest officials. Though now in a dilapidated state, this beautiful rest house is set amidst pine trees and offers complete solitude. On a clear day, you will be able to see spectacular views of **Nanda Ghunti** (6,309m) and **Trishul** (7,120m).

DAY FOUR

AKASHKHANDA-KUNJKHARAK
TIME 6-8 HOURS
LEVEL EASY-DIFFICULT

From Akashkhanda, the track meanders eastwards through dense temperate forests dominated by oak, chestnut and rhododendron. The rhododendron are a riot of red when in bloom. Birds commonly seen here include the colourful jays, magpies and thrushes. This area also supports rich mammal life; on the hill slopes you can try to spot the goral (goat antelope) and on the trail you stumble upon the occasional pugmarks of the leopard. About half-way to Kunjkharak or 2-3 hrs later, you descend to a gurgling mountain stream in an enchanting oak forest.

This is a great place to stop for lunch. The water in the stream is cool and crystal clear, surrounded by moss-covered rocks. The track then starts climbing gently due south, through forests of pine and oak, and then veers to the right or south to climb up into the fields of the small hamlet of **Harinagar**. Stop for a break here as the last leg up to Kunjkharak can be quite challenging, especially if you opt for the short-cut.

Walk past the homes and the little school building on the path heading straight across the small pasture. Look uphill to your left, and you will find a narrow track climbing sharply. This is the short-cut to **Kunjkharak**. Be

OTTO PFISTER

The sad fate of the Himalayan quail

Once found on the lower slopes of the western Himalayas around Nainital and Mussoorie, this bird was last recorded in June 1868. The Himalayan quail (*Ophrysia superciliosa*) was hunted indiscriminately during the colonial period. But it may have survived had it not been for "development" and "progress". After independence the sharp rise of population in Mussoorie and Nainital, the indiscriminate cutting of forests, frequent fires, excessive grazing, unplanned road and building construction, and above all, open cast mining for limestone wrought havoc with the quail's habitat.

In the miraculous and unlikely event that you locate one, you should know how to recognise it:

Males are greyish, with a black face and throat, white forehead and narrow supercilium (eyebrow). The female has marked dark-brown upperparts, buff coloured head-sides and underparts, contrasting dark mask and dark streaks on breast to vent. Both have red bill and legs. They grow to about 25 cm or 10" long.

The lack of records for over a century suggests that the species may be extinct, although there have been a few well-organised searches for it. The species is listed as critically endangered. The chances that a small population survives in some remote area in the lower or middle Himalayan range seem slim. However, the search to discover the Himalayan quail is still on. In fact, the BNHS (Bombay Natural History Society) has instituted a hefty sum of Rs 10 lakh to be offered to anyone who can provide evidence of its existence.

warned that you have to leave the track 15 mins later and negotiate a tough 60-degree climb up, due south-east. The more civilised path heads south past a small temple before climbing east gently. This will deposit you on the jeepable road a little past Kunjkharak. Simply turn left once you reach the roadhead and walk back towards the **Forest Rest House.** Camp here for the night in the compound of the bungalow.

Since the location is actually quite high, it can get very windy and winter temperatures may drop to 0 degrees, with occasional snowfall. The water source near Kunjkharak is about 300m away below the Forest Department nursery. Huge rocks in forested ridges make this a good place to sight high-altitude birds like the lammergeier, and the Himalayan and Eurasian griffon, the tawny eagle, steppe eagle and kestrel.

DAY FIVE
KUNJKHARAK-VINAYAK
TIME 5 HOURS
LEVEL EASY

From Kunjkharak, take the level jeepable road heading north along the ridge to Vinayak, 16 km away. Though this is a motorable track, chances of coming across any vehicle are very slim indeed and you can expect snow in the winter months. Barely a kilometre after Kunjkharak, there is a magnificent 380-km broad view of the

Taking a break after the long, hard climb up to Kunjkharak

Himalayan range. Visible are crests such as Nanda Devi, Trishul, Martoli and even some peaks further east in Nepal. A unique feature of the moist temperate forest that you walk through is the *jhoola* moss that carpets the forest floor underfoot. This moss absorbs water and helps retain moisture in the forest. There is good forest cover on both sides of the track all the

A red carpet welcome

way to Vinayak. At certain vantage points, you get great views of the meandering **Kosi River** to the north, while in the south, you can see the forests of **Ramnagar** and **Haldwani** that run parallel to the ridge. At **Vinayak** (2,600m) you can stay in the beautiful 🏠 **Forest Bungalow** or 🏕 camp out in the compound of the nursery. There is a ☕ tea-stall run by a friendly young man, who can rustle up a simple pahari meal for you.

DAY SIX
VINAYAK-PATHARIYA
TIME 4-5 HOURS
LEVEL EASY

Hike to the highest ridge of Vinayak that starts right in front of the bungalow. This day's trek takes us through one of the finest patches of cedar forest, criss-crossed by streams. Here is your best chance to find the elusive serow, and while you do, look out for signs of the Himalayan black bear. An hour's hike eastwards will lead to the top of the ridge for a stunning view of the Himalayas. From here, go along the ridge on the narrow trail due south-east to get to the main road at **Sigri** (2,350m). Walk the next 3 km on an unpaved road till a culvert before the **hamlet of Guhugu Khan**, from where a right turn onto a pony trail takes you to the tiny but well-stocked

Déjà Vu

If it is a slice of the sky, a heavenly lake or a Himalayan hideaway that you are looking for…find them all when you arrive at Déjà Vu, Naukuchiatal. A lake house in the hills, Déjà Vu's french windows open out onto the mountains with its terrace decking out over the Himalayas and Naukuchiatal's shimmering waters. This home away from home let's you live life as you like it with two roomsπ, a cozy hall, adjoining dining, an open kitchen and a wondrous terrace.

Equipped with the services of a cook and a cleaner, Déjà Vu, lets you bring in your provisions and set your own menus or organizes the provisions you need. And as the light breaks over the lake or as the stars rise over the mountains you can dine in or al fresco in the silence of the mountains. And succumb to enigma of the Himalayas at a sublime home you'll always want to return to - DÉJÀ VU...

Corbett Trails

Corbett Trails (India) is a continuing experiment in the discovery of new lands, their exotic cultures and of the wondrous wildlife far from hustle and bustle of the cities and highways.

Trekking
Wildlife Tours
Angling Trips
Jeep Safaris
Corporate and Incentive Tours
Hotel Reservations

C 29, Lajpat Nagar-II , New Delhi-110024 Phone: 011-5172 1601/02/03 Mobile: 9868 502185
Email: info@corbett-trails.com www.corbett-trails.com

Nanda Devi, Trishul and Martoli seen between Kunjkharak and Vinayak

market of **Pangot** (2,150 m). Situated at a pass, this market served as an important trading centre between the valleys in the old days. Today, there are a couple of resorts that cater to keen birders, and you could stop here for a couple of days if you like.

From Pangot, take the trail that goes along the southern end of the village along dense forests with undergrowth of ringal bamboo and ferns. This 4-hr hike offers the chance to encounter a variety of wildlife like the barking deer, the khaleej and koklass pheasants. This forest is of great ornithological importance as the once-considered extinct Himalayan quail was reported here. The trail leads to the popular **Naina Peak** (2,600 m), earlier known as **Cheena Peak**. From here take a trail to the right, heading downhill to the campsite of **Pathariya** (2,200m), a magical spot that offers a bird's eye-view of Nainital.

<table>
<tr><td colspan="2" align="center">DAY SEVEN</td></tr>
</table>

PATHARIYA-NAINITAL AND AROUND
TIME 1-2 HOURS
LEVEL EASY

If you have had enough of camping out you can leave **Pathariya** at the end of Day 6 and opt for the comforts of one of the many hotels at Nainital, which is just a short walk away. Pathariya, as the name suggests, is on a rocky ledge and forms the western flank of **Nainital**. From here you can sight the twin rocky mounds popularly known as **Camel's Back.** This quaint village comprises a few houses and from here, we take the trail leading south-east along the grassy ridge dotted with conifers. Along the way you get good views of the vast Terai plains to the south. A little over 2 km brings you to the junction of the Kaladhungi-Kilbury-Nainital Road, from where Nainital is a short walk away.

The main hub of Nainital is the **Naini Lake**, which, according to mythology, marks the spot where Sati's eye fell and thus reflects its emerald green colour. A temple dedicated to Naina Devi lies on the edge of the lake. While Nainital is a bustling township and offers tourist distractions like boating on the lake and shopping in its busy streets, you must take time out to visit **Guerney House**, the place where the legendary Jim Corbett was born.

TIP Taxi back to Ramnagar (70 km/ 2 hrs/ Rs 800-1,400) and spend a few days relaxing at Corbett

<table>
<tr><td align="center">TREKKING OPTION</td></tr>
</table>

If you don't fancy the uphill slogs on days 2 and 3, consider doing the trek in reverse, starting from **Pangot** and finishing at **Kumeria**. Or even just till **Kunjkharak**. This is particularly advisable if you have your kids along.

For rest house bookings and hotels, see Accommodation Listings on pages 533 (Corbett area), 538 (Pangot, Pathariya) and 539 (Vinayak) ✦

TREKKING HOLIDAYS IN INDIA

Almora to Jageshwar
The Kumaoni village trek

By Sonia Jabbar

Photographs by SONIA JABBAR

TIME	4 days
LEVEL	Easy
IDEAL SEASON	Oct to early Mar
LOCATION	Almora District, Kumaon Himalayas

Walking through a sea of ripening wheat near Deora

KALMATIA SANGAM-DEORA-DHAULACHINA-
JWALABANJ-JAGESHWAR

This is a perfect little hike for those who want a bit of nature and adventure over a long weekend break. From Delhi, the Ranikhet Express gets you into Kathgodam early in the morning and only a couple of hours later you find yourself in Almora, which means you can actually start walking the same day if you aren't too tired from the overnight train journey.

This low-altitude hike takes you over undulating country through beautiful terraced fields and forests into charming Kumaoni villages whose enterprising folk are now offering homestays. The rates are reasonable and this facility means you needn't carry a heavy pack loaded with tent,

stove and provisions. The rooms are simple: durrie on the floor and beds or camp-cots with bedding (though I recommend you carry your own sleeping bags). The biggest plus point is the clean, wholesome food, and the clean bathrooms on offer. In Dhaulachina there is the Eco Tourist Resort, with tented accommodation, perched on the lip of a hill with a lovely garden and equally lovely views. In Jwalabanj, the inn-keeper has fashioned a charming rock garden and sit-out with spectacular views of the Central Himalayas to be had post-monsoons, when the haze has lessened.

Besides the friendly village folk, the other attractions on the hike are the rhododendron trees, the birds, the ancient temple of Vridh (old) Jageshwar, the massive deodar trees and the temple complex at Jageshwar.

The best way to organise this trek is to stay a night or two at Kalmatia Sangam Resorts. It is advisable that you email Dieter Reeb of Kalmatia at least a week in advance and ask him to book the overnight stays at Deora, Dhaulachina and Jwalabanj. You can also ask him to provide you with a guide, if you need one. Alternatively, carry your sleeping bag and take a chance at the villages en route.

If you have a day at Kalmatia before the trek, you could ask Dieter for directions and visit the estate of the extraordinary Austrian Buddhist spiritual master, Lama Anagarika Govinda, and his partner, the Parsi photographer, Li Gotami. Govinda wrote the highly popular spiritual classic, *The Way of the White Clouds*. Also, try and visit the small but powerful Kasar Devi Temple. **WARNING** Carry some insect repellent to keep away the fleas/ticks. I would sit down to take a break in the forest and find myself covered in bites

Graphic by ANIS KHAN

DAY ONE
KALMATIA SANGAM–DEORA
DISTANCE 12 KM **TIME** 4 HOURS
LEVEL EASY

Between **Kalmatia Sangam Resorts** and the 🏠 chai shops, you will find a stone paved path running downhill, heading north past the village of **Matgaon**. The village is scattered, extending all the way down the hill to the bottom of the valley. Follow the path as it skirts the bottom of the hill and turns to the north-east. You will cross a little cemented bridge and skirt the edges of fields until you come to a larger bridge over a stream. Cross the river and head upstream, keeping to the true right of the valley. The guide told me that there was a lovely **waterfall**, and we climbed the hill to the north in search of it but found the winter drought had been so severe that the falls were a pathetic trickle. Apparently, if the monsoons are good and the winter snowfall plentiful, then

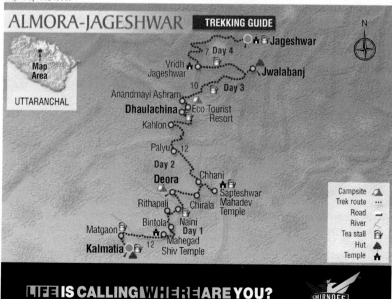

ALMORA-JAGESHWAR **TREKKING GUIDE**

Map Area

UTTARANCHAL

Jageshwar

7 Day 4

Vridh Jageshwar

Jwalabanj

10 Day 3

Anandmayi Ashram

Dhaulachina — Eco Tourist Resort

Kahlon

Palyu 12

Day 2

Deora — Chhani

Rithapali — Chirala — Sapteshwar Mahadev Temple

Bintola — Naini Day 1

Matgaon

Kalmatia — Mahegad Shiv Temple

12

Campsite	⌂
Trek route	···
Road	—
River	⟋
Tea stall	🏠
Hut	⛺
Temple	⛩

Umed Singh's gaily coloured guest house at Jwalabanj

GETTING THERE AND OUT

FROM ALMORA to Kalmatia Sangam Resort on the Upper Binsar Road, it's 20 km/ 40 mins by 🚗 (Rs 250). The hike begins near the shops outside the resort

RETURN From **Dhaulachina** on the third morning, get a taxi pick-up to **Kathgodam** which is 135 km/ 4 hrs by taxi (Rs 1,500) or 5 hrs by bus (Rs 135, infrequent service). Alternately, ask for taxi pick-up at **Jageshwar** at around lunchtime on Day 4 **Jageshwar to Almora** is 35 km/ 1½ hrs by taxi (Rs 600) or 2 hrs by bus (Rs 40, very limited service) **Jageshwar to Kathgodam** is 125 km/ 4 hrs by taxi (Rs 1,500) or 5 hrs by bus (Rs 130). Infrequent and uncomfortable bus services till Almora. From here, taxi to Kathgodam (90 km/ 2½ hrs) is Rs 900 approx. Or take a shared jeep (Rs 200 approx)

this is a lovely spot to spend an hour or so. Ascertain its health and, if the falls are full, perhaps you can plan to breakfast by them.

Continue upstream and if you haven't detoured at the falls, you should reach the lovely little **Mahegad Shiva Temple** just a couple of hours after leaving Kalmatia. Cross over to the left bank of the stream and climb the embankment following the water pipes, until you find a path across the stream heading uphill. Climb down and up the right bank again, descending to the **Bintola Fields** soon after. Walk on the parapet of the small irrigation channel as it's easier than walking through fields. After the **Bintola Village** the path turns left, or north, climbing gently up to a waterpoint and some abandoned buildings. Follow the path as it descends past **Rithapali** village and turns to the north-east, or right, to descend to the valley floor and the village of **Naini**. There are some spectacular old temples in the vicinity with beautifully carved stone idols of Shiva-Parvati. One of the smaller shrines has a four-headed Shiva. From Naini, cross the small stream over a pucca bridge and the cemented path ascends gently to the north-west, up the hill to the small village of **Deora**. ⚠ You can ask anyone for **Nar Singh's house** and bunk down for the night after a wholesome dinner of rotis and delicious local saag.

DAY TWO

DEORA-DHAULACHINA
DISTANCE 12 KM **TIME** 4-5 HOURS
LEVEL EASY

From the top of **Deora Village** follow the level path leading out to the east and then north-east, skirting the hill and then gently descending through groves of pine. It passes by the village of **Chirala** before descending sharply down to the valley floor. Follow the track heading north-northeast until you see a temple down by the stream on your right. Take the path on your right, heading to the old **Sapteshwar Mahadev Temple**. There is a ☕ teashop by the stream where you can stop for a break after visiting the temple. The walk from Deora should have taken no longer than 1-1$\frac{1}{2}$ hours. From the teashop backtrack to the point where you turned off on the path to the right. Now head north for a few minutes and then take a left into the valley heading to the north-west.

It is more convenient to walk on the cemented walls of the irrigation channel, but do this only if you have a head for heights. Otherwise, descend to the valley floor and walk up north-west, crossing the stream over a pucca bridge. The path ascends gently for about an hour to the small hamlet of **Palyu**, then goes level, still heading north-west for a short while through pine forests, before dropping down to a small shallow stream. Cross easily and climb up to the other bank. We had a sad experience here when we found a bull, half-eaten by wild animals, dying slowly. We tried to get help and even tried to put the animal out of its misery, but after an hour, we had to give up and leave it to its sorry fate.

From here, head north for about 5 mins and you will come to a wide ditch. Head left, up the ditch due north-west, for literally 2 mins, and you will find a path leading up the steep embankment to your right. A scramble up the steep slope will bring you onto the main road. From here scramble up the hill in front of you again, moving a few degrees to your left, or north, through forests until you come upon a clearing with a few houses. This is the hamlet of **Kahlon** and from here you will find the

Koklass pheasant

These pheasants are as big as a domestic fowl (51-61 cm) with a medium-sized tail. You may hear its loud kok-kok-kokha call at dawn and dusk. These are birds of dramatic appearance. Males have a metallic green head, a long brown crest and pointed chestnut-brown tail. It is largely silvery-grey with black streaks. The females have shorter crests and are brown and black. The

SANJEEVA PANDEY

species is found in the Western Himalayas, from Afghanistan, Pakistan, India, Nepal, to parts of China. In some parts of the Indian Himalayas, the species is still plentiful, though they are classified as vulnerable.

Koklass pheasants (*Pucrasia macrolopha*) are still being hunted for food in some parts in their native habitat. Deforestation and encroachment for agriculture appear to have considerable bearing on their conservation status in the wild.

Verdant fields near the village of Chirala

'cheh-footiya' path, which winds its way up to Dhaulachina.

The last section, from the first houses of **Dhaulachina** to the main road and the Eco Tourist Resort, is a bit of a climb. But you will be in Dhaulachina by lunchtime and so you can head straight for the up-scale dhaba, the **Hill View Hotel and Restaurant**, for a filling lunch of delicious dal-subzi and tandoori rotis. Head uphill a few hundred metres to the ▲ **Eco Tourist Resort** afterwards. You will still have the entire afternoon and evening free and that can be spent birding in the forests around Dhaulachina.

DAY THREE
DHAULACHINA-JWALABANJ
DISTANCE 10 KM **TIME** 3-4 HOURS
LEVEL EASY

Take the small track in front of the resort gate, which heads uphill to the north. In about 20-30 mins, you will come to the gates of the **Mata Anandmayi Ashram**. This serene spot sits on the top of the ridge commanding magnificent views all around. The buildings have a desolate air about them, apparently so since the Mataji passed away in 1982. Head east, past the buildings, and find a broad path leading eastwards out of the gate and descending gently through chir forests. The path skirts along the hill, and to your right and below is a bowl of pretty, green terraced fields and hamlets. After about an hour, you will come to a lone mud-hut, a 🍵 chai shop that is a good place for a break. From here the road turns gently to the north-east, ascending slowly through thick oak and rhododendron forests. It is a pretty route and, post-monsoons, offers great Himalayan views to your right. After about 2-3 hrs, when you find the road turning east again, look up to about one o'clock (north-east). On the top of the hill you will be able to see the glinting white houses of **Jwalabanj**. Now look to your left and find a narrow track leading off from the main road. The track climbs steeply up a couple of hundred metres and deposits you to ▲ **Umed Singh's home**, your night stay at Jwalabanj.

DAY FOUR
JWALABANJ-JAGESHWAR VIA VRIDH JAGESHWAR
DISTANCE 7 KM **TIME** 2½-3½ HOURS
LEVEL EASY

Wake early at dawn the next morning, head to the rock garden and look to the north-east. You will get a spectacular view of the Central Himalayas, right from **Neelkunth** in Garhwal to **Nampa** in Nepal. If you have the energy you can climb the hill behind the guest house for the 360-degree views. The climb up will take about 30 min to 1 hr, so factor that in when planning the day.

After breakfast, return to the point where the track brought you up to the ridge. You will see a split. Yesterday, you came up the track on your left. Today, take the track on your right. It soon becomes a wide jeepable road, taking you past a few ☕ tea-shops.

I stepped up on the roof of one of them and enjoyed the morning sun and the views to the north-west, over the tops of rhododendrons. Continue on the path heading north. At one point, perhaps 10-15 mins after the teashops, there is a short-cut, which leads off to the left. Climb up. The thin track goes parallel to the main road but here you get the views that are otherwise hidden by the hillside, if you continue on the road. The track has a couple of points where enormous boulders provide perfect picnic spots, so if you don't like early breakfasts you could pack rotis and have a picnic on the rocks. The track soon curves back to meet the road, onto which you descend gently to **Vridh Jageshwar.**

The Mahegad Shiv Temple

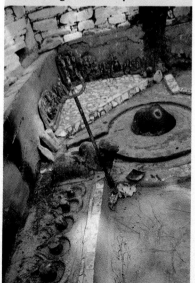

The route from **Jwalabanj** should not take you more than 1^1/$_2$-2 hrs even if you stopped for breakfast. Plan to spend a little time at the temple here. Even if you're an non-believer, it's difficult not to be impressed by the 1,200-year-old temple. Unlike the predatory mahants at Jageshwar, the old pandits here are gentle and welcoming. There is a palpable air of devotion and love, especially in the offerings of wild flowers beautifully arranged in the sanctum sanctorum.

The path to Jageshwar continues below the old temple, veers towards the east and drops down zig-zagging through the pine forests to the large temple complex of Jageshwar (9th-12th centuries), one of the 12 sites of the revered Jyotirlingas. You can spend a whole day wandering around among the hundred-odd stone temples and shrines. Get rid of the pesky pandits who offer nirvana for Rs 50 and take in the spirit of the place in solitude. For me the most spectacular sight was that of the ancient towering cedars, bestowing an ethereal majesty to the impressive complex. The silence of the place was broken only by the raucous cries of the huge, black ravens that circled the trees. But this is never so during Shivratri when thousands of devotees throng the complex and celebrate the festival.

From here, on your return to **Almora**, you can stop at the other old **temple of Dandeshwar**, and also check out the amazing prehistoric rock paintings at **Lakhudiar**.

TREKKING OPTION
On Day One, head to **Binsar Sanctuary** by taxi, stay overnight at the **Forest Rest House** and then head 14 km north-east to **Dhaulachina** on Day Two.

For rest house bookings and hotels, see Accommodation Listings on pages 533 (Binsar) and 534-535 (Jageshwar) ✦

NORTH-EAST

Graphic by ANIS KHAN

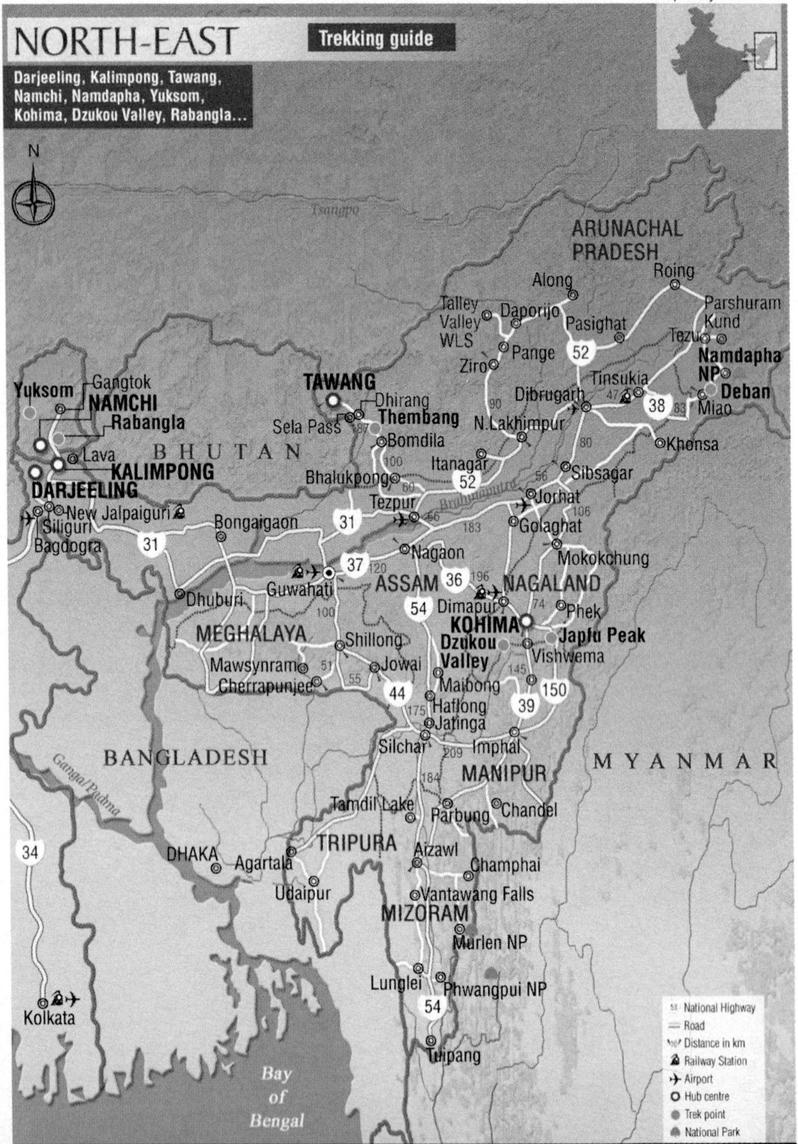

NORTH-EAST

Trekking guide

Darjeeling, Kalimpong, Tawang,
Namchi, Namdapha, Yuksom,
Kohima, Dzukou Valley, Rabangla...

N

ARUNACHAL PRADESH

Along
Roing
Talley Valley WLS
Daporijo
Pasighat
Parshuram Kund
Tezu
Ziro
Pange
52
Namdapha NP
Tinsukia
Deban
TAWANG
Dhirang
Dibrugarh
47
38 83 Miao
Yuksom
Gangtok
Yuksom
NAMCHI
Rabangla
Sela Pass
Thembang
N Lakhimpur
90
Khonsa
Bomdila
Lava
BHUTAN
100
Itanagar
80
Khonsa
KALIMPONG
Bhalukpong
52
56
Sibsagar
DARJEELING
Tezpur
Brahmaputra
Jorhat
New Jalpaiguri
Bongaigaon
31
66
60
183
Golaghat
106
Siliguri
Bagdogra
31
Nagaon
Mokokchung
Guwahati
37
120
ASSAM 36
196
NAGALAND
Dhuburi
100
54 Dimapur
74
Phek
MEGHALAYA
Shillong
KOHIMA
Japfu Peak
Dzukou Valley
Vishwema
Mawsynram
51
Jowai
Maibong
145
55
44
150
Cherrapunjee
175
Haflong
39
Jatinga
BANGLADESH
Silchar
209
Imphal
MYANMAR
184
MANIPUR
Tamdil Lake
Parbung
Chandel
34
DHAKA
Agartala
TRIPURA
Aizwal
Udaipur
Champhai
Vantawang Falls
MIZORAM
Murlen NP
Lunglei
Phwangpui NP
Kolkata
54
Tuipang
Bay of Bengal
Gangeo/Padma

51 National Highway
Road
Distance in km
Railway Station
Airport
Hub centre
Trek point
National Park

One day, in 1829, two British agents, sent to explore the region, stumbled upon a stunning view of Darjeeling and the breathtakingly rapturous beauty of the Kangchendzonga Range. It had been hitherto hidden by a thick jungle of oak and rhododendron, but it didn't take the British too long to make it habitable.

Today Darjeeling wears its 'Queen of the Hill Stations' title a bit wearily. But the tourists still come running, for 'Dorje Ling', or Place of the Thunderbolt, remains just as alluring, with its little villages, moss-laden rocks and tiny waterfalls hidden beneath fern thickets and wild roses.

MUST-VISITS

DOWNTOWN DARJEELING
Chowrasta, the main town square, is crowded with shops, restaurants, curio dealers, hawkers and pony-wallahs.

TOY TRAIN THRILLS
You should catch a ride on the lovely Darjeeling Toy Train (a UNESCO World Heritage Railway) as it chugs slowly from Kurseong to Ghoom.

MOUNTAINEERING HISTORY
Established in 1954, the Himalayan Mountaineering Institute (HMI) had the honour of having the Everest hero, Tenzing Norgay, as its first director. On Birch Hill Park, it is home to the fascinating Mountaineering Museum.

CHAI GARAM
Learn the difference between Flowery Golden Orange Pekoe and Fannings by dropping into world-famous tea estates around here — Runglee Rungliot, Happy Valley, Thurbo, Margaret's Hope and Castleton.

RARE EXOTICA
Padmaja Naidu Zoological Park has the Siberian Tiger and the Snow Leopard Breeding Centre. Timings 9-11 am, 2-3.30 pm; entry fee Rs 10.

WHERE TO STAY
The Windamere Hotel (Tel: 0354-2254041; Tariff: Rs 4,320-7,200) has comfortable rooms with fireplaces and bar but no TV. The New Elgin (Tel: 2254114; Tariff: Rs 3,800-4,100), over 100 years old, offers fine rooms with Burma teak floors, antique furniture and fireplaces. Lowis Jubilee Complex (Tel: 2256395; Tariff: Rs 150-180) offers h/c water and has a restaurant. Darjeeling Tourist Lodge (Tel: 2254411-13; Tariff: Rs 400-1,600) has a bar service.
For more hotels and details, see Accommodation Listings on pages 540-541

→ Darjeeling Facts

● **LOCATION** At the northern tip of West Bengal, Darjeeling (7,004 ft) is nestled in the Eastern Himalayas, close to Sikkim, Nepal and Bhutan
● **GETTING TO DARJEELING By air** Nearest airport: Bagdogra (94 km/ 3 hrs). Taxi Rs 1,200 **By rail** Nearest railhead: **New Jalpaiguri Junction** (90 km/ 3 hrs). Taxi Rs 1,200; bus Rs 65 **By road** From Siliguri (83 km), it's a 3-hr drive up the Hill Cart Road to Darjeeling
● **STD CODE** 0354
● **PERMITS** Foreigners do not need a permit upto 15 days in Darjeeling. For over 15 days, they must procure a permit from any Indian mission abroad or from the Foreigners' Regional Registration Office (FRRO) in Delhi (Tel: 011-26711384; website: immigrationindia. nic.in). However, if coming by air, they must report to the FRRO at Bagdogra Airport on arrival and departure, for endorsements on their passports

WHERE TO EAT
Breakfast at **Keventer's** on delicious eggs, cheese and bacon. **Supersoft Ice-Cream Parlour** has genuinely creamy handmade ice-creams and other yummy snacks. Visit **Glenary's** for homemade chocolates, gooey eclairs, cakes, pastries and soft warm bread. For steaming thukpa, momos and unforgettable chilli chutney, try **Dekevas**. You can dine at the **Darjeeling Planter's Club** or at the **Windamere Hotel** even if you don't stay there, with advance notice.

INPUTS FROM SHIBANI CHAUDHURY

Tiger Hill
The Darjeeling workout
By Tashi Tobgyal

Photographs by TASHI TOBGYAL

TIME	1 day
LEVEL	Easy
IDEAL SEASON	Mar to Apr, Oct to Nov
LOCATION	Near Ghoom, Darjeeling District

Visitors enjoying Tiger Hill

CHOWRASTA-TOONGSOONG-ALOO BARI-
JOREBUNGALOW-SENCHAL-TIGER HILL

Tiger Hill is a favourite early morning destination for holidaymakers in Darjeeling. Join them at your peril. You will be jostling with droves of loud tourists impatient to get their photos taken against the backdrop of the Kan-

Bharat Petroleum

GETTING THERE AND OUT

The hike starts from central Darjeeling (**Chowrasta**)
RETURN Get picked up at **Tiger Hill** (12 km/ 40 mins) for the return journey to Darjeeling, if you don't want to walk back. (Sumos, Maruti Vans, jeeps) charge Rs 600-700 approx. Book taxi in advance at Chowk Bazaar in Darjeeling. Shared taxis/ buses not available

gchendzonga Range. It is much more civilised to walk up and reach by late afternoon, catch the evening views and, if you aren't in too much of a hurry, you may even opt to spend the night and catch the sunrise before the big rush of tourists starts.

If you have indulged in too much food and drink, this day hike will help you get trim. Mountaineers and trekkers, scheduled for the higher altitude treks in Sikkim, usually do this walk as part of their acclimatisation, and to get their bodies into a comfortable rhythm. If you have your kids along on the trip, don't worry. Just rent a pony or two from the stables at Chowrasta, put them astride, and let them follow. They will happily play cowboy for the rest of the day.

Besides walking on this pretty nature trail along old forests, you can even get a glimpse of Tibetan Buddhist culture. Stop at the old Mag Dhog

Yolmowa Gompa, built by the Ven Sangay Lama of Yolmo, during the First World War in 1914. *Mag Dhog* means to ward off war, and that one is dedicated to world peace. The interior of the monastery has murals depicting the Buddha in different forms and mudras, painted with natural mineral and vegetable paints in the Tibetan art style prevalent in the region. It houses ancient Termas, the esoteric, secret teachings of the great Tibetan Buddhist masters. You can stop here and buy Tibetan and Sikkimese handicrafts and religious objects from the monks.

Another interesting stopover on this trail is the ancient Buddhist graveyard, two turns before you reach the monastery. In the old days, Tantric lamas used to practise the Chod ritual where they would allow spirits to 'feed' on their bodies to gain greater tantric powers. This was done in the middle of the night at this graveyard. Good thing the hike takes you past the

Graphic by ANIS KHAN

TIGER HILL | TREKKING GUIDE

Darjeeling
Chowrasta 2,134m
To Kalimpong
Toong Soong
To Manebhanjan
Aloo Bari
Jalapahar
Ghoom
Jorebungalow
Tiger Hill
Campsite
Trek
Road
Monastery
Tea stall
Senchal Lake 2,529m
NH 55
Map Area
N
To Siliguri
North-East

LIFE IS CALLING WHERE ARE YOU? SMIRNOFF
Cassettes and CDs

Sacred groves above the Satya Yug Cave temple

Thick forests above Senchal Lake

spot in broad daylight. Locals still believe that if you happen to walk past this route at dusk, evil spirits are likely to pounce on you! The tombs lie in an unkempt state, overrun by ferns and mosses, and the graveyard is full of beautiful, ageing Japanese pines (*Cryptomeria japonica*) and oak trees.

You wouldn't believe it when you see just how urbanised Darjeeling has become, but the woods of this area are home to a number of birds and animals. Look out for the endangered hill partridge, the broad-billed warbler and the white-tailed robin.

WARNING Stinging nettles en route!

THE TREK

DISTANCE 13-14 KM **TIME** 5 HOURS
LEVEL EASY

The hike starts from **Chowrasta** in Darjeeling (2,134m), going past the stables on the quiet but wide **Tenzing**

Norgay jeep track, past the settlements of **Toong Soong** and **Aloo Bari**, with its old monastery. The greenery around Aloo Bari thickens and you enter a peaceful area away from the mad rush of Darjeeling. Along the route to **Jorebungalow**, you will pass a few small hamlets, inhabited by the Tamangs, Rais and Bhutias, who trace their roots to Tibet. Stop here for a meal of local food. Besides the ubiquitous momos, try the *gundruk* with rice and the *sel* roti with dum aloo.

En route, there are many spots where you can just lie down in the bright sunlight and enjoy the solitude, particularly **Money Point**, marked by a cheery little brook, 3 km beyond the **Mag Dhog Monastery**. Just before you reach the dingy, damp town of Jorebungalow, there is a trail to the right, climbing up for about 2 km. It ends at the **Jalapahar Cantonment**, a British Raj remnant, and the way to St Paul's School. This area has been the training ground of the Gorkhas for centuries.

On returning from Tiger Hill, you can walk back to Darjeeling town via Jalapahar and catch lovely views of the **Kangchendzonga**, and the hills around Darjeeling, even the far away **Kurseong**, **Mirik**, and **Sandakphu**, and the distant plains of Bengal.

From Jorebungalow, you can hike up about a kilometre to visit the **Jathe Rinpoche Monastery**, associated with the Nyingmapa school of Buddhism. Or carry on to Tiger Hill. From Jorebungalow, you have two options to reach Tiger Hill. The first is to walk up the motorable route, but the second trail will have you move further outside the town and into wilderness.

A couple of hours climb through woods will bring you to **Senchal Lake** (2,529m), located on a plateau. It is the source of drinking water for Darjeeling. The forest here is evergreen and wooded, with a mix of the many species of the rhododendrons along with remnant oak, bamboo thickets,

Approaching the summit of Tiger Hill

ferns and wild orchids. Locals believe that the woods are enchanted. The forest spirit, called the *Banjhakri*, takes on different forms of animals and birds. Throughout the hike, one will come across miniature shrines devoted to the spirits of the woods.

Just before finally climbing up to the top of the hill, you will come across a creek from where you can see the terraces of Tiger Hill and the ancient temples above. A few minutes later, the trail joins the jeep track, which glides up from **Jorebungalow**. Another easy kilometre and **Tiger Hill** is reached.

As one stands atop the Tiger Hill, one is absolutely enchanted by the panoramic views of the guardians of Tibet. The tallest is the **Kangchendzonga**, to the left, as is the road to Lhasa, the ice-covered **Jelep La Pass** into Tibet. The top of **Everest** forms a straight line to Tiger Hill, 172 km away. **Chomolari**, on the border of Bhutan, and the **Yatung Valley** are also clearly seen. The other peaks visible are **Makalu,**

Offerings to female deities

Pandim, Kabru, Siniolochu, Kothang, Janu, Pandim, Simvu, Kumbakaran and Ratong. Also visible from here are the great rivers tumbling into the plains of Bengal — the **Teesta, Mahanadi, Balasun** and the **Mechi**, all meandering southwards.

Take a few minutes to hike uphill to the cave temples, said to be dated from the Satya Yug. Here resides the guardian deity of Tiger Hill. Even though it is a shrine devoted to Shiva, people of all faiths claim this as home of their favourite deities. One cave is believed to have its exit 76 km away, in Siliguri!

If you wish to see a sublime sunrise, camp overnight. There is abundant water and space in the grounds, to the right of the welcome gate. Early next morning, if you are lucky with the weather, hold your breath. You will see the most awesome sight of the sun gilding over the **Great Himalayan Range**.

On your return, either catch a jeep taxi or walk to Darjeeling via Jalapahar. ✦

The Singalila Trek
Come, see, be conquered

TIME	4-7 days
LEVEL	Easy to Moderate
IDEAL SEASON	Oct to mid-Dec, Apr to late-May
LOCATION	Darjeeling District, North Bengal

By Sujoy Das

The lovely views of the Kangchendzonga Range from Sandakphu

MANEBHANJAN-JAUBARI-SANDAKPHU-PHALUT-RAMAM-RIMBIK

Usually classified as an entry level 'first' trek, Sandakphu-Phalut is ideal for tourists who want an introduction to trekking but are not quite sure what to expect. There are bungalows and lodges along the way and food is also available, so there is no need for provisions and a lot of equipment. The trails are well defined and the trek can easily be handled without using porters if you can carry your own gear. The maximum altitude reached is about 3,600m so the problems of high-altitude sickness and acclimatisation are minimised.

Sandakphu was my first trek when I was in school. I still remember standing on the Singalila Ridge and gazing in awe at the ethereal beauty of Kangchendzonga dominating the entire horizon. From Phalut, the magnificent peak is at 'handshaking distance'. Subsequently, I have made about six trips to the Singalila Ridge in various seasons, including a winter visit in January, which, to my amazement, offered spectacular views right through the day with no clouds or haze! It is one of the few locations in the world that offers a view of four of the world's five highest mountains — Everest, Kangchendzonga, Lhotse and Makalu, amongst many others.

During late spring in April, the rhododendrons and magnolias are in bloom, and the hillsides are covered with red, pink, yellow and white blooms. Being primarily a 'ridge walk', there are views on all sides especially towards Nepal. An interesting sight is watching the cars at night, lit up like pinpricks on the distant Darjeeling hillside, their lights moving slowly against the black background many miles away to the south.

TIP It is possible to do this trek in a number of variants. Those with less time can complete it in four days

Graphic by ANIS KHAN

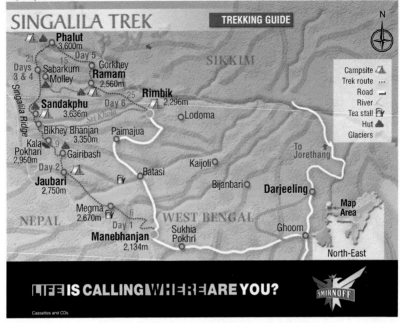

SINGALILA TREK

TREKKING GUIDE

N

Phalut
3,600m

Day 5

21
Days   15   Gorkhey
3 & 4   Sabarkum   Ramam
Molley   2,560m

SIKKIM

Campsite
Trek route
Road
River
Tea stall
Hut
Glaciers

Rimbik
25   2,296m

Sandakphu   Day 6
3,636m   Sri Khola   Lodoma

Bikhey Bhanjan   Paimajua
3,350m
Kala   9
Pokhari   Gairibash
2,950m
Day 2

To
Jorethang

Batasi
Kaijoli

Jaubari
2,750m

Bijanbari   Darjeeling

Map
Area

Megma
2,670m   6
Day 1
Manebhanjan
2,134m

WEST BENGAL

Ghoom

North-East

NEPAL

Sukhia
Pokhri

(Darjeeling-Manebhanjan-Jaubari-Sandakphu-Rimbik-Darjeeling). The trip to Phalut and back, via Ramam and Rimbik, described here, would take six to seven days, including travelling to and from Darjeeling

DAY ONE

MANEBHANJAN-JAUBARI
DISTANCE 6 KM **TIME** 4-5 HOURS
LEVEL EASY-MODERATE

The trail from **Manebhanjan** (2,134m) starts at the bazaar and, as you walk down the main road, there is a steep hill in front of you with a short-cut trail to the left. Above, the main road is clearly defined. Take this short-cut and immediately start climbing the hill to Chitre. The trail sometimes criss-crosses the jeepable road to Sandakphu, but it is advisable not to take the jeepable road as the distance and time taken will be far greater. After about 1½ hrs of climbing above Manebhanjan, you

reach a clearing with the monastery of **Chitre**. The trail passes the monastery to the left and continues to zig-zag up the hill in a northerly direction. About 3 hrs from Manebhanjan, you reach **Megma**, where tea shops are available for food and refreshments.

The start from Manebhanjan

Primulas

Drumstick primula

These pretty flowers are found in shrubberies and open slopes in moist situations, often along drains, between 1,500 and 4,500m. The plant is a perennial, usually growing 15-30 cm tall. It has purple to mauve-blue or, occasionally, white flowers. The drumstick primula (*Primula denticulata* [with small teeth]) flowers from May to June. The flowers are hermaphrodite (have both male and female organs) and are pollinated by insects. Flowers may be eaten raw after a thorough wash. They make a very attractive addition to salads.

Large-leaved primula

Found at elevations between 3,600 and 4,800m, the *Primula macrophylla* (large-leaved) is a perennial shrub growing to 12-25 cm. It bears an umbel of purple, violet or lilac flowers with dark centres. These primulas flower from July to August. The entire plant is used in Tibetan medicine. It has a bitter taste and a cooling potency. Anti-diarrhetic, anti-inflammatory and febrifuge, it is used variously in the treatment of diarrhoea, inflammation of the liver, gall bladder, stomach and intestines. It is especially used for children with high fever and diarrhoea.

Bharat Petroleum

GETTING THERE AND OUT

FROM DARJEELING to Mane-bhanjan, it's 25 km/ 1½ hrs by 🚙 (Rs 1,500/ shared jeep Rs 35) or 2 hrs by 🚌 (Rs 25). Buses leave Chowk Bazaar Bus Stand at 6.30 am but the service is erratic. The route goes via Ghoom and Sukhia Pokhri

RETURN Get picked up at **Rimbik** for **Darjeeling** (85 km/ 5 hrs) by pre-booked taxi (Rs 1,500) from Darj or Rimbik. Shared jeeps (Rs 80) and buses (6 hrs/ Rs 150) also available from Rimbik Bazaar, but very few and not in the afternoon. Buses run between 7 and 9 am. Plan on reaching Rimbik by noon if you wish to get back the same day. Else, pitch tent for the night in the Green View Hotel compound

The trail now levels out, skirts the hill to the left and climbs gently to the south-west to Jaubari. Megma to Jaubari would probably take 2 hrs of easy walking. **Jaubari** (2,750m) is a long village with open meadows and houses lined on either side.

Walk till the end of the village until you come to the hotels and guest houses. Food and spartan accommodation is available at Jaubari.

DAY TWO
JAUBARI-SANDAKPHU
DISTANCE 9 KM **TIME** 6-7 HOURS
LEVEL MODERATE

The trail passes through **Jaubari Village** and comes to a crossing. Proceeding straight would take you to Nepal so there is an arrow marked 'Sandakphu' and you should take the right hand fork at the crossing, which

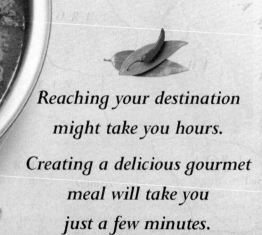

Reaching your destination might take you hours.

Creating a delicious gourmet meal will take you just a few minutes.

Next time you go on a trek don't forget to carry your favourite Kitchens of India curry pastes. So that when you take that well deserved break, making a delicious gourmet dish will take you all of a few minutes.

CURRY PASTE

A feast for the senses

MUTTON CURRY PASTE, **CHICKEN CURRY PASTE,** BUTTER CHICKEN CURRY PASTE, FISH CURRY PASTE, HYDERABADI BIRYANI PASTE & VEGETABLE BIRYANI PASTE.

For further information email us at kitchensofindia@itc.co.in

Fresh harvest of vegetables at Megma Village

proceeds due north-east. The trail then drops for about 30 mins to **Gairibash**, where there are ▲ **Trekkers' Huts** and **lodges**. Some trekkers prefer to skip Jaubari and make Gairibash the first night halt. The trail then climbs a hill for about 2 hrs through the forest and then descends to **Kala Pokhari** (2,950m), which has a lake with black waters and hence the name. From Kala Pokhari, there is a further climb of a couple of hours and then a descent to **Bikhey Bhanjan** (3,350m).

☞ Trekkers are advised to stop at Bikhey Bhanjan for refreshments as the steep climb to **Sandakphu** starts from here. The trail zig-zags its way up the hill, passing clumps of aconite (the poison plant). The path is now windswept and, to the west, the hills of Nepal can be clearly seen shimmering in the sunlight. Finally, after about 1¹/₂ hrs of stiff walking, the huts of Sandakphu can be seen on the ridge above.

▲ **Sandakphu** (3,636m) has a number of **Trekkers' Huts** and **bungalows**, so accommodation should not be a problem and bookings are not usually necessary, other than some days of the peak season in October. For those who do not wish to proceed to

Phalut, there is a route from Sandakphu to Rimbik, from where buses/shared taxis are available for Darjeeling. Retrace your footsteps down to **Bikhey Bhanjan**. From here there is a steep downhill trail through the forest heading east to Rimbik, taking about 6-7 hrs.

DAY THREE
REST DAY AT SANDAKPHU

It is advisable to have a rest day at Sandakphu, to savour the views of the mountains. There is a 180-degree view of open skies with snow-clad peaks dominating the horizon. To the west, you see **Lhotse** (8,501m), **Everest** (8,848m), **Makalu** (8,475m), **Chamlang** (7,319m), **Baruntse** (7,129m) and other peaks of the Nepal Himalayas.

Along the ridge, facing the north, are **Kokthang** (6,147m), **Rathong** (6,679m), **Kabru South** (7,317m), **Talung** (7,349m), **Janu** (7,710m) and the massive **Kangchendzonga** (8,586m). Further to the east is a breathtaking sight of the beautiful **Pandim** (6,691m) floating over the forested ridges of Sikkim, with **Simvu** (6,811m) and **Jobonu** (5,936m) peaks also visible.

EMBARK ON A WILD ADVENTURE

PENCH
BANDHAVGARH
RANTHAMBHORE

DAY FOUR

Sandakphu-Phalut

Distance 21 km **Time** 6-8 hours
Level Moderate

It is a 21-km walk from Sandakphu to Phalut, along the Singalila Ridge. The trail initially climbs north, above the cluster of bungalows at Sandakphu and then heads north-eastwards. This is the most beautiful part of the trek as the walk is largely level with magnificent views towards Nepal, as well as over Sikkim towards **Kangchendzonga**. During April and May, dwarf rhododendrons are in bloom as well as other Himalayan flora like primulas, anemones and crocuses. The silver-fir forest below the trail makes a beautiful sight. Overhead, one can spot birds like the lammergeier soaring over the peaks. After about 5 hrs of walking you come to **Sabarkum** (about 14 km from Sandakphu). **Molley** is 2 km to the east. There is a **Trekkers' Hut** at Molley if you need to stop overnight. But for Phalut, follow the trail northwards, keeping the Singalila Ridge on the left.

After about an hour the trail begins to climb through a series of zigzags till one reaches the 🔺 Trekkers' Hut. From the hut, the Phalut summit is about 20 minutes walk up the hill.

The steep slog up

Phalut (3,600m) is the tri-junction of Sikkim, West Bengal and Nepal. The view is the same as that at Sandakphu, except that the **Kangchendzonga Range** looks close enough to touch. The **Everest group** is also clearly visible to the west.

DAY FIVE

Phalut-Ramam

Distance 15 km **Time** 5-6 hours
Level Easy

Footprints mark a snow-covered Phalut in winter

The black redstart

The black and orange-chestnut colouring, the constantly shivering tail and dipping body distinguishes this sparrow-sized bird (*Phoenicurus ochruros*). The female redstart is brown and paler, but also has an orange-chestnut tail. They are found throughout the Himalayas, between 3,000 and 6,000m, even in Ladakh. In winter, they can be seen in the plains, more or less in all parts of India. They can be found in groves of trees, stony hummocks and dry scrub jungle, flitting from perch to perch, ceaselessly shivering their tails. Salim Ali delightfully describes their call as a, "sharp, mousy, whit…whit… reminiscent of a squeaking unoiled bicycle wheel revolving at moderate speed," though he concedes that in the breeding season the male "utters a pleasant little song".

From Phalut, the path descends the ridge through forests of chestnut, pine, hemlock and fir. The trail drops steeply south-eastwards for about 2 hrs till it reaches the meeting of two streams called the **Gorkhey Khola**, which is a tributary of the fast flowing **Ramam River**. It is a beautiful spot amidst thick, lush and green forest. Take a dip in the river and cool off, as there is a 1$^1/_2$-hr climb ahead to Samandin. Brown dippers, redstarts and forktails are often seen here, flitting by the sides of the stream.

Situated on a plateau, is the small village of **Samandin**. From here, the road descends to a small stream and again climbs up south for another hour and a half to the 🔺 **Ramam Trekkers' Hut** (2,560m).

TREKKING OPTION

There is an alternate route from Phalut to Ramam that goes via Sabarkum on the Singalila Ridge — from Sabarkum, turn left. This trail passes through virgin forest, which is a steep downhill to Ramam. This takes about 5 hrs and is about 16 km from Phalut. However, it is advisable not to take this trail in the late afternoon, especially in winter, as it gets dark by 4 pm and navigating through the forest is a difficult task then. The route via Gorkhey and Samandin is usually preferred.

DAY SIX

RAMAM-RIMBIK
DISTANCE 25 KM **TIME** 7-8 HOURS
LEVEL EASY

The first 2$^1/_2$ hrs is on a level pathway through the forest. This part of the trail is a paradise for birdwatchers with redstarts, tree pies and whistling thrushes being some of the species visible. The trail then leaves the forest and goes steeply downhill, due south for about an hour till it crosses the **Sri Khola Stream** over a bridge. From this point the road runs uphill at a gentle gradient, through forest and fields, till one reaches 🔺 **Rimbik** (2,296m) about 1$^1/_2$ hrs away. Stay overnight at Rimbik or if you've reached early, head back to Darjeeling or to Siliguri.

For Trekkers' Huts in Sandakphu, see
Accommodation Listings on page 543 ✦

SWAPAN NAYAK

Monks at Tharpa Choeling Monastery

Most of the drive to Kalimpong from Siliguri is along the Sevoke forests fringing the Teesta River. About halfway, the graceful Coronation Bridge leads off to the right towards the Dooars, Bengal's tea country and further upstream, magnificent river views are to be had. Once a transit point for Himalayan explorers, Kalimpong's alti-

cheese at the market, and visit **Dr Graham's Home** situated at the base of Deolo Hill. **St Theresa's Church**, built by local craftsmen to resemble a gompa, has woodcarvings on the walls that depict biblical scenes and sculpted figures resembling Buddhist monks.

FLOWER NURSERIES
One of Kalimpong's greatest USPs is that the area produces 80 per cent of India's gladioli. On offer are orchids, azaleas and other seasonal flowers.

RIVER CHALLENGE
The tossing waters of the Teesta invite the adventurous. **River rafting** here is both safe and thrilling.

→ Kalimpong Facts

- **LOCATION** Kalimpong (1,250m) is nestled in the north Bengal Himalayan foothills, east of Darjeeling across the stunning Teesta Gorge
- **GETTING TO KALIMPONG By air** Nearest airport: Bagdogra (80 km/2^1/$_2$ hrs), serviced by Indian Airlines and Jet Airways. Taxi Rs 1,000, shared jeep Rs 80 **By rail** Nearest railhead: New Jalpaiguri (74 km/ 2^1/$_2$ hrs). Taxi Rs 1,100; shared jeep Rs 100 **By road** From Siliguri (69 km/ 2^1/$_2$ hrs), it's a breathtaking if sometimes heart-stopping drive across the Teesta Gorge to Kalimpong. Drive on NH31 past the Coronation Bridge following the Teesta River. At Teesta Village, cross the bridge to the right and immediately take the turn-off up to Kalimpong. Buses and jeeps from Siliguri and Darjeeling to Kalimpong
- **STD CODE** 03552
- **TOURIST OFFICE** Morgan House, Kalimpong Tel: 255384

WHERE TO STAY
Two old colonial bungalows are **Morgan House** (Tel: 03552-255384; Tariff: Rs 500-2,600) and **Tashiding Tourist Lodge** (Tel: 255929; Tariff: Rs 750-1,600). **Himalayan Hotel** (Tel: 255248; Tariff: Rs 1,400-2,200) is surrounded by beautiful gardens. **Hotel Silver Oaks** (Tel: 255266-67; Tariff: Rs 3,500-3,800) has its own bakery. **Diki Lodge** (Tel: 255095; Tariff: Rs 250-900) has decent accommodation with a terrace garden.
For more hotels and details, see Accommodation Listings on pages 541-542

tude and location is ideal for a pleasant, relaxed getaway. Its clement weather is perfect for plants and Kalimpong's flower-nurseries, orchids and gladioli are world-renowned.

WHERE TO EAT
Kalimpong spoils you with steaming momos, thukpa, soup and chow stands at most busy corners. **Glenary's** has opened two eateries on Rishi Road and Ongden Road — both have cakes, pastries, patties, tea and coffee. **Mandarin Restaurant** is a popular eating option and is famous for its fish, roast pork and chicken balls. The **Kalsang Restaurant** on Link Road is a rustic place run by Tibetans.

MUST-VISITS
KALIMPONG SIGHTS
Take an afternoon stroll on the road to the cantonment and **Zang Dog Palri Fo-Brang Gompa**, which passes colonial houses with charming names like **Crookety** and **Morgan House** as well as the **Army Golf Club** (the highest in West Bengal). Buy the famous **Kalimpong**

INPUTS FROM SHIBANI CHAUDHURY

LIFE
IS CALLING
WHERE
ARE YOU?™
SMIRNOFF
STORM
Cassettes and CDs

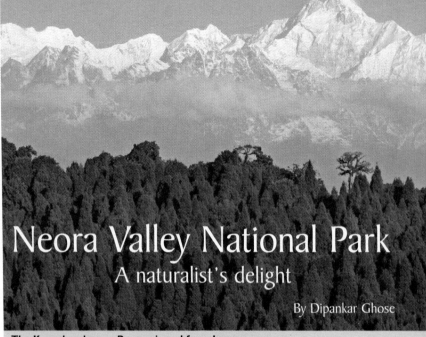

Neora Valley National Park
A naturalist's delight

By Dipankar Ghose

The Kangchendzonga Range viewed from Lava

TIME	4-5 days
LEVEL	Easy to Moderate
IDEAL SEASON	Mar to Jun, Oct to Dec
LOCATION	Darjeeling District, at the tri-junction of Bhutan, West Bengal and Sikkim

ZERO POINT (NEAR LAVA)-ALUBARI-RECHI LA-PANKHASARI-LAVA

Loud hoots, frantic as ambulance sirens, came through the thick lining of my sleeping bag and jolted me awake. I scrambled out of the tent to find the sound coming from the ridge below, then from the slope behind, and then from the hill to the north. As soon as I realised that it was the call of a male satyr tragopan, I ran off to record the time and other details. We were camping at Alubari within the Neora Valley National Park. This was to be

my home, and a source of great delight and excitement, for the next few weeks, as I mapped and researched the wildlife of the region.

The Neora National Park (183–3,200m) is named after the river that flows within the park. The park has a number of torrents and hill streams spread like a net, feeding the Neora River and sustaining a wonderful array of vegetation within the protected area. From tiny wild strawberries, wild white orchids (Kurseong white orchid) and primulas, to the towering Himalayan yew and hemlocks, the park has an amazing variety of flora which in turn supports an impressive population of birds and mammals. The area is home to more than 200 species of birds.

The patient trekker has every chance to see the flashy male satyr tragopan, kalij pheasant, golden eagle, Jerdon's baza, nutcracker, magpies and numerous finches and

GETTING THERE AND OUT

FROM KALIMPONG to Lava, it's 32 km/ 1 hr by 🚙 (Rs 800, shared jeep Rs 40) or 2½ hrs by 🚌 (Rs 30) **From Siliguri** you can approach Lava via **Damdim** and **Gorubathan** (100 km) in about 3 hrs (taxi Rs 1,500). Buses also available from Siliguri (5 hrs/ Rs 55) around morning and noon **RETURN** Book taxi in advance in Lava for return to **Kalimpong** or **Siliguri**. The Siliguri bus leaves at 6 am. If you return via Chalsa, you can catch one of the many buses (2 hrs/ Rs 35) to Siliguri (60 km) or take a taxi (1½ hrs/ Rs 600-800)

Graphic by ANIS KHAN

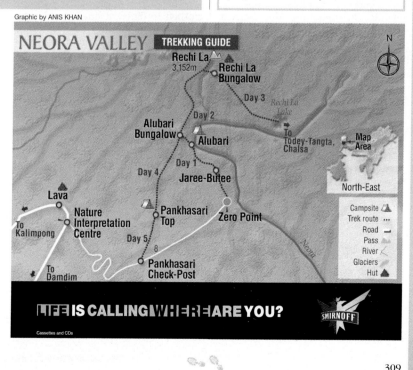

NEORA VALLEY — TREKKING GUIDE

Rechi La 3,152m / Rechi La Bungalow
Day 3
Rechi La Lake
Alubari Bungalow / Alubari
Day 2
To Todey-Tangta, Chalsa
Map Area
North-East
Day 1
Jaree-Butee
Day 4
Lava
Nature Interpretation Centre
Pankhasari Top
Zero Point
To Kalimpong
Day 5
8
Neora
Pankhasari Check-Post
To Damdim

Campsite
Trek route ···
Road
Pass
River
Glaciers
Hut

Morning mist rises off the lake near Todey Tangta

sunbirds. During spring and summer, the entire area is filled with the songs of different species of cuckoos, from the Indian cuckoo and the large hawk cuckoo to the oriental cuckoo and the lesser cuckoo. Mammals in the park include the tiger and the leopard, among the big cats. While pugmarks

Neora NP Entry Facts

● To enter the park, one must have **permission** from the wildlife authorities. Although, in theory, this is possible from the Range Officer in Lava, it is better to get your permissions from **Jalpaiguri** to avoid disappointment. Contact the office of the Divisional Forest Officer (Wildlife Division II), Aranya Bhawan, Jalpaiguri-735101. Tel: 03561-224907.

● **Park entry fee** Rs 20 per day per person, payable at the Forest Department (Wildlife) Range Office at Lava **Camping fee** Rs 200 per person per day, also to be paid here **Porters** Available in Lava town **Porter/ guide fee** Bargain as this could vary from a young lad, totally clueless about the park's conditions, asking for Rs 100 per day for a 25-kg load to Rs 250 per day for a professional porter-cum-guide-cum-cook

● **Trekking agents** See Listings on pages 515-516 for agents who organise treks to Neora NP

and scratch marks of the Asiatic black bear are common, sighting the rare red panda could be difficult. The goral and barking deer oblige by putting in regular appearances.

The higher ridges of the park are clothed in different hues of red, pink and white blooming rhododendrons during the spring and summer. About 10 species of rhododendrons have been recorded here, from the scarlet *gurans* to the milk-white *chimawl*. The trail near the Rechi La top is covered with a veritable red carpet of flowers shed from the trees during this season. Visible from the top of the pass is the magnificent Kangchendzonga Range, a sight that amply compensates for the long hike to the top. In close competition is the breathtaking view of cloud cover, over the valley of Bhutan, on the eastern side of Rechi La.

DAY ONE
ZERO POINT-ALUBARI
DISTANCE 6 KM **TIME** 4 HOURS
LEVEL EASY
On the **Lava-Damdim Road**, a bridle path heading south-east hugs the slope just below the **Nature Interpretation Centre**. An 8-km jeep-taxi drive through the oak-rhododendron-fir

Satyr tragopan or crimson-horned pheasant

Weighing 1 to 2 kg, this vividly coloured bird belongs to the pheasant family. It is listed as 'vulnerable' and it is estimated that there are less than 20,000 remaining in the wild, though out of the four species of tragopans or horned pheasants found in India, this is probably the most visible one. The satyr tragopan (*Tragopan satyra*) inhabits mountainous forests at altitudes of about 2,400-4,200m in summer, and 1,800m in winter.

It is so called because males have protruding fleshy outgrowths above their eyes, giving the appearance of horns. The male's horns and vivid red plumage are central to its courtship displays. Like many other bird species, satyr tragopans are 'monogamous'. They nest in pairs and the males play an active role in nurturing the young. April-June is the breeding season for this species, which is present in good numbers in the Neora Valley, especially around the Alubari camp and the forests further north-east. At dawn and dusk, the male satyr tragopan calls vociferously, cries that sound like a baby's wailing or an ambulance on full alert! Ask the forest guard or guide to look for this bird's droppings on the trail.

forest past the **Pankhasari Check-Post** will take you to a place called the **Zero Point**, where the road ends, and from where you will start walking.

Look for the trail going downhill on the left towards the pump house (today's walk is downhill all the way). This is steep at places so carry a bamboo staff to help stay steady.

En route to Jaree-Butee

About a kilometre away is the **Neora River**. There is also a pipeline that supplies water to the nearby settlements. Walk along the pipeline towards the north-west, entering an oak forest for a couple of kilometres until you arrive at a flat piece of land called **Jaree-Butee**. The place is full of wild strawberries and hidden amidst them are medicinal plants, hence the name Jaree-Butee. Alubari is about 3 km from here. The track continues along mountain streams and enters a moist, temperate forest with long mossy growths hanging down from large oak trees.

The camp at **Alubari** is near the river, and the large rocks provide good shelter for setting up a makeshift kitchen. Spend a night here to see the kalij pheasant, white-throated laughing thrush and chestnut-bellied tesia in the valley. Ask the guide to show you an Asiatic black bear's feeding place on an oak tree, popularly known as *bhalu-ka-gur* or the bear's nest.

311

Bullfinches

Lava and the Neora Valley complex are excellent areas for sighting the resident red-headed bullfinch (*Pyrrhula erythrocephala*) and the grey-headed bullfinch (*Pyrrhula erythaca*). About the size of the bulbul, the bird has a stout, conical, sparrow-like beak, which is used for breaking the cones of coniferous trees. Both species have a very soft voice that is heard in the ridges near Alubari and above. Unlike other passerines, bullfinches are somewhat bold and allow a patient photographer to come closer for a full-frame shot.

DAY TWO

ALUBARI-RECHI LA
DISTANCE 8 KM **TIME** 4-6 HOURS
LEVEL MODERATE

Be prepared for an uphill slog today. Walk out of **Alubari Camp** (3,152m), past an old wooden bungalow, heading north. Watch out for the red-headed bullfinch as they are found in good numbers here and can be a photographer's delight. From this point, the path heading north-east enters dense oak and rhododendron forest interspersed with bamboo groves, climbing uphill, and continuing for about 4 km. While walking, watch out for remnants of camouflaged bunkers, which

Setting up camp at Zero Point

were once used by the Indian Army for keeping an eye on Bhutan and Sikkim. The trail is full of fallen leaves, and goes in a northward direction through fir and hemlock forest and bamboo thickets. The final part of the climb is through rhododendron forest. During spring and summer, there is always a red-carpet welcome for visitors. Before reaching Rechi La, turn towards the east to get to the **Rechi La Bungalow**. ⚠ This is a concrete construction, with a long hall and a kitchen that can accommodate up to 10 people. The toilet, though, is in disrepair.

Rechi La Top can be reached by walking back and following the trail northwards. A short 10-15-min climb will bring you to the top (3,152m). Spend the evening on **Rechi La Top** to see the lights of **Gangtok Valley** and return early the next morning for the sunrise. This place is wonderful for sighting sunbirds and flowerpeckers. Also present is the spotted nutcracker.

DAY THREE

RECHI LA-LAKE (TODEY-TANGTA ROUTE)-RECHI LA
DISTANCE 8 KM **TIME** 6 HOURS
LEVEL MODERATE

Take the trail that goes past the **Rechi La Bungalow** towards the eastern side. It crosses three ridges in a series of switchbacks and goes down towards the villages of **Todey-Tangta** for about 4 km. It doesn't take more than 2 hrs to cross the three ridges and descend. On the right hand side of the trail is a big lake where you can spend some time checking for pugmarks of bear, leopard, goral, barking deer and lesser cats. The waters are clear and the reflection of the blooming rhododendron on its surface is an unforgettable sight. By the side of the trail are makeshift huts of shepherds, locally known as goth. Look out for small white-washed ritual figures on crevices of rocks or slope by the trail. Return to **Rechi La** following the same route for the night.

DAY FOUR

RECHI LA-PANKHASARI
DISTANCE 10 KM **TIME** 6 HOURS
LEVEL EASY-MODERATE

Today is an easy day going downhill all the way to **Alubari**. Follow the same trail from Rechi La Top to Alubari. Just before you reach Alubari, take the road that bypasses the camp and follows the main Pankhasari Ridge uphill in a south-westerly direction. A couple of kilometres from **Alubari Camp** is the area known as **Pankhasari Top**. You will find the ruins of a bungalow built by the Army during the British Raj.
The flat ground provides a good site for pitching tents, but it is advisable to locate the water source, which at times can be quite far from this ridge top. This place is famous for its white and cream-coloured rhododendron or *chimawl*. Spend the evening on the ridge's slopes to hear the hill partridge and satyr tragopan.

DAY FIVE

PANKHASARI-LAVA
DISTANCE 10 KM **TIME** 8 HOURS
LEVEL EASY

Trek downhill, due south-west, following the **Pankhasari Ridge** through the oak forest, and then pine-fir plantations, to reach just above the **Pankhasari Check-Post** on the **Lava-Zero Point** track. From Pankhasari to the check-post takes about 2 hrs, with

sightings of Himalayan greenfinches among the pine plantations. From the check-post, walk back towards Zero Point for some birdwatching. An occasional red panda is also not unusual. This place is full of kalij pheasants, hill partridges and hill barbets. The walk is mostly downhill and there is only one bridle path going down in a general south-westerly direction. The trek following the bridle path to Lava is easier. The other option is to use the *chorbato*, or the steep short-cuts to Lava. At Lava either stay overnight or return to Kalimpong the same day by taxi.

Ritual figures offered to the gods

TREKKING OPTIONS

Instead of returning to Lava from Rechi La, there are two other options that can be followed. With the help of a good guide, one could pass through **Todey-Tangta** to go further south to **Chalsa**, the roadhead in the **Dooars** about 20 km away. It is an easy walk on a motorable road through fields. It takes about an hour and a half by vehicle. So, if you don't feel like walking, a taxi ride is an option.

Seasoned trekkers could do the **Rechi La-Mouchouki-Samsing** route. This route requires some mountaineering experience. Cliff-scaling skills and ropes are useful. **Samsing** is an hour's drive from **Chalsa** town.

For rest house bookings and hotels, see Accommodation Listings on pages 540 (Chalsa) and 542 (Lava).

GOA
is a note of music

Soft and mellow like a jazz composition or loud and brash like a rock anthem... Goa is a harmonious blend of varied notes. There is something about Goa that makes people break into a song ! Some of the country's most gifted singers and musicians are from Goa, from **Surashree Kesarbai Kerkar, Moghubai Kurdikar, Master Dinanath Mangeshkar, Lata Mangeshkar, Pt. Jitendra Abhisheki, Kishori Amonkar, Asha Bhosle,**

DEPARTMENT OF TOURISM

GOVERNMENT OF GOA, Patto, Panaji, Goa - 403 001, India. Tel: 0832 - 24387

Shobha Gurtu, Remo Fernandes, Lorna, and Hema Sardesai.

There's something about Goa that makes the world's best musicians and DJ's want to perform here, year after year. Maybe it's the fact that music is a religion in Goa, a way of attaining salvation.

Music is the glue that binds one Goan to another.

And no one who comes here can remain untouched by it.

www.goatourism.org

A perfect holiday destination

f you don't relish spending long hours driving on mountain roads, consider a holiday in South Sikkim. Namchi is the district headquarters, located just 100 km away from Siliguri. Sky-high is what its name means, and though not quite that at 1,675m, it affords lovely views of the Kangchendzonga Range. It's also a convenient hub from where you can do the short hikes of Rabangla-Mainom Top, Damthang-Tendong and Hilley-Barsai. It also hosts an annual flower festival in April-May and the Namchi Mahotsav in October-November.

→ Namchi Facts

- **LOCATION** North-east of Darjeeling, Namchi is close to the Sikkim-West Bengal state border
- **GETTING TO NAMCHI By air** Nearest airport: Bagdogra (112 km/ 3^1/$_2$ hrs). Taxi Rs 1,750. Ask for taxi with a Namchi permit **By rail** Nearest railhead: New Jalpaiguri (107 km/ 3^1/$_2$ hrs) **By road** From Siliguri (102 km/ 3 hrs), drive on NH31A past Coronation Bridge, alongside the Teesta River. At Teesta Village, cross the bridge to the right and then cross the river again to Melli Bazaar. From Melli Check-Post, take the SPWD Road along the Rangit River to Jorethang (27 km/ 1 hr). Drive to the suspension bridge at town's end; before the bridge take the road on the right to Namchi (19 km/ 40 mins) **Siliguri to Namchi** Good bus connections to Jorethang (83 km/ 2^1/$_2$ hrs/ Rs 1,800). Jorethang to Namchi full taxi Rs 800, shared jeep Rs 45
- **STD CODE** 03595
- **SIKKIM PERMITS Foreigners** need an **Entry Permit** (15 days) for Sikkim, available against a valid passport and visa from any Indian mission abroad or Sikkim tourism offices in Delhi/ Kolkata. At Siliguri, Mr Adhikari, Jt Director, Sikkim Tourism (Siliguri Tel: 0353-2512646, 2512202), is particularly helpful. If visiting/ trekking in restricted areas, they require an **Inner Line Permit** (also known as **Restricted Area Permit**). This can be obtained by government-recognised travel agents, who can also arrange for any trekking permits, forest permits and the obligatory liaison officer required to accompany foreign nationals on treks and in restricted areas. Permit restrictions mean that trekkers can only follow well-beaten trails and within a limited period of time. It helps to carry photocopies of passport and visa along with passport-size photos

MUST-VISITS

BUDDHISM UNPLUGGED

Check out the new colossal 138-ft statue of Guru Padmasambhava at Samdruptse, the biggest in the world. Just below it is a pretty **Rock Garden**, a favourite spot for picnickers because of the gorgeous Kangchendzonga views. **Namchi Monastery**, located just above the town, houses a sculpture of Padmasambhava, dating to the 17th century. Hike through woods to the **Doling Gompa**, an old Nyingmapa monastery.

COTTAGE INDUSTRY

To experience authentic Sikkimese arts and crafts, visit this institution just 2 km from the town centre.

AROUND NAMCHI

A 500-m long vast cavern is a short 5-km hike from Rabangla. **Shar-chok Bé Phug** is known as the abode of the 'Peaceful White Deity'. Full of natural formations, locals come here to cleanse their sins and pray for a happy life.

ANGLING

Just 10 km from Namchi, on the banks of the **River Rangit** at **Sikip**, is an excellent fishing spot and river campsite.

WHERE TO STAY AND EAT

Namchi doesn't boast of many hotels or restaurants. **Hotel Mayal** (Tel: 03595-263588, 263711, 09434127322; Tariff: Rs 300-1,000) on Jorethang Road has a multi-cuisine restaurant, h/c running water and TV in its rooms and organises village tours.

Its restaurant serves regular Indian and Chinese food, and you can order everything from chowmein and momos to dishes typical of Sikkim, such as *shakbaley* (deep-fried meat bread, usually with a chicken filling). **Sam Dupcha**, a multi-cuisine restaurant next door to Hotel Mayal, has a similar menu.

For more hotels and details, see Accommodation Listings on page 542

INPUTS FROM SONIA JABBAR

Destination: North East

Backpackers' Paradise

Truly a heaven for the eco-tourist. With landscape that could be a snapshot of Eden. On the beaten track or off it, India's North East never fails to enthrall.

One of the primary focus areas of the North Eastern Council is to boost the Tourism industry in a sustainable manner for the 8 states of the Region - Arunachal Pradesh, Assam, Manipur, Meghalaya, Mizoram, Nagaland, Sikkim and Tripura. It has worked out an ecologically and culturally sound Draft Regional Tourism Policy for this bio-diversity hot spot.

SPPL-SHEEN/NEC-DIPV005/2005

The NEC is committed to all round development of the immensely potential Tourism Sector

Consider the 4,500-km International border the North East shares with four South East Asian countries. Or the caves - one of the most extensive in this part of the World.

Pick your destination - Cherrapunjee, the World's wettest place, or Majuli, the World's largest riverine Island.

Savour the rare exotic cuisine and enjoy the lyrical sound of the many dialects spoken in this part of the country. There are 10,000 other reasons that make the North East special.

The NEC is determined to create an enabling environment within the Region for a viable model, promoting rural tourism and cultural products while cataloguing internal resources for development of this Sector. With minimal investment and maximum returns - of funds and tourists!

Salient features of Draft Regional Tourism Policy

- Better telecommunication facilities to cover all villages identified as tourism areas to build up rural and eco-tourism
- Treating infrastructure development for tourism as an industry for funding
- Sponsoring exchange programmes to neighbouring countries to promote tourism and trade ties
- Emphasising need for each State to identify and develop its own tourist spots
- Focusing on conservation, preservation and promotion of cultural diversity, ethnicity, agronomy, water bodies
- Training manpower in professional travel and tourism management
- Promoting manufacture and marketing of tourism-oriented products; especially handloom and handicrafts.

NORTH EASTERN COUNCIL, SHILLONG
MINISTRY OF DEVELOPMENT OF THE NORTH EASTERN REGION
Government of India

www.necouncil.nic.in   e-mail: necsect@shillong.meg.nic.in
Phones: +91-364-222-2142/3982/3220   Fax: +91-364-222-2140/4270/7425/2364/6879

ISSUED BY DIPR, NEC

Rabangla to Mainom Top
Birder's paradise
By Sujoy Das

Prayer flags flutter gaily at the entrance to the Rabangla Monastery

TIME	I day
LEVEL	Moderate
IDEAL SEASON	Oct to mid-Dec, mid-Mar to end-May
LOCATION	South Sikkim

RABANGLA-MAINOM TOP-RABANGLA

This is a lovely little hike if you want to walk among ancient forests and see plenty of bird life without expending too much time or energy. Rabangla is located on the ridge between Mainom (3,230m) and Tendong (2,590m) peaks. It has a scrub forest, which is home to a number of Himalayan birds, including the verditer flycatcher, blue-fronted redstart, grey bushchat, dark-throated thrush, blue-whistling thrush, green-backed tit and white-browed fantail. The forest around Rabangla is home to the laughing thrush, babbler, cuckoo and hill partridge. If you are lucky, you may even get a glimpse of the rare satyr tragopan en route to Mainom. There are small hotels and lodges to stay at Rabangla, the best one being the cute Mt Narsing Resort with its wooden cottages on the hillside.

THE TREK
RABANGLA-MAINOM TOP-RABANGLA
TIME 6 HOURS
LEVEL EASY
Walk through the main **Rabangla Bazaar**, past all the shops on both sides and follow the jeepable road for about 20 mins. This is the road that

Graphic by ANIS KHAN

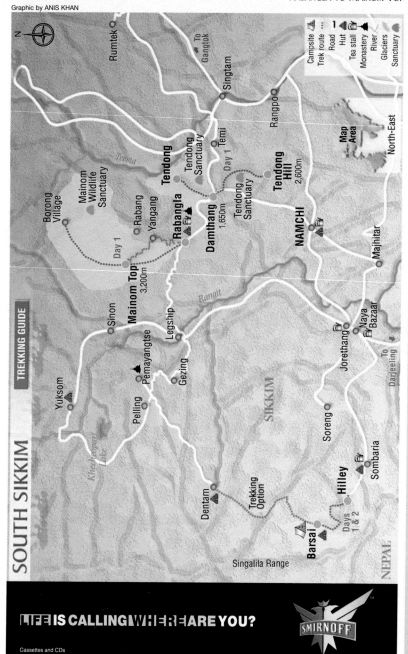

SOUTH SIKKIM

TREKKING GUIDE

N

To Ganglok

Rumtek

Singtam

Rangpo

Map Area

North-East

Teesta

Tendong

Tendong Sanctuary

Temi

Day 1

Tendong Hill
2,600m

Borong Village

Mainom Wildlife Sanctuary

Rabang

Yangang

Rabangla

Damthang
1,650m

Tendong Sanctuary

NAMCHI

Majhitar

Day 1

Mainom Top
3,200m

Sinon

Legship

Rangit

Jorethang

Naya Bazaar

To Darjeeling

Yuksom

Pemayangtse

Gezing

SIKKIM

Soreng

Khecheoperi lake

Pelling

Dentam

Trekking Option

Hilley

Sombaria

Barsai

Days 1 & 2

NEPAL

Singalila Range

Campsite
Trek route
Road
Hut
Tea stall
Monastery
River
Glaciers
Sanctuary

The Sikkim cuppa

If you are planning a visit to Damthang and Rabangla, you will pass through the **Temi Tea Estate**, located on the Gangtok-Rabangla Road. This is Sikkim's sole tea garden and connoisseurs will tell you that with a gem like this, the state doesn't need any more — it's a true solitaire. The tea produced here enjoys international repute, commanding premium prices in world auctions. The last Chogyal (king of Sikkim) initiated tea growing in Sikkim to provide employment for Tibetan refugees fleeing the Chinese invasion of their homeland. Initially, a small plantation was started in Kewzing. This later moved to Temi and a proper processing plant was constructed. The government-owned estate today produces about 1,00,000 kg of tea annually.

Temi is planted along steep hillsides ranging from 1,200-1,800m. The factory is situated at 1,500m and the road up to it is lined with cherry blossom trees. Driving up in November, when these trees are in bloom, is like moving through a pink mist beyond which one can glimpse the gleaming snows of **Kangchendzonga**. The drive up to Temi takes you through mountainsides lush with ferns. Numerous waterfalls rush down the slopes, some merely musical rills, others roaring cascades. All this natural verdant beauty feeds into the tea, giving it a subtle, multi-layered fragrance that gives it the unchallenged reputation of being the champagne among teas.

ARUNDHATI RAY

eventually leads to the **Ralang Monastery**. The road begins to climb and, after about 20 mins, there is a sign to the right marking the entrance to the **Mainom Wildlife Sanctuary**. The trail now leaves the jeepable road and begins to climb steeply through the forest full of oak, chestnut, magnolia, rhododendron, small bamboo and abundant flowers, moss, ferns and creepers. Watch out for the red panda, the Himalayan black bear and many species of deer.

The perfect little wild strawberry

TREKKING HOLIDAYS IN INDIA

Bharat Petroleum

GETTING THERE AND OUT

FROM NAMCHI to Rabangla, it's 22 km/ ¹/₂ hr by 🚙 (Rs 500) or shared jeep (Rs 30) and 40 mins by 🚌 (Rs 20), available from the bus stand **Siliguri to Rabangla** (120 km) is 4 hrs by jeep-taxi (Rs 2,000) and shared jeep (Rs 100). By bus it's 5 hrs and Rs 130

RETURN the same way to Namchi, from where you can head to Siliguri or Darjeeling via Jorethang

---

En route is a small hermitage containing the **image of Guru Padmasambhava**. The 4-hr steep climb along a well-trodden path brings the trekker to the top of **Mainom** (3,200m) that towers above the town. During spring, especially between March and April, the rhododendron display is quite spectacular. On a clear morning, the hilltop has a view of the peaks of the **Kangchendzonga Range**. The way down should not take longer than 2 hrs. Or, if you have a few more days, you may get a local agency to arrange

Guru Padmasambhava

Guru Padmasambhava, the most favoured icon in Sikkim, was a yogi from Uddiyan (present-day Swat in Pakistan) of the 8th or 9th century. Flying into Tibet astride a tiger, he awed the locals with his tantric powers, bound the local deities by oath to become servants and protectors of the Buddhadharma, and established Tibet's first monastery at **Samye**. He also founded the first of the four schools of Tibetan Buddhism, the Nyingma (each only differs in its approach to the path by the precepts and examples set by the founder-gurus of the schools).

Padmasambhava's hagiography shows him to be quite a controversial and colourful character. He is often depicted in thangkas and wall paintings wearing the three robes of the monk and a red cap.

SONIA JABBAR

---

a gentle hike from Mainom Hilltop to **Borong Village**, or follow the more treacherous trails taken by the famous British botanist, Sir Joseph Hooker, down to **Yangang Village**.

For hotels in Rabangla, see Accommodation Listings on pages 542-543 ✦

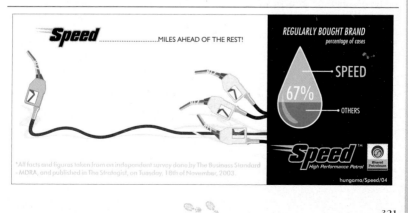

Damthang to Tendong
All in a day's walk
By Sujoy Das

TIME	1 day
LEVEL	Easy to Moderate
IDEAL SEASON	Oct to mid-Dec, mid-Mar to end-May
LOCATION	South Sikkim

On the trail to Tendong

DAMTHANG-TENDONG HILL-DAMTHANG

D amthang (1,650m) is one hour away from Rabangla and so this hike can be combined with the Mainom walk described earlier (*see Rabangla to Mainom Top on page 318*). In fact, it is better to stay at Namchi or Rabangla and travel to Damthang to do the hike as there is no suitable accommodation at Damthang.

Above Damthang, overlooking the South District headquarters of Namchi, there is a small, flat stretch of land at an altitude of 2,600m. It's surrounded by a lush green ancient forest, which is popularly known as the Tendong Hill — a small dormant volcano. Folklore has it that the Tendong Hill saved the Lepcha tribe from the ravages of the deluge when the whole world was flooded, a legend

Bharat Petroleum

GETTING THERE AND OUT

FROM NAMCHI to Damthang, it's 14 km/ $^1/_2$ hr by jeep (Rs 400) or $^3/_4$ hr by SNT (Rs 30), on the Gangtok-Namchi (via Temi) Road
RETURN Take the same route back

similar to the one in the Old Testament. Even today, Lepchas perform pujas to pay homage to the Tendong Hill. Pack a picnic lunch and climb this way on an invigorating day trek; it leads to some stunning vistas.

THE TREK
DAMTHANG-TENDONG HILL
TIME 3 HOURS
LEVEL EASY

Follow the main road from the town of Damthang, heading north-east, and then take the trail through the dense forests of the Tendong Sanctuary. Historically, this has been a place of retreat for Buddhist lamas who spend years in meditation amidst the silent peaks. The view from the top is something to be remembered, spanning the plains of Bengal upto the heights of the Himalayan ranges. Tendong is a great viewing point: to the east are the **Chola peaks**, to the west, the **Kangchendzonga** and the **Singalila Range**. It's tempting to linger. Remember, the way down should take about an hour and a half. ✦

Valley of Wails

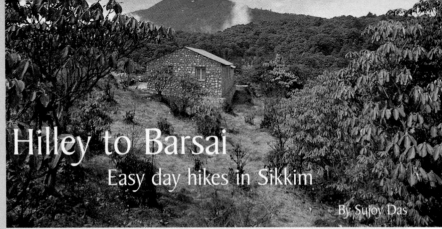

Hilley to Barsai
Easy day hikes in Sikkim

By Sujoy Das

The Shambala Rhododendron Resort at Barsai

TIME	1-2 days
LEVEL	Easy
IDEAL SEASON	Mar and Apr
LOCATION	West Sikkim

Speed **93**™
Experience Octane
The Hi-Octane High Performance petrol from Bharat Petroleum.

Bharat Petroleum

HILLEY-BARSAI-HILLEY

For those who love nature but don't relish sweating across long treks, the Barsai Rhododendron Sanctuary provides an ideal excursion. Located in the south-west corner of West Sikkim and spreading over 104 sq km across the ridge of the Singalila Range, it forms part of India's natural international border with Nepal. The protected forest is home to silver fir, hemlock, magnolia and the rhododendron. During March and April, the trail is ablaze with rhododendron blossoms and is a delightful day walk with stunning views of the high Himalayas. There's plenty of action for keen birdwatchers as well.
◆ **Entry permits** Can be obtained from the Wildlife Check-Post at Hilley **Park entry fee** Indians Rs 25 per day, foreigners Rs 50 per day **Local guide/porter** Rs 10 per day **Tent pitching charges** Rs 25 per tent per day **Still camera** Rs 10 per day **Video** Rs 500 per day

GETTING THERE AND OUT

FROM NAMCHI to Hilley, it's 77 km/ 3 hrs by jeep (Rs 1,600). You reach Hilley via Jorethang (19 km from Namchi), Sombaria (29 km from Jorethang). Only full taxis (Rs 1,100) ply from Sombaria to Hilley (26 km/1 hr). Bus and shared taxi till Sombaria
RETURN Get picked up at **Hilley** for Namchi or Siliguri (Rs 2,000) by taxi, booked in advance in Sombaria

DAY ONE

HILLEY-BARSAI
DISTANCE 4 KM **TIME** 1½ HOURS
LEVEL EASY
The bridle path from Hilley to Barsai heads due north along the Singalila Ridge, with views of the great **Kangchendzonga**. Being a gradual climb, the approx 4-km distance should take about 1½ hrs. While it is possible to leave Hilley early in the morning and be back by lunchtime, it is certainly

Rhododendron country

This is truly rhododendron country. This flower is the breathtaking glory of Sikkim and the land boasts of some 30 species, from the gigantic rhododendron grande — a tree that towers at 40 ft, to the diminutive nivale that rises barely 2 inches from the ground! Some, like the Dalhousie, are epiphytes growing on top of tall trees, barely visible from below. Others are painted prima donnas: like the conspicuous falconeri, with its large fleshy leaves covered with rust-coloured filaments on their underside. The rhododendron literally lives off its looks to attract bees and butterflies, as none of the species are fragrant.

These trails were also the favourite stamping ground of the man who systematically explored the land and documented the flora and fauna of the Eastern Himalayas. After Joseph Dalton Hooker obtained his MD from Glasgow University in 1839, young Hooker travelled exten-

SONIA JABBAR

sively for most of his life, going off on botanical expeditions to all corners of the world. He came to Sikkim for the first time in 1848, and his year-long travels resulted in an amazing record of the numerous species of animal and plant life, many of which turned out to be new discoveries. Numerous species of rhododendrons, ferns and orchids (like the spectacular golden yellow *Dendobrium hookeriana* with its deeply fringed lips and rich purple spots) are named after Hooker. He published *Rhododendrons of Sikkim* in 1849 (considered even today to be *the* authoritative text on the subject); while his *Himalayan Journals*, a travelogue, is a classic treasured by naturalists, historians and sociologists.

ARUNDHATI RAY

SUJOY DAS

more fun to stay at Barsai for a night to catch the views and enjoy the **rhododendron forests**.
🐾 Stay at the **Shambala Rhododendron Resort** (Tel: 0983-2005703; Tariff: Rs 200-800) in Barsai amidst the rhododendron forests. Book in Barsai or contact Help Tourism (*see Trekking Agents Listings on page 515*) in Siliguri.

TREKKING OPTION
BARSAI-DENTAM
LEVEL EASY
DISTANCE 10 KM **TIME** 2-3 HOURS
From Barsai, take the easy trail due north-east to Dentam. Check out the **Alpine Cheese Factory** here. Stay overnight at the 🐾 **Trekkers' Hut** or at **Alpine Guest House**. Or proceed to visit Pemayangtse monastery, or **Rabangla** (69 km), or return to **Sombaria** or **Namchi**. Irregular bus service, but shared taxis freely available.

For hotels, see Accommodation Listings on pages 540 (Barsai) and 543 (Sombaria) ✦

Dzongri and Goecha La Trek

Glacierland

By Sujoy Das

TIME	8-10 days
LEVEL	Moderate
IDEAL SEASON	Oct-mid Dec, Apr to mid-May
LOCATION	Western Sikkim

Sunset over Kangchendzonga from Dzongri

YUKSOM-TSOKHA-DZONGRI-THANSING-SAMITI-
GOECHA LA-KOKCHORUNG-DZONGRI-
CHAURIKHANG-TSOKHA-YUKSOM

This is undoubtedly the most popular trek in Sikkim, famed for its superb mountain views, a floral spectacle in summer, birds and views of pristine forest. It can get quite crowded on this route during October and sometimes during May as well, but trekkers who can brave early spring (April) and late autumn (mid-November to mid-December) would be suitably rewarded. The shorter version of the trek, which goes up to Dzongri, takes about five days, but the longer trek up to Goecha La Pass and back is described here. The trail initially meanders through dense forest and, in summer, flowering orchids can be seen clinging to the bark of the highest trees.

There is a lot of bird life as well in this part of the route — wagtails, redstarts, minivets, whistling thrushes, blue magpies, tree pies and more can be spotted along the way. For the intrepid, the monsoon must be the most beautiful time on the Dzongri alp. The weather is mild and the grass green and fresh. Numerous wild flowers including potentellias, saxifrage, anemones and primulas spread out in a colourful patchwork while sheep and yaks graze contentedly on the luxuriant vegetation.

The mountains are at their tantalising best — a sharp shower and the clouds lift for a few minutes to reveal the steep south face of Pandim. Sometimes at dawn the sky is clear and the entire chain of peaks is visible, only to be blanketed out by thick rain clouds by mid-morning. And, higher up, one can spot the reflection of Kangchendzonga in the still waters of the emerald blue lakes on the glacier.

TIP It is difficult to handle this trek alpine-style after Tsokha as food is not readily available and provisions, stoves etc have to be carried. It is necessary to arrange cooks, porters, provisions and kerosene at Yuksom, at one of the many hotels, before starting on the trek. Further, during the peak trekking

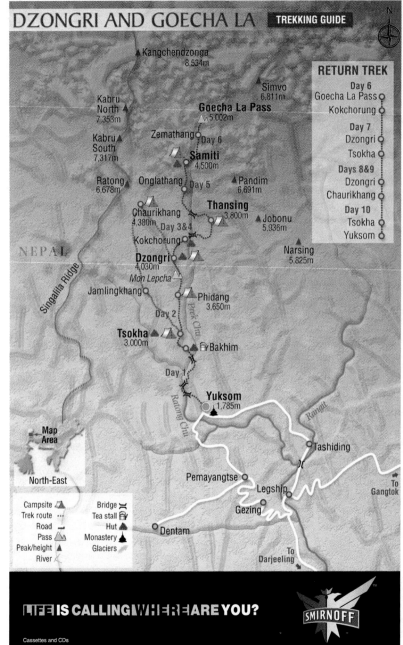

DZONGRI AND GOECHA LA

TREKKING GUIDE

N

Kangchendzonga
8,534m

Simvo
6,811m

Kabru
North
7,353m

Goecha La Pass
5,002m

Kabru
South
7,317m

Zemathang
Day 6

Samiti
4,500m

Pandim
6,691m

Ratong
6,678m

Onglathang
Day 5

Thansing
3,800m

Chaurikhang
4,380m
Day 3&4

Jobonu
5,936m

Kokchorung

Narsing
5,825m

NEPAL

Dzongri
4,030m

Mon Lepcha

Jamlingkhang

Phidang
3,650m

Day 2

Prek Chu

Singalila Ridge

Tsokha
3,000m

Bakhim

Day 1

Ratong Chu

Yuksom
1,785m

Rangit

Tashiding

Map
Area

North-East

Pemayangtse

Legship

To
Gangtok

Campsite
Trek route
Road
Pass
Peak/height
River

Bridge
Tea stall
Hut
Monastery
Glaciers

Gezing

Dentam

To
Darjeeling

RETURN TREK

Day 6
Goecha La Pass
Kokchorung

Day 7
Dzongri
Tsokha

Days 8&9
Dzongri
Chaurikhang

Day 10
Tsokha
Yuksom

327

Yellow-billed blue magpie

OTTO PFISTER

This is a pigeon-sized, purplish-blue bird with a black head, neck and breast, and a white patch on its nape and whitish underparts. The tail is long, with graduated black and white-tipped long streamers. Its bill is yellow, and the legs orange. Its call is usually loud and harsh, but it also has a repertoire of whistles. The blue magpie (*Urocissa flavirostris*) is omnivorous, eating insects and small frogs. They are sociable and hang out in groups of four to ten. There seems to be equality of sexes as both parents share duties towards the young. This magpie is found throughout the northern mountainous regions of the Indian sub-continent, from Hazara in Pakistan to Arunachal Pradesh in north-eastern India.

season of October, the Trekkers' Huts may become very busy and accommodation can sometimes pose a **problem, and tents will be needed.** There are a number of trekking companies in Gangtok and Siliguri who can make full arrangements for this trek

DAY ONE
YUKSOM-TSOKHA
TIME 6-7 HOURS
LEVEL MODERATE

The trail from Yuksom (1,785m) starts at the bazaar and follows the only main road northwards. It climbs gently out of the valley and hugs the right bank of the **Ratong Chu** river, which can be heard thundering through the gorge below. The trail crosses four bridges about 50 mins apart from each other. The last bridge is the longest and there is a camping spot here, on the banks of the river. In the monsoon, this part of the trail is inundated with leeches and salt is required to shake them off. From the fourth bridge, the trail climbs steeply to the north-west for an hour, to the **Forest Rest House** at **Bakhim**, which was the old halting point before Trekkers' Huts were built at Tsokha.

The **Bakhim FRH** is still used by the Himalayan Mountaineering Institute (HMI) for accommodation en route to their Base Camp at Chaurikhang, a day's march from

Bharat Petroleum

GETTING THERE AND OUT

FROM SILIGURI to Yuksom, via Teesta Bazaar, Melli, Jorethang, Legship and Tashiding, it's 141 km/ 5¹/₂ hrs) by jeep (Rs 2,400) or 4 hrs by to Jorethang (Rs 60). From here catch another bus to Yuksom (3 hrs/Rs 60) Plenty of taxis are available from the New Jalpaiguri railway station and in front of the Sikkim Nationalised Transport office on Hill Cart Road in Siliguri.

RETURN From **Yuksom**, return the same way by bus or taxi. As taxis are few, book in advance for a pick-up either in Siliguri or in Jorethang

Trekkers under the shadow of Ratong and Kabru South peaks

Dzongri. Trekkers can stay here by paying a small fee to the chowkidar, who can usually rustle up some 🍵 smoky tea. There is a good view from the bungalow down the valley towards Yuksom. Continue on the trail, passing behind the Bakhim bungalow, and climb in a north-westerly direction through forests of magnolia and rhododendron for about an hour to Tsokha, 3 km away.

🏕 The **Trekkers' Hut** at **Tsokha** (3,000 m) has a large camping ground behind it and groups usually pitch their tents here. There are a couple of private lodges in Tsokha, which also provide accommodation, including a new lodge just opposite the Trekkers' Hut.

DAY TWO
TSOKHA-DZONGRI
TIME 5-6 HOURS
LEVEL MODERATE-DIFFICULT
The path cuts through the village of **Tsokha** and continues its climb steeply northwards through forests of rhododendron to the alp of **Phidang**

(3,650m), taking around $2^1/_2$-3 hrs to complete the ascent. This is the steepest part of the trek as there is little respite in the form of descents. In wet weather, this part of the route becomes extremely muddy and slippery in parts. The clearing at **Phidang** is generally used as the spot for a lunch break and, in good weather, the peaks can be seen across the valley. During May and June, this part of the walk is exceptionally beautiful as rhododendrons, in their myriad hues, flower on either side of the trail.

🏕 Some groups may decide to camp in **Phidang** for the night to ensure acclimatisation but most trekkers stop for lunch and head on to Dzongri. The trail evens off a bit from Phidang before it climbs east again for Mon Lepcha, a pass which is higher than the Dzongri Trekkers' Hut (4,030m).

On a good day, **Mon Lepcha** commands an exceptional view of Pandim. The trail descends due north-west from Mon Lepcha before climbing north again, and the 🏕 **Dzongri Trekkers'**

Hut soon comes into view. The distance from Phidang to Dzongri should not take you more than 3 hrs, but remember that it is a stiff walk.

DAY THREE

REST DAY AT DZONGRI

It is advisable to have a rest day at Dzongri, both for acclimatisation as well as to savour the views of the mountains. Climb the hill above the bungalow referred to as **Dzongri Top**, and you will be rewarded with a panoramic view of **Kabru** (7,353m), **Ratong** (6,678m), **Kangchendzonga** (8,534 m), **Koktang** (6,147m), **Pandim** (6,691m) and **Narsing** (5,825m). Towards the west, the **Singalila Ridge**, which separates Sikkim from Nepal, can be seen.

In the afternoon, walk up to the Dzongri meadows and climb up to the ridge with the four chortens, at **Dablakhang**. The Dzongri meadow is a popular yak grazing ground and, on most days, large numbers of yaks can be seen grazing on the lush turf.

DAY FOUR

DZONGRI-THANSING

TIME 3-4 HOURS

LEVEL MODERATE

Step out from the Dzongri bungalow and take the right trail, which passes the building and then climbs east up along the right bank of the river. After cresting the hill, the path drops into the valley and then crosses a bridge over the **Prek Chu** river. During late May and June this part of the trail is full of dwarf rhododendron blossoms. **Thansing** (3,800m), an hour's climb due north from the bridge, is located below the slopes of **Mt Pandim**. This is usually an easy day and the more intrepid trekkers often travel to Samiti on the same day. This is, however, not recommended unless you are very well acclimatised and fit. There is a **Trekkers' Hut** at **Thansing** and groups often camp near the Prek Chu river.

DAY FIVE

THANSING-SAMITI

TIME 4-5 HOURS

LEVEL MODERATE-DIFFICULT

The trail from Thansing climbs gently north, up the valley, and follows a stream and alpine meadows. About an hour above Thansing, you reach **Onglathang**, which has a superb view of the south face of **Kangchendzonga**. Start early from Thansing so that you can catch the views before the clouds rush in. The trail then skirts a series of glacial moraines (an accumulation of earth and stones carried and finally deposited by a glacier) before crossing meadows again, and arrives at the

A welcome rest at the Trekkers' Hut at Dzongri

emerald green lake at **Samiti** (4,500m).  It is usually very cold at the **Trekkers' Hut** in Samiti and afternoon snowfall is a regular feature here, especially in the spring.

DAY SIX
SAMITI-GOECHA LA PASS-KOKCHORUNG
TIME 7-8 HOURS
LEVEL DIFFICULT

The climb to Goecha La begins with a gentle gradient eastwards for about half an hour and then, the real climbing starts. The trail follows the glacial moraine north-east and then drops to a dry lake at **Zemathang**. A rough scramble over rocks and boulders with a rise of about 400m will bring the trekker to the top of the pass. Most trekkers leave Samiti by first light so as to reach the top by 9.30 am or so. The climb from Samiti to **Goecha La** (5,002m) would take between 3¹/₂ and 4 hrs.

The pass is formed by a depression between **Pandim** and the **Kabru** spurs. It overlooks the **Talung Valley** and commands a very impressive view of the south face of **Kangchendzonga**. It is possible to go over the pass, into the valley, and follow the **Talung Glacier** for 2-3 days into North Sikkim, but this would be a mountaineering trip, requiring technical climbing skills and expedition support. Trekkers normally turn back at this point. The way down is quick. Follow your tracks back to

A cold winter at Dzongri

Thansing, which will take you 2-3 hrs, and then head for one hour towards Dzongri until you reach a clearing called **Kokchorung** (3,800m), which has a  **Trekkers' Hut**. One usually reaches here by late afternoon with enough time to set up camp.

DAY SEVEN
KOKCHURUNG-DZONGRI/ TSOKHA
TIME 5-6 HOURS
LEVEL MODERATE

It is possible to bypass Dzongri and reach Tsokha directly, though many of the guides and porters do not prefer this route as it travels through the forest and the trail is difficult to find, especially if it has snowed. From **Kokchorung**, head south-east on the

Sikkim's orchids: The prima donnas of paradise

Amongst the actors who form the cast of Sikkim's floral drama, it is the orchids who are the prima donnas. If any flower has learnt how to make the most of its presence, to strut its stuff to its best advantage, it is definitely this one.

Sikkim's orchids belong to two categories — epiphytes and terrestrial. Of the two, the epiphytes are better known and they include the famous *Dendrobrium* genus. The dazzling golden *Dendrobrium hookerianas*, with their rich purple spots, compete for top billing with the pouch-shaped *Calceolaria* whose wardrobe favours white, pink and yellow.

The *Cristata* species of the *Coelogyne* genus, on the other hand, spurns such

PRASHANT PANJIAR

showy displays. It goes for the virginal look, with snow-white flowers, and languidly drapes itself over tree stems and rocks. With jungle stripes and pouting lips, the *Arachanthe cathcarti* has attitude written all over its fleshy, large flowers. This variety likes it hot: choosing the moist warmth of tropical forests to display its chocolate-striped body and hinged lips.

The orchidarium outside Gangtok presents one with the chance to see several stunning orchid species. Commercial cultivation is becoming popular now. The growers are mainly individuals working on a small scale. They export almost all they produce.

ARUNDHATI RAY

well-marked trail for 4-5 hrs. Ask the chowkidar at Kokchorung or Thansing about the best route back, as the trail conditions change depending on the month, snowfall, rain and landslides. However, if you have the time, you may want to return via Dzongri and add a side trip to **Chaurikhang**.

TREKKING OPTION

DZONGRI-CHAURIKHANG-TSOKHA
TIME 5-6 HOURS EACH WAY (2 DAYS)
LEVEL MODERATE-TOUGH

It is a day's walk from Dzongri (4,030m) to the HMI Base Camp at Chaurikhang (4,380m). The camp is located on the edge of the **Ratong Glacier** with spectacular views of **Kabru, Kabru Dome, Koktang, Ratong** and **Frey's Peak**. A 2-hr walk along the glacier leads to **Dudh Pokhari**, with its milky white waters surrounded by peaks. The side trip to Chaurikhang would add 2 extra days to the trek. From the Dzongri bunga-

low, take the trail up the hill straight in front of the bungalow proceeding north-west. Do not take the right trail, which goes to Thansing. The trail climbs the hill and drops into the Dzongri meadows. Cross the meadows, continue to head north-west and follow the trail along the right bank of the **Ratong Chu river** with the black rock of **Kabru** (just below Kabru South peak) above you, to the right, until you can see the HMI huts in front of you. Pitch tent at **Chaurikhang**, and return to Tsokha the next day.

DAY EIGHT

TSOKHA-YUKSOM
TIME 4-5 HOURS
LEVEL EASY

Retrace your steps to Yuksom on the final day of the trek. The going is easier as the path is mainly downhill.

For hotel in Yuksom, see Accommodation Listings on page 544

Netherworld

Catacombs. Lairs. Caverns. Teeming with bats and other creepy crawlies. Say "cave" and that's the image the mind conjures up. Caves have always been associated with denizens of the underworld!

In reality, it's a whole different world deep in the bowels of the earth. Magnificent stalagtites and stalagmites that come to life under the faintest ray of light. Mesmerising rock formations that seem like works of art.

Meghalaya has one of the most extensive caving systems worldwide. It even boasts of the SE Asia's second longest living cave system. With 900 registered caves in the limestone rich hills, there are hundreds more just waiting to be found. Come. Explore. Who knows what you could discover. And even if you don't, wouldn't it be the adventure of a lifetime!

NORTH EASTERN COUNCIL, SHILLONG
MINISTRY OF DEVELOPMENT OF THE NORTH EASTERN REGION
Government of India

www.necouncil.nic.in   e-mail: necsect@shillong.meg.nic.in   Phones: +91-364-222-2142/3982/3220   Fax: +91-364-222-2140/4270/7425/2364/6879

I S S U E D   B Y   D I P R ,   N E C

SPPL-SHEEN/NEC-DIPR/009/2005

The largest state in the North-East, Arunachal is a sleepy giant, displaying few signs of the social or environmental crises that scar other parts of the country. Its topography is marked by a series of valleys that run from the Himalayas in the north to the Brahmaputra in the south. Arunachal's most popular tourist destination is in many ways its unlikeliest. Tawang only came under de facto Indian adminis-tration in the 1950s and then fell briefly to the Chinese in 1962. It's some 350 km of winding hill road from Tezpur, but nevertheless attracts tourists and trekkers alike with its natural beauty.

MUST-VISITS

NATURAL ATTRACTIONS

Try the 80-min **Tezpur-Tawang** helicopter ride, but for spectacular views, drive instead. En route lies **Sari Duar**, a traditional trading centre, the **Nameri Wildlife Reserve** and **Bhalukpong**, popular with anglers and picnickers. A 100 km later is **Bomdila**, from where the scenery gets interesting, climbing to the **Sela Pass** (4,215m). Other attractions include the **'Madhuri' Jheel** just outside Tawang, which was used as a location in the Shah Rukh starrer *Koyla*.

BUDDHIST CIRCUIT

Tawang Monastery, the largest in India, at 3,050m, dominates the skyline like a medieval fortress. To the south-east is **Urgeling**, birthplace of the 6th Dalai Lama. The **Sange Ryabgelling** shrine is close by, as is the **Khinme Monastery**. On the Tawang-Bumla Road is the **Singshur Nunnery**. **Taktsang Gompa** (12 km) is one of the holiest Buddhist shrines in Arunachal. And en route is the serene **Sangeshar Lake**.

WHERE TO STAY AND EAT

Take your pick from **Hotel Alpine** (Tel: 03794-222515; Tariff: Rs 400-700) and **Hotel Nefa** (Tel: 222419; Tariff: Rs 250-350) in Nehru Market, **Tourist Lodge** (Tel: 222359; Tariff: Rs 550-750) near the telephone exchange and **Hotel Shangrila** (Tel: 222224; Tariff: Rs 300-450), near the main bus stand. They have almost the same facilities including a restaurant. No credit cards accepted.

With no great restaurants either, stick to simple eateries and items (momos and butter-tea are always nice). *For more hotels and details, see Accommodation Listings on pages 543-544*

INPUTS FROM RAVI J. DEKA

→ Tawang Facts

- **LOCATION** In Arunachal Pradesh, at 3,400m, near the Tibet and Bhutan borders, 347 km from Tezpur and 187 km from Bomdila
- **GETTING TO TAWANG By air** Nearest airport: Tezpur (13 hrs), which has a morning Indian Airlines flight from Kolkata. Taxi Rs 3,500, shared jeep Rs 400. **Helicopter service** (1 hr 20 mins/ Rs 3,000) Tezpur to Tawang, Tue and Sat, weather permitting. Contact Dy Resident Commissioner, Arunachal Tourism, Guwahati (Tel: 0361-2412859) **By rail** Nearest railhead: Guwahati (473 km/ 17 hrs). Overnight journey to Tawang with a night halt at Tezpur or Bomdila. Taxi Rs 6,000 for a drop. Or take the ASTC bus (5 hrs/ Rs 90) to Tezpur from outside the Guwahati Railway Station. From Tezpur to Tawang, take a shared taxi (Rs 410) as the bus service is highly erratic and uncomfortable **By road** From Guwahati, take NH37 to Kuarital (163 km) via Nagaon. Turn left on NH37A to Tezpur (23 km). Then NH52 to Charduar and the long state highway into Arunachal to Tawang via Bhalukpong, Bomdila (overnight), Dhirang and the Se La Pass
- **STD CODE** 03794
- **PERMITS** • Indian nationals planning to visit restricted areas in Arunachal Pradesh require an **Inner Line Permit** (ILP) to do so. The ILP (Rs 25) can be obtained (carry valid ID and 2 photographs) from the Arunachal Tourism offices located in Delhi, Kolkata or Guwahati (see *Tourist Offices Listings on page 518*)
- • All visiting foreign nationals require a **Restricted Area Permit** (RAP). Available against a valid passport and visa, the RAP (US$ 50) can be obtained from any Indian mission abroad, the Home Ministry in New Delhi, and the office of the Home Commissioner, Itanagar (Tel: 0360-212339) for a period of 10 days only, for a minimum number of 4 people or more at a time

Arboreal stomping ground

The North East is covered by an intricate trellis of nature trails,
bridle paths and leaf-carpeted walkways that make
every trek a voyage of discovery.
Be it leisurely beginners' routes or
precarious gangways where one wrong step
could send you plummeting down a precipice
the North East is perfect for the footloose and fancyfree.
Or the adrenalin junkie with a bad case of wanderlust.
Beneath the forest canopy or in it.
If you want to commiserate with Mother Nature...
She's not going anywhere in a hurry!

NORTH EASTERN COUNCIL, SHILLONG
MINISTRY OF DEVELOPMENT OF THE NORTH EASTERN REGION
Government of India

www.necouncil.nic.in   e-mail: necsect@shillong.meg.nic.in   Phones: +91-364-222-2142/3982/3220   Fax: +91-364-222-2140/4270/7425/2364/6879
ISSUED BY DIPR, NEC   SPPL-SHEEN/NEC-DIPR/010/2005

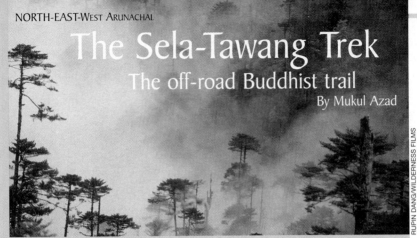

The Sela-Tawang Trek
The off-road Buddhist trail
By Mukul Azad

RUPIN DANG/WILDERNESS FILMS

Mists enshroud forests near the Sela Pass

TIME	8-9 days
LEVEL	Moderate
IDEAL SEASON	Oct-Apr. For flowers, late-May to end-Aug
LOCATION	West Kameng District of Arunachal Pradesh

THEMBANG-PANGAM-SEMNAK-LAGAM-NAMSHU-DHIRANG-SELA PASS-MUKTO-KIPI-TAWANG

This eastern-most state of India is the first to be kissed by the morning sun, therefore Arunachal Pradesh is also known as 'the land of the rising sun'. Bordered by China to the north, Myanmar to the east, Bhutan to the west and the states of Nagaland and Assam to the south, this is one of the most verdant and lush hill states amidst the seven sisters of the North-East, and also the largest. With 80 per cent of the state under forest cover, splendid wildlife and a vast network of rivers and streams, Arunachal possesses an unmatched beauty. Tribal culture and craft traditions crown the state's generous riches. Trekking in this unspoilt and unique region offers the trekker an enchanting peep into an

GETTING THERE AND OUT

FROM GUWAHATI to Bomdila, it's 346 km/ 11 hrs by 🚌 (Rs 4,000). For the 🚌-cum-shared taxi option, see *Tawang Facts* on page 334 **Tezpur to Bomdila** Shared Sumos (160 km/ 6 hrs/ Rs 160 per person) leave at 6 and 11.30 am daily from the Himalayan Holidays counter (Tel: 03712-223580, 09435082155). You can also get a reserved taxi (Rs 1,800-2,200) for **Bomdila** and on to **Thembang** (45 km/ 2 hrs), from where your trek begins. Between Bomdila and Thembang, the road is metalled only for the first 25 km and then starts deteriorating rapidly
RETURN From **Tawang** to **Tezpur** by taxi or shared jeep. Night halt at **Bomdila** recommended **Tezpur to Guwahati** ASTC buses run every 40 mins from the ASTC Bus Stand near Hotel Luit; or hire a taxi (no sharing)

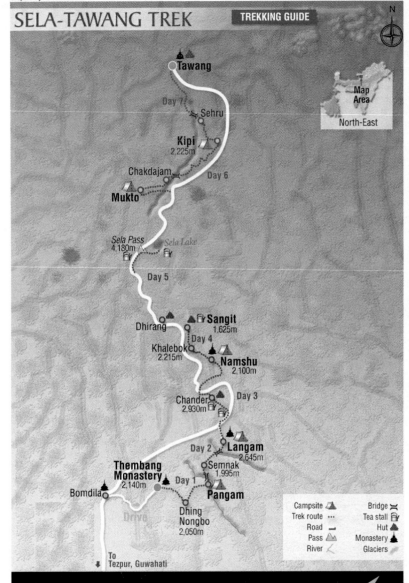

Graphic by ANIS KHAN

SELA-TAWANG TREK

TREKKING GUIDE

N

Tawang

Day 7

Sehru

Kipi
2,225m

Map Area

North-East

Chakdajam

Day 6

Mukto

Sela Pass
4,180m / *Sela Lake*

Day 5

Dhirang

Sangit
1,625m

Day 4

Khalebok
2,215m

Namshu
2,100m

Chander
2,930m

Day 3

Langam
2,645m

Day 2

Semnak
1,995m

Thembang Monastery
2,140m

Day 1

Pangam

Bomdila

Drive

Dhing Nongbo
2,050m

To
Tezpur, Guwahati

Campsite	Bridge
Trek route ···	Tea stall
Road —	Hut
Pass	Monastery
River	Glaciers

SUJAN CHATTERJEE

The red panda

Measuring 50-60cm and weighing 3-6 kg, the red panda (*Ailurus fulgens*) is one of the most striking creatures to be found in north-eastern India. It inhabits mixed forests with dense bamboo undergrowth. This endangered creature is sighted rarely. The red panda's chestnut-coloured body is offset by a white snout, inner ears and cheek patches. Its tail is ringed with light and dark chestnut bands. It has a wiry, white moustache, chestnut 'teardrop stains' along its cheeks, and large liquid brown eyes that make it very endearing.

The red panda marks its territory with urine, droppings and other powerful excretions from its anal glands. Other pandas detect these not by smell but taste! Communication is through a wide repertoire of squeaks, snorts and whistles. Unlike the giant panda of China, red pandas feed only on fresh bamboo leaves at the base of the stalk and do not eat the stalk itself.

VIVEK MENON

isolated and sparsely populated state where the ills of over-development and its consequent problems are nowhere in sight.

The trek follows the old Buddhist trail through Monpa villages dotted with beautiful monasteries, chortens and Mani walls. The trek is done in stages, covering the long distance to Tawang by taking sensible road support options in between. You have the choice of hiring a vehicle to meet you at appointed places and times for Rs 2,500 per day, or of just hopping on and off the many buses and shared taxis that ply the roads from sunrise to sunset. The motorable road runs all the way to Tawang, which was constructed after the 1962 war with China.

Main shrine of Tawang Monastery

Still used by Buddhist monks as they travel from one village and monastery to the next, the trail one takes winds through verdant valleys of rhododendron, oak and pine. Water is never a problem on this trek as you will find streams everywhere. This is a land where Buddhism thrives in all its colours — vibrant, real and living. And the trek transports you back in time to another world, which the road has not touched.

From Tezpur, drive 160 km (5-6 hrs) to Bomdila, the headquarters of West Kameng District, from where you can arrange porters and pick up supplies. Porters will charge Rs 225 per day plus one day return and bus fare. On the border of Arunachal, your permits will be checked.

Most travel agents of Arunachal have their offices here in Bomdila. The best place to stay is Hotel Shiphyangphong. There are a few other guest houses and a tourist lodge.

♦**Permits** Indians free, foreigners US$ 50 for a 10-day stay (*see Tawang Facts on page 334 for details*)

TIP The trail is a well-marked old stone track, almost 1-1^1/$_2$m wide all along, no matter where you get on or off it, making it extremely difficult to get lost on this trek. Water and camp-sites are mostly a non-issue unless otherwise mentioned

DAY ONE
BOMDILA-PANGAM
DISTANCE 8 KM **TIME** 2-3 HOURS
LEVEL MODERATE

The road winds its way up to the ridge, and just below the ridge, on the other side, lies the **Bomdila Monastery**, which is worth visiting. Then drive on to **Thembang** (2,140m), the seat of the **Gelugpa**, or the Yellow Hat school of Tibetan Buddhism. The monastery is run down, though interesting, as the gompa houses some relics from Lhasa. Your walk starts here.

Catch the trail behind the monastery, which skirts below the ridge and gently descends to a cluster of farms. The broad trail cuts through the farms and gently descends for an hour through dense forest to Dhing Nongbo (2,050m). Watch out for the elusive red panda while walking through the forest. **Dhing Nongbo** is a tiny village with a landmark white building hous-ing a large prayer wheel, which was made to ward off evil. The locals firmly believe that you should not travel on the trail in even numbers else one of you gets eaten by the evil spirit. If you are even in number, expect a porter to be thrust upon your group to make the numbers click. As

Sela Lake in winter

you face the building, take a left towards the school building. Beside it lies a beautiful, well-maintained chort-en called **Ghumtung**.

⚠️You can stay in the school building or take the path down to **Pangam Village**, which occupies both sides of the river. Cross the village and pick a suitable spot to camp.

DAY TWO
PANGAM-SEMNAK-LANGAM
DISTANCE 14 KM **TIME** 5-6 HOURS
LEVEL MODERATE

Cross the wooden bridge at Pangam and go upstream along the left bank of the river. It's an easy walk of about an hour to **Semnak Village** (1,995m). This unique village follows Drukpa Kunley, a famous Tibetan tantric mas-ter. Phallic symbols adorn entrances of home and the people are free-spirited and open. From Semnak, it's an easy descent through fields (about 30-40 mins) to a stream. Cross the

stream over a wooden bridge and follow the path rising steeply for about a kilometre to the village of **Langam** (2,645m). Initially, the trail passes through a thick bamboo forest before coming out to the **Panchsara Meadows**, a great spot for birdwatching. From Panchsara, it is a tough climb of about 500m through mossy ground and lush forest cover to Langam, the next village. A colourful gompa here houses the statue of Chamba, the future Buddha, as well as some old manuscripts.

There is a clearing near the monastery at Langam where you can camp.

DAY THREE
LANGAM-NAMSHU
DISTANCE 11 KM **TIME** 6 HOURS
LEVEL MODERATE

From Langam, walk on the non-jeep-able road for 300m till you meet the main road going to Tawang. Walk on the road for one hour till you come across some tea shops. A signboard here announces the trek to **Dhirang**. Leave the road and take the trail to your left going to Chander Village, perched on the ridge top. It is a steep climb of about 2 hrs to the top. Situated at 2,930m, **Chander** is a small village with a lodge, a few tea houses and a dhaba. From the ridge top above Chander, you can see spectacular views of **Gorichen**, Arunachal's highest mountain, amidst other snow-clad peaks. From Chander, follow the road, descending steeply for about 20 mins. At the first hairpin bend, you will notice a trail on your right. Take this trail, which descends gradually at first and then steeply over a series of switchbacks. An hour and a half into the descent, you will come upon a Mani wall with prayers inscribed on stones. Just a little ahead lies the village of **Namshu** (2,100m). The statue of Chamba dominates the monastery.

Camp near the monastery in Namshu Village.

DAY FOUR
NAMSHU-SANGIT
DISTANCE 10-12 KM **TIME** 6 HOURS
LEVEL MODERATE-DIFFICULT

Leave the monastery behind, heading to the smaller monastery 30 mins away. The trail, heading down, is flanked by chortens on both sides. The monastery has a statue of Shakya-muni Buddha. There are beautiful murals of Tsongkhapa (founder of Gelugpa School of Tibetan Buddhism). From the chorten, the trail climbs gently on some stretches and very steeply at others. One passes through densely forested mountainsides to the top, which takes about 1 hr. From the top, the trail descends on the other side for about 2 hrs, to the small village of **Khalebok** (2,215m). From here you can see Sangit Village below. Another tiring descent of about an hour brings you to **Sangit** (1,625m). At Sangit, cross the bridge to meet the Bomdila-Tawang Road.

You may opt to stay in Sangit, which has a few eateries and a guest house, or drive one hour to Dhirang, which has better accommodation. **Hotel Pemaling** or **Circuit House** are popular overnight places here.

DAY FIVE
DHIRANG-MUKTO VIA SELA PASS AND SELA LAKE
DISTANCE 8-10 KM **TIME** 3-4 HOURS
LEVEL EASY

Drive to Sela Pass (4,180m), getting off 3-5 km before the pass. The walk from here is amazing as you are above the tree line for the first time in the trek and the route affords spectacular views of the **Gorichen Peak**. At the top, there are few tea shops where you can take a break.

Hike up on any side of the **Sela Pass** to have fantastic views of the snow-clad mountains. The landscape here is barren and devoid of any trees. It's windy and cold on the pass, so keep a jacket handy.

Masked dancers at Tawang Monastery

From the pass, take the short-cut track which cuts through the winding main road. The track descends sharply for 30-40 mins to **Sela Lake**. There is a war memorial here at Jaswantgarh, dedicated to Jaswant Singh, the soldier who single-handedly held off the approaching Chinese troops from the pass during the 1962 Indo-China War. There are some army barracks here, from where you can get free ☕ tea and samosas. The jawans believe that the ghost of the dead Jaswant Singh visits them at night. They go to great lengths to prepare a bed, with food and water on it, to appease him. A crumpled bed in the morning bears testimony that the spirit did indeed occupy the dwelling!

From the lake, hop onto a taxi/bus, descending steeply to the river at the bottom of the valley. Then watch out for a board announcing Mukto Village, at which you get off. Take the trail going left and walk for about 3 km to reach **Mukto**. Tawang is visible from here further up on the slope.

🏕 Camp at **Mukto** for the night.

DAY SIX
MUKTO-KIPI
DISTANCE 9 KM **TIME** 5 HOURS
LEVEL MODERATE-DIFFICULT
From Mukto, trace your way back to the river. Then, take the downhill trail on the other side of the spur, and walk for about 30 mins to **Chakdajam**. The

trail meets with the road across the bridge. Cross the bridge and take off on your right on to the trail going uphill to Kipi. This is a 1-1½ hrs steep climb. **Kipi** (2,225m) is a uniquely traditional village with women always dressed in colourful ethnic clothes and adorned with jewellery studded with turquoise, jade and amber. Adjoining the village is an orchidarium housing rare species of orchids, some of which are on the verge of extinction.

🏕 Set up camp in or around **Kipi**.

DAY SEVEN
KIPI-TAWANG
DISTANCE 8-9 KM **TIME** 5-6 HOURS
LEVEL MODERATE
From Kipi, go ahead on the well-marked trail that gently descends to the river to a bridge. En route you will come across a small Mani wall and a chorten with a beautiful painting of Chamba. The last bit is over landslides to the river below at **Sehru Village**. The trek from **Kipi** to **Sehru** takes about 2 hrs. Cross the river and climb steeply for 1 hr, towards the ridge. The following 6 km is a gradual uphill trail to **Tawang**, which is right on top of the ridge. The **monastery** you'll find here is a centuries-old fortress, set against the dramatic setting of snow-mantled peaks. It is one of the largest living monasteries of the Gelugpa school, housing more than 200 monks. It closely resembles Lhasa's Potala Palace. From Tawang, you have valley views to both sides of the town. You can take the helicopter service (Rs 3,000) and fly back to Guwahati, or bus or taxi back.

TIP On your return, Luit Hotel at Tezpur offers the best accommodation, and a sunset cruise on the Brahmaputra is simply a must

For rest house bookings and hotels, see Accommodation Listings on pages 540 (Bomdila), 541 (Dhirang) and 544 (Tezpur) ✦

Namdapha National Park

In hornbill country

By Vikram Singh

Aerial view of the magnificent jungles of Namdapha

TIME	5-6 days
LEVEL	Easy to Moderate
IDEAL SEASON	Nov to Mar
LOCATION	Eastern Arunachal Pradesh

DEBAN-GIBBON'S LAND-DEBAN-HALDIBARI-HORNBILL GLADE-BULBULIA-RANI JHEEL-BULBULIA-DEBAN

If you ever wondered about a place that was still left to explore, try Namdapha. It has the sort of untouched wilderness where you can be the first to make a natural discovery. Tucked away in remote eastern Arunachal Pradesh, Namdapha is perhaps the most bio-diverse part of the sub-continent. The region's altitude varies from 200-4,578m. Its geographical boundaries with Myanmar, the Dapha Range (5,000m) and snow-fed rivers have kept the area well-protected and largely unexplored. Spread over 1,985 sq km, Namdapha is also a Project Tiger reserve — and the only such reserve, and one of the few national parks in India, where you explore only on foot. The trek is about exploration and you are never in too much of a hurry to get from point A to point B.

For keen nature and wildlife enthusiasts, this is perhaps the best experience offered anywhere in the country. The trek cuts through lush primary evergreen forests along well-defined trails, criss-crossed by numerous streams. The tall tree canopy rises 150m above and the undergrowth is impenetrable with the presence of bamboo and cane. You camp at pre-designated campsites and, unlike other treks, the camping sites here are only a short distance away from each other. It is advisable to cover the area in short stages to maximise your time for exploring this virgin terrain. The park is accessible only up to an altitude of 850m but Namdapha does throw in its share of challenges. Heavy rains can occur anytime, causing mudslides, and you have to keep a constant check on the ever-present leeches in the soil below.

Keep in mind that this is one of the country's largest virgin primary forests, so prepare accordingly and do not just drop in. Some of the first citizens of this lush terrain include tigers, leopards, elephants and wild dogs, so follow the advice of your accompanying forest guard, whose experience and resources in this area are invaluable. A pair of good binoculars is an absolute must for this trek as you would not want to miss out on the chance of viewing the amazing bird and mammal life present here. It's worth keeping a few extra days in hand for a trek like this, as nature may spring some pleasant surprises.

TIP The first thing to keep in mind when you set out to explore this area is that you must do it in the right season. We did it in mid-April, when the monsoons had set in, the leeches were out in the fields and the Neo Dhing River was nearly uncrossable because of the high water level. December and

Graphic by ANIS KHAN

January are the driest months and the best time to visit Namdapha

DAY ONE
DEBAN-GIBBON'S LAND-DEBAN
DISTANCE 22 KM **TIME** 8 HOURS
LEVEL MODERATE

You could walk right up to Gibbon's Land, 11 km away, on the motorable dirt road back towards **Miao**, or turn back a little earlier. Or get your taxi to drop you to Gibbon's Land and walk back to **Deban**. It is here that I got my first real taste of the spectacular bird life present here. In the streams we saw little and slaty-backed forktails, while the other birds included the flamboyant sultan's tit, scarlet minivets, lesser and greater yellownape woodpeckers and my first ever sighting of the red-tailed minla and collared treepie. In the area around **Gibbon's Land**, we sighted a large group of Assamese macaque, peacefully perched on top of a tree canopy. We walked back slowly

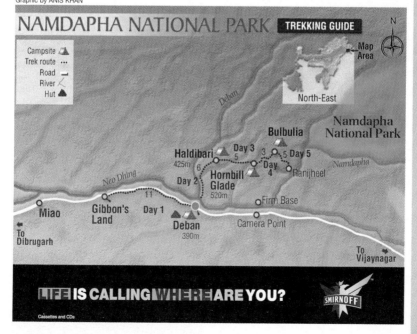

Namdapha's treasures

Namdapha is like the cauldron of a genetic soup that sometimes spills over to reveal its biological treasures. The unique blend of Indo-Burmese, Sino-Tibetan and Himalayan species has made Namdapha the most diverse habitat of the sub-continent. Three large mammals have been discovered in recent years, including the Javan rhino, the Malayan sun bear and the leaf deer. Declared a Project Tiger reserve in 1983, this is the only park in the world to harbour all the four big cats — tiger, leopard, clouded leopard and the snow leopard. The area is also home to rare mammals like the takin, Himalayan musk deer, slow loris and the Asian elephant. Namdapha is also home to India's only ape — the Hoolock gibbon. The bird life here is equally amazing, with almost 665 species recorded in the area so far, which is half the bird species present in the country! It is estimated that to complete a comprehensive study of the botanical resources present in Namdapha, it would take at least 50 years. This unspoilt and unexplored wilderness sustains diverse and incredibly varied life forms. It's the kind of stuff explorers dream of.

♦ **Entry fee** Indians Rs 10, foreigners Rs 50 **Vehicle fee** Rs 100 **Camera** Rs 75-800

and returned to the **Deban Rest House** by evening. It is also during this walk that we first realised that Namdapha is also home to at least five kinds of leeches, which are present in large numbers. Fortunately, with some help from our accompanying forest guard, we ordered for a pair of Leech Guards (a large, thick pair of socks, up to your knees, that prevents leeches from penetrating), which was picked up from an oncoming vehicle from Miao. 🔺 The **Forest Rest House** at **Deban** (390m) is where you camp the first night in Namdapha National Park. This picturesque rest house overlooks the Neo Dhing River.

DAY TWO
Deban-Haldibari
Distance 6 km **Time** 4 hours
Level Easy
This is one day when you do not want to sleep late as the excitement unfolds the moment you open your eyes. I woke early the next day to find the action had begun in the grounds of the rest house itself. A solitary barking deer was feeding a little distance away from the rest house and, moments later, the accompanying forest guard called for me to sight a fire-tailed sunbird. While sipping my first cup of tea I heard the loud whooping of **Hoolock gibbons**. I followed the evocative call leading to

Bharat Petroleum

GETTING THERE AND OUT

FROM DIBRUGARH to Deban, via Miao, it's 150 km/ 7 hrs by 🚗 (Rs 2,500). It's best to book your taxi (Sumo/ Mahindra jeep, minimum Rs 1,000 a day) in advance. No shared taxis available on this run. You could try the cheaper but unreliable 🚌 service to Miao, if you have ample time. But this is not a recommended option in these remote environs. From Miao, it's only an hour by taxi
RETURN Get picked up at **Deban** (25 km/ 1½ hrs from Miao) for **Dibrugarh** for your flight, or for **Tinsukia** (45 km/ 2 hrs/ Rs 1,600) for your train
TIP It is advisable to coordinate the entire logistics of this trip with your local tour operator in Arunachal Pradesh as you must have the arrangements for your permits, transportation, accommodation and trek in place before you get there

the forests behind the rest house — and came across a pair of these apes. They were swinging from one branch

to the other using their extended arms, stopping now and then to get a look at us below. It was barely seven in the morning and so much had already taken place. Such is the magic of the Namdapha National Park.

After breakfast at the rest house, we got ready to cross the **Neo Dhing River** for the trek onwards. A ferry boat waiting for us, plunged into the gushing torrent and before I knew it, the fast rapids combined with the skilled maneuvering of the experienced boatman had deposited us on the left bank, a considerable distance downstream. It is from here onwards that you are on your own, with the accompanying team of forest guard, cook and porters.

A trail from here takes you up an incline for about 300m, before you walk along a ridge to reach **Haldibari**, your next camping site. The walk to Haldibari is replete with birdcalls and we saw the magnificent great hornbill and great slaty woodpecker. After lunch at the Haldibari campsite, we explored the area only to be rewarded with yet another rarity — the Malayan giant squirrel. It was enough action for one day.

🏕 The campsite of **Haldibari** (425m) is reached before lunch. It houses a small shack amidst a clearing. We set up camp here in tents.

Tiger grass glows gold in the Namdapha National Park

DAY THREE
HALDIBARI-HORNBILL GLADE
DISTANCE 5 KM **TIME** 3 HOURS
LEVEL EASY

On the third morning, it felt as if I had gone to bed in Namdapha and had woken up in Vietnam. It was raining heavily, the army of leeches was out in the trenches and stepping out of the tent seemed impossible. Determined not to waste precious moments of the trip, I decided to brave a session of early morning birding. All signs of life had decreased considerably except for the streaked spiderhunters, which were present in large numbers.

We broke camp to carry on to our next site at **Hornbill Glade** (520m), a distance of 5 km from Haldibari. Within a few hours of continuous rain, the number of streams on the trails suddenly seemed to have increased and so had the leeches on the muddy track. Having covered hardly a kilometre, I decided to wade right through the streams on the path, rather than hop across the rocks, which were deceptive and slippery. In any case, it was pointless trying to stay dry under the given conditions. The hike was gentle though. It took 3 hrs of easy walking through mildly undulating terrain to reach **Hornbill Glade**.

This was the only point during the entire trek that I came across other travellers. Five American birders were camping the night here with an army of porters, local agents, cooks and other staff. It had stopped raining by late afternoon and I ventured out into the adjoining area. Hornbill really does live up to its name. Within 200m of the camp, I saw a rufous-necked hornbill, giving a short monosyllabic bark-like call at regular intervals, its distinct colours glowing in the fading light.

🔺 **Hornbill Glade** is an open patch with two large sheds and a makeshift hut, which serves as the kitchen.

Hoolock gibbon

Measuring less than a metre and weighing about 6-8 kg, the Hoolock gibbon is India's only ape. This tail-less primate is known more by its distinctive, haunting song, than by sight. Gibbon songs resound in the Namdapha forests at dawn. Vocalised as a loud "hookoo-hookoo-hookoo", the songs are sung by one group at a time, with other groups taking over in turns. The chorus continues till the sun is high up in the sky. The Hoolock gibbon is an extremely endangered primate.

SUJAN CHATTERJEE

The male is full black with white, silvery brows and young females are similarly coloured. Adult females, however, turn a golden blonde colour. Both are tail-less and have long arms, almost double the length of their bodies, helping them to swing from tree to tree using brachiation (hanging by the arms and swinging at high speed, hand over hand, from branch to branch). Gibbons can also stand upright and run along branches. These fascinating apes are said to be monogamous, mating for life.

VIVEK MENON

SNAPSHOTS FROM EDEN

(Also known as India's North East)

North East India is a veritable treasure trove of wildlife with many rare and endangered species making it their home. The region is home to the Brow Antlered Deer, the majestic Tragopan, the One-Horned Rhino, the Golden Langoor, the Hoolock Gibbon, the Great Indian Hornbill, the Clouded Leopard and myriad other furred and feathered species. It has a high density of elephant population. In the wilds of the North East you could be forgiven for imagining you were in Eden. Nature is beckoning. Heed its call! Be a part of this experience. Visit the North East!

NORTH EASTERN COUNCIL, SHILLONG
MINISTRY OF DEVELOPMENT OF THE NORTH EASTERN REGION
Government of India

www.necouncil.nic.in   e-mail: necsect@shillong.meg.nic.in   Phones: +91-364-222-2142/3982/3220   Fax: +91-364-222-2140/4270/7425/2364/6879

ISSUED BY DIPR, NEC   SPPL-SHEEN/NEC-DIPR/007/2005

Malayan giant squirrel

There are four species of giant squirrels in South and South-East Asia, of which three are found in India. These forest canopy dwellers rarely come down to the forest floor. They build multiple globe-shaped nests and use them for sleeping and as nurseries. They make shrill sounds and their high-pitched alarm calls rival those of monkeys.

The Malayan giant squirrel measures between 35 and 80 cm long and can be identified by its deep brown or black back and buff underparts. It has large black ears with hairy tufts, a black tail and black marks on its chin.

VIVEK MENON

SUJAN CHATTERJEE

DAY FOUR
HORNBILL GLADE-BULBULIA
DISTANCE 3 KM **TIME** 1½ HOURS
LEVEL EASY

Zipped inside a tent, you learn to identify birds and the jungle's creatures by their calls, and not by sight. The dense foliage also contributes to this. We moved to our next campsite at **Bulbulia**, a short hike away. The terrain got more undulating than the previous

One of many cooling brooks

days, with streams flowing across at regular intervals. The rain had come down heavily again and, after a little over an hour, we came to the base of a hill, atop which was our next camp.

Strategically located on top of a hill, the shack makes a perfect watchtower to check the stream below, giving you access to good views of the tree-top canopy. It's perfect for sightings of long-tailed sibias and greater racket-tailed drongos, who make regular halts on the perches close by. Being a marshland, thick undergrowth is missing here, making way for better viewing. Elephants often frequent the streams below. I spotted the rare black-backed forktail skimming the stream, and a hike up to the campsite yielded a solitary and rather lonely Hoolock gibbon. The excitement in **Bulbulia** continues past sunset and, if lucky, you could see flying squirrels gliding on the tree-top canopy. I went to bed wondering whether the owl hooting close by was a brown fish owl or a tawny fish owl. You realise that absorbing the throbbing jungle from the very perch of your bed is a lot better than being zipped up in a tent!

TREKKING HOLIDAYS IN INDIA

Rufous-necked hornbill

This large hornbill qualifies as 'vulnerable' because it has a small, rapidly declining population as a result of the destruction of evergreen forests, and hunting. The rufous-necked hornbill (*Aceros nipalensis*) originally occurred in mountainous regions between eastern Nepal and Vietnam. Although it is now absent from, or very rare, in much of its previous range, it still occurs in southern China, north-eastern India, Myanmar, Thailand, Laos and Vietnam. This huge bird measures over a metre long (48 inches). Males may be distinguished by a bushy crest, rufous (reddish-brown or reddish) on the neck and breast, maroon on abdomen. Its cheek, chin and upper throat are naked and scarlet, while it has a blue, naked eye-patch. The back and wings are black, with wings having white tips, and white on the lower half of the tail. The bill is a heavy, horn-shaped yellow, with striped upper parts. The female is less extravagantly coloured and is all black, except for white wing tips and lower tail.

The species is usually found in pairs or small flocks, except in the breeding season, when females are enclosed in tree cavities and males are often encountered foraging alone. The rufous-necked hornbill forages mainly on fruit in the canopy of tall trees. The calls of this hornbill are a variety of croaks, roars and cackles.

Bulbulia houses a large open-sided shack offering a spectacular view of a large aquifer below with several natural springs (*bulbule*), from which the place derives its name. What's even better is that the shack remains totally dry and leech-free. This is easily the Presidential Suite of Namdapha as it offers the luxury of a large bare wooden platform, which was to serve as my king-size bed for the next two days.

DAY FIVE
Bulbulia-Ranijheel-Bulbulia
Distance 5 km each way **Time** 7 hours
Level Easy

From Bulbulia, your trek carries on along the trail towards **Ranijheel**. Although there is a campsite at Ranijheel where you can pitch tents, we took the unanimous decision of exploring Ranijheel and returning back to the comfort of Bulbulia. The lack of any shade at Ranijheel makes camping a little more demanding. Cooking and other tasks can be a problem, especially if it rains.

In this walk, you face a few steep slopes on muddy tracks and the trail is broken in parts, though walkable. After 3 km of walking from Bulbulia, the trail suddenly caves under a thick bamboo patch for a good stretch. The forest guard warned of rogue elephants that often wandered here. It is advisable to stay close to your forest guard. This patch is popular with birders for species like great rufous-headed parrot-bill and red-billed scimitar babbler. It is in this walk that I saw some of the tallest trees in Namdapha, garlanded with orchids.

There were surprises everywhere. A grey peacock pheasant dashed across the trail, wreathed hornbills glided over the top tree canopy, and a pair of courting changeable hawk eagles

Photos SUJAN CHATTERJEE

The meandering Neo Dhing River

perched high up and gave out shrill calls. This walk is sure to take you in a state of trance. Soon enough, we stumbled across a clearing with the small lake of **Ranijheel** to the right. We explored the area and looked for the highly endangered white-winged duck, which was reported here. If you want to spend more time exploring Namdapha, it is possible to trek from here to **Firm Base**, **Embeong** and cross over the **Namdapha River** (if the water level permits) to complete a circular circuit back to **Deban** via **Camera Point**, in about 4-5 days. We headed back to Bulbulia after lunch, to reach before sundown.

Namdapha Facts

- **Contact** the Field Director in advance to inform him about your visit
- **Postal address** Field Director, Project Tiger, Namdapha National Park, Miao-792122, Dist Changlang, Arunachal Pradesh
- **Permits** Both Indians and foreigners require entry permits to visit Arunachal, which can be obtained from the Secretary, Govt of Arunachal Pradesh, Itanagar, or the Resident Commissioner of Arunachal Pradesh, Arunachal Bhavan, New Delhi (for more details see Tawang Facts on page 334)

DAY SIX
BULBULIA-DEBAN
DISTANCE 14 KM **TIME** 7 HOURS
LEVEL EASY

This is the last day of your trek, and it is best to start early to cover the entire distance back to the **Neo Dhing River** and cross over to **Deban**. It is advisable to reach the riverbank while there are still a few hours of light left. This will help you plan the return journey with your boatman.

The water level in the river can rise considerably by the evening, like in the case of any snow-fed river, and more so when it has been raining. This can make the river crossing on the ferry boat quite tricky and may require more than one run if there are over eight persons.

Stay overnight at the **Forest Rest House** at Deban.

TIP It is good to have a reliable local agent in Namdapha for booking of circuit houses, local transport, the Deban Forest Rest House and obtaining the necessary permits for visiting Arunachal Pradesh. You can contact **Tsering Wange** at himalayan-holidays.com

For rest house bookings in Deban, see Accommodation Listings on page 541 ✦

NILAYAN DUTTA

We drive up a mountain to look at the city below. The night has gone mad with stars and in front of us, spread over several hills, is beautiful Kohima. But it's really beautiful only at nights and early mornings. During the day, sadly, traffic and smog eclipse the high, surrounding mountains. Established by the British as a colonial outpost, though most of its old buildings were destroyed during the Second World War, it is here that the Japanese invasion was stopped in its tracks.

MUST-VISITS

COLONIAL HERITAGE

The **War Cemetery** was designed to create the effect of a serene garden in which visitors could feel a sense of peace. The red-roofed **Catholic Cathedral**, on Aradurah Hill, is the most prominent landmark in Kohima. What's most fun though is taking a walk in the **Super Market**. It's a narrow, climbing alley sidelined with shops that ends up in the huge Kohima Local Ground where traditional wrestling competitions are organised. Twenty kilometres away is **Khonoma**, the village of the warrior tribe,

School children near Kohima

the Agamis. And wherever you go in Nagaland, look out for birds. You will see none, not even crows. It's considered cool for a Naga male to bring them down with a single stone or a shot and they all practise a lot.

WHERE TO STAY

Kohima has a limited choice of hotels so book in advance. **Hotel Japfu Ashok** (Tel: 0370-2240211-13; Tariff: Rs 675-2,000) is the best here. **Hotel Fira** (Tel: 2245006; Tariff: Rs 400-600) has simple, clean rooms and a courteous staff. **Hotel Pine** (Tel: 2243129; Tariff: Rs 350-550) is a budget option.
For more hotels and details, see Accommodation Listings on page 542

WHERE TO EAT

Food, both at **Japfu** and **Fira**, is quite nice but their kitchens close by 8.30-9 pm, and it's impossible to get food in Kohima after that. A couple of Chinese restaurants have opened recently but they close by 4 pm!

INPUTS FROM ANURADHA KUMAR

→ Kohima Facts

● **LOCATION** About 400 km south-east of Guwahati, at 1,500m

● **GETTING TO KOHIMA By air** Nearest airport: Dimapur (74 km/ 2 hrs). Taxi Rs 500 **By rail** Nearest railhead: Dimapur **By road** NH37 till Nagaon via Jorbat and Raha. At Nagaon, turn right and take NH36 till Kohima via Howraghat, Bokajan and Dimapur

● **STD CODE** 0370

● **PERMITS** ● **Mandatory for Indians** (carry valid ID): Inner Line Permit from the Assistant Resident Commissioners, Delhi (Tel: 011-23017123/ 878) or Kolkata (Tel: 033-22825247/ 1967) or from the Department of Tourism, Kohima (Tel: 0370-2270107)
● **Mandatory for foreigners** Restricted Area Permit (US$ 50), for max 10 days for a group of 4 or more, from any Indian mission abroad, the Home Ministry in Delhi or the Assistant Resident Commissioners of Nagaland

Room with a view

Travel like a snail, slowly, with your dwelling on your back. Invite a neighbour to tea. Join a stag party at the nearest watering hole off a North Eastern nature trail!

Committed to promoting eco-tourism
...and preserving the environment

NORTH EASTERN COUNCIL, SHILLONG
MINISTRY OF DEVELOPMENT OF THE NORTH EASTERN REGION
Government of India

www.necouncil.nic.in   e-mail: necsect@shillong.meg.nic.in   Phones: +91-364-222-2142/3982/3220   Fax: +91-364-222-2140/4270/7425/2364/6879

ISSUED BY DIPR, NEC

SPPL-SHEEN/NEC-DIPR/011/2005

Dzukou Valley and Japfu Peak
The valley of eternal charm

By David Sayers and Mukul Azad

Wild flowers carpet the Dzukou Valley

TIME	4-5 days
LEVEL	Easy to Moderate
IDEAL SEASON	Late-May to end-Aug for flowers; Oct to Apr for trekking
LOCATION	Near Kohima

KOHIMA-DZUKOU TREKKERS' HUT/ DZUKOU VALLEY-VISHWEMA VILLAGE-JAPFU BASE CAMP-JAPFU PEAK

Known as one of the most charming valleys of Nagaland, the Dzukou Valley is a spectacular visual treat of emerald green hills, lush forests, serpentine streams that freeze in winter, and myriad colourful blooms that dot the vast caldera of the valley and its meadows. It is by far the best-known trekking area in Nagaland and, after one has completed the unremittingly steep climb and the subsequent 2-3 hrs walk through low bamboo scrub, one begins to understand why. The topography indicates that the valley is the bottom of a large crater or caldera of a long-extinct volcano, and one can look down upon it from the rim of the caldera. At 2,400m, there is a special kind of beauty, almost desolate, especially in the long shadows of early morning or late afternoon.

Above the valley is a huge mountain hut (more a shed). Behind the hut there is a small pocket of remnant oak and rhododendron forest, with the occasional *Magnolia campbellii*. Beyond this are some small, steep hills that tempt one to climb for a better view. Half-way up, any signs of tracks disappear and one is left fighting endless bamboo thickets. The only other thing to do is to descend by an easy route 150m

into the caldera, which is so big and open that it appears like a high-altitude mountain valley. It is very green, with extensive areas of bog and water plants and paths lined with primulas. In the monsoon season, tourist brochures understandably tell of richly flowering meadows and a locally abundant pink lily.

Sadly, bamboo and anything else that will catch fire is burnt, so there is little forest remaining around Dzukou Valley today. There are birds, but they are so conditioned to fear man that they are rarely to be seen. Locals are experts with catapults and rifles; indeed, we found one of our porters baking clay pellets over our cooking fire for catapult ammunition, and later discovered a woodpecker complete with feathers being slow-baked in the embers.

At present, it is a marvellous place for young people, travelling independently, to gain some trekking

Graphic by ANIS KHAN

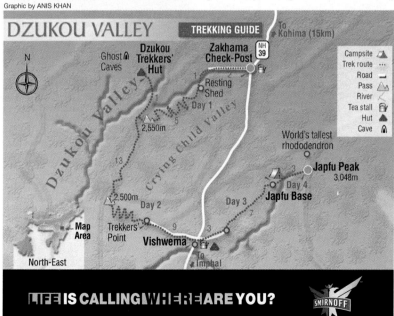

355

Bamboo trivia

Bamboo is a type of grass, and there are 1,500 species covering a variety of habitat. It's found on all the continents except Antarctica. Some are as short as 30 cm, while giant timber bamboo can grow to over 40m high. As a member of the grass family, bamboo can be recognised by the special structure of its stem, or 'culm', and also by its rapid rate of growth, and its flowering. (Bamboo does not flower every year, but once every 7-120 years, depending on the species, and usually dies after flowering).

Bamboo is flexible — it bends in strong winds but it rarely breaks. This flexibility is due to its hollow culm, and the nodes, or joints, between segments of the culm. The culm, branches and leaves stay green throughout the bamboo's life, even during winter. Some bamboo plants send runners out to establish new plants, while others, called 'clumpers', expand from the original plant. Usually, tropical bamboos are clumpers, while temperate bamboos are runners. The roots, called 'rhizomes', are where new plants are formed. New bamboo shoots are produced every year from these rhizomes.

With a tensile strength superior to mild steel, and a weight-to-strength ratio better than graphite, bamboo is the strongest growing woody plant on earth. It is also the fastest growing plant. Some varieties can grow as fast as *5 cm per hour*, or almost $1\frac{1}{2}$m per day! The lifespan of a single bamboo plant is not very long, only about 20 years. But it is very hardy — a stand of bamboo plants, near Ground Zero at Hiroshima in 1945, survived the atomic blast and sent up new shoots within days.

Madake is a type of bamboo that apparently flowers only once every 120 years. All types of bamboo flower infrequently, and remarkably, *all bamboo of a given species flower at exactly the same time.* This is so even if the bamboo plant is transplanted to different places.

experience. As foreigners we were very much heartened to see its popularity. It's clear that better maintained access trails, control over fires and hunting are badly needed. Ideally, there should be a resident warden based there, year round. interpretive information about the geology and natural history of the region would greatly enrich the visitor experience and enhance the status of the valley.

DAY ONE
KOHIMA-DZUKOU TREKKERS' HUT
DISTANCE 9 KM **TIME** 5 HOURS
LEVEL MODERATE

Start early morning and follow NH39 from Kohima to **Zakhama Check-Post** (15 km by road), marked by a small ☕ tea-stall. Here, a Rs 60 fee is charged for a good cause — the North Kohima Students Union uses it to maintain and keep the area clean. From the Zakhama Check-Post, walk along the stream on the 2-km jeepable road (jeeps not allowed), through forests of bamboo and deodar. Where the road ends, the path climbs steeply to the left spur along the stream, for 1 km. Follow the left bank that then meets with a resting shed. This is known as the **Crying Child Valley** as the beautiful tragopan pheasant, with its cry akin to a child's wailing, inhabits this area.

Walk along the right bank of the stream. From here onwards, the path is steep and, in places, you may need to get down on all fours. It is 5 km from the rest spot to the nameless 2,550m pass, which offers a breathtaking panoramic view into the **Dzukou Valley**. Uniquely gentle looking spurs and grassy meadows rise up from the

NILAYAN DUTTA

Old Naga lady near Kohima

GETTING THERE AND OUT

FROM DIMAPUR to Kohima, it's 74 km/ 2 hrs by 🚗 (reserved Maruti Rs 500, shared taxi Rs 100) or 3 hrs by 🚌 (Rs 50). Bus every hour from the NST Bus Stand, 5.30 am onwards. Indian Airlines offers direct connections to Dimapur from Kolkata on all days except Tuesdays, while the Dimapur railhead is connected to Delhi and Kolkata by the NE Express and the Bramhaputra Mail

RETURN From **Kohima** head back for Dimapur, preferably by pre-arranged or shared taxi to catch your train or flight

vast caldera of the valley floor, which abounds in colourful blooms during the monsoon months. Out of the 180-degree view on offer, 160 degrees is the Dzukou Valley alone.

From here on you are in a dwarf bamboo forest, which resembles tall grass from afar. Across the hairpin pass, the trail skirts below the ridge for 200m before coming to a split. Take the right one, which is a fairly easy short descent. After half an hour you will come across a tiny stream. Cross it to get to the **Dzukou Trekkers' Hut**, where the chowkidar can rustle up a good welcome meal.

⚠ The **Dzukou Trekkers' Hut** is about the size of a small factory or aircraft hanger, and as welcoming. It has a vast concrete floor with a few wooden platforms that serve as beds, where one can lay out sleeping bags for

The world's tallest rhododendron

The forests on the Japfu Range are replete with rhododendrons of various hues, ranging from purple, white to red and yellow. This valley also boasts of the tallest rhododendron tree in the world, a fact documented in the *Guinness Book of World Records*. With the average rhododendron growing from 10-15 ft, this remarkable tree was a reputed 108 ft tall when last measured in 1993, and is still growing! Two trekking routes exist for the approach to this tree. The earlier, tougher one was by the **Phesama River**, while a newer route now goes by **Aradura**, taking a total of five hours.

NEISATUO KEDITSU

the night. A small separate kitchen, a small but functioning toilet block and good water supply, complete the facilities. Local trekking clubs and school groups appear to be frequent visitors to the place.

DAY TWO
REST DAY (OPTIONAL)

Camp at the **Trekkers' Hut** and explore the wide and beautiful valley. Ahead of the Trekkers' Hut, you can do a walk to the **Ghost Caves** or 'Bhoot Gufa' as they are locally known. Remember to carry torches as the cave extends to almost a kilometre. Or simply descend around 30m from the hut, to the bottom of the vast caldera of the valley. You can explore the vast stretch of grasslands and rolling meadows, replete with flowers in the monsoon months.

DAY TWO
DZUKOU VALLEY-VISHWEMA VILLAGE
DISTANCE 14 KM TRAIL AND 9 KM ROAD
TIME 6-7 HOURS
LEVEL EASY-MODERATE

Take packed lunch and drinking water from the Trekkers' Hut for the day, as nothing is available on the route till the pass. Retrace your steps back to the split in the trail and this time take the right trail (it would have been the left when coming from **Zakhama**). It is a fairly level, easy trail that goes along the left side ridges of the valley through dwarf bamboo, which often have to be parted to be able to see the path in front. After a short series of zig-zags, you will reach another pass on the ridge from where you can see the highway to Imphal and the vast spread of the **Vishwema Village**. This is the point where you exit the **Dzukou Valley**. On the pass, you will come across a water pipe line, the water source for Vishwema Village. Follow it all the way down. The bamboo will come in useful as support for the initial bit of this downhill, which is very steep. At the bottom of the hill, the trail meets a road marked **'Trekkers' Point'**. From here, unless you have arranged in advance for a

Blossoms cover the valley floor

vehicle to pick you up, walk the level 9-km road which meets the NH61 at Vishwema Village.

You can spend the night in the community hall of the village (free), and procure food from the shops.

DAY THREE
VISHWEMA VILLAGE-JAPFU PEAK BASE
DISTANCE 10 KM **TIME** 4-5 HOURS
LEVEL EASY

Carry water, tents and food supplies from Vishwema. No water is available till the base of **Japfu Peak**. From the village, head 3 km on the main road heading north-west. The road morphs into a well-defined trail surrounded by lush forests over a 7-km stretch leading to the base of the peak. The trail gently skirts around the ridge, which is facing you, making it a gradual and easy ascent. There are plans afoot to build a hut though there are no visible signs of that yet. The forests here abound with rhododendrons of various hues.

A small clearing in the forest and a fresh water spring make for a good campsite at the base, marked by a 'Japfu Peak' signboard.

DAY FOUR
JAPFU BASE CAMP-JAPFU PEAK
DISTANCE 5-6 KM **TIME** 4 HOURS
LEVEL TOUGH

Ideally set out from camp at 2 am to get sunrise views from the peak which is essentially the highest point on the ridge. The trail is well defined all the way to the top. Initially leading through dense forest affording few views, the climb is steep. The last 150-m stretch of the trail opens out above the treeline and ascends smoothly to the peak. From the **Japfu Peak** (3,050m) you can see a vast spread of valleys, hills and villages. Half of Nagaland is visible from here, besides villages on the Arunachal side, and Dibrugarh in Assam. Retrace your way back on the trail, return to **Vishwema Village** and head on to **Kohima**. ✦

The interiors of Goa are as enchanting and attractive as its coastal belt. Nearly twenty per cent of this tiny state is covered by wildlife protected areas that provide richness and diversity in flora and fauna. It is a Goa that one should seek to discover, that is far removed from the sun and sand image so deftly crafted and promoted worldwide for decades. Be prepared to be won over by more than sun and sand.

Hugged by ghats and mountains, the lush green forests and wildlife regions are home to a variety of birds, animals and plants. The **Bhagwan Mahavir Wildlife Sanctuary** and the **Mollem National Park** jointly form the largest contiguous wildlife protected area in the state, covering 240 square kilometers. The dense vegetation provides ample cover to wildlife animals like the magnificent gaur, deer, wild boar and many more.

One of the most popular sanctuaries is the **Bondla Wildlife Sanctuary**. Though small in size, it boasts of a mini zoo, deer safari park, botanical garden and even eco-tourism cottages. Bondla is a paradise for the lovers of econ-tourism. Spend late evenings and nights here for an unforgettable experience. You will feel exhilaration and an uplifting of the spirits. The region is covered with moist deciduous forests with evergreens and canes alongside. Besides the state animal Gaur, frequently sighted are the panther, leopard, deer, porcupine, anteater and many other animals.

The **Cotigao Wildlife Sanctuary** is representative of the eco system in the Western Ghats region. Some of the tallest trees in the sanctuaries are found here, going up to 30 meters. Nearly 200 species of birds have made their home here, and they include the Pied Hornbill, Golden Backed

Woodpecker and the Great Indian Woodpecker.

The **Dr. Salim Ali Bird Sanctuary** is a treat for all bird lovers. Located along the river Mandovi, it has a dense vegetation of 14 different species of mangroves. During the winter months between November and January, migratory birds flock in thousands to feed on the banks of the river at the sanctuary. It is delight to watch and observe them in their full regalia. Watch towers there provide a truly bird's eye view of the region in full bloom. A boat ride in the backwaters in the early misty morning can create magic. This is when man is at peace with nature.

For the eco tourism enthusiast, there is even more than the notified sanctuary areas. The sacred groves located in Sattari taluka in north Goa is rich in medicinal plants. It also provides refuge to a unique forest community called the Myristica Swamp Forests having great ecological significance. The groves are said to be existing for over two centuries now and it has its own reigning deity named Nirankar. There are more sacred groves in Sanguem taluka in south Goa.

The Aravalem Falls and the Aravalem Caves in north Goa provide a perfect mix of mythology and ecology, and point to the bonding of Divinity with Nature. They are a must visit for the eco tourist.

There is so much more to explore and discover in wildlife Goa. One can spend the rest of one's life doing just that, and still be amazed at the constantly emerging new findings and excitement levels.

Come to Goa. Nature beckons.

For details please contact:

DEPARTMENT OF TOURISM
GOVERNMENT OF GOA,
Patto, Panaji, Goa - 403 001, India.
Tel: 0832 - 2438750 / 51 / 52
Fax: 0832 - 2438756

www.goatourism.org

GO GOA
A perfect holiday destination

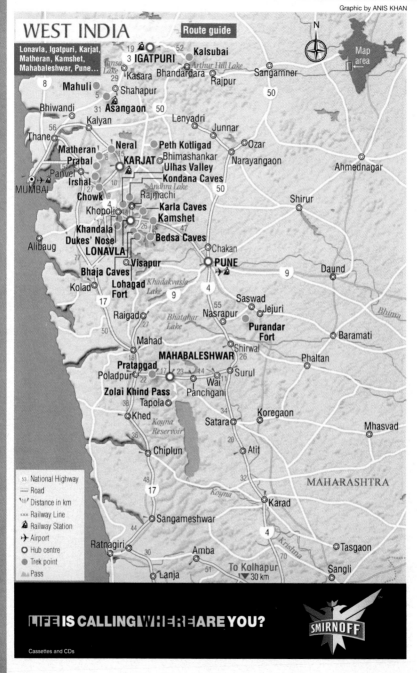

Graphic by ANIS KHAN

WEST INDIA Route guide

Lonavla, Igatpuri, Karjat,
Matheran, Kamshet,
Mahabaleshwar, Pune...

N

Map area

Kalsubai
19 52
3 IGATPURI
Tansa Lake
29 Kasara Bhandardara Arthur Hill Lake
Rajpur Sangamner
8 Mahuli 5 Shahapur 50
Bhiwandi 31 Asangaon 50
Kalyan Lenyadri Junnar
56 Thane Ozar
Matheran Neral Peth Kotligad Ahmednagar
Prabal 8 KARJAT Bhimashankar Narayangaon
Panvel Ulhas Valley
Irshal 10 Kondana Caves
MUMBAI 27 Andhra Lake 50
Chowk Rajmachi Shirur
Khopoli 14 Karla Caves
Khandala 26 Kamshet 47
Alibaug Dukes' Nose Bedsa Caves
LONAVLA Chakan
Bhaja Caves Visapur PUNE Daund
Kolad Lohagad Khadakvasla Lake 9
17 Fort 9 4
Raigad Bhatghar Lake Nasrapur 55 Saswad Jejuri
50 Purandar Baramati
Mahad Fort
MAHABALESHWAR Shirwal Phaltan
Pratapgad 26
Poladpur 22 17 23 44 Surul Mhasvad
Zolai Khind Pass Wai 11
38 Tapola Panchgani Koregaon
Khed 34
Koyna Reservoir Satara Atit
36 20
Chiplun 32 MAHARASHTRA
48
17
Koyna Karad
44 Sangameshwar 4 Krishna Tasgaon
Ratnagiri 30 Amba 70
Lanja 51 To Kolhapur Sangli
30 km

Legend:
- 53 National Highway
- Road
- 16 Distance in km
- Railway Line
- Railway Station
- Airport
- Hub centre
- Trek point
- Pass

Bhima

Mahuli
Wading through grass
By Andre Morris

A lone hiker makes her way through the grassland towards Mahuli

TIME	1 day or more
LEVEL	Easy
IDEAL SEASON	Jun to Oct
LOCATION	Kasara Range, in Igatpuri region, north-east of Mumbai, close to Tansa Lake

ASANGAON-MAHULI VILLAGE-MAHULI FORT

A walk up to Mahuli (762m) in the monsoon is the perfect way to return to nature. If you have the time, I recommend the whole walk from Asangaon, which is very picturesque and enjoyable, especially in the rains. The trail is easy, and there are open fields and meadows where a sea of grass sways gently in the breeze. Several streams gurgle and murmur as they run their course down to the sea. While travelling to or from Nasik, the Mahuli Range stands out and soars above the surrounding plains. Mahuli Fort is in the centre of the range and is the biggest of the three forts in the area. Mahuli Chanderi is

due south (or left while facing Mahuli) and Chhota Mahuli, as the name suggests, is a small hill on the right, due north of Mahuli Fort.

TIP Mahuli Village does not offer much in food and drink, so be prepared with your own supplies. The villagers will sometimes prepare a meal for you but this will be a simple affair of rice, dal and a vegetable with rotis and chutney (costing around Rs 50)

If you'd like a shorter walk, you could catch a bus or autorickshaw (Rs 70-100) from Asangaon to Mahuli Village, 5 km away.

DAY ONE
ASANGAON STATION-MAHULI FORT
DISTANCE 15-16 KM **TIME** 6-7 HOURS
LEVEL EASY

From Asangaon Station, walk along the railway tracks towards **Kasara** (due north) for about half a kilometre till you come to a bridge over the tracks. This is the **Mumbai-Nasik Highway**, or NH3. Turn left at this point and walk onto the road, heading west for 300m, and from here a tarred road branches off right and there is a sign-board for a Jain Teerth. Take the right turn and follow the road for 4 km to **Mahuli Village**.

There is a Forest Check-Post at the junction of the road from Asangaon and the road coming from **Shahapur**, which crosses the river (there is also a road to the Jain Temple that branches off to the right). The Forest Department now charges Rs 10 per head to enter the area but provides no facilities for water, toilets or other necessities.

From the Forest Check-Post, Mahuli is due north-west while the **Jain Teerth** is due north. The pinnacles and fort are now clearly visible but if you're hiking during the monsoon, they continue to play hide-and-seek with the clouds while on either side of the road you'll find lush green paddy fields. If you'd prefer a cross-country walk, you could leave the road 300m after exiting the highway and follow a footpath across a field and up a small

hillock to a tribal hamlet consisting of three huts (due north-west). Just past the hamlet, turn left (due north) and walk up the hillock from where **Mahuli Fort** is visible in the north-west. I usually prefer this route as it takes me through some lovely forest cover and across many streams and rivulets. Cross the small hills and ridges and you'll eventually come out near the Forest Check-Post.

TIP Your landmark should be the hill on the right of the three pinnacles or generally due north-west

From Mahuli Village, the tarred road continues due west to the base of the fort. Cross the river (via a bridge) and you'll reach the temples at the base of the fort. One can 🏕 camp at these temples or even at the **Hanuman Mandir** just across the bridge. There is a well just across the bridge on the left that has good drinking water. From the temples, a well-used trail leads off into the forest, goes past two streams and then climbs up a spur. This is the trail

Graphic by ANIS KHAN

MAHULI

TREKKING GUIDE

Tansa Lake

Map Area

Maharashtra

Lingi 540m

Chhota Mahuli 610m

Mahuli Fort 840m

Jain Teerth

To Igatpuri and Nasik

NH 3

Mahuli

| Fort 🏰 |
| Campsite 🏕 |
| Trek route ····· |
| Road |
| Railway line |
| Peak/height ▲ |
| River |
| Bridge ⋈ |
| Temple 🛕 |

Shahapur

To Bhiwandi and Mumbai

Asangaon

GETTING THERE AND OUT

FROM MUMBAI to Asangaon, it's 96 km/ 2 hrs by car, 2½ hrs by local 🚃 (Rs 20). There are regular Central Railway local trains from the Chhatrapati Shivaji Terminus (VT) to Asangaon. Besides these, all Kasara-bound local trains halt at Asangaon Station. NH3 passes through Asangaon Village but there is no scheduled bus stop. Unless you are driving, the train is the best option to get there and back **Asangaon to Mahuli** Auto till Mahuli Village, Rs 60-80 for a 6-km ride **RETURN** the same way

TREKKING HOLIDAYS IN INDIA

A fortified bond

Mahuli Fort was the bastion from where soldiers guarded an important trade route connecting the ghats to ports in the Konkan. The fort is also linked to legends about Chhatrapati Shivaji and his parents. His father Shahji Bhonsle and his maternal grandfather, Lakhuji Jadhava Rao, worked for the Nizamshah of Ahmadnagar. Jadhava Rao, it is said, did not approve of his daughter's marriage with Shahji. When the Mughal Emperor Shah Jahan laid siege to the fort — where Shahji had camped — Jadhava Rao used the opportunity to join hands with the enemy and turned against the Nizamshah. Shahji escaped from the fort and made his way to Shivneri Fort near Junnar. Jijabai apparently stayed behind at the camp to face her father and even rebuked him. She later escaped from the fort and joined her husband at Shivneri, where Shivaji was born.

PUNIT PARANJPE

to **Mahuli Fort** and this is where the climb begins. The trail climbs steeply up the spur (due north) and then tops out onto a flat stretch (30 mins).

The trail goes right for a couple of hundred metres and then turns left, going up steeply. An hour or more of uphill climbing will bring you to an iron ladder that leads into the fort. The trail (from the temples) is well marked with white arrows painted on rocks and boulders.

TIP If you are unsure of the way, hire a guide at Mahuli Village (Rs 100-150) to show you the way

There is very little in the fort to indicate that it once served as an impressive bastion. You'll find some water tanks (not potable) at the top and springs and ⚠ a few caves you could camp in after cleaning up. While there is another entrance to the fort via the **Kalyan Darwaza**, this involves rock climbing and is not advisable in the monsoon. You'll also find some ruins and remains of battlements, bastions and a large pond — all in a state of neglect. One underground water tank in the north has potable water all year round. From the western edge of the fort, you can get an excellent view of **Tansa Lake**, one of the major sources of water for Mumbai. **Return** Go down the same way you took to come up. The stream next to the temples is a great spot for a cool, refreshing dip after your climb and it's quite safe as the water is not very deep.

TREKKING OPTIONS

● You could camp up in the fort over a full moon weekend. The forests around and within the fort are full of animals and birds. Or make your way across to **Chhota Mahuli**, which is due south of Mahuli Fort, just beyond the pinnacles. A little-used trail connects the two. Take a guide along; it makes the walk easier.

● My preferred option is a laid-back trip, which allows me to enjoy just being out in the forests for a couple of days. I walk into **Mahuli Village** and then to the temple after the bridge. This becomes my base camp and I spend two days here making day trips to the forts or just walking around the forest. I have on occasion seen wild boar, porcupine, peacock and jungle fowl. If **birdwatching** is your passion, this is a great place to spot some. ✦

Hiking in Bhatsa River Valley

Igatpuri is not more than a dot of civilisation, on the very edge of a huge, breathtaking canvas that was meant for us to gape at and to marvel at. Silently.

MUST-VISITS

BHATSA RIVER AND CAMEL VALLEYS
On your way to Igatpuri from Mumbai, less than 3 km from Manas Resort, a landmark in the region, is the Bhatsa River Valley. It's a stunning depth of happy vegetation and rocks that run down a slope off the road. To the right of NH3, as you come in from Mumbai, is one of the most spectacular sights in this region — the Camel Valley. You will have to walk over and look down to find a slope that falls over 305m.

TRINGALWADI FORT
About 6 km from Manas Resort is the Tringalwadi Fort with a narrow pathway for a nice walk down to the calm Tringalwadi Lake that looks a trifle more beautiful from the fort.

WHERE TO STAY
Manas Resort (Tel: 02553-244030; Tariff: Rs 2,000-5,000) on the Mumbai-Nasik Highway, Talegaon, has a health club with sauna and jacuzzi, a swimming pool, a beauty parlour, badminton, table tennis and pool facilities. **Golden Resort** (Tel: 244849; Tariff: Rs 1,000-1,600) at Bortemba, and **Hotel Ashwin** (Tel: 243624/ 625; Tariff: Rs 400-900) are also good bets in Igatpuri. **Ganaka Motel** (Tel: 243204; Tariff: Rs 300) is a popular en route halt on NH3.
For more details, see Accommodation Listings on page 544

WHERE TO EAT
No great restaurants, except those found in hotels such as **Manas Resort** and **Golden Resort**. For less than Rs 300 for two, the restaurants here offer Indian, Chinese and Maharashtrian food. **Ganaka Motel's** 24-hr restaurant offers Maharashtrian cuisine and snacks.

INPUTS FROM MANU JOSEPH

Igatpuri is considered by some to be just another railway junction. Or, more kindly by others as a tiny town where meditators take a vow of silence for many days in the renowned Vipassana Centre — another junction on the way to a greater destination. But the truth is different. Igatpuri is cooler than the more popular destination of Khandala, and is guarded by tall green hills that are occasionally shrouded in mist.

In the monsoons, Igatpuri's hills and deep river valleys burst into many shades of green, covered by a mesh of criss-crossing streams and waterfalls.

→ Igatpuri Facts

- **LOCATION** Igatpuri (579m) is a tiny town embedded in the Western Ghats, north-east of Mumbai
- **GETTING TO IGATPURI By air** Nearest airport: Mumbai (138 km/ 2½ hrs). Taxi Rs 1,700-2,000 return fare, shared taxi Rs 200 **By rail** Igatpuri Junction **By road** From Mumbai, take NH3 to Igatpuri over the Kasara Ghat, via Shahapur. ST buses (3½ hrs, Rs 90) ply all day from Senapati Bapat Marg (Tulsi Pipe Road) Bus Stand in Mumbai to Nasik via Igatpuri
- **TIP** If you are driving during the monsoons, get fog lights installed in your car as the ghat sections get enveloped in thick mist
- **STD CODE** 02553

LIFE IS CALLING WHERE ARE YOU?

SMIRNOFF

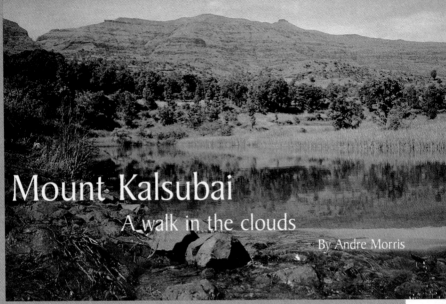

Mount Kalsubai
A walk in the clouds
By Andre Morris

Kalsubai view from the stream at the Bari Inspection Bungalow

TIME	1 day
LEVEL	Moderate
IDEAL SEASON	Sep to Feb
LOCATION	Igatpuri region, in the border between Nasik and Ahmadnagar districts

BARI-KALSUBAI-BARI

Beckoning climbers and trekkers from all over Western India is Mount Kalsubai (1,646m), the highest peak in Maharashtra and the Western Ghats. Highest, though, doesn't mean toughest, and Kalsubai is a trek for anyone who is reasonably fit. A breathtaking vista of shimmering waters and splendid forts awaits you, and making the trek even more exciting are the iron ladders that lead you up precarious paths and the series of pinnacles that lure you into thinking you've reached the top. Climb ahead, sip the delicious cool water of a well high up in the mountain, and be assured that the memories of this trek are going to stay with you for a long time.

THE TREK
BARI-KALSUBAI-BARI
DISTANCE 10 KM **TIME** 5-6 HOURS
LEVEL MODERATE

From behind the bus stop where you get off (there is only one bus stop in Bari), a footpath heads west across a field and joins a dirt road leading into **Bari Village** proper. Follow this for a kilometre. Just beyond the first section of the village, a path cuts across a stream and some rice paddies and climbs up a spur to disappear into the forest. This is the trail up. Initially, the climb is steep, then levels out onto a flat stretch with a few huts and open fields in 30 mins. Just past the huts, the path enters the courtyard of a temple. Some interesting stone pillars or lamp posts and carved Nandi bulls are scattered in the courtyard. The trees

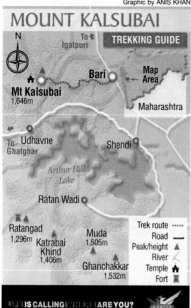

MOUNT KALSUBAI
TREKKING GUIDE

N
To Igatpuri
Bari
Map Area
Mt Kalsubai
1,646m
Maharashtra

To Ghatghar
Udhavne
Shendi

Arthur Hill Lake

Ratan Wadi

Ratangad
1,296m
Katrabai Khind
1,406m
Muda
1,505m
Ghanchakkar
1,532m

Trek route .....
Road
Peak/height ▲
River
Temple ♠
Fort

GETTING THERE AND OUT

FROM IGATPURI to Bari Village, it's 40 km/ 2 hrs by the Bhandardara State Transport (ST) 🚌 (Rs 36). All ST buses stop at Bari Village (about 12 km before **Bhandardara**); you can get off here. A better option is to catch a bus/ jeep 🚙 to **Ghoti**, which is 7 km away and get a jeep (Rs 350-500) from there to Bari **RETURN** the same way

around the temple make it an ideal oasis where you can take a break before continuing the climb. From here, the trail gets steeper and at three points iron ladders have been installed to assist you through.

Walk on behind the temple and climb up westwards to another flat stretch. You'll encounter some thick lantana bushes before climbing up a spur (30 mins). There are iron ladders fixed at two points and a couple of railings where the path is a little precarious. The second ladder is steep and leads up a rocky gully. From here, the trail is very dusty with lots of scree. Kalsubai's trademark is a series of false summits. Huffing and puffing to the top of the ridge, you are crestfallen to find that this is not the summit! About half a kilometre from the top is a small well. Even the fastidious will not be able to resist the cold clean water.

From the well, the summit rock is visible and a clear path leads up to an iron ladder that eventually brings you to the top. For the more adventurous, there is one iron chain still in place. This is on the left of the ladder. A short climb up the rock face will bring you to the top and a small temple dedicated to Devi Kalsubai.

The view from the top is the icing on the cake. Right below you is the vast expanse of **Arthur Hill Lake** or the backwaters of **Bhandardara Dam**. In the south one can see **Ghanchakkar**, **Katrabai Khind**, **Ratangad Fort** and Khutta Pinnacle while on the right or due west, one can see **Alang Fort**, Madangad and Kulang. Turning

En route to Ratangad Fort

Climbing the chain route to the summit of Kalsubai

around, in the north-east one can see the shimmering waters of **Beal Lake**, Aundha, Bitangad and Patta. Notice the offerings of many coins nailed to the wooden door-frame of the temple. There is no shade on the summit and the temple is not only too small but full of insects.

On the return, descend to Bari Village the way you came up but be careful as the scree makes the path rather slippery and the last thing you want is a sprained ankle. On two separate occasions, I have had the unfortunate

An enduring saas-bahu saga

Kalsubai, according to local legend, was the name of a tormented daughter-in-law who ran away to the top of a hill to escape harassment from her in-laws. She is believed to have disappeared here and the locals built a temple in her memory on the peak's summit. The hill is named **Kalsubai** after her.

experience of having to carry someone down to the village because of a badly sprained ankle or torn ligament.

TREKKING OPTIONS

● If you are keen on a long walk, you could descend all the way to **Bhandardara Dam**. From the well below the summit, follow a trail due south. This stays mostly on the left side of the hill and will bring you down to the **MTDC Holiday Resort**. Expect to take at least 4 hrs or more.

● An easier extension of your trek could be to walk along the road from **Bari to Warangushi** and then to Bhandardara (12 km), where, if you wish, you can spend the night at the **MTDC Resort**. Or from Warangushi, take a left turn and follow the Rajur Road till **Randha Falls** (14-15 km).

● One can also descend 10 km from the other side of the hill and reach **Udhavne Village**, from where it's a 15-16 km trek to **Bhandardara**.

For MTDC Resort in Bhandardara, see Accommodation Listings on page 544 ✦

Enjoy the best of nature with the best of its bounty.

The next time you go on a trek, don't forget to take the delicious fruit and spice conserves from Kitchens of India. Made from the juiciest fruits and fresh spices available, there's just no better way to be one with mother nature.

Kitchens of INDIA

FRUIT & SPICE CONSERVES

A feast for the senses

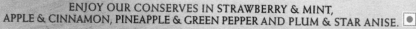

Recognising Karjat's potential as a relaxing weekend getaway, many wealthy Mumbaikars have built farmhouses here over the last two decades. Some cultivate flowers or mushrooms, others run poultry farms. And then there are those who have taken the city to the village and hold regular rave parties.

Karjat is where the coastal plain of the Konkan ends and the Bhor Ghat begins. Chance turned this unknown village into a railway hub. As a result, all trains heading this way stop at Karjat. While they halt, the passengers aboard get a few moments to grab a bite of the famous vada pav sold here.

ANIL DAVE/ DINODIA PHOTO LIBRARY

On the pretty road to Karjat

→ Karjat Facts

- **LOCATION** On the banks of the Ulhas River, south-east of Mumbai
- **GETTING TO KARJAT By air** Nearest airport: Mumbai (98 km/ 2½ hrs). Taxi Rs 1,100 **By rail** Karjat Station. Local trains connect CST Mumbai to Karjat (Rs 19 one way) every half hour from 2 am onwards **By road** Get to Panvel and drive past the NH17 junction on NH4, till Chowk. Turn left onto the Karjat Road, where there's a large sign indicating the turn for Matheran. A sign for Karjat also exists, but it's tiny and rather inconspicuous. Drive straight down for Karjat, which lies across the Ulhas River and just ahead of the left turn to Neral and Matheran. There are no direct buses to Karjat from Mumbai. You will have to switch buses at Panvel
- **STD CODE** 02148

MUST-VISITS

WHITE-WATER RAFTING
For an adrenaline-rush adventure, head to Karjat. During the monsoons it's possible to go white-water rafting on the upper sections of the Ulhas River, near Karjat. Outbound Adventures (see *Trekking Agents Listings on page 517*) organises rafting and canoeing trips here.

BIRDWATCHING
The best time for birdwatching on the banks of the Ulhas is during and just after the monsoon.

WHERE TO STAY
There are several guest houses and simple, down-to-earth budget places to stay in Karjat. The **Satya Health Farm Village Resort** (Tel: 02148-246154; Tariff: Rs 2,500) in Village Vanjerwadi has a meditation centre, gymnasium and a games room. **Dr Modi's Health Resort** (Tel: 222316; Tariff: Rs 2,200), located at Neral Road, has a health club with steam, sauna, jacuzzi and massages. **Hotel Kotligad** (Tel: 224920; Tariff: Rs 300) is a budget option in Village Kotligad and so is **Van Vihar** (Tel: 226844; Tariff: Rs 300). *For more details, see Accommodation Listings on pages 544-545*

WHERE TO EAT
Small stalls outside the station area serve vada pav as well as idlis, medu vadas, samosas, laddoos and sabudana vadas (with groundnuts). If you want to play it safe and avoid deep-fried food, ask for varan bhaat (Maharashtrian dal rice), usal pao or misal pao (also typically Maharashtrian). Karjat town itself has very little to offer by way of eating places. Most of the hotels and resorts have attached restaurants and you are probably best off eating there.

INPUTS FROM
NILOUFER VENKATRAMAN

TREKKING HOLIDAYS IN INDIA

Photographs by PUNIT PARANJPE

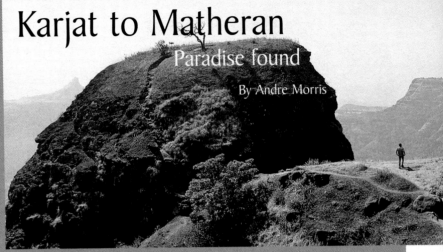

Karjat to Matheran
Paradise found

By Andre Morris

A lone walker at the One Tree Hill at Matheran

TIME	1-2 days
LEVEL	Easy
IDEAL SEASON	All year round
LOCATION	Karjat region, south-east of Mumbai, on the banks of Ulhas River, in Raigad District

KARJAT-VAVERLE-BHORGAON-AMBEWADI-ONE TREE HILL-MATHERAN-NERAL

With more than eight to ten different routes, Matheran (767m) is the ultimate destination for the trekker, naturalist and outdoor enthusiast. It is literally a forest on top of the hill (*mathe* means head and *raan* means forest). The dense forest cover, teeming bird life, long walks and flora and fauna make this an all-time favourite. The best part is that it's pollution-free as no vehicles are allowed in the hill station.

Apart from Bhimashankar, Matheran is the only other place where the giant red squirrel is to be found. It's also a haven for snakes, from the harmless keelbacks and pythons to the more deadly members of the clan such as cobras, kraits and vipers.

Sometime in 1982, I was bitten by a Russell's viper, and was fortunate enough not only to live to tell the

Ray-Ban

GENUINE SINCE 1937

CHANGE YOUR VIEW

EXPERIENCE THE RAY-BAN COLLECTION.

RB 3192 SIDESTREET RIMLESS RECTANGLE
M.R.P. Rs.4990/-

RB 4037 PREDATOR SHOT OVAL
M.R.P.Rs.3390/-

RB 3183 SIDESTREET TOP BAR SQUARE
M.R.P.Rs.4990/-

Choose from over 250 models at your nearest authorized Ray-Ban dealer.

888

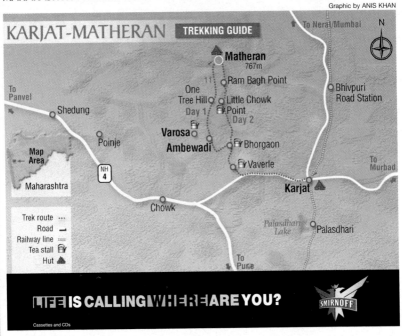

tale, but also to return to the place over 50 times after the event.

DAY ONE
KARJAT-AMBEWADI VILLAGE-MATHERAN
DISTANCE 10-11 KM **TIME** 4-5 HOURS **LEVEL** EASY

From Karjat, follow the **Karjat-Chowk Road** for 3 km until you see a signboard indicating a right turn, northwards, for **Vaverle Village**. Walk another 2 km along a tarred road from Vaverle to **Bhorgaon Village** (due north-east), which is at the base of Matheran. If you'd rather not walk along a tarred road, you could get a ride in an autorickshaw to Bhorgaon (*see Getting There and Out on page 376*). If you decide to take a cross-country route, remember that you will have to cross a wide stream to get to Bhorgaon. It may be difficult to ford during the monsoon.

Just before you enter Bhorgaon Village, a well-used footpath turns left (due west) and heads up a very gentle spur. It runs across some fields before turning north-west and climbing another spur, at the top of which you will come to **Ambewadi Village**. This is the last point where you will get water, so fill up your bottles as you pass the two village

Sunset point at Matheran

The drama unfolds before Alexander Point at Matheran

wells just beyond the village. The next watering hole is the cold drink stall at One Tree Hill in Matheran.

From Ambewadi, the trail is joined by another well-used path coming up from **Varosa Village**, on the other side of the spur. This is the final 3 km ascent to the top, climbing up a steep spur (due north) to a flat area. **Big Chowk Point** is clearly visible and looks like an elephant's head.

The track now heads into a stretch of thick forest, which is a welcome respite from the sun. As you near the end of the thick forest, you come to a mass of boulders and rocks into which the trail disappears. This is known as **Shivaji Steps** or the Shivaji Ladder. According to local legend, Shivaji rode up this route on horseback. From here, it's 500m to the top, up a stream bed that's dry except during the monsoon.

As you get to the top, you will see **One Tree Hill** on your left, connected to Matheran by a narrow ridge. On reaching the ridge take a right turn to come out at a cold drink stall. From the stall, it's an easy 3 km to the market place in **Matheran**. If you want to stay at Matheran overnight, there are numerous hotels and lodges to choose from, to suit all budgets.

However, if you want to head to Mumbai, your best bet is to head to **Dasturi Naka** (due north of the market place) and walk down along the road (11 km) to Neral. If you're in a mood for a quick descent, take the **Postman's Short-cut**. This route follows the road till the **Water Pipe Station**, then after half a kilometre, a footpath cuts across the railway line and follows a long spur, bringing you to the outskirts of **Neral** (5 or 6 km).

DAY TWO
MATHERAN-BHORGAON-KARJAT
DISTANCE 10-11 KM **TIME** 4-5 HOURS
LEVEL EASY

About $2^1/_2$-3 km from the Matheran market (due south-east) is **Ram Bagh Point**, which is on the way to **Little Chowk Point**, marked by a small cold drink/ tea-stall. From here, a broad trail paved with red stones, typical of Matheran, leads down the hillside in a gently meandering course. A kilometre along this trail, and you will come to a flat, thickly forested stretch.

When you are almost below Little Chowk Point, the path bifurcates. The path to the right heads due west, around the hill through some thick dense jungle.

Take the trail on the left, which leads down the ridge of a long spur for almost 2 km (due east) and then across some smaller hillocks and open fields ($2^1/_2$ km) before entering **Bhorgaon Village**. You can either follow the road to Karjat as given above or catch an autorickshaw to get to **Karjat**.

Another kilometre and you're at **Neral Station** from where you can get a Mumbai-bound local train.

If you'd rather not walk from Dasturi Naka to Neral, you can get a seat in a cab to Neral Station. Rates are fixed and currently stand at Rs 60 per seat.

TREKKING OPTIONS
There are numerous routes to get in or out of **Matheran**, as well as many long, pleasant walks around the hill station itself. You can come up with your own combinations. Here are a few ideas:

The black scorpion

Of all the insects and creatures to be found in the jungles of Matheran (and there are plenty — large spiders, beetles, snakes and their ilk), one that stands out is the black rock scorpion (*Androctonus crassicauda*). It's the largest of the known 350 species of scorpion, of which India has more than 80.

PORPOISE PHOTOSTOCK

This large, hairy creature can grow as long as eight or nine inches. It walks on its belly dragging its guided missile (or poison-filled tail) behind. The sting of this formidable creature is not as poisonous as its country cousin, the red scorpion. Yet the sting is very painful for a few hours, though not fatal. While walking around the hill station or scrambling around trees and boulders, keep an eye out for this scorpion. They usually want to be left alone just as much as you do, so give them a wide berth. If you are lucky, you may encounter a pair mating: the male holds the pincers of the female and drags her back and forth in a courtship dance. At the end of the mating, she usually kills and eats her suitor. Scorpions eat other insects, bugs and cockroaches. Even though the pincers look big and scary, remember it's the tail that has the sting.

● One enjoyable but long route (18-20 km) is to take a Karjat-bound local train from Mumbai and get down at **Vangani Station**. From there you can hike to Vaghachi Wadi, cross the Nakhind-Chanderi col and walk to **Panvel Lake**. From the lake, there are two routes up to Matheran. The first is via **Porcupine Point**, also called **Milk Trail** (locals use this to bring fresh milk up to the markets). The other route is less used and climbs a spur running due east. This first brings you to **Hashachi Patti**, a tribal hamlet, and then into Matheran via Malang Point.

● One can climb up to **Peb Fort** from **Neral** and then follow the railway line into Matheran.

● Another popular route starts at Bhivpuri Station and then goes via Thakurwadi up onto the **Garbet Plateau** and finally into Matheran via **Garbet Point**. This is a long trek (12-14 km) but enjoyable in the monsoon.

● From **Chowk Village** you can trek up to Varosa Village and then climb up to Matheran via the Shivaji Steps as described earlier (*see page 380*). You will join the main trail at Ambewadi.

● It's also possible to link Matheran into a 4- to 5-day trek starting at **Lonavla** and going on to Rajmachi, Bhairi Caves, Dhak Fort, Karjat and finally Matheran.

● Another interesting walk is from **Karnala** in the south-west, cross-country to Matheran.

● Opposite Matheran is **Prabal Fort** and Irshal (or **Vishalgad Fort**). You can either start at Irshal and then climb Prabal Fort, come down to Varosa and climb up to Matheran or do the trek in reverse (*see the Irshal-Prabal Trek on page 384*).

For hotels in Matheran, see Accommodation Listings on pages 547-548 ✦

Mark of Performance

Drive your Dream with Speed Fuels. Developed with internationally renowned fuel additive technology, you now have the satisfaction of indulging your vehicle with the best fuel available in the country today. At last, a fuel truly worthy of running your prized driving machine, a fuel that guarantees the ultimate driving experience.

World Class Fuels from

Bharat Petroleum

Irshal-Prabal Fort

High ground

By Andre Morris

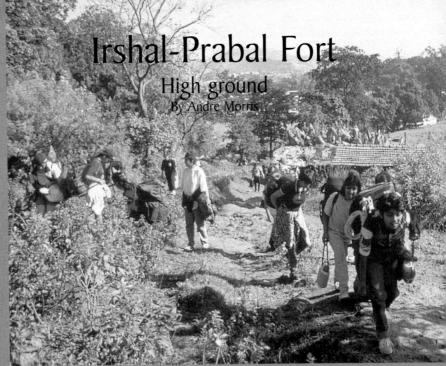

Young trekkers set off enthusiastically for the long day hike

TIME	1-2 days
LEVEL	Moderate to Difficult
IDEAL SEASON	Nov to Mar
LOCATION	Karjat region, Chowk area, south-east of Mumbai, in Raigad District

KARJAT-CHOWK-IRSHALWADI-IRSHAL-PRABAL-THAKURWADI-SHEDUNG

I t's the peak that always makes me stop and look up in awe. Though it was probably an important site guarding a trade route once upon a time, warning the mighty Marathas of approaching enemies, there is not much left of Irshal today. Even then, it's an exciting trek. Also known as Vishalgad (370m), Irshal looks like a cardboard cut-out, its two pinnacles resembling a pitch fork, and the large hole in the centre of the rock clearly visible from miles away. If you're not an experienced rock climber, do not take the risky route to the top. Instead, take a safer hike skirting the base of Irshal and walk across the ridge to Prabal Fort (707m).

The British once considered Prabal as a salubrious site for building a hill station, but the lack of water forced them to move across to Matheran in the north-east instead. The fort itself is in ruins, and overgrown by jungle, making for a very interesting walk. Look out for the petite mouse deer that is found in and around Prabal.

DAY ONE
IRSHAL-PRABAL FORT
DISTANCE 12-14 KM **TIME** 6-7 HOURS
LEVEL MODERATE

Alight at **Chowk** on the Mumbai-Pune Highway (NH4), at what is better known as the Matheran-Karjat turn-off. Walk along the highway towards Mumbai, due west, for a little more than a kilometre and take a right turn, due north-west. Follow a footpath that will lead across a couple of fields, across the new railway line and then up a long gentle spur. It's an easy 3-km walk up the spur to the plateau and to **Irshalwadi**, the village at the base of Irshal.

The pinnacle of Irshal rises from the middle of the plateau like an impregnable rock fortress. The trail to the top goes around the left (due west), across the ridge and then due north, to the other side of the hill (ensure the cliff walls are to your right). Then a narrow path climbs very steeply up a rock face and brings you to the hole in the rock. This trail continues a little further and brings you above the hole to an opening between the two

Bharat Petroleum

GETTING THERE AND OUT

FROM KARJAT, catch an ST 🚌 or a six-seater autorickshaw to **Chowk** (10 km/ Rs 10-15 per seat). The ride takes about 25 mins. If you are driving, take the Mumbai-Pune Expressway and get off at the first exit (Khopoli/ Shedung Exit) onto NH4. After driving for 12-14 km, stop at the sign indicating **Chowk Village**

RETURN From **Panvel** to **Mumbai** (51 km/ $1^1/_2$ hrs), either catch a 🚐 (Rs 550), or take one of the regular buses that run to Mumbai or catch a CST-bound Harbour Line local train

Graphic by ANIS KHAN

IRSHAL-PRABAL

TREKKING GUIDE

N

Kelve Teen ▲
Prabal Fort 707m
Matheran 767m ▲▲

Day 2

Pazar Lake

Shedung

To Panvel
NH 4

Poinje

Day 1

Nadhal Lake

12

Irshal 370m ▲

Irshalwadi

To Karjat
NH 4

Campsite ⛺
Trek route •••••
Road —
Peak/height ▲
River ⟨
Hut 🏠
Temple ⛩
Tea stall ☕

Chowk

Map Area

Maharashtra

pinnacles. There is one water tank with good drinking water available. If you go left from this gap, you will come to the base of the pinnacle. On the left of the rock face is another water tank and a very small natural cave-like shelter.

WARNING The route to the summit involves a 10-m rock climb to a sloping, exposed section full of loose scree. A small hole has been created in the rock face to anchor a rope, but this by no means reduces the danger. **Do not attempt this climb alone or if you have no climbing experience**

The view from the hole in the rock is breathtaking as much as it is fearsome, for you are on a very narrow stretch and there is often a strong breeze. On the rock wall, you'll find a stone plaque in memory of a climber who fell to his death while attempting the climb to the pinnacle.

Descend by retracing your steps to **Irshalwadi**. If you're tired, you could ⛺ camp out at Irshalwadi. Else, trek

Karvi bushes

Found all over the Sahyadris, karvi (*Carvia collosa* or *Strobilanthes callosus*) is also known as the Seven-year Plant. This is because they grow for seven years, flower in the eighth, and then die, dispersing the seeds so that new plants emerge the following year. Karvi grows very straight and is used by tribals and other villagers to make the walls of their homes, which are then plastered with cow dung. The karvi flower is purple in colour and attractive to bees. The honey acquired from bees that have fed off the karvi flower is coveted and considered to have medicinal properties. It is a dark, luminescent brown and not the usual golden colour. Karvi is also used as an insect repellent, and if while walking through the hills, you accidentally touch stinging nettle, pull off some karvi leaves and rub them on the itchy spot. Watch as the sting miraculously disappears!

up to Prabal Fort and camp at the **Ganesh Temple**. The ridge connecting **Prabal Fort** is due north-east and will take you to the lower plateau of the fort. Just before the start of the ridge, you'll find a spring, which has good water, though this usually dries up by the end of winter.

The walk across the ridge can take 2½-3 hrs and will bring you to the lower plateau of Prabal Fort. From this plateau, the trail moves due north along the base of the fort (ensure the fort is to your left). The route into the fort is over a faint trail up a steep gully into the fort (1-1½ hrs).

Along the way there is a water tank but this does not have water all the time. The top is initially covered with dense jungle, filled with karvi bushes and trees. The trail will lead through the forest and bring you to a Ganesh Temple.

TIP Not much is visible through the dense undergrowth and getting to the edge for a view is a little tricky. It is advisable to take a villager from Irshalwadi as a guide (they'll charge around Rs 100-150)

DAY TWO
PRABAL FORT-SHEDUNG
DISTANCE 6-7 KM **TIME** 3-4 HOURS
LEVEL MODERATE

From the **Ganesh Temple**, a faint trail leads north (1 km) and brings you to another entrance of the fort. On the opposite side is a pinnacle (due north) connected to Prabal by a col. A flight of steep rock steps leads out of the fort and down a spur to this col (½ hr/ 1 km).

From the col, turn left or south-west and then descend via a gully to **Thakurwadi** (1-1½ hrs). From here, it's another half an hour to **Vardoli Village** from where you can get transport (opt for either an ST bus or autorickshaw) to **Shedung**, located on NH4. **Panvel** is about 8 km away, and from there you can get a bus or local train back to Mumbai.

Prabal Fort stands tall in the haze of a warm spring afternoon

TREKKING OPTIONS

There are several options available depending on the time you have.

● You can start your trek at **Vardoli** and **Thakurwadi** and climb up to **Prabal Fort** first and then come across to **Irshal**. From here, go down to **Varosa Village** in the north-east and from there to **Matheran** via Shivaji Steps (*see page 380*).

● Proceed as above and then continue the trek due south to **Savna Lake**, Manekgad, Sankshi and **Karnala Fort**. Add at least 2-3 days to your plan.

● There are two lakes, **Nadhal** and **Pazar**, in the vicinity of **Irshal**, and there are plans for a new earthen dam on the eastern side at the base. These make for interesting walks and are great places to set up ⛺ camp. The thick forest around the lake is great for birdwatching too.

For hotels in Matheran, see Accommodation Listings on pages 547-548 ✦

Peth Fort Kotligad
The funnel mountain

By Andre Morris

TIME	1-2 days
LEVEL	Moderate
IDEAL SEASON	Jun to Mar
LOCATION	Karjat region, south-east of Mumbai, in Raigad District

Photographs by ANDRE MORRIS

The approach to Kotligad

KARJAT-AMBIVLI-PETH

The Peth Fort stands in splendid isolation in the Sahyadri mountain range, a solitary reaper rising like an inverted funnel above the surrounding landscape. The funnel is actually a volcanic plug, formed by the cooling lava flows that created the Deccan Plateau. The softer outer layers eroded over the ages, leaving pinnacles like Kotligad, as the Peth peak is called.

A long time ago, the fort was a watch-post for soldiers guarding the Bhor Ghat, which was once an important trade route between Pune and the port of Kalyan. The fort played a role in keeping trade routes open and was only captured by intrigue or by mistaken identity. Legend has it that the commander of the fort mistook the Mughals for the Marathas and allowed them to approach the fort.

Once at the fort, you're treated to a grand view of the Karjat and Bhimashankar Range, tunnels and pipelines, Matheran, several other hills and plains. In the monsoon, this is a particularly delightful hike and on weekends you'll find the route quite packed with trekkers. The sound of a waterfall cascading down the hillside and cicadas rejoicing in unison create a pleasant soundtrack accompanying you as you walk. Wild flowers sway in the breeze and small and large bullfrogs (*Rana tigrina*) hop about crisscrossing your path. There are plenty of birds and great views, which make the hike even more enjoyable. Dozens of fruit bats inhabit the caves at the base of the pinnacle, so if you don't mind the smell, take a peek at their habitat.

DAY ONE

AMBIVLI-PETH
DISTANCE 5-6 KM **TIME** 2-3 HOURS
LEVEL MODERATE
Take the right turn south-east just before Ambivli Village. There is a small restaurant at the junction here, called **Hotel Kotligad**, where you can get 🍴 refreshments. Here, you will find safe

Graphic by ANIS KHAN

PETH FORT

TREKKING GUIDE

To Murbad
Poshir
Khandas
Bhimashankar 1,005m
Padar Killa
Tungi
Ambivli
Maldev
Peth Fort 472m
Dhamni
Peth Village
To Karjat
Savale Khind
Jambuli
Map Area
Maharashtra

Campsite ⚑
Trek route ·····
Road ──
Pass ⛰
Peak/height ▲
River ∿
Hut ⛺
Temple ⛩
Tea stall ☕

GETTING THERE AND OUT

FROM KARJAT to Ambivli, it's 25-28 km/ 1 hr by State Transport (ST) 🚌 (Rs 15-20). Or hire a six-seater autorickshaw from Karjat Station (shared at Rs 30 per seat, among 10 people at least). The ride takes about 30-40 mins

TIP Hire the whole six-seater at Rs 300-450 and arrange for a pick-up when you return as well. No 🚗 available. If coming by car, follow the Karjat-Murbad Road and take the Jambuli turn-off (at a milestone indicating 'Karjat 18 km'). **Ambivli Village** is another 10 km from here

RETURN One can catch an ST bus back to **Karjat** (Ambivli to Karjat buses are turnaround ones and do not wait) or take a six-seater auto to Karjat and then a local train back to Mumbai

parking for your vehicle, arrangements for meals, guides and porters. All this comes at a very reasonable cost (contact Gopal Savant on Tel: 02148-224920; *also see Accommodation Listings on page 544*).

Half a kilometre later, the trail to Peth branches off to the east, or left. This is a metalled road until the base of the hill, from where a well-used trail leads up to Peth Village 3-4 km away.

This hike is very enjoyable, with many birds and good views of the surrounding area. Peth Fort itself appears to be very far off but don't worry. On reaching **Peth Village**, you can stop for ☕ a cup of tea and rest or even a hot meal at the branch of **Hotel Kotligad**. Also, don't miss checking out an unusual large brass cannon in the middle of the village.

The trail to the fort goes north or left of the base of the fort (remember the fort should be on your right). Walk through the village (until the

end) and turn right at the big red house. A path leads up north-east a little and then through fields. After a 10-min walk, look on your right (due south) for a trail leading through the jungle to the base of the pinnacle for a kilometre (30 mins).

Half-way up, take the trail leading off to the right or due west. It will bring you to an old cannon. At the base of the pinnacle is a large cave with five supporting pillars suggesting Buddhist monks hewed them, probably around 200 BC. At the end of this cave is a smaller cave (look out for the fruit bats that hang from the ceiling in this one).

The steep ascent to the top of the pinnacle is via a stone staircase tunnelled out of rock from near the water tank. This is the only way to the

LET YOUR
MIND TRAVEL
YOUR BODY
WILL FOLLOW...

OUTLOOK
traveller

Life is one incredible journey

traveller
COUNTRYSIDE
Green and Pleasant Holidays

traveller
Once and Future
Kingdoms

top. At the summit are some Maratha ruins that date back to the time when the fort was a watch-post for guarding the **Bhor Pass**.

Atop the pinnacle is a pleasant reward for the trudge up — panoramic views of the **Karjat** and **Bhimashankar ranges**, **Padar Killa**, lots of beautiful waterfalls (can be seen only in the monsoons), and in the distance, the hill station of **Matheran**.

The main cave at Kotligad

🛖 You can camp out in the caves at **Peth Fort**, but, during the monsoons, expect to have lots of company, especially on weekends. There's also some 🏠 lodging at the very rustic **Hotel Kotligad** at Peth Village. One could pitch a tent on top of the fort near the ruins, or just outside Peth Village, but only between end-October and May. Between June and mid-October during the monsoons, it's impossible to camp out in the open.

DAY TWO
PETH-AMBIVLI
DISTANCE 5-6 KM **TIME** 3 HOURS
LEVEL MODERATE
Walk back to **Ambivli** by retracing your steps to **Peth Village** and then follow the trail down. Alternatively,

you can take a lesser-known trail from just outside Peth Village down to **Jambuli Village**, which is a good tough walk in the monsoon. You should take a local guide (the charges will be between Rs 100 and 150), as the trail is often overgrown and indistinct. From Jambuli Village, there are several buses each day to Karjat as well as the odd six-seater autorickshaw.

TREKKING OPTIONS
● As **Peth Fort** is not connected to the main ghats running north to south, there is no direct route leading into the surrounding hills and one has to descend into the plains and then climb up again, whether you are going to **Bhimashankar** or **Padar Killa** or up to the **Bhivpuri Tunnels**.

● One interesting combination is to link your trek to Peth with one to **Bhimashankar**. From **Jambuli**, you'll need to take a bus to Kashele or Khandas and from there, begin your trek to Bhimashankar.

For hotels in Karjat, see Accommodation Listings on pages 544-545 ✦

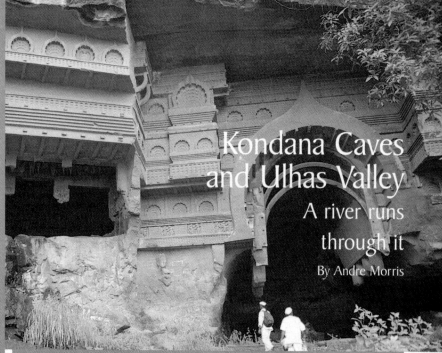

Kondana Caves and Ulhas Valley

A river runs through it

By Andre Morris

Visitors stand awe-struck at the magnificent entrance to the Kondana Caves

TIME	1-2 days
LEVEL	Easy
IDEAL SEASON	Jun to Jan
LOCATION	Karjat region, by the Ulhas River, near Rajmachi Fort in Raigad District

KONDANA VILLAGE-KONDANA CAVES-ULHAS VALLEY

At just 60m above sea level, Kondana Caves is not a challenging walk. But its location and easy accessibility make it one of the most pleasant hikes you can undertake near Mumbai. This is even more so in the monsoon as you'll come across a number of waterfalls, streams and pools along the way. The area's popularity can be gauged from the number of hikers and picnickers you'll find here during the monsoon. So if you want to have the caves all to yourself, then make your trip midweek when you'll almost certainly be the only one there.

DAY ONE

KONDANA VILLAGE-KONDANA CAVES
DISTANCE 4-5 KM **TIME** 1 1/2-2 HOURS
LEVEL EASY

Start at **Kondana Village** where the tarred road ends outside **Van Vihar**, a rustic lodge. Here there is safe parking (though it's on the road) for your vehicle, arrangements for meals, return transport to Karjat Station and guides and porters, if required. All this comes at a very reasonable cost (contact Anil or Vinayak Gogte on Tel: 02148-226844, 222930; *also see page 544*).

A dirt road due south leads further ahead along the Ulhas River, for about 500m (15 mins) and will bring you to

Photographs by ANDRE MORRIS

Graphic by ANIS KHAN

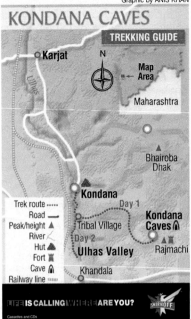

KONDANA CAVES
TREKKING GUIDE

Karjat N

Map Area

Maharashtra

Bhairoba Dhak

Kondana
Day 1

Trek route ·····
Road
Peak/height ▲
River
Hut ▲
Fort ⚔
Cave ⋒
Railway line

Kondana Caves ⋒
Tribal Village
Day 2
Ulhas Valley   Rajmachi
Khandala

GETTING THERE AND OUT

FROM KARJAT STATION to Kondivade, it's 14 km/ 45 mins by an ST 🚌. Alternatively, a six-seater autorickshaw charges Rs 10-15 per seat for the 30-min ride (but expect at least 10 people inside). You can also hire the whole six-seater at Rs 300-450 and arrange for a pick-up on the return as well. No 🚕 available. If coming by car, after turning left from NH4 for Matheran and Karjat, follow the Karjat-Murbad Road for about 15 km. Then take a right turn at the end of the bridge that crosses the Ulhas River in Karjat. A 14-km drive mostly along the banks of the river will bring you to **Kondana Village** and **Van Vihar** (a rustic lodge) **RETURN** Take an ST bus back to **Karjat** or a seat in a six-seater autorickshaw and then a local train back to Mumbai

a **tribal village**. Just beyond, a path turns left (due east) and winds its way across an open field with several eucalyptus trees along its border. Just beyond the field, the path climbs up a gentle spur and disappears into thick green forest. If it's raining, this part of the trail can be very slushy.

The trail is well used and crosses several streams and rivulets (in heavy downpours these can become raging torrents). A small detour will bring you to a lovely waterfall in the monsoon, which is also a great place to try out some rock climbing in dry weather (after October).

After 3 km (1 1/2 hrs), you'll come to a thick teak jungle. Here, another trail joins you from the left (make a note of this as you do not want to take a wrong turn while descending). At this junction, the trail turns right (due south), for about 100m. Keep your eyes focused on the left and get a glimpse, through the canopy, of the

simple but artistic **rock-cut caves of Kondana**. It will take another 5 mins before you actually reach the caves.

If you're trekking during the monsoon, a stream of water will cascade over the caves. No potable water is available, so remember to stock up at the beginning of the trek. Unfortunately, the entire cave area is often horribly littered; do make sure you take your garbage back with you.
Return the same way you ascended. Refresh yourself with a dip in the upper reaches of the Ulhas River. If you like, you could stay the night at **Van Vihar**, run by the very enterprising Gogtes at their home in **Kondana Village**. They provide very simple and rustic accommodation, hot meals at

Monsoon falls over Kondana Caves

just Rs 60 to 70 (for a thali lunch) and snacks which are home-cooked and served buffet-style. Their place is right on the banks of the river, so you can spend an evening sipping ☕ hot chai

gazing at the river after a long day of walking, swimming or rafting on the river. All this comes at a very reasonable cost (*see page 394*).

(*see page 394*)

DAY TWO

KONDANA VILLAGE–ULHAS VALLEY
DISTANCE 8-9 KM **TIME** 2¹/₂-3 HOURS
LEVEL EASY

Today you can walk up the **Ulhas Valley** for as long as you wish. This is an interesting hike, especially during and just after the monsoons. Once you have reached as far as you wish to go, turn back and return to **Van Vihar** for a hot meal or a lazy afternoon playing in the river.

From Van Vihar, follow the trail for **Kondana Caves** till the tribal village. From there follow the main dirt road straight ahead. After another kilometre you'll arrive at another tribal village. Head to the river from here and you will be able to see it cascade almost 25 ft down a steep slope. You'll see children from the village jumping off huge boulders into a deep pool at the bottom of the cascade, but don't attempt this yourself.

Kondana Caves

The ancient rock-cut caves of Kondana date back to the 2nd century BC. They are believed to be one of the region's oldest set of rock-cut cave monasteries. The main chaitya has a series of stone pillars suspended from the ceiling while the main stupa is broken and crumbling. The other caves further along are viharas and were the residential quarters for the monks.

Though in a state of ruin, the octagonal pillars (sloping inwards), wooden arches and interiors are very interesting.

Outside the main chaitya are some relief sculptures and the figure of a prince with the face damaged. An inscription next to this is said to be the name of the benefactor. The intricate details and proportions speak volumes of the artisans' skills.

In the vihara next to the chaitya, look closely at the ceiling and you will make out the remains of frescoes. On the walls, you'll find the remnants of the cow dung and husk used to plaster the walls before painting on them. Unfortunately, the caves are believed to have suffered major damage in the early 1900s, during an earthquake when the lower half of the pillars in the chaitya and much of the outer façade and water cisterns collapsed. You can still see sections of these ruins lying around the place.

TASHI TOBGYAL

Red silk cotton

Red silk cotton (*Bombax ceiba*) is found all over Naneghat and around Karjat and Kondana Caves. It's a tall deciduous tree that flowers between January and March after all its leaves have fallen. The flowers are large and red. The fruit pods are oval and contain a silky cotton with small black and brown seeds.

From here, paddy fields give way to scrub and thick jungle. It's best to stay along the river bank as there isn't much of a trail above the bank. In 1¹/₂ hrs, you will be deep in the **Ulhas Valley** amidst plenty of wildlife, birds and an assortment of plants and wild flowers. If you are on the left bank (right bank while facing upriver), you could take an obvious but little-used trail up the hillside (due south-west) to the railway line and **Thakurwadi Station** (not really a station, just a check-point where trains halt while climbing the ghat). You can catch a train to Karjat instead of heading back to Kondana Village.

TIP If you intend to go up to Thakurwadi, take a local as guide to ensure you don't get lost. The more adventurous can follow a steep, little-used trail on the left bank (due north-east) to **Rajmachi Fort** (not advisable during the monsoons)

TREKKING OPTIONS

● From Kondana Caves you could hike all the way up to **Rajmachi Fort** and then proceed to **Lonavla**.

● If it's not too hot and is between July and November, there's an interesting option I sometimes take to get back to **Karjat**. You could walk along the river up to **Palasdhari Station** and catch a local train back to Karjat or even to Mumbai. If you have the time you could also walk across to **Palasdhari Dam**, which is a small railway dam near the station.

For hotels in Karjat, see Accommodation Listings on pages 544-545 ✦

LIFE IS CALLING WHERE ARE YOU?
SMIRNOFF

Cassettes and CDs

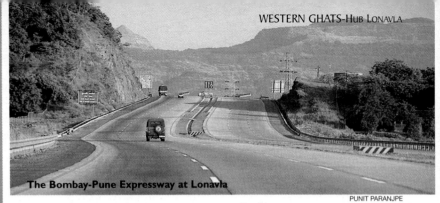

The Bombay-Pune Expressway at Lonavla

PUNIT PARANJPE

Bollywood filmmakers discovered the potential of this hill station as a shooting locale a long time ago. But Lonavla is much more than that. During the monsoons, it has lovely waterfalls that charm effortlessly, and hypnotic dark, rain clouds, racing over towering ghats.

MUST-VISITS

BUSHY DAM
Nestled in the forests just 6 km outside Lonavla (beyond Monsoon Lake) is this small and very popular dam. Swimming is not allowed.

ANGLING
Most lakes are open for fishing except those belonging to the Tata Electric Company. Check with officials beforehand.

→ Lonavla Facts

● **LOCATION** The hill station of Lonavla sits astride the ghats near the eastern extremity of the Deccan Plateau, a little more than half-way between Mumbai and Pune

● **GETTING TO LONAVLA By air** Nearest airport: Mumbai (102 km/ 2 hrs). Taxi Rs 1,100 **By rail** Lonavla Station. Deccan Queen and the Shatabdi are good options from Mumbai **By road** On the Mumbai-Pune Expressway, the travelling time to Lonavla is 2 hrs at the most. ST and Asiad buses (Rs 150-200) operating between Mumbai and Pune stop at Lonavla. A bus leaves every 15 mins from the Asiad Stand at Dadar, Mumbai

● **STD CODE** 02114

BIRDWATCHING
Lots of opportunity for spotting birds as this region is home to several local species and the nesting place for some migratory species as well.

WHERE TO STAY

Note that weekends are usually more expensive than weekdays. Advance bookings are a must.

Fariyas Holiday Resort (Tel: 02114-273852-253; Tariff: Rs 4,500-8,450), located on a hilltop, has a travel desk and swimming pool. **Hotel Rainbow Retreat** (Tel: 273445; Tariff: Rs 2,120-3,710), on Mumbai-Pune Road, has a travel desk, cable TV and room service. **Captans Resort** (Tel: 271313; Tariff: Rs 2,500-4,000), near Lonavla, has trekking, camping and yoga facilities. **Hotel Chandralok** (Tel: 272294; Tariff: Rs 390-1,350), off the Mumbai-Pune Highway, has a travel desk and room service.
For more hotels and details, see Accommodation Listings on page 546

WHERE TO EAT

Chandralok and Adarsh hotels serve Gujarati thalis (Rs 45-65). There are numerous Udupi-style eating houses as well. Along the main Mumbai-Pune Highway (near Lonavla), there are dozens of restaurants. Outside Lonavla Station (on the market side), you will find small restaurants serving everything from pav bhaji to biryani and burgers.

INPUTS FROM ANDRE MORRIS
AND NILOUFER VENKATRAMAN

TREKKING HOLIDAYS IN INDIA

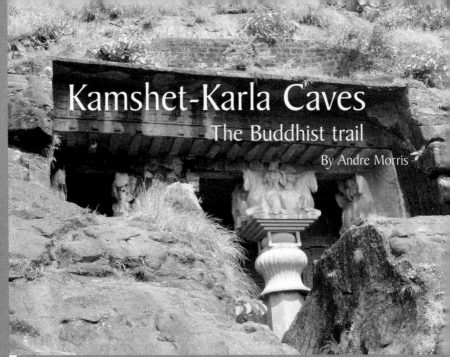

Kamshet-Karla Caves
The Buddhist trail

By Andre Morris

The overgrown entrance to the ancient Buddhist caves of Bedsa

TIME	2-4 days
LEVEL	Moderate
IDEAL SEASON	Sep to Mar/ Apr
LOCATION	South-east of Mumbai, beyond Lonavla-Khandala, in Pune District

KAMSHET-BEDSA CAVES-BEDSA HILL-VISAPUR FORT-LOHAGAD FORT-BHAJA CAVES-KARLA CAVES

The ancient Buddhist caves at Bhaja near Malavli have fascinated me ever since I first visited the place during a school excursion in 1977. Not only did the trip take me on a journey back 2,000 years, it also sparked my interest in Indian history and eventually prompted me to do my masters in the subject. In the course of my research, I

GETTING THERE AND OUT

FROM LONAVLA to Kamshet, it's 26 km/ 30 mins by jeep- (Rs 150), ST (Rs 10) or auto (Rs 100)
Mumbai to Lonavla by train is 3 hrs. Switch to local Pune-bound train and get off at Kamshet (20 mins). If coming by car, it's best to leave your vehicle in Lonavla and take the train to Kamshet
RETURN from **Karla Caves** by bus or auto to **Lonavla**, or catch a local train from Malavli to Lonavla. From Lonavla get bus, train or taxis/ jeeps to Mumbai

KAMSHET-KARLA CAVES · TREKKING GUIDE

Tungarli Lake

Valvan Lake

⋔ **Karla Caves**

Kamshet Station

N

Khandala ○ **Lonavla**

Valvan Exit **Day 4**

To Mumbai

NH 4

● **Kamshet** To Pune

Malavli ○

Mumbai-Pune Expressway

Microwave Tower

Bhaja Caves ○ ⋔

Day 2

Wageshwar Temple

Bedsa Hill Bedsa ⋔

Lohagad Fort

○ ⋔ 🏠 ⚑

Visapur Fort **Day 3**

Bedsa Caves

Bedsa ○

Day 1

Kale Colony

Pawna Lake

○ **Pawna Nagar**

Map Area

Tung Fort ○ ⚑

Maharashtra

Campsite ⛺		Bridge ⋈	
Trek route ···		Tea stall ☕	
Road ▭		Temple ⛩	
Pass ⛰		Cave ⋔	
River ≺		Railway line —	

Ramparts of the Lohagad Fort

discovered that some of the Buddhist rock-cut caves around the Western Ghats date back to the 2nd century BC. Most of these caves are situated along ancient trade routes that ran from the coastal plains of the Konkan through the ghats, into the Deccan Plateau.

While the more famous caves are big tourist attractions, there are many less known but equally interesting sites all over the Sahyadris. One such chain of caves is in the Lonavla region and trekking to these wonders is always a pleasure. From the elaborate caves lower in the hills, follow the trail up mountains. There, you'll find meditation and prayer halls giving way to forts and fortifications not seen elsewhere. In fact, many of the caves and water tanks in the numerous hill forts were actually built by Buddhists monks and were later occupied and worked upon to suit the needs of a garrison.

Some of the caves have the remains of frescoes and sculptures. Once, there were frescoes in the ceiling of the main chaitya of Bedsa Caves, but a village headman had the ceiling whitewashed. At Karla Caves, in front of the main chaitya, you'll find a Koli Temple where regular sacrifices of chickens and goats are made even as men and women dance in a religious trance.

This trek can be done in parts. Each place can be covered one at a time over different weekends, or completed over two, three or even five days. I have spread it over four days to give it a

Bedsa Caves

The Bedsa Caves are not elaborately sculptured or ornately decorated but their design and style, which have distinct Roman or Greek influences, are very interesting. Outside the main chaitya are two huge pillars with an elaborately carved capital of a bell. On top of this are animal and rider figures. Inside the chaitya is the stupa with pillars on either side (for circumambulation) and a sun window that catches the early morning rays. There are two rooms on either side of the main chaitya and some inscriptions above the doorways. The entrance to the chaitya is hewn out of rock leaving only a narrow passage. There is a large vihara to the right of the chaitya (when facing it) and six or seven water tanks (all potable). Further on the right are some unfinished caves, and on the left, several smaller stupas.

leisurely pace, with enough time to take in the atmosphere of these places.

DAY ONE
KAMSHET-BEDSA CAVES
DISTANCE 12-14 KM **TIME** 3-3¹/₂ HOURS
LEVEL 3 OPTIONS: TOUGH, MODERATE AND EASY

There are three options to get to Bedsa Caves starting from **Kamshet Station**, but getting there is a bit tricky, so if you are unsure, go to **Bedsa Village** and then climb up to the caves from there.

Inside the spectacular Bedsa Caves

THE EASY OPTION
From the station, walk 2 km to the ST Bus Station. A right turn here will bring you to the highway (NH4). Follow this road across NH4 towards **Kale Colony** for 10-12 km. Regular buses and jeeps ply from Kamshet to Kale Colony, so you can opt for these if you'd rather not walk on a tar road. You can also take a jeep (Rs 100-150 for the full jeep or Rs 10-15 per seat). There isn't much traffic on this road and the beauty of the hills makes the drive very enjoyable. I've often heard and seen peacock and jungle fowl in the early hours of the morning.

After passing a jeep track leading to the microwave tower, the road goes up a small ghat through a pass and then zigzags down the hill in a south-westerly direction. As you emerge out into the open, the **Bedsa Caves** are visible on your right, or to the north-west, and are easily recognisable by the pillars and towering sun window, which make it look like an ancient Roman monument. Walk on the road for 10-12 km (2-2¹/₂ hrs) till you see a sign for **Bedsa Village**. Here a road goes right or north and leads to Bedsa Village (this stretch is a motorable dirt road).

The lovely views from Lohagad Fort which include Pawna Dam and Tung Fort

From the village, a path leads off west, past rice fields and meadows, to the base of the hill. From here, a trail leads up to the caves (2 km from Bedsa Village). The easiest option is to drive this route right into Bedsa Village.

THE MODERATE OPTION

Walk from **Kamshet** on the road (due south) leading to Pawna Dam and Kale Colony for 5-6 km and then follow a jeep track (due west) leading up a long spur (on your right) for 2-3 km to the microwave tower.

From the base of the microwave hill (just before a hairpin bend with railings, when you can see the flat ridge below you, due north) a path leads off to the right or north-west and goes down the hill for 300-400m. From here, the trail goes south-west or left along the base of the hill (take the lower trail) and will eventually lead you to a pass (due west) with a temple dedicated to **Wageshwar**. The red and white BSNL Tower (not the microwave tower) and an electric pylon are visible throughout. From the temple, **Bedsa Village** is due south while the hill above the caves is south-west.

Walk south-west past the temple and the tower, along the ridge for 1 km. At the end of the ridge is a solitary fig tree. **Bedsa Caves** are 2 km away,

Bhaja Caves

The outstanding feature of these 2nd century caves is its chaitya (prayer hall), complete with original wooden arches and a stone stupa. There are 18 caves in all (most were living quarters and viharas), some interesting sculptures, inscriptions and a set of about 12 stupas. A big waterfall at the far end during the monsoon is an added attraction to the history lesson.

TREKKING HOLIDAYS IN INDIA

due south. The trail follows the contours of the hill before you descend eastwards. The descent from here to the caves is a little tricky and very steep in places (do not try it in the monsoon). Bedsa Caves are half-way down the hill and while it's only 2 km, it can take 1½ hrs or more. Bedsa Village will be visible to the right, or south-east, of the caves.

THE TOUGH OPTION

It's the trail of choice for those who want to get away from roads and vehicles. You will have a constant cool breeze, excellent views and a trail almost all to yourself, but for the wildlife. From **Kamshet**, walk back along the railway line or the road that runs parallel to it (towards Lonavla), or due west, for 1 km and then turn left or due south at the level crossing. A path leads up the hill for 300-400m and eventually comes out onto the **Mumbai-Pune Highway** (NH4).

Cross the highway and follow a path due south that climbs up a spur and then flattens out. In front of you (to the south) is a hill with a **microwave tower** (part of the railway communication network). Follow the crest of the ridge to the base of this hill for about 3 km, or just over 1 hr or 1½ hrs. This joins the trail, mentioned above, in the moderate route. Follow it to the caves.

Visapur Fort

The Visapur Fort is spread across 3 sq km and you can spend the whole day wandering around its ramparts. From two small hillocks at the top, you get excellent views of the fort, which has lots of water tanks, two large ponds, walls, ruins of houses, a couple of old cannons and the remains of a temple. The fort also has a large millstone where limestone and mortar were ground for fort wall construction. The views from the fort top are spectacular. On one side you can see **Pawna Dam**, **Tikona Fort**, **Tung Fort** (across the waters of Pawna Dam) and **Lohagad Fort**. According to local legend, a chieftain once promised a woman tightrope walker a reward to walk from Lohagad to Visapur forts. But when he found she had almost reached across to the other side, he cut the rope.

⚠ No camping is permitted in the caves. One can camp just outside the caves or down at the base of the hill.

DAY TWO
BEDSA CAVES-BEDSA HILL-VISAPUR FORT
DISTANCE 10-12 KM **TIME** 4-5 HOURS
LEVEL MODERATE

When facing the main chaitya of the Bedsa Caves, you'll find steps cut into the rock-face leading up the hill on your left (north-west). This is a very steep trail to the top of the hill (avoidable in the monsoons). Walk for $1\frac{1}{2}$ hrs up the path. It peters out in places, reappears, and is criss-crossed by other paths and finally reaches the base of a small hill. From here, turn left or south-west and follow the path for 1 km until you come to a small pass. **Bedsa Hill** is the one on your left (west) while facing the pass. From the pass, both routes (left and right) will bring you to **Malewadi Village**, also known as Visapur Village (a 6-7 km walk).

Alternatively, climb up the left side or west of the pass along a little-used but obvious path. This is a little steep initially but it brings you to the top of the hill (1 km) to an excellent walk along the flat top. This is a great walk at any time. There is a constant cool breeze as well as views of the surrounding area — **Tikona Fort** and **Pawna Lake** with **Visapur** and **Tung forts** on either side. On the right lie **Karla Ridge**, **Valvan Lake** and **Lonavla**. After walking past Bedsa Hill, you'll reach the end of the plateau ($1-1\frac{1}{2}$ hrs/ 4-5 km). The route down is on the right where you join the main trail at **Malewadi Village**. A broad trail from the village leads through the forest to the base of Visapur Fort. From here take the right trail (north) for 100m. This then turns west or right and will first bring you to a well $1\frac{1}{2}$ km away.

A little past the well, a path leads left or south-west up to a flat clearing (which makes a great ⚠ campsite), continues along the base of the fort

Looking out from the Visapur ruins

and seems to disappear into thick karvi bushes. It finally emerges at the base of a dry stream ($1\frac{1}{2}$ km). This is the path up to the fort. A 20-min walk due south-west and you're in **Visapur Fort**. ⚠ There are plenty of good campsites for the picking within the fort but make sure you are close to one of the many water tanks. Do not pollute them or leave garbage behind. If you'd rather camp indoors, there are two large caves just before you enter the fort. Personally, I prefer the open as the caves echo (even if you whisper), are musty and claustrophobic with no views and no water.

DAY THREE
VISAPUR FORT-LOHAGAD FORT
DISTANCE 5 KM **TIME** $1\frac{1}{2}$-2 HOURS
LEVEL EASY

Walk across (south) the two hillocks that mark the centre of the Visapur Fort. On emerging from the pass, go

Lohagad Fort

Lohagad, meaning iron fort, was, as its name suggests, impregnable. There is only one way into and out of the fort and this entails going through three or four entrance gates and several series of battlements, ramparts and steep walls. These defences look amazing viewed from above, from where you can marvel at the genius of those who built it.

As you enter the fort, you'll see a dargah and a huge rock-cut cave (once the residence of Buddhist monks, now occupied by a baba). Beyond the dargah (right) is an underground freshwater spring, some large ponds and rock-cut tanks. You can see the waters of **Pawna Dam** stretching all the way to **Lonavla**. At the western edge, a rock escarpment resembles a scorpion's sting (*vinchu kaanta*). Enjoy the grand view of the surrounding hills and lakes, **Tung** and **Tikona forts**, **Morvi Dongar** and more from the ramparts.

right or south-west (two caves here are a good landmark) and take a trail down (south-west) that will lead to Lohagad Fort about 4-5 km away. Precipitous fort walls rise sharply on either side as you walk down a steep path full of boulders.

The trail passes a stone water tank (good drinking water here) just before turning south-west and entering thick jungle and then emerges into the open onto a dirt road/ jeep track that leads to a col between Lohagad and Visapur forts. **Lohagad Wadi** is 1½ km (south-west) away. From the village, a path goes right (west) and leads into Lohagad Fort (1 km).

While one could find accommodation in Lohagad Wadi, this will be very rustic and basic. Within the fort, there is one large cave (now occupied by a baba) where one could camp. If you like your solitude and space, my advice would be to camp besides the talab (pond) in the middle of the fort. There are some trees and a flat open space that makes a good campsite, the night sky is quite amazing from here, as are the lights of Lonavla.

Return option to Lonavla An interesting option is to walk around **Lohagad Fort** (left or south from Lohagad Wadi)

Karla Caves

Karla provides the finest example of Buddhist rock-cut architecture in the Sahyadris. Great attention has been paid to the form of the carved mithuna figures on top of the columns. The vitality in these figures is not seen anywhere else and it indicates that these caves come from a period later than Bhaja and Bedsa (probably 50-70 AD). The main chaitya is elaborately carved and has exquisite pillars as well as inscriptions recording the names of patrons and donors. The wooden *chhatra* (umbrella) above the stupa is still intact. Outside the main chaitya, the verandah has a five-storeyed structure resting on life-sized elephants. Though initially Hinayana, the caves were taken over by Mahayana Buddhists and you'll find that images of the Buddha have been superimposed on many spaces. Notice the lion pillar outside the chaitya.

ABHIJIT BHATLEKAR

and follow a dirt road (due west) along the crest of the hill that brings you to a *khind* (pass). From here go right or north-west, follow the tarred road to Lonavla (about 4 hrs).

DAY FOUR
LOHAGAD FORT-BHAJA CAVES-KARLA CAVES-LONAVLA
DISTANCE 12-14 KM **TIME** 4 HOURS
LEVEL MODERATE-EASY

As there is only one route in and out of the fort, make your way back to Lohagad Wadi where some refreshments and a meal may be available. Then head to the saddle between the two forts, from where a broad, well-used trail leads down (north-west) to the left into a jungle and then down a gentle spur (3 km long). From here, **Bhaja Caves** are visible in the north-east or on your right.

At the bottom of the spur, the trail joins a jeep track which brings you to **Bhaja Village** (1½-2 km). Take a detour east (right) just before Bhaja Village and go up to the breathtaking Bhaja Caves (or walk up a flight of steps).

Return via Bhaja Village (1 km) and then along a metalled road due north to **Malavli Station** (3 km), where you cross the railway tracks. If this is your end-point, you can catch a local train to Lonavla, 15 km away. Or continue the trek on to **Karla Caves**, 7 km away. These are worth a visit to complete the Buddhist cave experience.

From Malavli, it's 3 km to NH4 along a tarred road. Cross the highway and walk another 3 km on a tar road due north to the base of **Karla Caves** and then walk up the flight of steps (1 km) to the caves. There are several State Transport (ST) buses out of Karla to Lonavla or you could get an auto (Rs 60-80) or a seat (Rs 10-15) in a six-seater auto to Lonavla.

For hotels, see Accommodation Listings on pages 545 (Kamshet) and 546 (Lonavla) ✦

Peak of Pain

The pain and sprain specialist. **IODEX**®

Duke's Nose

Climbing the cobra's hood

By Andre Morris

TIME	1 day
LEVEL	Easy
IDEAL SEASON	Jun to Feb
LOCATION	Near Khandala, in Pune District

Duke's Nose or Cobra's Hood stands proudly against the sky

Photographs by ANDRE MORRIS

KHANDALA-FORE BAY-DUKE'S NOSE

I have lost count of the number of times I have climbed Duke's Nose (1,005m) but I have never tired of this hike. This prominent peak, also known as Nagphani or Cobra's Hood, guards the Bhor Ghat and is visible from the train as well as the road. While climbing the Khandala Ghat, Duke's Nose looks like a formidable pinnacle. However, it's a very popular and easy hike and requires no special climbing skills. It takes an average of two hours to get to the top and the same to return.

Unlike other spots, this is a very enjoyable hike even in the monsoons. Though the top can get windy and cold, the clouds occasionally break to give you a fantastic view of the valley below. You can also sit and watch trains crawling in and out of the tunnels like giant worms.

TIP Remember to stock up on drinking water. Unless you are hiking in the monsoons or know the area very well, you are unlikely to find potable water along the way

THE TREK

KHANDALA-DUKE'S NOSE-KHANDALA

DISTANCE 8-10 KM **TIME** 4 HOURS
LEVEL Easy

From Khandala Station, walk back along the railway track for about 100m going towards Mumbai. Just past the level crossing (west), follow the old

DUKE'S NOSE — TREKKING GUIDE

(map showing Rajmachi Fort, Udhewadi, Khandala, Duke's Nose, Fore Bay, INS Shivaji, Valvan Lake, Valvan Exit, Lonavla, Malavli, Karla Caves, Bhaja Caves, Patan, Lohagad Fort, Visapur Fort, Tung Fort, Pawna Lake, Mumbai-Pune Expressway, NH4, To Mumbai, To Pune, Maharashtra Map Area)

Trek route .....
Road —
Fort 🏰
Cave ∩
River ∕
Railway line ┉

LIFE IS CALLING WHERE ARE YOU? SMIRNOFF
Cassettes and CDs

GETTING THERE AND OUT

FROM LONAVLA to Khandala, it's 3 km/ 15 mins by 🚗 (Rs 120) or auto (Rs 60-80) **Mumbai to Khandala** is 105 km/ 2½ hrs by car. If you are driving, take the Expressway and get off at the **Khandala Exit**. From Khandala, follow the old Mumbai-Pune Highway (NH4) for 400m (due west), then just past the large pond take a left turn. Turn left at the fork and left again at the next turn and continue up a steep narrow road to Fore Bay (where the Tata duct line ends). You can also take a 🚌 (Rs 200) or train (Rs 70-310) to Khandala from Mumbai **Khandala to Fore Bay** Autos charge Rs 30-40 **RETURN** It's best to make your way back to **Lonavla** to return to Mumbai. A non-AC Indica taxi to **Mumbai** costs Rs 1,100, shared non-AC taxi Rs 100-150 per seat, AC taxi Rs 250 per seat

unused railway track that climbs up the hill. Once the track ends, continue along the narrow tarred road going left (due south-west) for a kilometre or so, which will bring you to **Fore Bay**. This is where the Tata duct line water is stored before it's released down to Khopoli. This is private property but the Tata Electric Company has kept access open. This is also the last point where you will get water.

From Fore Bay, a footpath leads off into the jungle on the left (due south). This is really where the hike begins as one now leaves the beaten track and enters forests. About 5 mins into the trail, you'll leave the Tata property and pass through a turnstile-like gate, immediately after which the path

forks. The trail on the right is steep and full of scree, and the one on the left is gentle and easy. Take your pick, they both lead to the same col. A 15-min uphill trudge will bring you to the col with a large electric pylon. On the other side, you can see **INS Shivaji**, the naval training school, and **Koregad Fort** in the distance. Duke's Nose is not visible from here. This is a good place to take a break. If you look back along the way you have come up, you can see **Khandala Village**, **Rajmachi Fort** and **Dhak Plateau** in the distance.

From the col, follow the path going down towards INS Shivaji (due south-west) for a kilometre (10-15 mins). You will come out onto an open plain with **Duke's Nose** visible on the diagonal to your right (due west). Duke's Nose now looks like a small hillock because the entire area is at a higher elevation. It's a 2-km walk (due south-west) across the fields to the base of Duke's Nose (head for the low ridge that seems to

A nosey affair

Duke's Nose is named after Arthur Wellesley, the first Duke of Wellington (later general and British prime minister) who was famous, among other things, for his large aquiline nose. The large pinnacle, when seen from a distance, appears to be the nose of a person lying down. Locals call this peak **Nagphani** or Cobra's Hood, though it doesn't really have the fanned head of a cobra.

Duke's Nose has been a challenging technical climb from the valley as well as a daring rappel for intrepid adventurers over the years. Any one attempting any professional rock climbing should be aware that there are huge bee hives on the cliff side of Duke's Nose and that an accidental disturbance could cause major bee trouble.

connect Duke's Nose to INS Shivaji). In the monsoon, this can be a very enjoyable but wet walk and you will have to ford several small streams (not very swift, mostly knee deep).

From the base, a well-used path winds its way and leads to the top. The path climbs gradually at first and then gets steeper. You'll pass some **Nilgiri trees** and then take a rather steep trail ($1/_2$ hr/ 1 km) to find yourself at the top marked by a tiny Shiva temple, marvellous views and a sheer drop to the valley below. It can sometimes get quite windy at the top as there is very little vegetation, so watch your step.
Return You have to backtrack the way you came up.

A dramatic dusk at Khandala

TREKKING OPTIONS

● From Lonavla make your way past **Ryewood Park** to **Monsoon Lake** (also known as **Lonavla Lake**). Walk along the shores (on the right side or due south) till Duke's Nose comes into view, then head across to the base of the ridge and walk up to the top. This is a longer route.

● Another option is to take an auto-rickshaw from Lonavla to **Kurvanda Village** and then walk around the base of the hill (on your right or along the shores of Lonavla Lake) till Duke's Nose comes into view and head straight for the ridge.

● Yet another option is to head out to **INS Shivaji** (by bus or auto) from Lonavla and then hike cross-country to Duke's Nose. You could return by the easier route described above.

● The die-hard trekker can go past the old railway line. On reaching the road that leads to **Fore Bay**, follow the path going right that leads down into a thick jungle. Climb a little-used path to the base of Duke's Nose (the right-side base). Be warned this is a tough route and only those with rock-climbing skills should try it.

For hotels in Khandala and Lonavla, see Accommodation Listings on pages 545-546 ✦

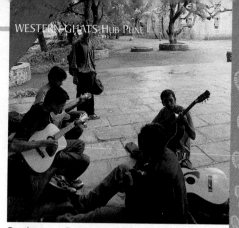

Students at Ferguson College

Pensioner's paradise, Oxford of the East, the cultural capital of Maharashtra. Old-time Punekars were happy enough to have the city thus described. But the new breed of young professionals would prefer a more hip label for their city – Cybercity maybe, or Shopper's Paradise. Yet, tucked somewhere between the spanking new glass and concrete, you will be able to find a rewarding glimpse of the erstwhile capital of the Peshwas and the Bombay Presidency.

MUST-VISITS

PESHWA VESTIGE

There isn't a lot left of **Shaniwarwada**, the once magnificent 18th century palace of the Peshwas, which was burnt down in a fire in 1827. Yet, it's an enduring symbol of the city's past. Next is the imposing Aga Khan Palace on Nagar Road at the other end of Pune, which houses the Gandhi National Memorial.

ADVENTURE OPTIONS

For airborne adventure, there's paragliding and powered paragliding at Hadapsur where Flying Safari (affiliated to the United India Paragliding Association) offers courses. Contact Eric Menezes or Mangesh Dighe on Tel: 020-5110795, 09822023790.

WHERE TO STAY

Quite the grandest of Pune's hotels, **Le Meridien's** (Tel: 020-26050505; Tariff: Rs 6,000-12,000) façade is a Pune landmark. **Hotel Panchshil** (Tel: 27472012-13; Tariff: Rs 1,150-2,000), on the outskirts, has cable TV and a 24-hr coffee shop. **Hotel Pearl** (Tel: 25534247-49; Tariff: Rs 600-900), located on Jangli Maharaj Road, has cable TV, a beauty parlour and laundry. You can also try **Hotel Homeland** (Tel: 26123203; Tariff: Rs 450-800), a colonial home turned into a family-run hotel, which also runs a multi-cuisine restaurant.
For more hotels and details, see Accommodation Listings on page 548

➜ Pune Facts

- **LOCATION** Pune (600m) sits on the cotton-rich Deccan Plateau, at the confluence of the Mula and Mutha rivers
- **GETTING TO PUNE By air** Lohegaon Airport, serviced by Jet, Sahara and Indian Airlines **By rail** Pune Junction **By road** The six-lane Mumbai-Pune Expressway has made driving the best option for getting to Pune. It's 163 km/ $3^1/_2$ hrs from Mumbai. Toll fee for cars Rs 100. The old NH4 via Khopoli is also very much in use. One-way taxi Rs 900. Volvo coaches (Rs 200) and MSRTC's Asiad buses (ordinary Rs 150, AC Rs 225; every 15 mins, 5 am to 2.30 pm) run daily from Dadar
- **STD CODE** 020

WHERE TO EAT

Shreyas, on Apte Road, with its long stainless-steel tables and prompt service is everyone's first port of call. Quiet and quaint is **Aamrapali**, tucked away behind its more popular neighbour **Roopali**, on Ferguson College Road. Not too far away, on Jangli Maharaj Road, **Mathura** has what it describes as a rustic Marathi thali. And, of course, Punekars swear by **Sweekar**, off Karve Road at Nal Stop. Roadside food is best at the tables set up along the stretch of the road near the police commissioner's office, popularly dubbed Chowpatty after its Mumbai cousin. It is better at night when there's less traffic.

INPUTS FROM SHERNA GANDHY

Life is one

Incredible Journey...

Purandar Fort

Capital story

By Andre Morris

School children take a break at the base of Purandar Fort

ABHIJIT BHATLEKAR

TIME	1 day (or more)
LEVEL	Easy
IDEAL SEASON	All year round, but can be hot in Apr and May
LOCATION	In the Bhuleshwar Range, in Pune District

NARAYANPETH-PURANDAR FORT

I first visited Purandar Fort (1,390m) on a cycling trip from school and was surprised to find out just how close it was to Pune and how wonderfully well-preserved and clean. I soon added it to my growing list of favourite escapes. The fort has an impressive past and has been witness to many a major battle. Believed to have been built between the Rashtrakuta and Yadava eras, Purandar changed hands several times and finally went to Adil Shah sometime in the early 17th century. He bequeathed the fort to one of the Adilshahi commanders, Mahadji Nilkanth. After Mahadji's death, his four sons began to fight over its possession, giving the Maratha king, Shivaji, the perfect opportunity to seize the fort in 1647.

THE TREK
NARAYANPUR VILLAGE-PURANDAR FORT
DISTANCE 5-6 KM **TIME** 2-3 HOURS
LEVEL EASY

Alight at **Narayanpur Village** and take time to visit the ancient **Narayaneshwar Mahadev Temple** here. This temple from the Rashtrakuta-Yadava period (753-1375 AD) is an important pilgrimage place. From Narayanpur, it's about 2 km along a tarred road to **Narayanpeth** at the base of the fort (some buses and jeeps run right up to Narayanpeth). There is a large banyan tree in the village square and ☕ a small tea-stall run by Mohan Darekar where you can get cold drinks, snacks, information booklets (only in Marathi) and a guide if you need one. Darekar has a wealth of knowledge on the fort and will also put you on the right path.

From the banyan tree, a path climbs a gentle spur due south-west and follows the electric poles most of the way. The fort walls and the motorable road are clearly visible on your right. The trail will come out onto the road going up. Follow this for 100m till a hairpin bend from where the trail goes off into the jungle due

Graphic by ANIS KHAN

PURANDAR FORT

TREKKING GUIDE

N

Map Area

Maharashtra

Saswad — To Pune

Narayanpur

Narayanpeth

To Pune

Khandkada ▲
Gadipathar

Purandar Fort
1,390m

Purandeshwar

Kedar

To Paltan

Campsite ⚠
Trek route ·····
Road —
Peak/height ▲
Temple ♠
Tea stall ⛺

LIFE IS CALLING WHERE ARE YOU?
Cassettes and CDs

Hi-Speed DIESEL

Bharat Petroleum

GETTING THERE AND OUT

FROM PUNE STATION to Narayanpur, it's 30 km. Take a 🚕 or autorickshaw from the station to Swargate Bus Stand, 6 km/ ¹/₂ hr. From here, regular PMT and ST buses (25 km/ 45 mins/ Rs 11) run till the base of Purandar Fort (called Purandar Paiyta or Narayanpeth), 2 km from Narayanpur where the trek begins. The buses run both via Katraj Ghat or Saswad. From Pune to Narayanpeth (32 km/ 1-1¹/₂ hrs), full 🚙 (jeep, Sumo) charges Rs 300-500. Seat-sharing jeeps (Rs 15-20) also available

RETURN On the way out, return to **Saswad** from where regular buses/ jeeps leave for Pune, about 25 km away. No direct buses to Swargate from Purandar Fort. So come down to Narayanpeth for bus/ jeep to Saswad, 10-15 mins away

The Purandeshwar Temple

east. From here, the entrance to the fort, as well as an old church are visible. The main gate, the walls and ramparts are very well preserved as **Purandar Fort** was occupied by the British after the defeat of the Marathas in the Third Maratha War of 1818. This is evident by the presence of a stone church just beyond the main entrance.

The entire structure is in excellent condition though it is neglected and used as a shelter for cattle. There are garrisons, barracks, resident quarters and bungalows, all in perfectly good condition. This is probably because the fort was in the possession of the defence services, which used it as a training base for the National Cadet Crops until a few years ago, and still maintain a presence here.

Just 100m beyond the old church is a small ⛺ tea-stall on the right side of the road. The path to the top of the fort and up to the *ballekilla* goes past this point. You first pass a temple

Photographs by ANDRE MORRIS

417

Shivaji's part-time capital

Shivaji's first battle against Adil Shah's army was fought from Purandar in 1648. According to one school of thought, Shivaji used Purandar Fort as his capital for almost 20 years because of its excellent defences and its proximity to Pune. His son Sambhaji was also born here.

The most notable event in the history of Purandar occurred when the Mughal commander Jai Singh besieged Shivaji in the fort. He cut off all the routes in and out of the fort and camped in Pune. After holding out for several months, Shivaji was forced to surrender and sign the famous treaty of Purandar in 1665. By this treaty, he surrendered 23 forts to the Mughals, retaining only 12. Five years later, Shivaji recaptured the fort, only to lose it again to Aurangzeb. After 1707, the fort was handed over to the Peshwas, who used it as their capital till it was handed over to the British in 1818.

dedicated to Purandeshwar, the deity of the fort, from where a well-used trail leads to the top and will take you through three more doorways and past several water tanks.

⚠ If you plan to spend the night in the fort, the temple is a good point to stop, but there are lots of other possibilities, so explore and take your pick.

TIP Just beyond the **Purandeshwar Temple** is an old British bungalow in near perfect condition, with fireplaces, chimneys, roof tiles and flooring intact. Though the only occupants seem to be cattle and goats, it's definitely worth a visit

From the top of the fort, one gets a grand view of the hills surrounding the city of Pune. One can see **Sinhagad Fort** in the north-west and **Torna** and **Rajgad** to the left of Sinhagad. The long ridge connecting Katraj to Sinhagad is also visible.

A complete walk or exploration of the fort can take 2-3 hrs. The fort walls, bastions and battlements on Purandar are all in good condition with several doors or entrances, and a dirt road on the southern side. There are three hillocks on Purandar called **Khandkada**, **Gadipathar** and **Kedar**. The last one has a flight of stone steps in good condition that lead to the top, where there is a temple dedicated to Kedareshwar.

Return The easiest way to return is to descend the way you came up and then get a bus back to Pune.

TOUGHER OPTION

Head to the **Konkani Darwaza** (due west) and descend by a path from there to the village of **Chinchewadi** (the Bhor-Saswad Road passes through this village). You can either walk along this road for 2 hrs till you reach Kapurval Village on the Pune-Bangalore Highway or just walk cross-country (due west) till you reach the highway. Catch a bus or jeep from here or hitch a ride in a truck.

Inside the church at Purandar

TREKKING OPTIONS

● You can make Purandar the last stage of a 3-day trip that can start with a trek to **Malhargad Fort**. Take a bus from Pune to Saswad that goes via Wadki Naka and Dive Ghat to Karha Plateau. Alight from the bus at the bottom of the ghat at **Phulewadi**. Malhargad Fort is due south-east about 3-4 km away. The fort walls are well preserved and it appears very imposing. On the *balle-killa*, there are two temples dedicated to Khandoba and Mahadev (Purandar is due south-west).

⚠ There is plenty of water in the fort, so you can camp here. From Malhargad, walk for 8 km (due west) along a ridge to the famous **Kanifnath Temple** (992m) and from there, it's a long cross-country walk of about 15-16 km to Purandar Fort.

● Yet another option is to visit **Purandar** first and then trek across to **Katraj Ghat**, which lies due north-west (there is no definite trail but there are several villages along the way). This is a long walk of over 5 hrs and will eventually bring you to the tunnel above Katraj Ghat and a good ⚠ campsite.

● One could undertake a trek for 2-3 days from **Purandar** to **Sinhagad** via Khed Shivapur and Kondanpur.

● A good long-haul trek would be Malhargad-Kanifnath Temple-Purandar-Katraj-Sinhgad-Rajgad-Torna and Raigad. This will take you 10-12 days or more. ✦

The summer capital of the erstwhile Bombay Presidency is striking not just because of its natural beauty. It also has some charming tales spun around its favourite points that take you back to a time when the hill station would officially and proudly down its shutters in the monsoons. Today, it's open throughout the year, but even now, Mahabaleshwar finds its true glory when the sun plays to the gallery, as it does willingly on many evenings.

The Mahabaleshwari Temple

MUST-VISITS

ARTHUR'S SEAT

Named after British actor Arthur Malet, this picturesque point was destroyed in a 1967 earthquake. The grilled area marks the point where Arthur would contemplate the nature of the wind.

HUNTER POINT

With 30 sightseeing spots, there's something to do every minute of your trip. There's Hunter Point, with its Pratapgad Fort views, and Mahabaleshwar's highest, Wilson Point, offering a spectacular view of the sunrise.

WHERE TO STAY

The best option is **Strawberry Country** (Tel: 02168-272101-02; Tariff: Rs 2,100-3,000) on Panchgani Road, which has a swimming pool and indoor games. **MTDC Holiday Resort** (Tel: 260318; Tariff: Rs 450-1,700) at Mahad Naka has a restaurant and indoor games. **Pratap Heritage** (Tel: 260778-79; Tariff: Rs 1,175-2,300) on Valley View Road has games, cable TV and room service. A budget option is **Hotel Blue Park** (Tel: 260375; Tariff: Rs 500-900) on Lodwick Point Road, which offers decent rooms with TV.
For more hotels and details, see Accommodation Listings on pages 546-547

WHERE TO EAT

Although eating out is not big in Mahabaleshwar, you're unlikely to go hungry on your holiday here. Several kinds of cuisine can be had – from Chinese to Indian, Continental and even Mexican. Try **Imperial Stores** for their pizzas and burgers. **Aman Restaurant** is good for kebabs and tandoori food.

INPUTS FROM PURBA DUTT

→ Mahabaleshwar Facts

● **LOCATION** Maharashtra's summer capital is located 1,372m ASL on the Shambhu Mahadeo Range in the Western Ghats, not too far from the Konkan Coast

● **GETTING TO MAHABALESHWAR By air**
Nearest airport: Pune (128 km/ 2$^{1}/_{2}$ hrs). Taxi Rs 1,500, shared taxi Rs 300-400; bus (Volvo, Asiad) 3 hrs/ Rs 150-225

TIP Look for a Mahabaleshwar taxi on its way up and a Pune taxi on the way down, it can work out cheaper
By rail Nearest railhead: Pune Station. Inter-City Express from Mumbai is the best option. From here, take a bus or Volvo coach to Mahabaleshwar **By road** From Mumbai, Mahabaleshwar is 291 km/ 5 hrs by taxi (Rs 3,000) and 6 hrs by bus (Volvo AC/ non-AC and regular ST and private, Rs 200-500). There are two routes to Mahabaleshwar, both equally scenic and popular. The NH4 route via Pune, Shirwal and Panchgani is longer but has better roads and is fast moving, especially since the Mumbai-Pune Expressway has been linked to the newly built bypass at Pune. Traffic moves fast and smoothly. The other is down NH17 via Pen, Mahad and Poladpur. Though shorter, one moves slowly up the ghats to Mahabaleshwar. At Poladpur police station (at the statue of Shivaji), take the road going left. Private vehicles need to pay (Rs 10) for the entry permit, valid for a week

● **STD CODE** 02168

● **TOURIST OFFICE** MTDC, Mahad Naka, Mahabaleshwar Tel: 02168-260318, 261318

NOW MAKE YOUR
SAFARI GO WILD

With Hi-Speed Diesel, your Safari will now go completely wild.
That's because Hi-Speed Diesel gives you a super smooth drive by cleaning out
harmful deposits from your engine and fuel-metering systems. This is made possible by the
patented Greenburn Combustion Technology and the multifunctional additives from
Afton Chemical Corporation (formerly Ethyl Corporation, USA).
Hi-Speed Diesel is backed by the Pure for Sure guarantee from Bharat Petroleum.
So the next time you tank up your Safari, be sure to use Hi-Speed Diesel.

PEAK PERFORMANCE. GREEN PERFORMANCE.

Hi-Speed Diesel is currently available in select Pure for Sure outlets in Mumbai, Delhi and Bangalore,
and available in major markets across the country. All brand names used here are trademarks of their respective owners.   SAATCHI & SAATCHI-469A/2004 M

Mahabaleshwar to Pratapgad
A trek back in time

By Andre Morris

TIME	2 days or more
LEVEL	Easy to Moderate
IDEAL SEASON	Oct to Mar
LOCATION	In the Koyna-Satara region, south-east of Mumbai, in the Western Ghats

The endless verdant valleys extending out around Mahabaleshwar

MAHABALESHWAR-ZOLAI KHIND-DUDHGAON-
CHATURBET-GHONASPUR-MAKARANDGAD-
HATLOT-PRATAPGAD

In 1803, Mahabaleshwar was a thickly forested, uninhabited, almost forgotten plateau that was part of the territory under Pratap Singh, the ruler of Satara. Its status changed after Governor Malcolm of Bombay exchanged a village for Mahabaleshwar in 1828. And thus began the development of the summer capital of the Bombay Presidency, now one of Maharashtra's most famous hill stations. It's also a place of religious interest for many. The ancient temples of Old Mahabaleshwar, after all, are said to be the sources of five rivers (Krishna, Koyna, Venna, Savitri and Gayatri).

GETTING THERE AND OUT

FROM PUNE to Mahabaleshwar, it's 128 km/ 2¹/₂ hrs by 🚗 (Rs 1,200-1,500) or 3 hrs by 🚌 (Volvo buses Rs 180, regular Rs 80-100). See *Mahabaleshwar Facts on page 420 for more details*

RETURN From **Mahabaleshwar**, there are several buses to Pune and also to Mumbai. Taxis are also available to both the cities

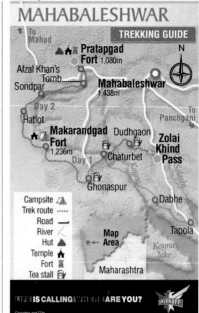

past made Mahabaleshwar my base and taken off on forays to one or two forts at a time, then returned to a hotel for the night before setting out on another trek. You can do each of these listed here as separate day treks, returning to Mahabaleshwar each evening, if you don't want to spend the night outdoors, particularly during the monsoons.

Even before the British arrived, the area was surrounded by several forts. In the west is the Pratapgad Fort, where Afzal Khan, general of Adil Shah of Bijapur, made a daring attack on Maratha king Chhatrapati Shivaji. In the south is Makarandgad (1,236m) and beyond it, Mahipatgad, Rasalgad, Vasota and Sumargad. Mahabaleshwar is a good starting point for a trek to some of these picturesque places. State Transport (ST) buses and jeeps run to several villages on the shores of Koyna Lake, from where you can take a ferry or launch across the backwaters of Koyna Dam and get closer to some of the forts.

The area is remote and surrounded by dense jungle. If wildlife interests you, there's wild boar, bear, deer, leopard and an abundance of bird life in the jungles around. I have in the

DAY ONE

MAHABALESHWAR-ZOLAI KHIND-DUDHGAON-CHATURBET-GHONASPUR-MAKARANDGAD

DISTANCE 12-15 KM **TIME** 6-7 HOURS
LEVEL MODERATE

TIP It's advisable to take a guide from **Chaturbet** if you are not sure of being able to find your own way up to **Makarandgad**, since the trail is through thick forest and it's easy to get lost. A guide will cost Rs 100-150 for the day and you'd need to share your food with him

423

At the top of Pratapgad Fort

From Mahabaleshwar, catch a bus or jeep going to **Tapola** and get off at **Zolai Khind Pass**. From the end of the pass, follow a well-used trail on the right or due north-west. Enter a dense forest and descend along a long spur to the village of **Dudhgaon** (2-2½hrs). **Makarandgad Fort** stands tall due west south-west, surrounded by thick forest cover.

If you'd like a shorter option, there are a few direct buses to Dudhgaon, but that would mean missing out on the lovely forests after Zolai Khind. From Dudhgaon, follow the dirt road due west, crossing the **Koyna River** before reaching **Chaturbet**. A footpath leads across fields and then up the hillside to disappear into the forest. The trail runs due south-west for 2-2½ hrs before coming to a flat stretch, where it joins another trail coming from the left.

TIP This trail comes up from **Dabhe Village** on the banks of the Koyna Lake. A launch service connects Dabhe with Tapola and other villages in the area, but check timings with locals, as these can be erratic

From the junction, walk another 30-45 mins, due south-west to **Ghonaspur Village**. Since much of the area in Makarandgad is filled with thick forests, the walk up with a constant cool breeze accompanying one is very pleasant. If you are quiet you may even spot jungle fowl and peacocks along the trail. From Ghonaspur, the trail into the fort goes due west and climbs another 30-45 mins before entering the *ballekilla* (big fort). Not much is known about **Makarandgad** and there are hardly any ruins or ramparts still standing. There is a large **Mahadev Temple** (renovated and maintained by local villagers). There's also a rock-cut cave that holds water and stretches far back with almost no end in sight (I tried using my torch but was unable to see the rear wall).

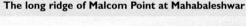

The long ridge of Malcom Point at Mahabaleshwar

the
OUTLOOKgroup

once again scores a winner

in the travel segment

with the

Outlook Traveller Getaways

being awarded the

"BEST TRAVEL PUBLICATION-ENGLISH"

by the Dept of Tourism,

Govt. of India.

The Largest Selling Travel Magazine in India

The Largest Selling Travel Guides in India

ABHIJIT BHATLEKAR

Jangam tribe

The people of this area are members of the Jangam tribe, which is a unique ethnic group. Unlike most of their neighbours, they bury their dead and then pile stones over the spot, much like gravestones. It's not clear whether they have been influenced by the practice of the English (after they took over Mahabaleshwar) or whether this is an ancient practice of the Jangam tribe.

One can camp in the temple (or just outside it if you have a tent), as the cave below has good drinking water. The nights are chilly but the sky, especially on a moonless night, is fantastic. You can see several constellations including **Cassiopeia**, **Orion the Hunter**, **The Great Bear** (Ursa Major), the **Pole Star** and **Sirius the Dog Star**, the brightest star in the sky. Depending on the time of the year, some planets are visible too.

DAY TWO
MAKARANDGAD-HATLOT-SHIRPOLI-KOYNA RIVER-PRATAPGAD
DISTANCE 10-11 KM **TIME** 4-5 HOURS
LEVEL MODERATE

From Makarandgad Fort, descend to **Hatlot Village** to the west. The trail descends along the right side following the base of the wall (due north). In about 30 mins, you will come to a temple set amidst thick forest. Follow a trail going left, or due south-west, that leads down to Hatlot (if you take the trail going right, you will reach Ghonaspur). After walking for 1-1½ hrs, you will come out of the jungle and to the first of four hamlets that make up Hatlot.

Past the first hamlet you will come to an iron bridge across which lies a **Maruti Temple**. Just past the last of the four hamlets, the trail turns due north-west and follows a dirt road (1 hr) that brings you down to the Koyna River and a dirt road that goes to Dudhgaon. Take a left, due north-west, at the road and follow it past **Shirpoli** and Dudhgaon Phata (junction). Walking along this road, you will pass **Parpar Village** (30-45 mins) and then **Sondpar Village**, from where a path leads up a gentle spur, due west. This will bring you to **Afzal Khan's Tomb** (1 hr). From here, follow the tarred road that will get you to the base of the fort in 10 mins.

TREKKING HOLIDAYS IN INDIA

CHANGE YOUR VIEW

EXPERIENCE THE RAY-BAN COLLECTION.

RB 3192 SIDESTREET RIMLESS RECTANGLE
M.R.P. Rs.4990/-

RB 4037 PREDATOR SHOT OVAL
M.R.P.Rs.3390/-

RB 3183 SIDESTREET TOP BAR SQUARE
M.R.P.Rs.4990/-

Choose from over 250 models at your nearest authorized Ray-Ban dealer.

In 1656, Shivaji annexed Jawli and turned his attention to building a fort on **Bhorpya Hill**, which was strategically located along the trade route from the Konkan to Wai. This became **Pratapgad Fort** (1,080m), which is one of the few forts in Maharashtra that is still in private hands. It remains with the Bhosale family of Satara and is fairly well maintained. This, plus its historical importance, and the fact that it is close to Mahabaleshwar makes it a big tourist attraction. You can engage the services of a guide who will narrate the history of the fort (with a twist) as he walks you around the different points (guide fee Rs 80).

As you enter the fort you will come across the watchtower and its protective walls. Further up there is the **Bhavani Mata Temple**, which houses an idol of Mahishasurmardini. This idol has been carved out of a single *saligram* stone (an ammonite fossil) that was brought by Shivaji all the way from the Kaligandaki River in Nepal in 1661. There is also an exquisite quartz Shivaling, believed to have been worshipped by Shivaji. Also, you can't miss the huge bronze statue of the famous Maratha chief.

From the western end of the fort, one can look down into the **Konkan**, while in the north one can see **Raigad**, **Torna**, **Rajgad** and several other forts. Mahabaleshwar is due north-east while **Makarandgad** is due south-east.

The fort walls are in excellent condition and its doors are still intact. Pratapgad is probably the only fort where, even today, the doors are closed and locked at 7 pm. It has all the trappings of a tourist destination with eating houses and stalls selling cold drinks, souvenirs, maps and information booklets (mostly in Hindi and

Tiger claws vs scorpion sting

In 1659, Aurangzeb and Adil Shah decided they had to get rid of Shivaji, and sent Afzal Khan, a giant of a man with a large army, to get rid of him. Afzal Khan, it seems, realised that Shivaji was no easy target and that his only chance was to use treachery and deceit. He arranged a meeting with Shivaji on the pretext of talking peace. Shivaji agreed to meet him at Pratapgad and secretly had his soldiers hiding in a small cave nearby. When they met, Afzal Khan embraced Shivaji and tried to stab him with a dagger, called a *vinchu kaanta* or scorpion's sting. Shivaji was well prepared — he was wearing *wagh nakh*, or tiger claws, on his right hand, with which he attacked and killed Afzal Khan. He then defeated Afzal Khan's army, hiding in valleys close by. This incident not only established Shivaji's status as a leader, but it also made him something of a stupendous legend in Maratha folklore.

ABHIJIT BHATLEKAR

Blue mormon
ANDRE MORRIS

Blue mormon (*Papilio polymnestor*) is a rare and pretty blue butterfly found around forested hilltops such as Matheran and Mahabaleshwar. The caterpillar of the blue mormon butterfly looks quite like the dangerous head of a snake! The two large 'eyes' are actually markings on its back while the actual small head is hidden underneath. It is also equipped with an osmeterium (scent gland), which releases a nasty smell if poked.

Marathi). Board and lodging are also available within the fort but be warned that they are very basic.

After exploring the fort, you can either spend the night ⛺ up in the fort or catch a bus or jeep that will take you up to Mahabaleshwar. It is also possible to get a bus back to Mumbai from the highway 7 km away.

TREKKING OPTIONS

● From **Pratapgad Fort**, you can walk down to Afzal Khan's Tomb and follow the trail you came up by till Dudhgaon Phata or Shirpoli. From here, there is a path that goes up the hillside through a dense jungle. It will bring you to **Mahabaleshwar** in 2-3 hrs. You will cross the road several times before reaching the top at **Bombay Point**.

● I have done this route in reverse and started my trek at Bombay Point, come down to Pratapgad and then gone to **Makarandgad**, descended to **Dabhe** to take a launch to **Tapola** and then to **Met Indavli** to visit **Vasota** (1,171m), **Chakdev** (984m) and **Rasalgad forts**. This requires an additional four days at least and much of the region is remote with very few facilities.

● Yet another option could be to trek across to **Raigad Fort**, due north from Pratapgad. You will have to factor at least one additional day for this. ✦

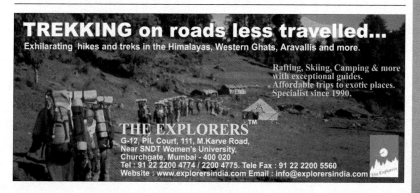

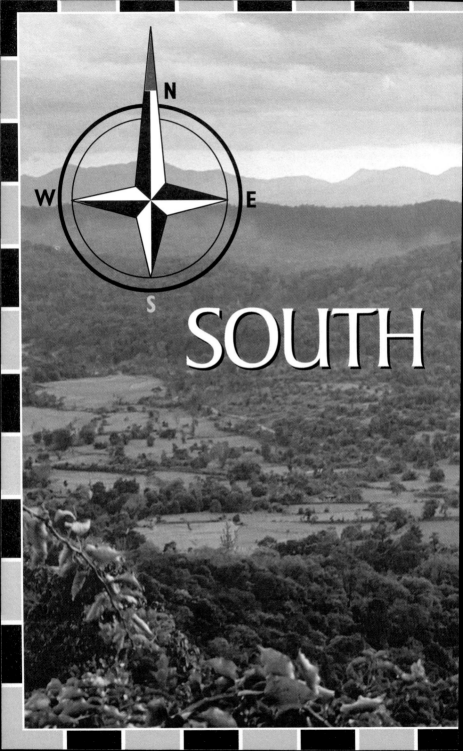

SOUTH

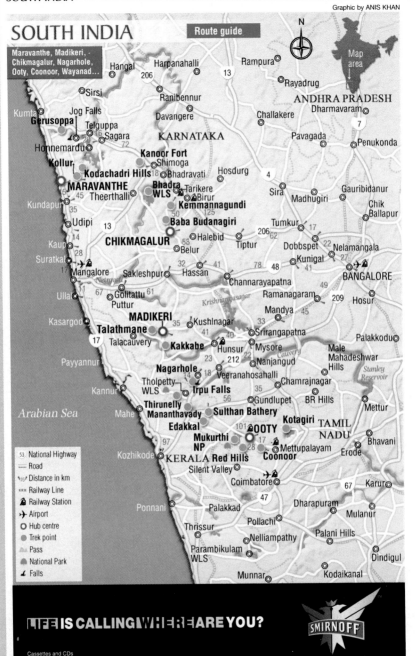

Graphic by ANIS KHAN

SOUTH INDIA

Route guide

Maravanthe, Madikeri, Chikmagalur, Nagarhole, Ooty, Coonoor, Wayanad...

N

Map area

ANDHRA PRADESH

Rampura
Rayadrug
Dharmavaram
7
Penukonda

Hangal
Harpanahalli
13
206
Sirsi
Ranibennur
Challakere
Pavagada
Jog Falls
Davangere
Kumta
Gerusoppa
Telguppa
Sagara
Honnemardu
Kollur
Kanoor Fort
Shimoga
Hosdurg
Sira
Madhugiri
Gauribidanur
Kodachadri Hills
Bhadravati
4
Chik Ballapur
MARAVANTHE
Bhadra
Tarikere
Theerthalli
WLS
Birur
Kemmannagundi
Kundapur
Baba Budanagiri
Tumkur
17
Udipi
13
Halebid
Tiptur
206
62
Dobbspet
22
Nelamangala
Kaup
CHIKMAGALUR
Belur
32
41
78
48
Kunigal
41
27
Suratkal
Mangalore
Sakleshpur
Hassan
Channarayapatna
49
BANGALORE
Ullal
Golitattu
Puttur
Ramanagaram
209
Hosur
Kasargod
MADIKERI
Kushlnagar
Mandya
45
Palakkodu
Talathmane
Talacauvery
Kakkabe
Hunsur
Srirangapatna
Male Mahadeshwar Hills
Payyannur
Nagarhole
Mysore
Stanley Reservoir
Tholpetty
WLS
Irpu Falls
Veeranahosahalli
Nanjangud
Chamrajnagar
Mettur
Kannur
Thirunelly
Gundlupet
BR Hills
Mahe
Mananthavady
Sulthan Bathery
Edakkal
Kotagiri
TAMIL NADU
Bhavani
Mukurthi NP
OOTY
Kozhikode
KERALA
Red Hills
Coonoor
Mettupalayam
Erode
Silent Valley
Karur
Coimbatore
47
Dharapuram
Ponnani
Palakkad
Pollachi
Mulanur
Thrissur
Nelliampathy
Palani Hills
Dindigul
Parambikulam WLS
Munnar
Kodaikanal

Arabian Sea

KARNATAKA

KERALA

Netravati

Krishnarajasagar

Cauvery

53 National Highway
Road
Distance in km
Railway Line
Railway Station
Airport
O Hub centre
Trek point
Pass
National Park
Falls

TREKKING HOLIDAYS IN INDIA

Kanoor Fort
From the pages of Jungle Book

By Vivek M

The first view of the lush green Western Ghats

TIME	3 days
LEVEL	Moderate
IDEAL SEASON	Oct to late Feb and the monsoons
LOCATION	Sharavathy Valley Wildlife Sanctuary in the Western Ghats

KANOOR FORT

TREKKING GUIDE

To Sagara

Gerusoppa N

Map Area

Karnataka

Day 3

Damaged Monument

Kanoor Fort

Shaale Mane

Day 2

Dabbe Falls

Doctor Mane

Day 1

Campsite
Trek route ·····
Road
River
Bridge
Falls

Hosagadde

To Bhatkal

LIFE IS CALLING WHERE ARE YOU?

SMIRNOFF

Cassettes and CDs

HOSAGADDE-SHAALE MANE-DOCTOR MANE-GERUSOPPA

Many treks lead to ancient forts in the Western Ghats of Karnataka, but the one to the Kanoor Fort is undoubtedly among the finest. This walk is the epitome of everything Shimoga promises for the city dweller who longs for nature: thick jungles teeming with wildlife, cataracts at every turn, lush green mountaintops and picture-perfect villages.

For a trek that begins on an unassuming jeep track, the journey's

433

Crossing a temporary bridge en route to Shaale Mane

an amazingly scenic one — I couldn't stop taking pictures as every turn introduced vistas that seemed better than the previous one. A hard day's work translated into a perfect night at the campsite of Shaale Mane. Perched on a little hill, I drank in the excellent views of the surrounding villages and paddy fields, watching the glow disappear beyond the high hills.

There's plenty of adventure too. At Dabbe Falls, I had to negotiate a steep descent to catch a glimpse of the thin, silvery thread falling down to the other side of the valley. You also get the chance to meet interesting people on the trail. I met Neel Kumar, for instance, a local lad with a fund of stories, who regaled me with tales of tigers and gaurs as I took a dip in the stream running through his paddy fields. On Day Two I met the 'doctor', an enthusiastic 80-year-old man who has a farm on the edge of the forest. Make sure you have a chat with him. He showed me around his beautiful farm filled with black peppers, arecanut,

banana plants and a curious 'vicks' plant that he had got from Nepal.

The trek, though, is not all a bed of roses. The section through the Govardhanagiri forest on the way to the fort is steep and tiring, but the occasional peacock will keep your enthusiasm high. The route also passes through sholas with leeches. So I suggest you bring a little cloth pouch with a concoction of rock salt, tobacco and lime to get rid of them.

On the last day I hurried towards Gerusoppa, past dark shola trees. The murmur of a distant stream kept me company as I traversed endless forests. But then when I finally saw the houses of Gerusoppa, heralding the end of this marvellous walk, I told myself that I should have gone slower.

TIP This trek needs complete self-sufficiency. Carry your tent and enough food for three days. You could use the Shaale Mane school verandah to curl up inside your sleeping bag, but it can get cold at nights. Since you will be crossing the Sharavathy Wildlife

Sanctuary, you need permission from the Deputy Conservator of Forests, Wildlife Division, DC Office Compound, Balraj Urs Road, Shimoga-577201. Tel: 08182-222983

DAY ONE

HOSAGADDE-SHAALE MANE

TIME 5 HOURS
LEVEL MODERATE

As soon as you reach **Hosagadde**, you'll see a small shop on the opposite side of the road. Pick up toffees from here to help you on your way and also — if it's the rainy season — huge plastic covers to protect yourself from the rains. The path begins just next to this shop and forks 10m later; keep to the left. This track is as big as a jeep road and heads north-west. After 20 mins, cross a small bridge over a stream and continue on the track for an hour or so until you hit a temporary bridge and the path divides.

Keep to the right, heading north. After 100m, you will cross a wooden bridge. From here onwards, the path turns into a foot track that heads north, along a wooden fence and descends into a stream. Just before you hit the stream, take a left. The foot track continues along the left side of the stream and gets quite narrow, passing through bamboo thickets. Climb over a wooden gate, and continue along the paddy fields,

GETTING THERE AND OUT

FROM BANGALORE to Sagara, it's 343 km/ 8 hrs by 🚆 (Rs 230). Take the night bus from Majestic Bus Stand. You will be there before 7 am **Sagara to Hosagadde** (52 km/ 3 hrs approx). Take the first private bus ('Gajanana' at 7.15 am; Rs 18) from Sagara towards Bhatkal (Kargal-Bilkandooru route) and get down at Hosagadde. If you miss this bus, there should be others almost every half-hour **RETURN** From **Gerusoppa**, there are buses to **Sagara** until 5.15 pm (2 hrs). Plenty of buses to **Bangalore** from Sagara that run until late in the night. You can take a detour to **Jog Falls** by taking the bus to **Maavinagundi** from Gerusoppa (27 km/ 1 hr/ Rs 25; last bus at 4 pm), reach Jog by a tempo (3 km/ 20 mins/ Rs 5), enjoy the spectacle and then catch a direct bus (374 km/ 10 hrs/ Rs 220) from **Jog to Bangalore**. Or, if you reach Gerusoppa late, hike down to the 'Circle' (T Junction) and get direct buses (11 hrs/ Rs 230) to Bangalore until 11 pm

Kanoor Kote

This 16th century forgotten fort in the dense jungles of the Sharavathy Valley is at the centre of many obscure tales. The last ruler over this part was the famous 'Pepper Queen' Chennabhairava-devi, one of the many Keladis of Kanoor. The Keladi kings were Jains and many of the locals here still follow the sect.

The reason for the Kanoor Fort being in ruins is the subject of many interesting stories. One tale says that an unknown epidemic caused people to flee this once busy and flourishing fort. Another speaks of how neighbouring rulers were jealous of the immense wealth the queen gained from trading black peppers with Portuguese colonists. This jealousy fuelled a battle and lead to the downfall of the empire. Either way, the fort now stands in utter ruins, slowly being swallowed by the jungle. A small exploration can spring a lot of pleasant surprises. Beautiful sculptures, tunnels, gateways and strong fort walls still remain, standing their ground against the forest.

crossing the stream and following the path past a house, heading north-west.

Cross a temporary bridge, walking on the right border of the paddy fields to reach a typical Malnad house. Take the path heading west past this house. Cross the stream and walk 10m, to where the path divides. Take the foot track heading west, which will turn into a jeep track. After 100m, you hit a permanent bridge, where you will see nice little waterfalls. Follow the jeep track, heading north.

The first house you get to is a certain Dabbe Gowdru's house. Ask permission before you enter his premises. **Dabbe Falls** can be seen from the edge of his fields overlooking the other side of the valley, but you have to descend sufficiently to get a glimpse of the waterfalls. Spend some leisure time there and then retrace your steps back to the pucca bridge. As you cross the bridge, take the foot track that ascends south-west to join a jeep track. Half a kilometre later, cross a stream and keep going straight (be sure not to take a right after the stream). Just after a

house, the track forks. Take the left. This jeep track ascends northwards.

You'll come across two houses; take the path going down and to the west, opposite them. Go down the path, cross a dam and the fields on the left side to arrive at a hut, and a path which continues behind it, ascending steeply. Follow this path to reach **Shaale Mane**, the village school. You can pitch your camp on the premises or sleep in the verandah. There is also water available from the tap on the premises.

DAY TWO
SHAALE MANE-DOCTOR MANE
TIME 6 HOURS
LEVEL MODERATE

Take the jeep track in front of the school heading south. After a short while the track forks; take a left. Where the jeep track ends at a house, take the footpath heading south-west, following the electric poles. Enter the fields through a small wooden gate on your left, and cross to the right side of the fields to get to a check dam. Cross the

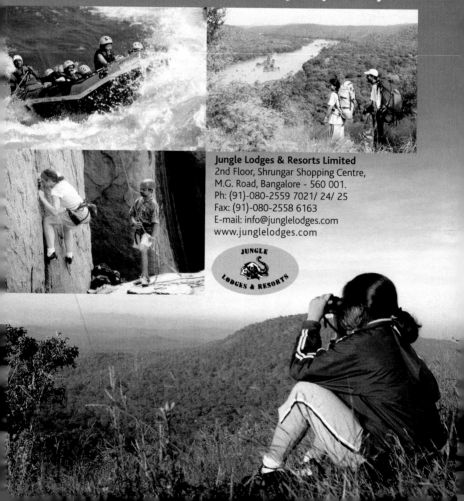

Jungle Lodges & Resorts Ltd.,
a Government of Karnataka
Undertaking, is India's largest
eco-tourism organization with
14 properties offering amazing
wildlife, adventure and
beach holidays.
Come, discover some of
Nature's best kept secrets,
preserved by JLR just for you.

Jungle Lodges & Resorts Limited
2nd Floor, Shrungar Shopping Centre,
M.G. Road, Bangalore - 560 001.
Ph: (91)-080-2559 7021/ 24/ 25
Fax: (91)-080-2558 6163
E-mail: info@junglelodges.com
www.junglelodges.com

JUNGLE
LODGES & RESORTS

dam and continue south-west on the path, following the electric poles.

Once the path descends, you can see the road. Skirt the fields to reach the road. Take a right to head towards **Kanoor**. The road is a pleasant 5-km walk, with hardly any vehicles and wonderful sights of the countryside. It ends at a permanent bridge. Note that the stream beneath is your last water source for the day and it's a great place for a dip too.

A jeep track continues north, with a forest signboard saying: 'Kanoor Fort 8 km'. The track is well defined from this point on and leads through some unbelievable forests. However, the first kilometre can be really taxing, so carry at least two bottles of water. Go past the unmanned forest gate and the couple of houses on the left (you could easily miss these as they nestle within thick foliage). The **Kanoor Fort** is just 1 km away. However, watch out for the spot when the track divides. A small wooden signpost hammered on a tree in the middle of the fork directs you to the track on your right. This track ascends south-west and leads you to the fort, which is just 100m away.

TIP Keep in mind the small, curious-looking broken stone arch on your left just before you hit the fork. A path right opposite this monument takes you to Gerusoppa, your third day's trek

The first sight of the fort is a huge stone wall on your right with a little arched doorway leading inside. Once you enter, a flight of stairs leads you further inside. Spend a few hours exploring the fort, and then go back to the fork, take the other route and head downwards. You will skirt around a jungle lake and cross a log bridge. The first house you see on your right ($1\frac{1}{2}$ km from the fort) is the old doctor's house. He is kind enough to let trekkers stay in his verandah (which can accommodate up to six people) but doesn't provide food. He prefers that his guests are well behaved and keep their noise levels to a minimum.

One of the many delightful streams that appear during the monsoons

Exploring the Kanoor Fort

TIP Leave early and take lots of water with you. This part can be quite tiring but the route is beautiful, and a chance of sighting wild animals is good

DAY THREE
DOCTOR MANE-GERUSOPPA
TIME 5 HOURS
LEVEL MODERATE

Retrace your steps back to the curious-looking piece of monument. The route opposite descends northwards. After about 1½ hrs, the path leads you out of the forest and divides into three, which can be confusing.

Take the path in the centre going north-west (not quite as defined as the other two), which heads uphill a little while. After 200m, you will cross a wooden gate. Head to the left of the house. The path leads down into a stream. Crossing this stream to get to the other side can be quite difficult, but not dangerous.

The track continues, skirts on the left of fields, and meets another path. Take a right and ascend north-west on a fairly well-defined jeep track. The hike is initially tiring, but you will pass a couple of streams that are perfect for a refreshing dip. The path finally ends on the banks of **River Sharavathy**. You can hop a boat to get across the river to the town of **Gerusoppa**, from where you can catch a bus to **Sagara**. ✦

PRASHANT PANJIAR

Enjoying the vistas at Maravanthe Beach

Maravanthe is beautiful. Period. Even in the monsoons under murky skies people stop on NH17, at the point where it cuts between the Sowparnika River and the Arabian Sea, to get views that are unmatched. Agitated waves lash against the shore even as on the opposite side, gentle ripples lap at the riverbank. For those who love beach holidays, Maravanthe holds some unexpected delights.

→ Maravanthe Facts

● **LOCATION** Maravanthe is a lovely strip of sand between the sea and NH17, near the backwaters of the Sowparnika River in Udupi District, in west Karnataka
● **GETTING TO MARAVANTHE By air** Nearest airport: Mangalore (109 km/ 2 hrs). Taxi Rs 800 **By rail** Nearest railhead: Mangalore **By road** The drive to Maravanthe from Mangalore, down coastal highway NH17 via Udupi and Kundapur, is beautiful
Bangalore to Maravanthe The best way to get to Maravanthe is to take a direct overnight luxury bus via Kundapur. Volvo coaches (AC Rs 400, non-AC Rs 280) do the 456-km journey in 9$^1/_2$ hrs. If you're driving by car, take NH4 till Nelamangala, then NH48 to Mangalore via Kunigal, Hassan and Mani and NH17 to Maravanthe via Udipi and Kundapur. Durgamba (Bangalore Tel: 080-23365871) and Sugama (Tel: 22283986), among others, operate daily night services from Bangalore to Maravanthe
● **STD CODE** 08254

MUST-VISITS
UNDERWATER SPORTS
Turtle Bay Resort and Soans Holidays make arrangements for and also have adequate facilities for scuba diving and snorkelling. For a group of six, the cost will be around Rs 1,000 for each person.

SEA RIDES
A boating trip around the Arabian Sea can be very enchanting. Hiring a boat for about an hour can cost you anywhere between Rs 800 and 1,000.

WHERE TO STAY
Maravanthe has the look of a rustic and simple beach, as there aren't many places to stay and rules prohibit the construction of any more resorts. Many also choose to stay in **Kundapur**, 12 km from Maravanthe.

The most luxurious option in Maravanthe is the **Turtle Bay Water Sports and Beach Resort** (Tel: 08254-265422; Tariff: Rs 500-1,000) on Kanchgodu Beach in Trasi. **Sagar Kinara Beach Resort** (Tel: 230136; Tariff: Rs 300-350), a lodge run by a local family, provides a home-stay option with Udupi food. **Isle of Amgol Resort** (Tel: 231683; Tariff: Rs 2,000) and **Hotel Sharon** (Tel: 230826; Tariff: Rs 160-750) in Kundapur offer trekking facilites.
For more hotels and details, see Accommodation Listings on pages 550-551

WHERE TO EAT
Maravanthe Beach has a few shacks that serve nice coffee and locally produced cashew nuts. Also, try some of the small hotels on the highway for the local fare, especially the *bangda* (mackerel) curry. Try kane (ladyfish) masala fry at **Banjara**, Hotel Sharon's non-vegetarian restaurant. JK Residency has a coastal speciality restaurant called **Coastal Heritage**. For the veggies, there is regular Udupi cuisine with *kottes* and neer dosa. And don't miss the masala dosa at **Harsha Refreshments** (Hotel Sharon).
Inputs from DEBARSHI DASGUPTA

TREKKING HOLIDAYS IN INDIA

LIFE IS CALLING WHERE ARE YOU?

SMIRNOFF

VIVEK M

Kodachadri
On table mountain

By Allen Mendonca

TIME	2 days
LEVEL	Easy
IDEAL SEASON	Oct to Mar
LOCATION	On the border of Shimoga and Udupi districts, in the Western Ghats

The long, hard route to the summit of Kodachadri

KOLLUR-KODACHADRI HILLS-KOLLUR

The Kodachadri Hills tower over the tiny pilgrim centre of Kollur. But there is still no mistaking Kodachadri (1,343m), the highest hill from which the range gets its name. It seems to rise high up into the clouds, greyish blue, with wreaths of green decorating it from the bottom to the top. It borders Kundapur in Udupi District. On its western portion, it drops almost perpendicular to the Mookambika Wildlife Sanctuary, which is the home of the endangered lion-tailed macaque.

The Sowparnika River flows in the valley beyond the hills and empties into the Arabian Sea near the famous Maravanthe Beach. The river has large stretches of mangrove forests rich in

Bharat Petroleum

GETTING THERE AND OUT

FROM MARAVANTHE to Kollur, via Kundapur, it's 57 km/ 1½ hrs by 🚗 (Rs 400) or 2 hrs by 🚌 (Rs 25) **ALTERNATIVE OPTION** Take NH4 from Bangalore to Tumkur and then NH206 to Shimoga (271 km/ 6 hrs). From Shimoga to the foothills is 120 km/ 3½ hrs via Theerthalli-Mastikatte Road. Trekkers favour this route **RETURN** the same way to Kundapur or Shimoga

aquatic delicacies like tiger prawns and crabs. Occasionally, fishermen are said to have come across crocodiles here.

DAY ONE
KOLLUR-KODACHADRI HILLS
DISTANCE 17 KM **TIME** 5-6 HOURS
LEVEL MODERATE

From Kollur catch a bus to **Koda-chadri**, getting off 12 km later at

Graphic by ANIS KHAN

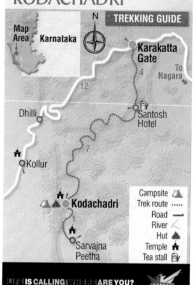

KODACHADRI
TREKKING GUIDE

Map Area — Karnataka

Karakatta Gate

To Nagara

4

12

Dhilli

Santosh Hotel

7

Kollur

Kodachadri

Sarvajna Peetha

Campsite
Trek route .....
Road —
River
Hut
Temple
Tea stall

Lion-tailed macaque

The lion-tailed macaque (*Macaca silenus*), with its characteristic long, brown-grey mane, has a black body and a black prehensile (adopted for seizing, especially by wrapping around) tail with a tuft of hair at the end.

The tail measures between half to a third of the length of the body. The spread of teak, coffee, tea and other plantations in the Western Ghats has spelt doom for this species, which has been unable to adapt to human habitation. The macaques live most of the time in the branches of tall trees, foraging at different levels of the forest, but seldom coming to the ground in search of food. They have developed an ingenious way to limit the amount of time needed to gather food, evolving cheek pouches that open beside their lower teeth and extend down the sides of their neck. When fully extended, these pouches can store an equivalent to the macaque's stomach capacity. It feeds on fruits, lizards, fledgling birds and stuffs them into their pouches.

The Kollur Mookambika Temple

The Mookambika Temple, in Kollur, nestled in the Kodachadri Hills, is an important religious place in the district. The 14-m high, centuries-old, iron Dwajasthamba (flag-staff) in front of the temple has been compared in quality to the Iron Pillar of Delhi, for it has withstood the vagaries of time without corroding. Atop the pillar is a trident that folklore claims belongs to the lion-riding Mother Goddess who slew the dumb (*mooka*) demon for terrorising the tribals who lived in the hills. The trident acts as a lightning conductor and has half-melted from repeated strikes. Next to it is another more recent pillar gilded in gold leaf and adorned with sculptures of various deities.

The noon puja here is very special because a priceless necklace of gold adorned with precious gems, including a 528-carat green sapphire, one of the biggest in the world, is placed around the neck of the deity. Alas, the spiritual alchemy is ruined by the presence of the old temple tusker cruelly chained to a stake next to the temple most of the year round. Lunch and dinner is served free to pilgrims and yes, trekkers too, from noon-2 pm and 7-9 pm respectively. The temple is open to visitors from 5.30 am-9.30 pm.

Karakatta Gate. If you are coming via Shimoga, then the hills are located 12 km west, down the **Theerthalli-Mastikatte Road**.

Whichever route you take, there's no mistaking Kodachadri, standing like a monolith. Pass through the concrete arch of the Karakatta Gate and walk on the level jeep track.

An hour's walk over the badly rutted road will bring you to 🏠 **Santosh Hotel** on your left. His puttu and channa are very popular with trekkers and if you're returning the next day, ensure that you order lunch before you proceed. Just behind the tea shop is a gently flowing stream of icy cold water, tumbling fresh from the hills. Take a dip and then get yourself a cup of tea and food. Thus fortified, walk towards the foothill of Kodachadri (remember you'll be climbing or getting down the mountain for the better part of the day, so ensure that you carry enough water and snacks).

Ten minutes from the tea shop, you'll see three paths leading upwards.

Take the middle one, because it has been hardened by centuries of movement of wild animals, cattle and people. This is the toughest portion of the hike as it is steep for the most part. There are brambles and thorn bushes and shrubs with spiky leaves that can leave nasty cuts. There are also cashew and berry trees crawling with vicious red ants, so watch out.

After $1^1/_2$ hrs the hill breaks into level ground on which is located a small temple. Rest awhile and then you can resume the hike.

The hill is so beautiful and the air so invigorating that one automatically walks slowly, taking in the sights of the green vistas and meadows on the surrounding hills and valleys and the **Mookambika Wildlife Sanctuary** nestling way below in the valley to the west. The left side of the hill is an almost perpendicular drop of 1,150m.

Sometimes, you'll catch a sparkle of silver from the river thundering through the valley. At other times, if you are lucky, you'll be able to witness

The magical waterfalls of Arshinagundi near Kollur

the blue of the Arabian Sea in the distant horizon. In the rainy season and post monsoon, one can see the grace of the **Agastya Teertha Waterfall** on the left face of the hill. About 2-3 hrs later, you reach **Kodachadri,** which has a PWD bungalow, a Shankaracharya Temple, and a couple of small houses with rooms on rent. If they have room, you can stay here or pitch your tents on the grounds around. There's plenty of water here.

It takes about 30-40 mins from here to reach the summit at a leisurely pace. There's a little temple-like structure here called the **Sarvajna Peetha** to mark the spot where Shankaracharya is said to have meditated. Trekkers love to reach the top in time for the sunrise or sunset which are both spectacular and make for great photographs.

DAY TWO

KODACHADRI-KOLLUR
DISTANCE 17 KM **TIME** 4 HOURS
LEVEL EASY

Walking down the same way is easier and should take 4 hrs. The slope towards Kundapur has steep faces and is not advisable unless one has undergone a rock-climbing course. On reaching the bottom, one can catch a bus or truck heading towards **Kundapur** or **Shimoga**. From here get onward transportation to head home.

For hotels in Kundapur, see Accommodation Listings on page 550 ✦

445

Baba Budanagiri Hills
Pligrimage in the clouds

By Allen Mendonca

The hills dissolve in the morning mist on the trail to Baba Budanagiri

TIME	4-5 days
LEVEL	Easy with some steep stretches
IDEAL SEASON	Sep to May
LOCATION	Chikmagalur District in West Karnataka

CHIKMAGALUR-MULLAIYANAGRI-BABA BUDANAGIRI-KEMMANNAGUNDI-BHADRA WILDLIFE SANCTUARY

The Iron Lady of India had a lot to be grateful for to Chikmagalur. Had the sleepy little town not voted her back into power in 1980, Indira Gandhi would have remained in the political wilderness because of the Emergency. Earlier, probably in 1650, a Sufi saint planted the first coffee saplings in the district and helped create India's finest coffee estates. These plantations in turn were nurtured and expanded by the British in the 19th and early part of the 20th century. Today, Indian planters and corporations own hundreds of acres of arabica and robusta plantations that cover the slopes of the hills. Pepper vines entwine over the silver oaks that provide shade to the coffee shrubs.

This is the district where the crescent-shaped Baba Budanagiri Range stretches for 80 km, rising majestically to an average height of 1,500-1,900m and blending seamlessly with the Western Ghats, designated as one of the 25 biodiversity hotspots of the world. This is the free range of the endangered tiger, bonnet macaque, gaur, elephant, spotted deer and nilgai. Over 250 bird species, over 300 precious medicinal plants and herbs, orchids and flowers and varieties of bamboo and timber trees flourish here. This is also the home of the great Bhadra River that begins as a series of streams on the hills and then tumbles onto the plains.

The Jagara Valley nestles between these hills. A folk song of the area captures the spirit of the place in these words: 'If the bamboo swings to the voice of the wind and the tiger wanders with gaiety, then it must be Jagara Valley.'

Trekking in these hills is sheer joy. In a matter of a few hours, one experiences a microcosm of the evolutionary tableaux, from the lichens and moss that cling onto the rocks to the dry deciduous sholas and grasslands.

TIP Carry water as one tends to get dehydrated during the trek. You can drink from the crystal clear springs when you reach higher ground. Carry salt to rub on leeches to get rid of them

DAY ONE
CHIKMAGALUR-MULLAIYANAGIRI
DISTANCE 14 KM **TIME** 3-4 HOURS
LEVEL EASY

Take any bus from the Chikmagalur Bus Station towards Kemmannagundi,

Graphic by ANIS KHAN

and just 6 km down the road, get off at the arch that says 'Sarpanadari', literally, the trail of the snake.

It will be better still to begin your trek from the town itself, heading north on the state road leading to **Kemmannagundi**. After 3 km, the road begins to twist and ascend. Coffee estates dot the hillside. Another 3 km and the 'Sarpanadari' arch beckons you to the left. There's a signboard that indicates the trail leading to the **Mullaiyanagiri Peak** (1,925m).

Avoid the motorable road that takes you three-fourths of the way to the peak. Instead, hit the trail on your right. You'll crest the first hill adorned with slippery rocks, bamboo and thorny shrubs in 45 mins. Take a breather and a swig of water. There's a plateau extending before you for about 30m. Cross it and the next hill towers 450m. The gradient now is around 45-40 degrees. Keep climbing and half-an-hour later, you'll come to

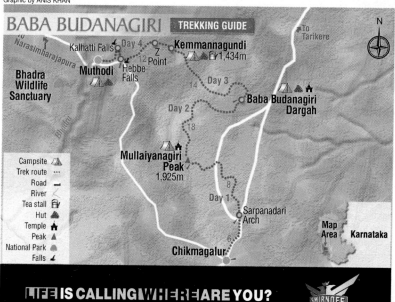

447

→ Chikmagalur Facts

For your Baba Budanagiri trek, make
Chikmagalur your base

● **LOCATION** A hill station in West Karnataka,
north-west of Bangalore

● **GETTING TO CHIKMAGALUR By air**
Nearest airport: Bangalore (245 km/ 6 hrs). Taxi
Rs 3,000 **By rail** Nearest railheads: Birur (46
km/ 1 hr by local bus) and Tarikere (56 km/
1½ hrs by local bus). The Janshatabdi Express
leaves Bangalore at 6 am via Birur (9.15 am)
and reaches Tarikere at 9.40 am **By road** Take
NH4 to Nelamangala, NH48 to Hassan via
Kunigal and Channarayapatna and state road to
Chikmagalur and the Baba Budanagiri Hills.
KSRTC buses (6 hrs) run every hour from the
Majestic Bus Stand in Bangalore (Express Rs 225,
Ultra Plus Rs 167). Last bus leaves at 11.30 pm.
This is the best because you'll reach
Chikmagalur early, right in time for the trek

● **STD CODE** 08262

● **MUST-VISITS** Chikmagalur has the topography of an ironing board — hills rise all
around it and coffee grows in the shade of
silver oaks. Stop by Panduranga at MG Road for
coffee beans or freshly ground powder minus
chicory. To arrange an estate visit, call
Mohammad Aseem on Tel: 09844168948 or
email: mohamedaseem@yahoo.com
Mullaiyanagiri, the highest peak in Karnataka, is
around 6 km from Chikmagalur town. Its 1,925m
height is ideal for watching sunsets. It also
makes for a nice 45-min trek to the top though
it's possible to drive most of the way.

● **WHERE TO STAY AND EAT** In Chikmagalur,
at **The Taj Garden Retreat** (Tel: 08262-
220202, 220404; Tariff: Rs 2,500-3,700), one
can take many things for granted — including a
stock of your cigarette brand. But the food here
is quite disappointing, though it's fun eating by
the pool. **The Planters Court** (Tel: 235881-
885; Tariff: Rs 375-1,100) is the next best thing
after Taj. They serve good South Indian breakfast
at their drive-in and do Chinese well too.
Aishwariya Regency (Tel: 224001-02; Tariff:
Rs 475-525) is a budget option and serves only
North Indian food.
*For more hotel details, see Accommodation Listings
on page 549*

a narrow ridge that provides panoramic views of the plains and the
Chikmagalur town and villages far
below. You'll also find laterite caves en
route with colonies of bats.

Follow the path as it winds uphill.
At 1,500m, one reaches a piece of level
ground, the size of a tennis court and
there, before you looms the Mullaiyanagiri Peak with a Shiva Temple
crowning the top. Climb the 50-plus
shaky stone steps and you can have a
darshan of the deity. ⚠ Camp here in
a tent, in the caves or in the courtyard
of the temple.

The hill is especially memorable in
the monsoon when winds reaching 60-
80 kmph whip across the hill and the
rain slices into the cliff face. On a clear
summer day, the 8-9 km route
(depending on how you traverse the
hills) will take you a little over 2 hrs to
cover, but in the monsoon it could
take over 3 hrs.

DAY TWO

MULLAIYANAGIRI-BABA BUDANAGIRI
DISTANCE 18 KM **TIME** 6-7 HOURS
LEVEL EASY WITH SOME STEEP CLIMBS

Kemmannagundi is to the north-west
of Chikmagalur, separated by the **Baba
Budanagiri Range**. Mullaiyanagiri,
the highest peak, lies almost half-way
along this range. The **Baba Budangiri
Dargah** lies 18 km to the north-east.
To reach there, descend a thousand
metres to the north-east of the Mullaiyanagiri Peak and then walk to the
junction of two trails that run almost
parallel to each other. One is used by
herdsmen who bring their cattle from
the plains to graze on the grassy
slopes, and the other by pilgrims and
trekkers. There are signboards pointing north-east to the dargah.

⚠ You can camp anywhere near the
dargah grounds or bunk down with
the pilgrims in a large hall in the dargah complex. If you want comfort,
taxi down to **Nature Nirvana Plantation Getaways** (Tel: 09844042152/

Smiles are still present despite the tough ascent to Mullaiyanagiri

09448364159; email: naturenirvana @yahoo.com/ naturenirvana.com), which is 15 km away in the Byne Khan and El Dorado coffee plantations.

DAY THREE
BABA BUDANAGIRI-KEMMANNAGUNDI
DISTANCE 14 KM **TIME** 4-5 HOURS
LEVEL EASY

Kemmannagundi is 14 km away to the north-west, but you first go around the shrine anti-clockwise and head south-west. You'll spot the trail easily. It leads through lush coffee estates and scrub forest, through large bare crevasses made by strip mining and then up north-west to the **Kemmannagundi Hill Station** (1,434m), made popular by Raja Krishna Rajendra Wodeyar IV, who spent his summers here in the 1930s.

You can camp at the **Kemmannagundi maidan**. Or stay in any one of the little 2-room lodges on the main road, which also claim to serve "brakfast". The hilltop **Horticulture Department Guest House** offers five cottages.

The healing touch of coffee

The **Inam Dattatreya Bababudan Swamy Dargah** is a cave shrine in the lower reaches of the Baba Budanagiri Range, 32 km from Chikmagalur by the state road. Legend has it that Hazrat Dada Hayat Mir Kalandar, a Sufi saint, arrived in these parts in the 1650s from Mecca, where he had gone on a Haj pilgrimage. There, in the cities of Arabia, he had tasted the popular aromatic coffee made from beans brought from Ethiopia. He collected seven beans and on his arrival in the hills, planted the seeds and nurtured the saplings. Soon he was cultivating a couple of acres on the hills and the brew caught the imagination and taste buds of the populace.

The saint was a teacher and healer who lived in a humble home in one of the laterite caves in the hills. His teachings, combined with his generosity with the refreshing brew, resulted in him being called Baba Budan, the saint who heals.

No one is quite sure how the cave where he lived also came to be known as the abode of Dattatreya, an incarnation of Brahma, Vishnu and Shiva.

What is certain is that both Hindus and Muslims have been worshipping this spot ever since the demise of the saint. The Muslims called him a disciple of the prophet while the Hindus considered him a reincarnation of Dattatreya. The shrine also spawned a syncretic belief that became an integral part of the region — the *awadhut* tradition that upholds a formless god and condemns caste and sacrificial rituals.

DAY FOUR

KEMMANNAGUNDI-BHADRA WILDLIFE SANCTUARY

DISTANCE 12 KM **TIME** 3-4 HOURS
LEVEL EASY

From the hill station, a number of trails head north-west to **Z Point**, a rocky promontory 3 km away, where one gets a panoramic view of the jungles covering the Western Ghats. To the left of Z Point, you'll spot a path. Trek along this steep and narrow path and after 5 km, you'll hear the booming sound of the 160m **Hebbe Waterfalls**. In the old days, hundreds of prisoners of the chieftains and kings of the region were pushed over the falls to their death, on the rocks in the rapids below.

Keep walking past Hebbe and climb another 2 km and you'll witness the 122-m cascade of the **Kalhatti Falls**. As you approach there, you'll spot a temple through the cloud of spray, nestling in the cliff over which the water tumbles. This should take you about 2 hrs. Refresh yourself in the cool water and march for $1^1/_2$ hrs parallel to the state road that takes off from near the falls and leads to the hamlet of **Muthodi** and the **Bhadra Wildlife Sanctuary**.

🔺 🔺 Camp at the **Muthodi Nature Camp** grounds or stay in their cottages or in the dorm. Join a safari to the sanctuary the next morning. Head home by the bus or taxi service available here for Chikmagalur.

For hotels, see Accommodation Listings on pages 549 (Baba Budanagiri), 550 (Kemmannagundi) and 551 (Muthodi) ✦

AASHIRVAAD
ReadyMeals

The one pack you need to carry on a trek.

Now food breaks on a trek can be as interesting and stimulating as the trek itself. Choose from Aashirvaad's wide range of ReadyMeals, simply heat and you've got yourself a delicious meal, ready in minutes. The best part, Aashirvaad ReadyMeals are made using no preservatives, making them as fresh as your trek is bound to be.

PRASHANT PANJIAR

Y ou'd think a travel agent possibly dreamed up this land. Picture this: 4,126 sq km carpeted in just about every shade of possible green. Paddy fields dot the countryside and the heady fragrance of cardamom and nutmeg rents the air. There are murmuring streams and rivulets, and the mighty Cauvery herself, wending her way through the countryside. Coorg is simply beautiful, an astonishing land, lush and fecund beyond belief.

The small, bustling Madikeri

MUST-VISITS

MADIKERI FORT

Originally a mud fort, Madikeri Fort was rebuilt with stone by Tipu Sultan. Inside the fort is the palace of the Lingayat rulers, a simple double-storey structure.

FISHING

A popular indulgence in these parts is fishing, as rivers are packed with mahseer. Many an anglers' meet has gone on to become an al fresco picnic.

WHERE TO STAY

Madikeri's best hotel is the **Coorg International** (Tel: 08272-228071-72; Tariff:

Rs 400-3,000), with indoor games, a health club and a swimming pool. Karnataka Tourism's **Mayura Valley View** (Tel: 228387; Tariff: Rs 430) is a good, clean, budget option, with great views of the valley. **Hill Town Hotel** (Tel: 223805; Tariff: Rs 500-750), centrally located, arranges sightseeing to places around. Mr Uthappa's **East End Hotel** (Tel: 229996; Tariff: Rs 210-700) has maintained a high standard through the years.

Capitol Village (Tel: 225492; Tariff: Rs 1,200-1,500) is located within a coffee and cardamom plantation, 5 km from the centre of Madikeri. With trekking, plantation tours and angling trips on offer, this is a good option for adventurers. Shanti Estate Bungalow (Tel: 223690; Tariff: Rs 300-500), 2$\frac{1}{2}$ km from Madikeri on the road to Virajpet, offers basic facilities in a homely atmosphere.
For more hotels and details, see Accommodation Listings on pages 550-551

WHERE TO EAT

The Coorgis have a way with pork (pandi curry), fowl (koli curry) and mango, and their akki rotis and *kadumputtus* are a treat. Coorg International has the multicuisine **Silver Oaks Restaurant, Lost Horizons Bar** and a pastry shop. **East End Hotel** has a bar and restaurant while **Capitol Village** offers Coorgi and Continental food. **Hill Town Hotel** and the **Mayura Valley View** offer a wide range, from Coorgi to North Indian, Chinese and Mughlai. All roadside stalls serve great coffee, but of course. **Amrit, Chitra** and **Brahmagiri** are the other favourites, serving food at a lower price.

INPUTS FROM SHEILA KUMAR

→ | Madikeri Facts

● **LOCATION** The capital of the Kodavas is at the heart of the Kodagu District, 237 km SW of Bangalore
● **GETTING TO MADIKERI By air** Nearest airport: Bangalore (237 km/ 5 hrs). Taxi Rs 1,500 **By rail** Nearest railhead: Hunsur (76 km/ 1$\frac{1}{2}$ hrs). Taxi Rs 700 **By road** Take SH17 to Srirangapatna via Maddur, then the bypass via Ranganathittu to Hunsur and SH88 to Madikeri via Kushalnagar and Suntikoppal. Cross the Cauvery just before Kushalnagar, then be prepared for not-so-smooth rides as the roads in Coorg are hardy. The destination and en route vistas will be well worth the bumpy rides though. KSTRC buses (6 hrs/ ordinary Rs 110, ultra deluxe Rs 165) run from the Majestic Bus Stand in Bangalore to Madikeri
● **STD CODE** 08272
● **TOURIST OFFICE** Karnataka Tourism, Hotel Mayura Valley View, Raja's Seat, Madikeri-571201. Tel: 08272-228387

TREKKING HOLIDAYS IN INDIA

...we see you, with your spirit of adventure, and know it's all you ever need to 'go beyond'... we know you have done that, be it the crack of morning just a night under the stars... we see it through you, a journey where you don't stop, not on beyond horizon, blazing new trails, the air thick with the smell of adventure...

on your adventure, we carry that spirit

WILDCRAFT™

proud to **journey** with you

Coorg Plantation Hikes
Short sojourns in paradise

By Anurag Mallick

Photographs by VIVEK M

TIME	2-10 days
LEVEL	Moderate
IDEAL SEASON	Sep-May, post monsoon for birdwatching
LOCATION	Coorg District in south-west Karnataka

At the summit of Thadiyendamol

Coorg has been internationally recognised as one of the most important biodiversity hotspots in the world. But the fact that now there's neither honey in Honey Valley, nor any orange in Orange County, speaks volumes about the fragile nature of Coorg's ecosystem and hence the need to preserve it. Here, the stem-borer challenges the robustness of robusta and the berry-borer wages a war against arabica. While this is no threat to democracy, Coorg's flora is in peril. Most of the fauna too has long been consigned to the walls of Kodava living rooms but the best way to appreciate the surviving bird life and natural beauty is a leisurely trek through the region.

In Coorg, the Western Ghats' main range extends from Subramanya in the north-west to the Brahmagiris in the south, the distance being a wide green swathe spanning over 100 km.

The Brahmagiris or Marenad Hills form a natural barrier between Coorg and Wayanad, which is another trek by itself. The small treks outlined here take you to the main peaks of the area, well-preserved plantations and remote organic farms. These farm stays make excellent trekking bases to explore Coorg's rich natural bounty and ensure that you also have an intellectually stimulating eco-holiday. But it is actually Coorg's relatively untouched

Graphic by ANIS KHAN

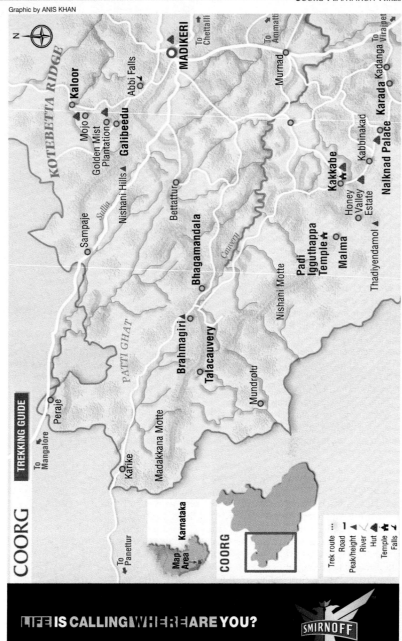

COORG

TREKKING GUIDE

N

KOTEBETTA RIDGE

Kaloor
Mojo
Golden Mist Plantation
Galibeedu
Nishani Hills
Sampaje
Sullia

MADIKERI
Abbi Falls
To Chettalli
To Ammatti
Murnad

Bettattur
Cauvery
Bhagamandala

PATTI GHAT
Brahmagiri
Talacauvery
Mundroti
Madakkana Motte
Karike
Peraje
To Mangalore
To Panettur

Nishani Motte
Padi Igguthappa Temple
Malma
Thadiyendamol

Kakkabe
Honey Valley Estate
Kabbinakad
Nalknad Palace
Karada Kadanga
To Virajpet

Karnataka
Map Area

COORG

Trek route
Road
Peak/height
River
Hut
Temple
Falls

455

Speed™
High Performance Petrol
Bharat Petroleum

GETTING THERE AND OUT

FROM MADIKERI to Mojo, the starting point of the trek, it's 11 km/ 30 mins by 🚗 (Rs 200). Mojo is north-west of Madikeri (Mercara). At Madikeri, ask for **Galibeedu Village** and following the signboard, take the right turn towards **Kaloor**. The isolated road to Mojo takes you through cardamom plantations and you get a view of the Kottebetta Hill to the right. Before reaching Kaloor, look out for the green eco-froggie Mojo logo and the bamboo gate on the left of the road **Bangalore to Mojo** If travelling by 🚌 from Bangalore, it's ideal that you book with **Mojo Rainforest Retreat** (*see page 459*) and they will arrange a pick-up from Madikeri **RETURN** Drive 25 km (30 mins by taxi/ Rs 450; 45 mins by bus/ Rs 15) from **Kakkabe** via Kadanga and Karada till you reach **Virajpet**, which is connected to SH88 and after Ranganathittu, you are back on the Mysore-Bangalore Highway

natural wilderness that makes it one of the best places in the world to get lost.

The catch is that to savour these well-preserved natural bastions of Coorg, you need to book with the people who safeguard it. It's a small price to pay for creature comforts in the middle of nowhere.

While it's not possible to pitch tents and trek through someone's property unless you book with them, there are neutral territories like Kottebetta Peak and the banks of the Cauvery where you can pitch tents. It might help to check with the Coorg Wildlife Society in Madikeri (*see contact details on page 465*). Also, make sure you call up the respective home-stays and check for availability.

DAY ONE
MOJO RAINFOREST TREK
TIME 1-3 HOURS
LEVEL EASY

Perched at 1,100m on the top of the rain-slope in Coorg's Western Ghats, **Mojo**, a 25-acre organic farm, lies tucked away in absolute isolation 12 km away from Madikeri.

Here, you will find the habanero (the world's second hottest chilli) and the southern birdwing (India's largest butterfly), not to mention the Atlas moth (the moth with the world's largest wingspan). Mojo also claims to have the best Blues collection in the country, hence its musical name. Many species of birds and several orchids are found in the farm too, making it a naturalist's paradise.

Trekkers cross the undulating landscape towards Thadiyendamol

Mojo is spread across four valleys, has a mountain stream and is criss-crossed by several moderate walks. Take a guided tour of the estate to understand the nuances of organic farming. An early morning walk to **Cardamom Valley** is extremely rich in birding, whereas an evening trudge to **Maya Hill** reveals a panoramic sunset view of the **Kotebetta Range**. It's also the only way you can make your mobile phone work.

🔺 MOJO RAINFOREST RETREAT

To get to Mojo, ask for **Galibeedu Village** and following the signboard, take the right turn towards Kaloor. A pick-up is possible from Madikeri if

The magic of the Western Ghats

The Western Ghats separate the western seaboard from the relatively dry, high tableland of the Deccan Plateau. It's a long patch of dense rainforests and shola forests stretching in a wide swathe of undulating green from Maharashtra, Goa, Karnataka and western Tamil Nadu till Kerala. The biological diversity found in the Western Ghats is unparalleled in the world and gives the region a dazzling array of birds, orchids and butterflies of every hue.

The southern part of the Western Ghats and its forests form the centre of distribution for 20 of India's endemic bird species and another 15 regional endemics common to Sri Lanka. Small wonder then that Bird Life International has recognised the Western Ghats as one of the most important endemic bird areas in Asia.

People of Kodagu have their own vocabulary to describe birds. While the racket-tailed drongo, with its majestic tail, is called bheemaraja-pakshi (big royal bird), the green barbet on account of its call is the guttar-pakshi, coucal for no apparent reason is chembuka and the black and orange scarlet minivet is called titte-kanda pakshi (glowing charcoal bird). Other species such as the Malabar parakeet, Malabar pied hornbill, Wayanad laughing thrush and Malabar trogon are endemic to the Western Ghats. The Malabar whistling thrush has a melodious but off-key whistle, which more than makes up for its dull blue appearance.

Apart from the Paris peacock, you can spot butterflies such as the bright yellow southern birdwing, the largest in India, which hovers around the canopy of trees. Kodagu also throws up its share of surprises — the furtive Malabar squirrel, beautiful orchids with unpronounceable names like Bulbophyllum fibriatum and swarms of fireflies that glow like decoration bulbs on trees in the warm nights of May and June.

The Pushpagiri Peak dominates the horizon

prior intimation is given. Discover Mojo — a heady mixture of eco-tourism and adventure. Mostly organic produce is used for the farm-fresh cuisine and the cottages too are an experience.

At Mojo, the Yin-Yang cottage comes at a cost of Rs 1,000 per person, the Brook-Side deluxe cottage at Rs 1,750 per person for the Maharaja room and Rs 1,500 for the standard room (all rates for double occupancy). All prices include full board and a guided tour of the plantation. For bookings, contact Anurag (Doc) or Sujata on 08272-265638.

DAY TWO
MOJO-GALIBEEDU RIDGE
DISTANCE 5 KM **TIME** 3-4 HOURS
LEVEL EASY

By road, Galibeedu is about 5 km from Mojo, but a better way to get there is the picturesque 3-km eastward walk, connecting the Mojo Rainforest Retreat to **Golden Mist Plantation**. The farm hands, Muthu Pandey or Suresh, can accompany you to Golden Mist. The trail leads north-west from Mojo, skirting past plantations of cardamom, coffee and patches of rainforest.

The estate is a good stopover for your walk to **Galibeedu Ridge**. A

The fern trail through charming Kakkabe

further 1-hr westward hike through open forest on a well-defined trail takes you to Galibeedu. It's only when you reach there that you realise why it's called Galibeedu. It's literally the 'windswept place', as the ridge area can get very breezy. Depending on your fatigue and comfort level, you can either return to Mojo to set out again for a more arduous climb the next morning or you can stop by at the Golden Mist for the night (see below).

🔺 GOLDEN MIST PLANTATION

The 20-acre organic coffee and tea plantation with its large, spacious cottage in a little clearing is unofficially called **Ludwig Mahal** after its German owner Ludwig Cremer. The place has six beds including a semi-private loft, all in one open unit, making it ideal for a close-knit group of friends who don't mind sharing the solitary but swanky bathroom. When Mr Cremer is in town, you have the honour of feasting on his lavish continental spreads. The tariff is Rs 2,500 per day per couple, including all meals and guide. There's a group rate of Rs 1,000 per person for three to six persons. Contact Ludwig or Vasu on Tel: 08272-265629.

DAY THREE
GOLDEN MIST-KALOOR RIDGE-KOTEBETTA
DISTANCE 15 KM **TIME** 5-6 HOURS
LEVEL MODERATE

From Golden Mist, take a guide and head south, crossing Mojo (1$\frac{1}{2}$ km) on the **Kaloor Ridge Road**. The road goes up to Kaloor Ridge and then moves in a south to south-east direction to enter the Kotebetta forest (9$\frac{1}{2}$ km), and then continues up to the **Kotebetta Ridge**, where you 🔺 camp for the night. Depending on whether there are herds of elephants in the vicinity, you pitch camp either in the safety of one of the farms or in the forest.

DAY FOUR
KOTEBETTA-GOLDEN MIST
DISTANCE 15 KM **TIME** 5-6 HOURS
LEVEL MODERATE

Return to **Golden Mist** the following day, retracing your route. Golden Mist also arranges an easier trek up to the **Nishani Hills**. If you leave early you can be up there in 3 hrs, catch the spectacular views of the **Sullia Valley** and return in time for a sumptuous lunch.

DAY FIVE

TALACAUVERY-BRAHMAGIRI PEAK-
TALACAUVERY
TIME 2 HOURS
LEVEL EASY

From Mojo, you get back to **Madikeri** and either take a bus from the bus stand or simply drive down to the twin religious outposts of Talacauvery and **Bhagamandala** that lie in the lap of the **Brahmagiri Mountain**. There are two Brahmagiri mountains: one at the southernmost point of Coorg on the border with Wayanad and the other near Bhagamandala (approx 50 km/ 1^1/$_2$ hrs from Mojo by taxi). This is where the rivers **Cauvery**, **Kannike** and **Sujyoti** meet, earning it the name, **Triveni Sangam**.

There are three temples above the confluence of the rivers dedicated to Subramanya, Vishnu and Bhagamandaleswara, a Shaivite shrine named after Sage Bhagyananda, who installed a linga here. To the north of Bhagamandala, you can trek to **Sampaje Valley**, which has dense forests, bamboo clumps and steep gorges.

Just 7 km away, situated at 1,276m on the slopes of Brahmagiri Hill, is **Talacauvery** (literally, the head of Cauvery), which is the birthplace of the sacred river. The place is marked by a *kundike* (pot) and from here the river emerges as a small perennial spring. Legend has it that the Goddess

The rolling hills of Coorg

Cauvery makes her appearance in the form of a gushing spring once a year during Tulamasa, when thousands gather to take a sacred dip. On Tula Sankramana (usually falls on October 16 every year), as the sun enters Libra, water gushes out from the *kundike* at a moment predicted by the priests.

From Talacauvery, steps lead up to the nearby **Brahmagiri Peak** (1 hr), where the seven great sages (sapta maharishi) had performed a special yagna. The peak offers excellent views of **Kudremukh, Chamundi Hills,**

Soft play of light at dusk en route to Thadiyendamol

Brahmagiri, **Wayanad** and the misty blue **Nilgiris**. Since it's a short climb, you can head down to your next base **Kakkabe** by late afternoon and check into Palace Estate (see below). Drive 2 km past Kakkabe to **Palace Junction** and look out for a black board saying 'Nalknad Palace'. There's a seemingly unending flight of steps that leads up to Palace Estate.

▲ PALACE ESTATE
Situated on a flat patch just above the Nalknad Palace, the estate offers a spectacular view of undulating plains. The 100-acre farm is located on the edge of a forest and has a wild mountain stream with a 15-m waterfall. Palace Estate is ideal for plantation treks and local tribal guides are available. There's traditional Coorgi cuisine such as *otti* (roti-like bread made of rice flour), *paputtu* (a semolina-

coconut sweet), curries and organically grown farm produce. Breakfast is served for Rs 65, lunch and dinner for Rs 105. Contact Apparanda Prakash Poovanna at Kakkabe on Tel: 08272-238446, 238346.

DAY SIX
KAKKABE-MALMA
TIME 1 ½ HRS
LEVEL EASY

Kakkabe was once the largest honey producer in South-East Asia. But a chance virus wiped out the resident bee population and, in a single stroke, it deflected the attention to something more than honey — the bountiful nature that produced it.

As you admire the beauty from your perch at Palace Estate, you can look down at **Nalknad Palace** to the right. Built in 1792 by Doddaveeraraja, it served as the royal hunting lodge

H SATISH

and summer home of the Kodava kings. As there were four villages in the vicinity, the place was called Nalaku-nadu (*nalu* stands for four), which over time got shortened to Nalaknad and finally Nalnad. Both names are used today. Call it what you may, but a palace it isn't. A double-storey structure with a conical roof, the building has intricate wooden friezes and murals.

From Nalknad Palace, you head back towards Kakkabe (2 km) and from the jeep stand go through the temple arch to the **Igguthappa Temple**. *Iggu* is grain, *thappa* means to give, hence Igguthappa is also worshipped as the Rain God. Igguthappa is supposed to

Trekking up to the clouds

have travelled with his four brothers and a sister to this area from Kerala until an archery contest decided the present seats of the different gods. A steep southwards climb from the temple is **Malma** (1$^{1}/_{2}$ hrs), a sacred spot, which has two natural ponds and marks the place from where Igguthappa descended. During the **Kaladcha Festival** in March, his idol is taken on a procession to the top of Malma and reinstalled in the temple, followed by various ceremonial dances.

Return to Palace Estate for the night.

<hr>

DAY SEVEN
THADIYENDAMOL AND AROUND
TIME 3$^{1}/_{2}$-4 HOURS
LEVEL EASY

At 1,747m, **Thadiyendamol** is the highest peak in Coorg and after Mullaiyanagiri in the Baba Budan Range, the second highest in Karnataka. Thadiyendamol lures trekkers with a glimpse of the coastline on a clear day. Depending on where you are climbing from, it takes about 2-3 hrs to get to the top and as long to come down. If you are short of time, the climb from Palace Estate is shorter but the longer route from Honey Valley passes through

thick rainforest and more scenic terrain. It is highly recommended.

To get to **Honey Valley** (2$^{1}/_{2}$ km from Kakkabe), drive from Palace Estate to Kabbinakad Junction (a tin-shed bus stop that's also referred to as Yavakapadi Post-Office). From here, turn right and then take the immediate steep mud road to your left. If you are not in an armoured car (or at least a jeep), do not even contemplate doing it in a humbler vehicle.

If you want serious adventure, try the uphill trudge to Honey Valley in heavy rain with a 30-kg backpack pulling at your shoulders. It takes a good hour for the 2-km climb. Jeeps can be hired from Kakkabe for Rs 250 (but not later than 6 pm). You can also park your vehicle in a secure parking lot off the main road and have the owner, Suresh, pick you up in his jeep. If it's not too late in the morning, you can easily do the **Thadiyendamol** trek in about 2$^{1}/_{2}$ hrs, walking east along a ridge until you reach the summit, before getting back, which is faster.

⚑ HONEY VALLEY ESTATE
Accommodation comprises of home-stay rooms and individual cottages ranging from Rs 200-1,500 and plantation huts available much cheaper at Rs 150 per day. Breakfast comes at Rs 60 and lunch/ dinner at Rs 90. For non-veg food, Rs 50 is charged extra. Contact Suresh and Susheela Chengappa, Honey Valley Estate (Tel: 08272-238339).

<hr>

DAY EIGHT
HONEY VALLEY AND BEYOND
TIME 2-3 HOURS
LEVEL EASY

At one time, Honey Valley was the only commercial apiary in Coorg, producing 6.5 tonnes annually. After honey crashed, Suresh and Susheela Chengappa turned their attention to coffee, cardamom, pepper, fruits and farm stays. The 56-acre farm, painstakingly built over two decades, is

TREKKING HOLIDAYS IN INDIA

Colourful tents come up at the campsite at Honey Valley

now a Mecca for mountain bikers, rock-climbers, trekkers and nature enthusiasts.

Apart from barking deer, pangolin and flying squirrel (whose calls you hear on full-moon nights), the estate is a good place to spot the elusive South Indian marten.

You could also interact with the local Adiya and Kudiya tribes who will help you explore the area in greater detail. A 1-hr walk to **Nilakandi Waterfall**, 3 km away, is one of the shorter treks. Suresh has marked out 27 other trekking routes that have varying levels of difficulty.

Continuing on the line of the Western Ghats are the well-wooded Tumbemale forests of Marenad. Just 1 1/2 hrs away from Honey Valley Estate

(5,262m) is **Chomamale**, the highest mountain in Kadiyatnad, in the Kabbe region. The ancient Kannada name is derived from Soma Male, named after its crescent-shaped appearance. It's believed that when clouds dip over the mountain enveloping it in a white fleece quilt, it is a sure sign of rain. If you have the time you can opt to extend your itinerary.

TIP Check with the Coorg Wildlife Society about campsites before making your trip. Contact the society at Kodagu Planters' Association, Post Box 111, Near DFO Quarters, Madikeri-571201 or on Tel: 08272-29873

For homestays and hotels, see Accommodation Listings on pages 549-550 (Kakkabe) and 550-551 (Madikeri) ✦

Blue skies and verdure dominate the Coorg landscape

The Talathmane Circuit
The woods are lovely, dark and deep…

By Sheetal Vyas

TIME	5 days
LEVEL	Moderate
IDEAL SEASON	Any time of the year except during monsoons
LOCATION	Around Madikeri, Kodagu District

TALATHMANE-DEVASTUR-MUKKODLU-KALOOR-
VANACHULU-TALATHMANE

Kodagu (also called Coorg) had been on my wish-list for a long time and it certainly lived up to my dreams. About 1,220m above sea level, this is mist-covered hill country that extends along the summits and slopes of the Western Ghats and is criss-crossed by a network of rivers. Most of this is virgin land and nearly 60 per cent of the district is still covered with rain forests.

The district leaves a melange of impressions with its never-ending plantations, the sounds and scents of the forest and the enchanting streams that you stumble upon ever so often. We spent one memorable afternoon in the waters of Kotte Abbi. After we had washed off the grime from the morning's hike, someone had a brilliant idea, which was unanimously agreed upon: lunch would be eaten in the water. We each found ourselves a shallow rock and, sitting waist deep in water, unpacked the lunches. The scrumptious *puliogare* (tamarind rice) made for a perfect meal.

Another source of delight were the campsites. Chosen for proximity to streams that abound in the district, each was verdant and thoroughly charming. One particular creek was reportedly a favourite with a herd of elephants and we were warned not to come out of our tents if we heard them at night. But nature intervened and we were caught in a raging, spectacular storm that threatened to blow our tents away. Needless to say, the elephants did not oblige us with an appearance.

On the other hand, there were plenty of leeches. These damp-loving creatures were numerous, quick and persistent; they also appear to have astounding powers of penetration, wriggling through shoes and fabric with slimy ease. Snuff or common salt

GETTING THERE AND OUT

FROM MADIKERI to Talathmane, it's 4 km/ 10 mins by 🚗 (Rs 100) or 15 mins by 🚌 (Rs 5). It's located on the road to Talacauvery
RETURN Take the same way back

repels the creatures, but we were unprepared. Before each bloodsucker-ridden stretch, the bellow would go up from the frontrunners and we would start to move rapidly, keeping a sharp lookout. Once in the sunlight, we'd haul off shoes and socks to check between our toes for the ones that were still undetected.

Graphic by ANIS KHAN

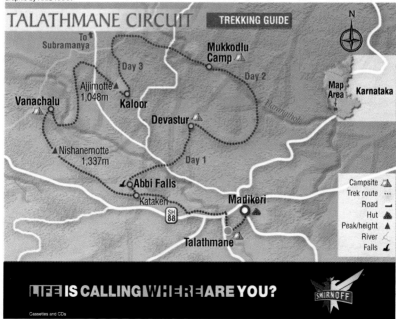

TALATHMANE CIRCUIT — TREKKING GUIDE

TRIBHUVAN TIWARI

The Asian elephant

Many species of elephant once roamed the Earth. Today, they are limited to just two species in Africa and the Asian elephant (*Elephas maximus*). In India, the wild Asian elephant population is estimated to be 25,000-27,000. Weighing 3,000 kg, the Asian elephant differs from the African one in a number of ways: it's smaller, has a rounded back as opposed to the saddle-shaped back of the African, its trunk ends in one tip, not two, its ears are smaller and it has a two-domed forehead.

Only male Asian elephants have tusks, while females have small 'tushes'. The tusks are prized for ivory, hence many animals are driven to extinction. Some males ('makhnas') are tuskless and can be distinguished from adult females by the penis bulge below the tail.

Elephants live in closely-knit family groups led by a matriarch. Adult males, however, are solitary and associate with the herd only for mating. All-male groups are occasionally seen. Elephants use a range of vocals to communicate, from tummy rumbles to low growls, infrasonic sounds and loud trumpeting.

Elephants migrate long distances in search of food, water and security, and use the same forest corridors for hundreds of years. If these corridors are blocked, they enter human settlements. Elephants are also attracted to crops in villages and to domestic alcoholic distilleries they are able to smell from miles away. The resulting conflict sadly often ends up cutting short the life of the elephant, which normally has a lifespan of 60 years.

TIP The Youth Hostel Association of India (YHAI), in association with local operators V-TRAK, organises this trek once every year. It is a rather convenient one: they supply guides, the tents, organise the campsites and the food. All you need to do is get your backpacks and trudge. If you choose to do this on your own, it is still advisable to coordinate with local operators to chalk out your exact route and organise permissions with plantation owners

View from the Madikeri Fort

PRASHANT PANJIAR

for the use of campsites. Contact V-TRAK, Friends Tours and Travels, College Road, Madikeri, Tel: 08272-229102, 229974 (*see Trekking Agents Listings on page 516*)

DAY ONE
TALATHMANE-DEVASTUR
DISTANCE 15 KM **TIME** 7-8 HOURS
LEVEL MODERATE

The V-Trak base camp at Talathmane is 500m from the Bhagamandala junction. The day starts early and there's a buzz in the air. The huts we spent the night in are charming. Everyone bustles about, packing lunch and filling bottles. Yashwant, a man with a ready grin, is our guide for the first three days. He knows the land like the proverbial back of his hand.

Our group comprises a motley crowd of nearly 15 people: a few experienced trekkers and quite a few first-timers. We start a little after 8.30 am, walking the first stretch through plantations. Coorg is ideal spice country and you'll pass through a lot of pepper and cardamom plantations and its world famous coffee plantations as well. Hit state highway SH88 and follow it for about half a kilometre before veering off onto a foot trail.

We wind our way north-ish to **Abbi Falls** today. The falls are about 4-5 km from Talathmane in the middle of a privately owned coffee estate. It takes us 3 hrs and quite a bit of energy to reach the falls by lunchtime. But I am disappointed, as the spot, with a steady stream of tourists, is not the most restful of places. This is where the Madikeri or **Muttaramutta stream** falls naturally from a 21-m high precipice. The water cascades from between huge boulders to a rocky, lush valley. The spot is a favourite with locals, tourists and film crews. The waters are deep and dangerous, however, and sitting below the waterfall for a spontaneous dunking is not recommended. The cataract is deafening and there is an abundance of natural flora. The British named the spot **Jessie Falls** in memory of the daughter of Madikeri's first chaplain, but the name 'Abbi' (Kodava for waterfall) has prevailed.

The next leg is glorious. We move north-east, and cross a narrow wooden log thrown across a stream and enter the forests. Tall stately trees flank our

The enchanting Abbi Falls

trail. I hear bird calls, but the foliage is too thick to see any. We have not yet stepped into rain forests, but the woods are thick, nonetheless. Every half an hour or so, we encounter another stream. The trail goes along one and it thins into a narrow brook, gurgling softly as it keeps us company for a bit. The path then widens into a mud track, which marks the beginning of a plantation.

It's nearly five in the evening before we troop into the △ campsite in **Devastur**. It is located next to a stream, which everyone jumps into.

The flowing water does much to soothe protesting muscles. After dinner, which includes jackfruit curry — a speciality in these parts — Yashwant gets a roaring campfire going and treats us to warm badam milk. The flames are hypnotic, but much to his disappointment, we slouch off in twos and threes to our tents for an early night.

DAY TWO

DEVASTUR-MUKKODLU
DISTANCE 14 KM **TIME** 6 HOURS
LEVEL EASY-MODERATE

Sleep has done its magic: I am raring to go. The first challenge of the day is to cross the stream we bathed in. I ford it barefoot, trousers rolled upto mid-thigh. Once booted, I set off and come to a fascinating log bridge high across a turbulent stream. It's so Indiana Jones-ish that it takes a while to cross: everyone wants a thrill of the view from up there, and to get photographed.

The trail then dips south and turns east along a well-marked footpath. The forests are hushed and lovely. The Devastur stream sloshes on and we climb uphill. The trails, on occasion, are so narrow that you have to cling to the mossy walls as you traverse them. I am told that wild elephants frequent this area, which makes me eager for an encounter with them.

That is not to be, though, for we hit a tar road after 2 hrs. This road connects Makkandur to Mukkodlu and we walk along it for about 4 km. The heat rising from the tar is uncomfortable and one has to stop at the many hospitable hamlets for water.

After 1½ hrs, we leave the road and turn right onto a trail. Moving eastwards for an hour, the trail leads one to a most delightful watering hole called **Kotte Abbi**. The waters of the **Hattihole stream** are clear and deep enough to allow raucous and splashy dives. The next part through the forests goes quickly. Then the trail

SRAVANAKUMAR/WILDERFILE

Shola forests

The sholas — as they are locally known — are located in montane evergreen rain forests. Occurring 1,900-2,220m along the southern Western Ghats, the shola-grassland ecosystem is a dense growth of trees in the depressions and folds of the ghats, surrounded by extensive areas (nearly 80 per cent) of grasslands. Thanks to the wind, the trees are stunted (15-20m) with spreading canopies, twiggy branches and multi-hued foliage.

This mountain eco-region is so species-rich that it is one of the 25 global biodiversity hotspots on earth. Rosewood and white cedar are common among several other wild species of trees; more than half the tree species found here are endemic. About 90 species of reptiles and almost 50 per cent of India's 206 species of amphibians are also endemic to this area. While the sholas are home to India's largest elephant population, they also shelter the endemic and endangered lion-tailed macaque.

Today, the sholas are threatened: nearly two-thirds of the natural forests in this eco-region have already been cleared. Threats come in the form of conversion of forests into plantations. It also comes from their being cleared for road construction, from tourism pressures, mining and from the grazing of livestock.

I BOUGHT the Bolero Invader way back in Aug '03 before it officially got launched in Bangalore. The reason is very simple; it was the vehicle I was looking for. Here was a vehicle, which could comfortably take me to any place I want ed to go, and not just that, thrill me with its 'go anywhere' capability once I reached there....one of the memorable trips I had in my Bolero Invader was to kemmanagundi and then to Hebbe waterfalls from there. This is an ideal spot where the Bolero Invader really played its dual roles nicely. Kemmanagundi is around 275kms away from Bangalore, A very scenic place with a cool climate even in top summer. 8 kms away from Kemmanagundi is the Hebbe falls. This 8kms is ideal for your first off-road experience. People usuallytrek this 8kms, which I have also done before but

this time I decided to cover the distance in my Bolero Invader. Toward the falls, it was all easy because there were no climbs and it is going down the hill. Being my first off-road drive with the Bolero Invader, I was a bit afraid of climbing up during my return from the falls. Down at the falls, people looked at us with admiration and surprise. The climb up also was a cakewalk. Even with just the two-wheel drive, the Bolero Invader climbs steep ascents very smoothly. The suspension, which feels a little bumpy on the tarmac, really shows up its capabilities during the off-road drive. It was a real satisfying experience and I started loving my Bolero Invader even more after the Kemmanagundy trip. To sum up, the Bolero Invader can take you through any surface and you can also show up a bit on the highway on your way back home. So far my Bolero Invader has never let me down. And not to mention, I use my Bolero Invader for the daily commutation too.

By Manoj Subramanium

Mahindra BOLERO
INVADER
getaway

PRASHANT PANJIAR

Coorg boasts of perfect green carpets of paddy fields fringed by thick forests

enters plantations again and descends into the ⛺ campsite at **Mukkodlu**. This is a truly beautiful place. A stream is in full torrent and the rice fields are pockmarked with elephant footprints. Dusk falls beautifully and the rising forests all around us are lit with dancing fireflies.

DAY THREE
Mukkodlu-Kalur via Mandalpatti
Distance 13 km **Time** 6½ hours
Level Moderate

Today the walk is due west and I get my first taste of the genuine shola forests. They are truly beautiful: thick canopies let in only thin strands of sunlight. The cicadas sing with gathering force as we step across a thick carpet of broad leaves. However, we are also introduced to the dreaded leeches.

The path through the forests isn't a permanent track and although we're not hacking through bush, we're progressing mainly because of Yashwant's uncanny sense of direction. The stint through the forests should take you about 1½ hrs, less if you try to outspeed the leeches, more if you stop to address the issue.

The next leg is leech-free but steep. I climb to overlook **Mandalpatti Road** and a lovely view of the hills. Among

them is **Pushpagiri**, the second highest peak in Kodagu (1,725m) and **Kottebetta**, the third highest (1,650m). As we change direction to turn south, there's a sharp difference in landscape — forests give way to rolling hills, dry scrub and rocks. We cross a few hillocks as dark clouds gather. The hills look breathtaking in the purple light. We stop for a quick lunch under the trees and trudge on under a light drizzle. The 2-hr descent to Kaloor is precarious. Rubble and mud loosen under my feet and I grasp desperately at anything in sight.

Once in the coffee and cardamom plantations, the campsite is still nearly an hour's walk away. We then come across a smallish patch of vanilla just before we arrive at 🏠 **Mr Prasanna's Farmhouse** (Tel: 08272-228693). It has three rooms and a hall and can accommodate upto 10 people. Bigger groups can pitch ⛺ tents near the river. Simple food is provided.

DAY FOUR
Kaloor-Vanachalu
Distance 14 km **Time** 7 hours
Level Moderate-Tough
Our new guide Vijay Kumar will lead us to Ajjimotte today. I slap on insect repellent and sprinkle salt generously

over my shoes. An hour north-north-west, we gather at the mouth of dense shola forests, take a deep breath and enter leech territory. We cover what would have normally taken us 45 mins in about 20, and rush out gasping into the sunlight. Next goal: **Ajjimotte** (1,048m).

The incline is steep and it takes about 1 hr 20 mins to reach the top, but the views are worth it. The peak overlooks several smaller mist-kissed peaks and the lush green plantation-covered valleys. The descent, of course, is tricky and slow, and it takes us almost 45 mins to get to the foot of the hill and head south.

Lunch stop is brief and not far from the **Madikeri-Subramanya Road**. We go onwards to the south for about one hour, past dry hills interspersed with dank forests. We then turn north-north-west again to reach the beautiful tea and cardamom **Vanachalu Plantations**. The  campsite is delightful, complete with its own waterfall made wonderfully private by a screen of foliage. Alternatively, you can stay at **Ramesh's** on the other side of the tea plantation, near the school.

DAY FIVE
VANACHALU-TALATHMANE VIA NISHANEMOTTE
DISTANCE 15 KM **TIME** 7 HOURS
LEVEL MODERATE

The trail out of Vanachalu goes south-east and is both muddy and steep. The rain has left heat and humidity in its wake. We leave the trail after about 15 mins and turn right to start climbing the hills. Half an hour later, we're walking south along the ridges of the Western Ghats. For nearly 1 hr and 20 mins, the track is mostly level and very pleasant. The steep climb to **Nishanemotte** (1,337m), however, compensates for any earlier lack of exercise.

The views of the valleys and the plantations are gorgeous but the descent towards the eastern side, which takes only 15 mins, is truly treacherous as Vijay Kumar sets a punishing pace. Next, still moving due south, is a 3-hr stretch through a veritable valley of spices that is truly remarkable. The mud road passes through almost every kind of spice and fruit plantation in the district — we find cardamom, pepper, coffee plants of both arabica and robusta varieties, orange gardens, cashew plants, ginger fields and vegetable gardens; a Kodagu microcosm, if you will. Our route rejoins SH88 at **Katakeri** and we retrace our way to the base camp at **Talathmane**. Camp for the night and head home the next morning after breakfast.

For homestays and hotels in Madikeri, see Accommodation Listings on pages 550-551 ✦

Brahmagiri Trek
In the footsteps of Lord Rama
By Anurag Mallick

TIME	3-4 days
LEVEL	Moderate
IDEAL SEASON	Sep to early Jun
LOCATION	Through the Brahmagiri Wildlife Sanctuary, from south-west Karnataka into Kerala

Irpu Falls early in the morning

IRPU-NARIMALBETTA-HANUMANBETTA-PAKSHIPATHALAM-THIRUNELLY

Perhaps the first trekker who left his footprints on Brahmagiri was Lord Rama on his return journey from Lanka. He crossed over this legendary hill range between the two nodal points of the Ishwara Temple at Irpu and Thirunelly in Kerala. With a star cast of Brahma, Rama, Hanuman, Parashuram, Krishna, Vishnu and Garuda, this short trek is, in a sense, a journey of epic proportions.

Located in the southern part of Karnataka's Coorg region, Irpu is a gateway to the Brahmagiris and showcases Coorg's biodiversity. Because of the variations in altitude, each step unravels myriad wonders. The mountain teems with rare orchids, medicinal herbs, butterflies of every hue and birds such as the Malabar trogon.

The trail, which passes through Brahmagiri Wildlife Sanctuary, fans out towards a range of peaks, each with their own mythology. Spread over 181 sq km, the Brahmagiri Wildlife Sanctuary stretches in a wide arc, ranging from lowland rainforests in the Makutta Wildlife Range to high-altitude shola grasslands in Srimangala. The sanctuary is adjacent to the Aralam Wildlife Sanctuary in

Photographs by H SATISH

A woman reaches out to pluck flowers near Brahmagiri

Kerala. A forested corridor punctuated by coffee plantations connects it to Wayanad and Nagarhole. This wild confluence of natural heritage constitutes, perhaps, one of the most untouched regions in India.

Graphic by ANIS KHAN

The forests abound with the Big Gang of Four — gaur (the largest bovine in the world), elephant, tiger and leopard, apart from other creatures such as sloth bear, jungle cat, wild dog, barking deer, Nilgiri langur,

bonnet macaque, lion-tailed macaque, Malabar giant squirrel, giant flying squirrel, civets, porcupine, pangolin, the elusive slender loris and the Nilgiri marten, whose call resounds through the hills on full moon nights. **TIP** Stop by at the Reserve Forest Office at Srimangala or Hunsur before you take the diversion to Irpu and Pakshi-pathalam so that you don't have to backtrack later (*for contact details see Brahmagiri Facts on page 478*). You'll be given written permission and, at a nominal cost, experienced guides will take you to the Forest Rest House on Brahmagiri's summit

There are various options at **Irpu** to stay overnight before starting your trek the following morning. This includes **Ramcad Estate Guest House** (Tel: 08274-244519), a 40-acre coffee and pepper plantation, where you pay Rs 195 whatever you opt for, be it one of the seven beds in an antique Coorg

A footnote from the Ramayana

While returning from Sri Lanka, the victorious brothers Rama and Lakshmana were crossing over the Brahmagiri Hills from Kerala to Kodagu. Lakshmana, in a rare display of disobe-dience, felt a sudden surge of frustra-tion, returned his bow and arrows to his elder brother and walked ahead. Oddly, the moment he stepped into Kodava land, his anger dissipated and Rama explained that Kerala's earth was such that it incited passions and Kodagu, on the other hand, bestowed calmness.

Overcome by remorse but unmoved by his brother's logic, Lakshmana shot an arrow into Brahmagiri's bowels and threatened to consign himself to the flames that shot forth. It was then that Rama created the Lakshmana Teertha, extinguished the fire and blessed its waters with the power to absolve a person of his sins. Some believe it was Laksh-mana's tears of remorse that became the Lakshmana Teertha.

Rama wished to consecrate the spot and instructed Hanuman to get a linga from Kashi. Hours flew by. When Hanuman didn't return and the appoint-ed time drew near, Rama shaped a linga out of mud and was about to install it, when Hanuman arrived.

Furious at his master's lack of faith, Hanuman wrapped his tail around a mountain and threatened to place it on Rama's head. In olden days, most dis-putes were solved either by shooting an arrow or hurling an axe. To appease an irate Hanuman, Rama shot an arrow from Irpu. It landed at Permad and this was where the linga from Kashi was established.

Rama further conceded that Hanu-man's Shiva Temple at Permad would rank higher than the Ishwara Temple at Irpu. Every Mahashivratri, before the puja commences at Irpu, a puja is performed a day earlier at Permad. Hanuman was pacified but the imprint of his tail was left forever on Hanuman-betta and is seen to this day.

The Brahmagiri Range is also the source of another stream called Rama-tirtha, which interestingly flows down the other side of the hill and meets the Laksh-mana Teertha at Srimangala, literally 'The Holy Place of Well-being'.

house, a wooden cottage, or a thatched cottage with a circular sit-out. The set-up is simple, the hospitality warm, the food reasonably priced and home-cooked. The place is a blast if you are in a big group. The owner also runs **Ramcad Home Needs** at Kutta (near Canara Bank). It's a great place to buy rations for the trek.

High Falls Holiday Home (Tel: 246027) is just off the road before Ramcad Guest House and offers newly built rooms on the first floor. Accommodation options are a three-bed suite with living room, three-bed family room and a double bedroom. Contact Bollera Venu/ Beena Poonacha for bookings.

Irpu Resorts (Tel: 426092) offers the best view of the Brahmagiri Hills, has a gracious lady as a host, delectable food and splendid estate walks. Pity it has just one double bedroom with attached bath for Rs 600 and a double bedroom with common bath for Rs 500. Extra bed comes at Rs 100. Contact Vanitha Bheemaiah for bookings.

DAY ONE
ISHWARA TEMPLE-IRPU FALLS-NARIMALBETTA
DISTANCE 10 KM **TIME** 3-5 HOURS
LEVEL MODERATE

It's said that the Shivaling in the **Ishwara Temple** was installed by Lord Rama on his return from Sri

GETTING THERE AND OUT

FROM BANGALORE to Irpu, it's 224 km/ 6 hrs by (Rs 1,300) or 7 hrs by (Rs 220). By car, take the Mysore Road bypass via Ranganathittu and get onto SH88. After **Hunsur**, turn towards Nagarhole via Murkal and head for Irpu via **Kutta**. The road passes through **Nagarhole National Park**, so no traffic is allowed after 6 pm. If you are late, stop by at Jungle Inn (Tel: 08222-246022) at Veeranahosahalli, 19 km after Hunsur towards Nagarhole **From Madikeri**, take the road to Gonikoppal, Ponnampet, Hudikeri and Srimangala. The diversion for Irpu is 2 km from here. If you want to go from Irpu to **Thirunelly** by road, take the turn from Kutta towards Mananthavady. After Tholpetty, you'll come to an intersection, from where Thirunelly is 13 km away
RETURN From **Thirunelly**, you backtrack the way you came, via Tholpetty, Nagarhole, Hunsur, Ranganathittu and Srirangapatana to Bangalore

→ Brahmagiri Facts

CONTACT POINTS

● Range Forest Officer, Brahmagiri Wildlife Sanctuary, Srimangala-571217 Coorg, Karnataka. Tel: 08274-426331

● Conservator of Forests, Madikeri Forest Office, Aranya Bhavan, Madikeri-571201 Tel: 08272-225708

● Deputy Conservator of Forests, Hunsur Wildlife Division, Hunsur. Tel: 08222-252041

● Dr SV Narasimhan (birdwatcher) Virajpet 571218 Coorg. Tel: 08274-238339 E-mail: vnsimhan@sancharnet.in

● Jayprasad, DFO, North Wayanad, Manathavady, Kerala. Tel: 04935-240233

The trek starts from the Ishwara Temple at Irpu. A short 1-km walk takes you to **Irpu Falls**, from where the forest trail climbs southwards up the **Brahmagiri** on an 8-km trek to the **Forest Rest House** at **Narimalbetta**.

Scarcely 1 km from the Ishwara Temple, the trail to the falls winds past a banyan tree before disappearing into the forest. Irpu is at its best after the rains, when the rainforest is glossy green and the 60-m drop, a raging torrent. Technically, you would be within the outer limits of the **Brahmagiri Wildlife Sanctuary**, but you don't need permission to go to the falls. If you are planning to go any further, get written permission from the Reserve Forest Office at Hunsur (*see Brahmagiri Facts alongside for contact details*).

The trek to Narimalbetta, to the south-west of the falls, is strewn with elephant and gaur droppings. After about an hour's climb, the route

Lanka, because of which it is also known as the **Rameshwar Temple**. It is customary to pay your respects here before you take a dip in the Lakshmana Teertha. The temple gates remain closed between 1 and 6 pm.

A trekker walks through the wild landscape of the Brahmagiri Sanctuary

The Pakshipathalam Caves

levels off and starts winding around the hillside instead of going right up the hill. At one point, the track crosses a stream and leads onto open grasslands and shola forests from where you can see the higher crests of the mountains. The Lakshmana Teertha stream has numerous stopover points to refresh you on your upward climb.

The camp is situated on a clearing 1,300m high up on the mountains, which are just below shola forests, home to wild elephants, tigers, leopards, sloth bear and gaur. It's not for nothing that the mountain is called Narimalbetta or Tiger Hill. 🏕️ Either camp out in tents or try the **Forest Rest House** (2 rooms, Rs 80, booked at the Hunsur Forest Office,

Tel: 08222-252041), a basic, British-built two-room with excellent views.

The trade-off is worth it. It comes equipped with a kitchen, so make sure you pick up supplies before you leave or you'll be left drawing lots as to who's going down. Solar cells on the roof help light up the inside and are the only source of electricity, so the electric light has to be used sparingly. After lunch, you can walk north-east up to **Narimal Peak**, about 2 km from the camp. You can see **Hanumanbetta**, an ordinary looking mountain with a strange ring near its crest that's believed to be an imprint left by Hanuman's tail.

DAY TWO

NARIMALBETTA-PAKSHIPATHALAM
DISTANCE 8 KM **TIME** 2-3 HOURS
LEVEL MODERATE

From the Forest Rest House at Narimalbetta, you can trek to Pakshipathalam, whose Kannada name is **Munikal**, via Brahmagiri Peak, which stands tall at 1,740m and is the highest point in the range. Get prior permission from the Forest Department at Hunsur (*refer Brahmagiri Facts alongside*). From Narimalbetta the path forks into two, with the right going southwards to **Pakshipathalam** (1,720m, literally Birds of the Subterranean World), and the left leading south-east to a T-junction

Kashi of the South

Thirunelly, known as 'Thekkankasi' or Kashi of the South, and its 3,000-year-old temple, are believed to be established by Brahma and visited in different yugas by Parashuram, Rama and Krishna.

According to mythology, when the Earth was weighed down by the sins committed by humans, Lord Brahma came to this quiet corner of the world and undertook penance under a

PRASHANT PANJIAR

gooseberry (neli) tree to redeem mankind, giving Thirunelly its name.

Lord Brahma also kindly lends his name to the Brahmagiri Hills. It's believed that when Brahma was consecrating Vishnu's idol in a temple dedicated to the preserver, Vishnu's mount Garuda was escaping with the kumbha amrita (pot of nectar) obtained from the Churning of the Cosmic Ocean. It is believed that drops of the amrita fell at Ujjain, Haridwar, Prayag and Nasik, sanctifying them as venues for the Kumbh Mela. Garuda reached Thirunelly just in time for the installation of his master's idol. He circled above thrice and a drop of amrita fell into the stream, endowing the Papanashini spring with amazing purifying powers.

Years later, when Parashuram came here in an attempt to expiate the sin of killing his mother at the behest of his father, his blood-stained hands were finally cleansed in the Papanashini, and Thirunelly became known for its miraculous powers to wash away a person's sins. When Rama came here, he offered two neli fruits to symbolise the pind-daan of his father Dasaratha, who had passed away after Rama had left for his exile, thus setting the trend for generations to follow.

from where you take a left to **Brahmagiri Peak**, about 4 km from the rest house. A short trek further south takes you right up to the borderline, lined by stones, and here you can stand with one foot in Karnataka and the other in Kerala. The green mountains of the Western Ghats stretch ahead as far as the eye can see. From Brahmagiri Peak, backtrack to the junction to continue southwards to Pakshipathalam.

The journey is no longer than about 2½ km, and from the junction

should take you about 15 mins. It's said that the ancient **caves of Pakshi-pathalam** are absolutely quiet; that no sound escapes from them and more importantly, no sound enters. Which is why, for centuries, **Munikal** (literally, Sage Rock) has been the most sought after site for contemplation by meditators. The network of rock caves perched at 1,740m at the northern end of the Brahmagiri Range, fall in Kerala.

Legend has it that after his aerial circumambulation, Garuda perched on Karimala, where today you can see a small projection shaped in the form

THE Peugeot XD3P engine is one brute of a mill with loads of torque. It really feels great to trudge along uneven ground and to cross speed breakers on the 3rd gear. The purr of the refined XD3P is music to the ears. The BA10 gear box, which also does duty on the Bolero GLX, does a wonderful job. The gear shifts are almost as smooth as a car.

The ride on tarmac is fairly comfortable. The suspension does a great job for the passengers. Once you go off road, the Invader is in its element. You really know what M&M means when they say that Bolero Invader – "Getaway". It has an insatiable appetite for bumps and potholes. The meaty 215/75 tyres, the good ground clearance and the huge torque make easy job of any terrain. I say this after taking the Invader across the jungles of Nagarhole National Park in Karnataka, driving all the way from Bangalore to Rajasthan and back and of course, pitting the Invader against the trickiest of terrains in the Western Ghats at the M&M Great Escape held in Goa in July '04.

Well, it is a vehicle for the young at heart, It is a vehicle which can take you to the Club on a Saturday night with as much grace as the ease with which it can take you to that camping site beyond that mountain. As I say it... " Bolero Invader. Get a life,..."

By Rahul Dubey

Mahindra BOLERO
INVADER getaway

Great views greet the trekker at the top of Brahmagiri

of an eagle. The rock is known as **Garudapara** and Garuda, the king of birds, stands guard over his subjects at Pakshipathalam, an avian paradise.

Rishipathalam, nearby, is another natural shelter, also said to be a meditation seat of the sages. A popular legend avers that two Brahmins walked across the Brahmagiri and reached Rishipathalam tired and hungry. The sages of the cave offered them an amla each. One Brahmin ate the fruit and died on the spot while the other thought he should purify himself in the sacred pond before eating. After his first dip, as he took his second plunge, he came out miles further in the Panchateertha Pond at Thirunelly, believed to be a sacred pond where five rivers meet.

There's no accommodation available at **Pakshipathalam**, so you must carry camping equipment and set up camp. If you are an avid birder, there's a watchtower that offers a good perch for birdwatching. In the monsoons, Pakshipathalam remains out of bounds as the path is faint, the trail is slippery and the forest teems with leeches and cold, irritated animals of varying sizes and appetites.

DAY THREE
PAKSHIPATHALAM-THIRUNELLY
DISTANCE 7 KM **TIME** 3 HOURS
LEVEL MODERATE

Getting to Thirunelly from Pakshipathalam involves trekking for 9 km south-east along winding paths, through dense forests. It's a sharp downhill trail and can be very tricky if it rains. From in between the dense mesh of ferns and creepers, the white speck in the distance that you can see down below is **Thirunelly Temple** playing hide and seek with you.

The rough, incomplete structure is the result of an unsolved dispute between the Malabar King of Kottayam and the Maharaja of Mysore, over who should construct the temple. It's shielded by 30 granite columns and faces east. There's an office and a counter to buy tokens for prasad/ puja. Male devotees are allowed to enter the temple only if

Invade the Mountains

By Kalim Ansari

THE mountains have always fascinated me. And the serpentine trails have enticed me to drive on. I waited for quite a many years to give in to this wish of mine.

I bought the Bolero Invader.

It's an open top, stylish vehicle with loads of attitude and power. I spent enough time contemplating between the thought of buying a comfortable small car or the rugged Invader. It isn't a city vehicle, but it still manages to get enough attention from the men who think cars are for the ladies.

But the rough terrains are what the Invader is made for. Such journeys give me a high. Nainital was about an 8 hour drive from Delhi. With the altitude everything changed, the weather, the colour of the sky, the roads and me also. But the Invader remained itself. The temperature was in single digits and mild fog had hit the region. But I still wanted to explore more. Driving through the curves and bends of the mountains I reached Mukteshwar, a picturesque location which is about 50 kms from Nainital. A night's halt was mandatory. Next morning, it took me some effort to creep out of the bed as the weather was really chilling. By the time I stepped out, I was wondering if my Invader will also take in so much of effort. And it surprised me with a smooth start.

Next on agenda was Ranikhet, which has a beautiful golf course and Almora. Throughout my drive, I could feel the cool wind on my face. Though I had an option of putting on the AC to avoid the smoke emitted by the trucks ahead of me, I was keen to look at the scenery without any interference. By evening I was already back in Nainital and the next morning was on my way back to Delhi.

I can hardly imagine myself in such a journey using any other vehicle. Hat's off to the Invader. Its powerful engine made the steep roads look like they were any other road of a city. The vehicle grips the road and is easy to manoeuvre on the treacherous mountain roads, while the suspension hardly made me feel the bad roads on those high altitudes. It brought me back safe and filled with memoirs of a drive I wished would never end.

It's been a year and a half since I thought of buying an Invader. And am I glad with my choice!

Mahindra BOLERO
INVADER getaway

Flowers and exotic plants adorn a farm at the base of Pakshipathalam

they are bare-chested. Inside the temple, there's a certain route to be followed, marked out by arrows. Most devotees come by evening, do a puja at night, have a bath in the **Papanashini** (literally, the destroyer of sins) spring in the morning and leave by afternoon. Steps behind the Thirunelly Temple lead to Panchateertha and the Papanashini spring.

TIP A good time to go is around Vishu, the Malayalam New Year, celebrated on April 14/ 15 at the Thirunelly Temple with great pomp. Apart from a Panchavadyam performance (percussion ensemble), there's Kathakali and Ottantullal (a traditional dance drama performance) within the temple precincts. That's when the district is also at its colourful best

Panchateertha is a sacred pond where five rivers are believed to have met. Nowadays, most of the water has dried up and the tank is covered by thick undergrowth. The only thing of interest is a mound at the centre, which can be reached by a short stone bridge. The mound has a slab of stone with what's said to be the imprint of Vishnu's feet, called **Vishnupad**.

Thirunelly deals with this quick flow of pilgrims efficiently. Shivali (the ceremonial three-lap pradakshina of the deity) takes place three times a day at 9 am, 12.30 pm and 8 pm while aarti is once a day, at 6.30 pm. The payasam (milk porridge served as prasad), at the Thirunelly Temple, is very delicious.

Make sure you pick up the take-away version (with jaggery instead of milk, so it stays fresh longer) from the *prasad* counter. For generous donations and details on puja, contact the executive officer, Sree Thirunelly Devaswom, Wayanad-670646 (Tel: 04935-2210210).

On the trail to Brahmagiri

In **Thirunelly**, there are only two eating joints, **Vishnu Padam** and **Nambisan**, which are vegetarian and offer a limited menu of masala dosa, plain dosa (roast) and chapati-peas for breakfast, lunch and dinner.

You can stay at the 57-room **Panchateertham Rest House** (Tel: 04935-2210210) in Thirunelly, the only place for tourists. It's one of those rare hotels where the view from the back is as good as the front. Charges are modest at Rs 125 per room bed, Rs 500 for the VIP room and Rs 20 for a bed in the dormitory. There's no restaurant but chai and food will be brought to your room if you ask. In peak season (Feb-May), the rest house is crowded, so book in advance.

The Forest Department also has a beautiful **Inspection Bungalow**, 1 km before Thirunelly. The view isn't as good as Panchateertham but there's absolute quiet and solitude. There's a signboard on the main road from where it is exactly 550m. Accommodation is limited and apart from 3 standard rooms, there's a VIP room available at Rs 450. It also has a 40-bedded dorm. Food is cooked by the caretaker and available for a nominal sum. For bookings, contact DFO, North Wayanad, Mananthavady (Tel: 04935-240233).

For rest house bookings, homestays and hotels, see Accommodation Listings on pages 549 (Irpu), 552 (Narimalbetta) and 552-553 (Thirunelly)

Wayanad Treks

Kerala's best kept secret, until now...

By Anurag Mallick

The densely forested Edakkal Hills wreathed in mist

TIME	2-7 days
LEVEL	Easy to Moderate
IDEAL SEASON	Sep to May
LOCATION	Wayanad District in north Kerala, south of Coorg in Karnataka

SULTHAN BATHERY-KUPAMUDI-EDAKKAL-
AMBUKUTHY-MEENMUTTY-CHEMBRA PEAK-
VYTHIRI-KURUVADWEEP-THIRUNELLY-
PAKSHIPATHALAM

If you haven't heard of Wayanad, or if you have and can't place it, don't blame yourself. Blame it on Kalpetta, the district headquarters. Unlike Kerala's other well-behaved district headquarters such as Kasargod, Kannur, Kottayam, Alappuzha and Ernakulam, this one is not named after the district. On a recent trip, the locals lamented that one could never find a bus that said Bangalore-Wayanad, and it was precisely because of this oversight in branding that Wayanad never made it big on the tourist circuit. It took me a while to digest that, but it's true. And in a way, it's a boon to travellers looking for something new, something untouched.

Located south of Coorg and sharing a boundary with the Nagarhole National Park, Wayanad lies bang in the middle of the Western Ghats. Perhaps its most famous inhabitant is the Wayanad laughing thrush, and the chance to hear its laugh-like call is incentive enough to be here.

The hilly district doesn't have any linear trek route like in the Himalayas; instead, it's fragmented into small one-day treks and walks that take a few hours. So plan your holiday according to time in hand. You can spend a weekend in one destination or spend a week tramping around all of them. While the number of days needed to cover Wayanad is just indicative of a bare-minimum itinerary, you'll find it tough to leave the excellent resorts tucked away in complete wilderness. To reach these far-flung nodes, you have to be at the

Graphic by ANIS KHAN

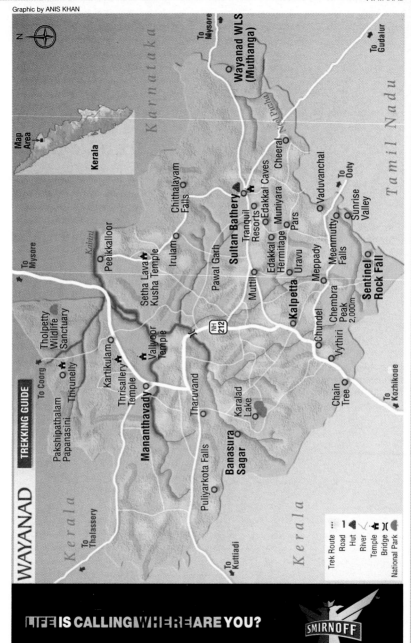

WAYANAD

TREKKING GUIDE

Map Area

Kerala

Karnataka

To Mysore

Wayanad WLS (Muthanga)

To Gudalur

Tamil Nadu

Neel Puzha

Chithalayam Falls

Cheeral

To Ooty

Sultan Bathery

Dakkal Caves

Tranquil Resorts

Edakkal Caves

Muniyara

Vaduvanchal

Pars

Irulam

Pawal Garh

Setha Lava Kusha Temple

Edakkal Hermitage

Uravu

Meenmutty Falls

Sunrise Valley

Peeikkalloor

Muttil

Meppady

Kalpetta

Sentinel Rock Fall

Kabini

To Mysore

NH 212

Chundel

Chembra Peak 2,000m

Tholpetty Wildlife Sanctuary

Kartikulam

Vallyoor Temple

Vythiri

To Coorg

Thrisallery Temple

Thiruvand

Chain Tree

To Kozhikode

Pakshipathalam Papanasini

Thrunelly

Mananthavady

Karalad Lake

Tharuvand

Banasura Sagar

Puliyarkota Falls

To Thalassery

Kerala

Kerala

To Kuttiadi

Trek Route
Road
Hut
River
Temple
Bridge
National Park

page 474), do the Wayanad trek in reverse and finally emerge at Sulthan Bathery on the eastern fringe.

→ Wayanad Facts

CONTACT POINTS
- EP Mohandas
District Tourist Promotion Council
North Kalpetta, Wayanad 673122.
Tel: 04936-202134, 09447072134
Email: layalakshmi@yahoo.co.in
- Jayprasad, Deputy Conservator of Forests
North Wayanad, Mananthavady.
Tel: 04936-240233
- Phanindra Kumar Rao, Wayanad Wildlife
Division, Sulthan Bathery, Wildlife Warden
Tel: 04936-220454, 270177

mercy of the public transport system, which isn't all that bad. But having your own vehicle saves time and also gives you flexibility.

In essence, you enter from Sulthan Bathery, east of Edakkal, do a circuitous trip through the south via Meenmutty and Soochipara waterfalls, climb Chembra Peak, cover Lakkidi and Vythiri in the west, get to the central headquarters of Kalpetta and then head north to Thirunelly and Pakshipathalam. If you have the luxury of time and the will to do an extended trip, you can trek across the Brahmagiri Hills from Irpu in Coorg, cross over to Thirunelly via Pakshipathalam (*also see Brahmagiri Trek on*

DAY ONE

KUPAMUDI ESTATE AND AROUND
DISTANCE AS FAR AS YOU WISH
LEVEL EASY

If Wayanad is the High School of Adventure, there can be no better preparatory course than 400 acres of Kupamudi Estate, which has as many as 11 well-marked walks within the estate itself. To get here, turn left 5 km before **Sulthan Bathery** on Ambalavayal Road towards **Edakkal**. Cross the hump, then a bridge and you'll find the estate's blue gate to your left.

For starters, you could try Indiana Jones (a moderate walk through coffee and bamboo clumps past rocky outcrops), Braveheart (an uphill climb for views of Wayanad) and walk past the old plantation bungalow to **Sitakully**, a pond where Sita is said to have bathed.

Once you have acclimatised, you can graduate to Cliffhanger (a steep hike to **Kupamudi Peak** for a 360-degree view), **Terminator** (an extreme downhill trudge) and **Anappara** (Elephant Rock), which lies outside the plantation.

Chembra Peak looms majestically over the Wayanad countryside

VIVEK M

Entrance to the Tranquil Resort

Since the area lies in the rain-shadow area, it gets limited rain and is great all year round, though the biggest advantage is the absolute absence of leeches. The catch is, to enjoy the estate walks, you need to avail the hospitality offered by Tranquil Plantation (see below). Which means, you can't camp outside the estate's boundary and do what would amount to a cross-border infiltration trek!

Billed as a top 'all-inclusive exclusive' hotel in the world, **Tranquil Plantation Hideaway** (Tel: 04936-220244; Tariff: Rs 4,000-5,500) is a

GETTING THERE AND OUT

FROM BANGALORE to Sulthan Bathery, it's 258 km/ 6 hrs by 🚗 (Rs 5,000), 7 hrs by 🚆 (Rs 175). Deluxe buses run from Bangalore's Majestic Bus Stand from 9 am-10 pm. If you're coming by car, drive down to Gundlupet via Mysore, then take the state highway to **Sulthan Bathery**. To reach your starting point **Kupamudi**, you need to cross Sulthan Bathery and take the left towards Ambalavayal. A 2-km drive will get you to your first stop, Tranquil Estate

RETURN From **Thirunelly**, head for **Mananthavady** (30 km), 1 hr by taxi (Rs 250) or 1½ hrs by bus (Rs 13). Buses run every hour from 6 am-5 pm. Taxis and buses available here for Bangalore via Mysore

plush resort with a swimming pool and rooms done up in wood. There's a buffet of Continental, Indian and farm-fresh fruits. Contact Victor or Jini, Tranquil Plantation, Kupamudi Coffee Estate, Kolagapara, for bookings.

DAY TWO
EDAKKAL-AMBUKUTHYMALA-EDAKKAL
DISTANCE 3 KM **TIME** 3-4 HOURS
LEVEL EASY

Just 5 km from Kupamudi via Amba-lavayal is the winding road to Edakkal and you can either take a bus or hike down the scenic stretch. From the makeshift parking lot at the base of the mountain, the **Edakkal Caves** are a 1-km uphill trudge through a hillside peppered with coffee and other plantation crops.

The climb takes 30-45 mins, though it's not the gradient but the scenic landscape that makes you catch your breath. Entry tickets can be picked up from the remotest ticket office you can ever hope to come across. Edakkal, perhaps on account of its precious **prehistoric drawings**, is guarded by an iron gate and kept under lock and key. Wilson Thomas, the security officer, accompanies visitors to the caves and doubles up as a guide. The steep climb from there is made easy by a couple of steel ladders. You need good footwear and the trek is avoidable during the rains when the trail becomes very slippery.
♦ **Entry fee** Adults Rs 5, children Rs 3
Timings 9.30 am-5 pm

From Edakkal Caves, a 305-m climb takes you through a lush boulder-strewn landscape to the top of **Ambukuthymala**, which takes

Edakkal Caves

The crowning glory of Wayanad is undoubtedly Edakkal. If it weren't for Fred Fawcett, the enterprising super-intendent of police of Malabar, it would have remained cloaked in the thick foliage of the Ambukuthy mountain range. During a hunting trip to Wayanad in 1890, he unearthed a Neolithic stone axe from a coffee estate, which led to his startling discovery of an ancient rock-shelter 1,219m up the mountain, replete with cave drawings.

Research showed that the caves were occupied by different sets of people at different points of time. Cave 1

acts as a drawing room of sorts, though the actual drawings are in Cave 2, a short climb up. The simplistic but detailed line drawings belong to the Neolithic Age and date back to 4,000-1,700 BC. You can easily make out images of a tribal king, a queen, a child, a wild dog, an elephant and deer. The filtered light and the shadow play give them depth, though it's believed that the original inhabitants drew inspiration from them by the firelight.

The second set, a little to the right, belongs to the Megalithic Age. On the other wall, you see a figure of a tall slender woman dating back to the 3rd century BC. A little to its right is a 1st century BC Pali inscription. There's a third cave a little higher up.

Cave 2, which is the biggest of the three, is 98 ft long, 30 ft wide and 93 ft high. And as you look up, you will see one boulder wedged in between two even bigger boulders, with its angular bottom protruding below. Edakkal (derived from 'eda' meaning 'between' and 'kal', which is 'stone') literally means 'The Stone in Between'.

Eddakal Hermitage: A welcome mark of civilisation in the middle of the forest

Photos SAIBAL DAS

about 1½ hrs. The trail is a lot firmer in this stretch and the absence of low-lying foliage gives a more panoramic view of the surrounding areas. Legend has it that an arrow shot by Lord Rama pierced the mountain causing a strange deep cleft. *Ambu* means arrow, *kuthy* is 'to pierce' and for sure, the gigantic fissure is there to be seen from Cave 2 down below in Edakkal. You can stay at **Edakkal Hermitage** (Tel: 04936-260123; Tariff: Rs 3,300-3,800), which is the only habitable dwelling available in the area — that's if you don't include camping out in the open on the top of Ambukuthy. This picturesque resort lies at the base of the Edakkal trail. The oldest cottage, which has two rooms, is named Fawcett after the

famous Malabar SP who excavated Edakkal, while another two-bed cottage, called Holtzsch after Fawcett's assistant, is on a higher elevation and hence commands the best view. On clear days, you can see your next goal, **Chembra**, the highest peak in Wayanad, looming in the distance. Contact Sibiraj or Shokraj Raveendran for bookings.

DAY THREE

VADUVANCHAL-MEENMUTTY

DISTANCE 7 KM **TIME** 3 HOURS
LEVEL MODERATE

Meenmutty may be no competition to Amazonian waterfalls, but trying to get to the place is no less than an adventure in the Amazon jungles. You have to first reach a tiny hamlet

The magnificent Meenmutty Falls

called **Vaduvanchal**, which is 13 km from Edakkal. From here, a 6-km dirt road takes you to **Chellangode**, a small junction where you can get a guide, and which takes you to a track, nearly obliterated by the heavy rains. In some patches, the undergrowth is so thick that it almost wipes out the track. Take a guide or trek alone at your peril!

A 1-hr walk takes you through undulating terrain and a perilously steep decline till you finally reach **Meenmutty**, but the effort is worthwhile. This majestic waterfall in the middle of nowhere cascades down in three steps and can be best experienced from the **Neelimala Viewpoint**.

From here, you could also check out **Kanthanpara** and **Soochipara** waterfalls, further south. It is near **Vellarimala Village** and the closest town/ base camp is **Chooralmala**. Named after a sharp needle-like (*soochi*) rock (*para*), over which the waterfall cascades down, Soochipara is also called Sentinel Rock after the Sentinel Tea Estate nearby. The District Tourism Promotion Council

(*DTPC, see Wayanad Facts on page 488*) sometimes organises rappelling down the rock face in November. The wide stretch of waterfalls ranges from 30-90m and the shallow pool that forms below is good for swimming and rafting. Soochipara also has tree-top huts that offer an excellent view of the Western Ghats.

For a place to stay, you'll have to head to **Meppady** via Vaduvanchal and stay at some of the modest hotels or the **PWD Rest House**. If you are looking for more comfort, from Vaduvanchal, drive or take a bus 22 km north to the district headquarters **Kalpetta**. Call the DTPC office at Kalpetta for more information.

DAY FOUR

MEPPADY-CHEMBRA PEAK-VYTHIRI

TIME 4-6 HOURS
LEVEL MODERATE

If you want to see the beauty of Wayanad, what better place to do it from than Chembra, the highest peak in the district. Standing majestically at 2,000m, Chembra is located near **Meppady**, and a trek to the top takes half the day. It's a hard climb, but the trail is well marked, making this the most popular hike in Wayanad.

TIP Take permission from the Ranger, Meppady Forest Department, before heading to the top

Once you reach the top, the land levels out into a grassy patch. The freshwater lake on the summit makes camping very easy. Day-trekkers are tempted to stay at **Chembra** for a couple of days, so make your plans accordingly. Provisions can be picked up from Meppady but it's better to hop across to the DTPC in **Kalpetta** (17 km away), from where you can hire guides and rent sleeping bags, canvas tents and trekking implements.

On your way out of Chembra, you can drive to **Pookot Lake** (3 km south of Vythiri), easily the most visited tourist spot in Wayanad. Surrounded

Vasota. Untouched.

By Irfan Mulla

THE route map was simple. Drive to Satara from Mumbai, head for Bamnoli village and a ferry to the Vasota fort. In the heart of Maharashtra the Mahindra Invader was my first choice. Other than the occasional Vada Pav stops, the drive took us straight to Satara. The Invader was a conscious decision borne out of need for a reliable, macho, good looking and economical vehicle.

Beyond Satara the uphill road in the late afternoon sun adds lovely highlights on the Wai mountain range. Soon the Invader looks like a school bus with 6 young school boys take a lift from us on the way to Bamnoli. We pass many colourful villages when the road turns downhill to expose a snaky water body. Our hopes soar. At Bamnoli the first house belongs to the Sarpanch's who I was told will provide food, water and directions to Vasota. Fortunately a government office in the village (Vasota is restricted) allows us to spend the night on the mountain range called Nageshwar.

We strike a deal to be ferried over 20kms of backwater to be dropped at the base of the fort and fetched the next morning. The back water is sweet and cold. The land on both sides casting green shadows on the water is simply refreshing. We were given strict instructions not to burst any fire crackers on the mountain since people do that to scare away the bears. Thus we found that the area was infested with great black bears.

The thrill great. The climb easy. At the top we turn to see the snake like backwater, the green forested land and an energizing wind. Powerful and mesmerizing. Fortunately just near the edge on the west we find the ruins of a Shiva temple. We eat dinner and sit admiring the movement in the great sky. I bet most of us were praying silently for protection against the bears and the cold. We retired inside a cramped room of the temple. No one slept

Morning brought such freshness and peace to the heart that we were overwhelmed with the golden light around us. Soon back at the base the hum of an engine could not be missed. A friend hugged the boatman-the saviour, when he anchored. The boatman suggested a dip near the shore and needless to say it was as refreshing as everything else Vasota had to offer.

Photos S SATISH KUMAR

The path to the Vythiri Resort

by lush, evergreen mountains, the 8-hectare natural freshwater lake offers boating and a lovely 2-km stroll on the pathway around it. The tourist complex has an aquarium, cafeteria, nursery and an Uravu Eco-Shoppe selling local handicrafts. During peak season (Sep-May), there's the added attraction of a half-a-kilometre horse-ride at Rs 15 per person.
◆**Boating fee** Rowboat for 4 costs Rs 50, rowboat for 8 Rs 100, pedal-boat for 2 Rs 30, pedal-boat for 4 Rs 50 **Timings** 9 am-5 pm **Entry fee** Adults Rs 5, children below 12, Rs 3 **Contact** Pookot Lake office, Tel: 04936-255207
🐾 At **Vythiri**, you can stay at **Green Magic Eco Resort** (Thiruvananthapuram Tel: 0471-2330437; Tariff: Rs 6,580-9,400), where a forest trail takes you deep inside the jungle. Perched above the canopy of trees, 30m from the jungle floor, is a tree house that would put Phantom and his Bandars to shame. Well-furnished, with a low maharaja-sized bed, a sit-out, bathroom with running water

and a fabulous view, Green Magic is easily the Attic of Wayanad. Those who find the tariff too high can try the much cheaper cottages below. It makes sense to book a day's stay and get picked up from Vythiri.

Vythiri Resort (Tel: 04936-255366; Tariff: Rs 3,500-4,250), with 18 cottages, 6 rooms and 9 huts and all the trappings of a tourist resort, is a slightly cheaper alternative. **Stream Valley Cottages** (Tel: 202787; Tariff: Rs 2,500), which has wooden cottages built on stilts, a fully equipped kitchenette (with food on demand) and a murmuring stream flowing nearby, is an eco-friendly option. There's also the picturesque **Rain Country Resorts** (Tel: 04936-255286; Tariff: Rs 2,500-3,600) in **Lakkidi** that has 8 rooms in conical heritage houses and a natural swimming pool.

DAY FIVE
Vythiri-Kalpetta
Distance As far as you wish
Level Easy
Since **Green Magic** lies in absolute seclusion, the area is very rich in birding. You can spend the morning bird-watching from the tree house and come down later to do the treks. You spot a lot of scarlet minivets, sunbirds, flycatchers, and some of the endemic birds you can see include the Malabar grey hornbill, Malabar parakeet, Wayanad laughing thrush and the Malabar whistling thrush.

A leisurely forest walk may throw up other surprises like the bright yellow butter snail and the Indian marten. **Vythiri** is perhaps one point in the whole itinerary where you find it extremely painful to leave and continuing onwards feels like a rudely broken dream. However, do not walk back in an attempt to savour the surroundings as it's a good 20 km from the main road. It makes more sense to take the jeep transfer to Vythiri, offered by the resort where you've

A state bus struggles uphill on the winding roads of Malabar

stayed and head onwards to **Kalpetta**.
🔺 Here, you can stay at **Hotel Green Gates** (Tel: 04936-202001; Tariff: Rs 1,000-2,750), just off NH212, the best that Kalpetta has to offer. It has spacious rooms, Internet and the excellent multi-cuisine Pazhassi Raja restaurant. Green Gates has an access-all authorisation from the DTPC for extensive exploration of Wayanad and provides tents, trekking equipment and guides. They also organise excursions to Chembra, Edakkal, Kuruva Island, Pakshipathalam and many other destinations, making it a one-stop shop for your holiday needs.

Since most tourists are weekend travellers and shops are usually closed on Sundays, the hotel has a boutique selling handicrafts at good rates. Contact Manjunath for bookings.

Another option is **The Royal Palm Holiday Home** (Tel: 206096; Tariff: Rs 1,500-2,000) with 6 cottages, Internet facility and a yoga-cum-meditation centre.

You can also shop at **Uravu**, a handicrafts village at Vellithol. About 4 km from Kalpetta towards Sulthan Bathery is a small town called **Muttil**, from where a right turn takes you 6 km to Uravu. It has a small artisan's

The more hostile the terrain, the better.

Mahindra BOLERO
INVADER

Wayanad laughing thrush

In the absence of any destination called 'Wayanad', where busloads of tourists could head to, what Wayanad needed was a brand reinforcer. The solution came in the form of the Wayanad laughing thrush (*Garrulax delesserti delesserti*).

But any self-respecting brand manager would call it a poor substitute. It flouts the basic laws of branding — the name is never consistent. Second, the bird remains difficult to spot. Third, in the rare event that you do manage to see it, you are presented by a brown blotch that can hardly be called spectacular. The bird is extremely finicky and disappears into the undergrowth at the slightest disturbance. Then, as you curse yourself for not having kept the camera ready, it utters shrieks of alarm, relayed one by one by its other hidden tribe members till it finally ends in a loud discordant 'laughter'. It is this garrulous act of ill humour that has earned the Wayanad laughing thrush its name. The bird is chestnut coloured with a white throat and a prominent black eye band. Displaying a trait common to most babblers, it stays in a group of 6 to 15 and can be found in dank undergrowths, cardamom sholas and, if you are lucky, along the edges of forest footpaths.

community (Tel: 04936-283244) that manufactures a wide range of pretty bamboo and clay handicrafts, sold at reasonable prices.

DAY SIX

KALPETTA-KURUVADWEEP
DISTANCE 10 KM **TIME** 4-5 HOURS
LEVEL EASY

From Kalpetta, you drive north and cross Mananthavady (35 km) to reach the Kartikulam-Palvelicham Road, from where a 5-km hike to your right takes you to **Kuruvadweep**. A good place to eat before you set off is **Asbe Restaurant** in Mananath-avady. Fish curry, chicken curry, fish fry, mutton fry, beef, prawn masala, mussels — this place serves it all. The food tastes home-cooked and the service is fast. A hearty meal for three will cost around Rs 200.

Kuruvadweep is 950 acres of evergreen forest on the tributaries of the east-flowing **Kabini**. The river is about 70m wide with no bridge, no boat and not even a bamboo raft to help you across. You simply have to wade across in knee-deep water, which in the monsoons becomes a raging current and for three months, Kuruvadweep becomes out of bounds.

If you are staying at Green Gates Hotel in Kalpetta, the hotel provides a naturalist, takes care of the logistics and can arrange guides. However, you can ask around at Mananthavady or Kartikulam for a local who'll double as a guide to Kuruvadweep. There are three islands here with a few submergible satellite islets. The main island has two freshwater lakes and several migratory birds can be seen here. These islands are uninhabited and hence have a well-preserved eco-system rich with various herbs, orchids and flowers. There's no place to stay but with prior permission from the Forest Department and with the help of their guides, you can camp and walk around on the

Vanilla flower

TREKKING HOLIDAYS IN INDIA

LIFE IS CALLING WHERE ARE YOUR SMIRNOFF

Quaint billboards on equally quaint buildings mark the town of Kalpetta

thickly forested island. After a day trip to Kuruvadweep, you can head for **Thirunelly** to stay for the night before you head out for **Pakshipathalam**.

🔺 You can stay at **Panchateertha Rest House** or the **Inspection Bungalow** in **Thirunelly** (*see Pakshipathalam-Thirunelly section in Brahmagiri Trek on page 482*).

DAY SEVEN
THIRUNELLY-PAKSHIPATHALAM
DISTANCE 7 KM **TIME** 3 HOURS
LEVEL EASY

The steps behind the Thirunelly Temple lead to Panchateertha and the Papanashini spring.

Legend has it that as Brahma was consecrating Vishnu's idol at Thirunelly, Garuda was escaping with the *amrita kumbha* (pot of nectar), arriving at Thirunelly just in time for the installation of his master's idol. He circled above thrice and a drop of *amrita* fell into the stream, endowing it with amazing purifying powers.

It is believed that after his aerial circumambulation, Garuda perched

on Karimala, where today you can see a small projection shaped in the form of an eagle. The rock is known as **Garudapara** and Garuda, the King of Birds, stands guard over his winged subjects at **Pakshipathalam**, a veritable avian paradise.

Pakshipathalam or 'Birds of the Subterranean' is a natural rock cave located at the northern end of the Brahmagiri Hills. A 7-km trek from Thirunelly takes you there through a dense jungle and can be covered in 3 hrs. There's no accommodation available, so most people do a day trip and trek back.

If you are an avid birder, you must carry camping equipment and take forest guides from **Appapara Forest Station** or a local from Thirunelly. There's a watchtower that offers a good perch for bird-watching.

♦ **Permit** Special permission has to be obtained from the Forest Department at Tholpetty/ Appapara or the DFO (Tel: 04935-240233) at Mananthavady to go to Pakshipathalam

In the monsoons, Pakshipathalam remains out of bounds as the path is faint, the trail is slippery and the forest teems with leeches and irritated animals of varying sizes.

For rest house bookings and hotels in the Wayanad region (Kerala), see Accommodation Listings on pages 552-553 ♦

Ooty, the Scotland of the East, is one of the most popular holiday destinations in India. In season, it's all about a crush of tourists on bad roads, taps running dry and shopkeepers trying to fleece you. But there's a secret to getting the best out of Ooty: go off-season. Ooty is then a series of piquant montages: the sun lights up one hill even as the other remains shrouded in green velvet. Mountain ponies contentedly chomp grass even as the fragrance of ghostly pines fill a mist-laden road. Enjoy the silence with a cup of hot filter coffee. Even the queen of the Blue Mountains, it is clear, enjoys the solitude.

→ Ooty Facts

● **LOCATION** Nestled in the middle of the Nilgiri Range, at a height of 2,268m
● **GETTING TO OOTY By air** Nearest airport: Coimbatore (88 km/ 2½ hrs). Serviced by Indian Airlines and Jet Airways. Taxi Rs 1,300 approx **By rail** Udhagamandalam Station on meter gauge; nearest broad gauge railheads: Mettupalayam (51 km/ 1½ hrs), Coimbatore **By road** State highway from Bangalore to Ooty (297 km/ 8 hrs) via Channapatna, Mysore, Nanjangud, Bandipur, Mudumalai and Gudalur
● **STD CODE** 0423
● **TOURIST OFFICE** Tamil Nadu Tourist Office, Wenlock Road, Ooty-643001. Tel: 0423-2443977

PRASHANT PANJIAR

Buildings from the Raj era

MUST-VISITS
BOTANICAL GARDENS
There are well laid-out lawns, tree-lined avenues and myriad ornamental plants and flowers. But the main attrac-

tion here is the fossilised tree trunk — it's 20 million years old.

PICNIC SPOT
Wenlock Downs, Ooty's most popular picnic spot, is a vast 20,000 acres of undulating landscape, once the venue for the Ooty Hunt. It's a great walk along grassy knolls and quiet roads.

WHERE TO STAY
The biggest hotel in town is the **Hotel Howard Johnson Monarch** (Tel: 0423-2444408/ 18/ 20; Tariff: Rs 1,200-6,000) on Havelock Road near the Botanical Gardens. **Willow Hill** (Tel: 2444037; Tariff: Rs 900-1,700), also located on Havelock Road, is a charming inn.

A large number of medium-budget hotels line Etiennes Road in Charing Cross, such as TTDC's **Hotel Tamil Nadu** (Tel: 2444370-7; Tariff: Rs 400-850), which has both rooms and cottages. Also on Etiennes Road are **Hotel Alkapuri** (Tel: 2440648; Tariff: Rs 450-900) and **Hotel Lakeview** (Tel: 2443580; Tariff: Rs 700-1,100). YWCA of India Project here (Tel: 2444262; Tariff: Rs 265-1,200) is another option. **Holiday Inn Gem Park** (Tel: 2441761; Tariff: Rs 1,950-2,995), on Sheddon Road, is well equipped.
For more hotels and details, see Accommodation Listings on pages 554-555

WHERE TO EAT
Ooty has several average Chinese restaurants, but **Shinkows**, opposite the elegant brick building of the Nilgiri Library, continues to occupy top place. **Kurinji**, on Commercial Road, serves up delicious South Indian fast food. Nilgiri Woodlands' **Toda Arch** has a multi-cuisine menu, as does Ooty Gate's **Aroma Delights**. Other multi-cuisine options are Sterling Fernhill's **Gulmohar Restaurant**, Hotel Lakeview's **Supper Club**, Hotel Khem's **Memory Lane** and the cafés at Hotel Mount View, Blue Hill International and The Willow Hill.

INPUTS FROM SHEILA KUMAR

TREKKING HOLIDAYS IN INDIA

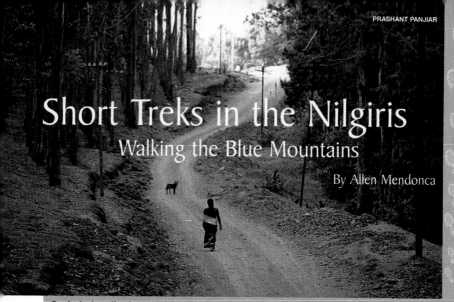

Short Treks in the Nilgiris
Walking the Blue Mountains

By Allen Mendonca

Secluded trails through pine forests mark the landscape around Ooty

The Nilgiris, also known as the Blue Mountains, constitute India's oldest mountain ranges and are located at the junction of the Western and Eastern Ghats, 2,500-2,600m above sea level. They stretch slightly into Kerala and Karnataka and are best suited for novice trekkers. These treks can be done all year round.

Three hugely popular hill stations, Ooty, Kotagiri and Coonoor, created by the British, offer ideal bases for interesting treks into the mountains where dense shola forests blend perfectly with tea estates, orange groves, coffee plantations, rolling meadows, bubbling brooks, tumbling waterfalls and crystal clear lakes.

The mountains are home to tribes such as the Todas, Kurumbhas and Irulas, each with colourful socio-cultural histories. The British considered the Nilgiris to be the Scotland of the East, built bungalows and rest houses on their estates and plantations and connected them through a network of winding mountain roads and even a railway. Half-a-dozen residential schools dot the area, which also boasts of a golf course and the Officers Training School in Wellington, a few kilometres out of Ooty.

OOTY-MUKURTHI LAKE TREK

TIME	3-4 days
LEVEL	Easy
IDEAL SEASON	Jun to Feb
LOCATION	West south-west of Ooty

DAY ONE

OOTY-PORTHIMUND
TIME 6-8 HOURS
LEVEL MODERATE

The town of Ooty is bisected by the state highway. So to begin the trek, you have to head towards the highway and then follow it westwards. After 3 km, look for a sign on the left that says **Parson's Peak**. Turn onto the dirt track winding upwards and west. Soon you'll be trekking across the upper reaches of the Nilgiris and meadows. After 8 km, you'll be on top of Parson's Peak overlooking the grassy knoll of **Parson's**

Valley. The mountain slopes gently towards the west. If you want to avoid the long slog, you could even take a bus from Ooty to the base of Parson's Peak and walk onwards from here.

From the peak, you'll be able to spot the tiny hamlet of **Porthimund**, with its red-tiled houses nestling in the mountains. But to get there, you have to first descend into the valley. Right after the summer rains in April-May, it's a spectacular sight to behold, for wild flowers of various hues carpet the valley as far as the eye can see. It takes about 3-4 hrs to get to Porthimund, where you can take 🗟 a tea/ coffee break. 🔺 Camp overnight here, but carry your own provisions.

GETTING THERE AND OUT
From Porthimund to Ooty Get picked up by a pre-arranged taxi (1 hr/ Rs 1,100) from Ooty. Bus service unreliable
Porthimund to Pykara Lake Arrange taxi pick-up (1 hr/ Rs 1,100). No bus service **Pykara to Ooty** by taxi is 1 hr 20 mins/ Rs 650 **Pykara to Mudumalai**, on the direct route via Talakunda (40 km), is

2 hrs by Sumo (Rs 1,300). No shared jeeps and buses available on this route
Mudumulai to Ooty is 1½ hrs by jeep (Rs 500-600). Buses for Ooty available from Masinagudi, 5 km from Theppakadu in Mudumalai Wildlife Sanctuary

DAY TWO
PORTHIMUND-MUKURTHI LAKE
TIME 2 HOURS
LEVEL EASY

From Porthimund, head 5 km west towards the Mukurthi Lake and dam. The walk takes you through eucalyptus plantations, coffee estates and a few small hamlets. It's a superb experience walking through this area and breathing the crisp mountain air. Although the lake is on the fringe of the Mukurthi National Park and one is tempted to explore the jungles, getting permissions for entry is near impossible. This is because the wildlife authorities want to preserve the pristine environment, quite like the Silent Valley National Park. But don't fret, there's plenty of pleasure to be had by the lake. Hire a boat or go fishing.

Graphic by SURAJ WADHWA

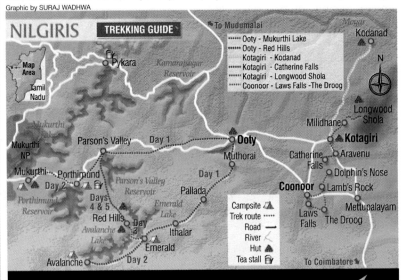

🏕 You can camp overnight on the premises of the dilapidated **Electricity Department Bungalow**, but with permission from the Superintendent Engineer, Generation Circle, Kunda (Tel: 0423-2509225, 09443048001). Or stay at the 🏠 **Nilgiris Wildlife and Environment Association Bungalow** (Tel: 0423-2447167 for bookings). Both are on the south side of the lake.

DAY 3
MUKURTHI LAKE-PORTHIMUND AND BEYOND
TIME 2 HOURS
LEVEL EASY

Return the same way to Porthimund, from where you can either get a taxi or bus back to **Ooty** or drive north-west to **Pykara Falls** and the **Pykara Lake**. You can have lunch at one of the lakeside eateries and then catch a bus or taxi back. Or drive another 20 km north over undulating terrain to the **Mudumalai National Park**.

The park is home to the tiger, bison, elephant, wild boar and other fauna (the endangered Nilgiri tahr lives in the upper reaches of the hills). There is an elephant safari every hour or so from the elephant camp at **Theppakadu** on the outskirts of the park. You can stay overnight at the 🏠 At the **Theppakadu Log Hut** and and **Theppakadu Sylvan Lodge** (for

Nilgiri tahr

Locally referred to as *varai adoo* (Tamil for cliff goat), these dusky brown or brownish grey goats with back-curving horns can be spotted gambolling high up in the mountains. They are a delight to watch as they leap nimbly from rock to rock. The tahr once roamed freely across the Nilgiris and the Western Ghats but were hunted down for their meat. They are now a protected species. Around 300-400 of them survive in these mountains and another 500 in sanctuaries in neighbouring Kerala.

E HANUMANTHA RAO/WILDERFILE

bookings contact Wildlife Warden Ooty, Tel: 0423-2444098; or DFO Kotagiri, Tel: 0423-2526235) and catch a bus or mini van, which ply regularly to Ooty.

OOTY-RED HILLS TREK

TIME	4-5 days
LEVEL	Easy
IDEAL SEASON	Oct to May
LOCATION	South of Ooty

DAY ONE

Ooty-Emerald
DISTANCE 12 KM **TIME** 4 HOURS
LEVEL Easy

Pack provisions, tents and water and head south-west from Ooty on the narrow **Muthorai Road**, and walk over meadows and hillocks parallel to the road towards **Red Hills**. After 8 km, you'll pass the villages of **Muthorai** and **Pallada**, and a little later, **Ithalar**. From here you'll have to trek across wide meadows keeping south till you reach the town of **Emerald** with its lovely lake. This is in fact the 'Lake District' with a total of eight lakes spread out in the valleys. Pitch your ⛺ tent anywhere along the shore of the lake.

DAY TWO

Emerald-Avalanche
DISTANCE 12 KM **TIME** 4 HOURS
LEVEL Easy

Head south for 12 km until you come across the **Avalanche Dam** and the **Avalanche Village** (named after a massive landslide in 1823). The village, home to the Toda tribe, is surrounded by forests of silver oak, pine, cypress and rhododendrons. There are also magnolias and orchids and a trout stream. Find a suitable spot and ⛺ camp overnight.

DAYS THREE TO FIVE

Retrace your way back to **Ooty** via **Parson's Valley**, or head to **Red Hills**. Head northwards along the lake on the Red Hills Road for 7 km, to the 🏔 **Red Hills Nature Resort**, where you can stay overnight. The next day, hike 14 km to Parson's Valley, and on the fifth day walk back to Ooty.

DAY HIKES AROUND KOTAGIRI

Kotagiri-Kodanad
DISTANCE 20 KM **TIME** 6-8 HOURS
LEVEL Moderate

Kotagiri, at a height of 1,982m plus, is the heart of the tea-growing area, east of Ooty. From Kotagiri head north-east of the town on the vast stretches of meadow parallel to the road to reach **Kodanad**, 20 km away. The place offers picture-postcard views of tea estates and the **Moyar River** winding its way in the valley below. If you wish to stay the night, there is the **Kodanad Forest Rest House** (for bookings contact DFO Nilgiris North Division, Tel: 0423-2443968). Or retrace your way back to Kotagiri or Ooty.

Kotagiri-St Catherine Falls
DISTANCE 8 KM **TIME** 2-3 HOURS
LEVEL Easy

Musically called Geddhehaada Halla, meaning 'foothill valley river' in the vernacular, this magnificent 250-ft double-cascaded waterfall is the second highest in the district. From Kotagiri, you'll need to take the Mettupalayam Road branching off at Aravenu and walk 8 km till the falls. Either return to Kotagiri or Ooty.

Kotagiri-Longwood Shola
DISTANCE 3 KM **TIME** 1 HOUR

Between August and September and then again in early December, the birder and wildlife enthusiast alike can head to Kotagiri. Just 3 km from here is the beautiful 20-hectare **Longwood Shola Forest**, a lush, wild tract that will definitely please nature lovers. Take written permission from the DFO, Nilgiri North Division, Mt Stuart Hill, Ooty-643001, before taking the road to **Milidhane**, which branches a short while later to Longwood. Explore the sholas with a guide or the forest guard who will check your papers at the entrance. Longwood also has a **Forest Rest House** (for bookings contact

Local women enjoying the sights from the Kodanad viewing point

Nilgiris DFO; *see facing page*). Also contact the **Nilgiris Wildlife and Environment Association** for more information (Tel: 0423-2447167).

GETTING THERE AND OUT
From Ooty to Kotagiri, it's 36 km/ 1¹/₂ hrs by taxi (Rs 500) or 2 hrs by bus (Rs 8). Buses run every 45 mins from the Ooty Bus Stand **Kotagiri to Kodanad** Get picked up at Kodanad by pre-arranged taxi (16 km/ ¹/₂ hr/ Rs 500) from Kotagiri **Kotagiri to St Catherine Falls** via Kattapettu is 20 km/ 1 hr by jeep (Rs 400) **St Catherine Falls to Ooty** is 56 km/ 2¹/₂ hrs by jeep (Rs 800-1,000)
RETURN the same way to Ooty from Kotagiri

COONOOR-LAW'S FALLS-THE DROOG TREK	
TIME	5-7 hours
LEVEL	Easy
DISTANCE	18 km
IDEAL SEASON	Apr to Jun, Sep to Oct
LOCATION	South-east of Ooty

Like in Ooty, the state road cuts through the middle of Coonoor. Head south-east on this state road to **Lamb's Rock** 9 km away. The rock, on a precipice, overlooks the **Coimbatore**

plains. Past this is **Lady Canning's Seat**, named after the Viceroy's wife.

Keep to the road and after 3 km you'll spot **Dolphin's Nose**, a greyish black rock remotely resembling a dolphin's snout and overlooking the valley. Take a break and retrace your steps. Five kilometres before Coonoor, you'll spot a detour to **Mettupalayam Road**, due south-east. **Law's Falls** are located at the junction of the Coonoor and Katteri streams, about 20 mins from Mettupalayam Road.

From here head east to **The Droog**, a ruined 16th century fort believed to have been used by Tipu Sultan. There are a number of springs holding promise of healing properties, the most famous being **Maan Sunai** (Deer Spring). You can see the state highway in the north. Trek down 2 km and take a bus to **Coonoor** as there are no hotels or guest houses close by.

GETTING THERE AND OUT
From Ooty to Coonoor, it's about 17 km/ 45 mins by taxi (Rs 350) or 1 hr 10 mins by bus (Rs 7)
RETURN Take the same route back. Keep a day for sightseeing in Ooty

For rest houses and hotels in the Nilgiris region (Tamil Nadu), see Accommodation Listings on pages 553-555 ✦

Health and first-aid
Sonia Jabbar

BEFORE THE TREK

The most important thing to take along on your hike is good health. Even if we have classified a trek as easy, ensure that you spend at least a couple of weeks training for the hike (*see page 19*). This will minimise the risk of sore muscles, strains and sprains. If you happen to develop a cold or diarrhoea before the trip, try and postpone it until you're feeling better. There is no point popping antibiotics and hoping it will clear up by the time you start walking. Minor illnesses are usually contracted when the body's natural resistance is low.

Going on a hike means first getting to the starting point, and if that is somewhere in the Himalayas, it would entail at least a day or two to get there. This not only means making your already handicapped body deal with the stresses of the journey, but also exposing it to the possibility of less-than-clean food and water. If you start out at a disadvantage, the physical stress of walking five to eight hours every day will only make you feel worse. So stay home, get better and then set out so that you can really enjoy your trek.

FIRST-AID KIT

What to carry in your first-aid kit depends on the kind of trek you are going on. If it is a day hike or a two-day hike, fairly close to civilisation, you'll only need to pack the bare essentials to tide you over until you can get proper medical attention. However, if you are in a place like Zanskar, where it may take you five days to get to basic medical facilities, you had better be well prepared. For long treks, I usually make a trip to a homeopathic store to add to my first-aid kit.

WHAT YOU SHOULD PACK
- Arnica homeopathic ointment or any other anti-inflammatory ointment: for sprains, bruises, aches and pains
- Crepe bandage: in case of sprains
- Calendula homeopathic cream: for cuts, stings, bites, rashes, sunburn and chafing
- Insect repellant: for mosquitoes, fleas, ticks and mites
- Needle, Swiss army knife: for puncturing blisters
- Tweezers: to pull out ticks and splinters
- Antiseptic ointment: for cuts and open blisters
- Blister pads or Band-Aids: for blisters
- Sterile gauze, sticking plaster and bandages: for cuts and wounds
- Nebasulf powder: for wounds
- Pudin Hara capsules: for indigestion, upset tummies
- Nux Vomica homeopathic pills: for indigestion, upset tummies
- Norfloxacin-400 or any other intestinal infection antibiotic as prescribed by your physician (for emergencies only)
- Isabgol: for indigestion, upset tummies

Peak of Pain

Valley of Wails

Mt. Misery

Bone Creek

Wrenching Range

The pain and sprain specialist. **IODEX**®

- Disprin and paracetamol: for headache, fever with body ache
- Antihistamine tablets: for coughs and colds, and bites and stings
- Cough drops: for sore throat
- Vicks Vaporub: for colds
- Multi-vitamins: very important, especially when you're eating less and exerting a great deal more than normal
- Tampons or sanitary towels: Women, keep some on you even if you're not expecting your periods. Sometimes, hard exercise can bring on unexpected menstruation.

WARNING If you are already on medication for some disease, whether asthma, diabetes, hypertension or any other ailment, consult with your physician thoroughly before you embark on the trek. Ensure that you carry all the medicines you need and know how to handle any emergency that may arise

FIRST-AID FOR COMMON AILMENTS

If you get sick in the mountains, the most important thing is to not panic. Discuss it with the rest of the group and see if you can factor in a rest day, rather than trying to play Rambo. Remember, the most important thing is not how high you climbed, but how much fun you had. The group may want to go ahead and pick you up on the way down. This is acceptable only if a responsible person is left behind to take care of you. Never agree to be left alone in the mountains, especially if you are unwell, even if it's only for a night.

Below are a few **first-aid tips** to deal with common health problems:

Blisters Get a good pair of walking shoes or hiking boots, and always wear a clean pair of socks. This will minimise your chance of getting blisters in the fist place. In the event you do get one, attend to it immediately. If you have a blister pad, put it on or devise one by putting a Band-Aid or sticking plaster over it. If it continues to grow, get a friend to puncture it, but **sterilise the needle** or Swiss army knife first. This can be done by holding it over a flame until it glows red and then cools. Wipe off any soot on the needle with a clean piece of gauze or cotton wool.

Clean the area thoroughly with water and soap. Dry it properly before puncturing the blister. To **lance the blister**, cut it on one side, allow the fluid to drain, lift the skin flap to **apply antiseptic cream**, then close it and put a Band-Aid or blister pad over it. If you're feeling squeamish about cutting, then puncture the blister by holding the needle almost parallel to the blister and gently inserting it, rather than trying to poke it from above. Make two punctures on opposite sides of the blister and squeeze to drain fluid. Liberally apply antiseptic cream before closing with Band-Aid or blister pad. Ensure you clean and dress it every day until it has healed.

Coughs and colds Drink plenty of fluids and **keep warm**. Pop those Vitamin C tabs; 1,000 mg a day will drive the cold away super-fast. **Gargle** with hot water and salt every morning and evening. You can try sniffing warm water up one nostril and then the other if your sinuses are congested, but ensure you blow your nose plenty of times so that no water remains in your sinuses. Carry some fresh ginger for ginger tea, which will definitely help the sore throat. Wear extra warm socks and a monkey cap at night. Keeping your head and feet warm will help the flu. Take an antihistamine tablet and a **paracetamol** before you sleep. You'll wake up feeling much better. Rest a day if your energy is low.

Tummy problems This is the most common problem on a hike, caused because of eating at greasy dhabas en route. In the hills, water is usually scarce, especially in summer, and the happy cooks dishing out rajma-chawal and aloo parathas don't really bother too much with hygiene. The second problem is drinking water on the hike itself. No matter how sparklingly clean a stream looks, desist from drinking untreated water (*see page 25 for purifying water*). In case you get the runs with gripes, eat very little, drink lots of boiled, clean water and see if Nux Vomica or three capsules a day of Pudin Hara and Isabgol at night doesn't settle it.

If the problem gets very bad, then you may want to take anti-biotics. I usually carry Norfloxacin-400 and take it twice a day for three days in an emergency. But check with your physician for the right drug for you before you leave. If you have very bad diarrhoea, and are feeling dehydrated, demand a rest day. Get someone to pitch your tent, and spend the day lying down. Ask someone in your group to make you **Oral Rehydation Salts** (ORS). In one litre of clean, boiled water, dissolve four teaspoons of sugar and half-a-teaspoon of salt. Keep sipping this through the day to keep from dehydration.

Sprains, aches and pains A twisted ankle or a wrenched knee is a serious thing if you're in the middle of nowhere. This could mean a ligament tear and months of care and rehabilitation before the injured part is fit again. If the ankle has swollen up and a rushing mountain stream is close by, hobble over with help from friends and submerge the foot and ankle into the cold water for 15-20 minutes. It will act like an ice-pack and bring down the swelling. Pat it dry and apply Arnica liberally. Bind it firmly, but not too tightly, with a crepe bandage. Sleep with your foot raised. You may put your jacket or backpack under your sleeping bag to raise your feet.

In most cases, unless the injury is a very minor one, consider your trek over. Try and come down the mountain slowly, using a friend's shoulder or a staff cut from a branch, and get back home ASAP. Show it to an orthopaedic specialist to check for hairline fractures. A liga-ment tear in the knee is extremely painful. I had one in Lahaul and the knee had gotten dislocated. A local shaman yanked it back into place while I yowled in pain. I don't suggest you try this. The knee had bal-looned painfully and I had to abandon my trek and return to Delhi. It took three weeks of Kerala Ayurvedic massage treatment before I could walk again. If any doctor recommends surgery, I would suggest try this wonderful and gentle treatment first before you let them cut you up.

Bites and stings I always carry a tube of Calendula Homeopathic cream but you can also carry a small bottle of Lacto Calamine. If you have been stung by a **honeybee**, in all likelihood you will be able to see the stinger left behind on your skin. Take it out gently by using your pen knife blade flat against your skin. Avoid tweezers or pressing down on the small dark venom sac as this will release the poison into your system. Once the stinger is out, wash the area thoroughly and apply Calendula. If you develop an allergic reaction, that is, the part swells up, pop an antihistamine pill. **Wasp bites** can be treated similarly but there won't be a stinger to remove.

Ticks and fleas If the **tick** is visible, take it out using a pair of tweezers, gripping it close to the head and twisting when pulling out. Be careful not to leave the head behind as this can cause infection and itching later. **Fleas** are extremely difficult to catch and the only sign of their presence will be red welts on your body. Wash with soap and water and apply Calendula. Sun your sleeping bag, clothes and backpack if you suspect infestation. Apply Odomos or any other insect repellent liberally on exposed parts to avoid bites.

Leeches If you are walking in leech country, try and protect yourself by applying insect repellent on your feet upto the ankles, wearing strong shoes and tucking your trousers into your socks. In case they still get through, carry a bag of salt on you. Applying salt will make them shrivel up and drop off. Never attempt to pull out a leech. It will leave behind anticoagulant on the puncture and you will continue to bleed profusely.

Stinging nettles can be painful. Remove any hair that may be left using some sticking plaster (the way women use wax to remove hair). Wash the area with soap and water and apply Calendula. The pain and rash should subside in a couple of hours at the maximum.

Cuts can be dealt with easily by applying a clean cloth, gauze or cotton wool to the wound and pressing down to stop the bleeding. Once the bleeding has stopped, wash the wound with clean water to remove dirt. Apply Nebasulf powder (I find it very useful in quickly drying out wounds) or antiseptic cream, cover with gauze or cotton wool and bandage or use tape to bind it up. Open, clean the wound and change the dressing after two days.

Serious wounds Once while trekking in Sikkim, I witnessed a young girl being gored by a dzo (cross between a yak and a cow). The wound on her thigh was the size of my fist. We were quick to act, plugging it by shoving my bandana into the wound and binding it up quickly. We applied a tourniquet on her upper thigh to stop the bleeding, devised a stretcher and sent her down the mountain for medical help. If you receive a deep wound, the most important thing is to stop the bleeding and then get medical help as soon as possible. Use a tourniquet only if the bleeding is severe and isn't stopping with pressure bandages.

WARNING Tourniquets can injure blood vessels and nerves if left in place too long, and can cause loss of an arm or leg. So use with extreme caution and get the victim to a hospital immediately. If medical aid is not available for over two hours, SLOWLY attempt to loosen the tourniquet 20 minutes after application.

Fractures are serious and have to be dealt with by a trained doctor. This would mean transporting the injured person down to civilisation, and so the injured part has to be immobilised to prevent jagged edges of the broken bone from cutting into tissue, muscle, blood vessels and nerves. Broken hands, arms, collar bones and legs are easier to deal with than broken skulls, necks and spines. A good website where you can learn more about dealing with serious fractures is http://www.wildernessmanuals.com/manual_4/chpt_4/10.html

The first thing to do is to determine whether there is a fracture to the injured part. If the bone hasn't broken through the skin and yet the part looks bruised and out of shape, treat it like a fracture. It's better to err on the side of caution.

Do not attempt to push back broken bones into place. If the skin is broken and bleeding, apply a pressure bandage to stop the bleeding and then bind it in a splint.

A splint is two rigid planes, which can sandwich the injured part. You can use tent poles or tree branches for fractured legs. The torso can be used as a splint for arm fractures. Tent pegs can be used for a broken wrist. Pad the injured arm or leg with a sweater or jacket before binding it between the splint. The splint can be bound with belts, bandages or material torn from clothing.

Apply the splint making sure that the injured part (arm, leg or bone) remains as immobile as possible. Place one splint on each side of the arm or leg. Make sure that the splints reach, if possible, beyond the joints above and below the fracture.

● Tie the splints *above* and *below* the fracture site with minimal motion to the injured areas. Tie all knots on the splint away from the casualty. DO NOT tie bandages directly over suspected fracture/dislocation site.

● You can make use of a sling suspended from the neck to support a broken arm or wrist. Slings can even be improvised by using a shirt, sweater or torn blanket. Remember that the casualty's hand should be higher than their elbow.

HEAT EXHAUSTION AND HEAT STROKE

Heat exhaustion happens if you have had prolonged physical exertion in hot, humid weather. If you find yourself breathing hard, feeling nauseous, headachy and exhausted, stop walking for the day. Find a cool, shady spot, remove unnecessary clothing, sponge yourself with water, particularly in the armpits, neck, groin and soles of feet. This will cool the body down. Drink plenty of water when the nausea has passed.

Attend to the first sign of heat exhaustion or it may turn into heat stroke, a far more serious condition. This occurs when the body's temperature regulation centre in the brain ceases to function causing the body temperature to rise continually. Brain damage and even death can result if it is not treated in time.

ACUTE MOUNTAIN SICKNESS (AMS), HIGH-ALTITUDE PULMONARY OEDEMA (HAPO) AND HIGH-ALTITUDE CEREBRAL OEDEMA (HACO)

The key to a successful trek is to have acclimatised well (*see page 16*), to a point where the body has adapted to decreasing levels of oxygen with increasing altitude. If you have gone from the plains up to the top of a mountain pass very quickly, you can suffer from AMS, a condition where there is mild swelling of brain tissue in response to lack of oxygen. This can happen easily in Ladakh if you have flown into Leh (3,353m) and started trekking the very next day.

You can tell you are suffering from AMS if after ascending to an altitude of over 2,500m, you suffer from a persistent headache, with any one or more of the following symptoms: loss of appetite, nausea, vomiting, fatigue or weakness, dizziness or light-headedness and difficulty in sleeping. Some trekkers pop Diamox pills for AMS and then carry on climbing. I don't recommend that. It's better to pitch camp and rest a day and let your body acclimatise naturally. The body usually recovers well enough for you to continue the trek the following day, but if it doesn't, you should come down to a lower altitude. Ignoring symptoms of AMS can lead to HACO and HAPO, the complications listed below.

HACO is when the brain tissue swells to a point where it can no longer function properly. Symptoms range from confusion and changes in behaviour or lethargy. There is also a characteristic loss of coordination called ataxia. This is a staggering walk that is similar to the way a person walks when very drunk. This is an extremely serious condition and may be fatal if ignored or not treated immediately. No matter what time of day or night, arrange for the person to be brought down the mountain with the help of porters or villagers to the last point they were feeling okay. This may mean returning to the campsite of the night before. The person should rest for a day until sufficiently recovered and then return home.

HAPO occurs when lack of oxygen in high altitudes causes constriction of some of the blood vessels in the lungs, shunting blood through a limited number of vessels that are not constricted. This dramatically elevates the blood pressure in these blood vessels and results in a high-pressure leak into the lungs. The symptoms can be any of the following: extreme fatigue, fever, breathlessness even at rest, fast, shallow breathing, cough with frothy or pink sputum, gurgling or rattling breath, chest tightness, fullness, or congestion, blue or grey lips or fingernails and drowsiness. If you suspect anyone to be suffering from HAPO, have them carried down immediately to a lower altitude (as in HACO above). This condition is as serious as HACO and can be fatal if not treated. The person will recover with rest at low altitude after a day or two and should return home thereafter.

Disclaimer The tips given here are based on the author's experience and no part of this article should be construed as expert medical advice. The publishers cannot accept responsibility for any consequences arising because of the use of information in this article. We recommend that you check with your doctor about medical treatment before leaving for your trek

TREKKING EQUIPMENT AGENCIES

LEGEND
Ⓗ Hire
Ⓢ For sale

BANGALORE
ADVENTUREWORKS Ⓗ Ⓢ
Location Near Bima Jewellers **Address** 121, 3rd Block, 8th Main, Jai Nagar. **Tel** 080-26538354, 26647036, 0944093570 **Email** adventureworks@touchtelindia.net **Contact** Raju

BHARMOUR
MOUNTAINEERING INSTITUTE SUB-CENTRE Ⓗ
Location Near bus stand **Address** Bharmour, Dist Chamba **Tel** 01895-225036
Contact Sanjay Nagrekar

DEHRA DUN
PARAMOUNT ENTERPRISES Ⓗ Ⓢ
Location Near Kotwali **Address** 16, Moti Bazaar **Tel** 0135-2658037, 09837036357 **Email** paramount_ent@vsnl.net **Website** paramountenterprises.com Contact Praveen Anand

DHARAMSALA
REGIONAL MOUNTAINEERING CENTRE Ⓗ
Address Swarga Ashram, McLeodganj, Dharamsala **Tel** 01892-221787 **Contact** S.R. Saini *Available for hire only when their courses are not on

KOLKATA
CHAKRA EQUIPMENTS Ⓗ Ⓢ
Location Near Deshbandhu Park **Address** 3A, Shyamlal Street, Shyam Bazaar, Kolkata
Tel 25300648, 09433111678
Email highequip@yahoo.co.in **Website** aboutadventures.org **Contact** Mrinmoy Saha

NEW DELHI
ADVENTURE 18 Ⓢ
Location Opp Venkateswara College **Address** 18, Satya Niketan, New Delhi
Tel 011-26878888, 09810043029
Email mo1@vsnlcom
Contact Mohit Oberoi

CARABIN INTERNATIONAL Ⓗ Ⓢ
Location Near Harkesh Nagar **Address** C 62/3 Okhla Industrial Area Phase II, New Delhi

Tel 51611082-83, 09810314563
Email carabin@vsnl.com **Website** carabinindia.com **Contact** Rajat Sethi

CHOGORI Ⓢ
Location Opp British Council Building **Address** 511, Kailash Building, KG Marg, New Delhi **Tel** 23312787/ 83 **Email** preeti@chogoriindia.com **Contact** Preeti Mishra *For bulk orders only

COLEMAN EAGLE SALES Ⓗ Ⓢ
Location Opp Sarvapriya Club **Address** 6/ 3 Sarvapriya Vihar, New Delhi **Tel** 26526273–75, 09313709329 **Email** eaglesales@eagle-grp.com **Website** eagle-grp.com **Contact** O P Tripathi

DIMENSIONS Ⓗ
Location Near Shiv Mandir
Address House No. 25, Chirag Dilli Main Road, New Delhi **Tel** 09811088290, 09350225713, 09350807888 **Email** gurriegeo@yahoo.com
Contact Gurminder

INDIAN MOUNTAINEERING FOUNDATION Ⓗ
Location Opp Anand Niketan
Address Benito Juarez Road, New Delhi
Tel 24671211/ 7935/ 1572 **Fax** 26883412
Email indmount@del2.vsnl.net.in

STIKAGE Ⓗ Ⓢ
Location In Momo Point Lane **Address** 7-UB, Jawahar Nagar, Kamla Nagar,
Delhi **Tel** 23850026, 23850036, 09868426655, 09868064114
Email stikage@yahoo.com
Website stikage.com, stikage.nav.to
Contact Surinder/ Ravi Sonik

TREKKO EQUIPMENT Ⓢ
Address Sector C-8, No. 8115, Vasant Kunj, New Delhi **Tel** 26890427, 09818003102
Fax 26895640 **Email** nageshsethi@yahoo.com
Contact Nagesh Sethi

ZANSKAR OUTDOOR EQUIPMENT Ⓗ Ⓢ
Location Opp Ryan International School
Address Pocket A2/ 110 Mayur Vihar Ph II, New Delhi **Tel** 22627453, 30961516, 09811676556 **Email** zanskar@hotmail.com
Contact Anil Kumar

DISCLAIMER: These listings should in no way be construed as a recommendation by the publisher

TREKKING AGENTS

NORTH HIMACHAL

DHARAMSALA STD 01892
SUMMIT ADVENTURES
Location Main Square, Bhagsu
Nag **Address** Upper
Dharamsala **Tel** 221679 220403,
09418021679 **Fax** 221681
Email office@summit
adventures.net **Website**
summit-adventures.net **Regions**
Kinnaur, Spiti **Services** Trekking,
rock and mountain climbing, jeep
tours **Contact** Milap, Subhash

MANALI STD 01902
HIMALAYAN ADVENTURES
Location Opp Tourist Info
Centre **Address** The Mall
Manali **Tel** 252750, 098162-
23004 **Fax** 252182 **Email**
roopu@sancharnet.in **Website**
himalayanadventurersindia.com
Regions J&K, Kinnaur, Lahaul &
Spiti, Garhwal **Services**
Trekking, jeep safaris, skiing
Contact Kapil and Roopu Negi

HIMALAYAN JOURNEYS
Location Opp SDM Office
Address The Mall, Manali
Tel 252365, 09816073355
Fax 253065 **Email**
himjon@del3.vsnl.net.in
Website himalayanjourneys
india.com **Regions** Lahaul &
Spiti, Ladakh, Zanskar **Services**
Trekking, rafting, skiing, jeep
safaris **Contact** Iqbal Sharma

HIMALAYAN SAGA
Location Near Manalsu Bridge
Address Club House Rd Manali
Tel 251848 09418005235
Email
travelinfo@himalayansaga.com
Website himalayansaga.com
Regions Lahaul and Spiti
Kinnaur **Services** Trekking,
rafting, skiing, jeep safaris

LADAKH AND ZANSKAR

LEH STD 01982
ADVENTURE NORTH
Location Near Main Market
Address Old Rd, Chulung, Leh
Tel 251227, 252139 **Fax** 252720
Email advnorth@sancharnet.in
Regions Ladakh, Zanskar
Services Trekking, jeep safaris
Contact Mohiuddin

DREAMLAND TREK & TOUR
Location Near Dreamland
Hotel **Address** Fort Rd, Leh **Tel**
250784, 253616, 09419178197
Email info@dream ladakh.com
Website dreamladakh.com
Region Ladakh **Services**
Trekking, mountaineering,
rafting, biking, safaris
Contact Javeed

KANG-YETSE EXPEDITIONS
Location Near the Mosque
Address Main Bazaar, Leh **Tel**
252131 **Regions** Ladakh,
Zanskar **Services** Trekking,
mountaineering **Contact** Bashir

RIMO EXPEDITIONS
Location Opp Police Station
Address Kanglachenchen Hotel
Complex, Leh **Tel** 253257/ 348
Gurgaon Tel 95124-2806027-
29 **Email** rimo@vsnl.com
Regions Ladakh, Uttaranchal,
Sikkim **Services** Trekking,
river rafting **Contact** Thinles
Dorjay in Leh

SNOW LEOPARD TRAILS
Location Opp Police Station
Address Kanglachenchen Hotel
Complex, Leh **Tel** 252355/ 074,
09419178039 **New Delhi Tel**
011-26133165, 26124788
09811119610 **Email**
leopard@nda.vsnl.net.in
Website indiamart.com

Regions J&K, Himachal
Services Treks, camping
Contact Wangshuk Kalon

UTTARANCHAL

JOSHIMATH STD 01389
ESKIMO ADVENTURES
Location Near GMVN Old
Complex **Address** Upper
Market, Joshimath **Tel** 222075
09412413714 **Telefax** 222630
Regions Garhwal, Kumaon
Services Trekking, rafting,
mountaineering, rock climbing,
Contact Manish Bhujvan

RISHIKESH STD 0135
ADVEN TOURS
Address Laxman Jhula, Tapovan
(Sarai), PO Tapovan, Via
Sivananda Nagar, Rishikesh **Tel**
2442023, 09412058891
Fax 2434066 **Email**
adventours5@hotmail.com/
sudhir_khanduri@yahoo.com
Regions Garhwal, Kumaon
Services Trekking, river
rafting, camping
Contact Sudhir Khanduri

**GARHWAL ADVENTURE
SPORTS**
Location Near GMVN office
Address Ranghar Bhavan Upper
Bazaar, Joshimath **Tel** 222459,
09412063262 **Regions** Garhwal,
Kumaon **Services** Trekking,
mountaineering, rafting, skiing,
wildlife **Contact** Madan Singh

MUSSOORIE STD 0135
TREK HIMALAYA TOURS
Location Opp Ropeway
Address The Upper Mall
Jhulaghar **Tel** 2630491
09837258589 **Email**
trekhimalaya@vsnl.com
Regions Garhwal, Ladakh
Service Trekking
Contact Neelambar Badoni

GARHWAL HIMALAYAN EXPLORATIONS
Location Opp Union Bank of India **Address** Kailash Gate Muni-ki-Reti, Rishikesh **Tel** 2433155, 09837055578 **Fax** 2431654 **Email** himalayas@sancharnet.in **Website** garhwal himalayas.com **Regions** Garhwal, Kumaon **Services** Trekking, rafting, mountaineering, rock climbing, jeep safaris, skiing **Contact** Rajiv Tiwari

RED CHILLI ADVENTURE SPORTS
Address Tapovan, Laxman Jhula Rd, Rishikesh **Tel** 2434021 2442421, 09412056021 **Email** redchilli@vsnl.com **Website** redchilliadventure.com **Regions** Garhwal, Kumaon **Services** Trekking, rafting, jeep safaris **Contact** Arvind

STEP HIMALAYAN ADVENTURE
Location Near GMVN Old Yatra Office **Address** Kailash Gate, Muni-ki-Reti, Rishikesh **Tel** 2432581, 09837069433 **Email** stephiml@vsnl.com **Regions** Garhwal, Kumaon **Services** Trekking, rafting, camping, skiing, wildlife tours **Contact** Mahesh Tiwari

NORTH-EAST
ARUNACHAL PRADESH

BOMDILA STD 03782
HIMALAYAN HOLIDAYS
Address ABC Bldg, Main Market, Bomdila **Tel** 222017 09436045063 **Fax** 223191 **Email** himalayan-holidays@india.com **Website** himalayan-holidays.com **Regions** Arunachal, Nagaland **Services** Trekking, mountain

climbing, angling, rafting, wildlife tours **Contact** Tsering Wange

NAGARLAGUN (NEAR ITANAGAR) STD 0360
DONYI HANGO ADVENTURE TOURS & TRAVEL
Address Sector C, Nagarlagun **Tel** 2244977, 09436043393 **Fax** 2247642 **Email** yanedai@sancharnet.in **Website** donyihango.net **Region** Arunachal **Service** Trekking **Contact** Yani Dai

TRIBAL VOYAGES
Address Ri Villa, Court Rd Sector D, Nagarlagun **Tel** 2350362-63, 09436044069 **Email** tribalvoyages @yahoo.co.in **Regions** Arunachal, Nagaland, Meghalaya **Services** Trekking, caving **Contact** Komkar Riba

NAGALAND

KOHIMA STD 0370
PEAK TRAVELS
Location Near Sun Book Store **Address** PR Hills **Tel** 2242993, 09436001694/ 05513 **Email** peaktravels@rediffmail.com **Region** Nagaland **Services** Trekking **Contact** Neisatuo Keditsu

SIKKIM

GANGTOK STD 03592
NAMGYAL TREKS & TOURS
Location Enchay Compound **Address** PO Box No. 75, Tibet Rd, Gangtok **Tel** 09434033122 **Fax** 203067 **Email** trekking@sancharnet.in **Website** namgyaltreks.net **Regions** Sikkim, Darjeeling **Services** Trekking, mountain-eering expedition **Contact** Namgyal P Sherpa

SIKKIM ADVENTURE
Address 6th Mile Tadong Gangtok **Telefax** 251250 **Mobile** 09832060555 **Email** sailesh@sikkim-adventure.com **Website** sikkim-adventure.com **Regions** Sikkim, Darjeeling, Bhutan **Services** Trekking, mountaineering **Contact** Sailesh Pradhan

TIBET TOURS AND TRAVELS
Location Enchay Compound **Address** Namnang Rd, Gangtok **Tel** 220322, 09434024070 09832087334 **Kolkata Tel** 033-24123873 **Email** tibettours@lhaso.com **Regions** Sikkim, Darjeeling, Bhutan, Dooars Nagaland **Services** Trekking, mountaineering expeditions, wildlife **Contact** Probir Sen

WEST BENGAL

DARJEELING STD 0354
TENZING NORGAY ADVENTURES
Address 1, DB Giri Rd, Darjeeling **Tel** 2256408, 09832037383 **Fax** 2253719 **Email** khangla@hotmail.com **Website** tenzing-norgay.com **Regions** Darjeeling, Kalimpong, Sikkim **Services** Trekking, rock and mountain climbing, whitewater rafting, kayaking **Contact** Jamling Tenzing

SILIGURI STD 0353
HELP TOURISM
Location Hill Cart Road **Address** 143, Hill Cart Road P O Box 67 Siliguri **Tel** 2535893, 09832066626, 09434046891 **Telefax** 2433683 **Email** helptourism@satyam.net.in **Regions** Darjeeling, Sikkim, Arunachal Pradesh, Nagaland

TREKKING AGENTS

Services Trekking, Birding, Culture Tours, Rafting, Wildlife Tours **Contact** Raj Basu

NATURE BEYOND
Location Near Siliguri College **Address** 3, Rajanikanto Sarani Hakimpara, Siliguri **Tel** 2532461 09434121162 **Email** info@east-himalaya.com **Website** east-himalaya.com **Regions** Darjeeling, Kalimpong, Sikkim **Services** Trekking, rafting, wildlife tours **Contact** Pallab

WEST
MAHARASHTRA

PUNE STD 020
PUGMARKS HOLIDAYS
Location Behind Sai Petrol Pump **Address** 595, Deccan Gymkhana Nandadeep Bldg Pune **Tel** 56014112-3 **Fax** 25539078 **Email** pugmarks@vsnl.net **Website** pugmarksholidays.com **Regions** Maharashtra **Services** Trekking, wildlife tours, rafting, scuba diving **Contact** Anil Gupte, Anirudh Chaoji

SOUTH
KARNATAKA

BANGALORE STD 080
NATURE ADMIRE
Location Near Hotel Sai Shakti **Address** 107, 8th Cross 6th Main, Malleswaram Bangalore **Tel** 23340065 09845079414 **Email** info@natureadmire.com **Website** natureadmire.com **Regions** Karnataka, Kerala, TN **Services** Trekking, rock and mountain climbing, whitewater rafting, parasailing **Contact** Dev Balaji

THE ADVENTURERS
Location Near Bhasyam Circle **Address** No. 142, 69th Cross

5th Block Rajaji Nagar, Bangalore **Tel** 23409712, 09448125298 **Fax** 23324338 **Email** honnemardu@satyam.net.in **Region** Karnataka **Services** Trekking, rock and mountain climbing, water sports **Contact** Swamy

MADIKERI STD 08272
V-TRAK FRIENDS TOURS & TRAVELS
Location Near FMC College **Address** College Rd, Madikeri **Tel** 229102, 229974 **Email** v_trak@rediffmail.com **Region** Karnataka **Services** Trekking, eco tours, birding **Contact** Ganesh

KERALA

COORG STD 08272
MOJO RAINFOREST RETREAT
Address Kaloor Rd, Galibeedu Village, Madikeri **Tel** 265638 **Telefax** 265636 **Email** wapred.india@vsnl.com **Website** rainforesttours.com **Region** Coorg **Services** Trekking, eco tours **Contact** Anurag Goel

KUNDAPUR STD 08254
SOANS HOLIDAYS
Address Grace Villa, CS Rd Kundapur **Tel** 231683 09448120826 **Fax** 232223 **Email** info@soans.com **Website** soans.com **Region** Karnataka **Services** Trekking, wildlife tours, cycling tours, birding **Contact** Vishwas Soans

METRO
AGENTS

CHENNAI STD 044
WILDTRAILS
Address 26, Thirunarayana Avenue, Off New Avadi Rd

Kilpauk, Chennai **Tel** 26442729, 09884045001 **Email** wilder@vsnl.com **Website** wildertrails.com **Regions** Tamil Nadu, Karnataka, Kerala **Services** Trekking, eco tours **Contact** Major A.S. Candade

KOLKATA STD 033
ENDEAVOUR TOURS AND TRAVELS
Location Opp Indira Cinema **Address** 1, Indra Rai Rd Kolkata **Tel** 24860583 09831107246 **Fax** 24765023 **Email** endeavour tours@vsnl.net **Region** Sikkim **Services** Trekking, rafting, angling, hang gliding **Contact** S.K. Bhaumik

HIMALAYAN FOOTPRINTS
Location Near Jessop & Co **Address** 77, Netaji Subhash Rd, Kolkata **Tel** 2431063 09830033896 **Fax** 22479163 **Email** neil1967@sify.com **Website** abouthimalayas.com **Regions** Sikkim, Darjeeling, Kalimpong **Services** Trekking, river-rafting **Contact** Neil Law

MUMBAI STD 022
COUNTRYSIDE OUTDOOR PROGRAMMES
Address Room No. 35, Vawda Building, 252, LJ Rd, Opp Shiv Sena Bhavan, Mumbai **Tel** 24441513, 09820125670 **Email** info@countryside india.com **Regions** Maharashtra, Himachal Pradesh, Ladakh, Sikkim **Services** Trekking, safari, river rafting, camping, skiing **Contact** Milind Bhide

INDIA OUTDOORS
Location Near Regal Metro Shoes **Address** 169/ C Outhouse, Neelkant Niwas,

Dr Ambedkar Rd, Dadar TT
Mumbai **Tel** 24186360
09820341803
Fax 24166944 **Email**
info@indiaoutdoors.com
Website indiaoutdoors.com
Regions Garhwal and Kumaon
Himalayas, Sikkim **Services**
Trekking, paragliding, sky-diving,
rafting, parasailing
Contact Pankaj Trivedi

OUTBOUND ADVENTURES
Address C-408, Ganga
Darshan, JP Rd, Versova,
Mumbai **Tel** 26315019 **Email**
outboundadventure@hotmail.
com **Website** outboundadven
ture.com **Region** Maharashtra
Services Trekking, whitewater
rafting, rock-climbing
Contact Andre Morris

YMCA
Location Opp Imperial Cinema
Address YMCA Student Branch
412, Lamington Rd, Mumbai **Tel**
23824534 09821643102 **Email**
melvin@bombayymcacamp.org
Region Sahyadris **Services**
Trekking, kayaking, canoeing,
rock climbing, rappelling
Contact Melvin Louis

NEW DELHI STD 011
AQUATERRA ADVENTURES
Location Near M Block Market
Address S-507, GF Greater
Kailash-II, New Delhi **Tel**
51636101, 09811103831 **Fax**
29212641 **Email**
aquatera@vsnl.com **Website**
aquaterraadventures.com
Regions Himachal Pradesh,
Darjeeling, Arunachal
Services Trekking, angling,
rafting, wildlife, Himalayan jeep
safaris **Contact** Vaibhav, Solil

BANJARA CAMPS & RETREATS
Address 1A, Hauz Khas Village,
New Delhi **Tel** 26861397
Telefax 26855152
09810645455 **Email**
banjara@vsnl.com **Website**
banjaracamps.com **Regions** HP,
Kinnaur, Spiti, Ladakh
Services Trekking, luxury
camps, jeep safaris
Contact Ajay Sud, Rajesh Ojha

IBEX EXPEDITIONS
Location Opp State Bank of
India Apartments **Address**
G-66, East of Kailash, New Delhi
Tel 26912641
Fax 26846403 **Email**
ibex@nde.vsnl.net.in **Website**
ibexexpeditions.com **Regions**
HP, Lahaul, Spiti, Kinnaur,
Ladakh, Uttaranchal **Services**
Trekking, eco tours, safaris,
rafting, mountain biking
Contact Mandip Singh Soin

SHIKHAR TRAVELS
Location Near Wimpy's
Address 209, Competent
House, F-14, Middle Circle
Connaught Place, New Delhi **Tel**
51523667-8, 09810024642 **Fax**
23323660 **Email**
india@shikhar.com **Regions**
Garhwal and Kumaon Himalayas
Services Trekking,
mountaineering, wildlife tours
Contact Capt Sudesh Kumar

WAYFARER TOURS AND TRAVELS
Location Near Sangam Cinema
Address 9/477, RK Puram,
New Delhi **Tel** 26107715,
09810261791 **Email**
wayfarerindia@hotmail.com
Website
wayfareradventures.com

Region Kumaon
Services Trekking
Contact Subroto Roy

WILDRIFT ADVENTURES
Location Close to PVR
Anupam **Address** E-47, Saket
New Delhi **Tel** 26850492
Fax 26962623
Email info@wildrift.com
Website wildrift.com
Regions Garhwal and Kumaon
Himalayas
Services Trekking, camping
Contact Balbir

WILD WORLD INDIA
Location Close to ISKON
Temple **Address** 26, Kailash
Hills, New Delhi **Tel** 26914417
9313772980 **Email**
vikram@wildworldindia.com
Website wildworldindia.com
Regions Arunachal,
Darjeeling, Kalimpong,
Sikkim, Garhwal and
Kumaon, West Bengal
Services Trekking, safaris,
angling, birding, wildlife
Contact Dipin, Gaurav,
Prasanna, Vikram

WISDOM TRAVELS
Location Opp Aurobindo
College **Address** Shop No. 13
1st floor, MMTC/ STC Market
Opp Aurobindo College New
Delhi **Tel** 26692036
09212001930 **Fax** 26692036
Email wisdom@vsnl.com
Website wisdomtravels.org
Regions Sikkim, Darjeeling,
Ladakh and Himachal Pradesh
Services Trekking, jeep
safaris, mountaineering, rafting,
rock climbing, bike tours,
Buddhist circuit tours
Contact Kelsang Phuntsok, Lalit

DISCLAIMER: These listings should in no way be construed as a recommendation by the publisher

INFORMATION ❶
INFORMATION & BOOKING ❶❿
TREKKING ❶

ARUNACHAL PRADESH
WEBSITE
arunachaltourism.com

ITANAGAR ❶
ARUNACHAL TOURISM
Pem Norbu, Ganga
Near Nirwachan Bhawan
Telefax 0360-2214745

DIBRUGARH, ASSAM
ARUNACHAL TOURISM DESK
Office of the Deputy
Resident Commissioner
Govt of AP, Mohanbari
Dibrugarh
Tel 0373-2382560

GUWAHATI
ARUNACHAL TOURISM ❶
Office of the Deputy
Resident Commissioner
Govt of AP, RG Baruah
Road, Baskar Nagar
Guwahati **Tel** 0361-
2412859, 09864016193

METRO/ CITY OFFICES
KOLKATA
ARUNACHAL TOURISM ❶
Office of the Deputy
Resident Commissioner
Govt of AP, 109, Sector 1
Salt Lake City, Kolkata
Tel 033-23341243

NEW DELHI
ARUNACHAL TOURISM ❶
Office of the Resident
Commissioner, Govt of
AP, Kautilya Marg
Chanakyapuri, New Delhi
Tel 011-23016177
Email
dtotour@yahoo.co.in

HIMACHAL PRADESH
WEBSITE hptdc.nic.in

SHIMLA
TOURIST INFO CENTRE
❶❿❶

Himachal Pradesh
Tourism Development
Corporation, The Mall
Shimla **Tel** 0177-2652561
Email
hptdc@sancharnet.in

DALHOUSIE
TOURIST INFO CENTRE ❶❿
HPTDC, Bus Stand
Dist Chamba, Dalhousie
Tel 01899-242136

YOUTH HOSTEL ❶❿
GROUP TREKKING
Tel 242189

DHARAMSALA
TOURIST INFO CENTRE ❶❿
HPTDC, Kotwali Bazaar
Dharamsala
Tel 01892-224928

MANALI
TOURIST INFO CENTRE ❶❿
HPTDC, The Mall, Manali
Tel 01902-253531 **Email**
mktmni@sancharnet.in

METRO OFFICES
CHENNAI
TOURIST INFO CENTRE ❶❿
HPTDC, Wallajah Road
Chennai **Tel** 044-
25385689 **Email**
hptourism_chennai@vsnl.
nic.in

KOLKATA
TOURIST INFO CENTRE ❶❿
HPTDC
Biplabi Anukul, Church
Street, Chandni Chowk
Kolkata **Tel** 033-
22126361 **Email**
hptdc_kolkata@vsnl.net

MUMBAI
TOURIST INFO CENTRE ❶❿
HPTDC, 36
World Trade Centre
Cuffe Parade

Mumbai
Telefax 022-22181123
Email hptdcmkt@vsnl.net

NEW DELHI
TOURIST INFO CENTRE ❶ ❿
HPTDC, Chandralok Bldg
36, Janpath
New Delhi
Tel 011-23324764
Email hpturism
@del2.vsnl.in

JAMMU & KASHMIR
WEBSITE jktourism.org

SRINAGAR
TOURIST RECEPTION
CENTRE ❶❿❶
J&K Tourist Development
Corporation
Residency Road
Srinagar
Tel 0194-2472644

LEH
TOURIST RECEPTION
CENTRE ❶❿❶
JKTDC, Leh
Tel 01982-252297

METRO OFFICES
CHENNAI
J&K TOURISM ❶
SF, 36/ 36A
North Usman Rd
Chennai
Telefax 044-28340958
Email tourjk@yahoo.com

KOLKATA
J&K TOURISM ❶
12, JL Nehru Road
Dharmatala
Kolkata
Telefax 033-22285791
Email
jktourism_kol@vsnl.net

MUMBAI
J&K TOURISM ❶❿
25, North Wing, World
Trade Centre, Cuffe
Parade, Colaba
Mumbai
Tel 022-22189040

NEW DELHI
TOURIST RECEPTION
CENTRE **❶**
JKTDC
Wazwan, Stall No. 3
Dilli Haat, New Delhi
Telefax 011-24670505
Mobile 09811693099

KARNATAKA

WEBSITE kstdc.nic.in

BANGALORE
CENTRAL RESERVATIONS
❶ ❶ ❶
Karnataka State Tourism
Development Corporation
Badami House, NR
Square, Bangalore
Tel 080-22275869
Email kstdc@vsnl.in

METRO OFFICES
MUMBAI
MYSORE SALES
INTERNATIONAL LTD **❶**
KSTDC
World Trade Centre
Cuffe Parade, Mumbai
Tel 022-22181658
Email
mysoresales@vsnl.com

NEW DELHI
MYSORE SALES
INTERNATIONAL LTD **❶ ❶**
KSTDC
C-4, State Emporia
Complex, Baba Kharak
Singh Marg, CP
New Delhi
Tel 011-23363863
Email
msildel@del3.vsnl.net.in

KERALA
WEBSITE ktdc.com

TRIVANDRUM
CENTRAL RESERVATIONS **❶ ❶**
Kerala Tourism
Development Corporation
Mascot Square
Trivandrum **Tel** 0471-
2316736 **Email**
centralreservations@ktdc.
com

METRO OFFICES
CHENNAI
KTDC TOURIST INFO **❶ ❶**
TTDC Complex
Wallajah Road, Chennai
Tel 044-25369789
Email ktdcchennai
@hotmail.com

MUMBAI
KTDC TOURIST RECEPTION
CENTRE **❶ ❶ ❶**
Kairali Nirmal Bldg, GF
Nariman Point
Mumbai
Telefax 022-22830491

NEW DELHI
KTDC TOURIST RECEPTION
CENTRE **❶ ❶**
Delhi Anantha
Dilli Haat, Opp INA
Market
New Delhi
Tel 011-24678360

MAHARASHTRA
WEBSITE
maharashtratourism.gov.in
mtdcindia.com

MUMBAI
CENTRAL RESERVATIONS **❶ ❶**
Maharashtra Tourism
Development Corporation
CDO Hutments
Opp LIC Building
Madame Cama Road
Mumbai
Tel 022 22026713/ 7762

PUNE
MTDC REGIONAL OFFICE
❶ ❶
I Block, Central Bldg
Pune
Tel 020-26126867

METRO OFFICES
NEW DELHI
MTDC TOURIST INFO
COUNTER **❶ ❶ ❶**
Maharashtra Food Stall
No. 20, Dilli Haat
New Delhi
Telefax 011-24672655
Mobile 09868342916

NAGALAND

KOHIMA
NAGALAND TOURISM **❶+**
PERMITS
Office of the Directorate
of Nagaland, Kohima
Tel 0370-2243124

METRO OFFICES
GUWAHATI
NAGALAND TOURISM **❶+**
PERMITS
Office of the Deputy
Resident Commissioner
Nagaland House, 6 Mile
Guwahati
Tel 0361-2332158

KOLKATA
NAGALAND TOURISM **❶+**
PERMITS
Office of the Assistant
Resident Commissioner
11, Shakespeare Sarani
Kolkata **Tel** 033-22825226

NEW DELHI
NAGALAND TOURISM **❶+**
PERMITS
Nagaland House
29, Aurangzeb Road
New Delhi
Tel 011-23016411

SIKKIM
WEBSITE sikkim.nic.in

GANGTOK
TOURISM DEPARTMENT
❶ ❶ ❶
Govt of Sikkim
MG Marg, Gangtok
Tel 03592-221634

METRO OFFICES
KOLKATA
SIKKIM TOURIST INFO **❶ ❶**
4/1, Middleton Street
Kolkata
Tel 033-22815328

NEW DELHI
SIKKIM TOURIST INFO **❶ ❶**
New Sikkim House
14, Panchseel Marg
Chanakyapuri

519

New Delhi
Tel 011-26115346/ 171

SILIGURI
Sikkim Tourist Info ❶ ❻
Sikkim Nationalised
Transport Colony
Hill Cart Road, Siliguri
Tel 0353-2512646

TAMIL NADU
Website
tamilnadutourism.org

CHENNAI
Tamil Nadu Tourism
Development
Corporation ❶ ❻
Tamil Nadu Tourism
Complex, 2, Wallajah
Road, Chennai
Tel 044-25383333 **Email**
ttdc@md3.vsnl.net.in

METRO OFFICES
BANGALORE
TTDC Tourist Info ❶ ❻
City Railway Station
Bangalore
Tel 080-26589683/ 172

KOLKATA
TTDC Tourist Info
G-26, Dakshinapan
Shopping Complex
No. 2, Gariyaghat Road
(South), Kolkata
Tel 033-24237432

MUMBAI
TTDC Tourist Info ❶ ❻
G-2A, Royal Grace
Lokmanya Tilak Colony
Marg No. 2, Dadar East
Mumbai
Tel 022-24110118

NEW DELHI
TTDC Tourist Info ❶ ❻
C-1, State Emporia
Complex, Baba Kharakh
Singh Marg, New Delhi
Tel 011-23745427

UTTARANCHAL
GARHWAL
Website gmvnl.com

KUMAON
Website kmvn.org

GMVN OFFICES
RISHIKESH
Trekking & Mountain-
eering Division ❶ ❻
Garhwal Mandal Vikas
Nigam Ltd
Muni-ki-Reti, Rishikesh
Tel 0135-2430799
Email gmvn@gmvnl.com

Central Reservations ❶ ❻
+ Yatra
GMVNL Shail Vihar,
Haridwar Bypass Road,
Rishikesh **Tel** 0135-
2431793/ 2648 **Email**
yatra@gmvnl.com

DEHRA DUN
GMVN Tourist Info ❶ ❻
74/1 Rajpur Road
Dehra Dun
Tel 0135-2746817/ 9308
Email gmvn@gmvnl.com

METRO OFFICES
BANGALORE
GMVN Tourist Info
❶ ❻ ❶
29/ 2, SF, Nanjappa
Mansion KH Road,
Shanti Nagar
Bangalore
Telefax 080-22249378
Mobile 09886180515
Email banglor@gmvn.com

CHENNAI
GMVN Tourist Info
❶ ❻ ❶
Wallajah Road, Chennai
Tel 044-25363524
Mobile 09444239796
Email gmvn@vsnl.com

KOLKATA
GMVN Tourist Info
❶ ❻ ❶
Room No. 224, Marshall
House, 33/1, Netaji
Subhash Road, Kolkata
Tel 033-22610554
09831110999 **Email**
prokolkatta@vsnl.net

MUMBAI
GMVN Tourist Info
❶ ❻ ❶
MTDC, CDO Hutments
Madame Cama Road
Mumbai
Telefax 022-22024415
09869341919 **Email**
mumbai@gmvnl.com

NEW DELHI
GMVN Tourist Info
❶ ❻ ❶
102, Indraprakash Bldg
31, Barakhamba Road
New Delhi
Tel 011-23350481/ 26620
Fax 23327713
Email gmvnl@bol.net.in

KMVN OFFICES
NAINITAL
Central Reservations ❶ ❻
Kumaon Mandal Vikas
Nigam, Tallital, Nainital
Tel 05942-235656 **Email**
crc_kmvn@rediffmail.com

DEHRA DUN
KMVN Tourist Info
❶ ❻ ❶
74/1, Rajpur Road
Dehra Dun
Tel 0135-2749720

METRO OFFICES
BANGALORE
KMVN Tourist Info
❶ ❻ ❶
304, Swiss Complex
33, Race Course Road
Bangalore
Tel 080-22263342

CHENNAI
KMVN Tourist Info
❶ ❻ ❶
Tamil Nadu Tourism
Complex, M-1, Wallajah
Road, Chennai
Tel 044-25362300 **Email**
subbayamma@yahoo.com

KOLKATA
KMVN Tourist Info
❶ ❻ ❶
12A, SF, Netaji Subhash

Road, Kolkata
Tel 033-22207855

MUMBAI
KMVN Tourist Info
❶ ❻ ❶
Core Communication
B/404, Royal Sands
Near City Mall
New Link Rd, Andheri (W)
Mumbai
Tel 022-26304880
Mobile 09869151829

NEW DELHI
KMVN Tourist Info
❶ ❻ ❶
103, Indraprakash Bldg
21, Barakhamba Road
New Delhi
Tel 011-23712246

WEST BENGAL
Website
westbengaltourism.com
wbtourism.com

KOLKATA
West Bengal Tourism Development Corporation ❶ ❻
1, Kiran Shankar Rai Road
C Block
Kolkata
Tel 033-22103194
Email wbtdc@vsnl.com

SILIGURI
West Bengal Tourist Info ❶ ❻
M-4 Building
Pradhan Road
Hill Cart Road
Siliguri
Tel 0353-2517561

DARJEELING
West Bengal Tourist Info ❶ ❻
1, Nehru Road
Tel 0354-2254102

Darjeeling Gorkha Hill Council Tourist Office
❶ ❻
Below Bellevue Hotel
Chowrasta

Darjeeling
Tel 0354-2255351

METRO OFFICES
CHENNAI
West Bengal Tourist Info ❶ ❻
West Bengal Youth Hostel
18, Wallajah Rd
Chennai
Tel 044-28532346

NEW DELHI
West Bengal Tourist Info ❶ ❻
State Emporia Bldg, Baba Kharak Singh Marg
New Delhi
Tel 011-23742840

MOUNTAINEERING INSTITUTES

BHARMOUR
Mountaineering Institute Sub-Centre
Bharmour
Dist Chamba
Tel 01895-225036

DARJEELING
Himalayan Mountaineering Institute
Jawahar Parbat
Darjeeling
West Bengal
Tel 0354-254083/ 087/ 088 Fax 253760

DHARAMSALA
Regional Mountaineering Centre
Swarga Ashram
McLeodganj
Dharamsala
Dist Kangra
Tel 01892-221787

GANGTOK
Sonam Gyatso Mountaineering Institute
(MHA) Govt of India
Ladakhi Mansion
Gangtok, Sikkim
Tel 03592-205620/ 202044

MANALI
Directorate of Mountaineering and Allied Sports
Left Bank, Manali
Tel 01902-252206
Email dmasmanali@yahoo.com
Website himachal.nic/dmas

NEW DELHI
Indian Mountaineering Foundation
6, Benito Juarez Rd
Tel 011-24671211/ 7935/ 1572
Email indmount@del2.vsnl.net.
Website indmount.org

RANIKHET
National Outdoor Leadership School
PO Bag No. 10
Ranikhet 263645
Tel 05966-222301
Email india@nols.edu
Contact Krishnan Kutty

UTTARKASHI
Nehru Institute of Mountaineering
Post Box No. 2
Uttarkashi
Tel 01374-222123
Email india.nim.
rediffmail.com

THE HIMALAYAN CLUB
Mumbai
D-18/ 155, MIG Colony
Bandra (E) Tel 022-26591387, 09322591636
Contact Divyesh Muni

New Delhi
G-66, East of Kailash
Tel 011-26912641
26828479 Contact
Mandeep Singh Soin

Kolkota
C/34, Jal Vayu Vihar
Block LB, Sector-3, Salt Lake Tel 033-22353896
Contact A Bhattacharyya

ACCOMMODATION LISTINGS

METRO RESERVATIONS
To book any State Tourism hotel in your city, see the detailed listing of Tourist Offices on pages 526-529

Legend
TE Taxes extra
NA Not accepted
CCF Chief Conservator of Forests
DFO Divisional Forest Officer

▷ HIMACHAL PRADESH

BAIJNATH STD 01894

PWD Rest House `PWD`
Address Baijnath, Dist Kangra
Rooms 2 **Tariff** Rs 100-150
Credit Cards NA **Facilities**
Caretaker can arrange food, attached bath, hot water
Reservations PWDC, Executive Engineer, Baijnath **Tel** 263035

BANJAR STD 01903

Forest Rest House `FRH`
Address Banjar, Dist Kullu
Rooms 2 **Tariff** Rs 250 **Credit Cards** NA **Facilities** Caretaker can arrange food, attached bath, hot water **Reservations** DFO, Banjar **Tel** 222226

BAROT

PWD Rest House `PWD`
Room 1 **Tariff** Rs 100-150
Credit Cards NA **Facilities**
Caretaker can arrange food, attached bath, hot water **Mandi Reservations** PWD, Deputy Commissioner's Office **Tel** 01905-224129

Accommodation type?
Spot these flags
`HOMESTAY`   `FRH/ PWD`

BHARMOUR STD 0190

Forest Rest House `FRH`
Rooms 4 **Tariff** Rs 250 **Credit Cards** NA **Facilities** Caretaker can arrange food, attached bath, hot water **Reservations** DFO, Bharmour **Tel** 225046

BIR/ BILLING STD 01894

Bara Bhangal Forest Rest House `FRH`
Rooms 2 **Tariff** Rs 250 **Credit Cards** NA **Facilities** Food on order, no bedding facility, attached bath, hot water **Palampur Reservations** DFO, Forest Department **Telefax** 01894-232630

Billing Forest Rest House `FRH`
Rooms 2 **Tariff** Rs 250 **Credit Cards** NA **Facilities** Food on order, no bedding facility, attached bath, hot water **Palampur Reservations** See above

Bir Forest Rest House `FRH`
Rooms 2 **Tariff** Rs 250 **Credit Cards** NA **Facilities** Food on order, attached bath, hot water **Palampur Reservations** See above

CHAMBA STD 01899

Akhand Chandi Hotel `BUDGET`
Address Near Govt College **Tel** 224072 **Fax** 224817 **Rooms** 8 **Tariff** Rs 300 **Credit Cards** NA **Facilities** Hot water, room service, TV

Special hotel facilities?
Spot these flags
`TREKKING`   `BIRDWATCHING`

Chamunda View
Location Hill-facing **Address** Near Bus Stand, Chamba **Tel** 222478 **Rooms** 21 **Tariff** Rs 450-750; TE **Credit Cards** NA **Facilities** Room service, hot water
Kolkata Reservations Diamond Tours and Travels, Jadu Nath Dey Road **Tel** 033-22259639

Hill View Guest House `BUDGET`
Location Central **Address** Behind Laxmi Talkies **Tel** 222027 **Rooms** 5 **Tariff** Rs 250-440 **Credit Cards** NA **Facilities** Parking, room service, TV

Himalayan Orchard Hut `TREKKING`
Location Central **Address** Near Laxmi Narayan Complex, Patnala Bazaar **Tel** 222507, 222607, 0941802401 **Email** manimahesh travels@yahoo.com **Rooms** 9, cottages 2 **Tariff** Rs 350-650 **Credit Cards** NA **Facilities** Restaurant, trekking, rock climbing, swimming pool, laundry, room service, hot water

Hotel Aroma Palace
Location Near Pink Palace **Address** Court Lane **Tel** 225577/777 **Fax** 222224 **Website** aroma-in-chambahp.com **Rooms** 26 **Tariff** Rs 500-3,000 **Credit Cards** Visa, Master **Facilities** Restaurant, Internet, doctor-on-call, room service, TV

Hotel Champak `HPTDC`
Location Hill-facing **Address** Near DC Office **Tel** 222774

Disclaimer Only a representative listing of hotels in each area has been given. The facilities listed may not be exhaustive. Tariff indicates the approx range (lowest to highest) of the rates prevailing at the time of going to press. The listings given here should not be construed as recommendations by the publisher

Rooms 7, dorm 1 **Tariff** Rs 75-300 **Credit Cards** NA **Metro Reservations** See page 518

Hotel Iravati HPTDC
Location Hill-facing **Address** Near DC Office **Tel** 222671 **Rooms** 19 **Tariff** Rs 600-1,200 **Credit Cards** NA **Facilities** Restaurant, parking, doctor-on-call, laundry, room service, TV **Metro Reservations** See page 518

Jamhar Forest Rest House FRH
Address PO Jamhar, Tehsil Chamba **Room** 1 **Tariff** Rs 250 **Credit Cards** NA **Facilities** Caretaker arranges food, attached bath, hot water **Reservations** DFO, Forest Department, Chamba **Tel** 222239, 222639

Jimmy's Inn BUDGET
Location Central **Address** Opp Bus Stand **Tel** 224748 **Rooms** 8 **Tariff** Rs 100-300; TE **Credit Cards** NA **Facilities** Room service, hot water, TV

River View Hotel
Location Hill-facing **Address** Near Bus Stand, Chamba **Tel** 222478, 224067 **Rooms** 21 **Tariff** Rs 350-750 **Credit Cards** NA **Facilities** Restaurant, TV

DALHOUSIE STD 01899

Alps Holiday Resort
Location Near DPS School **Address** Khajjiar Road **Tel** 240775 **Rooms** 16 **Tariff** Rs 1,200-2,400; TE **Credit Cards** AmEx, Visa, Master, BoB **Facilities** Restaurant, pool table, badminton, roller skates, travel desk, attached bath, hot water, room service, TV

Dalhousie Club BUDGET
Location Near Main Bus Stand **Tel** 242254 **Rooms** 6 **Tariff** Rs 410 **Credit Cards** NA **Facilities** Attached bath, hot water, room service

Fair View
Location Garam Sadak **Address** Malviya Road **Tel** 242206/ 825 **Fax** 242825 **Email** hotel_fair_view@yahoo.com **Rooms** 13 **Tariff** Rs 600; TE **Credit Cards** NA **Facilities** Restaurant, pool table, video arcade, hot water, room service, TV

Glory Hotel and Restaurant BUDGET
Location Near bus stand **Tel** 242533 **Rooms** 4 **Tariff** Rs 200-250; TE **Credit Cards** NA **Facilities** Attached bath, hot water

Hotel Craigs
Location Central **Address** Subhash Chowk **Tel** 242124 **Rooms** 7 **Tariff** Rs 350-550; TE **Credit Cards** NA **Facilities** Restaurant, room service, TV

Hotel Geetanjali HPTDC
Location Near The Mall **Tel** 242155 **Rooms** 10 **Tariff** Rs 550-800 **Credit Cards** NA **Facilities** Restaurant, attached bath, hot water, room service, TV **Metro Reservations** See page 518

Hotel Goher
Location Hill-facing **Address** Subhash Chowk **Tel** 242253 **Rooms** 26 **Tariff** Rs 800-1,200; TE **Credit Cards** NA **Facilities** Restaurant, parking, attached bath, hot water, room service, TV

Hotel Grand View
Location Hill-facing **Address** Near bus stand **Tel** 242823, 240760 **Fax** 240609 **Email** grandview@rediffmail.com **Rooms** 27 **Tariff** Rs 1,400-2,100; TE **Credit Cards** Visa, Master **Facilities** Restaurant, fridge, TV

Hotel Manimahesh HPTDC
Location Peak-facing **Tel** 242155 **Rooms** 18 **Tariff** Rs 800-1,500 **Credit Cards** NA

ACCOMMODATION LISTINGS

Facilities Restaurant, bar, drive-in, room service, TV **Metro Reservations** *See page 518*

Mehar Hotel
Location Central **Address** The Mall **Tel** 242179, 240079/ 179 **Rooms** 40 **Tariff** Rs 550-1,300; TE **Credit Cards** NA **Facilities** Restaurant, bar, laundry, attached bath, hot water, room service, TV **Delhi Reservations** Y-30, Hauz Khas **Tel** 011-26518455

Silverton Estate
Location Above Circuit House **Address** Moti Tibba **Telefax** 240674 **Mobile** 09418010674 **Website** heritagehotels.com **Rooms** 5 **Tariff** Rs 850-2,200; TE **Credit Cards** NA **Facilities** Restaurant, putting green, badminton, croquet, travel desk, hot water, room service, TV

Surkhigala Forest Rest House FRH
Location On the outskirts **Rooms** 2 **Tariff** Rs 250 **Credit Cards** NA **Facilities** Caretaker can arrange food, attached bath, hot water **Reservations** DFO, Dalhousie **Tel** 240616

Chonor House
Location Near Thekehen Choling **Address** McLeodganj, Dharamsala **Tel** 221006, 221077 **Telefax** 221468 **Email** chonorhs@norbulingka.org **Website** norbulingka.org **Rooms** 11 **Tariff** Rs 1,400-2,200; TE **Credit Cards** Visa, Master **Facilities** Restaurant, terrace, Internet, TV

Cloud's End Villa
Location Near the Tibetan

Library **Address** Khara Danda Road **Tel** 222109 **Email** tikaraj@rediffmail.com **Rooms** 7 **Tariff** Rs 1,200; TE **Credit Cards** AmEx **Facilities** Dining hall, heaters, TV **Delhi Reservations** Royal Expeditions, R-184, GK-1 **Telefax** 011-26475954

Forest Rest House FRH
Location Adjacent to office of Conservator of Forests **Address** Main Road **Rooms** 4 **Tariff** Rs 250 **Credit Cards** NA **Facilities** Caretaker arranges food, attached bath, hot water **Reservations** DFO, Forest Department, Dharamsala **Tel** 224887

Glenmoor Cottages
Location Valley view **Address** Upper Dharamsala **Tel** 221010 **Fax** 221021 **Website** glenmoor cottages.com **Rooms** 2, cottages 5 **Tariff** Rs 750-3,250; TE **Credit Cards** Visa, Master, BoB **Facilities** Dining hall, doctor-on-call, travel desk, horse riding, room service, TV

Hotel Bhagsu HPTDC
Location Near Namgyal Monastery **Address** McLeodganj, Upper Dharamsala **Tel** 221091-92 **Rooms** 20 **Tariff** Rs 800-1,650 **Credit Cards** NA **Facilities** Restaurant, parking, beer bar, skating, TV **Metro Reservations** *See page 518*

Hotel Tibet
Location Near Dalai Lama's residence **Address** PO McLeodganj **Tel** 221587 **Rooms** 20 **Tariff** Rs 550-990 **Credit Cards** Visa, Master, BoB **Facilities** Restaurant, bar, room service, TV

Loseling Guest House BUDGET
Location Central **Address** McLeodganj, Dharamsala **Tel**

220085, 221087 **Rooms** 17 **Tariff** Rs 150-250 **Credit Cards** NA **Facilities** Attached bath, room service

Pemathang Guest House
Location Valley view **Address** Hotel Bhagsu Road, McLeodganj **Tel** 221871, 09418044740 **Website** pemathang.com **Rooms** 15 **Tariff** Rs 600-900; TE **Credit Cards** NA **Facilities** Veg restaurant, rooms with kitchenette, hot water

Yatri Niwas HPTDC
Location Near bus stand **Tel** 223163 **Rooms** 30 **Tariff** Rs 300-750 **Credit Cards** NA **Facilities** Restaurant, drive-in, parking, room service, TV **Metro Reservations** *See page 518*

JANJHELI

Forest Rest House FRH
Rooms 2 **Tariff** Rs 250 **Credit Cards** NA **Facilities** Caretaker can arrange food, attached bath, hot water **Kullu Reservations** DFO, Kullu **Tel** 01902-222510

PWD Rest House FRH
Rooms 2 **Tariff** Rs 100-150 **Credit Cards** NA **Facilities** Caretaker can arrange food, attached bath, hot water **Kullu Reservations** PWD, Deputy Commissioner's Office **Tel** 01902-222226, 222486

JHIBI STD 01903

Dev Ganga Guest House
TREKKING BUDGET
Location River front **Address** PO Jhibi, Tehsil Banjar **Tel** 227005-6 **Rooms** 5 **Tariff** Rs 165-275 **Credit Cards** NA **Facilities** Hot water, veg meals, attached bath, trekking

Forest Rest House `FRH`
Rooms 2 **Tariff** Rs 250 **Credit Cards** NA **Facilities** Caretaker can arrange food, attached bath, hot water **Reservations** DFO, Banjar **Tel** 01903-222226

Hotel Uhl `HPTDC`
Location Near River Uhl **Tel** 222002 **Rooms** 15 **Tariff** Rs 400-600 **Credit Cards** NA **Facilities** Restaurant, laundry, room service, hot water, TV **Metro Reservations** See page 518

Forest Rest House `FRH`
Location Inside sanctuary **Rooms** 4 **Tariff** Rs 200 **Credit Cards** NA **Chamba Reservations** DFO, Wildlife Department **Tel** 01899-2226397

Hotel Khangsar
Tel 222275-6 **Rooms** 4 **Tariff** Rs 500-700 **Credit Cards** NA **Facilities** Attached bath, hot water, buffet meals

Kaza Retreat `HIGH-END`
Location Monastery precincts

Address Kaza, Dist Lahaul and Spiti **Rooms** 11 **Tariff** Rs 3,000 (includes meals) **Credit Cards** NA **Facilities** Restaurant, attached bath, hot water, TV **Delhi Reservations** Banjara Camps and Retreats, 1A, Hauz Khas Village **Tel** 011-26861397, 26855153 **Email** info@banjara camps.com **Website** banjara camps.com

New Circuit House `PWD`
Rooms 2 VIP, 8 ordinary **Tariff** Rs 100-150 **Credit Cards** NA **Facilities** Caretaker can arrange food, attached bath, hot water **Reservations** PWDC, Additional Deputy Commissioner's Office, PO Kaza, Dist Lahaul and Spiti **Tel** 222202 **Fax** 222215

Sakya's Abode
Tel 222254 **Rooms** 12 **Tariff** Rs 500-700 **Credit Cards** NA **Facilities** Attached bath, hot water, buffet meals

Tourist Lodge `HPTDC`
Address Kaza, Dist Lahaul and Spiti **Tel** 222566 **Rooms** 4, tents 5 **Tariff** Rs 350-500 **Credit Cards** NA **Facilities** Parking, drive-in, room service, attached bath, hot water **Metro Reservations** See page 518

Forest Rest House
Rooms 2 **Tariff** Rs 250 **Credit Cards** NA **Facilities** Food arranged, attached bath, hot water **Dalhousie Reservation** DFO, Dalhousie **Tel** 01899-240616

Hotel Devdar `HPTDC`
Location Hilltop **Address** Khajjiar **Tel** 236333 **Rooms** 18, 2 dorms **Tariff** Rs 75-1,500 **Credit Cards** NA **Facilities** Restaurant, sightseeing, drive-in, parking, TV **Metro Reservations** See page 518

PWD Rest House `PWD`
Rooms 2 **Tariff** Rs 100-150 **Credit Cards** NA **Facilities** Food arranged attached bath, hot water **Nirmand Reservations** Executive Engineer, PWD, Nirmand **Tel** 01904-255140

PWD Rest House `PWD`
Rooms 2 **Tariff** Rs 100-150 **Credit Cards** NA **Facilities** Food arranged attached bath, hot water

LIFE IS CALLING WHERE ARE

SMIRNOFF

Cassettes and CDs

ACCOMMODATION LISTINGS

Nirmand Reservations *See page 525*

LOSAR

PWD Rest House `PWD`
Rooms 2 **Tariff** Rs 100-150 **Credit Cards** NA **Facilities** Caretaker can arrange food, attached bath, hot water **Kaza Reservations** *See Kaza PWD on page 525*

MANALI STD 01902

Adventure Resort `HPTDC`
Location River front **Address** Raison, Dist Kullu **Tel** 240516 **Rooms** 14 huts **Tariff** Rs 650 **Credit Cards** NA **Facilities** Restaurant, parking, camping, lawn, adventure equipment, travel desk **Metro Reservations** *See page 518*

Banon Resorts
Location In the wilderness **Address** New Hope Orchards, Club House Road **Tel** 253026 **Email** banonresorts@vsnl.net **Rooms** 32 **Tariff** Rs 2,000-5,900; TE **Credit Cards** AmEx, Visa, Master, Diners **Facilities** Restaurant and bar, Internet, badminton, TT, room service **Delhi Reservations** E-888, Chittaranjan Park **Tel** 011-26270321

Hotel Beas `HPTDC`
Location River front **Address** Manali, Dist Kullu **Tel** 252832 **Rooms** 31 **Tariff** Rs 250-650 **Credit Cards** NA **Facilities** Dining hall, parking, doctor-on-call, room service, TV **Metro Reservations** *See page 518*

Hotel Sarvari `HPTDC`
Location Central **Address** Kullu **Tel** 222471 **Rooms** 17, dorm 1 **Tariff** Rs 450-1,500, dorm bed

Rs 75 **Credit Cards** NA **Facilities** Restaurant, parking, room service, doctor-on-call, TV **Metro Reservations** *See page 518*

HPTDC Log Huts `HPTDC`
Location Hill-facing **Address** Off Old Manali Road **Tel** 252407 **Rooms** 18 log huts, 2 cottages **Tariff** Rs 1,650-4,000 **Credit Cards** NA **Facilities** Kitchen facility, parking, doctor-on-call, room service, TV **Metro Reservations** *See page 518*

Johnson's Lodge
Location Central **Address** The Mall **Tel** 253764/ 023 **Rooms** 4 cottages **Tariff** Rs 1,000-3,500; TE **Credit Cards** NA **Facilities** Kids' playing area, café, fridge, lawn, room service, TV

Leela Huts
Location 1 km from Manali Bus Stand **Address** Club House Road **Tel** 252464, 253286 **Email** leelahuts@rediffmail.com **Website** leelahuts.com **Rooms** 5 huts **Tariff** Rs 2,500-4,500; TE **Credit Cards** NA **Facilities** Independent huts, kitchen, fireplace, hot water, room service, TV

Manali Resorts
Location Beside River Beas **Address** PO Box 63 **Tel** 252274, 253174 **Fax** 252174 **Website** manaliresorts.com **Rooms** 37 **Tariff** Rs 1,600-3,500; TE **Credit Cards** Master, Visa **Facilities** Restaurant and bar, billiards, gym, sauna, jacuzzi, room service, TV **Delhi Reservations** Manali Resorts, 90/22-B, Malviya Nagar **Telefax** 011-26689091 Online Reservations

New Hut Forest Rest House `FRH`
Location Near Manali Bus Stand

Rooms 2 **Tariff** Rs 250 **Credit Cards** NA **Facilities** Caretaker can arrange food, attached bath, hot water **Kullu Reservations** DFO, Kullu **Tel** 01902-222510

Sylvan Forest Rest House `FRH`
Location Near Manali Bus Stand **Rooms** 2 **Tariff** Rs 250 **Credit Cards** NA **Facilities** Caretaker can arrange food, attached bath, hot water **Kullu Reservations** *See above*

Sitaar Forest Rest House `FRH`
Location Near Manali Bus Stand **Room** 1 **Tariff** Rs 250 **Credit Cards** NA **Facilities** Caretaker can arrange food, attached bath, hot water **Kullu Reservations** *See above*

Snow Crest Manor
TROUT SAFARI
Location Overlooking Manalsu River **Address** Beyond Log Huts **Tel** 253351-4 **Fax** 253188 **Website** ushashriramhotels.com **Rooms** 32 **Tariff** Rs 2,300-9,300; TE **Credit Cards** AmEx, Visa, Master **Facilities** Multi-cuisine restaurant, bar, gym, indoor-outdoor games, trout safari, disco, Internet, room service, TV **Delhi Reservations** Usha Shriram Hotels, 19, Aditya Commercial Complex, Nangalraya, Delhi Cantt **Tel** 011-28520914-15 **Email** ushahtls@vsnl.com Online Reservations

Sunshine Guest House
Location 1 km from Manali Bus Stand **Address** Club House Road **Tel** 252320 **Rooms** 9 **Tariff** Rs 350 **Credit Cards** NA **Facilities** Dining hall, attached bath, hot water, room service

Timber Trail
Location Hilltop **Address**

Manali, Dist Kullu **Tel** 254181-84
Fax 253965 **Email** timbertrail
@glide.net.in **Rooms** 38 **Tariff**
Rs 2,800-3,200; TE **Credit
Cards** AmEx, Visa, Master
Facilities Restaurant and bar,
Internet, TT, badminton, travel
desk, laundry, room service, TV
Delhi Reservations A-459,
Defence Colony **Tel** 011-
24628575/ 77
Online Reservations

Whispering Rocks
Location En route to Rohtang
Address Manali-Rohtang Road,
Palchan **Tel** 256092/ 180 **Website** indiamart.com/whispering
resort **Rooms** 20 **Tariff** Rs
1,600-2,700; TE **Credit Cards**
NA **Facilities** Restaurant and
bar, children's park **Delhi Reservations** 2A/1, Taj Apartments,
Rao Tula Ram Marg **Tel** 011-
26167421/ 8563
Online Reservations

MANDI STD 01905

Hotel Evening Plaza
Location Central **Address** Near
Indra Market **Tel** 225123 **Rooms**
17 **Tariff** Rs 275-850; TE **Credit
Cards** NA **Facilities** Restaurant,
parking, attached bath, room
service, TV

Hotel Mandav HPTDC
Location Near bus stand **Tel**
235503 **Rooms** 13 **Tariff** Rs 300-
850 **Credit Cards** NA **Facilities**
Restaurant, bar, parking, doctor-
on-call, room service, attached
bath, hot water, TV **Metro
Reservations** See page 518

MANIMAHESH

PWD Rest House PWD
Rooms 2 **Tariff** Rs 100-150
Credit Cards NA **Facilities**
Caretaker arranges food,
attached bath, hot water
Chamba Reservations PWD,
Additional Deputy Commis-
sioner's Office **Tel** 01899-240606

MARGI

Forest Rest House FRH
Rooms 2 **Tariff** Rs 250 **Credit
Cards** NA **Facilities** Caretaker
can arrange food, attached bath,
hot water **Ani Reservations**
DFO, Ani, Luhri Office **Tel** 01782-
245874

NAGGAR STD 01902

Hotel Naggar Castle HPTDC
Location Valley-facing **Address**
Naggar **Tel** 248316 **Rooms** 12,
dorm 1 **Tariff** Rs 250-1,500,

dorm bed Rs 75 **Credit Cards**
NA **Facilities** Restaurant, park-
ing, art museum, TV **Metro
Reservations** See page 518

Hotel Ragini
Location Adjacent to Hotel Castle **Address** Naggar **Tel** 248119,
248185 **Email** raginitours@
hotmail.com **Rooms** 9 **Tariff**
Rs 500; TE **Credit Cards** NA
Facilities Restaurant, bar, German bakery, Internet, STD,
ayurvedic massage, yoga centre,
room service, TV

Poornima Rest House
Location Near Hotel Castle
Address Naggar **Tel** 248250,
248319 **Rooms** 6 **Tariff** Rs 550;
TE **Credit Cards** NA **Facilities**
Attached bath, hot water, room
service

Sheetal Guest House
Location Adjacent to Hotel
Castle **Address** Naggar **Tel**
248250, 248319 **Rooms** 14
Tariff Rs 400-1,000; TE **Credit
Cards** NA **Facilities** Restaurant,
room service, attached bath, hot
water, TV

Teji Devi Alliance Guest House
Location Near Hotel Castle
Address Naggar **Tel** 248263

ACCOMMODATION LISTINGS

Rooms 6 **Tariff** Rs 180-400 **Credit Cards** NA **Facilities** TV, room service, guide arranged

Circuit House
Location On a ridge **Address** Narkanda **Rooms** 5 **Tariff** Rs 100-150 **Credit Cards** NA **Facilities** Caretaker can arrange food, attached bath, hot water **Shimla Reservations** PWDC, Deputy Commissioner's Office, Shimla **Telefax** 0177-2653535

Hotel Hatu HPTDC
Location Hilltop **Address** Narkanda, Dist Shimla **Tel** 242430/ 509 **Rooms** 16 **Tariff** Rs 700-1,100 **Credit Cards** NA **Facilities** Restaurant, bar, children's park, electric heaters, geysers, hot water, TV **Metro Reservations** *See page 518*

POH

Circuit House
Rooms 1 VIP, 1 ordinary **Tariff** Rs 100-150 **Credit Cards** NA **Facilities** Caretaker can arrange food, attached bath, hot water **Kaza Reservations** *See Kaza PWD on page 525*

RAMPUR STD 01782

Hotel Bushehr Regency HPTDC
Location River front **Address** Rampur, Dist Shimla **Tel** 234103 **Rooms** 20 **Tariff** Rs 600-1,500 **Credit Cards** NA **Facilities** Restaurant, room service, TV **Metro Reservations** *See page 518*

Hotel Narendra
Location River front **Address** Near Rampur Bus Stand **Tel** 233155/ 655/ 755 **Fax** 234055

Rooms 15 **Tariff** Rs 165-550 **Credit Cards** NA **Facilities** Taxi arranged, attached bath, hot water, laundry, room service, TV

RUPI

Forest Rest House FRH
Rooms 2 **Tariff** Rs 250 **Credit Cards** NA **Facilities** Caretaker arranges food, attached bath, hot water **Sarahan Reservations** DFO, Sarahan **Tel** 01782-274232

PWD Rest House PWD
Rooms 2 **Tariff** Rs 200 **Credit Cards** NA **Facilities** Caretaker arranges food, attached bath, hot water **Reservations** PWDC, Addl Dy Commissioner's Office, Dist Kinnaur **Tel** 01786-222227

SANGLA STD 01786

Baikunth Adventure Camps TREKKING
Address Village Themgarang, Kinnaur **Tel** 242599, 09810672006 **Website** sangla.com **Rooms** 15 deluxe Swiss tents **Tariff** Rs 3,300 (per night/ 2 persons) **Credit Cards** NA **Facilities** Restaurant (multi-cuisine), barbecue, golf, campfire, sightseeing, day hikes and soft treks, river crossing **Delhi Reservations** The Caravan, 109, K-138, Kalkaji **Tel** 011-26451482, 26478096

Banjara Camps TREKKING
Location River front **Address** Batseri Village, Sangla **Tel** 242536 **Tents** 18 **Tariff** Rs 3,300 **Credit Cards** NA **Facilities** Buffet, attached bath, hot water **Delhi Reservations** Banjara Camps and Retreats, 1A, Hauz Khas Village **Tel** 011-26861397, 26855153

Forest Rest House FRH
Location Near Sangla forest **Rooms** 2 **Tariff** Rs 250 **Credit Cards** NA **Facilities** Caretaker can arrange food, attached bath, hot water **Kinnaur Reservations** DFO Kinnaur **Tel** 01786-223358

Mount Kailash Guest House
Location Central **Address** Sangla, Dist Kinnaur **Tel** 242390/ 527 **Rooms** 12 **Tariff** Rs 300-1,000; TE **Credit Cards** NA **Facilities** Restaurant, attached bath, room service, hot water, TV

PWD Rest House PWD
Rooms 2 **Tariff** Rs 200 **Credit Cards** NA **Facilities** Caretaker can arrange food, attached bath, hot water **Kinnaur Reservations** PWDC, Additional Deputy Commissioner's Office, Dist Kinnaur **Tel** 01786-222227

SHILLA

Forest Rest House FRH
Rooms 2 **Tariff** Rs 250 **Credit Cards** NA **Facilities** Caretaker can arrange food, attached bath, hot water **Ani Reservations** DFO, Ani, Luhri Office **Tel** 01782-245874

SHIMLA STD 0177

Bristol Resort
Location Below Hotel Cecil **Address** Chaura Maidan **Tel** 2651730, 2655254 **Rooms** 5 **Tariff** Rs 3,000-7,000 **Credit Cards** Visa, Master **Facilities** Restaurant, garden, drive-in parking

Camp Potter's Hill
Location In a forest **Address** Hotel Amber, Ram Bazaar **Tel** 09418065001 **Email** vibha@pottershill.com **Website**

pottershill.com **Rooms** 11 cottages **Tariff** 1,600-2,600; TE **Credit Cards** Visa, Master **Facilities** Restaurant, barbecue, children's park, indoor/ outdoor games, rappelling, rock climbing

Chapslee
Location Opp Auckland House **Address** Lakkar Bazaar **Tel** 2802542 **Fax** 2658663 **Email** chapslee@vsnl.com **Website** chapslee.com **Rooms** 6 **Tariff** Rs 5,500-7,500 **Credit Cards** Visa, Master **Facilities** Card room, drive-in parking, library, tennis court

Hotel Gulmarg
Location Near Main Bus Stand **Address** The Mall **Tel** 2653168, 2656968 **Fax** 2652380 **Rooms** 112 **Tariff** Rs 250-1,650; TE **Credit Cards** Visa, Master **Facilities** Parking, attached bath, hot water, room service, TV

Hotel Holiday Home `HPTDC`
Location Central **Tel** 2612890-97 **Fax** 2601705 **Rooms** 69 **Tariff** Rs 500-2,400 **Credit Cards** NA **Facilities** Restaurant, bar, coffee shop, billiards, car rental, health club, parking, sauna, video games, TV **Metro Reservations** *See page 518*

Hotel Mayur
Location Near Christ Church **Address** The Ridge **Tel** 2652392-3/ 98 **Fax** 2654919 **Rooms** 29 **Tariff** Rs 850-1,250; TE **Credit Cards** Visa, Master **Facilities** Room service, TV

Hotel Peterhoff `HPTDC`
Location Near State Museum **Tel** 2812236, 2652538 **Fax** 2613801 **Rooms** 19 **Tariff** 1,200-3,500 **Credit Cards** NA **Facilities** Restaurant, drive-in, parking, doctor-on-call, TV **Metro Reservations** *See page 518*

Madan Kunj
Location Near railway station **Address** Khud Cottage, Chaura Maidan **Tel** 2811837 **Fax** 2655480 **Email** rajmaidan@yahoo.com **Rooms** 6 **Tariff** Rs 693-1,750; TE **Credit Cards** NA **Facilities** Laundry, hot water, room service, TV

Springfield's
Location Valley-facing **Address** Opp Tibetan School, Chhota Shimla **Tel** 2621297 **Telefax** 2621298 **Website** ushashriram hotels.com **Rooms** 11 **Tariff** Rs 2,950-4,600; TE **Credit Cards** AmEx, Visa, Master **Facilities** Restaurant, billiards, indoor games, parking, room service **Delhi Reservations** Usha Shriram Hotels, 19, Aditya Commercial Complex, Nangalraya, Delhi Cantt **Tel** 011-25520914-15

The Cecil `HIGH-END`
Location Forest view **Address** Chaura Maidan **Tel** 2804848 **Fax** 2811024 **Email** reservations@thececil.com **Website** oberoi hotels.com **Rooms** 79 **Tariff** Rs 6,500-10,000; TE **Credit Cards** AmEx, Visa, Master **Facilities** Restaurant, bar, activities for children, billiards, indoor swimming pool, library, spa, TV **Delhi Reservations** Oberoi Hotels and Resorts, 7, Shamnath Marg **Tel** 011-23890606

Woodrina
Location Hillside **Address** Shimla-Kufri Road **Tel** 09816069315 **Rooms** 24 **Tariff** Rs 900-1,500 **Credit Cards** NA **Facilities** Restaurant, TV **Delhi Reservations** Classic Tours, K1/ 136, CR Park **Tel** 011-26421425-6

Woodville Palace
Location Hillside **Address** Raj Bhawan Road **Tel** 2623919 **Rooms** 25 **Tariff** Rs 2,200-7,000; TE **Credit Cards** AmEx, Visa, Master **Facilities** Restaurant,

room service, hot water, TV **Delhi Reservations** C-7, J-Block Market, Saket **Tel** 011-26868992/ 23

YMCA
Location Behind Christ Church **Address** The Ridge **Tel** 2650021 **Fax** 2811016 **Rooms** 40 **Tariff** Rs 346-660; TE **Credit Cards** NA **Facilities** Internet, billiards, gym, TT, rooms with and without attached bath, meals arranged (Rs 55-85); temporary membership Rs 40

YWCA
Location Near Post-office **Address** The Mall **Tel** 2803081, 09817065206 **Email** sumati999@rediffmail.com **Rooms** 13 **Tariff** Rs 300-1,000 **Credit Cards** NA **Facilities** Meals arranged (Rs 30); temporary membership Rs 20

SHOJA STD 01902

Shoja Retreat
Location Hilltop **Address** Village Shoja, PO Shoja, Tehsil Banjar **Tel** 238070 **Email** info@banjara camps.com **Website** banjara camps.com **Rooms** 8 **Tariff** Rs 3,200 **Credit Cards** NA **Facilities** Restaurant, attached bath, hot water, organised trips **Delhi Reservations** Banjara Camps and Retreats, 1A, Hauz Khas Village **Tel** 011-26855153

Forest Rest House FRH
Rooms 2 **Tariff** Rs 250 **Credit Cards** NA **Facilities** Caretaker can arrange food, attached bath, hot water **Banjar Reservations** DFO, Banjar **Tel** 01903-222226

PWD Rest House PWD
Rooms 2 **Tariff** Rs 100-150 **Credit Cards** NA **Facilities**

Caretaker can arrange food, attached bath, hot water **Kullu Reservations** PWD, Deputy Commissioner's Office, Kullu **Tel** 01902-222226, 222486

TABO STD 01906

Tabo Retreat
Location Near Tabo Gompa **Address** Village Tabo, Dist Spiti **Tel** 233381 **Rooms** 10 **Tariff** Rs 3,000 (including meals) **Credit Cards** NA **Facilities** Restaurant, attached bath, hot water **Delhi Reservations** *See Banjara Camps, Shoja left*

Tashi Khangsar
Tel 223346/ 77 **Rooms** 4 **Tariff** Rs 350-500 **Credit Cards** NA **Facilities** Hot water on request

Tabo Monastery
Address Tabo, Dist Spiti **Tel** 223403 **Rooms** 12 **Tariff** Rs 200-300 **Credit Cards** NA **Facilities** Attached bath, hot water

TAKRASI

Forest Rest House FRH
Rooms 2 **Tariff** Rs 250 **Credit Cards** NA **Facilities** Caretaker can arrange food, attached bath, hot water **Banjar Reservations** DFO, Banjar **Tel** 01903-222226

TARAGARH STD 01894

SATH Camps
TREKKING/ HANG GLIDING
Location Near tea country **Address** Bir Village **Tel** 268559 **Email** sath@sargroup.com **Website** sathcamps.com **Rooms** 8 Swiss tents **Tariff** Rs 1,500 **Credit Cards** NA **Facilities** Hot water, target shooting, equipment for fishing, organised treks, hang gliding, guide, STD/ ISD

Delhi Reservations SAR House, WZ–106/ 101, Rajouri Garden Extn, New Delhi **Tel** 011-25465002, 25934724

Taragarh Palace
Location Garden setting **Address** PO Taragarh **Tel** 242034 **Telefax** 243077 **Email** reservations@taragarh.com **Website** taragarh.com **Rooms** 16 **Tariff** Rs 1,100-2,750 **Credit Cards** AmEx **Facilities** In-room fridge, swimming pool, tennis, doctor-on-call, railway station/ airport pick-up on request **Delhi Reservations** 15, Institutional Area, Lodhi Road, New Delhi **Tel** 011-24643046

TARAL

Forest Rest House FRH
Rooms 2 **Tariff** Rs 250 **Credit Cards** NA **Facilities** Caretaker can arrange food, attached bath, hot water **Ani Reservations** DFO, Ani, Luhri Office **Tel** 01782-245874

TRIUND

Forest Rest House FRH
Location Ridge of the Dhauladhar **Rooms** 4 **Tariff** Rs 250 **Credit Cards** NA **Facilities** Caretaker can arrange food, attached bath, hot water **Dharamsala Reservations** DFO, Forest Department, Main Road **Tel** 01892-224887

▷ LADAKH AND ZANSKAR

ALCHI STD 01982

Choskar Guest House
Location 5 mins from Alchi Monastery **Address** Alchi Village **Tel** 227084 **Rooms** 12 **Tariff**

Rs 500-800 **Credit Cards** NA **Facilities** Restaurant, guide and pony arranged, attached bath, hot water, room service, TV **Leh Reservations** Contact Moruk Dorjay, Norgasling, Leh **Tel** 01982-254773 **Email** mdorjay@yahoo.co.in

Hotel Samdupling
Address Alchi **Tel** 253294, 227104, 09419178391 **Rooms** 14 **Tariff** Rs 2,100-2,700 **Credit Cards** NA **Facilities** Restaurant, hot water (open from Jun-Oct)

Zinskhang Holiday Home
Address Alchi **Tel** 227086 **Rooms** 16 **Tariff** Rs 1,500-2,700 **Credit Cards** NA **Facilities** Garden restaurant, hot water

LEH STD 01982

Hotel Dreamland TREKKING
Location Central **Address** Fort Road, Main Market **Tel** 252089, 09419178197 **Email** info@dreamladakh.com **Website** dreamladakh.com **Rooms** 12 **Tariff** Rs 450-850 **Credit Cards** Visa, Master **Facilities** Restaurant, travel desk, organise treks, TV

Hotel Green Land
Location Near Shanti Stupa

Address Changspa **Tel** 253156 **Rooms** 7 **Tariff** Rs 250 **Credit Cards** NA **Facilities** Room service, food against payment

Hotel Ibex TREKKING
Location Near Leh Taxi Stand **Address** Leh **Tel** 252281 **Rooms** 6 **Tariff** Rs 750 **Credit Cards** NA **Facilities** Restaurant, trekking, bar, room service, TV

Hotel Kanglachen TREKKING
Location Opp Police Station **Address** Leh **Tel** 252523, 250909 **Rooms** 25 **Tariff** Rs 2,100-2,700 **Credit Cards** AmEx **Facilities** Restaurant, travel desk, treks, room service, hot water, car park

Hotel Lharimo
Location Central **Address** Fort Road **Tel** 253345 **Rooms** 32 **Tariff** Rs 1,365-2,350 **Credit Cards** NA **Facilities** Restaurant, beer bar, room service, hot water, TV **Delhi Reservations** Welcome Travels, 209/88, Skipper Corner, Nehru Place **Tel** 011-26424638

Hotel Omasi La
Location Mountain-facing **Address** Changspa **Tel** 252119, 09419178815, 09419178472 **Rooms** 35 **Tariff** Rs 2,400-4,000;

including meals **Credit Cards** NA **Facilities** Restaurant, hot water, TV, phone, oxygen

Khangri Hotel
Location Central **Address** Main Bazaar **Tel** 252311/ 052 **Rooms** 35 **Tariff** Rs 1,600-2,500 **Credit Cards** Visa, Master, Diners **Facilities** Sightseeing, room service, attached bath, hot water, TV

Ladakh Sarai
Location Near airport **Address** Ayu Village **Tel** 244063 **Rooms** 14 **Tariff** Rs 2,048 **Credit Cards** AmEx, Visa, Master **Facilities** Restaurant, sightseeing, room service **Delhi Reservations** 33, Rani Jhansi Road **Tel** 011-23511483, 23671055 **Website** mountaintravelindia.com **Online Reservations**

Oriental Guest House
Location Below Shanti Stupa **Address** Changspa **Tel** 253153, 250516 **Fax** 252414 **Rooms** 24 **Tariff** Rs 100-600; TE **Credit Cards** NA **Facilities** Restaurant, travel desk, Internet, heating, room service, attached bath, hot water

Shambha-La TREKKING
Location In poplar tree grove

Cassettes and CDs

ACCOMMODATION LISTINGS

Address Skara **Tel** 251100, 253500 **Fax** 252607 **Rooms** 25 **Tariff** Rs 2,100-2,800 (including meals) **Credit Cards** AmEx **Facilities** Restaurant, arrange treks, sightseeing, doctor-on-call, free drop to town, hot water, heaters, laundry, room service, TV **Delhi Reservations** WelcomHeritage, C7, J-Block Market, Saket **Tel** 011-26561875, 09810035145

Snow View
Location Near orchards **Address** Upper Changspa **Tel** 250153, 252504 **Email** snowviewleh@hotmail.com **Rooms** 10 **Tariff** Rs 300-600 **Credit Cards** NA **Facilities** Restaurant, guides arranged, doctor-on-call, room service

NUBRA VALLEY

Shambha-La
Location Near river **Address** Tirith **Rooms** 25 beds **Tariff** Rs 2,760 (with meals) **Credit Cards** NA **Facilities** Catering **Delhi Reservations** K-40, Hauz Khas Enclave **Tel** 011-26867785, 09810035145 **Email** ladakh_shambala@vsnl.com

Yarab Tso
Location Near river **Address** Village Kyagar (Tiger) **Rooms** 12 **Tariff** Rs 1,400-1,800 with meals **Credit Cards** AmEx, Visa (accepted in Gurgaon only) **Facilities** Restaurant, doctor-on-call, room service **Gurgaon Reservations** 229/ DLF Galleria, Gurgaon **Tel** 0124-2806027-29

PADUM STD 01983

Hotel Ibex
Location Central **Address** Padum, Zanskar, Dist Kargil **Tel**

245012, 245021, 09418002171 **Email** zanskari@yahoo.co.in, **Rooms** 15 **Tariff** Rs 500-1,100 **Credit Cards** NA **Facilities** Restaurant, phone, room services

Marq Guest House
Location Central **Address** Padum, Zanskar **Tel** 245021/ 71, 09418002171 **Email** marq_guest house@yahoo.co.in **Rooms** 8 **Tariff** Rs 300-500 **Credit Cards** NA **Facilities** Restaurant, travel desk, room service, hot water

Tourist Bungalow **JKTDC**
Location Valley-facing **Address** Tourist Office, Zanskar **Rooms** 6 **Tariff** Rs 100 **Credit Cards** NA **Facilities** Room service, attached bath **Kargil Reservations** Tourist Office **Tel** 01985-232721/ 266 **Metro Reservations** See pages 518-519

◩ UTTARANCHAL

AGODA

Forest Rest House **FRH**
Address Agora **Rooms** 2 **Tariff** Rs 100 **Credit Cards** NA **Facilities** Caretaker arranges food, hot water **Uttarkashi Reservations** DFO, Uttarkashi **Tel** 01374-222444

ALMORA STD 05962

Deodar Resort
Location In the forest **Address** Papparsalle **Tel** 233025 **Email** rwheeler@rediffmail.com **Rooms** 3 **Tariff** Contact directly **Credit Cards** NA **Facilities** Dining hall, railway station pick-up (Rs 750), yoga classes

Gollu Devta Rest House
BUDGET
Location Central **Address** College Road, Papparsalle **Tel** 230250 **Rooms** 31 **Tariff** Rs 300-600 **Credit Cards** NA **Facilities** Dining hall, TV

Hotel Holiday Home **KMVN**
Location Near Almora University **Address** Mall Road **Tel** 230250 **Rooms** 17 **Tariff** Rs 450-750 **Credit Cards** NA **Facilities** Restaurant, travel desk, doctor-on-call, laundry, room service, hot water **Metro Reservations** See pages 520-21

Kalmatia Sangam Himalaya Resort **TREKKING** **HIGH-END**
Location Almora-Upper Binsar Road **Address** Kalimat Estate, PO Box 002 **Tel** 233625 **Email** geeta1@nde.vsnl.net.in **Website** kalmatia-sangam.com **Rooms** 9 **Tariff** Rs 9,800 (2N/ 3D, inclusive of all meals) **Credit Cards** Visa, Master **Facilities** Trekking, restaurant, travel desk, lockers on request, doctor-on-call, laundry, room service **Delhi Reservations** B-11, Gulmohar Park **Tel** 011-26862067

Kasaar Jungle Resort
HIGH-END
Address Binsar Road, Kasar Devi **Telefax** 251127 **Website** kasaarjungleresort.cjb.net **Rooms** 15 **Tariff** Rs 1,800-2,000 **Credit Cards** Visa, Master **Facilities** Restaurant, indoor games, travel desk, lockers, doctor-on-call, attached bath, hot water, TV **Delhi Reservations** E-74, Bharat Nagar, New Friends Colony **Tel** 011-26936948 **Fax** 26936945

New TRH Danya **KMVN**
Location Main Road **Address** Almora **Tel** 220588 **Rooms** 2, dorm 1 **Tariff** Rs 200-300, dorm bed Rs 50 **Credit Cards** NA **Facilities** Catering, hot water, TV

Metro Reservations *See pages 520-21*

Snow View Resort `HIGH-END`
Location Kasar Devi Binsar Road **Address** Papparsalle **Tel** 233650 **Rooms** 12 **Tariff** Rs 2,500-2,800; TE **Credit Cards** NA **Facilities** Restaurant, travel desk, sightseeing **Delhi Reservations** 40 Ashoka Avenue, Sainik Farms **Tel** 011-26518527

`BHOJBASA`

Tourist Rest House `GMVN`
Address Bhojbasa **Rooms** 2 dorms, tents 5 **Tariff** Rs 200 **Credit Cards** NA **Facilities** Caretaker arranges food **Metro Reservations** *See pages 520-21*

`BINSAR SANCTUARY`

Forest Rest House
Location Inside the forest **Rooms** 2 **Tariff** Rs 300 **Credit Cards** NA **Facilities** Attached bath, caretaker can prepare food **Reservations** Wildlife Warden, Binsar **Tel** 05962-252279

`CORBETT STD 05947`

Camp Forktail Creek `TREKKING`
Location Near tiger reserve **Address** Village Bhakrakot, PO Mohan **Tel** 287804 **Email** info@campforktailcreek.com **Website** campforktailcreek.com **Rooms** 11 tents **Tariff** Rs 1,625-2,250 **Credit Cards** AmEx **Facilities** Trekking, angling, day hikes, elephant and jungle safaris, overnight camping **Delhi Reservations** 26, Kailash Hills **Tel** 011-26914417 **Fax** 26832883

Claridges Corbett Hideaway `HIGH-END`
Location Near tiger reserve **Address** Garjia, Dhikuli, Ramnagar **Tel** 284132 **Fax** 284133 **Website** corbetthideaway. com **Rooms** 48 cottages **Tariff** Rs 4,250-4,750; TE **Credit Cards** AmEx, Master, Visa **Facilities** Gurney House Restaurant, bar, pool, Ayurvedic massage, safari, travel desk, doctor-on-call, heaters **Delhi Reservations** DD-29, Nehru Enclave, Kalkaji **Tel** 011-26413304

Corbett Riverside Resort
Location Overlooking Kosi River **Address** Gorjia, PO Dhikuli, Ramnagar **Tel** 284125, 09837067575 **Telefax** 284126 **Email** info@corbettriverside.com **Website** corbettriverside.com **Rooms** 28 **Tariff** Rs 2,500-4,000;TE **Credit Cards** AmEx, Visa, Master **Facilities** Multi-cuisine restaurant, indoor/ outdoor games, safari, attached bath, hot water, TV lounge **Delhi Reservations** A1, Cariappa Marg, Sainik Farms, Gate 2 **Tel** 011-26565191, 09891515188

Forest Rest Houses `FRH`
Location Inside park **Address** Corbett Tiger Reserve, Ramnagar **Tel** 251489 **Telefax** 253977 **Rooms** 70 **Tariff** Indians Rs 250-500, foreigners Rs 600-1,200 **Credit Cards** NA **Facilities** Attached bath, hot water on demand

Krishna Nidhi Corbett Inn
Address Ramnagar **Tel** 251755 **Rooms** 12 **Tariff** Rs 590-990 **Facilities** Restaurant, doctor-on-call, attached bath, hot water

Quality Inn `HIGH-END`
Location River front **Address** Kumeria Reserve Forest, PO Mohan **Tel** 287820 **Email** qicjr @hotmail.com **Rooms** 22 **Tariff** Rs 2,800-4,350 (meals included) **Credit Cards** Visa, Master **Facilities** Restaurant, Corbett safari, sightseeing, room service, attached bath, hot water, TV

ACCOMMODATION LISTINGS

DUGALBITTA

PWD Inspection Bungalow `PWD`
Address Dugalbitta **Rooms** 3
Tariff Rs 200 **Credit Cards** NA
Facilities Caretaker can prepare
food, hot water, attached bath
Rudraprayag Reservations
Deputy Manager's Office, PWD
Tel 01364-233300

GANGOTRI STD 013772

Forest Rest House `FRH`
Address Gangotri **Rooms** 2
Tariff Indians Rs 300-500, for-
eigners Rs 900-1,500 **Credit
Cards** NA **Facilities** Caretaker
can prepare food, hot water
Bhagirathi Reservations CCF
Office **Tel** 0135-2431159

TRH Gangotri `GMVN`
Location River front **Tel** 22221
Rooms 23, dorms 8 **Tariff**
Rs 140-1,200 **Credit Cards** NA
Facilities Restaurant, travel
desk, phone at reception, doc-
tor-on-call, room service, hot
water **Metro Reservations** See
pages 520-21
Online Reservations

`TIP` There are 2 GMVN Tourist
Rest Houses (TRHs) in Gangotri,
and both share the same phone
number and operate Apr-Oct

GAURIKUND STD 01364

Tourist Bungalow `GMVN`
Address Gaurikund **Tel** 269202,
09412913088 **Email**
gmvn@gmvnl.com **Website**
gmvnl.com **Rooms** 17, dorms 3
Tariff Rs 150-650 **Credit Cards**
NA **Facilities** Attached bath
Metro Reservations See pages
520-21
Online Reservations

GHANGARIA STD 01381

Tourist Rest House `GMVN`
Location Central **Tel** 226228
Rooms 7, dorms 2 **Tariff** Rs 60-
950 **Credit Cards** NA **Facilities**
Restaurant, sightseeing, laundry,
hot water, room service **Metro
Reservations** See pages 520-21

GOPESHWAR STD 01327

Tourist Rest House `GMVN`
Location Central **Address** PO
Gopeshwar **Tel** 252468 **Rooms**
4, dorms 2 **Tariff** Rs 60-450
Credit Cards NA **Facilities**
Restaurant, sightseeing, laundry,
hot water, room service **Metro
Reservations** See page 520-21
Online Reservations

GUPTKASHI STD 01364

Tourist Bungalow `GMVN`
Location Near bus stand **Tel**
267221 **Rooms** 18, dorms 3
Tariff Rs 140-650 **Credit Cards**
NA **Facilities** Restaurant, hot
water on request **Metro Reser-
vations** See page 520-21
Online Reservations

GWALDHAM STD 01363

Tourist Rest House `GMVN`
`TREKKING`
Location Near Kendriya
Vidyalaya **Tel** 274244 **Rooms** 6,
dorms 2 **Tariff** Rs 75-570 **Credit
Cards** NA **Facilities** Restaurant,
travel desk, trekking, guides
arranged, doctor-on-call, room
service, attached bath, hot water,
TV **Metro Reservations** See
pages 520-21

HANUMANCHATTI STD 01375

Tourist Rest House `GMVN`
Location River front **Address**

Near bus stand **Tel** 23371
Rooms 6, dorms 3 **Tariff** Rs
130-700 **Credit Cards** NA **Facilities** Restaurant, attached bath,
room service, hot water (open
from May to Nov) **Metro Reservations** See pages 520-21

HAR-KI-DUN

Forest Rest House `FRH`
Address Har-ki-Dun **Rooms** 2
Tariff Rs 250 **Credit Cards** NA
Facilities Hot water, attached
bath **Dehra Dun Reservations**
Director, Rajaji National Park **Tel**
0135-2621669

Tourist Rest House `GMVN`
Address TRH, Har-ki-Dun
Rooms 5, dorms 2 **Tariff** Rs
100-400; TE **Credit Cards** NA
Facilities Hot water, attached
bath **Metro Reservations** See
pages 520-21

HARSIL STD 01377

Tourist Rest House `GMVN`
Location Near bus stand
Address Harsil **Tel** 2332210
Rooms 12, dorm 1 **Tariff** Rs
100-700 **Credit Cards** NA **Facili-
ties** Restaurant, doctor-on-call,
travel desk **Metro Reservations**
See pages 520-21
Online Reservations

JAGESHWAR STD 05962

Forest Rest House `FRH`
Location Near bus stand
Address Jageshwar, PO
Punuwanola **Tel** 09412375567
Rooms 2 **Tariff** Rs 300-500
Almora Reservations CCF
Office **Tel** 05962-230229

Tourist Rest House Jagnath
`KMVN`
Location Near Jagnath Temple

Address PO Jageshwar **Tel** 263028 **Rooms** 9, dorm 1 **Tariff** Rs 400-700, dorm bed Rs 60 **Credit Cards** NA **Facilities** Restaurant, travel desk, attached bath, hot water **Metro Reservations** See pages 520-21

JOSHIMATH STD 01389

Hotel Dronagiri
Location Near Jyothi Vidyalaya **Address** Joshimath, Dist Chamoli **Tel** 222254 **Telefax** 222221 **Rooms** 17 **Tariff** Rs 750-3,000 **Credit Cards** NA **Facilities** Restaurant, laundry, room service, attached bath, hot water, TV **Rishikesh Reservations** Suri Enterprise, 47 Station Road **Tel** 0135-2430591 **Fax** 2430867

Hotel Kamat
Location Near ropeway **Address** Joshimath, Dist Chamoli **Tel** 222155 **Fax** 222100 **Rooms** 22 **Tariff** Rs 250-800 **Credit Cards** NA **Facilities** Restaurant, travel desk, doctor-on-call, laundry, room service, attached bath, hot water, TV

Old Tourist Rest House GMVN
Location Near bus stand **Address** Near Upper Bazaar **Tel** 222118 **Rooms** 22, dorm 1 **Tariff**

Rs 300-500, dorm bed Rs 70-100 **Credit** Cards NA **Facilities** Restaurant, laundry, room service, attached bath, hot water **Metro Reservations** See pages 520-21

Tourist Rest House GMVN
Location Above Gandhi Maidan **Address** Joshimath **Tel** 222226 **Rooms** 31 **Tariff** Rs 500-700 **Credit Cards** NA **Facilities** Canteen, travel desk, hot water **Metro Reservations** See pages 520-21

KARANPRAYAG STD 01363

Tourist Rest House GMVN
Location River front **Address** Opp Karanlok Lodge, Dist Chamoli **Email** gmvn@gmvnl. com **Website** gmvn.com **Tel** 244210 **Rooms** 16 **Tariff** Rs 200-600 **Facilities** Angling, rafting, restaurant, travel desk, trips organised, doctor-on-call, laundry, room service, attached bath, hot water **Metro Reservations** See pages 520-21

Online Reservations

KEDARNATH STD 01364

Tourist Rest House GMVN
Address TRH, Kedarnath **Tel**

263228 **Rooms** 16, dorms 2 **Tariff** Rs 150-1,200; TE **Credit Cards** NA **Facilities** Restaurant, hot water, attached bath, room service **Metro Reservations** See pages 520-21

MORI

HRR Camp
Location Near Tons River **Address** Village Mori **Rooms** tents 12 **Tariff** Rs 1,000 (stay only) **Credit Cards** AmEx, Visa, Master **Delhi Reservations** N-8 Green Park Main **Tel** 011-26852602, 26968169 **Website** hrrindia.com

Rafting Camp Lunagadh
Location Near Tons River **Address** Village Mori **Rooms** 25 tents **Tariff** Rs 4,000 (2D/ 2N meals and rafting trip inclusive) **Credit Cards** AmEx, Visa, Master **Delhi Reservations** Aquaterra Adventures, S-507, Greater Kailash II **Tel** 011-29212641/ 2760 **Website** aquaterra adventures.com 1

Online Reservations

MUSSOORIE STD 0135

Ambika Palace
Location Hill-top **Address**

LIFE IS CALLING WHERE ARE YOU?

SMIRNOFF

Cassettes and CDs

ACCOMMODATION LISTINGS

Waverley Convent Chowk **Tel** 2631229 **Rooms** 20 **Tariff** Rs 250-1,600 **Credit Cards** NA **Facilities** Laundry, intercom, room service, hot water, TV

Brentwood
Location Hill-top **Address** Kulri Bazaar **Tel** 2632126 **Rooms** 60 **Tariff** Rs 1,300-4,000; TE **Credit Cards** Visa, Master **Facilities** Restaurant, lockers, forex, room service, hot water, TV

Claridges Nabha HIGH-END
Location In a forest **Address** Barlowganj Road **Tel** 2631426-7 **Fax** 2631425 **Email** nabha claridges@rediffmail.com **Rooms** 20 **Tariff** Rs 3,950-4,950; TE **Credit Cards** AmEx, Visa, Master, Diners **Facilities** Dining hall, bar, gym, video game parlour **Delhi Reservations** Claridges, 12, Aurangzeb Road **Tel** 011-23010211

Cloud's End Forest Resort
Location Hill-top **Address** PO Box 1, Mussoorie **Tel** 2632242, 09412050242 **Email** info@cloudend.com **Website** cloudend.com **Rooms** 7 **Tariff** Rs 400-3,200; TE **Credit Cards** NA **Facilities** Restaurant, transport arranged, excursion trips, nature walks, room service, attached bath, hot water
Online Reservations

Ever Green
Location Near bus stand **Address** Picture Palace Road **Tel** 2632503, 2631503 **Rooms** 17 **Tariff** Rs 200-1,200 **Credit Cards** NA **Facilities** Restaurant, laundry, attached bath, hot water, TV

Garhwal Terrace GMVN
Location Near Library Bus Stand

Address The Mall **Tel** 2632682 **Fax** 2632683 **Website** gmvnl. com **Rooms** 29 **Tariff** Rs 700-1,700; TE **Credit Cards** Visa, Master **Facilities** Terrace Restaurant, bar, parking **Metro Reservations** See pages 520-21
Online Reservations

Green View BUDGET
Address Library **Tel** 2631361 **Rooms** 12 **Tariff** Rs 250-500 **Credit Cards** NA **Facilities** Phone, TV

Hamer International
Location Central **Address** The Mall, Kulri Bazaar **Tel** 2632818 **Rooms** 25 **Tariff** Rs 400-900;TE **Credit Cards** NA **Facilities** Hot water, parking, phone, laundry, room service, TV

Hotel Padmini Nivas
Address Library, The Mall **Tel** 2631093 **Telefax** 2632793 **Email** harshada@vsnl.com **Website** hotelpadmininivas.com **Rooms** 26 **Tariff** Rs 750-5,400 **Credit Cards** NA **Facilities** Veg restaurant, parking

Jaypee Residency Manor
LUXURY
Location Hill view **Address** Barlowganj **Tel** 2631800 **Website** jaypeehotels.com **Rooms** 90 **Tariff** Rs 5,500-12,000; TE **Credit Cards** AmEx, Visa, Master, Diners **Facilities** Restaurant, health club **Delhi Reservations** Hotel Vasant Continental, Vasant Vihar **Tel** 011-26148800
Online Reservations

Kasmanda Palace
Location Valley facing **Address** The Mall Road **Tel** 2632424, 2633949 **Website** indian heritagehotels.com **Rooms** 15 **Tariff** Rs 2,300- 3,000; TE **Credit**

Cards AmEx, Visa, Master **Facilities** Restaurant, doctor-on-call, golf course, horse riding, TV **Delhi Reservations** Welcom Heritage Hotels, 31, 1st Floor, Sri Fort Road **Tel** 011-26266650-55

Savoy Hotel
Location Hill-facing **Address** Near Library Chowk **Tel** 2632120/ 010 **Rooms** 35 **Tariff** Rs 800-2,500; TE **Credit Cards** NA **Facilities** Restaurant, travel desk, room service, laundry, TV

NAINITAL STD 05942

Alka The Lake Side Hotel
Location Near Naini Lake **Address** The Mall **Tel** 236626-28 **Website** alkahotel.com **Rooms** 45 **Tariff** Rs 1,700-4,500; TE **Credit Cards** AmEx, Visa, Master **Facilities** Restaurant, central heating, travel desk, TV **Delhi Reservations** Pathfinders, S-325, Greater Kailash-II **Tel** 011-29219325
Online Reservations

Balrampur House
Location Above High Court **Address** Mallital **Tel** 236236 **Fax** 239902 **Rooms** 19 **Tariff** Rs 1,200-3,500 **Credit Cards** NA **Facilities** Multi-cuisine restaurant, room service, hot water, TV **Delhi Reservations** Balrampur House Annex, 16, Tilak Marg **Tel** 011-23384495
Online Reservations

Chevron Fairhavens
BIRDWATCHING
Location Adjacent to GPO **Address** Mallital **Tel** 236057 **Telex** 236604 **Website** chevron-hotels.com **Rooms** 30 **Tariff** Rs 2,000-3,200; TE **Credit Cards** AmEx, Visa, Master, Diners **Facilities** Hiking, multi-cuisine

restaurant, parking, horse riding, nature walk, birdwatching, boating, doctor-on-call **Delhi Reservations** Chevron Hotels, D-9/C, Acharya Niketan, Mayur Vihar-I **Tel** 22753151 **Email** hotels@bol.net.in
Online Reservations

Claridges Naini Retreat
HIGH-END

Location Near The Mall **Address** Ayarpatta Slopes **Tel** 235105 **Fax** 235103 **Rooms** 33 **Tariff** Rs 3,200-6,000; TE **Credit Cards** AmEx, Visa, Master **Facilities** Restaurant, bar, central heating, forex, room service **Delhi Reservations** Leisure Hotels Ltd, DD 29, Nehru Enclave, Kalkaji **Tel** 011-26293905

Evelynn Hotel

Location Lake view **Address** Mall Road **Tel** 235467 **Fax** 236457 **Rooms** 60 **Tariff** Rs 600-3,500; TE **Credit Cards** AmEx, Visa, Master **Facilities** Restaurant, travel desk, Internet, doctor-on-call, room service **Mumbai Reservations** Anand Travels, 14 Wawda Building, 252, Lady Jamshedji Tata Road **Tel** 022-24443487 **Fax** 2446467
Online Reservations

Hotel Arif Castle **HIGH-END**

Location Near Balika Vidya Mandir **Address** Near The Mall **Tel** 236231 **Fax** 236231 **Email** arifcastlesnts@hotmail.com **Rooms** 66 **Tariff** Rs 3,600-4,900; TE **Credit Cards** AmEx, Visa, Master, BoB **Facilities** Coffee shop, billiards, forex, Internet **Delhi Reservations** A-100, Lajpat Nagar-I **Tel** 011-32403110, 09818261720 **Email** hotelarif@vsnl.com
Online Reservations

Hotel Krishna

Location Lake front **Address** Central Mall **Tel** 231646 **Fax** 237550 **Rooms** 22 **Tariff** Rs 1,200-2,400; TE **Credit Cards** Visa, Master **Facilities** Restaurant, travel desk, doctor-on-call, laundry, room service, TV

Hotel Langdale Manor

Location Near lake **Address** Langdale Estate, Mallital **Tel** 235447 **Fax** 231362 **Rooms** 27 **Tariff** Rs 900-1,400; TE **Credit Cards** NA **Facilities** Restaurant, sightseeing, travel desk, doctor-on-call, laundry, room service, hot water, TV

Hotel Pratap Regency

Location Lake front **Address** The Mall **Tel** 235865-6 **Fax** 238003 **Rooms** 36 **Tariff** Rs 1,000-1,750; TE **Credit Cards** Visa, Master **Facilities** Restaurant, travel desk, doctor-on-call, laundry, room service, hot water, TV **Mumbai Reservations** Amar, Sanjay **Tel** 022-26326717

Manu Maharani **HIGH-END**

Location Lake-facing **Address** Grasmere Estate, Mallital **Tel** 237341-8 **Fax** 237350 **Email** manumaharani@vsnl.com **Rooms** 66 **Tariff** Rs 3,500-6,500; TE **Credit Cards** AmEx, Visa, Master, Diners **Facilities** Restaurant, laundry, doctor-on-call, room service, hot water, TV **Delhi Reservations** 4828/ 24, Prahlad Lane, Ansari Road, Daryaganj **Tel** 011-3242446
Online Reservations

Palace Belvedere **HIGH-END**

Location Lake-facing **Address** Awagarh Estate, Mallital **Tel** 237434 **Fax** 235082 **Website** palacebelvedere.com **Rooms** 21 **Tariff** Rs 2,600-3,900; TE **Credit Cards** AmEx, Visa, Master **Facilities** Restaurant, parking, TV **Delhi Reservations** 31, Siri Fort Road **Tel** 011-26266650-7
Online Reservations

ACCOMMODATION LISTINGS

Sarovar Tourist Rest House
KMVN
Location Lake-facing **Address**
Tallital **Tel** 235570 **Fax** 236374
Email kmvn@yahoo.com **Rooms**
17 **Tariff** Rs 1,000-2,100 **Credit
Cards** Visa, Master **Facilities**
Multi-cuisine restaurant, travel
desk, doctor-on-call, laundry,
room service, hot water **Metro
Reservations** *See pages 520-21*

Shalimar Hotel **BUDGET**
Location Near Library Address
Mall Road **Tel** 235721 **Fax**
235493 **Rooms** 72 **Tariff** Rs 400-
800; TE **Credit Cards** NA **Facilities** Restaurant, room service

Snow View Tourist Rest House
KMVN
Location Snow View Hill
Address TRH, Snow View **Tel**
238570 **Rooms** 4 **Tariff** Rs 500-
600; TE **Credit Cards** NA **Facilities** Food on order, phone, room
service, hot water, TV **Metro
Reservations** *See pages 520-21*

TRH Sukhtal **KMVN**
Location Near Ramnagar Bus
Stand **Address** Sukhtal, Mallital
Tel 235400, 236111 **Fax** 236897
Email kmvn@yahoo.com **Rooms**
42 **Tariff** Rs 675-1,500, dorm
bed Rs 100; TE **Credit Cards**
Visa, Master, BoB **Facilities**
Restaurant, food on order,
phone, laundry, room service,
hot water, TV **Metro Reserva-
tions** *See pages 520-21*
Online Reservations

Vikram Vintage Inn **HIGH-END**
Location Central **Address** Near
ATI, Mallital **Tel** 236179 **Rooms**
37 **Tariff** Rs 3,105-4,600 **Credit
Cards** AmEx, Visa, Master **Facil-
ities** Restaurant, travel desk,TV
Delhi Reservations Vikram
Hotels, 182, Ring Road, Lajpat

Nagar **Tel** 011-26436451 **Email**
hotelvikram@vsnl.com
Online Reservations

OKHIMATH STD 01364

Tourist Rest House **GMVN**
Address PO Okhimath,
Rudraprayag **Tel** 264236 **Web-
site** gmvnl.com **Rooms** 2, huts 5
Tariff Rs 150-500 **Credit Cards**
NA **Facilities** Travel desk, doc-
tor-on-call, laundry, room serv-
ice, hot water **Metro Reserva-
tions** *See pages 520-21*
Online Reservations

OSLA

Forest Rest House **FRH**
Address FRH, Osla **Rooms** 4,
dorms 2 **Tariff** Rs 150-350; TE
Credit Cards NA **Facilities** Hot
water, attached bath **Dehra Dun
Reservations** Director, Rajaji
National Park **Tel** 0135-2621669

PANGOT

Jungle Lore Birding Lodge
BIRDWATCHING
Location In the forest **Address**
Village Pangot, via Nainital **Email**
indianwildlife@vsnl.com **Website**
tiger_camp.com **Rooms** 5 **Tariff**
Rs 1,250 **Credit Cards** NA **Facil-
ities** Dining hall, hot water,
nature walk and trek **Delhi
Reservations** Asian Adventure,
B-9, Sector-27, Noida **Tel** 95120-
2524874-78 **Fax** 9394878

PATHARIYA

Forest Rest House **FRH**
Address Pathariya **Rooms** 2
suites **Tariff** Rs 100 **Credit
Cards** NA **Facilities** Hot water,
attached bath, caretaker can
prepare food **Almora Reserva-

tions** DFO, Civil and Soyam Forest Division **Tel** 05962-230229

RAMBARA

Tourist Rest House **GMVN**
Address TRH, Rambara **Rooms**
6, dorms 2 **Tariff** Rs 100-550
Credit Cards NA **Facilities** Canteen, room service, hot water on
request **Metro Reservations**
See pages 520-21

RUDRAPRAYAG STD 01364

Monal Resort **HIGH-END**
Location Near river **Address**
Dist Rudraprayag **Tel** 233901-05
Fax 233906 **Rooms** 50 **Tariff** Rs
1,600-3,500; TE **Credit Cards**
NA **Facilities** Restaurant **Delhi
Reservations** 801-802, Nirmal
Tower, 26, Barakhamba Road **Tel**
011-23312804

Tourist Rest House **GMVN**
Address TRH, Rudraprayag **Tel**
233347 **Rooms** 18, dorms 3
Tariff Rs 110-1,400; TE **Credit
Cards** NA **Facilities** Dining
room, hot water, attached bath
Metro Reservations *See pages
520-21*

SONPRAYAG

Forest Rest House **FRH**
Address Sonprayag **Rooms** 2
Tariff Rs 100 **Facilities** Attached
bath, hot water, caretaker can
prepare food **Kedarnath Reservations** DFO, Kedarnath Wildlife
Tel 01372-252149

SUYAL SAUR STD 01364

Tourist Rest House **GMVN**
Address TRH, Syal Saur **Tel**
258228 **Rooms** 10 huts **Tariff** Rs
500-750 **Credit Cards** NA **Facilities** Canteen, room service, hot

water on request **Metro Reservations** *See pages 520-21*

Tourist Rest House GMVN
Address TRH, Taluka **Rooms** 4, dorms 2 **Tariff** Rs 150-400; TE **Credit Cards** NA **Facilities** Hot water, attached bath **Metro Reservations** *See pages 520-21*

UTTARKASHI STD 01374

Amba Hotel BUDGET
Location Next to post-office **Address** Main Market **Tel** 222646, 09412984189 **Rooms** 7 **Tariff** Rs 150-450 **Credit Cards** NA **Facilities** Adventure sports equipment provided, restaurant, travel desk, central heating, sightseeing, doctor-on-call, laundry, room service, attached bath, hot water, TV

Forest Rest House FRH
Address Uttarkashi **Rooms** 3 **Tariff** 100 **Credit Cards** NA **Facilities** Attached bath, hot water on demand **Reservations** DFO, Uttarkashi **Tel** 01374-222444

Hanslok Hotel BUDGET
Location Near Oriental Bank

Address Hanuman Chowk, Main Market **Tel** 222157 **Rooms** 36 **Tariff** Rs 100-350 **Credit Cards** NA **Facilities** Travel desk, doctor-on-call, laundry, room service, attached bath, hot water, TV

Hotel Akash Ganga TREKKING
Location Near Suspension Bridge **Address** Joshiyara **Tel** 09412077688 **Email** akashgangauki@yahoo.co.in **Rooms** 35 **Tariff** Rs 400-750 **Credit Cards** NA **Facilities** Trekking, meals on request, travel desk, phone, doctor-on-call, laundry, room service, attached bath, hot water, TV

Hotel Natraj BUDGET
Location Near State Bank of India **Address** Main Bazaar **Tel** 222035 **Rooms** 7 **Tariff** Rs 100-200 **Credit Cards** NA **Facilities** Laundry, room service, attached bath, hot water (on request)

Hotel Relax TREKKING
Location Near Shishu Mandir School **Address** NIM Road, Joshiyara **Tel** 09412026305 **Email** amodsingh@yahoo.com **Rooms** 25 **Tariff** Rs 300-850 **Credit Cards** NA **Facilities** Treks arranged, restaurant, travel desk, central heating, doctor-on-call, attached bath, hot water, TV

Monal Tourist Home TREKKING
Location Near Darga Temple **Address** Kot Bungalow Road **Tel** 222270, 09412984183 **Email** monaluttarkashi@rediffmail.com **Rooms** 5 **Tariff** Rs 500-800 **Credit Cards** NA **Facilities** Trekking arranged, meals on request, travel desk, sightseeing, doctor-on-call, laundry, room service, attached bath, hot water, TV

Sahaj Villa
Location Opp Maheshwari School **Address** Main Market, Gyansu **Tel** 222783 **Rooms** 12 **Tariff** Rs 500-900 **Credit Cards** NA **Facilities** Laundry, room service, attached bath, hot water

Forest Rest House FRH
Address Vinayak **Rooms** 2 suites **Tariff** Rs 300 **Credit Cards** NA **Facilities** Attached bath, hot water on demand **Nainital Reservations** DFO, Nainital **Tel** 05942-236469

Tourist Rest House GMVN
Address TRH, Wan **Rooms** 2 dorms **Tariff** Rs 60-100; TE **Credit Cards** NA **Facilities** Hot

ACCOMMODATION LISTINGS

water, attached bath **Metro Reservations** *See pages 520-21*

▷ NORTH-EAST

BARSAI

Shambala Rhododendron Resort
Location Inside the Sanctuary **Tel** 09832005703 **Rooms** 1, dorm 1 **Tariff** Rs 200-600 **Credit Cards** NA **Facilities** Hot water, dining hall **Siliguri Reservations** Help Tourism **Tel** 0353-2535893

BOMDILA STD 03782

Hotel Shangrila `BUDGET`
Location Outskirts **Tel** 222226 **Rooms** 5 **Tariff** Rs 220-350 **Credit Cards** NA **Facilities** Restaurant, hot water, room service, TV

Hotel Shipyangphong `BUDGET`
Location Near Buddha Stadium **Tel** 222286 **Rooms** 24 **Tariff** Rs 400-750 **Credit Cards** NA **Facilities** Restaurant, hot water, room service, TV

CHALSA STD 03562

Sinclairs Retreat Dooars
`HIGH-END`
Address Chalsa Hill Top, Dist Jalpaiguri **Tel** 260282 **Website** sinclairshotels.com **Rooms** 72 cottages **Tariff** Rs 1,900-3,700; TE **Credit Cards** AmEx, Visa, Master, Diners **Facilities** River rafting, restaurant, bar, swimming pool, hot water, TV

DARJEELING STD 0354

Darjeeling Tourist Lodge
`WB TOURISM`
Location Central **Address** Bhanu Sarani **Tel** 2254411/ 13

Telefax 2254412 **Rooms** 23 **Tariff** Rs 400-1,600; TE **Credit Cards** NA **Facilities** Bar, attached bath, hot water, room service, TV **Metro Reservations** *See page 521*

Hotel Dekeling
Location Central **Address** 51, Gandhi Road **Tel** 2254149 **Telefax** 2253298 **Website** dekeling. com **Rooms** 22 **Tariff** Rs 650-1,250 **Credit Cards** Visa, Master **Facilities** Restaurant, laundry, room service, hot water, TV

Hotel Denzongpa `BUDGET`
Location Near railway station **Address** JP Sharma Road **Tel** 2256061 **Rooms** 22 **Tariff** Rs 300-600 **Credit Cards** NA **Facilities** Hot water, room service, TV

Hotel Garuda `TREKKING`
Location Near Mahakal Market **Address** 64, Ladenla Road **Tel** 2254563, 09434024070 **Email** tibettours@lhaso.com **Rooms** 26 **Tariff** Rs 1,400-2,500 **Credit Cards** NA **Facilities** Trekking, restaurant, travel desk, laundry, hot water, room service, TV **Kolkata Reservations** Tibet Tours and Travels, 53, Ananda-pally **Tel** 033-24123873

Hotel Mohit
Location Near United Bank **Address** HD Lama Road **Tel** 2254818 **Website** hotelmohit.com **Rooms** 28 **Tariff** Rs 1,150-2,800 **Credit Cards** Visa, Master **Facilities** Restaurant, attached bath, bar, room service, TV **Kolkata Reservations** Diamond Tours and Travels, 30 Jadunath Dey Road **Tel** 033-22259639

Hotel Opal Inn `BUDGET`
Location Near bus stand

Address 116, TN Road **Tel** 2254463 **Rooms** 16 **Tariff** Rs 550 **Credit Cards** NA **Facilities** Lodging only, attached bath, hot water

Hotel Seven Seventeen
Location Central **Address** HD Lama Road **Tel** 2255099 **Fax** 2254717 **Rooms** 33 **Tariff** Rs 1,100-1,300; TE **Credit Cards** Visa, Master **Facilities** Restaurant, bar, room service, TV

Lowis Jublee Complex `DGHC`
Location Below railway station **Address** Dr SK Paul Road **Tel** 2256395 **Rooms** 9 **Tariff** Rs 150-180; TE **Credit Cards** NA **Facilities** Restaurant, hot water **Kolkata Reservations** Darjeeling Gorkha Hill Council, Middleton Street **Tel** 033-22821715

Park Lane Hotel
Location Near railway station **Address** Tamang Buddhist Monastery Road, Judge Bazaar **Tel** 2256902 **Email** slg_park lane@sancharnet.in **Rooms** 17 **Tariff** Rs 1,000-1,500 **Credit Cards** Visa **Facilities** Restaurant, room service, travel desk, TV

Pine Ridge Hotel `BUDGET`
Location Central **Address** The Mall **Tel** 2254074 **Email** pine ridge@yahoo.com **Rooms** 33 **Tariff** Rs 500-800 **Credit Cards** AmEx **Facilities** Restaurant, sightseeing, attached bath, hot water, room service, TV

The Cedar Inn
Location Near St Paul's School **Address** Jalapahar Road, PO 102 **Tel** 2254446 **Fax** 2256764 **Email** slg_cedar@sancharnet.in **Rooms** 22 **Tariff** Rs 3,200-4,400 **Credit Cards** Visa, Master **Facilities** Restaurant, health club

The New Elgin
Location Near Mall Road
Address 18 HD Lama Road **Tel**
2254114 **Fax** 2254267 **Email**
newelgin@cal.vsnl.net.in **Website**
elginhotels.com **Rooms** 25 **Tariff**
Rs 3,800-4,100; TE **Credit
Cards** AmEx, Visa, Master **Facilities** Multi-cuisine restaurant, tea
lounge, bar, forex, lockers, parking, laundry, room service, TV
Kolkata Reservations 5 Park
Row, 47 Park Street **Tel** 033-
22269878 **Fax** 2466388
Online Reservations

The Windamere Hotel
`HIGH-END`
Location Near Chowrasta
Address Observatory Hill **Tel**
2254041-42 **Fax** 2254043 **Web-
site** windamerehotel.com
Rooms 37 **Tariff** Rs 4,320-7,200
(including meals); TE **Credit
Cards** AmEx, Master, Diners
Facilities Restaurant, bar, TV
Online Reservations

`DEBAN`

Forest Rest House `FRH`
Address Deban, Dist Changlang
Rooms 6, huts 2, dorm 1 **Tariff**
Rs 30-190 **Credit Cards** NA
Facilities Attached bath, hot
water, caretaker arranges food

Namdapha Reservations Field
Director, Project Tiger, Nam-
dapha Tiger Reserve, Miao
Telefax 03807-222249

`DHIRANG STD 03780`

Dhirang Resort
Location Near Main Market
Address Medical Road **Tel**
242352, 09436045063 **Email**
dhirangresort@yahoo.com
Rooms 5, suites 4 **Tariff** Rs 500-
1,000 **Credit Cards** NA **Facilities**
Restaurant, attached bath, TV

Hotel Pemaling
Address Narangchilo **Tel** 242615
Rooms 5, suites 2 **Tariff** Rs 800-
1,500 **Credit Cards** NA **Facilities** Restaurant, attached bath,
room service, TV

Circuit House `BUDGET`
Location 2 km from Main Bazaar
Address Narangchilo **Tel** 242157
Rooms 4 **Tariff** Rs 300 **Credit
Cards** NA **Facilities** Dining hall,
attached bath **Reservations**
Arunachal Pradesh Tourist Info
Officer, Dhirang **Tel** 242324

`KALIMPONG STD 03552`

Bethlehem Lodge `BUDGET`
Location Near DB Giri Street

Address Rishi Road, 10th Mile
Tel 255185 **Rooms** 6 **Tariff** Rs
350-600 **Credit Cards** NA **Facilities** Lodging only

Cloud Nine
Location Above Rishi Bankim
Park **Address** Ringking Pong
Road **Tel** 259554 **Email**
cloud9kpg@yahoo.com **Rooms**
5 **Tariff** Rs 800; TE **Credit Cards**
NA **Facilities** Restaurant,
attached bath, TV **Kolkata
Reservations** Help Tourism, 67A
Kali Temple Road, Kalighat **Tel**
033-24550917

Diki Lodge
Location 10 mins from bus
stand **Address** 10th Mile, Tripai
Road **Tel** 255095 **Fax** 256935
Email dikilodge@hotmail.com
Rooms 18 **Tariff** Rs 250-900
Credit Cards NA **Facilities**
Multi-cuisine restaurant, parking,
room service, hot water, TV

Hilltop Tourist Lodge
`WB TOURISM`
Address Hill Tourist Lodge,
Kalimpong **Tel** 255654 **Rooms** 7,
dorms 2 **Tariff** Rs 825-1,100,
dorm bed Rs 275 **Credit Cards**
NA **Facilities** Attached bath, hot
water, room service, TV **Metro
Reservations** See page 521

ACCOMMODATION LISTINGS

Hotel Silver Oak `HIGH-END`
Location Hillside **Address**
Ringking Pong Road **Tel** 255266-
67 **Telefax** 255368 **Website**
elginhotels.com **Rooms** 20 **Tariff**
Rs 3,500-3,800 **Credit Cards**
AmEx, Visa, Master, Diners, BoB
Facilities Restaurant, bar, forex,
room service, TV **Kolkata**
Reservations Elgin Hotels, 5,
Park Row, 47 Park Street **Tel**
033-22463884
Online Reservations

Kalimpong Park Hotel
Location Hill-facing **Address**
Ringking Pong Road **Tel** 255304
Email parkhotel@satyam.net.in
Rooms 19 **Tariff** Rs 1,300-2,000;
TE **Credit Cards** Master, Visa
Facilities Multi-cuisine restau-
rant, bar, room service, TV

Kalimpong Himalayan Hotel
Location Near Municipality
Office **Address** Upper Cart Road
Tel 255248 **Fax** 255122 **Rooms**
16 **Tariff** Rs 1,400-2,200 **Credit**
Cards AmEx, Visa, Master
Facilities Restaurant, parking,
laundry, hot water

Morgan House Tourist Lodge
`WB TOURISM`
Address Ringkingpong Road **Tel**
255384 **Rooms** 7 **Tariff** Rs 500-
2,600 **Credit Cards** NA **Facili-**
ties Bar, attached bath, hot
water, room service, TV **Metro**
Reservations See page 521

Paramount Inn `BUDGET`
Location Near Police Station
Address Main Road **Tel** 255037
Rooms 9 **Tariff** Rs 250-500
Credit Cards NA **Facilities**
Multi-cuisine restaurant, parking,
room service, hot water, TV

Tashiding Hotel `WB TOURISM`
Address Tashiding Lodge **Tel**

255929 **Rooms** 6 **Tariff** Rs 750-
1,600 **Credit Cards** NA **Facili-**
ties Dining room, attached bath,
hot water, room service **Metro**
Reservations See page 521

The Himalayan Hotel
Location Near Municipality
Office **Address** Upper Cart Road
Tel 255248 **Fax** 255122 **Rooms**
16 **Tariff** Rs 1,400-2,200 **Credit**
Cards AmEx, Visa, Master **Facil-**
ities Multi-cuisine restaurant,
parking, laundry, hot water

`KOHIMA STD 0370`

Hotel Fira
Location Near Old Yatri Niwas
Address Old Minister's Hill **Tel**
2245006 **Rooms** 16, dorm 1 **Tar-**
iff Rs 400-600, dorm bed Rs 200
Credit Cards NA **Facilities**
Restaurant, attached bath, room
service, TV

Hotel Japfu Ashok
Location Near taxi stand
Address PR Hills **Tel** 2240211-
13 **Fax** 2243439 **Rooms** 25
Tariff Rs 675-2,000 **Credit**
Cards NA **Facilities** Restaurant,
coffee shop, handicrafts shop,
Internet, fridge, hot water, room
service, TV **Delhi Reservations**
Shikhar Travels, 209, Competent
House, Connaught Circle
Tel 011-23323660

Hotel Pine `BUDGET`
Location Near MLA Hostel
Address Midland **Tel** 2243129
Rooms 7 **Tariff** Rs 350-550
Credit Cards NA **Facilities**
Attached bath, room service, TV

Tourist Lodge
Location Above the cathedral
Address New Minister's Hill **Tel**
(caretaker) 2241056,
09436010245 **Rooms** 16 **Tariff**

Rs 500-1,000 **Credit Cards** NA
Facilities Restaurant, hot water
on request

`LAVA`

Forest Rest House `FRH`
Location Central **Address** Lava
Rooms 24 **Tariff** Rs 700-1,200
Credit Cards NA **Facilities** Can-
teen, attached bath, room serv-
ice, TV **Kolkata Reservations**
Forest Division, Dharmatala **Tel**
033-22370060-61

`NAMCHI STD 03595`

Hotel Kesang `BUDGET`
Location Central **Address** Namchi Bazaar, South Sikkim **Tel**
263746 **Rooms** 6 **Tariff** Rs 250-
350 **Credit Cards** NA **Facilities**
Restaurant, room service, hot
water on request

Hotel Mayal
Location Central **Address**
Jorethang Road, South Sikkim
Tel 263588, 09434127322
Email wongdi_sonam@yahoo.
co.in **Website** sikkiminfo.net/
hotelmayal **Rooms** 20
Tariff Rs 300-1,000 **Credit**
Cards NA **Facilities** Restaurant,
room service, attached bath, hot
water, TV

`RABANGLA STD 03595`

Hotel Manokamona
Location Central **Address**
Kewzing Road **Tel** 260804
Rooms 12 **Tariff** Rs 525-700
Credit Cards NA **Facilities**
Restaurant, attached bath, hot
water, room service, TV

Hotel Menamla
Location Central **Address**
Kewzing Road **Tel** 260666
Rooms 12, dorm 1 **Tariff** Rs

400-1,000, dorm bed Rs 100
Credit Cards NA **Facilities**
Restaurant, bar, travel desk, doctor-on-call, attached bath, hot
water, room service, TV

Hotel Ravangla Star
Location Hill-facing **Address**
Kewzing Road **Tel** 260733
Rooms 10 **Tariff** Rs 600-1,050
Credit Cards NA **Facilities** Rest-
aurant, sightseeing, room serv-
ice, attached bath, hot water, TV

Hotel Zumthang TREKKING
Location Below Power Guest
House **Address** Rabangla
Bazaar **Tel** 260870,
09434318047 **Email** wangbhutia
@rediffmail.com **Rooms** 11 **Tariff**
Rs 500-1,050 **Credit Cards** NA
Facilities Trekking, restaurant,
travel desk, parking, doctor-on-
call, laundry, hot water, TV

Mt Narsing Village Resort
Location Pelling-Pemayangtse
Highway **Address** 15th Mile, PO
Rabangla **Tel** 226822 ,
09434026822 **Fax** 220960 **Email**
takapa@sancharnet.in **Website**
yuksom-tours.com **Rooms** 11
Tariff Rs 550-1,250 **Credit**
Cards NA **Facilities** Restaurant,
travel desk, laundry, attached
bath, hot water, room service, TV

Trekkers' Hut A
Location Inside Singalila National Park **Rooms** 6, dorm 1 **Tar-**
iff Rs 80-400 **Credit Cards** NA
Facilities Food provided, common toilet **Darjeeling Reserva-**
tions Glenary's, Nehru Rd, Near
Chowrasta **Tel** 0354-2257554

Trekkers' Hut B
Location Inside Singalila Nat-
ional Park **Rooms** 1 dorm **Tariff**
Dorm bed Rs 50 **Credit Cards**
NA **Facilities** Food provided,
common toilet **Darjeeling**
Reservations See above

Trekkers' Hut C
Location Inside Singalila Nat-
ional Park **Rooms** 1 dorm **Tariff**
Dorm bed Rs 50 **Credit Cards**
NA **Facilities** Food provided,
common toilet **Darjeeling**
Reservations See above

SOMBARIA STD 03595

Prashanti Guest House
Location Near SNT Office
Address Sombaria Bazaar **Tel**
254236 **Rooms** 6 **Tariff** Rs 100-
400 **Credit Cards** NA **Facilities**
Home cooked meals, hot water,
attached bath, taxi arranged

TAWANG STD 03794

Hotel Alpine
Location Hill-facing **Address**
Nehru Market **Tel** 222515
Rooms 8 **Tariff** Rs 400-700
Credit Cards NA **Facilities**
Restaurant, hot water, room
service, TV

Hotel Gangchin BUDGET
Location Central **Address** Old
Market **Tel** 222431 **Rooms** 7
Tariff Rs 150-200 **Credit Cards**
NA **Facilities** Hot water, room
service

Hotel Nefa BUDGET
Location Central **Address**
Nehru Market **Tel** 222419
Rooms 9 **Tariff** Rs 250-350
Credit Cards NA **Facilities**
Restaurant, hot water, room
service, TV

Hotel Shangrila BUDGET
Location Near Main Bus Stand
Address Old Market **Tel** 222224
Rooms 15 **Tariff** Rs 300-450
Credit Cards NA **Facilities**
Restaurant, hot water, room
service, TV

Tourist Lodge
Location Central **Address** Near
Telephone Exchange **Tel** 222359

ACCOMMODATION LISTINGS

Rooms 8 **Tariff** Rs 550-750
Credit Cards NA **Facilities**
Restaurant, hot water, room
service, TV

TEZPUR STD 03712

Hotel Anirudha
Location Near Himmat Singh
Petrol Pump **Address** NT Road
Tel 252595 **Rooms** 36 **Tariff** Rs
130-1000: TE **Credit Cards** NA
Facilities Restaurant, laundry,
parking, attached bath, hot
water, room service, TV

Hotel Luit
Location Near Anwar Cinema
Address RS Road **Telefax**
222083 **Rooms** 38 **Tariff** Rs 250-
1,300 **Credit Cards** NA
Facilities Restaurant, bar, TV

YUKSOM STD 03595

Hotel Tashi Ghang
Location Lakeside **Address**
Beside Lake Karthok **Tel**
241202-03 **Rooms** 18
Tariff Rs 650-1,500; TE
Credit Cards NA **Facilities**
Restaurant, travel desk, room
service, hot water, attached bath,
TV **Siliguri Reservations** Nature
Beyond **Tel** 0353-2532461
Email info@east-himalaya.com
Website east-himalaya.com

▷ WEST

BHANDARDARA STD 02424

MTDC Holiday Resort MTDC
Location Lake view **Tel** 257032,
257171 **Fax** 257170 **Rooms** 35
Tariff Rs 500-2,500; TE
Credit Cards NA **Facilities**
Restaurant, travel desk,
laundry, attached bath, room
service, TV **Metro Reservations**
See page 519

IGATPURI STD 02553

Ganaka Motel BUDGET
Location Valley front **Address**
Near Manas Resort, NH3 **Tel**
243204 **Email** anuja_kamat@
rediffmail.com **Rooms** 15 **Tariff**
Rs 300 **Credit Cards** NA **Facilities** Restaurant, sightseeing
arranged, attached bath, hot
water, room service **Mumbai
Reservations** Laxmi Niketan,
K Dhuru Road **Tel** 022-24306030

Golden Resort
Location Hill-facing **Address**
68-69, Opp petrol pump,
Bortemba **Tel** 244849 **Email**
goldenresort@rediffmail.com
Rooms 22 **Tariff** Rs 1,000-1,600;
TE **Credit Cards** NA **Facilities**
Restaurant, bar, room service, TV
Mumbai Reservations Hotel
Golden Palace Pvt Ltd, 9, Shastri
Marg **Tel** 022-25146879

Hotel Ashwin
Location On the highway
Address Near Mahindra &
Mahindra, Mumbai-Agra High-
way **Tel** 243624-5 **Email** hotel
ashwin@hotelashwin.com **Web-
site** hotelashwin.com **Rooms** 42
Tariff Rs 400-900; TE **Credit
Cards** NA **Facilities** Restaurant,
travel desk, doctor-on-call, park-
ing, laundry, room service,
attached bath, hot water, TV
Mumbai Reservations 130,
M Karve Road **Tel** 022-22834437

Manas Resort HIGH-END
Location Opp Bharat Distillery
Address 303-A, Mumbai-Nasik
Highway **Tel** 244030 **Email**
info@manasresort.com
Website manasresort.com
Rooms 46 **Tariff** Rs 2,000-5,000;
TE **Credit Cards** AmEx, Visa,
Master, Diners **Facilities** Restau-
rant, bar, coffee shop, health

club, gym, indoor games, swimming pool, travel desk, doctor-
on-call, Internet, room service,
TV **Mumbai Reservations**
Camelley Hotel Pvt Ltd, Jewel
Arcade, TPS 4, 1st Road **Tel**
022-26403704

KARJAT STD 02148

Dr Modi's Health Resort
HIGH-END
Location In the foothills
Address Neral Road, Village
Wanjale **Tel** 222316 **Rooms** 40
Tariff Rs 2,200; TE **Credit Cards**
Visa, Master, Diners **Facilities**
Restaurant, gym, health club,
yoga, meditation games, health
cuisine **Mumbai Reservations**
14, Jolly Maker Apartment, No.
3, Cuffe Parade Road **Telefax**
022-22161520

Hotel Kotligad BUDGET
Location In the foothills
Address Village Kotligad **Tel**
224920 **Rooms** 3 **Tariff** Rs 300
Facilities Meals arranged, hot
water

**Satya Health Farm Village
Resort** HIGH-END
Location River front **Address**
Village Vanjerwadi **Tel** 246154
Email konarkhospitality@hot
mail.com **Website** satyahealth
farm.com **Rooms** 30 **Tariff** Rs
2,500; TE **Credit Cards** NA
Facilities Restaurant, meditation
centre, Kerala message centre,
gym **Mumbai Reservations** 266,
Patel Building, Opp Central
Plaza, Girgaum **Tel** 022-
56348501

Van Vihar BUDGET
Location Outskirts **Address**
Kondhavni, Karjat **Tel** 226844
Rooms 1 dorm **Tariff** Dorm bed
Rs 300 (meals included) **Credit**

HOTELS

Cards NA **Facilities** Attached bath, hot water, meals

KAMSHET STD 02114

Native Place Getaway TREKKING PARAGLIDING
Location Water front **Address** LV 41/42, Golden Glades, Village Uksan **Tel** 266187, 266278, 09821430798 **Email** info@native-place.com **Website** nativeplace.com **Rooms** 3, dorms 4 **Tariff** 1,800 (meals included), dorm bed Rs 600 (meals included) per person **Credit Cards** NA **Facilities** Paragliding, trekking, travel desk, attached bath **Mumbai Reservations** Nirvana Adventures, 2A, Takshila Apartments, Tagore Road, Santacruz (W) **Tel** 022-26493110, 0932708809

Nirvana Base Camp TREKKING PARAGLIDING
Location In shady groves **Address** LV 41/42, Golden Glades, Village Uksan **Tel** 266187, 09821430798 **Email** sanjay@nirvanaadventures.com **Rooms** 10 tents **Tariff** Rs 600 (meals included) per person **Credit Cards** NA **Facilities** Paragliding, trekking, travel desk, laundry, attached bath **Mumbai Reservations** See above

Nirvana Cottages TREKKING PARAGLIDING
Location Secluded **Address** LV 41/42, Golden Glades, Village Uksan **Tel** 266187, 09821430798 **Rooms** 2 cottages **Tariff** Rs 700-1,000 (meals included) per person **Credit Cards** NA **Facilities** Paragliding, trekking, travel desk, laundry, attached bath **Mumbai Reservations** See below left

PG Ashram PARAGLIDING
Location Lake front **Address** Govitri Village, Golden Glades, Taluka Maval **Tel** 266122, 09822635579 **Website** pgashram.com **Rooms** 2, dorms 2 **Tariff** Rs 1,400 (meals included), dorm bed Rs 450 (meals included) **Credit Cards** NA **Facilities** Paragliding, buffet lunch, camping, phone

YMCA Camp Lakeside KAYAKING PARAGLIDING BUDGET
Location Lake-facing **Address** Nilshi Village, Maval Taluk, Dist Pune **Tel** 09823239729 **Website** bombayymcacamp.org **Rooms** 5 cabins, 10 tents **Tariff** Rs 250 **Credit Cards** NA **Facilities** Kayaking, paragliding **Mumbai Reservations** Melvin Louis, YMCA Student Branch, 12 Nathala Parekh Marg, Colaba

Tel 022-22020079 **Email** melvin@bombayymcacamp.org

KHANDALA STD 02114

Convent Villa BUDGET
Location Hill-facing **Address** Convent of Jesus and Mary, Bombay House, Nuns' Hill **Tel** 269131 **Rooms** 12 **Tariff** Rs 175 per bed **Credit Cards** NA **Facilities** Lodging only

Hotel Fun-n-Food BUDGET
Location Hill-facing **Address** 61, Hilltop Colony, Mumbai-Pune Road **Mobile** 09422545639 **Email** indiatravel@vsnl.com **Rooms** 32 **Tariff** Rs 550 **Credit Cards** AmEx, Visa, Master **Facilities** Multi-cuisine restaurant, room service, attached bath, hot water **Mumbai Reservations** Mrs Jatiani, A-1 Apartments, 270, Valkeshwar Road **Tel** 022-23620518

Velvet Hills Retreat
Location Valley-facing **Address** Vikas Valley, Near PWD Guest House, Khandala **Tel** 270149 **Fax** 270154 **Website** velvethills.com **Rooms** 25 **Tariff** Rs 925-2,650; TE **Credit Cards** AmEx, Visa, Master, Diners **Facilities** Swimming pool, gym, STD, TV

Introducing Plum and Star Anise Conserves. Kitchens of India. FRUIT & SPICE CONSERVES. A feast for the senses. For further information email us at kitchensofindia@itc.co.in

ACCOMMODATION LISTINGS

Mumbai Reservations 106, Vikas Centre, Vivekananda Road, Santacruz **Tel** 022-26115842, 56939333

LONAVLA STD 02114

Captans Resort `TREKKING`
Location Hillside **Address** Beyond Thakurwadi Village, Tungarli Dam **Tel** 271313 **Fax** 272007 **Email** captans@vsnl.net **Website** captans.com **Rooms** 6, **Tariff** Rs 2,500-4,000 **Credit Cards** NA **Facilities** Trekking, camping, travel desk, Internet, yoga, doctor-on-call

Fariyas Holiday Resort
`HIGH-END`
Location Hilltop **Address** Post Box 8, Frichley Hill, Tungarli **Tel** 273852-53 **Fax** 272080 **Email** fhrl@pn3.vsnl.net.in **Website** fariyas.com **Rooms** 103 **Tariff** Rs 4,500-8,450 **Credit Cards** AmEx, Visa, Master **Facilities** Restaurant, coffee shop, swimming pool, travel desk, doctor-on-call, hot water, mini-bar, room service, STD/ ISD, TV **Mumbai Reservations** Fariyas Hotel Pvt Ltd, Off Arthur Bunder Road **Tel** 022-22876526-27
Online Reservations

Hari International `BUDGET`
Location Hill-facing **Address** Old Mumbai-Pune Highway **Tel** 271488 **Rooms** 25 **Tariff** Rs 750-950; TE **Credit Cards** NA **Facilities** Restaurant, attached bath, hot water, room service, TV

Hotel Chandralok `BUDGET`
Location Near ST Bus Stand **Address** Off Mumbai-Pune Highway **Tel** 272294 **Telefax** 272921 **Email** hotelchandralok@vsnl.com **Website** hotelchandralok.com

Rooms 23 **Tariff** Rs 390-1,350; TE **Credit Cards** NA **Facilities** Restaurant, travel desk, lockers, doctor-on-call, room service, TV

Hotel Rainbow Retreat
Location Near Lonavla Market **Address** Opp Valvan Dam, Mumbai-Pune Road **Tel** 273445 **Fax** 274533 **Email** rainbow retreat@vsnl.com **Rooms** 48 **Tariff** Rs 2,120-3,710 **Credit Cards** AmEx, Visa, Master, BoB **Facilities** Travel desk, doctor-on-call, room service, TV **Mumbai Reservations** 340, J Jeejibhoy Road **Tel** 022-23083121

Hotel Ramakrishna
Location Hill-facing **Address** Old Mumbai-Pune Highway **Tel** 273600 **Rooms** 40 **Tariff** Rs 1,000-1,700; TE **Credit Cards** NA **Facilities** Restaurant, attached bath, hot water, room service

Maharaja Lodge `BUDGET`
Location Central **Address** Old Mumbai-Pune Highway **Tel** 272919 **Rooms** 17 **Tariff** Rs 450-1,100; TE **Credit Cards** NA **Facilities** Attached bath, hot water, room service, TV

The Duke's Retreat
Location Hill-facing **Address** Mumbai-Pune Highway, Khandala **Tel** 273826-27 **Fax** 273836 **Email** dukes@pn2.vsnl.net.in **Website** dukesretreat.com **Rooms** 62 **Tariff** Rs 4,800-5,300 **Credit Cards** AmEx, Visa, Master **Facilities** Multi-cuisine restaurant, Coffee shop, bar, swimming pool, health club, ayurvedic massage, doctor-on-call, room service, STD/ ISD, TV **Mumbai Reservations** Off Sadhana Rayon House, Dr Naoroji Road **Tel** 022-22618293

MAHABALESHWAR STD 02168

Anand Van Bhavan
Location Outskirts **Address** Opp Krishna Valley, Duchess Road **Tel** 260030-31 **Fax** 260641 **Website** hotelanandvanbhuvan.com **Rooms** 20 **Tariff** Rs 500-1,600 **Credit Cards** Visa, Master **Facilities** Dining hall, pick-up and drop, travel desk, doctor-on-call, room service, TV **Mumbai Reservations** Bhagat Gully, Mahim **Tel** 022-24306687

Brightland Holiday Village
`HIGH-END`
Location River valley front **Address** Kate's Point Road **Tel** 260700 **Fax** 260707 **Email** brightland@vsnl.com **Website** brightlandholiday.com **Rooms** 65 **Tariff** Rs 2,200-20,000; TE **Credit Cards** Visa, Master **Facilities** Restaurant, pub, swimming pool, health club, Ayurvedic health centre, travel desk, doctor-on-call, room service, TV **Mumbai Reservations** Clark House, 8 Nathalal Parekh Marg, Opp Sahakari Bhandar, Colaba **Tel** 022-22872590-93
Online Reservations

Holiday Resort `MTDC`
Location Bombay Point **Address** Mahad Naka, Mahabaleshwar **Tel** 260318 **Fax** 260300 **Email** mahatour@ bol.net.in **Rooms** 110, 6 dorms **Tariff** Rs 450-1,700, dorm bed Rs 100; TE **Credit Cards** AmEx, Visa, Master **Facilities** Restaurant **Metro Reservations** *See page 519*

Hotel Blue Park `BUDGET`
Location Near Madhu Sagar Factory **Address** Lodwick Point Road **Tel** 260375 **Rooms** 26 **Tariff** Rs 500-900 **Credit Cards**

NA **Facilities** Doctor-on-call, room service, TV **Mumbai Reservations** SH4, GF, Saraswati Niwas, Rokadia Lane, Borivli (W) **Tel** 022-28904545

Hotel Parijat BUDGET
Location Near Bagbinton Point **Address** Dr Sabane Road **Tel** 260196 **Rooms** 11 **Tariff** Rs 750-1,500; TE **Credit Cards** NA **Facilities** Attached bath, room service, TV

Hotel Ripon BUDGET
Location Lake front **Tel** 260257 **Telefax** 260623 **Rooms** 6 **Tariff** Rs 600-1,500 **Credit Cards** NA **Facilities** Fridge, TV

Hotel Sai Regency
Location Central **Address** Dr Sabane Road, Poonam Chowk **Tel** 260157 **Rooms** 21 **Tariff** Rs 1,000-1,200; TE **Credit Cards** NA **Facilities** Restaurant, attached bath, room service, TV

Kalpana Excellency BUDGET
Location Central **Address** Murry Peth **Tel** 260419, 09422039912 **Rooms** 20 **Tariff** Rs 400-900 (meals included); TE **Credit Cards** NA **Facilities** Attached bath, STD, room service, travel desk, doctor-on-call, TV

Pratap Heritage
Location Valley-facing **Address** Valley View Road **Tel** 260778-79 **Fax** 260777 **Email** prataperitage@vsnl.net **Rooms** 36 **Tariff** Rs 1,175-2,300; TE **Credit Cards** Visa, Master **Facilities** Travel desk, games, doctor-on-call, room service, TV **Mumbai Reservations** Lokhandwala Complex **Tel** 022-26326717, 09821355306

Strawberry Country
Location Near Lingmala Waterfall **Address** Panchgani Road, Metgutad **Tel** 272101-02 **Rooms** 28 **Tariff** Rs 2,100-3,000; TE **Credit Cards** Master **Facilities** Swimming pool, doctor-on-call, room service, TV **Mumbai Reservations** C/o SM Beharay and Company, 108, Habib Building, JSS Road, Opp Girgaum Church **Tel** 022-26455687

MATHERAN STD 02148

Hanjar House BUDGET
Location Central **Address** Near Railway Station **Tel** 230229 **Rooms** 15 **Tariff** Rs 600 (meals included); TE **Credit Cards** NA **Facilities** Attached bath, room service

Hope Hall Hotel BUDGET
Location Valley view **Address** MG Road **Tel** 230193 **Rooms** 14 **Tariff** Rs 600-800; TE **Credit Cards** NA **Facilities** Restaurant, attached bath, indoor/ outdoor games, room service

Janata Happy Home BUDGET
Location Central **Address** Kasturba Road **Tel** 230229 **Rooms** 11 **Tariff** Rs 500-600 (meals included); TE **Credit Cards** NA **Facilities** Attached bath, room service, TV

Matheran Holiday Resort MTDC
Location Outskirts **Address** Dasturi Naka **Tel** 230277 **Fax** 230566 **Rooms** 40 **Tariff** Rs 450-1,300 **Credit Cards** Master, Visa **Facilities** Doctor-on-call, hot water, room service, TV **Metro Reservations** See page 519

Regal Hotel
Location Near railway station **Address** Kasturba Road **Tel** 230243 **Telefax** 230143 **Email** regalmatheran@yahoo.com **Website** regalmatheran.com **Rooms** 43 **Tariff** Rs 1,300-3,600; TE **Credit Cards** AmEx, Visa, Master, BoB **Facilities** Multi-cuisine restaurant, swimming pool,

ACCOMMODATION LISTINGS

health club, indoor and outdoor games **Mumbai Reservations** SH4, Irla Society Road, Vile Parle (W) **Tel** 022-26285020

Richie Rich Resorts `HIGH-END`
Location Near Matheran Market **Address** Bazaar Peth, MG Road **Tel** 230007-8 **Fax** 230111 **Email** richierichresorts@hotmail.com **Website** richierichresorts.com **Rooms** 40 **Tariff** Rs 3,300-6,600 **Credit Cards** Visa, Master, Diners **Facilities** Restaurant, lounge, swimming pool, shopping arcade **Mumbai Reservations** 236/ 38, Samuel Street, Masjid Bunder **Tel** 022-23403333

The Byke Retreat
Location 10 mins from Main Market **Address** MG Road **Tel** 230365-6 **Fax** 230316 **Email** byke@vsnl.com **Website** the-byke.com **Rooms** 51 **Tariff** Rs 3,300-4,500; TE **Credit Cards** Visa, Master **Facilities** Multi-cuisine restaurant, bar, swimming pool, health club, TV **Mumbai Reservations** 202, Chartered House, 293, Dr Cawasji Hormasji Street **Tel** 022-22068602

`PUNE STD 020`

Best Western The Pride Hotel
`HIGH-END`
Location Central **Address** 5, University Road, Shivajinagar **Tel** 25534567 **Fax** 25533228 **Website** book.bestwestern.com/bestwestern **Rooms** 108 **Tariff** Rs 5,200-10,350 **Credit Cards** AmEx, Visa, Master **Facilities** Multi-cuisine restaurant, bar, room service, health club, laundry, attached bath, hot water, TV
Online Reservations

Central Lodge `BUDGET`
Location Near railway station

Address 13, Wilson Garden **Tel** 26125229 **Rooms** 69 **Tariff** Rs 170-300; TE **Credit Cards** NA **Facilities** Common bathroom, room service

Hotel Ashirwad
Location Near railway station **Address** 16, Connaught Road **Tel** 26128585 **Fax** 26126121 **Email** hotelash@vsnl.com **Rooms** 45 **Tariff** Rs 1,600-2,150; TE **Credit Cards** Visa, Master, Diners **Facilities** Veg restaurant, travel desk, laundry, room service, TV

Hotel Chetak `BUDGET`
Location Near Deccan Gymkhana **Address** 1100/ 2, Model Colony **Tel** 25652681 **Fax** 25654078 **Email** chetak@pn2.vsnl.net.in **Rooms** 18 **Tariff** Rs 650-800; TE **Facilities** Attached bath, tea, coffee on request

Hotel Homeland `BUDGET`
Location Near Pune Railway Station **Address** 18, Wilson Garden **Tel** 26123203 **Fax** 6132622 **Email** homeland@satyam.net.in **Rooms** 22 **Tariff** Rs 450-800; TE **Credit Cards** Visa, Master **Facilities** Multi-cuisine restaurant, laundry, attached bath, TV

Hotel Panchshil
Location Near Industrial Area **Address** C-32, Near MIDC Office, Chinchwad **Tel** 27472012-13 **Fax** 27464474 **Email** panchshil@vsnl.com **Rooms** 47 **Tariff** Rs 1,150-2,000; TE **Credit Cards** AmEx, Visa, Master **Facilities** Coffee shop, travel desk, doctor-on-call, room service, TV

Hotel Pearl `BUDGET`
Location Opp Balgandharva

Rangmandir **Address** Jangli Maharaj Road **Tel** 25534247 **Fax** 25671815 **Email** dilipborawake @hotmail.com **Rooms** 15 **Tariff** Rs 600-900 **Credit Cards** Visa, Master **Facilities** Restaurant, bar, laundry, hot water

Hotel Woodland
Location Near railway station **Address** Sadhu Vaswani Circle **Tel** 26125454 **Fax** 26123131 **Email** tghotels@hotmail.com **Website** tghotels.com **Rooms** 100 **Tariff** Rs 1,000-2,200; TE **Credit Cards** Visa, Master **Facilities** Restaurant, laundry, doctor-on-call, airport/ station transfer, hot water, TV
Online Reservations

Le Meridien `HIGH-END`
Location Central **Address** 5, RBM Road **Tel** 26050505 **Fax** 26050506 **Email** reservations@ lemeridienpune.com **Website** lemeridienpune.com **Rooms** 176 **Tariff** Rs 6,000-12,000; TE **Credit Cards** AmEx, Visa, Master, Diners **Facilities** Multi-cuisine restaurants, bar, pool, health club, travel desk, doctor-on-call, Internet, TV
Online Reservations

The Sagar Plaza
Location Opp Planet M **Address** 1, Bund Garden Road **Tel** 26122622 **Fax** 26122633 **Website** sarovarparkplaza.com **Rooms** 76 **Tariff** Rs 3,200-7,000; TE **Credit Cards** AmEx, Visa, Master, Diners **Facilities** Multi-cuisine restaurant, bar, pool, gym, travel desk, room service, TV **Mumbai Reservations** Sarovar Park Plaza Hotels, 42, Mittal Chambers, Nariman Point **Tel** 022-22350800 **Fax** 22352766
Online Reservations

⊠ KARNATAKA

BABA BUDANAGIRI STD 08262

Nature Nirvana TREKKING BIRDWATCHING
Location In the jungle **Address** 1353, Prabhu Street, Church Road, Chikmagalur **Tel** 234904, 09844042152, 09448364152 **Email** naturenirvana@yahoo.com **Website** naturenirvana.com **Tariff** Rs 1,150 **Credit Cards** NA **Facilities** Restaurant, travel desk, coracle rides, fishing, bonfires, barbecues, nature walks, wildlife safari, plantation tours, birdwatching

CHIKMAGALUR STD 08262

Aishwariya Regency BUDGET
Address KM Road, Parvaphipura **Tel** 224001-02, 09341010238 **Rooms** 17 **Tariff** Rs 475-525 **Credit Cards** NA **Facilities** Restaurant, parking, hot water

The Planters Court
Location Opp KSRTC Bus Depot **Address** Kountheya Hotel Pvt Ltd, KM Road **Tel** 235881-85 **Rooms** 31 **Tariff** Rs 411-1,232 **Credit Cards** Visa **Facilities** Restaurant, travel desk, laundry, hot water, attached bath, TV

Bangalore Reservations 29/1, Kaverappa Layout, Vasant Nagar **Tel** 080-22351387 **Email** kounthey@sancharnet.in

The Taj Garden Retreat
HIGH-END
Location Central **Address** KM Road, Opp Pavitravana, Jyothinagar **Tel** 220202, 220404 **Fax** 220222 **Website** tajhotels.com **Rooms** 29 **Tariff** Rs 2,500-3,700 **Credit Cards** AmEx, Visa, Master **Facilities** Restaurant, indoor swimming pool, Ayurvedic massage centre, games room, outdoor central court, room service, coffee maker, mini bar, TV

IRPU FALLS STD 08274

High Falls Holiday House
HOMESTAY
Location In the forest **Address** Irpu Falls, Kurchi Post, Srimangala, South Coorg **Tel** 246027, 09448720527 **Email** highfalls_info@yahoo.co.in **Rooms** 3, cottages 4 **Tariff** Rs 850-1,300 **Credit Cards** NA **Facilities** Restaurant, travel desk, room service, hot water, wildlife safari

Irpu Resorts BUDGET
HOMESTAY
Location In the jungle **Address** Irpu Falls, Kurchi Post, Srimangala, South Coorg **Tel** 09448475222 **Rooms** 2 **Tariff** Rs 600 **Credit Cards** NA **Facilities** Room service, hot water

Ramcad Estate Guest House
TREKKING HOMESTAY
Location 1 km from Irpu Falls **Address** Near Irpu Temple, Kodagu **Tel** 246228, 244982, 09448144982 **Rooms** 3 **Tariff** Rs 160 **Credit Cards** NA **Facilities** Trekking, restaurant, doctor-on-call, laundry, room service

KAKKABE STD 08272

Honey Valley Estate TREKKING HOMESTAY BIRDWATCHING
Location Plantation **Address** Honey Valley Estate, Yavakapadi Post **Tel** 238339, 09448720689 **Email** honeyvalley_2000@yahoo.com **Website** honeyvalleyindia.com **Rooms** 8, cottages 5 **Tariff** Rs 200-1,500 **Credit Cards** NA **Facilities** Trekking, birdwatching, hot water, common dining hall

Palace Estate TREKKING BUDGET HOMESTAY
Location Edge of forest **Address** AP Poovanna, Kakkabe **Tel** 238446 **Rooms** 6 **Tariff**

ACCOMMODATION LISTINGS

Rs 225-700 **Credit Cards** NA **Facilities** Trekking, traditional Coorgi food

---

KEMMANNAGUNDI STD 08261

Horticulture Department Guest House `TREKKING` `BUDGET`
Location In the jungle **Tel** 237126 **Rooms** 25, cottages 5, dorms 5 **Tariff** Rs 300-800, dorm bed Rs 100 **Credit Cards** NA **Facilities** Trekking, restaurant, hot water **Reservations** Special Officer, Krishbarajendra Hill Station, Kemmannagundi Post, Tarikere Taluk **Bangalore Reservations** Director of Horticulture, Lalbagh **Tel** 080-26571925

KUNDAPUR STD 08254

Anugraha Tourist Home `BUDGET`
Address NH17, Hemmady, Kundapur **Tel** 278343 **Rooms** 10 **Tariff** Rs 200-250 **Credit Cards** NA **Facilities** Restaurant, hot water, room service, travel desk

Hotel Sharon `TREKKING`
Location On the highway **Address** NH17, Opp Shastri Park, Kundapur **Tel** 230826, 09448120826 **Fax** 230723 **Email** info@soans.com **Website** soans.com **Rooms** 54 **Tariff** Rs 160-750; TE **Credit Cards** Visa **Facilities** Trekking, restaurant, travel desk

Hotel Shashidhara `BUDGET`
Location Near bus stand **Address** Opp Shantha Market **Tel** 233244 **Rooms** 38 **Tariff** Rs 250 **Credit Cards** NA **Facilities** Restaurant, hot water, room service, travel desk

Isle of Amgol Resort `TREKKING`
Location Island **Address** Basrur Village, Kundapur **Tel** 231683, 09448120826 **Fax** 232223 **Email** info@soans.com **Website** soans.com **Rooms** 5, dorm 1 **Tariff** Rs 2,000, dorm bed Rs 500; TE **Credit Cards** NA **Facilities** Trekking, kayaking, rafting, restaurant, doctor-on-call, hot water, parking, travel desk

Turtle Bay Water Sports and Beach Resort
Location On the beach **Address** Gujjadi Post, Kanchgodu, Kundapur **Tel** 265422 **Fax** 2345761 **Email** turtlebayindia@yahoo.com **Website** turtlebayeco.com **Rooms** 15, dorms 20 **Tariff** Rs 500-1,000, dorm bed Rs 200; TE **Credit Cards** NA **Facilities** Restaurant, water sports, travel desk, hot water

---

MADIKERI STD 08272

Capitol Village
Location Coffee plantation **Address** School Road, Madikeri **Tel** 225492 **Fax** 229455 **Rooms** 19 **Tariff** Rs 1,200-1,500; TE **Credit Cards** NA **Facilities** Restaurant, room service, attached bath, hot water

Coorg International
Location 1 km from bus stand **Address** Convent Road, Madikeri **Tel** 229390, 228071-72 **Fax** 228073 **Email** hcicoorg@sancharnet.in **Website** coorg hotels.com **Rooms** 25 **Tariff** Rs 400-3,000 **Credit Cards** AmEx, Visa, Master **Facilities** Restaurant, health club, room service, travel desk

East End Hotel `BUDGET`
Location Central **Address** General Thimmaih Road, Madikeri **Tel** 229996, 09884125690 **Rooms** 7 **Tariff** Rs 210-700

Credit Cards NA **Facilities** Restaurant, room service, attached bath, hot water, TV

Golden Mist Plantation & Resorts `HOMESTAY`
Location In an organic farm **Address** Galibeedu Village Post, Madikeri **Tel** 265629 **Email** lud wigorganic@hotmail.com **Website** goldenmist.4t.com **Rooms** Cottage 1 **Tariff** Rs 2,500; TE **Credit Cards** NA **Facilities** Room service, hot water **Bangalore Reservations** C/o PV Company, Fraser Town, Mosque Road Cross **Tel** 080-25485705, 09448406469

Hill Town Hotel
Location Central **Address** Daswal Road, Near Vivys Hospital **Tel** 223805 **Rooms** 38 **Tariff** Rs 500-750; TE **Credit Cards** NA **Facilities** Multi-cuisine restaurant, sightseeing, attached bath, room service, TV

Mayura Valley View `KSTDC`
Location Valley view **Address** Near Raja's Seat, Madikeri **Tel** 228387 **Rooms** 6 **Tariff** Rs 430 **Credit Cards** NA **Facilities** Restaurant, room service, hot water, attached bath **Metro Reservations** *See page 519*

Mr Prasanna's Farmhouse `TREKKING` `HOMESTAY`
Location In a plantation **Address** Nandethi Estate, Kalur Village and Post, Via Madikeri **Tel** 228693 **Rooms** 1, tents 10 **Tariff** Rs 500-1,000 (meals included) **Credit Cards** NA **Facilities** Trekking

Mojo Rainforest Retreat `TREKKING` `HOMESTAY`
Location In the forest **Address** Kaloor Road, Galibeedu Village,

Madikeri **Tel** 265638 **Telefax** 265636 **Email** wapred.india@vsnl.com **Website** rainforestours.com **Rooms** 4 **Tariff** Rs 1,000-1,750; TE **Credit Cards** NA **Facilities** Treks and jeep excursions arranged, attached bath

Shanti Estate Bungalow
TREKKING
Location In the valley **Address** PO Box 26, Madikeri **Tel** 223690, 594290 **Email** vgopal31@yahoo.co.in **Rooms** 2 **Tariff** Rs 300-500; TE **Credit Cards** NA **Facilities** Trekking, attached bath, food on request

MUTHODI STD 08262

Muthodi Nature Camp **FRH**
BUDGET
Location In the jungle **Address** Range Forest Officer, Muthodi Wildlife Range, Jagara Post **Rooms** 2 cottages, 2 dorms **Tariff** Rs 450-700, dorm bed Rs 50-100 **Email** dcfbadra@sancharnet.in **Website** karnatakawildernesstourism.org **Facilities** Caretaker can arrange food, hot water, vehicle available **Chikmagalur Reservations** Field Director, Bhadra Tiger Reserve **Tel** 08262-234904, 230751 **Email** dcfbadra@sancharnet.in

MARAVANTHE STD 08254

Sagar Kinara Beach Resort
TREKKING **BUDGET**
Location On the beach **Address** Trasi-Maravanthe Beach **Tel** 230136, 09448724861 **Email** sgr_kinara@yahoo.co **Rooms** 7 rooms **Tariff** Rs 300-350 **Credit Cards** NA **Facilities** Trekking, restaurant, hot water, parking, room service, travel desk

NAGARHOLE STD 08274

Cauvery Guest House
Location In the forest **Address** Nagarhole National Park, Dist Kodagu **Tel** 2444221 **Rooms** 2 **Tariff** Rs 1,000-2,000 **Credit Cards** NA **Facilities** Food on request, laundry, hot water **Mysore Reservations Tel** 0821-2480901 **Bangalore Reservations Tel** 080-2334556 **Email** pccfwl@vsnl.com

Chilligiri Estate **TREKKING**
BUDGET
Tel 244265 **Rooms** 3 **Tariff** Rs 200-300 **Credit Cards** NA **Facilities** Trekking, restaurant, doctor-on-call, laundry, room service,

sightseeing trips **Mercara Reservations** Coorg Tourist Office, Near Raja's Seat **Tel** 08272-225817

Jungle Inn **TREKKING**
Location Overlooking NNP **Address** 19th km, Hunsur-Nagarhole Road, Veeranahosahalli, Hunsur Taluk **Tel** 08222-246022, 246160, 09448271975 **Fax** 247016 **Email** info@jungleinnnagarhole.com, jungle_inn123@rediffmail.com **Website** jungleinnnagarhole.com **Rooms** 8, tent cottages 4 **Tariff** Rs 1,800-2,500 (meals and safari included) **Credit Cards** NA **Facilities** Trekking in Coorg only, coracle rides, elephant rides, wildlife sanctuary tour, wildlife safaris, hot water, attached bath **Mysore Reservations** 432, 8th Cross Neeti Marga, Siddarth Nagar **Tel** 0821-2470161, 09448271975

Vana Atithi
Location Adjoining Nagarhole National Park **Address** Nanch Estate, PB No. 17, Keeta, Kodagu **Tel** 2444228, 2444888 **Rooms** 3 **Tariff** Rs 1,500 **Credit Cards** NA **Facilities** Restaurant, guide, hot water, taxi arranged

ACCOMMODATION LISTINGS

NARIMALBETTA STD 08274

Forest Rest House `FRH`
Location In the forest **Address** Deputy Conservator of Forests, Hunsur Wildlife Division **Tel** 08222-252041 **Rooms** 3 **Tariff** Rs 750 **Facilities** Attached bath, only lodging

▷ KERALA

EDAKKAL STD 04936

Edakkal Hermitage `HIGH-END` `TREKKING`
Location Hill-top **Address** Near Edakkal Caves, Ambalavayal **Tel** 260123 **Email** edakkal@hotmail.com **Website** edakkal.com **Rooms** 7, tree house 1 **Tariff** Rs 3,300-3,800 **Credit Cards** NA **Facilities** Trekking, restaurant, café, room service, attached bath, hot water
Online Reservations

KALPETTA STD 04936

Hotel Green Gates `TREKKING`
Location On a hillock **Address** TB Road, Kalpetta **Tel** 202001-04 **Fax** 203975 **Email** greengates@sify.com **Website** greengateshotel.com **Rooms** 18, cottages 4 **Tariff** Rs 1,000-2,750 **Credit Cards** AmEx, Visa, Master, BoB **Facilities** Trekking, multi-cuisine restaurants, Ayurvedic spa, sightseeing, swimming, health club, Internet, laundry, room service, attached bath, TV
Online Reservations

The Royal Palm Holiday Home
Location Hill-top **Address** Guodalai Kunnu, Kalpetta **Tel** 206096 **Email** cheriyathotham@eth.net **Website** royalpalmwayanad.com

Rooms 6 cottages **Tariff** Rs 1,500-2,000 **Credit Cards** NA **Facilities** Internet café, travel desk, yoga, doctor-on-call

KOLAGAPARA STD 04936

Tranquil Plantation Hideaway
Location In a coffee estate **Address** Tranquil Plantation, Kupamudi Coffee Estate, Kolagapara **Tel** 220244, 09847865824 **Email** homestay @vsnl.com **Rooms** 8 **Tariff** Rs 4,000-5,500 **Credit Cards** NA **Facilities** Food on request, swimming pool, attached bath

LAKKIDI STD 04936

Rain Country Resorts `TREKKING`
Location In a valley **Address** Lakkidi **Tel** 255286-7, 09447245288 **Email** resorts@raincountryresort.com **Website** raincountryresort.com **Rooms** 8 cottages **Tariff** Rs 2,500-3,600 **Credit Cards** NA **Facilities** Trekking, multi-cuisine restaurant, sightseeing, shop, fishing, room service, attached bath

MEPPADY STD 04936

PWD Rest House `PWD` `BUDGET`
Location In the jungle **Address** Meppady Post, Wayanad **Rooms** 1 **Tariff** Rs 220 **Credit Cards** NA **Facilities** Attached bath, caretaker can prepare food **Kalpetta Reservations** Dist Collector, Civil Station, Kalpetta North **Tel** 04936-202251

SULTHAN BATHERY STD 04936

Forest Inspection Bungalow `FRH` `BUDGET`
Location Main road **Address** Near Wildlife Warden's Office, Sulthan Bathery **Rooms** 2 **Tariff**

Rs 200-300 **Credit Cards** NA **Facilities** Hot water could be arranged **Reservations** Deputy Conservator of Forests, Wildlife Division, Sulthan Bathery **Tel** 220454

Hotel High Lord `BUDGET`
Address Highland Building, Chunga **Tel** 220358 **Rooms** 21 **Tariff** Rs 150-780; TE **Credit Cards** NA **Facilities** Restaurant, travel desk, bar, parking, laundry, room service, hot water

Hotel Resort `BUDGET`
Location Central **Address** PB 42, Sulthan Bathery, Wayanad Dist **Tel** 220510-12 **Telefax** 220583 **Email** theresort@sify.com **Rooms** 12 **Tariff** Rs 375-800 TE **Credit Cards** AmEx, Visa, Master **Facilities** Restaurant, sightseeing, taxi arranged, parking, room service, TV

Jaya Hotel `BUDGET`
Location Main road **Address** Sulthan Bathery, Wayanad Dist **Tel** 220245 **Rooms** 18 **Tariff** Rs 70-120 **Credit Cards** NA **Facilities** Restaurant, laundry, parking, room service, hot water

Motel Anam `BUDGET` `KSTDC`
Location 2 km from town **Address** Ooty Road, Sulthan Bathery, Wayanad Dist **Tel** 222150 **Rooms** 1 **Tariff** Rs 200 **Credit Cards** NA **Facilities** Room service

THIRUNELLY STD 04935

Forest Inspection Bungalow `FRH` `BUDGET`
Location Secluded **Tel** 240233, 09447373726 **Rooms** 4 **Tariff** Rs 450 **Credit Cards** NA **Facilities** Attached bath, hot water, caretaker can arrange food

Wayanad Reservations DFO, North Wayanad, Mananthavady, Kerala **Tel** 04935-240233

Panchateertham Rest House
Location Near Thirunelly Temple **Rooms** 57 **Tariff** Rs 125-500, dorm bed Rs 20 **Credit Cards** NA **Facilities** Only lodging, attached bath, hot water **Reservations** Executive Officer, Thirunelly Temple **Tel** 210055, **Wayanad Reservations** DFO, North Wayanad **Tel** 04935-240233, 09447373726

VYTHIRI STD 04936

Green Magic Eco Resort
TREKKING **HIGH-END**
Address Vythiri **Tel** 2330437 **Email** tourindia@vsnl.com **Website** tourindiakerala.com **Rooms** Tree houses 4, eco lodges 4 **Tariff** Rs 6,580-9,400; TE **Credit Cards** NA **Facilities** Trekking, guide service, common bath, traditional Kerala cuisine **Thiruvananthapuram Reservations** PB No. 163, near SMV High School, MG Road **Tel** 0471-2330437 **Fax** 2331407

Stream Valley Cottages
TREKKING **GUIDES** **HOMESTAY**
Location Near Thalipuzha Junc-

tion **Address** Vythiri, Lakkidi PO **Tel** 202787, 09847502787 **Email** thmkpt@satyam.net.in **Website** streamvalleycottages.com **Rooms** Cottages 11, tree house 1 **Tariff** Rs 2,500-4,000 **Credit Cards** NA **Facilities** Trekking, guides, open air rest house, sightseeing, Intercom, laundry, attached bath, hot water, TV

Vythiri Resort **HIGH-END**
TREKKING
Location Near Gandhi Gramam **Address** Lakkidi PO, Wayanad **Tel** 255366-67 **Fax** 255368 **Website** vythiriresort.com **Rooms** 6, cottages 18, huts 9 **Tariff** Rs 3,500-4,250 **Credit Cards** AmEx, Visa, Master, BoB **Facilities** Trekking, multi-cuisine restaurant, swimming pool, sightseeing, Ayurvedic centre-cum-spa, hot water, TV

▷ TAMIL NADU

COONOOR STD 0423

Hotel Blue Hills
Location Near bus stand **Address** Mount Road, Coonoor **Tel** 2230103, 2230174 **Rooms** 31 **Tariff** Rs 450-900; TE **Credit Cards** NA **Facilities** Restaurant, laundry, hot water, travel desk

Taj Garden Retreat
Location Overlooking the hills **Address** Church Road, Upper Coonoor **Tel** 2230021/42 **Fax** 2232775 **Email** retreat.coonoor @tajhotels.com **Website** taj hotels.com **Rooms** 32 **Tariff** Rs 3,500-6,400; TE **Credit Cards** AmEx, Visa, Master, Diners **Facilities** Restaurant, bar, gym, activity centre, indoor games, volleyball, cricket, Ayurvedic centre, travel desk, room service, laundry, pick-up and drop to station/ airport

YWCA Wyoming Holiday Home
Location Central **Address** Bedford, Coonoor **Tel** 2234426 **Rooms** 9, dorms 2 **Tariff** Rs 200-400, dorm Rs 600; TE **Credit Cards** NA **Facilities** Restaurant, laundry, taxi arranged, room service, yoga class arranged, attached toilets

---

KODANAD

Kodanad Forest Rest House
FRH
Location Inside the jungle **Address** Kodanad, Kotagiri **Rooms** 2 **Tariff** Rs 150 **Credit Cards** NA **Facilities** Cooking facility, caretaker arranges food too, attached bath, hot water

ACCOMMODATION LISTINGS

Ooty Reservations DFO Nilgiris (North) Tel 0423-2443968

KOTAGIRI STD 04266

Blue Star
Location Central Address Top Hill Complex Tel 271473 Rooms 22 Tariff Rs 180-660; TE Credit Cards NA Facilities Restaurant, parking, room service, doctor, sightseeing trips, taxis arranged, laundry

Hotel New Hills BUDGET
Location Near bus stand Address Police Station Road Tel 272073 Rooms 14 Tariff Rs 100-300 Credit Cards NA Facilities Restaurant, room service, sightseeing trips, taxis arranged

Misty Heights HOMESTAY
Location Nestled in the hills Address Kotagiri Tel 279353 Email mistyheightsindia@hot mail.com Website misty heightsindia.com Rooms Cottages 2 Tariff Rs 2,500-3,000 Credit Cards NA Facilities Internet, golfing, outdoor games

LONGWOOD SHOLA

Forest Rest House FRH
Location Inside the jungle Address Longwood Shola, Kotagiri Rooms 3 Tariff Rs 150 Credit Cards NA Facilities Cooking facility, caretaker arranges food too, attached bath, hot water Ooty Reservations See Kodanad above

MUDUMALAI STD 0423

Forest Rest Houses FRH
Location Inside Mudumalai Wildlife Sanctuary Address Forest Range Office, Reception Range, Theppakadu Tel 2526235

Rest Houses 7, dorms 2 Tariff Rs 330, dorm bed Rs 35 Credit Cards NA Facilities Cook available, attached bath Ooty Reservations Conservator of Forests Tel 0423-2444098

MUKURTHI LAKE

Forest Rest House FRH
Location Inside the jungle Address Mukurthi Lake Rooms 2, dorm 1 Tariff Rs 150 Credit Cards NA Facilities Cooking facility, caretaker arranges food, attached bath, hot water Ooty Reservations Nilgiris Wildlife and Environment Association Tel 0423-2447167

OOTY STD 0423

Holiday Inn Gem Park
Location Near city centre Address Sheddon Road, Ooty Tel 2441761-62 Fax 2444302 Website holiday-inn.com Rooms 95 Tariff Rs 1,950-2,995; TE Credit Cards AmEx, Visa, Master, Diners Facilities Restaurant, swimming pool, health club, room service, TV Bangalore Reservations Golden Square Business Centre, 102 Eden Park, No. 20, Vittal Mallya Road Tel 080-2996524
Online Reservations

Hotel Alkapuri
Address 36, Ettines Road, Charing Cross Tel 2440648 Email alkapurihotel@rediffmail.com Rooms 49 Tariff Rs 450-900; TE Credit Cards Visa, Master Facilities Restaurant, sightseeing, hot water, room service, TV

Hotel Blue Hill International
Location Near Collectorate Office Address Near SBI, Hospital Road Tel 2444466 Rooms 88

Tariff Rs 400-1,750; TE Credit Cards NA Facilities Travel desk, parking, laundry, attached bath, room service, TV

Hotel Highland Lodge BUDGET
Location Central Address Shoreham Palace Road, Off Ettines Road Tel 2443718 Email vssvvp@sancharnet.in Rooms 10 Tariff Rs 400-600; TE Credit Cards NA Facilities Sightseeing, attached bath, hot water, room service, TV

Hotel Howard Johnson Monarch TREKKING
Location Hill top Address Havelock Road Tel 2444408/18 Website hojoindia.com Rooms 62 Tariff Rs 1,200-6,000; TE Credit Cards Visa, Master, Diners Facilities Trekking, restaurant, room service, travel desk
Online Reservations

Hotel Lakeview
Location Near railway station Address West Lake Road Tel 2443580-82, Fax 2443579 Website hotellakeview.com Rooms 123 cottages Tariff Rs 700-1,100; TE Credit Cards AmEx, Visa, Master, BoB, Diners Facilities Restaurant, travel desk, gift shop, horse riding, laundry, room service

Hotel Nahar Nilgiris
Location Central Address 52 A, Charing Cross Tel 2442173, 2443685 Fax 2452253 Email nahar@md5.vsnl.net.in Rooms 88 Tariff Rs 1,200-3,000; TE Credit Cards Visa, Master Facilities Restaurant, travel desk, doctor-on-call, laundry, hot water

Hotel Sinclairs TREKKING
Location Hill-facing Address 444 Gorishola Road, PO Box 81

554

Tel 2441376-80 **Fax** 2444229 **Email** sinooty@sancharnet.in **Website** sinclairshotels.com **Rooms** 88 **Tariff** Rs 1,480-1,970; TE **Credit Cards** AmEx, Visa, Master **Facilities** Trekking, restaurant, bar, health centre, parking, room service, TV **Bangalore Reservations** West Minister Building, Cunningham Road **Tel** 080-22269336 Online Reservations

Hotel Tamil Nadu TTDC
Location Central **Address** Charing Cross Road **Tel** 2444370-7 **Fax** 2444369 **Rooms** 65 **Tariff** Rs 400-850; TE **Credit Cards** Visa, Master **Facilities** Restaurant, laundry, sightseeing **Metro Reservations** See page 520

Mayura Sudarshan KSTDC
Location Inside horticultural garden **Address** Fernhill **Tel** 2443828 **Website** kstdc.nic.in **Email** kstdc@vsnl.in **Rooms** 17 **Tariff** Rs 275-850; TE **Facilities** Restaurant, travel desk, room service, hot water, TV **Metro Reservations** See page 519

Nilgiri Woodlands
Location Near bus stand **Address** Ettines Road, Opp Race Course Road **Tel** 2442551

Fax 2442530 **Email** nilgiris_woodlands@yahoo.com **Rooms** 30 **Tariff** Rs 400-1,045; TE **Credit Cards** Visa, Master **Facilities** Restaurant, travel desk, massage centre, doctor-on-call, laundry, room service

Preethi Palace BUDGET
Location Central **Address** Ettines Road, Charing Cross **Tel** 2442789 **Fax** 2444469 **Rooms** 52 **Tariff** Rs 350-650; TE **Credit Cards** NA **Facilities** Restaurant, travel desk, laundry, TV

Sterling Days Inn TREKKING
Location Near lake **Address** PO No. 73, Kundha House Road, Fern Hill **Tel** 2441073-74 **Fax** 2445890 **Website** sterlingresorts.org **Rooms** 175 **Tariff** Rs 1,700-2,950; TE **Credit Cards** AmEx, Visa, Master, Diners **Facilities** Trekking, restaurant, **Bangalore Reservations** Sterling Resorts, Talreja Niwas, 3-4, 8th Cross, Lakshmi Road, Shanthi Nagar **Tel** 080-22270044

The Willow Hill
Location Hill top **Address** 58/1, Havelock Road **Tel** 2444037 **Website** thewillowhill.com **Rooms** 10 **Tariff** Rs 900-1,700; TE **Credit Cards** AmEx, Visa,

Master, Diners **Facilities** Restaurant, children's garden, carom room, chess

Youth Hostel TTDC
Location Near Botanical Garden **Address** Botanical Garden Road **Tel** 2443665 **Rooms** 4 **Tariff** Rs 250-650, dorm bed Rs 75 **Credit Cards** NA **Facilities** Restaurant **Metro Reservations** See page 520

YWCA
Location Town centre **Address** Anandgiri, Ettines Road **Tel** 2444262 **Rooms** 33 **Tariff** Rs 265-1,200 **Credit Cards** NA **Facilities** Restaurants, travel desk, doctor-on-call, laundry, room service

RED HILLS STD 0423

Red Hills Nature Resort TREKKING BIRDWATCHING
Location In the bio-reserves **Address** Emerald, Nilgiris **Tel** 2595755, 09842259554 **Email** vijayredhill@yahoo.co.in **Website** indianjungle.com **Rooms** 8 **Tariff** Rs 2,200-3,000 (meals included) **Credit Cards** NA **Facilities** Trekking, mountain biking, birdwatching, fishing, sightseeing, massages

LADAKH & ZANSKAR

Summer Treks June-August

Day Temp 20⁰-25⁰C **Night Temp** 5⁰-14⁰C

Weather conditions Warm to hot dry days, fierce sun, cool-cold nights. July-August rivers in spate. No monsoons. Can get snow in higher areas and passes in May and September. Pack fleece or light woolies and windproof jacket. Carry good sleeping bag and mat.

UTTARANCHAL & HIMACHAL

Low-altitude treks

Day Temp 18⁰-25⁰C **Night Temp** 12⁰-15⁰C

Weather conditions Pleasant days, cool nights; cold nights only in early spring or late autumn. No rain. Ideal for trekking. Light woolies. Jacket only in early spring and late autumn.

Monsoon Treks June-September

Day Temp 25⁰-26⁰C **Night Temp** 18⁰-19⁰C

Weather conditions Warm humid days. Heavy afternoon and evening showers usually between July and September. Cool, humid days if there is cloud cover. Light clothing and raingear.

High-altitude treks

Day Temp 15⁰-25⁰C **Night Temp** 11⁰-16⁰C

Weather conditions Warm, pleasant days. Cool to cold nights. Humidity 35-50%. Snow on passes till May. Light woolies and jacket. Carry good sleeping bag and mat.

Trekking Holidays in India

NORTH-EAST

LOW-ALTITUDE TREKS
Day Temp 15^0-25^0C **Night Temp** 10^0-12^0C
Weather conditions Warm, pleasant days and cool nights. March-May can be humid. Rain in summer. Drier in post-monsoon months. Frost in December-January.

HIGH-ALTITUDE TREKS
Day Temp 10^0-18^0C **Night Temp** 6^0-12^0C
Weather conditions Warm, clear days. March-May can get humid, some rain in the afternoons. Nights can be cool. Carry rain gear. Snow in December.

WEST

Day Temp 30^0-38^0C **Night Temp** 21^0-27^0C **Weather conditions** Summer: Hot, clear days; humidity 58% Monsoons: Cloudy, windy. Heavy rainfall, so carry raingear. Winter: Clear, sunny days. Cool nights. Humidity 50%.

SOUTH

Day Temp 25^0-33^0C **Night Temp** 18^0-22^0C **Weather conditions** October-March: Warm days, cool nights. Pre-monsoon rains in May. Southwest monsoon in June-September: Humid, warm days. Cloudy or rainy. North-east monsoon in October.

WEATHER

GLOSSARY

ASL Above Sea Level
BSNL Bharat Sanchar Nigam Limited
FRH Forest Rest House
HMI Himalayan Mountaineering Institute
INS Indian Naval Ship/ Indian Naval School
NH National Highway
NP National Park
ST State Transport
SNT Sikkim National Transport
84 Mahasiddhas the 'great realised ones' or 'great perfected ones', practitioners of Tantra in Buddhism. The number 84 is symbolic and signifies completeness
aarti a special prayer performed in temples, as per a daily schedule and involving the offering of lamps
agarbattis incense sticks
atta flour
babas mendicants, holy men
bandobast arrangements, often involving planning and large-scale organisation
bhojpatra birch trees, considered sacred in the hills
baksheesh tip; a voluntary monetary emolument for services or favours rendered
ballekilla big fort, citadel
Bodhisattvas spiritually advanced embodiments of virtues, the Bodhisattvas delay their ascent to Nirvana in order to stay in the world and save other beings. Bodhisattvas are essentially Buddhas in the making. Manjushri (the Bodhisattva of Wisdom) and Avalokiteshwara (the Bodhisattva of Compassion) together make up the essence of a Buddha
bugyal alpine flowering meadow
cairns a heap of stones piled up as a memorial or a landmark
chaitya sacred place; in Buddhism, it means a stupa (*see stupa*) and a building containing a stupa is called a chaitya hall
cheh-footiya/ cheh futta six-footer; a path that is six feet wide
chir one of the five types of pines occurring naturally in India and the only one commercially tapped for resin
chorten stupa

chos-khor religious enclave
chowkidar watchman
chungi check-post
col the lowest point of a ridge or saddle between two peaks, providing a pass from one side of the mountain to another
dalia broken wheat semolina
dandis palanquins
dargah tomb or shrine of a Muslim saint
darshan viewing of a revered deity
devta god
dhabas rustic roadside restaurants famous for hot, wholesome food
dham shrine
dharamshalas rest house with basic facilities, attached to religious sites or temples, where people stay for a nominal fee or donation
Dhyani Buddhas *see Pancha Tathagathas*
dhurrie/ durrie rug
dodi trout
dogris summer houses
du khang interior of the main temple/ assembly hall
Gaddis shepherd community
ghats a mountain range/ pass; flight of steps leading down to a river
gompa monastery, hermitage
Gorkhas Nepalese warriors, originally recruited and trained by the British for their armies in India, some of whom eventually migrated and settled in India
gufa/ gupha cave
gundruk delicacy made of dried and dehydrated radish cooked with appropriate seasonings into a hot, popular broth, served with rice
guru teacher, mentor, guide
Gujjars pastoralists, members of a semi-nomadic community that migrates from lowland plains to the upper reaches of the Himalayas in the summer
Hinayana early school of Buddhism. Also called Theravada (doctrine of the elders), it's one of two main branches of Buddhism (Mahayana came later; *see Mahayana Buddhism*). The ideal of early

Buddhism was the perfected saintly sage, 'arahant' or 'arhat', who attained liberation by purifying the self of all defilement and desires

jo curd made with yak's milk

jhula seat attached to a ropeway for river crossings

khal mountain pass

kothas temporary mud dwellings of the Gujjar shepherd community

kund tank/ pond

kuchha rough, unpaved (path), or not permanent (bridge)

la pass

lama monk or priest in Tibetan-Buddhism

langar free community kitchen in a gurudwara (Sikh shrine), which is open to everyone regardless of caste or religious background

lingam/ Shivalingam/ Shivaling phallic representation of Shiva; most often unadorned and set upon a circular base, which is indicative of the female yoni

mahant head priest of a temple

Mahayana Buddhism literally, the 'Greater Vehicle', the later school of Buddhism. Different from Hinayana as it shifts focus from personal salvation to attaining wisdom for the sake of sentient beings

mandalas mystical, circular diagrams that symbolise the cosmos in both Hinduism and Buddhism

mandir temple

Mani walls stone tablets carved with Buddhist prayers and piled into a wall, often on trail junctions or near villages

mithuna erotic sculpted pairs of men and women seen in temple architecture

mudras hand gestures in statues or images of deities or the Buddha, signifying a particular quality

nag serpent

navratras nine-day festival celebrated in honour of Goddess Durga, held twice a year, in spring and autumn

nirvana enlightenment; release from the cycle of life and death

nallah narrow gorge with mountain stream or dry river bed

palkis palanquins

Panch Tathagathas known as the Five Buddha families, these images of the Tibetan Buddhist pantheon have the central Shakyamuni or Vairochana ('Illuminator'), the Akshobhaya ('Unshakeable'), Ratnasambhava ('Jewel-born One'), Amitabha ('Infinite Light') and Amoghasiddhi ('Fearless One')

pahari that which belongs to the mountains

parikrama/ pradakshina circum-ambulatory path, circumambulation

pind-daan ritual offerings to ancestors

prasad offerings of food to the gods, later partaken of by the devout

puja prayer

pullus camping grounds where water is available

saag edible greens

sadhu holy man, ascetic

sadhu-sarai lodgings for holy men

sarai wayside inn

scree small loose stones that cover a mountain slope

sel dough of rice flour deep-fried in rings

shaman a priest or priestess who uses magic for the purpose of curing the sick

Shivratri annual night-long festival in praise of Shiva, the god of the gods

stupa domed or beehive-shaped Buddhist monument, erected to enshrine a relic or commemorate a sacred site

tal lake

thali plate; a nourishing and simple or elaborate selection of dishes served in fixed or unlimited quantities

thangkas Tibetan or Ladakhi Buddhist religious scroll painting

tos fir trees

tsampa barley flour

vihara monastery, a place for monks to stay, often excavated caves

yagna a ritualistic fire sacrifice

yatra sacred journey, pilgrimage

yogi meditator and or master of yoga

About the Authors

Allen Mendonca is a Bangalore-based writer, columnist, actor and musician. He served in senior positions in a number of national dailies before deciding to travel to wherever his dreams take him. He is presently busy with the final edit of his first novel, to be launched later this year.

Andre Morris taught history at Mumbai's Wilson College before walking the wild side. He lives in Mumbai but spends half his life in the outdoors — hiking, rock climbing, rafting, canoeing and birdwatching. He also runs Outbound Adventure, an outdoor education and adventure outfit.

From copywriting to travel writing and a rock band to a radio station, **Anurag Mallick** is a nomad at heart and writer by choice. He has trekked in the Himalayas, taken a dip at the Maha Kumbh, meditated in a Buddhist monastery, documented the Ranthambhore Tiger Census and several bird surveys. Currently based in Delhi, he is working on a book.

Ashok Dilwali trained as a chartered accountant before becoming a full-time photographer. Excelling in his art, he has had numerous solo exhibitions and published 13 books. Armed with his Linhof, Hasselblad and Nikon cameras, he is today one of India's best-known photographers.

Born in Scotland (1934), **Bill Aitken** studied comparative religion at Leeds University. He hitch-hiked to India in 1959 and became a naturalised citizen in 1972. He loves steam engine and motorbike travel and has written travelogues on India's mountains, rivers and railways. Aitken lives in Mussoorie.

Born in France in 1973, **David Ducoin** discovered India in 1989 and fell in love with the Zanskar Valley. He has since looked for excuses to return: as trekking guide, photographer and documentary filmmaker for French TV. He has published four books on Zanskar and helps NGOs working on education and Tibetan medicine in Ladakh.

David Sayers is a botanical horticulturist who, after an international career in botanic gardens, established David Sayers Travel, a UK company specialising in botanical travel. He is the author of *The Bradt Travelguide to the Azores*.

Deepak Sanan is an IAS officer, Himachal Pradesh cadre, who has trekked extensively in the state. His writings include a book on exploring Kinnaur and Spiti, as well as numerous articles about Himachal in travel magazines and books.

Dipankar Ghose, a wildlife biologist, is well travelled across the Eastern Himalayas and North-East India. He has authored numerous scientific articles and travelogues in regional and international journals and magazines. At present he is involved in field-based conservation work in the Eastern Himalayas. Birdwatching, nature photography, trekking and illustrating are his hobbies.

Minakshi Chaudhry has trekked throughout Himachal over the last one decade and authored two books: *Exploring Pangi Himalaya: A World Beyond Civilization* and *A Guide to Trekking in Himachal*. Her interest in studying nature and people's lifestyle grew in Nigeria, West Africa, where she spent her formative years. This was nurtured on her return to Himachal Pradesh where she travelled extensively as a correspondent of *The Indian Express*.

Much of **Mohit Satyanand's** life is spent in his Kumaon garden looking at the snow-peaks of the Nanda Devi cluster. He delights in introducing children and first-time trekkers to the joys of the wilderness. In the city, he is a strategic management adviser to corporates and non-profit organisations.

Mukul Azad, an adventure tour planner and operator, has travelled extensively in India, and trekked and climbed all over the Himalayas. He also enjoys water sports, skiing and nature photography.

Rakesh Shukla was born in Kasauli and spent part of his childhood in Chakrata, Dehra Dun and Madhopur, on the banks of the Ravi. Now, he spends his time doing, as he puts it, "a bit of writing, a bit of lawyering, a bit of music and a bit of engagement with social issues". Travelling, though, is his "special passion".

Sheetal Vyas is a freelance journalist/ writer/ editor based in Hyderabad. Her earlier work included television, documentaries, publishing and journalism. A keen traveller, birder and adventure sports enthusiast, she has big plans for a novel or script, whichever comes first.

Sujoy Das has trekked and photographed in the Himalayas for the last 25 years. He is the co-author of *Sikkim — A Traveller's Guide*, nominated in the Banff Mountain Book

Festival Awards, and is represented by the international photo-agency, Stock Boston USA. His photographs have been widely published in books and magazines worldwide.

Born in Darjeeling, **Tashi Tobgyal** has always been a trekking enthusiast. He has explored much of the Himalayas, including remote areas like Mustang and Dolpo on the Nepal-Tibet border. His present work as photo researcher at *Outlook Traveller Getaways* keeps him in Delhi, but doesn't prevent him from dreaming about making a documentary on the salt traders of Dolpo.

After an MBA and a stint in advertising, **Vikram Singh** switched to travel and currently runs Wild World India, a wildlife promotion company. He has conducted bird surveys in the North-East, undertaken wildlife explorations in the Western Ghats, spoken on 'Wildlife Films as a Conservation Tool' at Sunderbans and is developing Uttaranchal as a premium sport fishing destination through the Mahseer Conservation Society.

Vivek M divides time between being a doctor and planning the next trek in the Western Ghats, something he has been doing for the past six years. He dreams of doing serious photo-journalism sometime in the future.

ABOUT THE PROJECT AND PHOTO EDITOR

Sonia Jabbar is a writer, journalist and photographer. Writing, editing and photo-editing this guide book has been, for her, an act of thanksgiving to the Himalayas for providing so much wonder and delight over the years.

INDEX - THE TREKS

TREKKING HOLIDAYS IN INDIA

INDEX

INDEX - THE TREKS

GENERAL INDEX

TREKKING HOLIDAYS IN INDIA

GENERAL INDEX

INDEX

GENERAL INDEX

INDEX

571

GENERAL INDEX

Boxes in the book

PHOTO CREDITS

Front Cover Photograph: **SUMAN DUBEY**
Caption: **Looking over the Dhel pastures in the Great Himalayan National Park, Himachal**

Back Cover Photograph: **ASHOK DILWALI**
Caption: **En route to Chanderkhani Pass, Kullu Valley**

ABHIJIT BHATLEKAR
CONTENTS *Page 6* Entrance to the Karla Caves (below)

AKRANT VICHITRA
CONTENTS *Page 4* (top) Campsite at Norbu Sumdo; *Page 4* (centre) Norbu Sumdo

ANDRE MORRIS
CONTENTS *Page 7* Taking a break en route to Mahuli Fort (below)

H SATISH
CONTENTS *Page 7* Morning mist over the Wayanad Hills (above)

MANU BAHUGUNA/ photoindia.com
SPREADS *Pages 38-39* Glacial flow in Ladakh; *Pages 430-431* View of Coorg from Madikeri; *Pages 290-291* View of the Lohit River

PRASHANT PANJIAR
WEATHER *Page 557* After a monsoon shower over

the Lachung Valley (top); *Page 557* En route to the Nandi Hills (below) **CONTENTS** *Page 6* At the Enchey Monastery in Gangtok (above)

PUNIT PARANJPE
WEATHER *Page 557* Monsoon greenery along the Igatpuri railway route (centre) **SPREADS** *Pages 362-363* Igatpuri landscape

SANJEEV SAITH
Page 221 Devotee at Gaumukh

SONIA JABBAR
WEATHER *Page 556* (above) Horses grazing at Tso Kar in Kiyul, Ladakh; *Page 556* White blanket of snow over Wildflower Hall, Mashobra (below)
CONTENTS *Page 4* Pathway through the fresh snow at Mashobra (below); *Page 5* Kaladunghi landscape

PHOTO COURTESY
Page 200 Heinrich-Harrer Museum (Hüttenberg/Austria)
Page 496 Tranquil Plantation Hideaway

ACKNOWLEDGEMENTS

Outlook Traveller Getaways would like to thank Ajay Sood and Rajesh Ojha, Banjara Camps & Retreats; Akbar Ahmed, Corbett Riverside Resort; Andre Morris, Outbound Adventures; Anurag Goel, Mojo Rainforest Retreat; Arvind Bhardwaj, Red Chilli Adventure Sports; Bishwapriyo Rahut, Thirdeye Tours & Treks; Butaram, Triveni Travels; Capt Swadesh Kumar, Shikhar Travels; Chandrashekhar, Escape; David Sonam, Snow View Hotel; Dev Balaji, Nature Admire; Dr SK Vohra; EP Mohandas, DTPC North Kalpetta; Garhwal Mandal Vikas Nigam (Delhi & Uttaranchal); Garhwal Motor Union; Himachal Tourism; Jamling Tenzing, Tenzing Norgay Adventures; Javeed, Dreamland Trek & Tour; Kumaon Mandal Vikas Nigam (Delhi & Uttaranchal); Mandip Singh Soin, Ibex Expeditions; Milind Bhide, Countryside; Neelambar Badoni, Trek Himalaya Tours; Nilgiris Wildlife and Environment Association; Pallab, Naturebeyond; Prabeer Sen, Tibet Tours and Travel; Prakash Thakur, Banjara Orchard; Adven Tours; Suresh Chengappa, Honey Valley; Tsering Wange, Himalayan Holidays; T Dorjee, Khangri Tours & Treks; Thomas Ringma, Asst Director Tourism, Nagaland; Yani Dai, Donyi Hango Adventure Tours; the DFOs, Conservators of Forests and Wildlife Wardens of Karnataka, Kerala, Himachal Pradesh, Tamil Nadu and Uttaranchal; Jai Shankar (Travel Desk) and Murli (Activity Department) of Sterling Days Inn, Ooty; Victor Dey, Tranquil Plantation Hideaway; Vivek M, Vishwas Soans, Soans Holidays and many others for their support and assistance

REFERENCES

WEBSITES
Birdlife International-Threatened Birds of Asia www.rdb.or.id/index.html
Birds of Kolkata www.kolkatabirds.com **Convention On International Trade In Endangered Species** www.ukcites.gov.uk **Plants For A Future** www.pfaf.org, **Oriental Bird Club** www.orientalbirdclub.org
Royal Botanic Gardens, Kew www.rbgkew.org.uk **Royal Geographic Society** www.rgs.org

BOOKS
The Book of Indian Birds Dr Salim Ali **Birds of the Himalayas-A Photographic Guide** Bikram Grewal & Otto Pfister **Flowers of the Western Himalayas** Rupin Dang **A Field Guide to Indian Mammals** Vivek Menon